THE TRIBES AND CASTES

OF THE

CENTRAL PROVINCES OF INDIA

MACMILLAN AND CO., Limited
LONDON · BOMBAY · CALCUTTA
MADRAS · MELBOURNE

THE MACMILLAN COMPANY
NEW YORK · BOSTON · CHICAGO
DALLAS · SAN FRANCISCO

THE MACMILLAN CO. OF CANADA, Ltd.
TORONTO

THE
TRIBES AND CASTES
OF THE
CENTRAL PROVINCES OF INDIA

BY

R. V. RUSSELL
OF THE INDIAN CIVIL SERVICE
SUPERINTENDENT OF ETHNOGRAPHY, CENTRAL PROVINCES

ASSISTED BY

RAI BAHĀDUR HĪRA LĀL
EXTRA ASSISTANT COMMISSIONER

PUBLISHED UNDER THE ORDERS OF THE CENTRAL PROVINCES ADMINISTRATION

IN FOUR VOLUMES

VOL. IV

MACMILLAN AND CO., LIMITED
ST. MARTIN'S STREET, LONDON

1916

306.09543
R966t
Vol.4

COPYRIGHT

CONTENTS OF VOLUME IV

ARTICLES ON CASTES AND TRIBES OF THE CENTRAL PROVINCES IN ALPHABETICAL ORDER

The articles which are considered to be of most general interest are shown in capitals

	PAGE
KUMHĀR (*Potter*)	3
KUNBI (*Cultivator*)	16
Kunjra (*Greengrocer*)	50
Kuramwār (*Shepherd*)	52
KURMI (*Cultivator*)	55
Lakhera (*Worker in lac*)	104
Lodhi (*Landowner and cultivator*)	112
Lohār (*Blacksmith*)	120
Lorha (*Growers of* san-*hemp*)	126
Mahār (*Weaver and labourer*)	129
Mahli (*Forest tribe*)	146
Majhwār (*Forest tribe*)	149
Māl (*Forest tribe*)	153
Māla (*Cotton-weaver and labourer*)	156
MĀLI (*Gardener and vegetable-grower*)	159
Mallāh (*Boatman and fisherman*)	171
Māna (*Forest tribe, cultivator*)	172
Mānbhao (*Religious mendicant*)	176
Māng (*Labourer and village musician*)	184
Māng-Garori (*Criminal caste*)	189
Manihār (*Pedlar*)	193
Mannewār (*Forest tribe*)	195
MARĀTHA (*Soldier, cultivator and service*)	198

CONTENTS

	PAGE
MEHTAR (*Sweeper and scavenger*)	215
Meo (*Tribe*)	233
Mīna or Deswāli (*Non-Aryan tribe, cultivator*)	235
Mirāsi (*Bard and genealogist*)	242
MOCHI (*Shoemaker*)	244
Mowār (*Cultivator*)	250
Murha (*Digger and navvy*)	252
Nagasia (*Forest tribe*)	257
Nāhal (*Forest tribe*)	259
NAI (Barber)	262
Naoda (*Boatman and fisherman*)	283
Nat (*Acrobat*)	286
Nunia (*Salt-refiner, digger and navvy*)	294
Ojha (*Augur and soothsayer*)	296
ORAON (*Forest tribe*)	299
Pāik (*Soldier, cultivator*)	321
Panka (*Labourer and village watchman*)	324
PANWĀR RĀJPŪT (*Landowner and cultivator*)	330
Pardhān (*Minstrel and priest*)	352
Pārdhi (*Hunter and fowler*)	359
Parja (*Forest tribe*)	371
Pāsi (*Toddy-drawer and labourer*)	380
Patwa (*Maker of silk braid and thread*)	385
PINDĀRI (*Freebooter*)	388
Prabhu (*Writer and clerk*)	399
Rāghuvansi (*Cultivator*)	403
Rājjhar (*Agricultural labourer*)	405
RĀJPŪT (*Soldier and landowner*)	410

RĀJPŪT CLANS

Baghel.	Chauhān.	Pāik.
Bāgri.	Dhākar.	Parihār.
Bais.	Gaharwār.	Rāthor.
Baksaria.	Gaur.	Sesodia.
Banāphar.	Haihaya.	Solankhi.
Bhadauria.	Hūna.	Somvansi.
Bisen.	Kachhwāha.	Sūrajvansi.
Bundela.	Nāgvansi.	Tomara.
Chandel.	Nikumbh.	Yādu.

CONTENTS

	PAGE
Rajwār (*Forest tribe*)	470
Rāmosi (*Village watchmen and labourers, formerly thieves*)	472
Rangrez (*Dyer*)	477
Rautia (*Forest tribe and cultivators, formerly soldiers*)	479
Sanaurhia (*Criminal thieving caste*)	483
Sānsia (*Vagrant criminal tribe*)	488
Sānsia (Uria) (*Mason and digger*)	496
Savar (*Forest tribe*)	500
Sonjhara (*Gold-washer*)	509
Sudh (*Cultivator*)	514
SUNĀR (*Goldsmith and silversmith*)	517
Sundi (*Liquor distiller*)	534
Tamera (*Coppersmith*)	536
Taonla (*Soldier and labourer*)	539
TELI (*Oilman*)	542
THUG (*Criminal community of murderers by strangulation*)	558
Turi (*Bamboo-worker*)	588
Velama (*Cultivator*)	593
VIDUR (*Village accountant, clerk and writer*)	596
Wāghya (*Religious mendicant*)	603
Yerūkala (*Criminal thieving caste*)	606

ILLUSTRATIONS IN VOLUME IV

		PAGE
97.	Potter and his wheel	4
98.	Group of Kunbis	16
99.	Figures of animals made for Pola festival	40
100.	Hindu boys on stilts	42
101.	Throwing stilts into the water at the Pola festival	46
102.	Carrying out the dead	48
103.	Pounding rice	60
104.	Sowing	84
105.	Threshing	86
106.	Winnowing	88
107.	Women grinding wheat and husking rice	90
108.	Group of women in Hindustāni dress	92
109.	*Coloured Plate*: Examples of spangles worn by women on the forehead	106
110.	Weaving : sizing the warp	142
111.	Winding thread	144
112.	Bride and bridegroom with marriage crowns	166
113.	Bullocks drawing water with *mot*	170
114.	Māng musicians with drums	186
115.	Statue of Marātha leader, Bīmbāji Bhonsla, in armour	200
116.	Image of the god Vishnu as Vithoba	248
117.	Coolie women with babies slung at the side	256
118.	Hindu men showing the *choti* or scalp-lock	272
119.	Snake-charmer with cobras	292
120.	Transplanting rice	340
121.	Group of Pardhāns	352
122.	Little girls playing	400

		PAGE
123.	Gujarāti girls doing figures with strings and sticks	402
124.	Ornaments	524
125.	Teli's oil-press	544
126.	The Goddess Kāli	574
127.	Wāghya mendicants	604

PRONUNCIATION

a	has the sound of	u in *but* or *murmur*.
ā	,,	,,	a in *bath* or *tar*.
e	,,	,,	é in *écarté* or ai in *maid*.
i	,,	,,	i in *bit*, or (as a final letter) of y in *sulky*.
ī	,,	,,	ee in *beet*.
o	,,	,,	o in *bore* or *bowl*.
u	,,	,,	u in *put* or *bull*.
ū	,,	,,	oo in *poor* or *boot*.

The plural of caste names and a few common Hindustāni words is formed by adding *s* in the English manner according to ordinary usage, though this is not, of course, the Hindustāni plural.

NOTE.—The rupee contains 16 annas, and an anna is of the same value as a penny. A pice is a quarter of an anna, or a farthing. Rs. 1-8 signifies one rupee and eight annas. A lakh is a hundred thousand, and a krore ten million.

PART II

ARTICLES ON CASTES AND TRIBES

KUMHĀR—YEMKALA

KUMHĀR

LIST OF PARAGRAPHS

1. *Traditions of origin.*
2. *Caste subdivisions.*
3. *Social customs.*
4. *The Kumhār as a village menial.*
5. *Occupation.*
6. *Breeding pigs for sacrifices.*
7. *The goddess Demeter.*
8. *Estimation of the pig in India.*
9. *The buffalo as a corn-god.*
10. *The Dasahra festival.*
11. *The goddess Devi.*

Kumhār, Kumbhār.—The caste of potters, the name being derived from the Sanskrit *kumbh*, a water-pot. The Kumhārs numbered nearly 120,000 persons in the Central Provinces in 1911 and were most numerous in the northern and eastern or Hindustāni-speaking Districts, where earthen vessels have a greater vogue than in the south. The caste is of course an ancient one, vessels of earthenware having probably been in use at a very early period, and the old Hindu scriptures consequently give various accounts of its origin from mixed marriages between the four classical castes. " Concerning the traditional parentage of the caste," Sir H. Risley writes,[1] " there seems to be a wide difference of opinion among the recognised authorities on the subject. Thus the Brahma Vaivārtta Purāna says that the Kumbhakār or maker of water-jars (*kumbha*), is born of a Vaishya woman by a Brāhman father ; the Parāsara Samhita makes the father a Mālākār (gardener) and the mother a Chamār ; while the Parāsara Padhati holds that the ancestor of the caste was begotten of a Tili woman by a Pattikār or weaver of silk cloth. Sir Monier Williams again, in his Sanskrit Dictionary, describes them as the offspring of a Kshatriya woman by a Brāhman. No importance can of course be attached to

1. Traditions of origin.

---

[1] *Tribes and Castes of Bengal*, art. Kumhār.

such statements as the above from the point of view of actual fact, but they are interesting as showing the view taken of the formation of castes by the old Brāhman writers, and also the position given to the Kumhār at the time when they wrote. This varies from a moderately respectable to a very humble one according to the different accounts of his lineage. The caste themselves have a legend of the usual Brāhmanical type: "In the Kritayuga, when Maheshwar (Siva) intended to marry the daughter of Hemvanta, the Devas and Asuras [1] assembled at Kailās (Heaven). Then a question arose as to who should furnish the vessels required for the ceremony, and one Kulālaka, a Brāhman, was ordered to make them. Then Kulālaka stood before the assembly with folded hands, and prayed that materials might be given to him for making the pots. So Vishnu gave his Sudarsana (discus) to be used as a wheel, and the mountain of Mandāra was fixed as a pivot beneath it to hold it up. The scraper was Adi Kūrma the tortoise, and a rain-cloud was used for the water-tub. So Kulālaka made the pots and gave them to Maheshwar for his marriage, and ever since his descendants have been known as Kumbhakār or maker of water-jars."

2. Caste sub-divisions.

The Kumhārs have a number of subcastes, many of which, as might be expected, are of the territorial type and indicate the different localities from which they migrated to the Central Provinces. Such are the Mālwi from Mālwa, the Telenga from the Telugu country in Hyderābād, the Pardeshi from northern India and the Marātha from the Marātha Districts. Other divisions are the Lingāyats who belong to the sect of this name, the Gadhewāl or Gadhere who make tiles and carry them about on donkeys (*gadha*), the Bardia who use bullocks for transport and the Sungaria who keep pigs (*suar*). Certain endogamous groups have arisen simply from differences in the method of working. Thus the Hāthgarhia [2] mould vessels with their hands only without using the wheel; the Goria [3] make white or red pots only and not black ones; the Kurere mould their vessels on a stone slab revolving on a stick and not on a wheel; while the Chakere are Kumhārs who use the wheel (*chāk*) in

---

[1] Gods and demons.   [2] *Hāth*, hand and *garhna*, to make or mould.
[3] *Gora*, white or red, applied to Europeans.

POTTER AND HIS WHEEL.

Bemrose, Collo., Derby.

localities where other Kumhārs do not use it. The Chhutakia and Rakhotia are illegitimate sections, being the offspring of kept women.

Girls are married at an early age when their parents can afford it, the matches being usually arranged at caste feasts. In Chānda parents who allow a daughter to become adolescent while still unwed are put out of caste, but elsewhere the rule is by no means so strict. The ceremony is of the normal type and a Brāhman usually officiates, but in Betūl it is performed by the Sawāsa or husband of the bride's paternal aunt. After the wedding the couple are given kneaded flour to hold in their hands and snatch from each other as an emblem of their trade. In Mandla a bride-price of Rs. 50 is paid.

The Kumhārs recognise divorce and the remarriage of widows. If an unmarried girl is detected in criminal intimacy with a member of the caste, she has to give a feast to the caste-fellows and pay a fine of Rs. 1-4 and five locks of her hair are also cut off by way of purification. The caste usually burn the dead, but the Lingāyat Kumhārs always bury them in accordance with the practice of their sect. They worship the ordinary Hindu deities and make an offering to the implements of their trade on the festival of Deothān Igāras. The village Brāhman serves as their priest. In Bālāghāt a Kumhār is put out of caste if a dead cat is found in his house. At the census of 1901 the Kumhār was ranked with the impure castes, but his status is not really so low. Sir D. Ibbetson said of him: " He is a true village menial; his social standing is very low, far below that of the Lohār and not much above the Chamār. His association with that impure beast, the donkey, the animal sacred to Sitala, the smallpox goddess, pollutes him and also his readiness to carry manure and sweepings." As already seen there are in the Central Provinces Sungaria and Gadheria subcastes which keep donkeys and pigs, and these are regarded as impure. But in most Districts the Kumhār ranks not much below the Barhai and Lohār, that is in what I have designated the grade of village menials above the impure and below the cultivating castes. In Bengal the Kumhārs have a much higher status and Brāhmans will

3. Social customs.

take water from their hands. But the gradation of caste in Bengal differs very greatly from that of other parts of India.

4. The Kumhār as a village menial.

The Kumhār is not now paid regularly by dues from the cultivators like other village menials, as the ordinary system of sale has no doubt been found more convenient in his case. But he sometimes takes the soiled grass from the stalls of the cattle and gives pots free to the cultivator in exchange. On Akti day, at the beginning of the agricultural year, the village Kumhār of Saugor presents five pots with covers on them to each cultivator and receives $2\frac{1}{2}$ lbs. of grain in exchange. One of these the tenant fills with water and presents to a Brāhman and the rest he reserves for his own purposes. On the occasion of a wedding also the bridegroom's party take the bride to the Kumhārin's house as part of the *sohāg* ceremony for making the marriage propitious. The Kumhār seats the bride on his wheel and turns it round with her seven times. The Kumhārin presents her with seven new pots, which are taken back to the house and used at the wedding. They are filled with water and are supposed to represent the seven seas. If any two of these pots accidentally clash together it is supposed that the bride and bridegroom will quarrel during their married life. In return for this the Kumhārin receives a present of clothes. At a funeral also the Kumhār must supply thirteen vessels which are known as *ghāts*, and must also replace the broken earthenware. Like the other village menials at the harvest he takes a new vessel to the cultivator in his field and receives a present of grain. These customs appear to indicate his old position as one of the menials or general servants of the village ranking below the cultivators. Grant-Duff also includes the potter in his list of village menials in the Marātha villages.[1]

5. Occupation.

The potter is not particular as to the clay he uses and does not go far afield for the finer qualities, but digs it from the nearest place in the neighbourhood where he can get it free of cost. Red and black clay are employed, the former being obtained near the base of hills or on high-lying land, probably of the laterite formation, and the latter in the beds of tanks or streams. When the clay is thoroughly kneaded

---

[1] *History of the Marāthas*, edition 1878, vol. i. p. 26.

and ready for use a lump of it is placed on the centre of the wheel. The potter seats himself in front of the wheel and fixes his stick or *chakrait* into the slanting hole in its upper surface. With this stick the wheel is made to revolve very rapidly, and sufficient impetus is given to it to keep it in motion for several minutes. The potter then lays aside the stick and with his hands moulds the lump of clay into the shape required, stopping every now and then to give the wheel a fresh spin as it loses its momentum. When satisfied with the shape of his vessel he separates it from the lump with a piece of string, and places it on a bed of ashes to prevent it sticking to the ground. The wheel is either a circular disc cut out of a single piece of stone about a yard in diameter, or an ordinary wooden wheel with spokes forming two diameters at right angles. The rim is then thickened with the addition of a coating of mud strengthened with fibre.[1] The articles made by the potter are ordinary circular vessels or *gharas* used for storing and collecting water, larger ones for keeping grain, flour and vegetables, and *surāhis* or amphoras for drinking-water. In the manufacture of these last salt and saltpetre are mixed with the clay to make them more porous and so increase their cooling capacity. A very useful thing is the small saucer which serves as a lamp, being filled with oil on which a lighted wick is floated. These saucers resemble those found in the excavations of Roman remains. Earthen vessels are more commonly used, both for cooking and eating purposes among the people of northern India, and especially by Muhammadans, than among the Marāthas, and, as already noticed, the Kumhār caste musters strong in the north of the Province. An earthen vessel is polluted if any one of another caste takes food or drink from it and is at once discarded. On the occasion of a death all the vessels in the house are thrown away and a new set obtained, and the same measure is adopted at the Holi festival and on the occasion of an eclipse, and at various other ceremonial purifications, such as that entailed if a member of the household has had maggots in a wound. On this account cheapness is an indispensable quality in pottery, and there is

---

[1] The above description is taken from the Central Provinces *Monograph* on *Pottery and Glassware* by Mr. Jowers, p. 4.

no opening for the Kumhār to improve his art. Another product of the Kumhār's industry is the *chilam* or pipe-bowl. This has the usual opening for inhaling the smoke but no stem, an impromptu stem being made by the hands and the smoke inhaled through it. As the *chilam* is not touched by the mouth, Hindus of all except the impure castes can smoke it together, passing it round, and Hindus can also smoke it with Muhammadans.

It is a local belief that, if an earthen pot is filled with salt and plastered over, the rains will stop until it is opened. This device is adopted when the fall is excessive, but, on the other hand, if there is drought, the people sometimes think that the potter has used it to keep off the rain, because he cannot pursue his calling when the clay is very wet. And on occasions of a long break in the rains, they have been known to attack his shop and break all his vessels under the influence of this belief. The potter is sometimes known as Prājapati or the 'The Creator,' in accordance with the favourite comparison made by ancient writers of the moulding of his pots with the creation of human beings, the justice of which will be recognised by any one who watches the masses of mud on a whirling wheel growing into shapely vessels in the potter's creating hands.

6. Breeding pigs for sacrifices.

Certain Kumhārs as well as the Dhīmars make the breeding of pigs a means of subsistence, and they sell these pigs for sacrifices at prices varying from eight annas (8d.) to a rupee. The pigs are sacrificed by the Gonds to their god Bura Deo and by Hindus to the deity Bhainsāsur, or the buffalo demon, for the protection of the crops. Bhainsāsur is represented by a stone in the fields, and when crops are beaten down at night by the wind it is supposed that Bhainsāsur has passed over them and trampled them down. Hindus, usually of the lower castes, offer pigs to Bhainsāsur to propitiate him and preserve their crops from his ravages, but they cannot touch the impure pig themselves. What they have to do, therefore, is to pay the Kumhār the price of the pig and get him to offer it to Bhainsāsur on their behalf. The Kumhār goes to the god and sacrifices the pig and then takes the body home and eats it, so that his trade is a profitable one, while conversely to sacrifice a pig without partaking of its flesh must necessarily be bitter to the frugal Hindu mind, and this indicates the importance of the deity who is to be propitiated by the offering. The first question which arises in connection with this curious custom is why pigs should be sacrificed for the preservation of the crops; and the reason appears to be that the wild pig is the animal which, at present, mainly damages the crops.

In ancient Greece pigs were offered to Demeter, the corn-goddess, for the protection of the crops, and there is good reason to suppose that the conceptions of Demeter herself and the lovely Proserpine grew out of the worship of the pig, and that both goddesses were in the beginning merely the deified pig. The highly instructive passage in which Sir J. G. Frazer advances this theory is reproduced almost in full:[1] "Passing next to the corn-goddess Demeter, and remembering that in European folklore the pig is a common embodiment of the corn-spirit, we may now ask whether the pig, which was so closely associated with Demeter, may not originally have been the goddess herself in animal form? The pig was sacred to her; in art she was portrayed carrying or accompanied by a pig; and the pig was regularly sacrificed in her mysteries, the reason assigned being that the pig injures the corn and is therefore an enemy of the goddess. But after an animal has been conceived as a god, or a god as an animal, it sometimes happens, as we have seen, that the god sloughs off his animal form and becomes purely anthropomorphic; and that then the animal which at first had been slain in the character of the god, comes to be viewed as a victim offered to the god on the ground of its hostility to the deity; in short, that the god is sacrificed to himself on the ground that he is his own enemy. This happened to Dionysus and it may have happened to Demeter also. And in fact the rites of one of her festivals, the Thesmophoria, bear out the view that originally the pig was an embodiment of the corn-goddess herself, either Demeter or her daughter and double Proserpine. The Thesmophoria was an autumn festival celebrated by women alone in October, and appears to have represented with mourning rites the descent of Proserpine (or Demeter) into the lower world, and with joy her return

7. The goddess Demeter.

[1] *Golden Bough*, ii. pp. 299, 301.

from the dead. Hence the name Descent or Ascent variously applied to the first, and the name *Kalligeneia* (fair-born) applied to the third day of the festival. Now from an old scholium on Lucian we learn some details about the mode of celebrating the Thesmophoria, which shed important light on the part of the festival called the Descent or the Ascent. The scholiast tells us that it was customary at the Thesmophoria to throw pigs, cakes of dough, and branches of pine-trees into 'the chasms of Demeter and Proserpine,' which appear to have been sacred caverns or vaults.

"In these caverns or vaults there were said to be serpents, which guarded the caverns and consumed most of the flesh of the pigs and dough-cakes which were thrown in. Afterwards—apparently at the next annual festival—the decayed remains of the pigs, the cakes, and the pine-branches were fetched by women called 'drawers,' who, after observing rules of ceremonial purity for three days, descended into the caverns, and, frightening away the serpents by clapping their hands, brought up the remains and placed them on the altar. Whoever got a piece of the decayed flesh and cakes, and sowed it with the seed-corn in his field, was believed to be sure of a good crop.

"To explain this rude and ancient rite the following legend was told. At the moment when Pluto carried off Proserpine, a swineherd called Eubuleus chanced to be herding his swine on the spot, and his herd was engulfed in the chasm down which Pluto vanished with Proserpine. Accordingly, at the Thesmophoria pigs were annually thrown into caverns to commemorate the disappearance of the swine of Eubuleus. It follows from this that the casting of the pigs into the vaults at the Thesmophoria formed part of the dramatic representation of Proserpine's descent into the lower world ; and as no image of Proserpine appears to have been thrown in, we may infer that the descent of the pigs was not so much an accompaniment of her descent as the descent itself, in short, that the pigs were Proserpine. Afterwards, when Proserpine or Demeter (for the two are equivalent) became anthropomorphic, a reason had to be found for the custom of throwing pigs into caverns at her festival; and this was done by saying that when Pluto carried off Proserpine, there happened to be some swine browsing near, which were swallowed up along with her. The story is obviously a forced and awkward attempt to bridge over the gulf between the old conception of the corn-spirit as a pig and the new conception of her as an anthropomorphic goddess. A trace of the older conception survived in the legend that when the sad mother was searching for traces of the vanished Proserpine, the footprints of the lost one were obliterated by the footprints of a pig ; originally, we may conjecture, the footprints of the pig were the footprints of Proserpine and of Demeter herself. A consciousness of the intimate connection of the pig with the corn lurks in the legend that the swineherd Eubuleus was a brother of Triptolemus, to whom Demeter first imparted the secret of the corn. Indeed, according to one version of the story, Eubuleus himself received, jointly with his brother Triptolemus, the gift of the corn from Demeter as a reward for revealing to her the fate of Proserpine. Further, it is to be noted that at the Thesmophoria the women appear to have eaten swine's flesh. The meal, if I am right, must have been a solemn sacrament or communion, the worshippers partaking of the body of the god."

8. Estimation of the pig in India.

We thus see how the pig in ancient Greece was worshipped as a corn-deity because it damaged the crops and subsequently became an anthropomorphic goddess. It is suggested that pigs are offered to Bhainsāsur by the Hindus for the same reason. But there is no Hindu deity representing the pig, this animal on the contrary being regarded as impure. It seems doubtful, however, whether this was always so. In Rājputāna on the stone which the Regent of Kotah set up to commemorate the abolition of forced taxes were carved the effigies of the sun, the moon, the cow and the hog, with an imprecation on whoever should revoke the edict.[1] Colonel Tod says that the pig was included as being execrated by all classes, but this seems very doubtful. It would scarcely occur to any Hindu nowadays to associate the image of the impure pig with those of the sun, moon and cow, the representations of three of his greatest deities. Rather it gives some reason for

[1] *Rājasthān*, ii. p. 524.

supposing that the pig was once worshipped, and the Rājpūts still do not hold the wild boar impure, as they hunt it and eat its flesh. Moreover, Vishnu in his fourth incarnation was a boar. The Gonds regularly offer pigs to their great god Bura Deo, and though they now offer goats as well, this seems to be a later innovation. The principal sacrifice of the early Romans was the Suovetaurilia or the sacrifice of a pig, a ram and a bull. The order of the words, M. Reinach remarks,[1] is significant as showing the importance formerly attached to the pig or boar. Since the pig was the principal sacrificial animal of the primitive tribes, the Gonds and Baigas, its connection with the ritual of an alien and at one time hostile religion may have strengthened the feeling of aversion for it among the Hindus, which would naturally be engendered by its own dirty habits.

9. The buffalo as a corn-god.

It seems possible then that the Hindus reverenced the wild boar in the past as one of the strongest and fiercest animals of the forest and also as a destroyer of the crops. And they still make sacrifices of the pig to guard their fields from his ravages. These sacrifices, however, are not offered to any deity who can represent a deified pig but to Bhainsāsur, the deified buffalo. The explanation seems to be that in former times, when forests extended over most of the country, the cultivator had in the wild buffalo a direr foe than the wild pig. And one can well understand how the peasant, winning a scanty subsistence from his poor fields near the forest, and seeing his harvest destroyed in a night by the trampling of a herd of these great brutes against whom his puny weapons were powerless, looked on them as terrible and malignant deities. The sacrifice of a buffalo would be beyond the means of a single man, and the animal is now more or less sacred as one of the cow tribe. But the annual joint sacrifice of one or more buffaloes is a regular feature of the Dasahra festival and extends over a great part of India. In Betūl and other districts the procedure is that on the Dasahra day, or a day before, the Māng and Kotwār, two of the lowest village menials, take a buffalo bull and bring it to the village proprietor, who makes a cut on its nose and draws blood. Then it is taken all round the village and to the shrines of

[1] *Orpheus*, p. 152.

the gods, and in the evening it is killed and the Māng and Kotwār eat the flesh. It is now believed that if the blood of a buffalo does not fall at Dasahra some epidemic will attack the village, but as there are no longer any wild buffaloes except in the denser forests of one or two Districts, the original meaning of the rite might naturally have been forgotten.[1]

10. The Dasahra festival.

The Dasahra festival probably marks the autumnal equinox and also the time when the sowing of wheat and other spring crops begins. Many Hindus still postpone sowing the wheat until after Dasahra, even though it might be convenient to begin before, especially as the festival goes by the lunar month and its date varies in different years by more than a fortnight. The name signifies the tenth day, and prior to the festival a fast of nine days is observed, when the pots of wheat corresponding to the gardens of Adonis are sown and quickly sprout up. This is an imitation of the sowing and growth of the real crop and is meant to ensure its success. During these nine days it is said that the goddess Devi was engaged in mortal combat with the buffalo demon Mahisāsur or Bhainsāsur, and on the tenth day or the Dasahra she slew him. The fast is explained as being observed in order to help her to victory, but it is really perhaps a fast in connection with the growing of the crops. A similar nine days' fast for the crops was observed by the Greeks.[2]

11. The goddess Devi.

Devi signifies '*the* goddess' *par excellence*. She is often the tutelary goddess of the village and of the family, and is held to have been originally Mother Earth, which may be supposed to be correct. In tracts where the people of northern and southern India meet she is identified with Anna Pūrna, the corn-goddess of the Telugu country; and in her form of Gauri or 'the Yellow One' she is perhaps herself the yellow corn. As Gauri she is worshipped at weddings in conjunction with Ganesh or Ganpati, the god of Good Fortune; and it is probably in honour of the harvest colour that Hindus of the upper castes wear yellow at

---

[1] The sacrifice is now falling into abeyance, as landowners refuse to supply the buffalo.
[2] Dr. Jevons, *Introduction to the History of Religion*, p. 368.

their weddings and consider it lucky. A Brāhman also prefers to wear yellow when eating his food. It has been seen [1] that red is the lucky colour of the lower castes of Hindus, and the reason probably is that the shrines of their gods are stained red with the blood of the animals sacrificed. High-caste Hindus no longer make animal sacrifices, and their offerings to Siva, Vishnu and Devi consist of food, flowers and blades of corn. Thus yellow would be similarly associated with the shrines of the gods. All Hindu brides have their bodies rubbed with yellow turmeric, and the principal religious flower, the marigold, is orange-yellow. Yellow is, however, also lucky as being the colour of Vishnu or the Sun, and a yellow flag is waved above his great temple at Rāmtek on the occasion of the fair. Thus Devi as the corn-goddess perhaps corresponds to Demeter, but she is not in this form an animal goddess. The Hindus worshipping Mother Earth, as all races do in the early stage of religion, may by a natural and proper analogy have ascribed the gift of the corn to her from whom it really comes, and have identified her with the corn-goddess. This is by no means a full explanation of the goddess Devi, who has many forms. As Pārvati, the hill-maiden, and Durga, the inaccessible one, she is the consort of Siva in his character of the mountain-god of the Himalayas; as Kāli, the devourer of human flesh, she is perhaps the deified tiger; and she may have assimilated yet more objects of worship into her wide divinity. But there seems no special reason to hold that she is anywhere believed to be the deified buffalo; and the probable explanation of the Dasahra rite would therefore seem to be that the buffalo was at first venerated as the corn-god because, like the pig in Greece, he was most destructive to the crops, and a buffalo was originally slaughtered and eaten sacramentally as an act of worship. At a later period the divinity attaching to the corn was transferred to Devi, an anthropomorphic deity of a higher class, and in order to explain the customary slaughter of the buffalo, which had to be retained, the story became current that the beneficent goddess fought and slew the buffalo-demon which injured the crops, for the benefit of her worshippers, and the fast was observed and the

---

[1] *Vide* article on Lakhera.

buffalo sacrificed in commemoration of this event. It is possible that the sacrifice of the buffalo may have been a non-Aryan rite, as the Mundas still offer a buffalo to Deswāli, their forest god, in the sacred grove; and the Korwas of Sargūja have periodical sacrifices to Kāli in which many buffaloes are slaughtered. In the pictures of her fight with Bhainsāsur, Devi is shown as riding on a tiger, and the uneducated might imagine the struggle to have resembled that between a tiger and a buffalo. As the destroyer of buffaloes and deer which graze on the crops the tiger may even be considered the cultivator's friend. But in the rural tracts Bhainsāsur himself is still venerated in the guise of a corn-deity, and pig are perhaps offered to him as the animals which nowadays do most harm to the crops.

KUNBI

[This article is based on the information collected for the District Gazetteers of the Central Provinces, manuscript notes furnished by Mr. A. K. Smith, C.S., and from papers by Pandit Pyāre Lāl Misra and Munshi Kanhya Lāl. The Kunbis are treated in the *Poona* and *Khāndesh* volumes of the *Bombay Gazetteer*. The caste has been taken as typical of the Marāthi-speaking Districts, and a fairly full description of the marriage and other ceremonies has therefore been given, some information on houses, dress and food being also reproduced from the *Wardha* and *Yeotmal District Gazetteers*.]

LIST OF PARAGRAPHS

1. *Distribution of the caste and origin of name.*
2. *Settlement in the Central Provinces.*
3. *Subcastes.*
4. *The cultivating status.*
5. *Exogamous septs.*
6. *Restrictions on marriage of relatives.*
7. *Betrothal and marriage.*
8. *Polygamy and divorce.*
9. *Widow-marriage.*
10. *Customs at birth.*
11. *Sixth- and twelfth-day ceremonies.*
12. *Devices for procuring children.*
13. *Love charms.*
14. *Disposal of the dead.*
15. *Mourning.*
16. *Religion.*
17. *The Pola festival.*
18. *Muhammadan tendencies of Berār Kunbis.*
19. *Villages and houses.*
20. *Furniture.*
21. *Food.*
22. *Clothes and ornaments.*
23. *The Kunbi as cultivator.*
24. *Social and moral characteristics.*

1. Distribution of the caste and origin of name.

Kunbi.—The great agricultural caste of the Marātha country. In the Central Provinces and Berār the Kunbis numbered nearly 1,400,000 persons in 1911; they belong to the Nāgpur, Chānda, Bhandāra, Wardha, Nimār and Betūl Districts of the Central Provinces. In Berār their strength was 800,000, or nearly a third of the total population. Here they form the principal cultivating class over the whole area except in the jungles of the north and south, but muster most strongly in the Buldāna District to the west, where in some tāluks nearly half the population

GROUP OF KUNBIS.

belongs to the Kunbi caste. In the combined Province they are the most numerous caste except the Gonds. The name has various forms in Bombay, being Kunbi or Kulambi in the Deccan, Kulwādi in the south Konkan, Kanbi in Gujarāt, and Kulbi in Belgaum. In Sanskrit inscriptions it is given as Kutumbika (householder), and hence it has been derived from *kutumba*, a family. A chronicle of the eleventh century quoted by Forbes speaks of the Kutumbiks or cultivators of the *grāms* or small villages.[1] Another writer describing the early Rājpūt dynasties says:[2] "The villagers were Koutombiks (householders) or husbandmen (Karshuks); the village headmen were Putkeels (patels)." Another suggested derivation is from a Dravidian root *kul*, a husbandman or labourer; while that favoured by the caste and their neighbours is from *kun*, a root, or *kan*, grain, and *bi*, seed; but this is too ingenious to be probable.

It is stated that the Kunbis entered Khāndesh from Gujarāt in the eleventh century, being forced to leave Gujarāt by the encroachments of Rājpūt tribes, driven south before the early Muhammadan invaders of northern India.[3] From Khāndesh they probably spread into Berār and the adjoining Nāgpur and Wardha Districts. It seems probable that their first settlement in Nāgpur and Wardha took place not later than the fourteenth century, because during the subsequent period of Gond rule we find the offices of Deshmukh and Deshpāndia in existence in this area. The Deshmukh was the manager or headman of a circle of villages and was responsible for apportioning and collecting the land revenue, while the Deshpāndia was a head *patwari* or accountant. The Deshmukhs were usually the leading Kunbis, and the titles are still borne by many families in Wardha and Nāgpur. These offices[4] belong to the Marātha country, and it seems necessary to suppose that their introduction into Wardha and Berār dates from a period at least as early as the fourteenth century, when these territories were included in the dominions of the Bahmani kings of Bījapur. A subsequent large influx of Kunbis into Wardha

2. Settlement in the Central Provinces.

---

[1] *Rāsmāla*, i. p. 100.
[2] *Ibidem*, p. 241.
[3] *Khāndesh Gazetteer*, p. 62.
[4] *Bombay Gazetteer*, vol. i. part ii. p. 34.

and Nāgpur took place in the eighteenth century with the conquest of Raghūji Bhonsla and the establishment of the Marātha kingdom of Nāgpur. Traces of these separate immigrations survive in the subdivisions of the caste, which will now be mentioned.

3. Sub-castes.

The internal structure of the Kunbi caste in the Central Provinces shows that it is a mixed occupational body recruited from different classes of the population. The Jhāre or jungly[1] Kunbis are the oldest immigrants and have no doubt an admixture of Gond blood. They do not break their earthen vessels after a death in the house. With them may be classed the Mānwa Kunbis of the Nāgpur District; these appear to be a group recruited from the Mānas, a primitive tribe who were dominant in Chānda perhaps even before the advent of the Gonds. The Mānwa Kunbi women wear their cloths drawn up so as to expose the thigh like the Gonds, and have some other primitive practices. They do not employ Brāhmans at their marriages, but consult a Mahār Mohtūria or soothsayer to fix the date of the ceremony. Other Kunbis will not eat with the Mānwas, and the latter retaliate in the usual manner by refusing to accept food from them; and say that they are superior to other Kunbis because they always use brass vessels for cooking and not earthen ones. Among the other subcastes in the Central Provinces are the Khaire, who take their name from the *khaīr*[2] or catechu tree, presumably because they formerly prepared catechu; this is a regular occupation of the forest tribes, with whom it may be supposed that the Khaire have some affinity. The Dhanoje are those who took to the occupation of tending *dhan*[3] or small stock, and they are probably an offshoot of the Dhangar or shepherd caste whose name is similarly derived. Like the Dhangar women they wear cocoanut-shell bangles, and the Mānwa Kunbis also do this; these bangles are not broken when a child is born, and hence the Dhanojes and Mānwas are looked down on by the other subcastes, who refuse to remove their leaf-plates after a feast. The name of the

---

[1] From *jihār*, a tree or shrub.

[2] *Acacia catechu*.

[3] *Dhan* properly means wealth, *cf.* the two meanings of the word stock in English.

Khedule subcaste may be derived from *kheda* a village, while another version given by Mr. Kitts[1] is that it signifies 'A beardless youth.' The highest subcaste in the Central Provinces are the Tirole or Tilole, who now claim to be Rājpūts. They say that their ancestors came from Therol in Rājputāna, and, taking to agriculture, gradually became merged with the Kunbis. Another more probable derivation of the name is from the *til* or sesamum plant. The families who held the hereditary office of Deshmukh, which conferred a considerable local position, were usually members of the Tirole subcaste, and they have now developed into a sort of aristocratic branch of the caste, and marry among themselves when matches can be arranged. They do not allow the remarriage of widows nor permit their women to accompany the wedding procession. The Wāndhekars are another group which also includes some Deshmukh families, and ranks next to the Tiroles in position. Mr. Kitts records a large number of subcastes in Berār.[2] Among them are some groups from northern India, as the Hindustāni, Pardesi, Dholewār, Jaiswār and Singrore; these are probably Kurmis who have settled in Berār and become amalgamated with the Kunbis. Similarly the Tailanges and Munurwārs appear to be an offshoot of the great Kāpu caste of cultivators in the Telugu country. The Wanjāri subcaste is a fairly large one and almost certainly represents a branch of the Banjāra caste of carriers, who have taken to agriculture and been promoted into the Kunbi community. The Lonhāre take their name from Lonār Mehkar, the well-known bitter lake of the Buldāna District, whose salt they may formerly have refined. The Ghātole are those who dwelt above the *ghāts* or passes of the Saihadri range to the south of the Berār plain. The Baone are an important subcaste both in Berār and the Central Provinces, and take their name from the phrase Bāwan Berār,[3] a term applied to the province by the Mughals because it paid fifty-two lakhs of revenue, as against only eight lakhs realised from the adjoining Jhādi or hill country in the Central Provinces. In Chhindwāra is found a small local

---

[1] *Berār Census Report* (1881), para. 180.
[2] *Ibidem.*
[3] *Bāwan* = fifty-two.

subcaste called Gādhao because they formerly kept donkeys, though they no longer do so; they are looked down on by the others who will not even take water from their hands. In Nimār is a group of Gujarāti Kunbis who are considered to have been originally Gūjars.[1] Their local subdivisions are Leve and Karwa and many of them are also known as Dālia, because they made the *dāl* or pulse of Burhānpur, which had a great reputation under native rule. It is said that it was formerly despatched daily to Sindhia's kitchen.

4. The cultivating status.

It appears then that a Kunbi has in the past been synonymous with a cultivator, and that large groups from other castes have taken to agriculture, have been admitted into the community and usually obtained a rise in rank. In many villages Kunbis are the only ryots, while below them are the village menials and artisans, several of whom perform functions at weddings or on other occasions denoting their recognition of the Kunbi as their master or employer; and beneath these again are the impure Mahārs or labourers. Thus at a Kunbi betrothal the services of the barber and washerman must be requisitioned; the barber washes the feet of the boy and girl and places vermilion on the foreheads of the guests. The washerman spreads a sheet on the ground on which the boy and girl sit. At the end of the ceremony the barber and washerman take the bride and bridegroom on their shoulders and dance to music in the marriage-shed; for this they receive small presents. After a death has occurred at a Kunbi's house the impurity is not removed until the barber and washerman have eaten in it. At a Kunbi's wedding the Gurao or village priest brings the leafy branches of five trees, the mango, *jāmun*,[2] *umar*[3] and two others and deposits them at Māroti's temple, whence they are removed by the parents of the bride. Before a wedding again a Kunbi bride must go to the potter's house and be seated on his wheel while it is turned round seven times for good luck. At seed-time and harvest all the village menials go to the cultivator's field and present him with a specimen of their wares or make obeisance to him, receiving in return a small present of

---

[1] *Bombay Gazetteer, Hindus of Gujarāt*, p. 490, App. B, Gūjar.

[2] *Eugenia jambolana*.
[3] *Ficus glomerata*.

grain. This state of things seems to represent the primitive form of Hindu society from which the present widely ramified system of castes may have expanded, and even now the outlines of the original structure may be discernible under all subsequent accretions.

5. Exogamous septs.

Each subcaste has a number of exogamous septs or clans which serve as a table of affinities in regulating marriage. The vernacular term for these is *kul*. Some of the septs are named after natural objects or animals, others from titles or nicknames borne by the reputed founder of the group, or from some other caste to which he may have belonged, while others again are derived from the names of villages which may be taken to have been the original home of the sept or clan. The following are some septs of the Tirole subcaste : Kole, jackal; Wānkhede, a village; Kadu, bitter; Jagthāp, famous; Kadam, a tree; Meghe, a cloud; Lohekari, a worker in iron; Ughde, a child who has been exposed at birth; Shinde, a palm-tree; Hagre, one who suffers from diarrhœa; Aglāwe, an incendiary; Kalamkār, a writer; Wāni (Bania), a caste; Sutār, a carpenter, and so on. A few of the groups of the Bāone subcaste are :—Kāntode, one with a torn ear; Dokarmāre, a killer of pigs; Lūte, a plunderer; Titarmāre, a pigeon-killer; and of the Khedule : Patre, a leaf-plate; Ghoremāre, one who killed a horse; Bāgmare, a tiger-slayer; Gadhe, a donkey; Burāde, one of the Burud or Basor caste; Nāktode, one with a broken nose, and so on. Each subcaste has a number of septs, a total of 66 being recorded for the Tiroles alone. The names of the septs confirm the hypothesis arrived at from a scrutiny of the subcastes that the Kunbis are largely recruited from the pre-Aryan or aboriginal tribes. Conclusions as to the origin of the caste can better be made in its home in Bombay, but it may be noted that in Canara, according to the accomplished author of *A Naturalist on the Prowl*,[1] the Kunbi is quite a primitive forest-dweller, who only a few years back lived by scattering his seed on patches of land burnt clear of vegetation, collecting myrobalans and other fruits, and snaring and trapping animals exactly like the Gonds and Baigas of the Central Provinces. Similarly in Nāsik it is stated that a large proportion of the Kunbi

[1] See the article entitled 'An Anthropoid.'

caste are probably derived from the primitive tribes.[1] Yet in the cultivated plains which he has so largely occupied, he is reckoned the equal in rank of the Kurmi and other cultivating castes of Hindustān, who in theory at any rate are of Aryan origin and of so high a grade of social purity that Brāhmans will take water from them. The only reasonable explanation of this rise in status appears to be that the Kunbi has taken possession of the land and has obtained the rank which from time immemorial belongs to the hereditary cultivator as a member and citizen of the village community. It is interesting to note that the Wanjāri Kunbis of Berār, who, being as already seen Banjāras, are of Rājpūt descent at any rate, now strenuously disclaim all connection with the Banjāra caste and regard their reception into the Kunbi community as a gain in status. At the same time the refusal of the Marātha Brāhmans to take water to drink from Kunbis may perhaps have been due to the recognition of their non-Aryan origin. Most of the Kunbis also eat fowls, which the cultivating castes of northern India would not usually do.

6. Restrictions on marriage of relatives. A man is forbidden to marry within his own sept or *kul*, or in that of his mother or either of his grandmothers. He may marry his wife's younger sister but not her elder sister. Alliances between first and second cousins are also prohibited except that a sister's son may be married to a brother's daughter. Such marriages are also favoured by the Marātha Brāhmans and other castes, and the suitability of the match is expressed in the saying *Ato ghari bhāsi sūn*, or 'At a sister's house her brother's daughter is a daughter-in-law.' The sister claims it as a right and not unfrequently there are quarrels if the brother decides to give his daughter to somebody else, while the general feeling is so strongly in favour of these marriages that the caste committee sometimes imposes a fine on fathers who wish to break through the rule. The fact that in this single case the marriage of near relatives is not only permitted but considered almost as an obligation, while in all other instances it is strictly prohibited, probably points to the conclusion that the custom is a survival of the matriarchate, when a brother's property would pass to his sister's son. Under such a law of inheritance

[1] *Bombay Gazetteer, Nāsik*, p. 26.

he would naturally desire that his heir should be united to his own daughter, and this union might gradually become customary and at length almost obligatory. The custom in this case may survive when the reasons which justified it have entirely vanished. And while formerly it was the brother who would have had reason to desire the match for his daughter, it is now the sister who insists on it for her son, the explanation being that among the Kunbis as with other agricultural castes, to whom a wife's labour is a valuable asset, girls are expensive and a considerable price has to be paid for a bride.

Girls are usually married between the ages of five and eleven and boys between ten and twenty. The Kunbis still think it a mark of social distinction to have their daughters married as young as possible. The recognised bride-price is about twenty rupees, but much larger sums are often paid. The boy's father goes in search of a girl to be married to his son, and when the bride-price has been settled and the match arranged the ceremony of Māngni or betrothal takes place. In the first place the boy's father proceeds to his future daughter-in-law's house, where he washes her feet, smears her forehead with red powder and gives her a present of a rupee and some sweetmeats. All the party then eat together. This is followed by a visit of the girl's father to the boy's house where a similar ceremony is enacted and the boy is presented with a cocoanut, a *pagri* and cloth, and a silver or gold ring. Again the boy's relatives go to the girl's house and give her more valuable presents of jewellery and clothing. A Brāhman is afterwards consulted to fix the date of the marriage, but the poorer Kunbis dispense with his services as he charges two or three rupees. Prior to the ceremony the bodies of the bride and bridegroom are well massaged with vegetable oil and turmeric in their respective houses, partly with a view to enhance their beauty and also perhaps to protect them during the trying period of the ceremony when maleficent spirits are particularly on the alert. The marriage-shed is made of eleven poles festooned with leaves, and inside it are placed two posts of the *sāleh* (*Boswellia serrata*) or *umar* (*Ficus glomerata*) tree, one longer than the other, to represent the bride and bridegroom. Two jars

7. Betrothal and marriage.

filled with water are set near the posts, and a small earthen platform called *baola* is made. The bridegroom wears a yellow or white dress, and has a triangular frame of bamboo covered with tinsel over his forehead, which is known as *bāsing* and is a substitute for the *maur* or marriage-crown of the Hindustāni castes. Over his shoulder he carries a pick-axe as the representative implement of husbandry with one or two wheaten cakes tied to it. This is placed on the top of the marriage-shed and at the end of the five days' ceremonies the members of the families eat the dried cakes with milk, no outsider being allowed to participate. The *barāt* or wedding procession sets out for the bride's village, the women of the bridegroom's family accompanying it except among the Tirole Kunbis, who forbid the practice in order to demonstrate their higher social position. It is received on the border of the girl's village by her father and his friends and relatives, and conducted to the *janwāsa* or temporary lodging prepared for it, with the exception of the bridegroom, who is left alone before the shrine of Māroti or Hanumān. The bridegroom's father goes to the marriage-shed where he washes the bride's feet and gives her another present of clothes, and her relatives then proceed to Māroti's temple where they worship and make offerings, and return bringing the bridegroom with them. As he arrives at the marriage pavilion he touches it with a stick, on which the bride's brother who is seated above the shed pours down some water and is given a present of money by the bridegroom. The bridegroom's feet are then washed by his father-in-law and he is given a yellow cloth which he wears. The couple are made to stand on two wooden planks opposite each other with a curtain between them, the bridegroom facing east and the bride west, holding some Akshata or rice covered with saffron in their hands. As the sun sets the officiating Brāhman gets on to the roof of the house and repeats the marriage texts from there. At his signal the couple throw the rice over each other, the curtain between them is withdrawn, and they change their seats. The assembled party applaud and the marriage proper is over. The Brāhman marks their foreheads with rice and turmeric and presses them together. He then seats them on the earthen platform or *baola*, and ties their clothes together, this being known as the Brahma Gānthi or Brāhman's knot. The wedding usually takes place on the day after the arrival of the marriage procession and another two days are consumed in feasting and worshipping the deities. When the bride and bridegroom return home after the wedding one of the party waves a pot of water round their heads and throws it away at a little distance on the ground, and after this some grain in the same manner. This is a provision of food and drink to any evil spirits who may be hovering round the couple, so that they may stop to consume it and refrain from entering the house. The expenses of the bride's family may vary from Rs. 60 to Rs. 100 and those of the bridegroom's from Rs. 160 to Rs. 600. A wedding carried out on a lavish scale by a well-to-do man is known as Lāl Biāh or a red marriage, but when the parties are poor the expenses are curtailed and it is then called Safed Biāh or a white marriage. In this case the bridegroom's mother does not accompany the wedding procession and the proceedings last only two days. The bride goes back with the wedding procession for a few days to her husband's house and then returns home. When she arrives at maturity her parents give a feast to the caste and send her to her husband's house, this occasion being known as Bolvan (the calling). The Karwa Kunbis of Nimār have a peculiar rule for the celebration of marriages. They have a *guru* or priest in Gujarāt who sends them a notice once in every ten or twelve years, and in this year only marriages can be performed. It is called *Singhast ki sāl* and is the year in which the planet Guru (Jupiter) comes into conjunction with the constellation Sinh (Leo). But the Karwas themselves think that there is a large temple in Gujarāt with a locked door to which there is no key. But once in ten or twelve years the door unlocks of itself, and in that year their marriages are celebrated. A certain day is fixed and all the weddings are held on it together. On this occasion children from infants in arms to ten or twelve years are married, and if a match cannot be arranged for them they will have to wait another ten or twelve years. A girl child who is born on the day fixed for weddings may, however, be married twelve days afterwards, the twelfth night being called Māndo Rāt, and on this occasion any other weddings which may have been unavoidably postponed owing to a death or illness in the families may also be completed. The rule affords a loophole of escape for the victims of any such *contretemps* and also insures that every girl shall be married before she is fully twelve years old. Rather than not marry their daughter in the *Singhast ki sāl* before she is twelve the parents will accept any bridegroom, even though he be very poor or younger than the bride. This is the same year in which the celebration of marriages is forbidden among the Hindus generally. The other Kunbis have the general Hindu rule that weddings are forbidden during the four months from the 11th Asārh Sudi (June) to the 11th Kārtik Sudi (October). This is the period of the rains, when the crops are growing and the gods are said to go to sleep, and it is observed more or less as a time of abstinence and fasting. The Hindus should properly abstain from eating sugarcane, brinjals, onions, garlic and other vegetables for the whole four months. On the 12th of Kārtik the marriage of Tulsi or the basil plant with the Sāligrām or ammonite representing Vishnu is performed and all these vegetables are offered to her and afterwards generally consumed. Two days afterwards, beginning from the 14th of Kārtik, comes the Diwāli festival. In Betūl the bridal couple are seated in the centre of a square made of four plough yokes, while a leaf of the pīpal tree and a piece of turmeric are tied by a string round both their wrists. The untying of the string by the local Brāhman constitutes the essential and binding portion of the marriage. Among the Lonhāre subcaste a curious ceremony is performed after the wedding. A swing is made, and a round pestle, which is supposed to represent a child, is placed on it and swung to and fro. It is then taken off and placed in the lap of the bride, and the effect of performing this symbolical ceremony is supposed to be that she will soon become a mother.

8. Polygamy and divorce.

Polygamy is permitted but rarely practised, a second wife being only taken if the first be childless or of bad character, or destitute of attractions. Divorce is allowed, but in some localities at any rate a divorced woman cannot marry again unless she is permitted to do so in writing by her first husband. If a girl be seduced before marriage a fine is imposed on both parties and they are readmitted to social intercourse, but are not married to each other. Curiously enough, in the Tirole and Wāndhekar, the highest subcastes, the keeping of a woman is not an offence entailing temporary exclusion from caste, whereas among the lower subcastes it is.[1]

The Kunbis permit the remarriage of widows, with the exception of the Deshmukh families of the Tirole subcaste who have forbidden it. If a woman's husband dies she returns to her father's house and he arranges her second marriage, which is called *choli-pātal*, or giving her new clothes. He takes a price for her which may vary from twenty-five to five hundred rupees according to the age and attractions of the woman. A widow may marry any one outside the family of her deceased husband, but she may not marry his younger brother. This union, which among the Hindustāni castes is looked upon as most suitable if not obligatory, is strictly forbidden among the Marātha castes, the reason assigned being that a wife stands in the position of a mother to her husband's younger brothers. The contrast is curious. The ceremony of widow-marriage is largely governed by the idea of escaping or placating the wrath of the first husband's ghost, and also of its being something to be ashamed of and contrary to orthodox Hinduism. It always takes place in the dark fortnight of the month and always at night. Sometimes no women are present, and if any do attend they must be widows, as it would be the worst of omens for a married woman or unmarried girl to witness the ceremony. This, it is thought, would lead to her shortly becoming a widow herself. The bridegroom goes to the widow's house with his male friends and two wooden seats are set side by side. On one of these a betel-nut is placed which represents the deceased husband of the widow. The new bridegroom advances with a small wooden sword, touches the nut with its tip, and then kicks it off the seat with his right toe. The barber picks up the nut and burns it. This is supposed to lay the deceased husband's spirit and prevent his interference with the new union.

9. Widow-marriage.

---

[1] This is the rule in the Nāgpur District.

The bridegroom then takes the seat from which the nut has been displaced and the woman sits on the other side to his left. He puts a necklace of beads round her neck and the couple leave the house in a stealthy fashion and go to the husband's village. It is considered unlucky to see them as they go away because the second husband is regarded in the light of a robber. Sometimes they stop by a stream on the way home, and, taking off the woman's clothes and bangles, bury them by the side of the stream. An exorcist may also be called in, who will confine the late husband's spirit in a horn by putting in some grains of wheat, and after sealing up the horn deposit it with the clothes. When a widower or widow marries a second time and is afterwards attacked by illness, it is ascribed to the illwill of their former partner's spirit. The metal image of the first husband or wife is then made and worn as an amulet on the arm or round the neck. A bachelor who wishes to marry a widow must first go through a mock ceremony with an *ākra* or swallow-wort plant, as the widow-marriage is not considered a real one, and it is inauspicious for any one to die without having been properly married once. A similar ceremony must be gone through when a man is married for the third time, as it is held that if he marries a woman for the third time he will quickly die. The *ākra* or swallow-wort (*Calotropis gigantea*) is a very common plant growing on waste land with mauve or purple flowers. When cut or broken a copious milky juice exudes from the stem, and in some places parents are said to poison children whom they do not desire to keep alive by rubbing this on their lips.

10. Customs at birth.

During her monthly impurity a woman stays apart and may not cook for herself nor touch anybody nor sleep on a bed made of cotton thread. As soon as she is in this condition she will untie the cotton threads confining her hair and throw them away, letting her hair hang down. This is because they have become impure. But if there is no other woman in the house and she must continue to do the household work herself, she does not throw them away until the last day.[1] Similarly she must not sleep on

---

[1] From a note by Mr. A. K. Smith, C.S.

a cotton sheet or mattress during this time because she would defile it, but she may sleep on a woollen blanket as wool is a holy material and is not defiled. At the end of the period she proceeds to a stream and purifies herself by bathing and washing her head with earth. When a woman is with child for the first time her women friends come and give her new green clothes and bangles in the seventh month; they then put her into a swing and sing songs. While she is pregnant she is made to work in the house so as not to be inactive. After the birth of a child the mother remains impure for twelve days. A woman of the Māng or Mahār caste acts as midwife, and always breaks her bangles and puts on new ones after she has assisted at a birth. If delivery is prolonged the woman is given hot water and sugar or camphor wrapped in a betel-leaf, or they put a few grains of gram into her hand and then someone takes and feeds them to a mare, as it is thought that the woman's pregnancy has been prolonged by her having walked behind the tethering-ropes of a mare, which is twelve months in foal. Or she is given water to drink in which a Sulaimāni onyx or a rupee of Akbar's time has been washed; in the former case the idea is perhaps that a passage will be made for the child like the hole through the bead, while the virtue of the rupee probably consists in its being a silver coin and having the image or device of a powerful king like Akbar. Or it may be thought that as the coin has passed from hand to hand for so long, it will facilitate the passage of the child from the womb. A pregnant woman must not look on a dead body or her child may be still-born, and she must not see an eclipse or the child may be born maimed. Some believe that if a child is born during an eclipse it will suffer from lung-disease; so they make a silver model of the moon while the eclipse lasts and hang it round the child's neck as a charm. Sometimes when delivery is delayed they take a folded flower and place it in a pot of water and believe that as its petals unfold so the womb will be opened and the child born; or they seat the woman on a wooden bench and pour oil on her head, her forehead being afterwards rubbed with it in the belief that as the oil falls so the child will be born. If a child is a long time before learning to speak they give it leaves of the pīpal tree to eat, because the leaves of this tree make a noise by rustling in the wind; or a root which is very light in weight, because they think that the tongue is heavy and the quality of lightness will thus be communicated to it. Or the mother, when she has kneaded dough and washed her hands afterwards, will pour a drop or two of the water down the child's throat. And the water which made her hands clean and smooth will similarly clear the child's throat of the obstruction which prevented it from speaking. If a child's neck is weak and its head rolls about they make it look at a crow perching on the house and think this will make its neck strong like the crow's. If he cannot walk they make a little triangle on wheels with a pole called *ghurghuri*, and make him walk holding on to the pole. The first teeth of the child are thrown on to the roof of the house, because the rats, who have especially good and sharp teeth, live there, and it is hoped that the child's second teeth may grow like theirs. A few grains of rice are also thrown so that the teeth may be hard and pointed like the rice; the same word, *kani*, being used for the end of a grain of rice and the tip of a tooth. Or the teeth are placed under a water-pot in the hope that the child's second teeth may grow as fast as the grass does under water-pots. If a child is lean some people take it to a place where asses have lain down and rolled in ashes; they roll the child in the ashes similarly and believe that it will get fat like the asses are. Or they may lay the child in a pigsty with the same idea. People who want to injure a child get hold of its coat and lay it out in the sun to dry, in the belief that the child's body will dry up in a similar manner. In order to avert the evil eye they burn some turmeric and juāri flour and hold the newly-born child in the smoke. It is also branded on the stomach with a burning piece of turmeric, perhaps to keep off cold. For the first day or two after birth a child is given cow's milk mixed with water or honey and a little castor oil, and after this it is suckled by the mother. But if she is unable to nourish it a wet-nurse is called in, who may be a woman of low caste or even a Muhammadan. The mother is given no regular food for the first two days, but only some sugar and spices. Until the child is six months old its head and body are oiled every second or third day and the body is well hand-rubbed and bathed. The rubbing is meant to make the limbs supple and the oil to render the child less susceptible to cold. If a child when sitting soon after birth looks down through its legs they think it is looking for its companions whom it has left behind and that more children will be born. It is considered a bad sign if a child bites its upper teeth on its underlip; this is thought to prognosticate illness and the child is prevented from doing so as far as possible.

On the sixth day after birth they believe that Chhathi or Satwai Devi, the Sixth-day Goddess, comes at midnight and writes on the child's forehead its fate in life, which writing, it is said, may be seen on a man's skull when the flesh has come off it after death. On this night the women of the family stay awake all night singing songs and eating sweetmeats. A picture of the goddess is drawn with turmeric and vermilion over the mother's bed. The door of the birth-room is left open, and at midnight she comes. Sometimes a Sunār is employed to make a small image of Chhathi Devi, for which he is paid Rs. 1-4, and it is hung round the child's neck. On this day the mother is given to eat all kinds of grain, and among flesh-eating castes the soup of fish and meat, because it is thought that every kind of food which the mother eats this day will be easily digested by the child throughout its life. On this day the mother is given a second bath, the first being on the day of the birth, and she must not bathe in between. Sometimes after childbirth a woman buys several bottles of liquor and has a bath in it; the stimulating effect of the spirit is supposed to remedy the distension of the body caused by the birth. If the child is a boy it is named on the twelfth and if a girl on the thirteenth day. On the twelfth day the mother's bangles are thrown away and new ones put on. The Kunbis are very kind to their children, and never harsh or quick-tempered, but this may perhaps be partly due to their constitutional lethargy. They seldom refuse a child anything, but taking advantage of its innocence will by dissimulation make it

11. Sixth- and twelfth-day ceremonies

12. Devices for procuring children.

forget what it wanted. The time arrives when this course of conduct is useless, and then the child learns to mistrust the word of its parents. Minute quantities of opium are generally administered to children as a narcotic.

If a woman is barren and has no children one of the remedies prescribed by the Sarodis or wandering soothsayers is that she should set fire to somebody's house, going alone and at night to perform the deed. So long as some small part of the house is burnt it does not matter if the fire be extinguished, but the woman should not give the alarm herself. It is supposed that the spirit of some insect which is burnt will enter her womb and be born as a child. Perhaps she sets fire to someone else's house so as to obtain the spirit of one of the family's dead children, which may be supposed to have entered the insects dwelling on the house. Some years ago at Bhāndak in Chānda complaints were made of houses being set on fire. The police officer[1] sent to investigate found that other small fires continued to occur. He searched the roofs of the houses, and on two or three found little smouldering balls of rolled-up cloth. Knowing of the superstition he called all the childless married women of the place together and admonished them severely, and the fires stopped. On another occasion the same officer's wife was ill, and his little son, having fever, was sent daily to the dispensary for medicine in charge of a maid. One morning he noticed on one of the soles of the boy's feet a stain of the juice of the *bhilawa*[2] or marking-nut tree, which raises blisters on the skin. On looking at the other foot he found six similar marks, and on inquiry he learned that these were made by a childless woman in the expectation that the boy would soon die and be born again as her child. The boy suffered no harm, but his mother, being in bad health, nearly died of shock on learning of the magic practised against her son.

Another device is to make a *pradakshana* or pilgrimage round a pīpal tree, going naked at midnight after worshipping Māroti or Hanumān, and holding a necklace of *tulsi* beads in the hand. The pīpal is of course a sacred tree, and is the abode of Brahma, the original creator of the world.

[1] Circle Inspector Ganesh Prasād.   [2] *Semicarpus anacardium*.

Brahma has no consort, and it is believed that while all other trees are both male and female the pīpal is only male, and is capable of impregnating a woman and rendering her fertile. A variation of this belief is that pīpal trees are inhabited by the spirits of unmarried Brāhman boys, and hence a woman sometimes takes a piece of new thread and winds it round the tree, perhaps with the idea of investing the spirit of the boy with the sacred thread. She will then walk round the tree as a symbol of the wedding ceremony of walking round the sacred post, and hopes that the boy, being thus brought to man's estate and married, will cause her to bear a son. But modest women do not go naked round the tree. The Amāwas or New Moon day, if it falls on a Monday, is specially observed by married women. On this day they will walk 108 times round a pīpal tree, and then give 108 mangoes or other fruits to a Brāhman, choosing a different fruit every time. The number 108 means a hundred and a little more to show there is no stint, 'Full measure and flowing over,' like the customary present of Rs. 1-4 instead of a rupee. This is also no doubt a birth-charm, fruit being given so that the woman may become fruitful. Or a childless woman will pray to Hanumān or Mahābīr. Every morning she will go to his shrine with an offering of fruit or flowers, and every evening will set a lamp burning there; and morning and evening, prostrating herself, she makes her continuous prayer to the god: '*Oh, Mahābīr, Mahārāj! hamko ek batcha do, sirf ek batcha do.*'[1] Then, after many days, Mahābīr, as might be anticipated, appears to her in a dream and promises her a child. It does not seem that they believe that Mahābīr himself directly renders the woman fertile, because similar prayers are made to the River Nerbudda, a goddess. But perhaps he, being the god of strength, lends virile power to her husband. Another prescription is to go to the burying-ground, and, after worshipping it, to take some of the bone-ash of a burnt corpse and wear this wrapped up in an amulet on the body. Occasionally, if a woman can get no children she will go to the father of a large family and let him beget a child upon her, with or without the connivance of her husband. But only the more immodest women do this. Or

---

[1] 'Oh, Lord Mahābīr, give me a child, only one child.'

she cuts a piece off the breast-cloth of a woman who has children, and, after burning incense on it, wears it as an amulet. For a stronger charm she will take a piece of such a woman's cloth and a lock of her hair and some earth which her feet have pressed and bury these in a pot before Devi's shrine, sometimes fashioning an image of the woman out of them. Then, as they rot away, the child-bearing power of the fertile woman will be transferred to her. If a woman's first children have died and she wishes to preserve a later one, she sometimes weighs the child against sugar or copper and distributes the amount in charity. Or she gives the child a bad name, such as Dagharia (a stone), Kachria (sweepings), Ukandia (a dunghill).

13. Love charms.

If a woman's husband is not in love with her, a prescription of a *Mohani* or love-charm given by the wise women is that she should kill an owl and serve some of its flesh to her husband as a charm. "It has not occurred," Mr. Kipling writes, "to the oriental jester to speak of a boiled owl in connection with intoxication, but when a husband is abjectly submissive to his wife her friends say that she has given him boiled owl's flesh to eat."[1] If a man is in love with some woman and wishes to kindle a similar sentiment in her the following method is given: On a Saturday night he should go to a graveyard and call out, 'I am giving a dinner to-morrow night, and I invite you all to attend.' Then on the Sunday night he takes cocoanuts, sweetmeats, liquor and flowers to the cemetery and sets them all out, and all the spirits or Shaitāns come and partake. The host chooses a particularly big Shaitān and calls to him to come near and says to him, 'Will you go with me and do what I ask you.' If the spirit assents he follows the man home. Next night the man again offers cocoanuts and incense to the Shaitān, whom he can see by night but not by day, and tells him to go to the woman's house and call her. Then the spirit goes and troubles her heart, so that she falls in love with the man and has no rest till she goes to him. If the man afterwards gets tired of her he will again secretly worship and call up the Shaitān and order him to turn the woman's inclination

[1] *Beast and Man in India*, p. 44. But, according to the same writer, the Hindus do say, 'Drunk as an owl' and also 'Stupid as an owl.'

away. Another method is to fetch a skull from a graveyard and go to a banyan tree at midnight. There, divesting himself of his clothes, the operator partially cooks some rice in the skull, and then throws it against the tree; he gathers all the grains that stick to the trunk in one box and those that fall to the ground in another box, and the first rice given to the woman to eat will turn her inclination towards him, while the second will turn it away from him. This is a sympathetic charm, the rice which sticks to the tree having the property of attracting the woman.

The Kunbis either bury or burn the dead. In Berār sepulture is the more common method of disposal, perhaps in imitation of the Muhammadans. Here the village has usually a field set apart for the disposal of corpses, which is known as Smashān. Hindus fill up the earth practically level with the ground after burial and erect no monument, so that after a few years another corpse can be buried in the same place. When a Kunbi dies the body is washed in warm water and placed on a bier made of bamboos, with a network of *san*-hemp.[1] Ordinary rope must not be used. The mourners then take it to the grave, scattering almonds, sandalwood, dates, betel-leaf and small coins as they go. These are picked up by the menial Mahārs or labourers. Halfway to the grave the corpse is set down and the bearers change their positions, those behind going in front. Here a little wheat and pulse which have been tied in the cloth covering the corpse are left by the way. On the journey to the grave the body is covered with a new unwashed cloth. The grave is dug three or four feet deep, and the corpse is buried naked, lying on its back with the head to the south. After the burial one of the mourners is sent to get an earthen pot from the Kumhār; this is filled with water at a river or stream, and a small piece is broken out of it with a stone; one of the mourners then takes the pot and walks round the corpse with it, dropping a stream of water all the way. Having done this, he throws the pot behind him over his shoulder without looking round, and then all the mourners go home without looking behind them. The stone with which the hole has been made in the earthen pot is held to represent

14. Disposal of the dead.

---

[1] *Crotalaria juncea.*

the spirit of the deceased. It is placed under a tree or on the bank of a stream, and for ten days the mourners come and offer it *pindas* or balls of rice, one ball being offered on the first day, two on the second, and so on, up to ten on the tenth. On this last day a little mound of earth is made, which is considered to represent Mahādeo. Four miniature flags are planted round, and three cakes of rice are laid on it; and all the mourners sit round the mound until a crow comes and eats some of the cake. Then they say that the dead man's spirit has been freed from troubling about his household and mundane affairs and has departed to the other world. But if no real crow comes to eat the cake, they make a representation of one out of the sacred *kusha* grass, and touch the cake with it and consider that a crow has eaten it. After this the mourners go to a stream and put a little cow's urine on their bodies, and dip ten times in the water or throw it over them. The officiating Brāhman sprinkles them with holy water in which he has dipped the toe of his right foot, and they present to the Brāhman the vessels in which the funeral cakes have been cooked and the clothes which the chief mourner has worn for ten days. On coming home they also give him a stick, umbrella, shoes, a bed and anything else which they think the dead man will want in the next world. On the thirteenth day they feed the caste-fellows and the head of the caste ties a new *pagri* on the chief mourner's head backside foremost; and the chief mourner breaking an areca-nut on the threshold places it in his mouth and spits it out of the door, signifying the final ejectment of the deceased's spirit from the house. Finally, the chief mourner goes to worship at Māroti's shrine, and the household resumes its ordinary life. The different relatives of the deceased man usually invite the bereaved family to their house for a day and give them a feast, and if they have many relations this may go on for a considerable time. The complete procedure as detailed above is observed only in the case of the head of the household, and for less important members is considerably abbreviated. The position of chief mourner is occupied by a man's eldest son, or in the absence of sons by his younger brother, or failing him by the eldest son of an elder brother, or failing male relations by the widow. The chief mourner is considered to have a special claim to the property. He has the whole of his head and face shaved, and the hair is tied up in a corner of the grave-cloth. If the widow is chief mourner a small lock of her hair is cut off and tied up in the cloth. When the corpse is being carried out for burial the widow breaks her *mangalsūtram* or marriage necklace, and wipes off the *kunku* or vermilion from her forehead. This necklace consists of a string of black glass beads with a piece of gold, and is always placed on the bride's neck at the wedding. The widow does not break her glass bangles at all, but on the eleventh day changes them for new ones.

The period of mourning for adults of the family is ten days, and for children three, while in the case of distant relatives it is sufficient to take a bath as a mark of respect for them. The male mourners shave their heads, the walls of the house are whitewashed and the floor spread with cow-dung. The chief mourner avoids social intercourse and abstains from ordinary work and from all kinds of amusements. He debars himself from such luxuries as betel-leaf and from visiting his wife. Oblations are offered to the dead on the third day of the light fortnight of Baisākh (June) and on the last day of Bhādrapad (September). The Kunbi is a firm believer in the action of ghosts and spirits, and never omits the attentions due to his ancestors. On the appointed day he diligently calls on the crows, who represent the spirits of ancestors, to come and eat the food which he places ready for them ; and if no crow turns up, he is disturbed at having incurred the displeasure of the dead. He changes the food and goes on calling until a crow comes, and then concludes that their previous failure to appear was due to the fact that his ancestors were not pleased with the kind of food he first offered. In future years, therefore, he changes it, and puts out that which was eaten, until a similar *contretemps* of the non-appearance of crows again occurs. The belief that the spirits of the dead pass into crows is no doubt connected with that of the crow's longevity. Many Hindus think that a crow lives a thousand years, and others that it never dies of disease, but only when killed by violence. Tennyson's 'many-wintered crow' may indicate some similar

15. Mourning.

idea in Europe. Similarly if the Gonds find a crow's nest they give the nestlings to young children to eat, and think that this will make them long-lived. If a crow perches in the house when a woman's husband or other relative is away, she says, ' Fly away, crow; fly away and I will feed you'; and if the crow then flies away she thinks that the absent one will return. Here the idea is no doubt that if he had been killed his spirit might have come home in the shape of the crow perching on the house. If a married woman sees two crows breeding it is considered a very bad omen, the effect being that her husband will soon die. It is probably supposed that his spirit will pass into the young crow which is born as a result of the meeting which she has seen.

Mr. A. K. Smith states that the omen applies to men also, and relates a story of a young advocate who saw two crows thus engaged on alighting from the train at some station. In order to avert the consequences he ran to the telegraph office and sent messages to all his relatives and friends announcing his own death, the idea being that this fictitious death would fulfil the omen, and the real death would thus become unnecessary. In this case the belief would be that the man's own spirit would pass into the young crow.

16. Religion. The principal deities of the caste are Māroti or Hanumān, Mahādeo or Siva, Devi, Satwai and Khandoba. Māroti is worshipped principally on Saturdays, so that he may counteract the evil influences exercised by the planet Saturn on that day. When a new village is founded Māroti must first be brought and placed in the village and worshipped, and after this houses are built. The name Māroti is derived from Marut, the Vedic god of the wind, and he is considered to be the son of Vāyu, the wind, and Anjini. Khandoba is an incarnation of Siva as a warrior, and is the favourite deity of the Marāthas. Devi is usually venerated in her incarnation of Marhai Māta, the goddess of smallpox and cholera—the most dreaded scourges of the Hindu villager. They offer goats and fowls to Marhai Devi, cutting the throat of the animal and letting its blood drop over the stone, which represents the goddess; after this they cut off a leg and hang it to the tree above her shrine, and eat the

remainder. Sometimes also they offer wooden images of human beings, which are buried before the shrine of the goddess and are obviously substitutes for a human sacrifice; and the lower castes offer pigs. If a man dies of snake-bite they make a little silver image of a snake, and then kill a real snake, and make a platform outside the village and place the image on it, which is afterwards regularly worshipped as Nāgoba Deo. They may perhaps think that the spirit of the snake which is killed passes into the silver image. Somebody afterwards steals the image, but this does not matter. Similarly if a man is killed by a tiger he is deified and worshipped as Bāghoba Deo, though they cannot kill a tiger as a preliminary. The Kunbis make images of their ancestors in silver or brass, and keep them in a basket with their other household deities. But when these get too numerous they take them on a pilgrimage to some sacred river and deposit them in it. A man who has lost both parents will invite some man and woman on Akshaya Tritiya,[1] and call them by the names of his parents, and give them a feast. Among the mythological stories known to the caste is one of some interest, explaining how the dark spots came on the face of the moon. They say that once all the gods were going to a dinner-party, each riding on his favourite animal or *vāhan* (conveyance). But the *vāhan* of Ganpati, the fat god with the head of an elephant, was a rat, and the rat naturally could not go as fast as the other animals, and as it was very far from being up to Ganpati's weight, it tripped and fell, and Ganpati came off. The moon was looking on, and laughed so much that Ganpati was enraged, and cursed it, saying, ' Thy face shall be black for laughing at me.' Accordingly the moon turned quite black; but the other gods interfered, and said that the curse was too hard, so Ganpati agreed that only a part of the moon's face should be blackened in revenge for the insult. This happened on the fourth day of the bright fortnight of Bhādon (September), and on that day it is said that nobody should look at the moon, as if he does, his reputation will probably be lowered by some false charge or

---

[1] The 3rd Baisākh (May) Sudi, the commencement of the agricultural year. The name means, ' The day of immortality.'

libel being promulgated against him. As already stated, the Kunbi firmly believes in the influence exercised by spirits, and a proverb has it, 'Brāhmans die of indigestion, Sunārs from bile, and Kunbis from ghosts'; because the Brāhman is always feasted as an act of charity and given the best food, so that he over-eats himself, while the Sunār gets bilious from sitting all day before a furnace. When somebody falls ill his family get a Brāhman's cast-off sacred thread, and folding it to hold a little lamp, will wave this to and fro. If it moves in a straight line they say that the patient is possessed by a spirit, but if in a circle that his illness is due to natural causes. In the former case they promise an offering to the spirit to induce it to depart from the patient. The Brāhmans, it is said, try to prevent the Kunbis from getting hold of their sacred threads, because they think that by waving the lamp in them, all the virtue which they have obtained by their repetitions of the Gāyatri or sacred prayer is transferred to the sick Kunbi. They therefore tear up their cast-off threads or sew them into clothes.

17. The Pola festival.

The principal festival of the Kunbis is the Pola, falling at about the middle of the rainy season, when they have a procession of plough-bullocks. An old bullock goes first, and on his horns is tied the *makhar*, a wooden frame with pegs to which torches are affixed. They make a rope of mango-leaves stretched between two posts, and the *makhar* bullock is made to break this and stampede back to the village, followed by all the other cattle. It is said that the *makhar* bullock will die within three years. Behind him come the bullocks of the proprietors and then those of the tenants in the order, not so much of their wealth, but of their standing in the village and of the traditional position held by their families. A Kunbi feels it very bitterly if he is not given what he considers to be his proper rank in this procession. It has often been remarked that the feudal feeling of reverence for hereditary rights and position is as strong among the Marātha people as anywhere in the world.

18. Muhammadan tendencies of Berār Kunbis.

In Wardha and Berār the customs of the Kunbis show in several respects the influence of Islām, due no doubt to the long period of Muhammadan dominance in the country. To this may perhaps be attributed the prevalence of burial

FIGURES OF ANIMALS MADE FOR POLA FESTIVAL.

Bemrose, Colio., Derby.

of the dead instead of cremation, the more respectable method according to Hindu ideas. The Dhanoje Kunbis commonly revere Dāwal Mālik, a Muhammadan saint, whose tomb is at Uprai in Amraoti District. An *urus* or fair is held here on Thursdays, the day commonly sacred to Muhammadan saints, and on this account the Kunbis will not be shaved on Thursdays. They also make vows of mendicancy at the Muharram festival, and go round begging for rice and pulse ; they give a little of what they obtain to Muhammadan beggars and eat the rest. At the Muharram they tie a red thread on their necks and dance round the *alāwa*, a small hole in which fire is kindled in front of the *tāzias* or tombs of Hussain. At the Muharram [1] they also carry horseshoes of silver or gilt tinsel on the top of a stick decorated with peacock's feathers. The horseshoe is a model of that of the horse of Hussain. The men who carry these horseshoes are supposed to be possessed by the spirit of the saint, and people make prayers to them for anything they want. If one of the horseshoes is dropped the finder will keep it in his house, and next year if he feels that the spirit moves him will carry it himself. In Wardha the Kunbis worship Khwāja Sheikh Farīd of Girar, and occasionally Sheikh Farīd appears to a Kunbi in a dream and places him under a vow. Then he and all his household make little imitation beggars' wallets of cloth and dye them with red ochre, and little hoes on the model of those which saises use to drag out horses' dung, this hoe being the badge of Sheikh Farīd. Then they go round begging to all the houses in the village, saying, ' *Dam*,[2] *Sāhib, dam.*' With the alms given them they make cakes of *malīda*, wheat, sugar and butter, and give them to the priest of the shrine. Sometimes Sheikh Farīd tells the Kunbi in the dream that he must buy a goat of a certain Dhangar (shepherd), naming the price, while the Dhangar is similarly warned to sell it at the same price, and the goat is then purchased and sacrificed without any haggling. At the end of the sacrifice the priest releases the Kunbi from his vow, and he must then shave the whole of his head and distribute liquor to the caste-fellows in order to

---

[1] Furnished by Inspector Ganesh Prasād.
[2] *Dam* : breath or life.

be received back into the community. The water of the well at Sheikh Farīd's shrine at Girar is considered to preserve the crops against insects, and for this purpose it is carried to considerable distances to be sprinkled on them.

19. Villages and houses.

An ordinary Kunbi village[1] contains between 70 and 80 houses or some 400 souls. The village generally lies on a slight eminence near a *nullah* or stream, and is often nicely planted with tamarind or pīpal trees. The houses are now generally tiled for fear of fire, and their red roofs may be seen from a distance forming a little cluster on high-lying ground, an elevated site being selected so as to keep the roads fairly dry, as the surface tracks in black-soil country become almost impassable sloughs of mud as soon as the rains have broken. The better houses stand round an old mud fort, a relic of the Pindāri raids, when, on the first alarm of the approach of these marauding bands, the whole population hurried within its walls. The village proprietor's house is now often built inside the fort. It is an oblong building surrounded by a compound wall of unbaked bricks, and with a gateway through which a cart can drive. Adjoining the entrance on each side are rooms for the reception of guests, in which constables, chuprāssies and others are lodged when they stay at night in the village. *Kothas* or sheds for keeping cattle and grain stand against the walls, and the dwelling-house is at the back. Substantial tenants have a house like the proprietor's, of well-laid mud, whitewashed and with tiled roof; but the ordinary cultivator's house is one-roomed, with an *angan* or small yard in front and a little space for a garden behind, in which vegetables are grown during the rains. The walls are of bamboo matting plastered over with mud. The married couples sleep inside, the room being partitioned off if there are two or more in the family, and the older persons sleep in the verandahs. In the middle of the village by the biggest temple will be an old pīpal tree, the trunk encircled by an earthen or stone platform, which answers to the village club. The respectable inhabitants will meet here while the lower classes go to the liquor-shop nearly every

---

[1] These paragraphs are largely based on a description of a Wardha village by Mr. A. K. Smith, C.S.

HINDU BOYS ON STILTS.

night to smoke and chat. The blacksmith's and carpenter's shops are also places of common resort for the cultivators. Hither they wend in the morning and evening, often taking with them some implement which has to be mended, and stay to talk. The blacksmith in particular is said to be a great gossip, and will often waste much of his customer's time, plying him for news and retailing it, before he repairs and hands back the tool brought to him. The village is sure to contain two or three little temples of Māroti or Mahādeo. The stones which do duty for the images are daily oiled with butter or *ghī*, and a miscellaneous store of offerings will accumulate round the buildings. Outside the village will be a temple of Devi or Māta Mai (Smallpox Goddess) with a heap of little earthen horses and a string of hens' feet and feathers hung up on the wall. The little platforms which are the shrines of the other village gods will be found in the fields or near groves. In the evening the elders often meet at Māroti's temple and pay their respects to the deity, bowing or prostrating themselves before him. A lamp before the temple is fed by contributions of oil from the women, and is kept burning usually up to midnight. Once a year in the month of Shrāwan (July) the villagers subscribe and have a feast, the Kunbis eating first and the menial and labouring castes after them. In this month also all the village deities are worshipped by the Joshi or priest and the villagers. In summer the cultivators usually live in their fields, where they erect temporary sheds of bamboo matting roofed with juāri stalks. In these most of the household furniture is stored, while at a little distance in another funnel-shaped erection of bamboo matting is kept the owner's grain. This system of camping out is mainly adopted for fear of fire in the village, when the cultivator's whole stock of grain and his household goods might be destroyed in a few minutes without possibility of saving them. The women stay in the village, and the men and boys go there for their midday and evening meals.

Ordinary cultivators have earthen pots for cooking purposes and brass ones for eating from, while the well-to-do have all their vessels of brass. The furniture consists of a few stools and cots. No Kunbi will lie on the ground,

20. Furniture.

probably because a dying man is always laid on the ground to breathe his last; and so every one has a cot consisting of a wooden frame with a bed made of hempen string or of the root-fibres of the *palās* tree (*Butea frondosa*). These cots are always too short for a man to lie on them at full length, and are in consequence supremely uncomfortable. The reason may perhaps be found in the belief that a man should always lie on a bed a little shorter than himself so that his feet project over the end. Because if the bed is longer than he is, it resembles a bier, and if he lies on a bier once he may soon die and lie on it a second time. For bathing they make a little enclosure in the compound with mats, and place two or three flat stones in it. Hot water is generally used and they rub the perspiration off their bodies with a flat stone called Jhāwar. Most Kunbis bathe daily. On days when they are shaved they plaster the head with soft black earth, and then wash it off and rub their bodies with a little linseed or sesamum oil, or, if they can afford it, with cocoanut oil.

21. Food.

" The Kunbis eat three times a day, at about eight in the morning, at midday and after dark. The morning meal is commonly eaten in the field and the two others at home. At midday the cultivator comes home from work, bathes and takes his meal, having a rest for about two hours in all. After finishing work he again comes home and has his evening meal, and then, after a rest, at about ten o'clock he goes again to the fields, if the crops are on the ground, and sleeps on the *mara* or small elevated platform erected in the field to protect the grain from birds and wild animals; occasionally waking and emitting long-drawn howls or pulling the strings which connect with clappers in various parts of the field. Thus for nearly eight months of the year the Kunbi sleeps in his fields, and only during the remaining period at home. Juāri is the staple food of the caste, and is eaten both raw and cooked. The raw pods of juāri were the provision carried with them on their saddles by the marauding Marātha horsemen, and the description of Sivaji getting his sustenance from gnawing at one of these as he rode along is said to have struck fear into the heart of the Nizām. It is a common custom among well-to-do tenants and proprietors to invite their friends to a picnic in the fields when the crop is ripe to eat *hurda* or the pods of juāri roasted in hot ashes. For cooking purposes juāri is ground in an ordinary handmill and then passed through a sieve, which separates the finer from the coarser particles. The finer flour is made into dough with hot water and baked into thick flat *chapātis* or cakes, weighing more than half a pound each; while the coarse flour is boiled in water like rice. The boiled pulse of *arhar* (*Cajanus indicus*) is commonly eaten with juāri, and the *chapātis* are either dipped into cold linseed oil or consumed dry. The sameness of this diet is varied by a number of green vegetables, generally with very little savour to a European palate. These are usually boiled and then mixed into a salad with linseed or sesamum oil and flavoured with salt or powdered chillies, these last being the Kunbi's indispensable condiment. He is also very fond of onions and garlic, which are either chopped and boiled, or eaten raw. Butter-milk when available is mixed with the boiled juāri after it is cooked, while wheat and rice, butter and sugar are delicacies reserved for festivals. As a rule only water is drunk, but the caste indulge in country liquor on festive occasions. Tobacco is commonly chewed after each meal or smoked in leaf cigarettes, or in *chilams* or clay pipe-bowls without a stem. Men also take snuff, and a few women chew tobacco and take snuff, though they do not smoke. It is noticeable that different subdivisions of the caste will commonly take food from each other in Berār, whereas in the Central Provinces they refuse to do so. The more liberal usage in Berār is possibly another case of Muhammadan influence. Small children eat with their father and brothers, but the women always wait on the men, and take their own food afterwards. Among the Dālia Kunbis of Nimār, however, women eat before men at caste feasts in opposition to the usual practice. It is stated in explanation that on one occasion when the men had finished their meal first and gone home, the women on returning were waylaid in the dark and robbed of their ornaments. And hence it was decided that they should always eat first and go home before nightfall. The Kunbi is fairly liberal in the matter of food. He will eat the flesh of goats, sheep and deer, all kinds of fish and fowls, and will drink liquor. In Hoshangābād and Nimār the higher subcastes abstain from flesh and wine. The caste will take food cooked without water from Brāhmans, Banias and Sunārs, and that mixed with water only from Marātha Brāhmans. All castes except Marātha Brāhmans will take water from the hands of a Kunbi.

22. Clothes and ornaments.

The dress of the ordinary cultivator is most commonplace and consists only of a loin-cloth, another cloth thrown over the shoulders and upper part of the body, which except for this is often bare, and a third rough cloth wound loosely round the head. All these, originally white, soon assume a very dingy hue. There is thus no colour in a man's everyday attire, but the gala dress for holidays consists of a red *pagri* or turban, a black, coloured or white coat, and a white loin-cloth with red silk borders if he can afford it. The Kunbi is seldom or never seen with his head bare; this being considered a bad omen because every one bares his head when a death occurs. Women wear *lugras*, or a single long cloth of red, blue or black cotton, and under this the *choli*, or small breast-cloth. They have one silk-bordered cloth for special occasions. A woman having a husband alive must not wear a white cloth with no colour in it, as this is the dress of widows. A white cloth with a coloured border may be worn. The men generally wear shoes which are open at the back of the heel, and clatter as they move along. Women do not, as a rule, wear shoes unless these are necessary for field work, or if they go out just after their confinement. But they have now begun to do so in towns. Women have the usual collection of ornaments on all parts of the person. The head ornaments should be of gold when this metal can be afforded. On the finger they have a miniature mirror set in a ring; as a rule not more than one ring is worn, so that the hands may be free for work. For a similar reason glass bangles, being fragile, are worn only on the left wrist and metal ones on the right. But the Dhanoje Kunbis, as already stated, have cocoanut shell bangles on both wrists. They smear a mark of red powder on the forehead or have a spangle there. Girls are generally tattooed in childhood when the skin is tender, and the

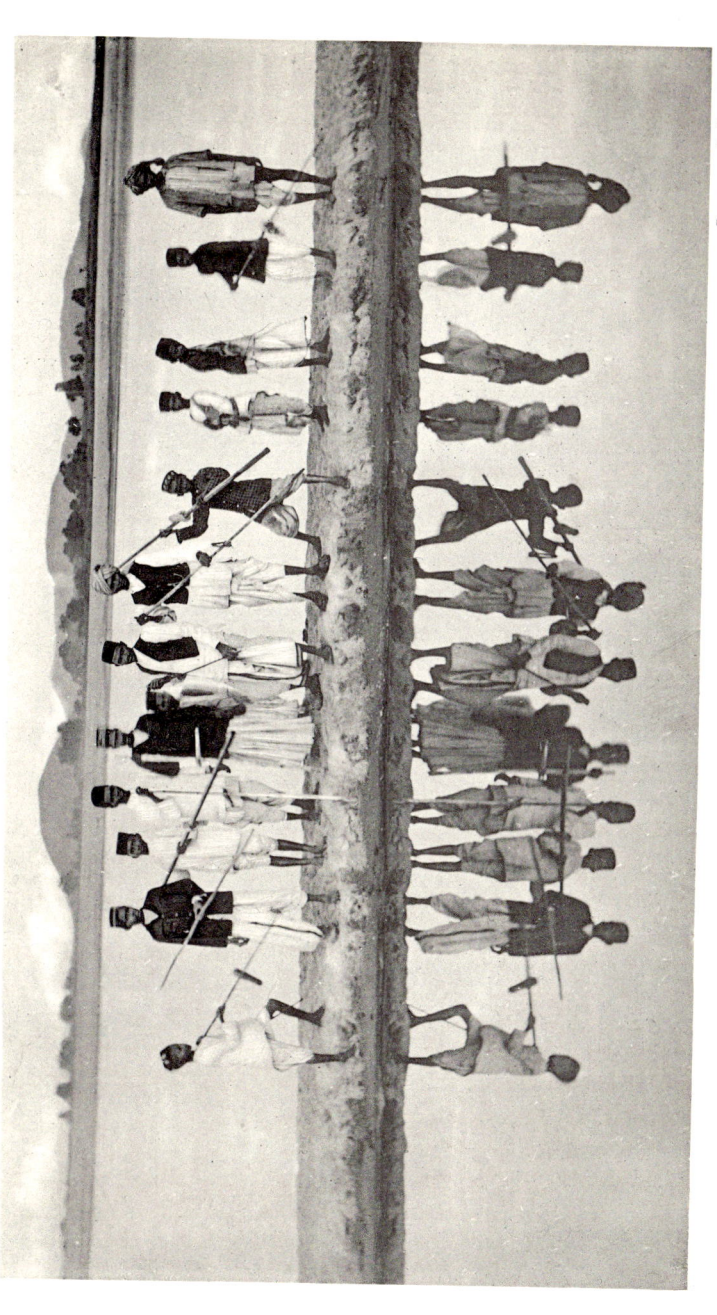

THROWING STILTS INTO THE WATER AT THE POLA FESTIVAL.

operation is consequently less painful. They usually have a small crescent and circle between the brows, small circles or dots on each temple and on the nose, cheeks and chin, and five small marks on the back of the hands to represent flies. Some of the Deshmukh families have now adopted the sacred thread; they also put caste marks on the forehead, and wear the shape of *pagri* or turban formerly distinctive of Marātha Brāhmans.

23. The Kunbi as cultivator.

The Kunbi has the stolidity, conservative instincts, dulness and patience of the typical agriculturist. Sir R. Craddock describes him as follows:[1] "Of the purely agricultural classes the Kunbis claim first notice. They are divided into several sections or classes, and are of Marātha origin, the Jhāri Kunbis (the Kunbis of the wild country) being the oldest settlers, and the Deshkar (the Kunbis from the Deccan) the most recent. The Kunbi is certainly a most plodding, patient mortal, with a cat-like affection for his land, and the proprietary and cultivating communities, of both of which Kunbis are the most numerous members, are unlikely to fail so long as he keeps these characteristics. Some of the more intelligent and affluent of the caste, who have risen to be among the most prosperous members of the community, are as shrewd men of business in their way as any section of the people, though lacking in education. I remember one of these, a member of the Local Board, who believed that the land revenue of the country was remitted to England annually to form part of the private purse of the Queen Empress. But of the general body of the Kunbi caste it is true to say that in the matter of enterprise, capacity to hold their own with the moneylender, determination to improve their standard of comfort, or their style of agriculture, they lag far behind such cultivating classes as the Kirār, the Rāghvi and the Lodhi. While, however, the Kunbi yields to these classes in some of the more showy attributes which lead to success in life, he is much their superior in endurance under adversity, he is more law-abiding, and he commands, both by reason of his character and his caste, greater social respect among the people at large. The wealthy Kunbi proprietor is occasionally rather

---

[1] *Nāgpur Settlement Report*, para. 45.

spoilt by good fortune, or, if he continues a keen cultivator, is apt to be too fond of land-grabbing. But these are the exceptional cases, and there is generally no such pleasing spectacle as that afforded by a village in which the cultivators and the proprietors are all Kunbis living in harmony together." The feeling[1] of the Kunbi towards agricultural improvements has hitherto probably been something the same as that of the Sussex farmer who said, ' Our old land, it likes our old ploughs' to the agent who was vainly trying to demonstrate to him the advantages of the modern two-horse iron plough over the great wooden local tool ; and the emblem ascribed to old Sussex—a pig couchant with the motto ' I wun't be druv '—would suit the Kunbi equally well. But the Kunbi, too, though he could not express it, knows something of the pleasure of the simple outdoor life, the fresh smell of the soil after rain, the joy of the yearly miracle when the earth is again carpeted with green from the bursting into life of the seed which he has sown, and the pleasure of watching the harvest of his labours come to fruition. He, too, as has been seen, feels something corresponding to " That inarticulate love of the English farmer for his land, his mute enjoyment of the furrow crumbling from the ploughshare or the elastic tread of his best pastures under his heel, his ever-fresh satisfaction at the sight of the bullocks stretching themselves as they rise from the soft grass."

24. Social and moral characteristics.

Some characteristics of the Marātha people are noticed by Sir R. Jenkins as follows :[2] "The most remarkable feature perhaps in the character of the Marāthas of all descriptions is the little regard they pay to show or ceremony in the common intercourse of life. A peasant or mechanic of the lowest order, appearing before his superiors, will sit down of his own accord, tell his story without ceremony, and converse more like an equal than an inferior ; and if he has a petition he talks in a loud and boisterous tone and fearlessly sets forth his claims. Both the peasantry and the better classes are often coarse and indelicate in their

---

[1] The references to English farming in this paragraph are taken from an article in the *Saturday Review* of 22nd August 1908.
[2] *Report on the Territories of the Rāja of Nāgpur.*

Bemrose, Collo., Derby

CARRYING OUT THE DEAD.

language, and many of the proverbs, which they are fond of introducing into conversation, are extremely gross. In general the Marāthas, and particularly the cultivators, are not possessed of much activity or energy of character, but they have quick perception of their own interest, though their ignorance of writing and accounts often renders them the dupes of the artful Brāhmans." "The Kunbi," Mr. Forbes remarks,[1] "though frequently all submission and prostration when he makes his appearance in a revenue office, is sturdy and bold enough among his own people. He is fond of asserting his independence and the helplessness of others without his aid, on which subject he has several proverbs, as : 'Wherever it thunders there the Kunbi is a landholder,' and 'Tens of millions are dependent on the Kunbi, but the Kunbi depends on no man.'" This sense of his own importance, which has also been noticed among the Jāts, may perhaps be ascribed to the Kunbi's ancient status as a free and full member of the village community. "The Kunbi and his bullocks are inseparable, and in speaking of the one it is difficult to dissociate the other. His pride in these animals is excusable, for they are most admirably suited to the circumstances in which nature has placed them, and possess a very wide-extended fame. But the Kunbi frequently exhibits his fondness for them in the somewhat peculiar form of unmeasured abuse. 'May the Kāthis[2] seize you!' is his objurgation if in the peninsula of Surat ; if in the Idar district or among the mountains it is there 'May the tiger kill you!' and all over Gujarāt, 'May your master die!' However, he means by this the animal's former owner, not himself; and when more than usually cautious he will word his chiding thus—'May the fellow that sold you to me perish.'" But now the Kāthis raid no more and the tiger, though still taking good toll of cattle in the Central Provinces, is not the ever-present terror that once he was. But the bullock himself is no longer so sacrosanct in the Kunbi's eyes, and cannot look forward with the same certainty to an old age of idleness, threatened only by starvation in the hot weather or death by surfeit of the new

[1] *Rāsmālā*, ii. 242.
[2] A freebooting tribe who gave their name to Kāthiawār.

moist grass in the rains; and when therefore the Kunbi's patience is exhausted by these aggravating animals, his favourite threat at present is, 'I will sell you to the Kasais' (butchers); and not so very infrequently he ends by doing so. It may be noted that with the development of the cotton industry the Kunbi of Wardha is becoming much sharper and more capable of protecting his own interests, while with the assistance and teaching which he now receives from the Agricultural Department, a rapid and decided improvement is taking place in his skill as a cultivator.

Kunjra.[1]—A caste of greengrocers, who sell country vegetables and fruit and are classed as Muhammadans. Mr. Crooke derives the name from the Sanskrit *kunj*, ' a bower or arbour.' They numbered about 1600 persons in the Central Provinces in 1911, principally in the Jubbulpore Division. The customs of the Kunjras appear to combine Hindu and Muhammadan rites in an indiscriminate medley. It is reported that marriage is barred only between real brothers and sisters and foster brothers and sisters, the latter rule being known as *Dudh bachāna*, or ' Observing the tie of the milk.' At their betrothal presents are given to the parties, and after this a powder of henna leaves is sent to the boy, who rubs it on his fingers and returns it to the girl that she may do the same. As among the Hindus, the bodies of the bridal couple are anointed with oil and turmeric at their respective houses before the wedding. A marriage-shed is made and the bridegroom goes to the bride's house wearing a cotton quilt and riding on a bullock. The barber holds the umbrella over his head and must be given a present before he will fold it, but the wedding is performed by the Kāzi according to the Nikāh ceremony by the repetition of verses from the Korān. The wedding is held at four o'clock in the morning, and as a preliminary to it the bride is presented with some money by the boy's father, which is known as the Meher or dowry. On its conclusion a cup of sherbet is given to the bridegroom, of which he drinks

---

[1] This article is partly based on papers by Nanhe Khān, Sub-Inspector of Police, Khurai, Saugor, and Kesho Rao, Headmaster, Middle School, Seoni-Chhapāra.

half and hands the remainder to the bride. The gift of the Meher is considered to seal the marriage contract. When a widow is married the Kāzi is also employed, and he simply recites the Kalama or Muhammadan profession of belief, and the ceremony is completed by the distribution of dates to the elders of the caste. Divorce is permitted and is known as *talāq*. The caste observe the Muhammadan festivals, and have some favourite saints of their own to whom they make offerings of *gulgula*, a kind of pudding, with sacrifices of goats and fowls. Participation in these rites is confined to members of the family. Children are named on the day of their birth, the Muhammadan Kāzi or a Hindu Brāhman being employed indifferently to select the name. If the parents lose one or more children, in order to preserve the lives of those subsequently born, they will allow the *choti* or scalp-lock to grow on their heads in the Hindu fashion, dedicating it to one of their Muhammadan saints. Others will put a *hasli* or silver circlet round the neck of the child and add a ring to this every year; a strip of leather is sometimes also tied round the neck. When the child reaches the age of twelve years the scalp-lock is shaved, the leather band thrown into a river and the silver necklet sold. Offerings are made to the saints and a feast is given to the friends of the family. The dead are buried, camphor and attar of roses being applied to the corpse. On the *Tīja* and *Chālisa*, or third and fortieth days after a death, a feast is given to the caste-fellows, but no mourning is observed, neither do the mourners bathe nor perform ceremonies of purification. On the *Tīja* the Korān is also read and fried grain is distributed to children. For the death of a child the ordinary feasts need not be given, but prayers are offered for their souls with those of the other dead once a year on the night of Shab-i-Barāt or the fifteenth day of the month Shabān,[1] which is observed as a vigil with prayer, feasts

[1] Literally 'The Month of Separation.' It is the eighth month of the Muhammadan year and is said to be so called because in this month the Arabs broke up their encampments and scattered in search of water. On the night of Shab-i-Barāt God registers all the actions of men which they are to perform during the year; and all the children of men who are to be born and die in the year are recorded. Though properly a fast, it is generally observed with rejoicings and a display of fireworks. Hughes' *Dictionary of Islam*, p. 570.

and illuminations and offerings to the ancestors. Kunjra men are usually clean-shaven with the exception of the beard, which is allowed to grow long below the chin. Their women are not tattooed. In the cities, Mr. Crooke remarks,[1] their women have an equivocal reputation, as the better-looking girls who sit in the shops are said to use considerable freedom of manners to attract customers. They are also very quarrelsome and abusive when bargaining for the sale of their wares or arguing with each other. This is so much the case that men who become very abusive are said to be behaving like Kunjras; while in Dacca Sir H. Risley states[2] that the word Kunjra has become a term of abuse, so that the caste are ashamed to be known by it, and call themselves Mewa-farosh, Sabzi-farosh or Bepāri. When two women are having an altercation, their husbands and other male relatives are forbidden to interfere on pain of social degradation. The women never sit on the ground, but on small wooden stools or *pīrhis*. The Kunjras belong chiefly to the north of the Province, and in the south their place is taken by the Marārs and Mālis who carry their own produce for sale to the markets. The Kunjras sell sugarcane, potatoes, onions and all kinds of vegetables, and others deal in the dried fruits imported by Kābuli merchants.

Kuramwār.[3]—The shepherd caste of southern India, who are identical with the Tamil Kurumba and the Telugu Kuruba. The caste is an important one in Madras, but in the Central Provinces is confined to the Chānda District where it numbered some 4000 persons in 1911. The Kuramwārs are considered to be the modern representatives of the ancient Pallava tribe whose kings were powerful in southern India in the seventh century.[4]

The marriage rules of the Kuramwārs are interesting. If a girl reaches adolescence while still single, she is finally expelled from the caste, her parents being also subjected to a penalty for readmission. Formerly it is said that such a girl was sacrificed to the river-goddess by being placed in a small hut on the river-bank till a flood came and swept

---

[1] *Tribes and Castes of the N.W.P.*, art. Kunjra.
[2] *Tribes and Castes of Bengal, ibidem.*
[3] This article is compiled from notes taken by Mr. Hīra Lāl and by Pyāre Lāl Misra, Ethnographic clerk.
[4] *North Arcot Manual*, vol. i. p. 220.

her away. Now she is taken to the river and kept in a hut, while offerings are made to the river-goddess, and she may then return and live in the village though she is out of caste. In Madras, as a preliminary to the marriage, the bridegroom's father observes certain marks or 'curls' on the head or hair of the bride proposed. Some of these are believed to forecast prosperity and others misery to the family into which she enters. They are therefore very cautious in selecting only such girls as possess curls (*sūli*) of good fortune. The writer of the *North Arcot Manual*,[1] after recording the above particulars, remarks: "This curious custom obtaining among this primitive tribe is observed by others only in the case of the purchase of cows, bulls and horses." In the Central Provinces, however, at least one parallel instance can be given from the northern Districts where any mark resembling the V on the head of a cobra is considered to be very inauspicious. And it is told that a girl who married into one well-known family bore it, and to this fact the remarkable succession of misfortunes which has attended the family is locally attributed. Among the Kuramwārs marriages can be celebrated only on four days in the year, the fifth day of both fortnights of Phāgun (February), the tenth day of the second fortnight of the same month and the third day of Baisākh (April). At the marriage the bride and bridegroom are seated together under the canopy, with the shuttle which is used for weaving blankets between them, and they throw coloured rice at each other. After this a miniature swing is put up and a doll is placed in it in imitation of a child and swung to and fro. The bride then takes the doll out and gives it to the bridegroom, saying: 'Here, take care of it, I am now going to cook food'; while after a time the boy returns the doll to the girl, saying, 'I must now weave the blanket and go to tend the flock.' The proceeding seems a symbolic enactment of the cares of married life and the joint tending of the baby, this sort of symbolism being particularly noticeable in the marriage ceremonies of the people of Madras. Divorce is not permitted even though the wife be guilty of adultery, and if she runs away to her father's house her husband cannot use force to bring her back if she refuses to

---

[1] Vol. i. p. 224.

return to him. The Kuramwārs worship the implements of their calling at the festival of Ganesh Chaturthi, and if any family fails to do this it is put out of caste. They also revere annually Mallana Deva and Mallani Devi who guard their flocks respectively from attacks of tigers and epidemics of murrain. The shrines of these deities are generally built under a banyan tree and open to the east. The caste are shepherds and graziers and also make blankets. They are poor and ignorant, and the Abbé Dubois [1] says of them: "Being confined to the society of their woolly charge, they seem to have contracted the stupid nature of the animal, and from the rudeness of their nature they are as much beneath the other castes of Hindus as the sheep by their simplicity and imperfect instruction are beneath the other quadrupeds." Hence the proverbial comparison 'As stupid as a Kuramwār.' When out of doors the Kuramwār retains the most primitive method of eating and drinking; he takes his food in a leaf and licks it up with his tongue, and sucks up water from a tank or river with his mouth. They justify this custom by saying that on one occasion their god had taken his food out of the house on a leaf-plate and was proceeding to eat it with his hands when his sheep ran away and he had to go and fetch them back. In the meantime a crow came and pecked at the food and so spoilt it. It was therefore ordained that all the caste should eat their food straight off the leaf, in order to do which they would have to take it from the cooking-pot in small quantities and there would be no chance of leaving any for the crows to spoil. The story is interesting as showing how very completely the deity of the Kuramwārs is imagined on the principle that god made man in his own image. Or, as a Frenchman has expressed the idea, '*Dieu a fait l'homme à son image, mais l'homme le lui a bien rendu.*' The caste are dark in colour and may be distinguished by their caps made from pieces of blankets, and by their wearing a woollen cord round the waist over the loin-cloth. They speak a dialect of Canarese.

---

[1] *Hindu Manners, Customs and Ceremonies.*

KURMI

LIST OF PARAGRAPHS

1. *Numbers and derivation of name.*
2. *Functional character of the caste.*
3. *Subcastes.*
4. *Exogamous groups.*
5. *Marriage rules. Betrothal.*
6. *The marriage-shed or pavilion.*
7. *The marriage cakes.*
8. *Customs at the wedding.*
9. *Walking round the sacred post.*
10. *Other ceremonies.*
11. *Polygamy, widow-marriage and divorce.*
12. *Impurity of women.*
13. *Pregnancy rites.*
14. *Earth-eating.*
15. *Customs at birth.*
16. *Treatment of mother and child.*
17. *Ceremonies after birth.*
18. *Suckling children.*
19. *Beliefs about twins.*
20. *Disposal of the dead.*
21. *Funeral rites.*
22. *Burning the dead.*
23. *Burial.*
24. *Return of the soul.*
25. *Mourning.*
26. *Shaving, and presents to Brāhmans.*
27. *End of mourning.*
28. *Anniversaries of the dead.*
29. *Beliefs in the hereafter.*
30. *Religion. Village gods.*
31. *Sowing the Jawaras or gardens of Adonis.*
32. *Rites connected with the crops. Customs of cultivation.*
33. *Agricultural superstitions.*
34. *Houses.*
35. *Superstitions about houses.*
36. *Furniture.*
37. *Clothes.*
38. *Women's clothes.*
39. *Bathing.*
40. *Food.*
41. *Caste feasts.*
42. *Hospitality.*
43. *Social customs. Tattooing.*
44. *Caste penalties.*
45. *The cultivating status.*
46. *Occupation.*
Appendix. List of exogamous clans.

Kurmi.[1]—The representative cultivating caste of Hindustān or the country comprised roughly in the United Provinces, Bihār and the Central Provinces north of the

1. Numbers and derivation of name.

[1] In this article some account of the houses, clothes and food of the Hindus generally of the northern Districts has been inserted, being mainly reproduced from the District Gazetteers.

55

Nerbudda. In 1911 the Kurmis numbered about 300,000 persons in the Central Provinces, of whom half belonged to the Chhattīsgarh Division and a third to the Jubbulpore Division; the Districts in which they were most numerous being Saugor, Damoh, Jubbulpore, Hoshangābād, Raipur, Bilāspur and Drūg. The name is considered to be derived from the Sanskrit *krishi*, cultivation, or from *kurma*, the tortoise incarnation of Vishnu, whether because it is the totem of the caste or because, as suggested by one writer, the Kurmi supports the population of India as the tortoise supports the earth. It is true that many Kurmis say they belong to the Kashyap *gotra*, Kashyap being the name of a Rishi, which seems to have been derived from *kachhap*, the tortoise; but many other castes also say they belong to the Kashyap *gotra* or worship the tortoise, and if this has any connection with the name of the caste it is probable that the caste-name suggested the *gotra*-name and not the reverse. It is highly improbable that a large occupational caste should be named after an animal, and the metaphorical similitude can safely be rejected. The name seems therefore either to come from *krishi*, cultivation, or from some other unknown source.

2. Functional character of the caste.

There seems little reason to doubt that the Kurmis, like the Kunbis, are a functional caste. In Bihār they show traces of Aryan blood, and are a fine-looking race. But in Chota Nāgpur Sir H. Risley states: "Short, sturdy and of very dark complexion, the Kurmis closely resemble in feature the Dravidian tribes around them. It is difficult to distinguish a Kurmi from a Bhumij or Santāl, and the Santāls will take cooked food from them."[1] In the Central Provinces they are fairly dark in complexion and of moderate height, and no doubt of very mixed blood. Where the Kurmis and Kunbis meet the castes sometimes amalgamate, and there is little doubt that various groups of Kurmis settling in the Marātha country have become Kunbis, and Kunbis migrating to northern India have become Kurmis. Each caste has certain subdivisions whose names belong to the other. It has been seen in the article on Kunbi that this caste is of very diverse origin, having assimilated large bodies of persons

[1] *Tribes and Castes of Bengal*, art. Kurmi.

from several other castes, and is probably to a considerable extent recruited from the local non-Aryan tribes; if then the Kurmis mix so readily with the Kunbis, the presumption is that they are of a similar mixed origin, as otherwise they should consider themselves superior. Mr. Crooke gives several names of subcastes showing the diverse constitution of the Kurmis. Thus three, Gaharwār, Jādon and Chandel are the names of Rājpūt clans; the Kori subcaste must be a branch of the low weaver caste of that name; and in the Central Provinces the names of such subcastes as the Agaria or iron-workers, the Lonhāre or salt-refiners, and the Khaira or catechu-collectors indicate that these Kurmis are derived from low Hindu castes or the aboriginal tribes.

3. Subcastes.

The caste has a large number of subdivisions. The Usrete belonged to Bundelkhand, where this name is found in several castes; they are also known as Havelia, because they live in the rich level tract of the Jubbulpore Haveli, covered like a chessboard with large embanked wheat-fields. The name Haveli seems to have signified a palace or headquarters of a ruler, and hence was applied to the tract surrounding it, which was usually of special fertility, and provided for the maintenance of the chief's establishment and household troops. Thus in Jubbulpore, Mandla and Betūl we find the forts of the old Gond rulers dominating an expanse of rich plain-country. The Usrete Kurmis abstain from meat and liquor, and may be considered as one of the highest subcastes. Their name may be derived from *a-sreshtha*, or not the best, and its significance would be that formerly they were considered to be of mixed origin, like most castes in Bundelkhand. The group of Sreshtha or best-born Kurmis has now, however, died out if it ever existed, and the Usretes have succeeded in establishing themselves in its place. The Chandnāhes of Jubbulpore or Chandnāhus of Chhattīsgarh are another large subdivision. The name may be derived from the village Chandnoha in Bundelkhand, but the Chandnāhus of Chhattīsgarh say that three or four centuries ago a Rājpūt general of the Rāja of Ratanpur had been so successful in war that the king allowed him to appear in Durbār in his uniform with his forehead marked with sandalwood, as a special honour.

When he died his son continued to do the same, and on the king's attention being drawn to it he forbade him. But the son did not obey, and hence the king ordered the sandalwood to be rubbed from his forehead in open Durbār. But when this was done the mark miraculously reappeared through the agency of the goddess Devi, whose favourite he was. Three times the king had the mark rubbed out and three times it came again. So he was allowed to wear it thereafter, and was called Chandan Singh from *chandan*, sandalwood ; and his descendants are the Chandnāhu Kurmis. Another derivation is from Chandra, the moon. In Jubbulpore these Chandnāhes sometimes kill a pig under the palanquin of a newly married bride. In Bilāspur they are prosperous and capable cultivators, but are generally reputed to be stingy, and therefore are not very popular. Here they are divided into the Ekbahinyas and Dobahinyas, or those who wear glass bangles on one or both arms respectively. The Chandrāha Kurmis of Raipur are probably a branch of the Chandnāhus. They sprinkle with water the wood with which they are about to cook their food in order to purify it, and will eat food only in the *chauka* or sanctified place in the house. At harvest when they must take meals in the fields, one of them prepares a patch of ground, cleaning and watering it, and there cooks food for them all.

The Singrore Kurmis derive their name from Singror, a place near Allahābād. Singror is said to have once been a very important town, and the Lodhis and other castes have subdivisions of this name. The Desha Kurmis are a group of the Mungeli tahsīl of Bilāspur. Desh means one's native country, but in this case the name probably refers to Bundelkhand. Mr. Gordon states[1] that they do not rear poultry and avoid residing in villages in which their neighbours keep poultry. The Santore Kurmis are a group found in several Districts, who grow *san*-hemp,[2] and are hence looked down upon by the remainder of the caste. In Raipur the Mānwa Kurmis will also do this ; Māna is a word sometimes applied to a loom, and the Mānwa Kurmis may be so called because they grow hemp and weave sacking from the fibres. The

[1] *Indian Folk Tales*, p. 8.
[2] *Crotalaria juncea.* See article on Lorha for a discussion of the Hindus' prejudice against this crop.

Pataria are an inferior group in Bilāspur, who are similarly despised because they grow hemp and will take their food in the fields in *patris* or leaf-plates. The Gohbaiyān are considered to be an illegitimate group; the name is said to signify 'holding the arm.' The Bāhargaiyan, or 'those who live outside the town,' are another subcaste to which children born out of wedlock are relegated. The Palkiha subcaste of Jubbulpore are said to be so named because their ancestors were in the service of a certain Rāja and spread his bedding for him; hence they are somewhat looked down on by the others. The name may really be derived from *palal*, a kind of vegetable, and they may originally have been despised for growing this vegetable, and thus placing themselves on a level with the gardening castes. The Masūria take their name from the *masūr* or lentil, a common cold-weather crop in the northern Districts, which is, however, grown by all Kurmis and other cultivators; and the Agaria or iron-workers, the Kharia or catechu-makers, and the Lonhāre or salt-makers, have already been mentioned. There are also numerous local or territorial subcastes, as the Chaurasia or those living in a Chaurāsi[1] estate of eighty-four villages, the Pardeshi or foreigners, the Bundelkhandi or those who came from Bundelkhand, the Kanaujias from Oudh, the Gaur from northern India, and the Marāthe and Telenge or Marāthas and Telugus; these are probably Kunbis who have been taken into the caste. The Gabel are a small subcaste in Sakti State, who now prefer to drop the name Kurmi and call themselves simply Gabel. The reason apparently is that the other Kurmis about them sow *san*-hemp, and as they have ceased doing this they try to separate themselves and rank above the rest. But they call the bastard group of their community Rakhaut Kurmis, and other people speak of all of them as Gabel Kurmis, so that there is no doubt that they belong to the caste. It is said that formerly they were pack-carriers, but have now abandoned this calling in favour of cultivation.

Each subcaste has a number of exogamous divisions and these present a large variety of all types. Some groups have

4. Exogamous groups.

---

[1] There are several Chaurāsis, a grant of an estate of this special size being common under native rule.

the names of Brāhman saints as Sāndil, Bhāradwaj, Kausil and Kashyap; others are called after Rājpūt septs, as Chauhān, Rāthor, Panwār and Solanki; other names are of villages, as Khairagarhi from Khairagarh, Pandariha from Pandaria, Bhadaria, and Harkotia from Harkoti; others are titular, as Sondeha, gold-bodied, Sonkharchi, spender of gold, Bimba Lohir, stick-carrier, Banhpagar, one wearing a thread on the arm, Bhandāri, a store-keeper, Kumaria, a potter, and Shikāria, a hunter; and a large number are totemistic, named after plants, animals or natural objects, as Sadāphal, a fruit; Kathail from *kath* or catechu; Dhorha, from *dhor*, cattle; Kānsia, the *kāns* grass; Karaiya, a frying-pan; Sarang, a peacock; Samundha, the ocean; Sindia, the date-palm tree; Dudhua from *dudh*, milk, and so on. Some sections are subdivided; thus the Tidha section, supposed to be named after a village, is divided into three subsections named Ghurepake, a mound of cowdung, Dwarparke, doorjamb, and Jangi, a warrior, which are themselves exogamous. Similarly the Chaudhri section, named after the title of the caste headman, is divided into four subsections, two, Majhgawān and Bamuria, named after villages, and two, Purwa Thok and Pascham Thok, signifying the eastern and western groups. Presumably when sections get so large as to bar the marriage of persons not really related to each other at all, relief is obtained by subdividing them in this manner. A list of the sections of certain subcastes so far as they have been obtained is given at the end of the article.

5. Marriage rules. Betrothal.

Marriage is prohibited between members of the same section and between first and second cousins on the mother's side. But the Chandnāhe Kurmis permit the wedding of a brother's daughter to a sister's son. Most Kurmis forbid a man to marry his wife's sister during her lifetime. The Chhattīsgarh Kurmis have the practice of exchanging girls between two families. There is usually no objection to marriage on account of religious differences within the pale of Hinduism, but the difficulty of a union between a member of a Vaishnava sect who abstains from flesh and liquor, and a partner who does not, is felt and expressed in the following saying:

POUNDING RICE.

> *Vaishnava purush avaishnava nāri*
> *Unt beil ki jot bichāri,*

or 'A Vaishnava husband with a non-Vaishnava wife is like a camel yoked with a bullock.' Muhammadans and Christians are not retained in the caste. Girls are usually wedded between nine and eleven, but well-to-do Kurmis, like other agriculturists, sometimes marry their daughters when only a few months old. The people say that when a Kurmi gets rich he will do three things: marry his daughters very young and with great display, build a fine house, and buy the best bullocks he can afford. The second and third methods of spending his money are very sensible, whatever may be thought of the first. No penalty is imposed for allowing a girl to exceed the age of puberty before marriage. Boys are married between nine and fifteen years, but the tendency is towards the postponement of the ceremony. The boy's father goes and asks for a bride and says to the girl's father, 'I have placed my son with you,' that is, given him in adoption; if the match be acceptable the girl's father replies, 'Yes, I will give my daughter to collect cowdung for you'; to which the boy's father responds, 'I will hold her as the apple of my eye.' Then the girl's father sends the barber and the Brāhman to the boy's house, carrying a rupee and a cocoanut. The boy's relatives return the visit and perform the '*God bharna,*' or 'Filling the lap of the girl.' They take some sweetmeats, a rupee and a cocoanut, and place them in the girl's lap, this being meant to induce fertility. The ceremony of betrothal succeeds, when the couple are seated together on a wooden plank and touch the feet of the guests and are blessed by them. The auspicious date of the wedding is fixed by the Brāhman and intimation is given to the boy's family through the *lagan* or formal invitation, which is sent on a paper coloured yellow with powdered rice and turmeric. A bride-price is paid, which in the case of well-to-do families may amount to as much as Rs. 100 to Rs. 400.

6. The marriage-shed or pavilion.

Before the wedding the women of the family go out and fetch new earth for making the stoves on which the marriage feast will be cooked. When about to dig they worship the earth by sprinkling water over it and offering flowers and rice. The marriage-shed is made of the wood of the *sāleh* tree,[1] because this wood is considered to be alive. If a pole of *sāleh* is cut and planted in the ground it takes root and sprouts, though otherwise the wood is quite useless. The wood of the *kekar* tree has similar properties and may also be used. The shed is covered with leaves of the mango or *jāmun*[2] trees, because these trees are evergreen and hence typify perpetual life. The marriage-post in the centre of the shed is called Magrohan or Khām; the women go and worship it at the carpenter's house; two pice, a piece of turmeric and an areca-nut are buried below it in the earth and a new thread and a *toran* or string of mango-leaves is wound round it. Oil and turmeric are also rubbed on the marriage-post at the same time as on the bride and bridegroom. In Saugor the marriage-post is often a four-sided wooden frame or a pillar with four pieces of wood suspended from it. The larger the marriage-shed is made the greater honour accrues to the host, even though the guests may be insufficient to fill it. In towns it has often to be made in the street and is an obstacle to traffic. There may be eight or ten posts besides the centre one.

7. The marriage-cakes.

Another preliminary ceremony is the family sacrament of the Meher or marriage-cakes. Small balls of wheat-flour are kneaded and fried in an earthen pan with sesamum oil by the eldest woman of the family. No metal vessel may be used to hold the water, flour or oil required for these cakes, probably because earthen vessels were employed before metal ones and are therefore considered more sacred. In measuring the ingredients a quarter of a measure is always taken in excess, such as a seer[3] and a quarter for a seer of wheat, to foreshadow the perpetual increase of the family. When made the cakes are offered to the Kul Deo or household god. The god is worshipped and the bride and bridegroom then first partake of the cakes and after them all members of the family and relatives. Married daughters and daughters-in-law may eat of the cakes, but not widows, who are probably too impure to join in a sacred sacrament. Every person admitted to partake of the marriage-cakes is held to belong to the family, so that all other members of

---

[1] *Boswellia serrata.*   [2] *Eugenia jambolana.*   [3] 2 lbs.

it have to observe impurity for ten days after a birth or death has occurred in his house and shave their heads for a death. When the family is so large that this becomes irksome it is cut down by not inviting persons beyond seven degrees of relationship to the Meher sacrament. This exclusion has sometimes led to bitter quarrels and actions for defamation. It seems likely that the Meher may be a kind of substitute for the sacrificial meal, at which all the members of the clan ate the body of the totem or divine animal, and some similar significance perhaps once attached to the wedding-cake in England, pieces of which are sent to relatives unable to be present at the wedding.

Before the wedding the women of each party go and anoint the village gods with oil and turmeric, worshipping them, and then similarly anoint the bride and bridegroom at their respective houses for three days. The bridegroom's head is shaved except for his scalp-lock; he wears a silver necklet on his neck, puts lamp-black on his eyes, and is dressed in new yellow and white clothes. Thus attired he goes round and worships all the village gods and visits the houses of his relatives and friends, who mark his forehead with rice and turmeric and give him a silver piece. A list of the money thus received is made and similar presents are returned to the donors when they have weddings. The bridegroom goes to the wedding either in a litter or on a horse, and must not look behind him. After being received at the bride's village and conducted to his lodging, he proceeds to the bride's house and strikes a grass mat hung before the house seven times with a reed-stick. On entering the bride's house the bridegroom is taken to worship her family gods, the men of the party usually remaining outside. Then, as he goes through the room, one of the women who has tied a long thread round her toe gets behind him and measures his height with the thread without his seeing. She breaks off the thread at his height and doubling it once or twice sews it round the top of the bride's skirt, and they think that as long as the bride wears this thread she will be able to make her husband do as she likes. If the girls wish to have a joke they take one of the bridegroom's shoes which he has left

8. Customs at the wedding.

outside the house, wrap it up in a piece of cloth, and place it on a shelf or in a cupboard, where the family god would be kept, with two lamps burning before it. Then they say to the bridegroom, ' Come and worship our household god ' ; and if he goes and does reverence to it they unwrap the cloth and show him his own shoe and laugh at him. But if he has been to one or two weddings and knows the joke he just gives it a kick. The bride's younger brother steals the bridegroom's other shoe and hides it, and will not give it back without a present of a rupee or two. The bride and bridegroom are seated on wooden seats, and while the Brāhman recites texts, they make the following promises. The bridegroom covenants to live with his wife and her children, to support them and tell her all his concerns, consult her, make her a partner of his religious worship and almsgiving, and be with her on the night following the termination of her monthly impurity. The bride promises to remain faithful to her husband, to obey his wishes and orders, to perform her household duties as well as she can, and not to go anywhere without his permission. The last promise of the bridegroom has reference to the general rule among Hindus that a man should always sleep with his wife on the night following the termination of her menses because at this time she is most likely to conceive and the prospect of a child being born must not be lost. The Shāstras lay it down that a man should not visit his wife before going into battle, this being no doubt an instance of the common custom of abstinence from conjugal intercourse prior to some important business or undertaking ; but it is stated that if on such an occasion she should have just completed a period of impurity and have bathed and should desire him to come in to her, he should do so, even with his armour on, because by refusing, in the event of his being killed in battle, the chance of a child being born would be finally lost. To Hindu ideas the neglect to produce life is a sin of the same character, though in a minor degree, as that of destroying life ; and it is to be feared that it will be some time before this ingrained superstition gives way to any considerations of prudential restraint. Some people say that for a man not to visit his wife at this time is as great a sin as murder.

9. Walking round the sacred post.

The binding ceremony of the marriage is the walking seven times round the marriage-post in the direction of the sun. The post probably represents the sun and the walk of the bridal couple round it may be an imitation of the movement of the planets round the sun. The reverence paid to the marriage-post has already been noticed. During the procession the bride leads and the bridegroom puts his left hand on her left shoulder. The household pounding-slab is near the post and on it are placed seven little heaps of rice, turmeric, areca-nut, and a small winnowing-fan. Each time the bride passes the slab the bridegroom catches her right foot and with it makes her brush one of the little heaps off the slab. These seven heaps represent the seven Rishis or saints who are the seven large stars of the constellation of the Great Bear.

10. Other ceremonies.

After the wedding the bride and bridegroom resume their seats and the parents of the bride wash their feet in a brass tray, marking their foreheads with rice and turmeric. They put some silver in the tray, and other relations and friends do the same. The presents thus collected go to the bridegroom. The Chandnāhu Kurmis then have a ceremony known as *palkachār*. The bride's father provides a bed on which a mattress and quilt are laid and the bride and bridegroom are seated on it, while their brother and sister sprinkle parched rice round them. This is supposed to typify the consummation of the marriage, but the ceremony is purely formal as the bridal couple are children. The bridegroom is given two lamps and he has to mix their flames, probably to symbolise the mixing of the spirits of his wife and himself. He requires a present of a rupee or two before he consents to do so. During the wedding the bride is bathed in the same water as the bridegroom, the joint use of the sacred element being perhaps another symbolic mark of their union. At the feasts the bride eats rice and milk with her husband from one dish, once at her own house and once after she goes to her husband's house. Subsequently she never eats with her husband but always after him. She also sits and eats at the wedding-feasts with her husband's relations. This is perhaps meant to mark her admission into her husband's clan. After the wedding the Brāhmans on either side recite Sanskrit verses, praising their respective families and displaying their own learning. The competition often becomes bitter and would end in a quarrel, but that the elders of the party interfere and stop it.

The expenses of an ordinary wedding on the bridegroom's side may be Rs. 100 in addition to the bride-price, and on the bride's Rs. 200. The bride goes home for a day or two with the bridegroom's party in Chhattīsgarh but not in the northern Districts, as women accompany the wedding procession in the former but not in the latter locality. If she is too small to go, her shoes and marriage-crown are sent to represent her. When she attains maturity the *chauk* or *gauna* ceremony is performed, her husband going to fetch her with a few friends. At this time her parents give her clothes, food and ornaments in a basket called *jhanpi* or *tipara* specially prepared for the occasion.

11. Polygamy, widow-marriage and divorce.

A girl who becomes pregnant by a man of the caste before marriage is wedded to him by the rite used for widows. If the man is an outsider she is expelled from the community. Women are much valued for the sake of their labour in the fields, and the transgressions of a wife are viewed with a lenient eye. In Damoh it is said that a man readily condones his wife's adultery with another Kurmi, and if it becomes known and she is put out of caste, he will give the penalty feasts himself for her admission. If she is detected in a *liaison* with an outsider she is usually discarded, but the offence may be condoned should the man be a Brāhman. And one instance is mentioned of a mālguzār's wife who had gone wrong with a Gond, and was forgiven and taken back by her husband and the caste. But the leniency was misplaced as she subsequently eloped with an Ahīr. Polygamy is usual with those who can afford to pay for several wives, as a wife's labour is more efficient and she is a more profitable investment than a hired servant. An instance is on record of a blind Kurmi in Jubbulpore, who had nine wives. A man who is faithful to one wife, and does not visit her on fast-days, is called a Brahmachari or saint and it is thought that he will go to heaven. The remarriage of widows is permitted and is usual. The widow goes to a well on some night in the dark fortnight, and leaving her old clothes there puts on new ones which are given to her by the barber's wife. She then fills a pitcher with water and takes it to her new husband's house. He meets her on the threshold and lifts it from her head, and she goes into the house and puts bangles on her wrists. The following saying shows that the second marriage of widows is looked upon as quite natural and normal by the cultivating castes :

"If the clouds are like partridge feathers it will rain, and if a widow puts lamp-black on her eyes she will marry again ; these things are certain."[1]

A bachelor marrying a widow must first go through the ceremony with a ring which he thereafter wears on his finger, and if it is lost he must perform a funeral ceremony as if a wife had died. If a widower marries a girl she must wear round her neck an image of his first wife. A girl who is twice married by going round the sacred post is called Chandelia and is most unlucky. She is considered as bad or worse than a widow, and the people sometimes make her live outside the village and forbid her to show them her face. Divorce is open to either party, to a wife on account of the impotency or ill-treatment of her husband, and to a husband for the bad character, ill-health or quarrelsome disposition of his wife. A deed of divorce is executed and delivered before the caste committee.

During her periodical impurity, which lasts for four or five days, a woman should not sleep on a cot. She must not walk across the shadow of any man not her husband, because it is thought that if she does so her next child will be like that man. Formerly she did not see her husband's face for all these days, but this rule was too irksome and has been abandoned. She should eat the same kind of food for the whole period, and therefore must take nothing special on one day which she cannot get on other days. At this time she will let her hair hang loose, taking out all the cotton strings by which it is tied up.[2] These strings, being cotton, have become

12. Impurity of women.

[1] Elliot, *Hoshangābād Settlement Report*, p. 115.
[2] The custom is pointed out by Mr. A. K. Smith, C.S.

impure, and must be thrown away. But if there is no other woman to do the household work and she has to do it herself, she will keep her hair tied up for convenience, and only throw away the strings on the last day when she bathes. All cotton things are rendered impure by her at this time, and any cloth or other article which she touches must be washed before it can be touched by anybody else; but woollen cloth, being sacred, is not rendered impure, and she can sleep on a woollen blanket without its thereby becoming a defilement to other persons. When bathing at the end of the period a woman should see no other face but her husband's; but as her husband is usually not present, she wears a ring with a tiny mirror and looks at her own face in this as a substitute.

If a woman desires to procure a miscarriage she eats a raw *papāya* fruit, and drinks a mixture of ginger, sugar, bamboo leaves and milk boiled together. She then has her abdomen well rubbed by a professional *masseuse*, who comes at a time when she can escape observation. After a prolonged course of this treatment it is said that a miscarriage is obtained. It would seem that the rubbing is the only treatment which is directly effective. The *papāya*, which is a very digestible fruit, can hardly be of assistance, but may be eaten from some magical idea of its resemblance to a foetus. The mixture drunk is perhaps designed to be a tonic to the stomach against the painful effects of the massage.

13. Pregnancy rites.

As regards pregnancy Mr. Marten writes as follows:[1] " A woman in pregnancy is in a state of taboo and is peculiarly liable to the influence of magic and in some respects dangerous to others. She is exempt from the observance of fasts, is allowed any food she fancies, and is fed with sweets and all sorts of rich food, especially in the fifth month. She should not visit her neighbour's houses nor sleep in any open place. Her clothes are kept separate from others. She is subject to a large number of restrictions in her ordinary life with a view of avoiding everything that might prejudice or retard her delivery. She should eschew all red clothes or red things of any sort, such as suggest blood, till the third or

[1] *Central Provinces Census Report* (1911), p. 153.

fourth month, when conception is certain. She will be careful not to touch the dress of any woman who has had a miscarriage. She will not cross running water, as it might cause premature delivery, nor go near a she-buffalo or a mare lest delivery be retarded, since a mare is twelve months in foal. If she does by chance approach these animals she must propitiate them by offerings of grain. Nor in some cases will she light a lamp, for fear the flame in some way may hurt the child. She should not finish any sowing, previously begun, during pregnancy, nor should her husband thatch the house or repair his axe. An eclipse is particularly dangerous to the unborn child and she must not leave the house during its continuance, but must sit still with a stone pestle in her lap and anoint her womb with cowdung. Under no circumstances must she touch any cutting instrument as it might cause her child to be born mutilated.

"During the fifth month of pregnancy the family gods are worshipped to avoid generally any difficulties in her labour. Towards the end of that month and sometimes in the seventh month she rubs her body with a preparation of gram-flour, castor-oil and turmeric, bathes herself, and is clothed with new garments and seated on a wooden stool in a space freshly cleaned and spread with cowdung. Her lap is then filled with sweets called *pakwān* made of cocoanut. A similar ceremony called Boha Jewan is sometimes performed in the seventh or eighth month, when a new *sāri* is given to her and grain is thrown into her lap. Another special rite is the *Pansavan* ceremony, performed to remove all defects in the child, give it a male form, increase its size and beauty, give it wisdom and avert the influence of evil spirits."

14. Earth-eating.

Pregnant women sometimes have a craving for eating earth. They eat the earth which has been mixed with wheat on the threshing-floor, or the ashes of cowdung cakes which have been used for cooking. They consider it as a sort of medicine which will prevent them from vomiting. Children also sometimes get the taste for eating earth, licking it up from the floor, or taking pieces of lime-plaster from the walls. Possibly they may be attracted by the saltish taste, but the result is that they get ill and their stomachs are distended. The Panwār women of Bālāghāt eat red and white clay in order that their children may be born with red and white complexions.

15. Customs at birth.

During the period of labour the barber's wife watches over the case, but as delivery approaches hands it over to a recognised midwife, usually the Basorin or Chamārin, who remains in the lying-in room till about the tenth day after delivery. "If delivery is retarded," Mr. Marten continues,[1] "pressure and massage are used, but coffee and other herbal decoctions are given, and various means, mostly depending on sympathetic magic, are employed to avert the adverse spirits and hasten and ease the labour. She may be given water to drink in which the feet of her husband[2] or her mother-in-law or a young unmarried girl have been dipped, or she is shown the *swastik* or some other lucky sign, or the *chakra-vyuha*, a spiral figure showing the arrangement of the armies of the Pāndavas and Kauravas which resembles the intestines with the exit at the lower end."

The menstrual blood of the mother during child-birth is efficacious as a charm for fertility. The Nāin or Basorin will sometimes try and dip her big toe into it and go to her house. There she will wash her toe and give the water to a barren woman, who by drinking it will transfer to herself the fertility of the woman whose blood it is. The women of the family are in the lying-in room and they watch her carefully, while some of the men stand about outside. If they see the midwife coming out they examine her, and if they find any blood exclaim, 'You have eaten of our salt and will you play us this trick'; and they force her back into the room where the blood is washed off. All the stained clothes are washed in the birth-room, and the water as well as that in which the mother and child are bathed is poured into a hole dug inside the room, so that none of it may be used as a charm.

16. Treatment of mother and child.

The great object of the treatment after birth is to prevent the mother and child from catching cold. They appear to confuse the symptoms of pneumonia and infantile lockjaw in a disease called *sanpāt*, to the prevention of which their efforts are directed. A *sigri* or stove is kept alight under the bed, and in this the seeds of *ajwāin* or coriander are

---

[1] *C.P. Census Report* (1911), p. 153.   [2] Or his big toe.

burnt. The mother eats the seeds, and the child is waved over the stove in the smoke of the burning *ajwāin*. Raw asafoetida is put in the woman's ears wrapped in cotton-wool, and she eats a little half-cooked. A freshly-dried piece of cowdung is also picked up from the ground and half-burnt and put in water, and some of this water is given to her to drink, the process being repeated every day for a month. Other details of the treatment of the mother and child after birth are given in the articles on Mehtar and Kunbi. For the first five days after birth the child is given a little honey and calf's urine mixed. If the child coughs it is given *bans-lochan*, which is said to be some kind of silicate found in bamboos. The mother does not suckle the child for three days, and for that period she is not washed and nobody goes near her, at least in Mandla. On the third day after the birth of a girl, or the fourth after that of a boy, the mother is washed and the child is then suckled by her for the first time, at an auspicious moment pointed out by the astrologer. Generally speaking the whole treatment of child-birth is directed towards the avoidance of various imaginary magical dangers, while the real sanitary precautions and other assistance which should be given to the mother are not only totally neglected, but the treatment employed greatly aggravates the ordinary risks which a woman has to take, especially in the middle and higher castes.

17. Ceremonies after birth.

When a boy is born the father's younger brother or one of his friends lets off a gun and beats a brass plate to proclaim the event. The women often announce the birth of a boy by saying that it is a one-eyed girl. This is in case any enemy should hear the mention of the boy's birth, and the envy felt by him should injure the child. On the sixth day after the birth the Chhathi ceremony is performed and the mother is given ordinary food to eat, as described in the article on Kunbi. The twelfth day is known as Barhon or Chauk. On this day the father is shaved for the first time after the child's birth. The mother bathes and cuts the nails of her hands and feet; if she is living by a river she throws them into it, otherwise on to the roof of the house. The father and mother sit in the *chauk* or space marked out for worship with cowdung and flour; the woman is on the man's left side, a woman being known as Bāmangi or the left limb, either because the left limb is weak or because woman is supposed to have been made from man's left side, as in Genesis. The household god is brought into the *chauk* and they worship it. The Bua or husband's sister brings presents to the mother known as *bharti*, for filling her lap: silver or gold bangles if she can afford them, a coat and cap for the boy; dates, rice and a breast-cloth for the mother; for the father a rupee and a cocoanut. These things are placed in the mother's lap as a charm to sustain her fertility. The father gives his sister back double the value of the presents if he can afford it. He gives her husband a head-cloth and shoulder-cloth; he waves two or three pice round his wife's head and gives them to the barber's wife. The latter and the midwife take the clothes worn by the mother at child-birth, and the father gives them each a new cloth if he can afford it. The part of the navel-string which falls off the child's body is believed to have the power of rendering a barren woman fertile, and is also intimately connected with the child's destiny. It is therefore carefully preserved and buried in some auspicious place, as by the bank of a river.

In the sixth month the Pasni ceremony is performed, when the child is given grain for the first time, consisting of rice and milk. Brāhmans or religious mendicants are invited and fed. The child's hair and nails are cut for the first time on the Shivrātri or Akti festival following the birth, and are wrapped up in a ball of dough and thrown into a sacred river. If a child is born during an eclipse they think that it will suffer from lung disease; so a silver model of the moon is made immediately during the eclipse, and hung round the child's neck, and this is supposed to preserve it from harm.

18. Suckling children.

A Hindu woman will normally suckle her child for two to three years after its birth, and even beyond this up to six years if it sleeps with her. But they think that the child becomes short of breath if suckled for so long, and advise the mother to wean it. And if she becomes pregnant again, when she has been three or four months in this condition, she will wean the child by putting *nīm* leaves or some other bitter thing on her breasts. A Hindu should not visit his wife for the last six months of her pregnancy nor until the child has been fed with grain for the first time six months after its birth. During the former period such action is thought to be a sin, while during the latter it may have the effect of rendering the mother pregnant again too quickly, and hence may not allow her a sufficiently long period to suckle the first child.

Twins, Mr. Marten states, are not usually considered to be inauspicious.[1] "It is held that if they are of the same sex they will survive, and if they are of a different sex one of them will die. Boy twins are called Rāma and Lachhman, a boy and a girl Mahādeo and Pārvati, and two girls Ganga and Jamuni or Sīta and Konda. They should always be kept separate so as to break the essential connection which exists between them and may cause any misfortune which happens to the one to extend to the other. Thus the mother always sleeps between them in bed and never carries both of them nor suckles both at the same time. Again, among some castes in Chhattīsgarh, when the twins are of different sex, they are considered to be *pāp* (sinful) and are called Pāpi and Pāpin, an allusion to the horror of a brother and sister sharing the same bed (the mother's womb)." Hindus think that if two people comb their hair with the same comb they will lose their affection for each other. Hence the hair of twins is combed with the same comb to weaken the tie which exists between them, and may cause the illness or death of either to follow on that of the other.

19. Beliefs about twins.

The dead are usually burnt with the head to the north. Children whose ears have not been bored and adults who die of smallpox or leprosy are buried, and members of poor families who cannot afford firewood. If a person has died by hanging or drowning or from the bite of a snake, his body is burnt without any rites, but in order that his soul may be saved, the *hom* sacrifice is performed subsequently to the cremation. Those who live near the Nerbudda and Mahānadi sometimes throw the bodies of the dead into these rivers and think that this will make them go to heaven.

20. Disposal of the dead.

---

[1] *C.P. Census Report* (1911), p. 158.

The following account of a funeral ceremony among the middle and higher castes in Saugor is mainly furnished by Major W. D. Sutherland, I.M.S., with some additions from Mandla, and from material furnished by the Rev. E. M. Gordon:[1] "When a man is near his end, gifts to Brāhmans are made by him, or by his son on his behalf. These, if he is a rich man, consist of five cows with their calves, marked on the forehead and hoofs with turmeric, and with garlands of flowers round their necks. Ordinary people give the price of one calf, which is fictitiously taken at Rs. 3-4, Rs. 1-4, ten annas or five annas according to their means. By holding on to the tail of this calf the dead man will be able to swim across the dreadful river Vaitarni, the Hindu Styx. This calf is called Bachra Sānkal or 'the chain-calf,' as it furnishes a chain across the river, and it may be given three times, once before the death and twice afterwards. When near his end the dying man is taken down from his cot and laid on a woollen blanket spread on the ground, perhaps with the idea that he should at death be in contact with the earth and not suspended in mid-air as a man on a cot is held to be. In his mouth are placed a piece of gold, some leaves of the *tulsi* or basil plant, or Ganges water, or rice cooked in Jagannāth's temple. The dying man keeps on repeating 'Rām, Rām, Sitārām.'"

21. Funeral rites.

As soon as death occurs the corpse is bathed, clothed and smeared with a mixture of powdered sandalwood, camphor and spices. A bier is constructed of planks, or if this cannot be afforded the man's cot is turned upside down and the body is carried out for burial on it in this fashion, with the legs of the cot pointing upwards. Straw is laid on the bier, and the corpse, covered with fine white cloth, is tied securely on to it, the hands being crossed on the breast, with the thumbs and great toes tied together. When a married woman dies she is covered with a red cloth which reaches only to the neck, and her face is left open to the view of everybody, whether she went abroad unveiled in her life or not. It is considered a highly auspicious thing for a woman to die in the lifetime of her husband and children, and the corpse is sometimes dressed like a bride and

[1] In *Indian Folk Tales*.

ornaments put on it. The corpse of a widow or girl is wrapped in a white cloth with the head covered. At the head of the funeral procession walks the son of the deceased, or other chief mourner, and in his hand he takes smouldering cowdung cakes in an earthen pot, from which the pyre will be kindled. This fire is brought from the hearth of the house by the barber, and he sometimes also carries it to the pyre. On the way the mourners change places so that each may assist in bearing the bier, and once they set the bier on the ground and leave two pice and some grain where it lay, before taking it up again. After the funeral each person who has helped to carry it takes up a clod of earth and with it touches successively the place on his shoulder where the bier rested, his waist and his knee, afterwards dropping the clod on the ground. It is believed that by so doing he removes from his shoulder the weight of the corpse, which would otherwise press on it for some time.

At the cremation-ground the corpse is taken from the bier and placed on the pyre. The cloth which covered it and that on which it lay are given to a sweeper, who is always present to receive this perquisite. To the corpse's mouth, eyes, ears, nostrils and throat is applied a mixture of barley-flour, butter, sesamum seeds and powdered sandal-wood. Logs of wood and cowdung cakes are then piled on the body and the pyre is fired by the son, who first holds a burning stick to the mouth of the corpse as if to inform it that he is about to apply the fire. The pyre of a man is fired at the head and of a woman at the foot. Rich people burn the corpse with sandalwood, and others have a little of this, and incense and sweet-smelling gum. Nowadays if the rain comes on and the pyre will not burn they use kerosine oil. When the body is half-consumed the son takes up a piece of wood and with it strikes the skull seven times, to break it and give exit to the soul. This, however, is not always done. The son then takes up on his right shoulder an earthen pot full of water, at the bottom of which is a small hole. He walks round the pyre three times in the direction of the sun's course and stands facing to the south, and dashes the pot on the ground, crying out in his grief, 'Oh, my father.' While this is going on *mantras* or

22. Burning the dead.

sacred verses are recited by the officiating Brāhman. When the corpse is partly consumed each member of the assembly throws the *Pānch lakariya* (five pieces of wood or sprigs of basil) on to the pyre, making obeisance to the deceased and saying, '*Swarg ko jao*,' or 'Ascend to heaven.' Or they may say, 'Go, become incarnate in some human being.' They stay by the corpse for $1\frac{1}{4}$ *pahars* or watches or some four hours, until either the skull is broken by the chief mourner or breaks of itself with a crack. Then they bathe and come home and after some hours again return to the corpse, to see that it is properly burnt. If the pyre should go out and a dog or other animal should get hold of the corpse when it is half-burnt, all the relatives are put out of caste, and have to give a feast to all the caste, costing for a rich family about Rs. 50 and for a poor one Rs. 10 to Rs. 15. Then they return home and chew *nīm* leaves, which are bitter and purifying, and spit them out of their mouth, thus severing their connection with the corpse. When the mourners have left the deceased's house the women of the family bathe, the bangles of the widow are broken, the vermilion on the parting of her hair and the glass ornament (*tikli*) on her forehead are removed, and she is clad in white clothing of coarse texture to show that henceforth she is only a widow.

On the third day the mourners go again and collect the ashes and throw them into the nearest river. The bones are placed in a silken bag or an earthen pot or a leaf basket, and taken to the Ganges or Nerbudda within ten days if possible, or otherwise after a longer interval, being buried meantime. Some milk, salt and calf's urine are sprinkled over the place where the corpse was burnt. These will cool the place, and the soul of the dead will similarly be cooled, and a cow will probably come and lick up the salt, and this will sanctify the place and also the soul. When the bones are to be taken to a sacred river they are tied up in a little piece of cloth and carried at the end of a stick by the chief mourner, who is usually accompanied by several caste-fellows. At night during the journey this stick is planted in the ground, so that the bones may not touch the earth.

23. Burial. Graves are always dug from north to south. Some people say that heaven is to the north, being situated in the

Himalayas, and others that in the Satyug or Golden Age the sun rose to the north. The digging of the grave only commences on the arrival of the funeral party, so there is of necessity a delay of several hours at the site, and all who attend a funeral are supposed to help in digging. It is considered to be meritorious to assist at a burial, and there is a saying that a man who has himself conducted a hundred funerals will become a Rāja in his next birth. When the grave has been filled in and a mound raised to mark the spot, each person present makes five small balls of earth and places them in a heap at the head of the grave. This custom is also known as *Pānch lakariya*, and must therefore be an imitation of the placing of the five sticks on the pyre; its original meaning in the latter case may have been that the mourners should assist the family by bringing a contribution of wood to the pyre. As adopted in burial it seems to have no special significance, but somewhat resembles the European custom of the mourners throwing a little dust into the grave.

On the third day the *pindas* or sacrificial cakes are offered and this goes on till the tenth day. These cakes are not eaten by the priest or Mahā-Brāhman, but are thrown into a river. On the evening of the third day the son goes, accompanied by a Brāhman and a barber, and carrying a key to avert evil, to a pīpal[1] tree, on whose branches he hangs two earthen pots: one containing water, which trickles out through a hole in the bottom, and the other a lamp. On each succeeding night the son replenishes the contents of these pots, which are intended to refresh the spirit of the deceased and to light it on its way to the lower world. In some localities on the evening of the third day the ashes of the cooking-place are sifted, and laid out on a tray at night on the spot where the deceased died, or near the cooking-place. In the morning the layer of ashes is inspected, and if what appears to be a hand- or footprint is seen, it is held that the spirit of the deceased has visited the house. Some people look for handprints, some for footprints, and some for both, and the Nais look for the print of a cow's hoof, which when seen is held to prove that the deceased in consideration of his singular merits has been reborn a cow. If

24. Return of the soul.

---

[1] *Ficus R.*

a woman has died in child-birth, or after the birth of a child and before the performance of the sixth-day ceremony of purification, her hands are tied with a cotton thread when she is buried, in order that her spirit may be unable to rise and trouble the living. It is believed that the souls of such women become evil spirits or *Churels*. Thorns are also placed over her grave for the same purpose.

25. Mourning. During the days of mourning the chief mourner sits apart and does no work. The others do their work but do not touch any one else, as they are impure. They leave their hair unkempt, do not worship the gods nor sleep on cots, and abjure betel, milk, butter, curds, meat, the wearing of shoes, new clothes and other luxuries. In these days the friends of the family come and comfort the mourners with conversation on the shortness and uncertainty of human life and kindred topics. During the period of mourning when the family go to bathe they march one behind the other in Indian file. And on the last day all the people of the village accompany them, the men first and after they have returned the women, all marching one behind the other. They also come back in this manner from the actual funeral, and the idea is perhaps to prevent the dead man's spirit from following them. He would probably feel impelled to adopt the same formation and fall in behind the last of the line, and then some means is devised, such as spreading thorns in the path, for leaving him behind.

26. Shaving, and presents to Brāhmans. On the ninth, tenth or eleventh day the males of the family have the front of the head from the crown, and the beard and moustaches, shaved in token of mourning. The Mahā-Brāhman who receives the gifts for the dead is shaved with them. This must be done for an elder relation, but a man need not be shaved on the death of his wife, sister or children. The day is the end of mourning and is called Gauri Ganesh, Gauri being Pārvati or the wife of Siva, and Ganesh the god of good fortune. On the occasion the family give to the Mahā-Brāhman[1] a new cot and bedding with a cloth, an umbrella to shield the spirit from the sun's rays, a copper vessel full of water to quench its thirst, a brass lamp to guide it on its journey, and if the family is well-to-do a

---

[1] He is also known as Katia or Kattaha Brāhman and as Mahāpātra.

horse and a cow. All these things are meant to be for the use of the dead man in the other world. It is also the Brāhman's business to eat a quantity of cooked food, which will form the dead man's food. It is of great spiritual importance to the dead man's soul that the Brāhman should finish the dish set before him, and if he does not do so the soul will fare badly. He takes advantage of this by stopping in the middle of the meal, saying that he has eaten all he is capable of and cannot go on, so that the relations have to give him large presents to induce him to finish the food. These Mahā-Brāhmans are utterly despised and looked down on by all other Brāhmans and by the community generally, and are sometimes made to live outside the village. The regular priest, the Malai or Purohit, can accept no gifts from the time of the death to the end of the period of mourning. Afterwards he also receives presents in money according to the means of his clients, which it is supposed will benefit the dead man's soul in the next world ; but no disgrace attaches to the acceptance of these.

27. End of mourning.

When the mourning is complete on the Gauri-Ganesh day all the relatives take their food at the chief mourner's house, and afterwards the *panchāyat* invest him with a new turban provided by a relative. On the next bazār day the members of the *panchāyat* take him to the bazār and tell him to take up his regular occupation and earn his livelihood. Thereafter all his relatives and friends invite him to take food at their houses, probably to mark his accession to the position of head of the family.

28. Anniversaries of the dead.

Three months, six months and twelve months after the death presents are made to a Brāhman, consisting of Sīdha, or butter, wheat and rice for a day's food. The anniversaries of the dead are celebrated during Pitripaksh or the dark fortnight of Kunwār (September-October). If a man died on the third day of any fortnight in the year, his anniversary is celebrated on the third day of this fortnight and so on. On that day it is supposed that his spirit will visit his earthly house where his relatives reside. But the souls of women all return to their homes on the ninth day of the fortnight, and on the thirteenth day come the souls of all those who have met with a violent death, as by a fall, or have been killed by wild animals or snakes. The spirits of such persons are supposed, on account of their untimely end, to entertain a special grudge against the living.

29. Beliefs in the hereafter.

As regards the belief in the hereafter Mr. Gordon writes :[1] "That they have the idea of hell as a place of punishment may be gathered from the belief that when salt is spilt the one who does this will in Pātāl or the infernal region have to gather up each grain of salt with his eyelids. Salt is for this reason handed round with great care, and it is considered unlucky to receive it in the palm of the hand; it is therefore invariably taken in a cloth or vessel. There is a belief that the spirit of the deceased hovers round familiar scenes and places, and on this account, whenever possible, a house in which any one has died is destroyed or deserted. After the spirit has wandered round restlessly for a certain time it is said that it will again become incarnate and take the form either of man or of one of the lower animals." In Mandla they think that the soul after death is arraigned and judged before Yama, and is then chained to a flaming pillar for a longer or shorter period according to its sins. The gifts made to Brāhmans for the dead somewhat shorten the period. After that time it is born again with a good or bad body and human or animal according to its deserts.

30. Religion. Village gods.

The caste worship the principal Hindu deities. Either Bhagwān or Parmeshwar is usually referred to as the supreme deity, as we speak of God. Bhagwān appears to be Vishnu or the Sun, and Parmeshwar is Siva or Mahādeo. There are few temples to Vishnu in villages, but none are required as the sun is daily visible. Sunday or Rawiwār is the day sacred to him, and some people fast in his honour on Sundays, eating only one meal without salt. A man salutes the sun after he gets up by joining his hands and looking towards it, again when he has washed his face, and a third time when he has bathed, by throwing a little water in the sun's direction. He must not spit in front of the sun nor perform the lower functions of the body in its sight. Others say that the sun and moon are the eyes of God, and the light of the sun is the effulgence of God, because by its light and heat all moving and immobile creatures sustain their life and all

---

[1] *Indian Folk Tales*, p. 54.

corn and other products of the earth grow. In his incarnations of Rāma and Krishna there are temples to Vishnu in large villages and towns. Khermāta, the mother of the village, is the local form of Devi or the earth-goddess. She has a small hut and an image of Devi, either black or red. She is worshipped by a priest called Panda, who may be of any caste except the impure castes. The earth is worshipped in various ways. A man taking medicine for the first time in an illness sprinkles a few drops on the earth in its honour. Similarly for the first three or four times that a cow is milked after the birth of a calf the stream is allowed to fall on the ground. A man who is travelling offers a little food to the earth before eating himself. Devi is sometimes considered to be one of seven sisters, but of the others only two are known, Marhai Devi, the goddess of cholera, and Sitala Devi, the goddess of smallpox. When an epidemic of cholera breaks out the Panda performs the following ceremony to avert it. He takes a kid and a small pig or chicken, and some cloth, cakes, glass bangles, vermilion, an earthen lamp, and some country liquor, which is sprinkled all along the way from where he starts to where he stops. He proceeds in this manner to the boundary of the village at a place where there are cross-roads, and leaves all the things there. Sometimes the animals are sacrificed and eaten. While the Panda is doing this every one collects the sweepings of his house in a winnowing-fan and throws them outside the village boundary, at the same time ringing a bell continuously. The Panda must perform his ceremony at night and, if possible, on the day of the new moon. He is accompanied by a few other low-caste persons called Gunias. A Gunia is one who can be possessed by a spirit in the temple of Khermāta. When possessed he shakes his head up and down violently and foams at the mouth, and sometimes strikes his head on the ground. Another favourite godling is Hardaul, who was the brother of Jujhār Singh, Rāja of Orchha, and was suspected by Jujhār Singh of loving the latter's wife, and poisoned in consequence by his orders. Hardaul has a platform and sometimes a hut with an image of a man on horseback carrying a spear in his hand. His shrine is outside the village, and two days before a marriage the women of the family visit his shrine and cook and eat their food there and invite him to the wedding. Clay horses are offered to him, and he is supposed to be able to keep off rain and storms during the ceremony. Hardaul is perhaps the deified Rājpūt horseman. Hanumān or Mahābīr is represented by an image of a monkey coloured with vermilion, with a club in his hand and a slain man beneath his feet. He is principally worshipped on Saturdays so that he may counteract the evil influences exercised by the planet Saturn on that day. His image is painted with oil mixed with vermilion and has a wreath of flowers of the cotton tree; and *gugal* or incense made of resin, sandalwood and other ingredients is burnt before him. He is the deified ape, and is the god of strength and swiftness, owing to the exploits performed by him during Rāma's invasion of Ceylon. Dūlha Deo is another godling whose shrine is in every village. He was a young bridegroom who was carried off by a tiger on his way to his wedding, or, according to another account, was turned into a stone pillar by a flash of lightning. Before the starting of a wedding procession the members go to Dūlha Deo and offer a pair of shoes and a miniature post and marriage-crown. On their return they offer a cocoanut. Dūlha Deo has a stone and platform to the east of the village, or occasionally an image of a man on horseback like Hardaul. Mirohia is the god of the field boundary. There is no sign of him, but every tenant, when he begins sowing and cutting the crops, offers a little curds and rice and a cocoanut and lays them on the boundary of the field, saying the name of Mirohia Deo. It is believed among agriculturists that if this godling is neglected he will flatten the corn by a wind, or cause the cart to break on its way to the threshing-floor.

31. Sowing the *Jawaras* or Gardens of Adonis.

The sowing of the Jawaras, corresponding to the gardens of Adonis, takes place during the first nine days of the months of Kunwār and Chait (September and March). The former is a nine days' fast preceding the Dasahra festival, and it is supposed that the goddess Devi was during this time employed in fighting the buffalo-demon (Bhainsāsur), whom she slew on the tenth day. The latter is a nine days' fast at the new year, preceding the triumphant entry of Rāma into Ajodhia on the tenth day on his return from Ceylon. The first period comes before the sowing of the spring crop of wheat and other grains, and the second is at the commencement of the harvest of the same crop. In some localities the Jawaras are also grown a third time in the rains, probably as a preparation for the juāri sowings,[1] as juāri is planted in the baskets or 'gardens' at this time. On the first day a small room is cleared and whitewashed, and is known as the *diwāla* or temple. Some earth is brought from the fields and mixed with manure in a basket, and a male member of the family sows wheat in it, bathing before he does so. The basket is kept in the *diwāla* and the same man attends on it throughout the nine days, fasting all day and eating only milk and fruit at night. A similar nine days' fast was observed by the Eleusinians before the sacramental eating of corn and the worship of the Corn Goddess, which constituted the Eleusinian mysteries.[2] During the period of nine days, called the Naorātra, the plants are watered, and long stalks spring up. On the eighth day the *hom* or fire offering is performed, and the Gunias or devotees are possessed by Devi. On the evening of the ninth day the women, putting on their best clothes, walk out of the houses with the pots of grain on their heads, singing songs in praise of Devi. The men accompany them beating drums and cymbals. The devotees pierce their cheeks with long iron needles and walk in the procession. High-caste women, who cannot go themselves, hire the barber's or waterman's wife to go for them. The pots are taken to a tank and thrown in, the stalks of grain being kept and distributed as a mark of amity. The wheat which is sown in Kunwār gives a forecast of the spring crops. A plant is pulled out, and the return of the crop will be the same number of times the seed as it has roots. The woman who gets to the tank first counts the number of plants in her pot, and this gives the price of wheat in rupees per *māni*.[3] Sometimes marks of red rust appear on the plants, and this shows that the crop will suffer from rust. The ceremony performed in Chait is said to be a sort of

---

[1] *Sorghum vulgare*, a large millet.
[2] Dr. Jevons, *Introduction to the History of Religion*, p. 365.
[3] A measure of 400 lbs.

harvest thanksgiving. On the ninth day of the autumn ceremony another celebration called 'Jhinjhia' or 'Norta' takes place in large villages. A number of young unmarried girls take earthen pots and, making holes in them and placing lamps inside, carry them on their heads through the village, singing and dancing. They receive presents from the villagers, with which they hold a feast. At this a small platform is erected and two earthen dolls, male and female, are placed on it; rice and flowers are offered to them and their marriage is celebrated.

32. Rites connected with the crops. Customs of cultivation. The following observances in connection with the crops are practised by the agricultural castes in Chhattīsgarh:

The agricultural year begins on Akti or the 3rd day of Baisākh (April-May). On that day a cup made of *palās*[1] leaves and filled with rice is offered to Thākur Deo. In some villages the boys sow rice seeds before Thākur Deo's shrine with little toy ploughs. The cultivator then goes to his field, and covering his hand with wheat-flour and turmeric, stamps it five times on the plough. The mālguzār takes five handfuls of the seed consecrated to Thākur Deo and sows it, and each of the cultivators also sows a little. After this regular cultivation may begin on any day, though Monday and Friday are considered auspicious days for the commencement of sowing. On the Hareli, or festival of the fresh verdure, which falls on the 15th day of Shrāwan (July-August), balls of flour mixed with salt are given to the cattle. The plough and all the implements of agriculture are taken to a tank and washed, and are then set up in the courtyard of the house and plastered with cowdung. The plough is set facing towards the sun, and butter and sugar are offered to it. An earthen pot is whitewashed and human figures are drawn on it with charcoal, one upside down. It is then hung over the entrance to the house and is believed to avert the evil eye. All the holes in the cattle-sheds and courtyards are filled and levelled with gravel. While the rice is growing, holidays are observed on five Sundays and no work is done. Before harvest Thākur Deo must be propitiated with an offering of a white goat or a black fowl. Any one who begins to cut his crop before this

[1] *Butea frondosa.*

SOWING.

Bemrose, Collo., Derby.

offering has been made to Thākur Deo is fined the price of a goat by the village community. Before threshing his corn each cultivator offers a separate sacrifice to Thākur Deo of a goat, a fowl or a broken cocoanut. Each evening, on the conclusion of a day's threshing, a wisp of straw is rubbed on the forehead of each bullock, and a hair is then pulled from its tail, and the hairs and straw made into a bundle are tied to the pole of the threshing-floor. The cultivator prays, 'O God of plenty! enter here full and go out empty.' Before leaving the threshing-floor for the night some straw is burnt and three circles are drawn with the ashes, one round the heap of grain and the others round the pole. Outside the circles are drawn pictures of the sun, the moon, a lion and a monkey, or of a cart and a pair of bullocks. Next morning before sunrise the ashes are swept away by waving a winnowing-fan over them. This ceremony is called *anjan chadhāna* or placing lamp-black on the face of the threshing-floor to avert the evil eye, as women put it on their eyes. Before the grain is measured it must be stacked in the form of a trapezium with the shorter end to the south, and not in that of a square or oblong heap. The measurer stands facing the east, and having the shorter end of the heap on his left hand. On the larger side of the heap are laid the *kalara* or hook, a winnowing-fan, the *dauri*, a rope by which the bullocks are tied to the threshing-pole, one or three branches of the *ber* or wild plum tree, and the twisted bundle of straw and hair of the bullocks which had been tied to the pole. On the top of the heap are placed five balls of cowdung, and the *hom* or fire sacrifice is offered to it. The first *kātha*[1] of rice measured is also laid by the heap. The measurer never quite empties his measure while the work is going on, as it is feared that if he does this the god of abundance will leave the threshing-floor. While measuring he should always wear a turban. It is considered unlucky for any one who has ridden on an elephant to enter the threshing-floor, but a person who has ridden on a tiger brings luck. Consequently the Gonds and Baigas, if they capture a young tiger and tame it, will take it round

---

[1] A measure containing 9 lb. 2 oz. of rice.

the country, and the cultivators pay them a little to give their children a ride on it. To enter a threshing-floor with shod feet is also unlucky. Grain is not usually measured at noon but in the morning or evening.

33. Agricultural superstitions.

The cultivators think that each grain should bear a hundredfold, but they do not get this as Kuvera, the treasurer of the gods, or Bhainsāsur, the buffalo demon who lives in the fields, takes it. Bhainsāsur is worshipped when the rice is coming into ear, and if they think he is likely to be mischievous they give him a pig, but otherwise a smaller offering. When the standing corn in the fields is beaten down at night they think that Bhainsāsur has been passing over it. He also steals the crop while it is being cut and is lying on the ground. Once Bhainsāsur was absent while the particular field in the village from which he stole his supply of grain was cut and the crop removed, and afterwards he was heard crying that all his provision for the year had been lost. Sometimes the oldest man in the house cuts the first five bundles of the crop, and they are afterwards left in the field for the birds to eat. And at the end of harvest the last one or two sheaves are left standing in the field, and any one who likes can cut and carry them away. In some localities the last stalks are left standing in the field and are known as *barhona* or the giver of increase. Then all the labourers rush together at this last patch of corn and tear it up by the roots; everybody seizes as much as he can and keeps it, the master having no share in this patch. After the *barhona* has been torn up all the labourers fall on their faces to the ground and worship the field. In other places the *barhona* is left standing for the birds to eat. This custom arises from the belief demonstrated by Sir J. G. Frazer in *The Golden Bough* that the corn-spirit takes refuge in the last patch of grain, and that when it is cut he flies away or his life is extinguished. And the idea is supported by the fact that the rats and other vermin, who have been living in the field, seek shelter in the last patch of corn, and when this is cut have to dart out in front of the reapers. In some countries it is thought, as shown by Sir J. G. Frazer, that the corn-spirit takes refuge in the body of one of these animals.

THRESHING.

Bemrose, Collo., Derby.

The house of a mālguzār or good tenant stands in a courtyard or *angan* 45 to 60 feet square and surrounded by a brick or mud wall. The plan of a typical house is shown below:—

34. Houses.

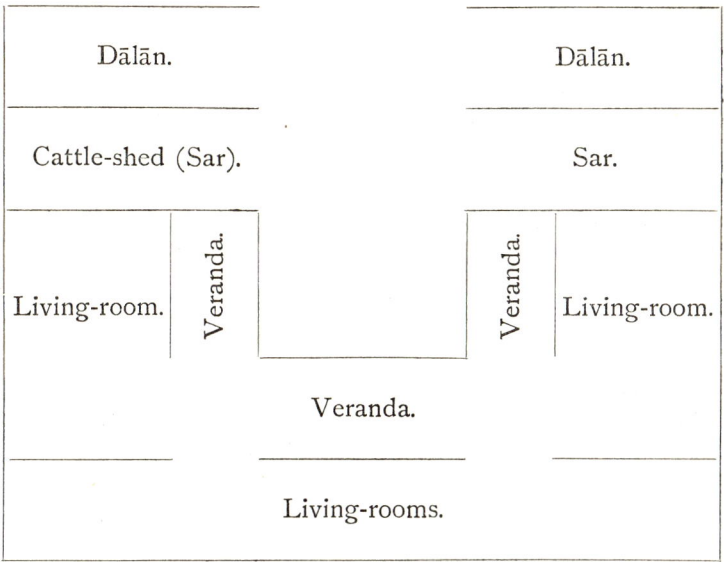

The *dālān* or hall is for the reception of visitors. One of the living-rooms is set apart for storing grain. Those who keep their women secluded have a door at the back of the courtyard for their use. Cooking is done in one of the rooms, and there are no chimneys, the smoke escaping through the tiles. They bathe either in the *chauk* or central courtyard, or go out and bathe in a tank or river or at a well. The family usually sleep inside the house in the winter and outside in the hot weather. A poor mālguzār or tenant has only two rooms with a veranda in front, one of which is used by the family, while cattle are kept in the other; while the small tenants and labourers have only one room in which both men and cattle reside. The walls are of bamboo matting plastered on both sides with mud, and the roof usually consists of single small tiles roughly baked in an improvised kiln. The house is surrounded by a mud wall or hedge, and sometimes has a garden behind in which tobacco, maize or vegetables are grown. The interior is dark, for light is admitted only by the low door, and the smoke-stained ceiling contributes to the gloom. The floor is of beaten earth well plastered with cowdung, the plastering being repeated weekly.

35. Superstitions about houses.

The following are some superstitious beliefs and customs about houses. A house should face north or east and not south or west, as the south is the region of Yama, the god of death, who lives in Ceylon, and the west the quarter of the setting sun. A Muhammadan's house, on the other hand, should face south or west because Mecca lies to the south-west. A house may have verandas front and back, or on the front and two sides, but not on all four sides. The front of a house should be lower than the back, this shape being known as *gai-mukh* or cow-mouthed, and not higher than the back, which is *singh-mukh* or tiger-mouthed. The front and back doors should not be in a straight line, which would enable one to look right through the house. The *angan* or compound of a house should be a little longer than it is wide, no matter how little. Conversely the building itself should be a little wider along the front than it is long from front to rear. The kitchen should always be on the right side if there is a veranda, or else behind. When an astrologer is about to found a house he calculates the direction in which Shesh Nāg, the snake on whom the world reposes, is holding his head at that time, and plants the first brick or stone to the left of that direction, because snakes and elephants do not turn to the left but always to the right. Consequently the house will be more secure and less likely to be shaken down by Shesh Nāg's movements, which cause the phenomenon known to us as an earthquake. Below the foundation-stone or brick are buried a pice, an areca-nut and a grain of rice, and it is lucky if the stone be laid by a man who has been faithful to his wife. There should be no echo in a house, as an echo is considered to be the voice of evil spirits. The main beam should be placed in position on a lucky day, and the carpenter breaks a cocoanut against it and receives a present. The width of the rooms along the front of a house should be five cubits each, and if there is a staircase it must have an uneven

WINNOWING.

number of steps. The door should be low so that a man must bend his head on entering and thus show respect to the household god. The floor of the verandas should be lower than that of the room inside; the Hindus say that the compound should not see the veranda nor the veranda the house. But this rule has of course also the advantage of keeping the house-floor dry. If the main beam of a house breaks it is a very bad omen, as also for a vulture or kite to perch on the roof; if this should happen seven days running the house will inevitably be left empty by sickness or other misfortune. A dog howling in front of the house is very unlucky, and if, as may occasionally happen, a dog should get on to the roof of the house and bark, the omen is of the worst kind. Neither the pīpal nor banyan trees should be planted in the yard of a house, because the leavings of food might fall upon them, and this would be an insult to the deities who inhabit the sacred trees. Neither is it well to plant the *nīm* tree, because the *nīm* is the tree of anchorites, and the frequent contemplation of it will take away from a man the desire of offspring and lead to the extinction of his family. Bananas should not be grown close to the house, because the sound of this fruit bursting the pod is said to be audible, and to hear it is most unlucky. It is a good thing to have a *gular*[1] tree in the yard, but at a little distance from the house so that the leavings of food may not fall upon it; this is the tree of the saint Dattatreya, and will cause wealth to increase in the house. A plant of the sacred *tulsi* or basil is usually kept in the yard, and every morning the householder pours a vessel of water over it as he bathes, and in the evening places a lamp beside it. This holy plant sanctifies the air which passes over it to the house.

No one should ever sit on the threshold of a house; this is the seat of Lakshmi, the goddess of wealth, and to sit on it is disrespectful to her. A house should never be swept at twilight, because it is then that Lakshmi makes her rounds, and she would curse it and pass by. At this time a lamp should be lighted, no one should be allowed to sleep, and even if a man is sick he should sit up on his bed. At

---

[1] *Ficus glomerata.*

this time the grinding-mill should not be turned nor grain be husked, but reverence should be paid to ancestors and to the household deities. No one must sit on the grinding-mill; it is regarded as a mother because it gives out the flour by which the family is fed. No one must sit on cowdung cakes because they are the seat of Saturn, the Evil One, and their smell is called *Sanīchar ke bās*. No one must step on the *chūlha* or cooking-hearth nor jar it with his foot. At the midday meal, when food is freshly cooked, each man will take a little fire from the hearth and place it in front of him, and will throw a little of everything he eats on to the fire, and some *ghī* as an offering to Agni, the god of fire. And he will also walk round the hearth, taking water in his hand and then throwing it on the ground as an offering to Agni. A man should not sleep with his feet to the south, because a corpse is always laid in that direction. He should not sleep with his feet to the east, nor spit out water from his mouth in the direction of the east.

36. Furniture.

Of furniture there is very little. Carefully arranged in their places are the brass cooking-pots, water-pots and plates, well polished with mud and water applied with plenty of elbow-grease by the careful housewife. Poor tenants frequently only have one or two brass plates and cups and an iron girdle, while all the rest of their vessels are of earthenware. Each house has several *chūlhas* or small horseshoe erections of earth for cooking. Each person in the house has a sleeping-cot if the family is comfortably off, and a spare one is also kept. These must be put out and exposed to the sun at least once a week to clear them of fleas and bugs. It is said that the Jains cannot adopt this method of disinfecting their beds owing to the sacrifice of insect life thereby involved; and that there are persons in Calcutta who make it their profession to go round and offer to lie on these cots for a time; they lie on them for some hours, and the little denizens being surfeited with their blood subsequently allow the owner of the cot to have a quiet night. A cot should always be shorter than a man's length, so that his legs project over the end; if it is so long as to contain his whole length it is like a bier, and it is feared that lying on a cot of this kind will cause him shortly to lie

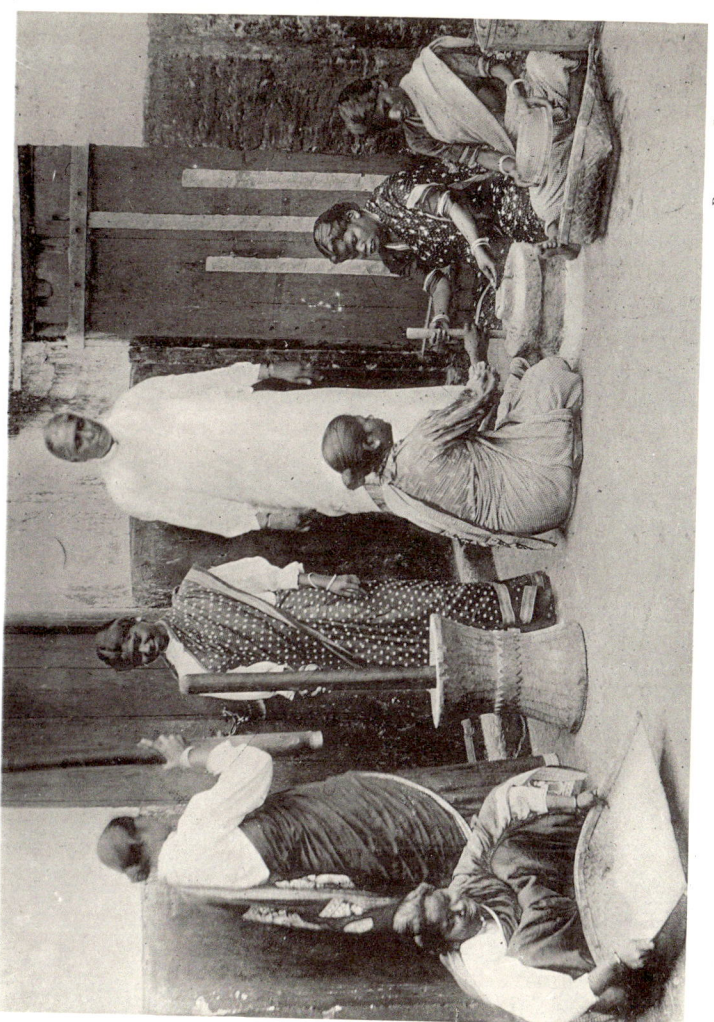

WOMEN GRINDING WHEAT AND HUSKING RICE.

Bemrose, Collo., Derby.

on a bier. Poor tenants do not usually have cots, but sleep on the ground, spreading kodon-straw on it for warmth. They have no bedding except a *gudri* or mattress made of old rags and clothes sewn together. In winter they put it over them, and sleep on it in summer. They will have a wooden log to rest their heads on when sleeping, and this will also serve as a seat for a guest. Mālguzārs have a *razai* or quilt, and a *doria* or thick cloth like those used for covering carts. Clothes and other things are kept in *jhāmpis* or round bamboo baskets. For sitting on there are *machnīs* or four-legged stools about a foot high with seats of grass rope or *pīrhis*, little wooden stools only an inch or two from the ground. For lighting, wicks are set afloat in little earthen saucers filled with oil.

Landowners usually have a long coat known as *angarkha* reaching to the knees, with flaps folding over the breasts and tied with strings. The *bandi* is a short coat like this but coming only to the hips, and is more popular with cultivators. In the cold weather it is frequently stuffed with cotton and dyed dark green or dark blue so as not to show the dirt. For visits of ceremony a pair of *paijāmas* are kept, but otherwise the *dhoti* or loin-cloth is commonly worn. Wearing the *dhoti* pulled half-way up to the thighs is called 'cultivator's fashion.' A shirt may be worn under the coat; but cultivators usually have only one garment, nowadays often a sleeveless coat with buttons in front. The proper head-dress is the *pagri*, a piece of coloured cloth perhaps 30 feet long and a foot wide, twisted tightly into folds, which is lifted on and off the head and is only rarely undone. Twisting the *pagri* is an art, and a man is usually hired to do it and paid four annas. The *pagris* have different shapes in different parts of the country, and a Hindu can tell by the shape of a man's *pagri* where he comes from. But nowadays cultivators usually wear a *dupatta* or short piece of cloth tied loosely round the head. The tenant arranges his head-cloth with a large projection on one side, and in it he carries his *chilam* or pipe-bowl, and also small quantities of vegetables, salt or condiments purchased at the bazār. In case of necessity he can transform it into a loin-cloth, or tie up a bundle of grass with it, or tie his *lota* to it to draw water from a well.

37. Clothes.

'What can the washerman do in a village where the people live naked?' is a Chhattīsgarhi proverb which aptly indicates that scantiness is the most prominent feature of the local apparel. Here a cloth round the loins, and this usually of meagre dimensions, constituted, until recently, the full dress of a cultivator. Those who have progressed a stage farther throw a cloth loosely over one shoulder, covering the chest, and assume an apology for a turban by wrapping another small rag carelessly round the head, leaving the crown generally bare, as if this part of the person required special sunning and ventilation. Hindus will not be seen out-of-doors with the head bare, though the Gonds and other tribes only begin to wear head-cloths when they are adopting Hinduism. The Gondi fashion was formerly prevalent in Chhattīsgarh. Some sanctity attaches to the turban, probably because it is the covering of the head. To knock off a man's turban is a great insult, and if it drops off or he lets it fall, it is a very bad omen.

38. Women's clothes.

Women in the northern Districts wear a skirt made of coarse cloth, usually red or blue, and a shoulder-cloth of the same material. Hand-woven cloth is still commonly used in the interior. The skirt is sometimes drawn up through the legs behind so as to give it a divided appearance; this is called *kachhota*. On the upper part of the body they wear an *angia* or breast-cloth, that is a short, tight, sleeveless jacket reaching only to below the breasts. The *angia* is tied behind, while the Marātha *choli*, which is the same thing, is buttoned or tied in front. High-caste women draw their shoulder-cloth right over the head so that the face cannot be seen. When a woman goes before a person of position she covers her head, as it is considered immodest to leave it bare. Women of respectable families wear a sheet of fine white, yellow, or red cloth drawn over the head and reaching to the ankles when they go on a journey, this being known as *pichhora*. In Chhattīsgarh all the requirements of fashion among women are satisfied by one cloth from 8 to 12 yards long and about a yard wide, which envelops the person in one fold from the waist to below the knee, hanging somewhat loosely. It is tied at the waist, and the remaining half is spread over the breast and drawn across the right shoulder,

GROUP OF WOMEN IN HINDUSTĀNI DRESS.

the end covering the head like a sheet and falling over the left shoulder. The simplicity of this solitary garment displays a graceful figure to advantage, especially on festival days, when those who can afford it are arrayed in tasar silk. When a girl is married the bridegroom's family give her expensive clothes to wear at festivals and her own people give her ordinary clothes, but usually not more than will last a year. Whenever she goes back to her father's house after her marriage, he gives her one or two cloths if he can afford it. Women of the middle and lower classes wear ornaments of bell-metal, a mixture of copper and zinc, which are very popular. Some women wear brass and zinc ornaments, and well-to-do persons have them of silver or gold.

39. Bathing.

Hot water is not used for bathing in Saugor, except by invalids, but is customary in Betūl and other Districts. The bathing-place in the courtyard is usually a large square stone on which the bather sits; he has a big circular brass vessel by him called *gangāl*,[1] and from this he takes water either in a cup or with his hands and throws it over himself, rubbing his body. Where there is a tank or stream people go to bathe in it, and if there is none the poorer classes sometimes bathe at the village well. Each man or woman has two body- or loin-cloths, and they change the cloth whenever they bathe—going into the water in the one which they have worn from the previous day, and changing into the other when they come out; long practice enables them to do this in public without any undue exposure of the body. A good tank or a river is a great amenity to a village, especially if it has a *ghāt* or flight of stone steps. Many people will spend an hour or so here daily, disporting themselves in the water or on the bank, and wedding and funeral parties are held by it, owing to the facilities for ceremonial bathing.

40. Food.

People who do not cultivate with their own hands have only two daily meals, one at midday and the other at eight or nine in the evening. Agriculturists require a third meal in the early morning before going out to the fields. Wheat and the millets juāri and kodon are the staple foods of the cultivating classes in the northern Districts, and rice is kept for festivals. The millets are made into thick *chapātis* or

[1] From Ganga, or the Ganges, and *āla* a pot.

cakes, their flour not being sufficiently adhesive for thin ones, and are eaten with the pulses, lentils, arhar,[1] mung[2] and urad.[3] The pulses are split into half and boiled in water, and when they get soft, chillies, salt and turmeric are mixed with them. Pieces of *chapāti* are broken off and dipped into this mixture. Various vegetables are also eaten. When pulse is not available the *chapātis* are simply dipped into buttermilk. If *chapātis* cannot be afforded at both meals, *ghorna* or the flour of kodon or juār boiled into a paste with water is substituted for them, a smaller quantity of this being sufficient to allay hunger. Wheat-cakes are fried in *ghī* (clarified butter) as a luxury, and at other times in sesamum oil. Rice or ground gram boiled in buttermilk are other favourite foods.

In Chhattīsgarh rice is the common food: it is eaten with pulses at midday and with vegetables cooked in *ghī* in the evening. In the morning they drink a rice-gruel, called *bāsi*, which consists of the previous night's repast mixed with water and taken cold. On festivals rice is boiled in milk. Milk is often drunk at night, and there is a saying, " He who drinks water in the morning and milk at night and takes *harra* before he sleeps will never need a doctor." A little powdered *harra* or myrobalan acts as an aperient. The food of landowners and tenants is much the same, except that the former have more butter and vegetables, according to the saying, ' *Rāja praja ka ekhi khāna*,' or ' The king and peasant eat the same food.' Those who eat flesh have an occasional change of food, but most Kurmis abstain from it. Farmservants eat the gruel of rice or kodon boiled in water when they can afford it, and if not they eat mahua flowers. These are sometimes boiled in water, and the juice is then strained off and mixed with half-ground flour, and they are also pounded and made into *chapātis* with flour and water. The leaves of the young gram-plants make a very favourite vegetable and are eaten raw, either moist or dried. In times of scarcity the poorer classes eat tamarind leaves, the pith of the banyan tree, the seeds of the bamboo, the bark of the *semar* tree,[4] the fruit of the *babūl*,[5] and other articles. A

---

[1] *Cajanus indicus.*   [2] *Phaseolus mungo.*   [3] *Phaseolus radiatus.*
[4] *Bombax malabaricum.*   [5] *Acacia arabica.*

cultivator will eat 2 lbs. of grain a day if he can get it, or more in the case of rice. Their stomachs get distended owing to the large quantities of boiled rice eaten at one time. The leaves of the *chirota* or *chakora*, a little plant [1] which grows thickly at the commencement of the rains near inhabited sites, are also a favourite vegetable, and a resource in famine time. The people call it 'Gaon ka thākur,' or 'lord of the village,' and have a saying:

> *Amarbel aur kamalgata,*
> *Gaon ka thākur, gai ka matha,*
> *Nagar sowāsan, unmen milai,*
> *Khāj, dād, sehua mīt jāwe.*

Amarbel is an endless creeper, with long yellow strings like stalks, which infests and destroys trees; it is called *amarbel* or the immortal, because it has no visible root. *Kamalgata* is the seed of the lotus; *gai ka matha* is buttermilk; *nagar sowāsan*, 'the happiness of the town,' is turmeric, because married women whose husbands are alive put turmeric on their foreheads every day; *khāj, dād* and *sehua* are itch, ringworm and some kind of rash, perhaps measles; and the verse therefore means:

"Eat *amarbel*, lotus seeds, chirota, buttermilk and turmeric mixed together, and you will keep off itch, ringworm and measles." Chirota is good for the itch.

At the commencement of a marriage or other ceremonial feast the host must wash the feet of all the guests himself. If he does not do this they will be dissatisfied, and, though they will eat at his house, will consider they have not been properly welcomed. He takes a large brass plate and placing the feet of his guest on it, pours water over them and then rubs and dries them; the water is thrown away and fresh water poured out for the next guest unless they should be brothers. Little flat stools about three inches high are provided for the guests, and if there are not enough of them a carpet is spread; or *baithkis* or sitting-mats plaited from five or six large leaves are set out. These serve as a mark of attention, as it would be discourteous to make a man sit on the ground, and they also prevent the body-

41. Caste-feasts.

---

[1] *Cassia tora.*

cloth from getting wet. The guests sit in the *chauk* or yard of the house inside, or in the *angan* or outside yard, either in lines or in a circle; members of the same caste sit with their crossed knees actually touching those of the man on either side of them to emphasise their brotherhood; if a man sat even a few inches apart from his fellows people would say he was out of caste—and this is how a man who is put out of caste actually does sit. Before each guest may be set two plates of leaves and eight *donas* or leaf-cups. On the plates are heaped rice, cakes of wheat fried in butter, and of husked urad pulse cooked with tilli or sesamum oil, and the pulse of gram and lentils. In the cups will be sugar, *ghī*, *dahi* or curded milk, various vegetables, pumpkins, and *besin* or ground gram cooked with buttermilk. All the male members of the host's family serve the food and they take it round, heaping and pouring it into each man's plates or cups until he says enough; and they continue to give further helpings as required. All the food is served at once in the different plates and cups, but owing to the number of guests a considerable time elapses before all are fully served, and the dinner lasts about two hours. The guests eat all the different dishes together with their fingers, taking a little of each according to their fancy. Each man has his *lota* or vessel of water by him and drinks as he eats. When the meal is finished large brass plates are brought in, one being given to about ten guests, and they wash their hands over these, pouring water on them from their vessels. A fresh carpet is then spread in the yard and the guests sit on it, and betel-leaf and tobacco are distributed. The huqqa is passed round, and *chilams* and *chongis* (clay pipe-bowls and leaf-pipes) are provided for those who want them. The women do not appear at the feast but stay inside, sitting in the *angan* or inner court, which is behind the *purda*.

42. Hospitality.

The people still show great hospitality, and it is the custom of many mālguzārs, at least in Chhattīsgarh, to afford food and a night's rest to all travellers who may require it. When a Brāhman comes to the village such mālguzārs will give him one or two annas, and to a Pandit or learned man as much as a rupee. Formerly it is said that when any stranger came through the village he was at once offered a cup of milk and told to drink it or throw it away. But this custom has died out in Chhattīsgarh, though one has met with it once or twice in Sambalpur. When District Officers go on tour, well-to-do landowners ask to be allowed to supply free provisions for the whole camp at least for a day, and it is difficult to refuse them gracefully. In Mandla, Banias and mālguzārs in villages near the Nerbudda sometimes undertake to give a pound of grain to every *parikramawāsi* or pilgrim perambulating the Nerbudda. And as the number of these steadily increases in consequence, they often become impoverished as a result of such indiscriminate charity.

The Kurmis employ Brāhmans for their ceremonies. They have *gurus* or spiritual preceptors who may be Brāhmans or Bairāgis; the *guru* is given from 8 annas to Rs. 5 when he initiates a neophyte, as well as his food and a new white cloth. The *guru* is occasionally consulted on some religious question, but otherwise he does nothing for his disciple except to pay him an occasional visit, when he is hospitably entertained. The Kurmis of the northern Districts do not as a rule eat meat and also abstain from alcohol, but in Chhattīsgarh they eat the flesh of clean animals and fish, and also of fowls, and drink country liquor. Old men often give up flesh and wine as a mark of piety, when they are known as Bhagat or holy. They will take food cooked with water only from Brāhmans, and that cooked without water from Rājpūts, Banias and Kāyasths as well. Brāhmans and Rājpūts will take water from Kurmis in the northern Districts though not in Chhattīsgarh. Here the Kurmis do not object to eating cooked food which has been carried from the house to the fields. This is called *rengai roti*, and castes which will eat it are considered inferior to those who always take their food in the *chauka* or purified place in the house. They say 'Rām, Rām' to each other in greeting, and the Raipur Kurmis swear by a dog or a pig. Generally they do not plough on the new or full moon days. Their women are tattooed after marriage with dots on the cheeks, marks of flies on the fingers, scorpions on the arms, and other devices on the legs.

43. Social customs. Tattooing.

44. Caste penalties. Permanent expulsion from caste is inflicted for a change of religion, taking food or having sexual intercourse with a member of an impure caste, and for eating beef. For killing a man, a cow, a buffalo, an ass, a horse, a squirrel, a cat or a monkey a man must purify himself by bathing in the Ganges at Allahābād or Benāres and giving a feast to the caste. It will be seen that all these are domestic animals except the monkey, who is the god Hanumān. The squirrel is counted as a domestic animal because it is always about the house, and the souls of children are believed to go into squirrels. One household animal, the dog, is omitted, and he appears to be less sacred than the others. For getting maggots in a wound the offender must bathe in a sacred river, such as the Nerbudda or Mahānadi, and give a feast to the caste. For eating or having intercourse with a member of any caste other than the impure ones, or for a *liaison* within the caste, or for divorcing a wife or marrying a widow, or in the case of a woman for breaking her bangles in a quarrel with her husband, a penalty feast must be given. If a man omits to feast the caste after a death in his family a second feast is imposed, and if he insults the *panchāyat* he is fined.

45. The cultivating status. The social status of the Kurmi appears to be that of the cultivator. He is above the menial and artisan castes of the village and the impure weaving and labouring castes; he is theoretically equal to the artisan castes of towns, but one or two of these, such as the Sunār or goldsmith and Kasār or brass-worker, have risen in the world owing to the prosperity or importance of their members, and now rank above the Kurmi. The Kurmi's status appears to be that of the cultivator and member of the village community, but a large proportion of the Kurmis are recruited from the non-Aryan tribes, who have obtained land and been admitted into the caste, and this tends to lower the status of the caste as a whole. In the Punjab Kurmis apparently do not hold land and are employed in grass-cutting, weaving, and tending horses, and are even said to keep pigs.[1] Here their status is necessarily very low as they follow the occupations of the impure castes. The reason why the

---

[1] *Punjab Census Report* (1881), p. 340.

Kurmi as cultivator ranks above the village handicraftsmen may perhaps be that industrial pursuits were despised in early times and left to the impure Sūdras and to the castes of mixed descent; while agriculture and trade were the occupations of the Vaishya. Further, the village artisans and menials were supported before the general use of current coin by contributions of grain from the cultivators and by presents of grain at seed-time and harvest; and among the Hindus it is considered very derogatory to accept a gift, a man who does so being held to admit his social inferiority to the giver. Some exception to this is made in the case of Brāhmans, though even with them the rule partly applies. Of these two reasons for the cultivator's superiority to the menial and artisan castes the former has to a large extent lost its force. The handicrafts are no longer considered despicable, and, as has been seen, some of the urban tradesmen, as the Sunār and Kasār, now rank above the Kurmi, or are at least equal to him. Perhaps even in ancient times these urban artificers were not despised like the village menials, as their skill was held in high repute. But the latter ground is still in full force and effect in the Central Provinces at least: the village artisans are still paid by contributions from the cultivator and receive presents from him at seed-time and harvest. The remuneration of the village menials, the blacksmith, carpenter, washerman, tanner, barber and waterman is paid at the rate of so much grain per plough of land according to the estimated value of the work done by them for the cultivators during the year. Other village tradesmen, as the potter, oilman and liquor-vendor, are no longer paid in grain, but since the introduction of currency sell their wares for cash; but there seems no reason to doubt that in former times when no money circulated in villages they were remunerated in the same manner. They still all receive presents, consisting of a sowing-basketful of grain at seed-time and one or two sheaves at harvest. The former are known as *Bījphuti*, or 'the breaking of the seed,' and the latter as *Khanvār*, or 'that which is left.' In Bilāspur the Kamias or village menials also receive as much grain as will fill a winnowing-fan when it has been threshed. When the peasant has harvested his grain all come and beg from him. The Dhīmar brings waternut, the Kāchhi or market-gardener some chillies, the Teli oil and tobacco, the Kalār some liquor if he drinks it, the Bania some sugar, and all receive grain in excess of the value of their gifts. The village menials come for their customary dues, and the Brāhman, the Nat or acrobat, the Gosain or religious mendicant, and the Fakīr or Muhammadan beggar solicit alms. On that day the cultivator is like a little king in his fields, and it is said that sometimes a quarter of the crop may go in this way; but the reference must be only to the spring crop and not to the whole holding. In former times grain must have been the principal source of wealth, and this old custom gives us a reason for the status of the cultivator in Hindu society. There is also a saying :

> *Uttam kheti, madhyam bān,*
> *Kanisht chākri, bhīk nidān,*

or 'Cultivation is the best calling, trade is respectable, service is menial, and begging is degraded.'

46. Occupation.
The Kurmi is the typical cultivator. He loves his land, and to lose it is to break the mainspring of his life. His land gives him a freedom and independence of character which is not found among the English farm-labourers. He is industrious and plodding, and inured to hardship. In some Districts the excellent tilth of the Kurmi's fields well portrays the result of his persevering labour, which he does not grudge to the land because it is his own. His wife is in no way behind him; the proverb says, "Good is the caste of the Kurmin; with a hoe in her hand she goes to the fields and works with her husband." The Chandnāhu Kurmi women are said to be more enterprising than the men, keeping them up to their work, and managing the business of the farm as well as the household.

APPENDIX

List of Exogamous Clans

Sections of the Chandnāhu subcaste :

Chānwar bambar .	Fly fan.
Sandil . .	Name of a Rishi.

APPENDIX

Gaind	Ball.
Sadāphal	A fruit.
Sondeha	Gold-bodied.
Sonkharchi	Spender of gold.
Kathail	*Kath*, wood, or *kaththa*, catechu.
Kāshi	Benares. The Desha Kurmis are all of this *gotra*. It may also be a corruption of Kachhap, tortoise.
Dhorha	*Dhor*, cattle.
Sumer	A mountain.
Chatur Midalia	*Chatur*, clever.
Bhāradwāj	After the Rishi of that name; also a bird.
Kousil	Name of a Rishi.
Ishwar	God.
Samund Karkari	A particle in an ocean.
Akālchuwa	*Akāl*, famine.
Padel	Fallow.
Bāghmār	Tiger-slayer.
Hardūba	Green grass.
Kānsia	*Kāns*, a kind of grass.
Ghiu Sāgar	Ocean of *ghī*.
Dharam Dhurandar	Most charitable.
Singnāha	*Singh*, a lion.
Chimangarhia	Belonging to Chimangarh.
Khairagarhia	Belonging to Khairagarh.
Gotam	A Rishi.
Kāshyap	A Rishi.
Pandariha	From Pandaria, a village.
Paipakhār	One who washes feet.
Bānhpakhār	One who washes arms.
Chauria	Chaurai, a vegetable.
Sānd Sathi	*Sānd*, bullock.
Singhi	*Singh*, lion or horn.
Agra—Chandan	Sandalwood.
Tek Sanichar	Saturday.
Karaiya	Frying-pan.
Pukharia	Pond.
Dhubinha	Dhobi, a caste.
Pāwanbare	*Pāwan*, air.
Modganga	Ganges.

Sections of the Gabel subcaste:

Gangajal	Ganges water.
Bimba Lohir	Bearer of a *lāthi* (stick).
Sarang	Peacock.
Rāja Rāwat	Royal prince.
Singār	Beauty.
Bānh pagar	With a thread on the arm.
Samundha	Ocean.
Parasrām	Rishi.

Katārmal	*Katār*, dagger.
Chauhān	Sept of Rājpūts.
Pātan	Village.
Gajmani	Elephant.
Deori Sumer	Village.
Lahura Samudra	Small sea.
Hansbimbraon	*Hans*, goose.
Sunwāni	Purifier.

Sections of the Santora subcaste :

Narvaria	Narwar, a town in Gwalior State.
Mundharia	Mundhra, a village.
Naigaiyan	Naogaon, a town in Bundelkhand.
Pipraiya	Piparia, a village.
Dindoria	Dindori, a village in Mandla District.
Baheria	A village.
Bāndha	*Bāndh*, embankment.
Ktmūsar	Wooden pestle.

Sections of the Tirole subcaste :

Baghele	*Bāgh*, tiger, or a sept of Rājpūts.
Rāthor	Clan of Rājpūts.
Panwār	Clan of Rājpūts.
Solanki	Clan of Rājpūts.
Aulia	*Aonla*, a fruit-bearing tree.
Sindia	*Sindi*, date-palm tree.
Khusia	*Khusi*, happiness.
Sanoria	*San*, hemp.
Gora	Fair-coloured.
Bhākrya	*Bhākar*, a thick bread.

Sections of the Gaur subcaste :

Bhandāri	Storekeeper.
Dudhua	*Dūdh*, milk.
Patele	A headman.
Lonia	Salt-maker.
Kumaria	A potter.
Sionia	Seoni town.
Chhaparia	Chhapāra, a town.
Bijoria	A tree.
Simra	A village.
Ketharia	*Keth*, a fruit.
Usargaiyan	Perhaps a village.
Bhadoria	Village.
Rurgaiyan	Village.
Musrele	*Mūsar*, a pestle.

Sections of the Usrete subcaste :

Shikāre	Hunter.
Nāhar	Tiger.

Gursaraiyan	Gursarai, a town.
Bardia	A village.
Sandia	*Sānd*, a bull.
Sirwaiyan	Sirwai, a village.
Itguhān	A village.
Sengaiyan or *Singaiyan*	Sengai, a village.
Harkotia	Harkoti, a village.
Noria	Norai, a village.
Larent	Lareti, a village.
Rabia	Rabai, a village.
Lakhauria	(Lakori village. It is said that whoever utters the name of this section early in the morning is sure to remain hungry the whole day, or at least will get into some trouble that day.)
Dhandkonya	*Dhandakna*, to roll.
Badgaiyan	*Badagaon*, a large village.
Kotia	*Kot*, a fort.
Bilwār	*Billi*, cat.
Thutha	Stump of a tree.

Sections of the Kanaujia subcaste:

Tidha.—From Tidha, a village. This section is subdivided into (*a*) *Ghureparke* (of the cow-dung hill); (*b*) *Dwārparke* (of the door); and (*c*) *Jangi* (warrior).

Chamania.—From Chamyani (village). This is also subdivided into:
  (*a*) *Gomarhya.*
  (*b*) *Mathuria* (Muttra town).

Chaudhri (caste headman). This is divided as follows:

(*a*) *Majhgawān*	A village.
(*b*) *Purva thok*	Eastern group.
(*c*) *Pashchim thok*	Western group.
(*d*) *Bamurya*	A village.
Rāwat	Title.
Malha	Perhaps sailor or wrestler.
Chiloliān	Chiloli, a village.
Dhanuiyan	Dhanu Kheda, a village.

LAKHERA

LIST OF PARAGRAPHS

1. *General notice.*
2. *Social customs.*
3. *The lac industry.*
4. *Lac bangles.*
5. *Red, a lucky colour.*
6. *Vermilion and spangles.*
7. *Red dye on the feet.*
8. *Red threads.*
9. *Lac toys.*

1. General notice.

Lakhera, Laheri.—The small caste whose members make bangles and other articles of lac. About 3000 persons were shown as belonging to the caste in the Central Provinces in 1911, being most numerous in the Jubbulpore, Chhīndwāra and Betūl Districts. From Berār 150 persons were returned, chiefly from Amraoti. The name is derived from the Sanskrit *laksha-kara*, a worker in lac. The caste are a mixed functional group closely connected with the Kacheras and Patwas; no distinction being recognised between the Patwas and Lakheras in some localities of the Central Provinces. Mr. Baillie gives the following notice of them in the *Census Report of the North-Western Provinces* (1891): "The accounts given by members of the caste of their origin are very various and sometimes ingenious. One story is that like the Patwas, with whom they are connected, they were originally Kāyasths. According to another account they were made from the dirt washed from Pārvati before her marriage with Siva, being created by the god to make bangles for his wife, and hence called Deobansi. Again, it is stated, they were created by Krishna to make bangles for the Gopis or milkmaids. The most elaborate account is that they were originally Yāduvansi Rājpūts, who assisted the Kurus to make a fort of lac, in which the Pāndavas were to be treacherously burned. For this traitorous conduct they were degraded and compelled eternally to work in lac or glass."

The bulk of these artisan and manufacturing castes tell stories showing that their ancestors were Kāyasths and Rājpūts, but no importance can be attached to such legends, which are obviously manufactured by the family priests to minister to the harmless vanity of their clients. To support their claim the Lakheras have divided themselves like the Rājpūts into the Sūrajvansi and Somvansi subcastes or those who belong to the Solar and Lunar races. Other subdivisions are the Mārwāri or those coming from Mārwār in Rājputāna, and the Tarkhera or makers of the large earrings which low-caste women wear. These consist of a circular piece of wood or fibre, nearly an inch across, which is worked through a large hole in the lobe of the ear. It is often the stalk of the *ambāri* fibre, and on the outer end is fixed a slab decorated with little pieces of glass. The exogamous sections of the Lakheras are generally named after animals, plants and natural objects, and indicate that the caste is recruited from the lower classes of the population. Their social customs resemble those of the middle and lower Hindustāni castes. Girls are married at an early age when the parents can afford the expense of the ceremony, but no penalty is incurred if the wedding is postponed for want of means. The remarriage of widows and divorce are permitted. They eat flesh, but not fowls or pork, and some of them drink liquor, while others abstain. Rājpūts and Banias will take water from them, but not Brāhmans. In Bombay, however, they are considered to rank above Kunbis.

2. Social customs.

The traditional occupation of the Lakheras is to make and sell bangles and other articles of lac. Lac is regarded with a certain degree of superstitious repugnance by the Hindus because of its red colour, resembling blood. On this account and also because of the sin committed in killing them, no Hindu caste will propagate the lac insect, and the calling is practised only by Gonds, Korkus and other primitive tribes. Even Gonds will often refuse employment in growing lac if they can make their living by cultivation. Various superstitions attach to the propagation of the insects to a fresh tree. This is done in Kunwār (September) and

3. The lac industry.

always by men, the insects being carried in a leaf-cup and placed on a branch of an uninfected tree, usually the *kusum*.[1] It is said that the work should be done at night and the man should be naked when he places the insects on the tree. The tree is fenced round and nobody is allowed to touch it, as it is considered that the crop would thus be spoiled. If a woman has lost her husband and has to sow lac, she takes her son in her arms and places the cup containing the insects on his head; on arriving at the tree she manages to apply the insects by means of a stick, not touching the cup with her own hands. All this ritual attaches simply to the infection of the first tree, and afterwards in January or February the insects are propagated on to other trees without ceremony. The juice of onions is dropped on to them to make them healthy. The stick-lac is collected by the Gonds and Korkus and sold to the Lakheras; they clear it of wood as far as possible and then place the incrusted twigs and bark in long cotton bags and heat them before a fire, squeezing out the gum, which is spread out on flat plates so as to congeal into the shape of a pancake. This is again heated and mixed with white clay and forms the material for the bangles. They are coloured with *chapra*, the pure gum prepared like sealing-wax, which is mixed with vermilion, or arsenic and turmeric for a yellow colour. In some localities at least only the Lakheras and Patwas and no higher caste will sell articles made of lac.

4. Lac bangles.

The trade in lac bangles has now greatly declined, as they have been supplanted by the more ornamental glass bangles. They are thick and clumsy and five of them will cover a large part of the space between the elbow and the wrist. They may be observed on Banjāra women. Lac bangles are also still used by the Hindus, generally on ceremonial occasions, as at a marriage, when they are presented to and worn by the bride, and during the month of Shrāwan (July), when the Hindus observe a fast on behalf of the growing crops and the women wear bangles of lac. For these customs Mr. Hīra Lāl suggests the explanation that lac bangles were at one time generally worn by the

---

[1] *Schleichera trijuga*.

EXAMPLES OF SPANGLES WORN BY WOMEN ON THE FOREHEAD.

Hindus, while glass ones are a comparatively recent fashion introduced by the Muhammadans. In support of this it may be urged that glass bangles are largely made by the Muhammadan Turkāri or Sīsgar, and also that lac bangles must have been worn prior to glass ones, because if the latter had been known the clumsy and unornamental bracelet made of lac and clay could never have come into existence. The wearing of lac bangles on the above occasions would therefore be explained according to the common usage of adhering on religious and ceremonial occasions to the more ancient methods and accessories, which are sanctified by association and custom. Similarly the Holi pyre is often kindled with fire produced by the friction of wood, and temples are lighted with vegetable instead of mineral oil.

It may be noted, however, that lac bangles are not always worn by the bride at a wedding, the custom being unknown in some localities. Moreover, it appears that glass was known to the Hindus at a period prior to the Muhammadan invasions, though bangles may not have been made from it. Another reason for the use of lac bangles on the occasions noticed is that lac, as already seen, represents blood. Though blood itself is now repugnant to the Hindus, yet red is pre-eminently their lucky colour, being worn at weddings and generally preferred. It is suggested in the *Bombay Gazetteer*[1] that blood was lucky as having been the first food of primitive man, who learnt to suck the blood of animals before he ate their flesh. But it does not seem necessary to go back quite so far as this. The earliest form of sacrifice, as shown by Professor Robertson Smith,[2] was that in which the community of kinsmen ate together the flesh of their divine or totem animal god and drank its blood. When the god became separated from the animal and was represented by a stone at the place of worship and the people had ceased to eat raw flesh and drink blood, the blood was poured out over the stone as an offering to the god. This practice still obtains among the lower castes of Hindus and the primitive tribes, the blood of animals offered to Devi and other village deities being allowed to drop on to the stones representing them. But the higher

5. Red, a lucky colour.

---

[1] *Hindus of Gujarāt*, App., art. Vāghri, footnote. [2] *Religion of the Semites.*

castes of Hindus have abandoned animal sacrifices, and hence cannot make the blood-offering. In place of it they smear the stone with vermilion, which seems obviously a substitute for blood, since it is used to colour the stones representing the deities in exactly the same manner. Even vermilion, however, is not offered to the highest deities of Neo-Hinduism, Siva or Mahādeo and Vishnu, to whom animal sacrifices would be abhorrent. It is offered to Hanumān, whose image is covered with it, and to Devi and Bhairon and to the many local and village deities. In past times animal sacrifices were offered to Bhairon, as they still are to Devi, and though it is not known that they were made to Hanumān, this is highly probable, as he is the god of strength and a mighty warrior. The Mānbhao mendicants, who abhor all forms of bloodshed like the Jains, never pass one of these stones painted with vermilion if they can avoid doing so, and if they are aware that there is one on their road will make a circuit so as not to see it.[1] There seems, therefore, every reason to suppose that vermilion is a substitute for blood in offerings and hence probably on other occasions. As the places of the gods were thus always coloured red with blood, red would come to be the divine and therefore the propitious colour among the Hindus and other races.

6. Vermilion and spangles.

Among the constituents of the Sohāg or lucky *trousseau* without which no Hindu girl of good caste can be married are *sendur* or vermilion, *kunku* or red powder or a spangle (*tikli*), and *mahāwar* or red balls of cotton-wool. In Chhattīsgarh and Bengal the principal marriage rite is usually the smearing of vermilion by the bridegroom on the parting of the bride's hair, and elsewhere this is commonly done as a subsidiary ceremony. Here also there is little reason to doubt that vermilion is a substitute for blood; indeed, in some castes in Bengal, as noted by Sir H. Risley, the blood of the parties is actually mixed.[2] This marking of the bride with blood is a result of the sacrifice and communal feast of kinsmen already described; only those who could join in the sacrificial meal and eat the flesh of the sacred animal god

---

[1] Mackintosh, *Report on the Mānbhaos*.

[2] See articles on Khairwār and Kewat.

were kin to it and to each other; but in quite early times the custom prevailed of taking wives from outside the clan; and consequently, to admit the wife into her husband's kin, it was necessary that she also should drink or be marked with the blood of the god. The mixing of blood at marriage appears to be a relic of this, and the marking of the forehead with vermilion is a substitute for the anointing with blood. *Kunku* is a pink powder made of turmeric, lime-juice and borax, which last is called by the Hindus 'the milk of Anjini,' the mother of Hanumān. It seems to be a more agreeable substitute for vermilion, whose constant use has probably an injurious effect on the skin and hair. *Kunku* is used in the Marātha country in the same way as vermilion, and a married woman will smear a little patch on her forehead every day and never allow her husband to see her without it. She omits it only during the monthly period of impurity. The *tikli* or spangle is worn in the Hindustāni Districts and not in the south. It consists of a small piece of lac over which is smeared vermilion, while above it a piece of mica or thin glass is fixed for ornament. Other adornments may be added, and women from Rājputāna, such as the Mārwāri Banias and Banjāras, wear large spangles set in gold with a border of jewels if they can afford it. The spangle is made and sold by Lakheras and Patwas; it is part of the Sohāg at marriages and is affixed to the girl's forehead on her wedding and thereafter always worn; as a rule, if a woman has a spangle it is said that she does not smear vermilion on her forehead, though both may occasionally be seen. The name *tikli* is simply a corruption of *tīka*, which means a mark of anointing or initiation on the forehead; as has been seen, the basis of the *tikli* is vermilion smeared on lac-clay, and it is made by Lakheras; and there is thus good reason to suppose that the spangle is also a more ornamental substitute for the smear of vermilion, the ancient blood-mark by which a married woman was admitted into her husband's clan. At her marriage a bride must always receive the glass bangles and the vermilion, *kunku*, or spangle from her husband, the other ornaments of the Sohāg being usually given to her by her parents. Unmarried girls now also sometimes wear small ornamental spangles, and put *kunku* on their foreheads.

But before marriage it is optional and afterwards compulsory. A widow may not wear vermilion, *kunku*, or spangles.

7. Red dye on the feet. The Lakheras also sell balls of red cotton-wool known as *māhur ki guleli* or *mahāwar*. The cotton-wool is dipped in the melted lac-gum and is rubbed on to the feet of women to colour them red or pink at marriages and festivals. This is done by the barber's wife, who will colour the feet of the whole party, at the same time drawing lines round the outside of the foot and inward from the toes. The *mahāwar* is also an essential part of the Sohāg of marriage. Instead of lac the Muhammadans use *mehndi* or henna, the henna-leaves being pounded with catechu and the mixture rubbed on to the feet and hands. After a little time it is washed off and a red dye remains on the skin. It is supposed that the similar custom which prevailed among the ancient Greeks is alluded to in the epithet of 'rosy-fingered Aurora.' The Hindus use henna dye only in the month Shrāwan (July), which is a period of fasting; the auspicious *kunku* and *mahāwar* are therefore perhaps not considered suitable at such a time, but as special protection is needed against evil spirits, the necessary red colouring is obtained from henna. When a married woman rubs henna on her hands, if the dye comes out a deep red tinge, the other women say that her husband is not in love with her; but if of a pale yellowish tinge, that he is very much in love.

8. Red threads. The Lakheras and Patwas also make the *kardora* or waist-band of red thread. This is worn by Hindu men and women, except Marātha Brāhmans. After he is married, if a man breaks this thread he must not take food until he has put on a fresh one, and the same rule applies to a woman all her life. Other threads are the *rākhis* tied round the wrists for protection against evil spirits on the day of Rakshābandhan, and the necklets of silk or cotton thread wound round with thin silver wire, which the Hindus put on at Anant Chaudas and frequently retain for the whole year. The colour of all these threads is generally red in the first place, but they soon get blackened by contact with the skin.

9. Lac toys. Toys of lac are especially made during the fast of Shrāwan (July). At this time for five years after her marriage a Hindu bride receives annually from her husband a present called Shrāoni, or that which is given in Shrāwan. It consists of a *chakri* or reel, to which a string is attached, and the reel is thrown up into the air and wound and unwound on the string; a *bhora* or wooden top spun by a string; a *bansuli* or wooden flute; a stick and ball, lac bangles and a spangle, and cloth, usually of red chintz. All these toys are made by the carpenter and coloured red with lac by the Lakhera, with the exception of the bangles which may be yellow or green. For five years the bride plays with the toys, and then they are sent to her no longer as her childhood has passed. It is probable that some, if not all of them, are in a manner connected with the crops, and supposed to have a magical influence, because during the same period it is the custom for boys to walk on stilts and play at swinging themselves; and in these cases the original idea is to make the crops grow as high as the stilts or swing. As in the other cases, the red colour appears to have a protective influence against evil spirits, who are more than usually active at a time of fasting.

LODHI

LIST OF PARAGRAPHS

1. *Origin and traditions.*
2. *Position in the Central Provinces.*
3. *Subdivisions.*
4. *Exogamous groups.*
5. *Marriage customs.*
6. *The Gauna ceremony. Fertility rites.*
7. *Widow-marriage and puberty rite.*
8. *Mourning impurity.*
9. *Social customs.*
10. *Greetings and method of address.*
11. *Sacred thread and social status.*

1. Origin and traditions.

Lodhi, Lodha.—An important agricultural caste residing principally in the Vindhyan Districts and Nerbudda valley, whence they have spread to the Wainganga valley and the Khairāgarh State of Chhattīsgarh. Their total strength in the Province is 300,000 persons. The Lodhis are immigrants from the United Provinces, in whose Gazetteers it is stated that they belonged originally to the Ludhiāna District and took their name from it. Their proper designation is Lodha, but it has become corrupted to Lodhi in the Central Provinces. A number of persons resident in the Harda tahsīl of Hoshangābād are called Lodha and say that they are distinct from the Lodhis. There is nothing to support their statement, however, and it is probable that they simply represent the separate wave of immigration which took place from Central India into the Hoshangābād and Betūl Districts in the fifteenth century. They spoke a different dialect of the group known as Rājasthāni, and hence perhaps the caste-name did not get corrupted. The Lodhis of the Jubbulpore Division probably came here at a later date from northern India. The Mandla Lodhis are said to have been brought to the District by Rāja Hirde Sāh of the Gond-Rājpūt dynasty of Garha-Mandla in the seventeenth century, and they were given large grants of the waste land in the interior in order that they might clear it of forest.[1] The Lodhis are a good instance of a caste who have obtained a great rise in social status on migrating to a new area. In northern India Mr. Nesfield places them lowest among the agricultural castes and states that they are little better than a forest tribe. He derives the name from *lod*, a clod, according to which Lodhi would mean clodhopper.[2] Another suggestion is that the name is derived from the bark of the *lodh* tree,[3] which is collected by the Lodhas in northern India and sold for use as a dyeing agent. In Bulandshahr they are described as " Of short stature and uncouth appearance, and from this as well as from their want of a tradition of immigration from other parts they appear to be a mixed class proceeding from aboriginal and Aryan parents. In the Districts below Agra they are considered so low that no one drinks water touched by them; but this is not the case in the Districts above Agra."[4] In Hamīrpur they appear to have some connection with the Kurmis, and a story told of them in Saugor is that the first Lodhi was created by Mahādeo from a scarecrow in a Kurmi woman's field and given the vocation of a farmservant. But the Lodhis themselves claim Rājpūt ancestry and say that they are descended from Lava, the eldest of the two sons of Rāja Rāmchandra of Ajodhya.

2. Position in the Central Provinces.

In the Central Provinces they have become landholders and are addressed by the honorific title of Thākur, ranking with the higher cultivating castes. Several Lodhi landholders in Damoh and Saugor formerly held a quasi-independent position under the Muhammadans, and subsequently acknowledged the Rāja of Panna as their suzerain, who conferred on some families the titles of Rāja and Diwān. They kept up a certain amount of state and small contingents of soldiery, attended by whom they went to pay their respects to the representative of the ruling power. " It would be difficult," says Grant,[5] " to recognise the descendants of the

---

[1] Colonel Ward's *Mandla Settlement Report*, p. 29.
[2] *Brief View of the Caste System*, p. 14.
[3] *Symplocos racemosa*.
[4] Rāja Lachman Singh's *Bulandshahr Memo*, p. 182, quoted in Mr. Crooke's *Tribes and Castes*, art. Lodha.
[5] *Narsinghpur Settlement Report* (1866), p. 28.

peaceful cultivators of northern India in the strangely accoutred Rājas who support their style and title by a score of ragged matchlock-men and a ruined mud fort on a hillside." Sir B. Fuller's *Damoh Settlement Report* says of them: " A considerable number of villages had been for long time past in the possession of certain important families, who held them by prescription or by a grant from the ruling power, on a right which approximated as nearly to the English idea of proprietorship as native custom permitted. The most prominent of these families were of the Lodhi caste. They have developed tastes for sport and freebooting and have become decidedly the most troublesome item in the population. During the Mutiny the Lodhis as a class were openly disaffected, and one of their proprietors, the Tālukdār of Hindoria, marched on the District headquarters and looted the treasury." Similarly the Rāmgarh family of Mandla took to arms and lost the large estates till then held by them. On the other hand the village of Imjhira in Narsinghpur belonging to a Lodhi mālguzār was gallantly defended against a band of marauding rebels from Saugor. Sir R. Craddock describes them as follows: " They are men of strong character, but their constant family feuds and love of faction militate against their prosperity. A cluster of Lodhi villages forms a hotbed of strife and the nearest relations are generally divided by bitter animosities. The Revenue Officer who visits them is beset by reckless charges and counter-charges and no communities are less amenable to conciliatory compromises. Agrarian outrages are only too common in some of the Lodhi villages."[1] The high status of the Lodhi caste in the Central Provinces as compared with their position in the country of their origin may be simply explained by the fact that they here became landholders and ruling chiefs.

3. Subdivisions. In the northern Districts the landholding Lodhis are divided into a number of exogamous clans who marry with each other in imitation of the Rājpūts. These are the Mahdele, Kerbania, Dongaria, Narwara, Bhadoria and others. The name of the Kerbanias is derived from Kerbana, a village in Damoh, and the Bālākote family of that District are the

[1] *Nāgpur Settlement Report*, p. 24.

head of the clan. The Mahdeles are the highest clan and have the titles of Rāja and Diwān, while the others hold those of Rao and Kunwar, the terms Diwān and Kunwar being always applied to the younger brother of the head of the house. These titles are still occasionally conferred by the Rāja of Panna, whom the Lodhi clans looked on as their suzerain. The name of the Mahdeles is said to be derived from the *mehndi* or henna plant. The above clans sometimes practise hypergamy among themselves and also with the other Lodhis, taking daughters from the latter on receipt of a large bridegroom-price for the honour conferred by the marriage. This custom is now, however, tending to die out. There are also several endogamous subcastes ranking below the clans, of whom the principal are the Singrore, Jarha, Jāngra and Mahālodhi. The Singrore take their name from the old town of Singraur or Shrengera in northern India, Singrore, like Kanaujia, being a common subcaste name among several castes. It is also connected more lately with the Singrām Ghat or ferry of the Ganges in Allahābād District, and the title of Rāwat is said to have been conferred on the Singrore Lodhis by the emperor Akbar on a visit there. The Jarha Lodhis belong to Mandla. The name is probably a form of Jharia or jungly, but since the leading members of the caste have become large landholders they repudiate this derivation. The Jāngra Lodhis are of Chhattīsgarh, and the Mahālodhis or 'Great Lodhis' are an inferior group to which the offspring of irregular unions are or were relegated. The Mahālodhis are said to condone adultery either by a man or woman on penalty of a feast to the caste. Other groups are the Hardiha, who grow turmeric (*haldi*), and the Gwālhare or cowherds. The Lodhas of Hoshangābād may also be considered a separate subcaste. They disclaim connection with the Lodhis, but the fact that the parent caste in the United Provinces is known as Lodha appears to establish their identity. They abstain from flesh and liquor, which most Lodhis consume.

This division of the superior branch of a caste into large exogamous clans and the lower one into endogamous subcastes is only found, so far as is known, among the Rājpūts and one or two landholding castes who have imitated them. Its origin is discussed in the Introduction.

4. Exogamous groups. The subcastes are as usual divided into exogamous groups of the territorial, titular and totemistic classes. Among sections named after places may be mentioned the Chāndpuria from Chāndpur, the Kharpuria from Kharpur, and the Nāgpuriha, Raipuria, Dhamonia, Damauha and Shāhgariha from Nāgpur, Raipur, Dhamoni, Damoh and Shāhgarh. Two-thirds of the sections have the names of towns or villages. Among titular names are Saulākhia, owner of 100 lakhs, Bhainsmār, one who killed a buffalo, Kodonchor, one who stole kodon,[1] Kumharha perhaps from Kumhār a potter, and Rājbhar and Barhai (carpenter), names of castes. Among totemistic names are Baghela, tiger, also the name of a Rājpūt sept; Kutria, a dog; Khajūria, the date-palm tree; Mirchaunia, chillies; Andwār, from the castor-oil plant; Bhainsaiya, a buffalo; and Nāk, the nose.

5. Marriage customs. A man must not marry in his own section nor in that of his mother. He may marry two sisters. The exchange of girls between families is only in force among the Bilāspur Lodhis, who say, 'Eat with those who have eaten with you and marry with those who have married with you.' Girls are usually wedded before puberty, but in the northern Districts the marriage is sometimes postponed from desire to marry into a good family or from want of funds to pay a bridegroom-price, and girls of twenty or more may be unmarried. A case is known of a man who had two daughters unmarried at twenty-two and twenty-three years old, because he had been waiting for good *partis*, with the result that one of them went and lived with a man and he then married off the other in the Singhast[2] year, which is forbidden among the Lodhis, and was put out of caste. The marriage and other ceremonies of the Lodhis resemble those of the Kurmis, except in Chhattīsgarh where the Marātha fashion is followed. Here, at the wedding, the bride and bridegroom hold between them a doll made of dough with 21 cowries inside, and as the priest repeats the marriage texts they pull it apart like a cracker and see how many cowries each has got. It is

---

[1] A small millet.
[2] Every twelfth year when the planet Jupiter is in conjunction with the constellation Sinh (Leo).

considered auspicious if the bridegroom has the larger number. The priest is on the roof of the house, and before the wedding he cries out:

'Are the king and queen here?' And a man below answers, 'Yes.'
'Have they shoes on their feet?' 'Yes.'
'Have they bracelets on their hands?' 'Yes.'
'Have they rings in their ears?' 'Yes.'
'Have they crowns on their heads?' 'Yes.'
'Has she glass beads round her neck?' 'Yes.'
'Have they the doll in their hands?' 'Yes.'

And the priest then repeats the marriage texts and beats a brass dish while the doll is pulled apart. In the northern Districts after the wedding the bridegroom must untie one of the festoons of the marriage-shed, and if he refuses to do this, it is an indelible disgrace on the bride's party. Before doing so he requires a valuable present, such as a buffalo.

When the girl becomes mature the Gauna or going-away ceremony is performed. In Chhattīsgarh before leaving her home the bride goes out with her sister and worships a *palās* tree.[1] Her sister waves a lighted lamp seven times over it, and the bride goes seven times round it in imitation of the marriage ceremony. At her husband's house seven pictures of the family gods are drawn on a wall inside the house and the bride worships these, placing a little sugar and bread on the mouth of each and bowing before them. She is then seated before the family god while an old woman brings a stone rolling-pin[2] wrapped up in a piece of cloth, which is supposed to be a baby, and the old woman imitates a baby crying. She puts the roller in the bride's lap saying, 'Take this and give it milk.' The bride is abashed and throws it aside. The old woman picks it up and shows it to the assembled women saying, 'The bride has just had a baby,' amid loud laughter. Then she gives the stone to the bridegroom who also throws it aside. This ceremony is meant to induce fertility, and it is supposed that by making believe that the bride has had a baby she will quickly have one.

The higher clans of Lodhis in Damoh and Saugor pro-

6. The Gauna ceremony. Fertility rites.

[1] *Butea frondosa.*   [2] This is known as *lodha.*

7. Widow-marriage and puberty rite.

hibit the remarriage of widows, but instances of it occur. It is said that a man who marries a widow is relegated to the Mahālodhi subcaste or the Lahuri Sen, an illegitimate group, and the Lodhis of his clan no longer acknowledge his family. But if a girl's husband dies before she has lived with him she may marry again. The other Lodhis freely permit widow-marriage and divorce. When a girl first becomes mature she is secluded, and though she may stay in the house cannot enter the cook-room. At the end of the period she is dressed in red cloth, and a present of cocoanuts stripped of their shells, sweetmeats, and a little money, is placed in her lap, while a few women are invited to a feast. This rite is also meant to induce fertility, the kernel of the cocoanut being held to resemble an unborn baby.

8. Mourning impurity.

The higher clans consider themselves impure for a period of 12 days after a birth, and if the birth falls in the Mūl asterism or Nakshatra, for 27 days. After death they observe mourning for 10 days; on the 10th day they offer ten *pindas* or funeral cakes, and on the 11th day make one large *pinda* or cake and divide it into eleven parts; on the 12th day they make sixteen *pindas* and unite the spirit of the dead man with the ancestors; and on the 13th day they give a feast and feed Brāhmans and are clean. The lower subcastes only observe impurity for three days after a birth and a death. Their funeral rites are the same as those of the Kurmis.

9. Social customs.

The caste employ Brāhmans for weddings, but not necessarily for birth and death ceremonies. They eat flesh and fish, and the bulk of the caste eat fowls and drink liquor, but the landowning section abjures these practices. They will take food cooked with water from Brāhmans, and that cooked without water also from Rājpūts, Kāyasths and Sunārs. In Narsinghpur they also accept cooked food from such a low caste as Rājjahrs,[1] probably because the Rājjhars are commonly employed by them as farmservants, and hence have been accustomed to carry their master's food. A similar relation has been found to exist between the Panwār Rājpūts and their Gond farmservants. The higher class Lodhis make an inordinate show of hospitality at their

---

[1] The Rājjhars are a low caste of farmservants and labourers, probably an offshoot of the Bhar tribe.

weddings. The plates of the guests are piled up profusely with food, and these latter think it a point of honour never to refuse it or say enough. When melted butter is poured out into their cups the stream must never be broken as it passes from one guest to the other, or it is said that they will all get up and leave the feast. Apparently a lot of butter must be wasted on the ground. The higher clans seclude their women, and these when they go out must wear long clothes covering the head and reaching to the feet. The women are not allowed to wear ornaments of a cheaper metal than silver, except of course their glass bangles. The Mahālodhis will eat food cooked with water in the cook-room and carried to the fields, which the higher clans will not do. Their women wear the *sāri* drawn through the legs and knotted behind according to the Marātha fashion, but whenever they meet their husband's elder brother or any other elder of the family they must undo the knot and let the cloth hang down round their legs as a mark of respect. They wear no breast-cloth. Girls are tattooed before adolescence with dots on the chin and forehead, and marks on one hand. Before she is tattooed the girl is given sweets to eat, and during the process the operator sings songs in order that her attention may be diverted and she may not feel the pain. After she has finished the operator mutters a charm to prevent evil spirits from troubling the girl and causing her pain.

10. Greetings and method of address.

The caste have some strict taboos on names and on conversation between the sexes. A man will only address his wife, sister, daughter, paternal aunt or niece directly. If he has occasion to speak to some other woman he will take his daughter or other female relative with him and do his business through her. He will not speak even to his own women before a crowd. A woman will similarly only speak to her father, son or nephew, and father-, son- or younger brother-in-law. She will not speak to her elder brother-in-law, and she will not address her husband in the presence of his father, elder brother or any other relative whom he reveres. A wife will never call her husband by his name, but always address him as father of her son, and, if she has no son, will sometimes speak to him through his younger brother. Neither the father nor mother will call their eldest son by his name, but will use some other name. Similarly a daughter-in-law is given a fresh name on coming into the house, and on her arrival her mother-in-law looks at her for the first time through a *guna* or ring of baked gram-flour. A man meeting his father or elder brother will touch his feet in silence. One meeting his sister's husband, sister's son or son-in-law, will touch his feet and say, ' *Sāhib, salaam.*'

11. Sacred thread and social status.

The higher clans invest boys with the sacred thread either when they are initiated by a Guru or spiritual preceptor, or when they are married. The thread is made by a Brāhman and has five knots. Recently a large landholder in Mandla, a Jarha Lodhi, has assumed the sacred thread himself for the first time and sent round a circular to his caste-men enjoining them also to wear it. His family priest has produced a legend of the usual type showing how the Jarha Lodhis are Rājpūts whose ancestors threw away their sacred threads in order to escape the vengeance of Parasurāma. Generally in social position the Lodhis may be considered to rank with, but slightly above, the ordinary cultivating castes, such as the Kurmis. This superiority in no way arises from their origin, since, as already seen, they are a very low caste in their home in northern India, but from the fact that they have become large landholders in the Central Provinces and in former times their leaders exercised quasi-sovereign powers. Many Lodhis are fine-looking men and have still some appearance of having been soldiers. They are passionate and quarrelsome, especially in the Jubbulpore District. This is put forcibly in the saying that ' A Lodhi's temper is as crooked as the stream of a bullock's urine.' They are generally cultivators, but the bulk of them are not very prosperous as they are inclined to extravagance and display at weddings and on other ceremonial occasions.

1. Legends of the caste.

Lohār, Khāti, Ghantra, Ghisāri, Panchāl.—The occupational caste of blacksmiths. The name is derived from the Sanskrit *Lauha-kāra*, a worker in iron. In the Central Provinces the Lohār has in the past frequently combined the occupations of carpenter and blacksmith, and in such a capacity he is known as Khāti. The honorific designations applied to the caste are Karīgar, which means skilful, and

Mistri, a corruption of the English 'Master' or 'Mister.' In 1911 the Lohārs numbered about 180,000 persons in the Central Provinces and Berār. The Lohār is indispensable to the village economy, and the caste is found over the whole rural area of the Province.

"Practically all the Lohārs," Mr. Crooke writes,[1] "trace their origin to Visvakarma, who is the later representative of the Vedic Twashtri, the architect and handicraftsman of the gods, 'The fashioner of all ornaments, the most eminent of artisans, who formed the celestial chariots of the deities, on whose craft men subsist, and whom, a great and immortal god, they continually worship.' One[2] tradition tells that Visvakarma was a Brāhman and married the daughter of an Ahīr, who in her previous birth had been a dancing-girl of the gods. By her he had nine sons, who became the ancestors of various artisan castes, such as the Lohār, Barhai, Sunār, and Kasera."

The Lohārs of the Uriya country in the Central Provinces tell a similar story, according to which Kamar, the celestial architect, had twelve sons. The eldest son was accustomed to propitiate the family god with wine, and one day he drank some of the wine, thinking that it could not be sinful to do so as it was offered to the deity. But for this act his other brothers refused to live with him and left their home, adopting various professions; but the eldest brother became a worker in iron and laid a curse upon the others that they should not be able to practise their calling except with the implements which he had made. The second brother thus became a woodcutter (Barhai), the third a painter (Mahārana), the fourth learnt the science of vaccination and medicine and became a vaccinator (Suthiār), the fifth a goldsmith, the sixth a brass-smith, the seventh a coppersmith, and the eighth a carpenter, while the ninth brother was weak in the head and married his eldest sister, on account of which fact his descendants are known as Ghantra.[3] The Ghantras are an inferior class of blacksmiths,

[1] *Tribes and Castes of the N.W.P. and Oudh*, art. Lohār.
[2] Dowson, *Classical Dictionary*, s.v.
[3] In Uriya the term *Ghantrabela* means a person who has illicit intercourse with another. The Ghantra Lohārs are thus probably of bastard origin, like the groups known as half-castes and others which are frequently found.

probably an offshoot from some of the forest tribes, who are looked down on by the others. It is said that even to the present day the Ghantra Lohārs have no objection to eating the leavings of food of their wives, whom they regard as their eldest sisters.

2. Social position of the Lohār.

The above story is noticeable as indicating that the social position of the Lohār is somewhat below that of the other artisan castes, or at least of those who work in metals. This fact has been recorded in other localities, and has been explained by some stigma arising from his occupation, as in the following passage: "His social position is low even for a menial, and he is classed as an impure caste, in so far that Jāts and others of similar standing will have no social communion with him, though not as an outcast like the scavenger. His impurity, like that of the barber, washerman and dyer, springs solely from the nature of his employment; perhaps because it is a dirty one, but more probably because black is a colour of evil omen. It is not improbable that the necessity under which he labours of using bellows made of cowhide may have something to do with his impurity."[1]

Mr. Nesfield also says: "It is owing to the ubiquitous industry of the Lohār that the stone knives, arrow-heads and hatchets of the indigenous tribes of Upper India have been so entirely superseded by iron-ores. The memory of the stone age has not survived even in tradition. In consequence of the evil associations which Hinduism has attached to the colour of black, the caste of Lohār has not been able to raise itself to the same social level as the three metallurgic castes which follow." The following saying also indicates that the Lohār is of evil omen:

Ar, Dhār, Chuchkār.
In tinon se bachāwe Kartār.

Here *Ar* means an iron goad and signifies the Lohār; *Dhār* represents the sound of the oil falling from the press and means a Teli or oilman; *Chuchkār* is an imitation of the sound of clothes being beaten against a stone and denotes the Dhobi or washerman; and the phrase thus runs, 'My Friend, beware of the Lohār, Teli, and Dhobi, for they

[1] *Punjab Census Report* (1881), para. 624. (Ibbetson.)

are of evil omen.' It is not quite clear why this disrepute should attach to the Lohār, because iron itself is lucky, though its colour, black, may be of bad omen. But the low status of the Lohār may partly arise from the fact of his being a village menial and a servant of the cultivators; whereas the trades of the goldsmith, brass-smith and carpenter are of later origin than the blacksmith's, and are urban rather than rural industries; and thus these artisans do not commonly occupy the position of village menials. Another important consideration is that the iron industry is associated with the primitive tribes, who furnished the whole supply of the metal prior to its importation from Europe: and it is hence probable that the Lohār caste was originally constituted from these and would thus naturally be looked down upon by the Hindus. In Bengal, where few or no traces of the village community remain, the Lohār ranks as the equal of Koiris and Kurmis, and Brāhmans will take water from his hands;[1] and this somewhat favours the argument that his lower status elsewhere is not due to incidents of his occupation.

3. Caste subdivisions.

The constitution of the Lohār caste is of a heterogeneous nature. In some localities Gonds who work as blacksmiths are considered to belong to the caste and are known as Gondi Lohārs. But Hindus who work in Gond villages also sometimes bear this designation. Another subdivision returned consists of the Agarias, also an offshoot of the Gonds, who collect and smelt iron-ore in the Vindhyan and Satpūra hills. The Panchāls are a class of itinerant smiths in Berār. The Ghantras or inferior blacksmiths of the Uriya country have already been noticed. The Ghisāris are a similar low class of smiths in the southern Districts who do rough work only, but sometimes claim Rājpūt origin. Other subcastes are of the usual local or territorial type, as Mahūlia, from Māhul in Berār; Jhāde or Jhādia, those living in the jungles; Ojha, or those professing a Brāhmanical origin; Marātha, Kanaujia, Mathuria, and so on.

4. Marriage and other customs.

Infant-marriage is the custom of the caste, and the ceremony is that prevalent among the agricultural castes of the locality. The remarriage of widows is permitted, and

[1] *Tribes and Castes of Bengal*, art. Lohār.

they have the privilege of selecting their own husbands, or at least of refusing to accept any proposed suitor. A widow is always married from her father's house, and never from that of her deceased husband. The first husband's property is taken by his relatives, if there be any, and they also assume the custody of his children as soon as they are old enough to dispense with a mother's care. The dead are both buried and burnt, and in the eastern Districts some water and a tooth-stick are daily placed at a cross-road for the use of the departed spirit during the customary period of mourning, which extends to ten days. On the eleventh day the relatives go and bathe, and the chief mourner puts on a new loin-cloth. Some rice is taken and seven persons pass it from hand to hand. They then pound the rice, and making from it a figure to represent a human being, they place some grain in its mouth and say to it, 'Go and become incarnate in some human being,' and throw the image into the water. After this the impurity caused by the death is removed, and they go home and feast with their friends. In the evening they make cakes of rice, and place them seven times on the shoulder of each person who has carried the corpse to the cemetery or pyre, to remove the impurity contracted from touching it. It is also said that if this be not done the shoulder will feel the weight of the coffin for a period of six months. The caste endeavour to ascertain whether the spirit of the dead person returns to join in the funeral feast, and in what shape it will be born again. For this purpose rice-flour is spread on the floor of the cooking-room and covered with a brass plate. The women retire and sit in an adjoining room while the chief mourner with a few companions goes outside the village, and sprinkles some more rice-flour on the ground. They call to the deceased person by name, saying, 'Come, come,' and then wait patiently till some worm or insect crawls on to the floor. Some dough is then applied to this and it is carried home and let loose in the house. The flour under the brass plate is examined, and it is said that they usually see the footprints of a person or animal, indicating the corporeal entity in which the deceased soul has found a resting-place. During the period of mourning members of the bereaved family do not follow their ordinary business, nor eat flesh, sweets or other delicate food. They may not make offerings to their deities nor touch any persons outside the family, nor wear head-cloths or shoes. In the eastern Districts the principal deities of the Lohārs are Dūlha Deo and Somlai or Devi, the former being represented by a knife set in the ground inside the house, and the latter by the painting of a woman on the wall. Both deities are kept in the cooking-room, and here the head of the family offers to them rice soaked in milk, with sandal-paste, flowers, vermilion and lamp-black. He burns some melted butter in an earthen lamp and places incense upon it. If a man has been affected by the evil eye an exorcist will place some salt on his hand and burn it, muttering spells, and the evil influence is removed. They believe that a spell can be cast on a man by giving him to eat the bones of an owl, when he will become an idiot.

In the rural area of the Province the Lohār is still a village menial, making and mending the iron implements of agriculture, such as the ploughshare, axe, sickle, goad and other articles. For doing this he is paid in Saugor a yearly contribution of twenty pounds of grain per plough of land[1] held by each cultivator, together with a handful of grain at sowing-time and a sheaf at harvest from both the autumn and spring crops. In Wardha he gets fifty pounds of grain per plough of four bullocks or forty acres. For making new implements the Lohār is sometimes paid separately and is always supplied with the iron and charcoal. The hand-smelting iron industry has practically died out in the Province and the imported metal is used for nearly all purposes. The village Lohārs are usually very poor, their income seldom exceeding that of an unskilled labourer. In the towns, owing to the rapid extension of milling and factory industries, blacksmiths readily find employment and some of them earn very high wages. In the manufacture of cutlery, nails and other articles the capital is often found by a Bhātia or Bohra merchant, who acts as the capitalist and employs the Lohārs as his workmen. The women help their husbands by blowing the bellows and dragging the hot iron

5. Occupation.

[1] About 15 acres.

from the furnace, while the men wield the hammer. The Panchāls of Berār are described as a wandering caste of smiths, living in grass mat-huts and using as fuel the roots of thorn bushes, which they batter out of the ground with the back of a short-handled axe peculiar to themselves. They move from place to place with buffaloes, donkeys and ponies to carry their kit.[1] Another class of wandering smiths, the Ghisāris, are described by Mr. Crooke as follows: "Occasional camps of these most interesting people are to be met with in the Districts of the Meerut Division. They wander about with small carts and pack-animals, and, being more expert than the ordinary village Lohār, their services are in demand for the making of tools for carpenters, weavers and other craftsmen. They are known in the Punjab as Gādiya or those who have carts (*gādi, gāri*). Sir D. Ibbetson[2] says that they come up from Rājputāna and the North-Western Provinces, but their real country is the Deccan. In the Punjab they travel about with their families and implements in carts from village to village, doing the finer kinds of iron-work, which are beyond the capacity of the village artisan. In the Deccan[3] this class of wandering blacksmiths are called Saiqalgar, or knife-grinders, or Ghisāra, or grinders (Hindi, *ghisāna*, 'to rub'). They wander about grinding knives and tools."

Lorha.[4]—A small caste of cultivators in the Hoshangābād and Nimār Districts, whose distinctive occupation is to grow *san*-hemp (*Crotalaria juncea*) and to make sacking and gunny-bags from the fibre. A very strong prejudice against this crop exists among the Hindus, and those who grow it are usually cut off from their parent caste and become a separate community. Thus we have the castes known as Kumrāwat, Patbīna and Dāngur in different parts of the Province, who are probably offshoots from the Kurmis and Kunbis, but now rank below them because they grow this crop; and in the Kurmi caste itself a subcaste of Santora (hemp-picking) Kurmis has grown up. In Bilāspur the

---

[1] *Berār Census Report*, 1881 (Kitts).
[2] *Punjāb Ethnography*, para. 624.
[3] *Bombay Gazetteer*, xvi. 82.
[4] This article is partly based on papers by Mr. P. B. Telang, Munsiff Seoni-Mālwa, and Mr. Wāman Rao Mandloi, nāib-tahsīldār, Harda.

Pathāria Kurmis will grow *san*-hemp and ret it, but will not spin or weave the fibre ; while the Athāria Kurmis will not grow the crop, but will spin the fibre and make sacking. The Saugor Kewats grow this fibre, and here Brāhmans and other high castes will not take water from Kewats, though in the eastern Districts they will do so. The Narsinghpur Mallāhs, a branch of the Kewats, have also adopted the cultivation of *san*-hemp as a regular profession. The basis of the prejudice against the *san*-hemp plant is not altogether clear. The Lorhas themselves say that they are looked down upon because they use wheat-starch (*lapsi*) for smoothing the fibre, and that their name is somehow derived from this fact. But the explanation does not seem satisfactory. Many of the country people appear to think that there is something uncanny about the plant because it grows so quickly, and they say that on one occasion a cultivator went out to sow hemp in the morning, and his wife was very late in bringing his dinner to the field. He grew hungry and angry, and at last the shoots of the hemp-seeds which he had sown in the morning began to appear above the ground. At this he was so enraged that when his wife finally came he said she had kept him waiting so long that the crop had come up in the meantime, and murdered her. Since then the Hindus have been forbidden to grow *san*-hemp lest they should lose their tempers in the same manner. This story makes a somewhat excessive demand on the hearer's credulity. One probable cause of the taboo seems to be that the process of soaking and retting the stalks of the plant pollutes the water, and if carried on in a tank or in the pools of a stream might destroy the village supply of drinking-water. In former times it may have been thought that the desecration of their sacred element was an insult to the deities of rivers and streams, which would bring down retribution on the offender. It is also the case that the proper separation of the fibres requires a considerable degree of dexterity which can only be acquired by practice. Owing to the recent increase in the price of the fibre and the large profits which can now be obtained from hemp cultivation, the prejudice against it is gradually breaking down, and the Gonds, Korkus and lower Hindu castes have waived their religious scruples and are glad to turn an honest penny by sowing hemp either on their own account or for hire. Other partially tabooed crops are turmeric and *āl* or Indian madder (*Morinda citrifolia*), while onions and garlic are generally eschewed by Hindu cultivators. For growing turmeric and *āl* special subcastes have been formed, as the Alia Kunbis and the Hardia Mālis and Kāchhis (from *haldi*, turmeric), just as in the case of *san*-hemp. The objection to these two crops is believed to lie in the fact that the roots which yield the commercial product have to be boiled, and by this process a number of insects contained in them are destroyed. But the preparation of the hemp-fibre does not seem to involve any such sacrifice of insect life. The Lorhas appear to be a mixed group, with a certain amount of Rājpūt blood in them, perhaps an offshoot of the Kirārs, with whose social customs their own are said to be identical. According to another account, they are a lower or illegitimate branch of the Lodha caste of cultivators, of whose name their own is said to be a corruption. The Nimār Gūjars have a subcaste named Lorha, and the Lorhas of Hoshangābād may be connected with these. They live in the Seoni and Harda tahsīls of Hoshangābād, the *san*-hemp crop being a favourite one in villages adjoining the forests, because it is not subject to the depredations of wild animals. Cultivators are often glad to sublet their fields for the purpose of having a crop of hemp grown upon them, because the stalks are left for manure and fertilise the ground. String and sacking are also made from the hemp-fibre by vagrant and criminal castes like the Banjāras and Bhāmtas, who formerly required the bags for carrying their goods and possessions about with them.

MAHĀR

LIST OF PARAGRAPHS

1. *General notice.*
2. *Length of residence in the Central Provinces.*
3. *Legend of origin.*
4. *Subcastes.*
5. *Exogamous groups and marriage customs.*
6. *Funeral rites.*
7. *Childbirth.*
8. *Names.*
9. *Religion.*
10. *Adoption of foreign religions.*
11. *Superstitions.*
12. *Social rules.*
13. *Social subjection.*
14. *Their position improving.*
15. *Occupation.*

Mahār, Mehra, Dhed.—The impure caste of menials, labourers and village watchmen of the Marātha country, corresponding to the Chamārs and Koris of northern India. They numbered nearly 1,200,000 persons in the combined Province in 1911, and are most numerous in the Nāgpur, Bhandāra, Chānda and Wardha Districts of the Central Provinces, while considerable colonies are also found in Balāghāt, Chhindwāra and Betūl. Their distribution thus follows largely that of the Marāthi language and the castes speaking it. Berār contained 400,000, distributed over the four Districts. In the whole Province this caste is third in point of numerical strength. In India the Mahārs number about three million persons, of whom a half belong to Bombay. I am not aware of any accepted derivation for the word Mahār, but the balance of opinion seems to be that the native name of Bombay, Mahārāshtra, is derived from that of the caste, as suggested by Wilson. Another derivation which holds it to be a corruption of Maha Rāstrakūta, and to be so called after the Rāshtrakūta Rājpūt dynasty of the eighth and ninth centuries, seems less probable because countries are very seldom named after ruling

1. General notice.

dynasties.[1] Whereas in support of Mahārāshtra as 'The country of the Mahārs,' we have Gujarāshtra or Gujarāt, the country of the Gūjars, and Saurāshtra or Surat, the country of the Sauras. According to Platts' Dictionary, however, Mahārāshtra means 'the great country,' and this is what the Marātha Brāhmans themselves say. Mehra appears to be a variant of the name current in the Hindustāni Districts, while Dheda, or Dhada, is said to be a corruption of Dharadas or hillmen.[2] In the Punjab it is said to be a general term of contempt meaning 'Any low fellow.'[3]

Wilson considers the Mahārs to be an aboriginal or pre-Aryan tribe, and all that is known of the caste seems to point to the correctness of this hypothesis. In the *Bombay Gazetteer* the writer of the interesting Gujarāt volume suggests that the Mahārs are fallen Rājpūts; but there seems little to support this opinion except their appearance and countenance, which is of the Hindu rather than the Dravidian type. In Gujarāt they have also some Rājpūt surnames, as Chauhān, Panwār, Rāthor, Solanki and so on, but these may have been adopted by imitation or may indicate a mixture of Rājpūt blood. Again, the Mahārs of Gujarāt are the farmservants and serfs of the Kunbis. "Each family is closely connected with the house of some landholder or *pattidār* (sharer). For his master he brings in loads from the fields and cleans out the stable, receiving in return daily allowances of buttermilk and the carcases of any cattle that die. This connection seems to show traces of a form of slavery. Rich *pattidārs* have always a certain number of Dheda families whom they speak of as ours (*hamāra*), and when a man dies he distributes along with his lands a certain number of Dheda families to each of his sons. An old tradition among Dhedas points to some relation between the Kunbis and Dhedas. Two brothers, Leva and Deva, were the ancestors, the former of the Kunbis, the latter of the Dhedas."[4] Such a relation as this

---

[1] This derivation is also negatived by the fact that the name Mahāratta was known in the third century B.C. or long before the Rāstrakūtas became prominent.

[2] *Bombay Gazetteer, Gujarāt Hindus*, p. 338.

[3] Ibbetson, *Punjab Census Report* (1881).

[4] *Bombay Gazetteer, l.c.* text and footnote by R. v. J. S. Taylor.

in Hindu society would imply that many Mahār women held the position of concubines to their Kunbi masters, and would therefore account for the resemblance of the Mahār to Hindus rather than the forest tribes. But if this is to be regarded as evidence of Rājpūt descent, a similar claim would have to be allowed to many of the Chamārs and sweepers. Others of the lowest castes also have Rājpūt sept names, as the Pārdhis and Bhīls; but the fact can at most be taken, I venture to think, to indicate a connection of the 'Droit de Seigneur' type. On the other hand, the Mahārs occupy the debased and impure position which was the lot of those non-Aryan tribes who became subject to the Hindus and lived in their villages; they eat the flesh of dead cattle and this and other customs appear to point decisively to a non-Aryan origin.

Several circumstances indicate that the Mahār is recognised as the oldest resident of the plain country of Berār and Nāgpur. In Berār he is a village servant and is the referee on village boundaries and customs, a position implying that his knowledge of them is the most ancient. At the Holi festival the fire of the Mahārs is kindled first and that of the Kunbis is set alight from it. The Kāmdar Mahār, who acts as village watchman, also has the right of bringing the *toran* or rope of leaves which is placed on the marriage-shed of the Kunbis; and for this he receives a present of three annas. In Bhandāra the Telis, Lohārs, Dhīmars and several other castes employ a Mahār *Mohturia* or wise man to fix the date of their weddings. And most curious of all, when the Panwār Rājpūts of this tract celebrate the festival of Nārāyan Deo, they call a Mahār to their house and make him the first partaker of the feast before beginning to eat themselves. Again in Berār[1] the Mahār officiates at the killing of the buffalo on Dasahra. On the day before the festival the chief Mahār of the village and his wife with their garments knotted together bring some earth from the jungle and fashioning two images set one on a clay elephant and the other on a clay bullock. The images are placed on a small platform outside the village site and worshipped; a young he-buffalo is bathed

2. Length of residence in the Central Provinces.

---
[1] Kitts' *Berār Census Report* (1881), p. 143.

and brought before the images as though for the same object. The Patel wounds the buffalo in the nose with a sword and it is then marched through the village. In the evening it is killed by the head Mahār, buried in the customary spot, and any evil that might happen during the coming year is thus deprecated and, it is hoped, averted. The claim to take the leading part in this ceremony is the occasion of many a quarrel and an occasional affray or riot. Such customs tend to show that the Mahārs were the earliest immigrants from Bombay into the Berār and Nāgpur plain, excluding of course the Gonds and other tribes, who have practically been ousted from this tract. And if it is supposed that the Panwārs came here in the tenth century, as seems not improbable,[1] the Mahārs, whom the Panwārs recognise as older residents than themselves, must have been earlier still, and were probably numbered among the subjects of the old Hindu kingdoms of Bhāndak and Nagardhan.

3. Legend of origin.

The Mahārs say they are descended from Mahāmuni, who was a foundling picked up by the goddess Pārvati on the banks of the Ganges. At this time beef had not become a forbidden food; and when the divine cow, Tripād Gayatri, died, the gods determined to cook and eat her body and Mahāmuni was set to watch the pot boiling. He was as inattentive as King Alfred, and a piece of flesh fell out of the pot. Not wishing to return the dirty piece to the pot Mahāmuni ate it; but the gods discovered the delinquency, and doomed him and his descendants to live on the flesh of dead cows.[2]

4. Sub-castes.

The caste have a number of subdivisions, generally of a local or territorial type, as Daharia, the residents of Dāhar or the Jubbulpore country, Baonia (52) of Berār, Nemādya or from Nimār, Khāndeshi from Khāndesh, and so on; the Katia group are probably derived from that caste, Katia meaning a spinner; the Bārkias are another group whose name is supposed to mean spinners of fine thread; while the Lonārias are salt-makers. The highest division are the Somvansis or children of the moon; these claim to have taken part with the Pāndavas against the Kauravas in the

---

[1] See article on Panwār Rājpūt.
[2] *Berār Census Report* (1881), p. 144.

war of the Mahābhārata, and subsequently to have settled in Mahārāshtra.¹ But the Somvansi Mahārs consent to groom horses, which the Baone and Kosaria subcastes will not do. Baone and Somvansi Mahārs will take food together, but will not intermarry. The Ladwān subcaste are supposed to be the offspring of kept women of the Somvansi Mahārs; and in Wardha the Dhārmik group are also the descendants of illicit unions and their name is satirical, meaning 'virtuous.' As has been seen, the caste have a subdivision named Katia, which is the name of a separate Hindustāni caste; and other subcastes have names belonging to northern India, as the Mahobia, from Mahoba in the United Provinces, the Kosaria or those from Chhattīsgarh, and the Kanaujia from Kanauj. This may perhaps be taken to indicate that bodies of the Kori and Katia weaving castes of northern India have been amalgamated with the Mahārs in Districts where they have come together along the Satpūra Hills and Nerbudda Valley.

5. Exogamous groups and marriage customs.

The caste have also a large number of exogamous groups, the names of which are usually derived from plants, animals, and natural objects. A few may be given as examples out of fifty-seven recorded in the Central Provinces, though this is far from representing the real total; all the common animals have septs named after them, as the tiger, cobra, tortoise, peacock, jackal, lizard, elephant, lark, scorpion, calf, and so on; while more curious names are—Darpan, a mirror; Khānda Phari, sword and shield; Undrimāria, a rat-killer; Aglāvi, an incendiary; Andhāre, a blind man; Kutramāria, a dog-killer; Kodu Dūdh, sour milk; Khobragāde, cocoanut-kernel; Bhājikhai, a vegetable eater, and so on.

A man must not marry in his own sept, but may take a wife from his mother's or grandmother's. A sister's son may marry a brother's daughter, but not vice versa. A girl who is seduced before marriage by a man of her own caste or any higher one can be married as if she were a widow, but if she has a child she must first get some other family to take it off her hands. The custom of *Lamjhana* or serving for a wife is recognised, and the expectant bridegroom will live with his father-in-law and work for him for a period

¹ Kitts' *Berār Census Report*, p. 144.

varying from one to five years. The marriage ceremony follows the customary Hindustāni or Marātha ritual[1] as the case may be. In Wardha the right foot of the bridegroom and the left one of the bride are placed together in a new basket, while they stand one on each side of the threshold. They throw five handfuls of coloured rice over each other, and each time, as he throws, the bridegroom presses his toe on the bride's foot; at the end he catches the girl by the finger and the marriage is complete. In the Central Provinces the Mohtūria or caste priest officiates at weddings, but in Berār, Mr. Kitts states,[2] the caste employ the Brāhman Joshi or village priest. But as he will not come to their house they hold the wedding on the day that one takes place among the higher castes, and when the priest gives the signal the dividing cloth (Antarpat) between the couple is withdrawn, and the garments of the bride and bridegroom are knotted, while the bystanders clap their hands and pelt the couple with coloured grain. As the priest frequently takes up his position on the roof of the house for a wedding it is easy for the Mahārs to see him. In Mandla some of the lower class of Brāhmans will officiate at the weddings of Mahārs. In Chhindwāra the Mahārs seat the bride and bridegroom in the frame of a loom for the ceremony, and they worship the hide of a cow or bullock filled with water. They drink together ceremoniously, a pot of liquor being placed on a folded cloth and all the guests sitting round it in a circle. An elder man then lays a new piece of cloth on the pot and worships it. He takes a cup of the liquor himself and hands round a cupful to every person present.

In Mandla at a wedding the barber comes and cuts the bride's nails, and the cuttings are rolled up in dough and placed in a little earthen pot beside the marriage-post. The bridegroom's nails and hair are similarly cut in his own house and placed in another vessel. A month or two after the wedding the two little pots are taken out and thrown into the Nerbudda. A wedding costs the bridegroom's party about Rs. 40 or Rs. 50 and the bride's about Rs. 25.

---

[1] Described in the articles on Kurmi and Kunbi.
[2] *Loc. cit.*

They have no going-away ceremony, but the occasion of a girl's coming to maturity is known as Bolāwan. She is kept apart for six days and given new clothes, and the caste-people are invited to a meal. When a woman's husband dies the barber breaks her bangles, and her anklets are taken off and given to him as his perquisite. Her brother-in-law or other relative gives her a new white cloth, and she wears this at first, and afterwards white or coloured clothes at her pleasure. Her hair is not cut, and she may wear *patelas* or flat metal bangles on the forearm and armlets above the elbow, but not other ornaments. A widow is under no obligation to marry her first husband's younger brother; when she marries a stranger he usually pays a sum of about Rs. 30 to her parents. When the price has been paid the couple exchange a ring and a bangle respectively in token of the agreement. When the woman is proceeding to her second husband's house, her old clothes, necklace and bangles are thrown into a river or stream and she is given new ones to wear. This is done to lay the first husband's spirit, which may be supposed to hang about the clothes she wore as his wife, and when they are thrown away or buried the exorcist mutters spells over them in order to lay the spirit. No music is allowed at the marriage of a widow except the crooked trumpet called *singāra*. A bachelor who marries a widow must first go through a mock ceremony with a cotton-plant, a sword or a ring. Divorce must be effected before the caste *panchāyat* or committee, and if a divorced woman marries again, her first husband performs funeral and mourning ceremonies as if she were dead. In Gujarāt the practice is much more lax and "divorce can be obtained almost to an indefinite extent. Before they finally settle down to wedded life most couples have more than once changed their partners."[1] But here also, before the change takes place, there must be a formal divorce recognised by the caste.

6. Funeral rites.

The caste either burn or bury the dead and observe mourning for three days,[2] having their houses whitewashed and their faces shaved. On the tenth day they give a feast

---

[1] *Bombay Gazetteer, Gujarāt Hindus*, loc. cit.

[2] In Berār for ten days—Kitts' *Berār Census Report, l.c.*

to the caste-fellows. On the Akshaya Tritia[1] and the 30th day of Kunwār (September) they offer rice and cakes to the crows in the names of their ancestors. In Berār Mr. Kitts writes:[2] "If a Mahār's child has died, he will on the third day place bread on the grave; if an infant, milk; if an adult, on the tenth day, with five pice in one hand and five betel-leaves in the other, he goes into the river, dips himself five times and throws these things away; he then places five lighted lamps on the tomb, and after these simple ceremonies gets himself shaved as though he were an orthodox Hindu."

7. Childbirth.

In Mandla the mother is secluded at childbirth in a separate house if one is available, and if not they fence in a part of the veranda for her use with bamboo screens. After the birth the mother must remain impure until the barber comes and colours her toe-nails and draws a line round her feet with red *mahur* powder. This is indispensable, and if the barber is not immediately available she must wait until his services can be obtained. When the navel-string drops it is buried in the place on which the mother sat while giving birth, and when this has been done the purification may be effected. The Dhobi is then called to wash the clothes of the household, and their earthen pots are thrown away. The head of the newborn child is shaved clean, as the birth-hair is considered to be impure, and the hair is wrapped up in dough and thrown into a river.

8. Names.

A child is named on the seventh or twelfth day after its birth, the name being chosen by the Mohtūria or caste headman. The ordinary Hindu names of deities for men and sacred rivers or pious and faithful wives for women are employed; instances of the latter being Ganga, Godāvari, Jamuna, Sīta, Laxmi and Rādha. Opprobrious names are sometimes given to avert ill-luck, as Damdya (purchased for eight cowries), Kauria (a cowrie), Bhikāria (a beggar), Ghusia (from *ghus*, a mallet for stamping earth), Harchatt (refuse), Akāli (born in famine-time), Langra (lame), Lula (having an arm useless); or the name of another low caste is given, as Bhangi (sweeper), Domari (Dom sweeper), Chamra (tanner), Basori (basket-maker). Not infrequently children are named

---

[1] 3rd Baisākh (April) Sudi, commencement of agricultural year.
[2] *Berār Census Report, l.c.*

after the month or day when they were born, as Pusau, born in Pus (December), Chaitu, born in Chait (March), Manglu (born on Tuesday), Buddhi (born on Wednesday), Sukka (born on Friday), Sanīchra (born on Saturday). One boy was called Mulua or 'Sold' (*mol-dena*). His mother had no other children, so sold him for one pice (farthing) to a Gond woman. After five or six months, as he did not get fat, his name was changed to Jhuma or 'lean,' probably as an additional means of averting ill-luck. Another boy was named Ghurka, from the noise he made when being suckled. A child born in the absence of its father is called Sonwa, or one born in an empty house.

The great body of the caste worship the ordinary deities Devi, Hanumān, Dūlha Deo, and others, though of course they are not allowed to enter Hindu temples. They principally observe the Holi and Dasahra festivals and the days of the new and full moon. On the festival of Nāg-Panchmi they make an image of a snake with flour and sugar and eat it. At the sacred Ambāla tank at Rāmtek the Mahārs have a special bathing-ghāt set apart for them, and they may enter the citadel and go as far as the lowest step leading up to the temples; here they worship the god and think that he accepts their offerings. They are thus permitted to traverse the outer enclosures of the citadel, which are also sacred. In Wardha the Mahārs may not touch the shrines of Mahādeo, but must stand before them with their hands joined. They may sometimes deposit offerings with their own hands on those of Bhīmsen, originally a Gond god, and Māta Devi, the goddess of smallpox. 9. Religion.

In Berār and Bombay the Mahārs have some curious forms of belief. "Of the confusion which obtains in the Mahār theogony the names of six of their gods will afford a striking example. While some Mahārs worship Vithoba, the god of Pandharpur, others revere Varuna's twin sons, Meghoni and Deghoni, and his four messengers, Gabriel, Azrael, Michael and Anādin, all of whom they say hail from Pandharpur."[1] The names of archangels thus mixed up with Hindu deities may most probably have been obtained from the Muhammadans, as they include Azrael; 10. Adoption of foreign religions.

[1] *Berār Census Report, l.c.*

but in Gujarāt their religion appears to have been borrowed from Christianity. "The Karia Dhedas have some rather remarkable beliefs. In the Satya Yug the Dhedas say they were called Satyas; in the Dvāpar Yug they were called Meghas; in the Treta Yug, Elias; and in the Kali Yug, Dhedas. The name Elias came, they say, from a prophet Elia, and of him their religious men have vague stories; some of them especially about a famine that lasted for three years and a half, easily fitting into the accounts of Elijah in the Jewish Scriptures. They have also prophecies of a high future in store for their tribe. The king or leader of the new era, Kuyām Rai by name, will marry a Dheda woman and will raise the caste to the position of Brāhmans. They hold religious meetings or *ochhavas*, and at these with great excitement sing songs full of hope of the good things in store for them. When a man wishes to hold an *ochhava* he invites the whole caste, and beginning about eight in the evening they often spend the night in singing. Except perhaps for a few sweetmeats there is no eating or drinking, and the excitement is altogether religious and musical. The singers are chiefly religious Dhedas or Bhagats, and the people join in a refrain '*Avore Kuyām Rai Rāja*, Oh! come Kuyām Rai, our king.'"[1] It seems that the attraction which outside faiths exercise on the Mahārs is the hope held out of ameliorating the social degradation under which they labour, itself an outcome of the Hindu theory of caste. Hence they turn to Islām, or to what is possibly a degraded version of the Christian story, because these religions do not recognise caste, and hold out a promise to the Mahār of equality with his co-religionists, and in the case of Christianity of a recompense in the world to come for the sufferings which he has to endure in this one. Similarly, the Mahārs are the warmest adherents of the Muhammadan saint Sheikh Farīd, and flock to the fairs held in his honour at Girar in Wardha and Partāpgarh in Bhandāra, where he is supposed to have slain a couple of giants.[2]

---

[1] *Bombay Gazetteer, Gujarāt Hindus.*

[2] It was formerly suggested that the fact of the Mahārs being the chief worshippers at the shrines of Sheikh Farīd indicated that the places themselves had been previously held sacred, and had been annexed by the Muhammadan priests; and the legend of the giant, who might represent the demonolatry of the aboriginal faith, being slain by the saint might be a parable, so to say, expressing this process. But in

In Berār[1] also they revere Muhammadan tombs. The remains of the Muhammadan fort and tank on Pimpardol hill in Jalgaon tāluk are now one of the sacred places of the Mahārs, though to the Muhammadans they have no religious associations. Even at present Mahārs are inclined to adopt Islām, and a case was recently reported when a body of twenty of them set out to do so, but turned back on being told that they would not be admitted to the mosque.[2] A large proportion of the Mahārs are also adherents of the Kabīrpanthi sect, one of the main tenets of whose founder was the abolition of caste. And it is from the same point of view that Christianity appeals to them, enabling European missionaries to draw a large number of converts from this caste. But even the Hindu attitude towards the Mahārs is not one of unmixed intolerance. [Once in three or four years in the southern Districts, the Panwārs, Mahārs, Pankas and other castes celebrate the worship of Nārāyan Deo or Vishnu, the officiating priest being a Mahār. Members of all castes come to the Panwār's house at night for the ceremony, and a vessel of water is placed at the door in which they wash their feet and hands as they enter; and when inside they are all considered to be equal, and they sit in a line and eat the same food, and bind wreaths of flowers round their heads. After the cock crows the equality of status is ended, and no one who goes out of the house can enter again.] At present also many educated Brāhmans recognise fully the social evils resulting from the degraded position of the Mahārs, and are doing their best to remove the caste prejudices against them.

11. Superstitions.

They have various spells to cure a man possessed of an evil spirit, or stung by a snake or scorpion, or likely to be in danger from tigers or wild bears; and in the Morsi tāluk of Berār it is stated that they so greatly fear the effect of an enemy

---

view of the way in which the Mehtars worship Musalmān saints, it seems quite likely that the Mahārs might do so for the same reason, that is, because Islām partly frees them from the utter degradation imposed by Hinduism. Both views may have some truth. As regards the legends themselves, it is highly improbable that Sheikh Farīd, a well-known saint of northern India, can ever have been within several hundred miles of either of the places with which they connect him.

[1] From Mr. C. Brown's notes.

[2] *C.P. Police Gazette.*

writing their name on a piece of paper and tying it to a sweeper's broom that the threat to do this can be used with great effect by their creditors.[1] To drive out the evil eye they make a small human image of powdered turmeric and throw it into boiled water, mentioning as they do so the names of any persons whom they suspect of having cast the evil eye upon them. Then the pot of water is taken out at midnight of a Wednesday or a Sunday and placed upside down on some cross-roads with a shoe over it, and the sufferer should be cured. Their belief about the sun and moon is that an old woman had two sons who were invited by the gods to dinner. Before they left she said to them that as they were going out there would be no one to cook, so they must remember to bring back something for her. The elder brother forgot what his mother had said and took nothing away with him; but the younger remembered her and brought back something from the feast. So when they came back the old woman cursed the elder brother and said that as he had forgotten her he should be the sun and scorch and dry up all vegetation with his beams; but the younger brother should be the moon and make the world cool and pleasant at night. The story is so puerile that it is only worth reproduction as a specimen of the level of a Mahār's intelligence. The belief in evil spirits appears to be on the decline, as a result of education and accumulated experience. Mr. C. Brown states that in Malkāpur of Berār the Mahārs say that there are no wandering spirits in the hills by night of such a nature that people need fear them. There are only tiny *pari* or fairies, small creatures in human form, but with the power of changing their appearance, who do no harm to any one.

12. Social rules.

When an outsider is to be received into the community all the hair on his face is shaved, being wetted with the urine of a boy belonging to the group to which he seeks admission. Mahārs will eat all kinds of food including the flesh of crocodiles and rats, but some of them abstain from beef. There is nothing peculiar in their dress except that the men wear a black woollen thread round their necks.[2] The women may be recognised by their bold carriage, the

---

[1] Kitts, *l.c.* [2] *Ibidem*.

absence of nose-rings and the large irregular dabs of vermilion on the forehead. Mahār women do not, as a rule, wear the *choli* or breast-cloth. An unmarried girl does not put on vermilion nor draw her cloth over her head. Women must be tattooed with dots on the face, representations of scorpions, flowers and snakes on the arms and legs, and some dots to represent flies on the hands. It is the custom for a girl's father or mother or father-in-law to have her tattooed in one place on the hand or arm immediately on her marriage. Then when girls are sitting together they will show this mark and say, 'My mother or father-in-law had this done,' as the case may be. Afterwards if a woman so desires she gets herself tattooed on her other limbs. If an unmarried girl or widow becomes with child by a man of the Mahār caste or any higher one she is subjected after delivery to a semblance of the purification by fire known as Agnikāsht. She is taken to the bank of a river and there five stalks of juāri are placed round her and burnt. Having fasted all day, at night she gives a feast to the caste-men and eats with them. If she offends with a man of lower caste she is finally expelled. Temporary exclusion from caste is imposed for taking food or drink from the hands of a Māng or Chamār or for being imprisoned in jail, or on a Mahār man if he lives with a woman of any higher caste; the penalty being the shaving of a man's face or cutting off a lock of a woman's hair, together with a feast to the caste. In the last case it is said that the man is not readmitted until he has put the woman away. If a man touches a dead dog, cat, pony or donkey, he has to be shaved and give a feast to the caste. And if a dog or cat dies in his house, or a litter of puppies or kittens is born, the house is considered to be defiled; all the earthen pots must be thrown away, the whole house washed and cleaned and a caste feast given. The most solemn oath of a Mahār is by a cat or dog and in Yeotmāl by a black dog.[1] In Berār, the same paper states, the pig is the only animal regarded as unclean, and they must on no account touch it. This is probably owing to Muhammadan influence. The worst social sin which a Mahār can commit is to get vermin in a wound, which is

---

[1] Stated by Mr. C. Brown.

known as Deogan or being smitten by God. While the affliction continues he is quite ostracised, no one going to his house or giving him food or water; and when it is cured the Mahārs of ten or twelve surrounding villages assemble and he must give a feast to the whole community. The reason for this calamity being looked upon with such peculiar abhorrence is obscure, but the feeling about it is general among Hindus.

13. Social subjection.

The social position of the Mahārs is one of distressing degradation. Their touch is considered to defile and they live in a quarter by themselves outside the village. They usually have a separate well assigned to them from which to draw water, and if the village has only one well the Mahārs and Hindus take water from different sides of it. Mahār boys were not until recently allowed to attend school with Hindu boys, and when they could not be refused admission to Government schools, they were allotted a small corner of the veranda and separately taught. When Dher boys were first received into the Chānda High School a mutiny took place and the school was boycotted for some time. The people say, '*Mahār sarva jātīcha bāhar*,' or 'The Mahār is outside all castes.' Having a bad name, they are also given unwarrantably a bad character; and '*Māhar jātīchā*' is a phrase used for a man with no moral or kindly feelings. But in theory at least, as conforming to Hinduism, they were supposed to be better than Muhammadans and other unbelievers, as shown by the following story from the Rāsmāla:[1] A Muhammadan sovereign asked his Hindu minister which was the lowest caste. The minister begged for leisure to consider his reply and, having obtained it, went to where the Dhedas lived and said to them: "You have given offence to the Pādishāh. It is his intention to deprive you of caste and make you Muhammadans." The Dhedas, in the greatest terror, pushed off in a body to the sovereign's palace, and standing at a respectful distance shouted at the top of their lungs: "If we've offended your majesty, punish us in some other way than that. Beat us, fine us, hang us if you like, but don't make us Muhammadans." The Pādishāh smiled, and turning to his minister who sat by him affecting to hear

[1] Vol. ii. p. 237.

WEAVING—SIZING THE WARP.

nothing, said, 'So the lowest caste is that to which I belong.' But of course this cannot be said to represent the general view of the position of Muhammadans in Hindu eyes; they, like the English, are regarded as distinguished foreigners, who, if they consented to be proselytised, would probably in time become Brāhmans or at least Rājpūts. A repartee of a Mahār to a Brāhman abusing him is: The Brāhman, '*Jāre Mahārya*' or 'Avaunt, ye Mahār'; the Mahār, '*Kona dīushi neīn tumchi goburya*' or 'Some day I shall carry cow-dung cakes for you (at his funeral)'; as in the Marātha Districts the Mahār is commonly engaged for carrying fuel to the funeral pyre. Under native rule the Mahār was subjected to painful degradations. He might not spit on the ground lest a Hindu should be polluted by touching it with his foot, but had to hang an earthen pot round his neck to hold his spittle.[1] He was made to drag a thorny branch with him to brush out his footsteps, and when a Brāhman came by had to lie at a distance on his face lest his shadow might fall on the Brāhman. In Gujarāt[2] they were not allowed to tuck up the loin-cloth but had to trail it along the ground. Even quite recently in Bombay a Mahār was not allowed to talk loudly in the street while a well-to-do Brāhman or his wife was dining in one of the houses. In the reign of Sidhrāj, the great Solanki Rāja of Gujarāt, the Dheras were for a time at any rate freed from such disabilities by the sacrifice of one of their number.[3] The great tank at Anhilvāda Pātan in Gujarāt had been built by the Ods (navvies), but Sidhrāj desired Jusma Odni, one of their wives, and sought to possess her. But the Ods fled with her and when he pursued her she plunged a dagger into her stomach, cursing Sidhrāj and saying that his tank should never hold water. The Rāja, returning to Anhilvāda, found the tank dry, and asked his minister what should be done that water might remain in the tank. The Pardhān, after consulting the astrologers, said that if a man's life were sacrificed the curse might be removed. At that time the Dhers or outcastes were compelled to live at a distance from

---

[1] *Bombay Gazetteer*, vol. xii. p. 175.
[2] Rev. A. Taylor in *Bombay Gazetteer*, *Gujarāt Hindus*, p. 341 f.
[3] The following passage is taken from Forbes, *Rāsmāla*, i. p. 112.

the towns; they wore untwisted cotton round their heads and a stag's horn as a mark hanging from their waists so that people might be able to avoid touching them. The Rāja commanded that a Dher named Māyo should be beheaded in the tank that water might remain. Māyo died, singing the praises of Vishnu, and the water after that began to remain in the tank. At the time of his death Māyo had begged as a reward for his sacrifice that the Dhers should not in future be compelled to live at a distance from the towns nor wear a distinctive dress. The Rāja assented and these privileges were afterwards permitted to the Dhers for the sake of Māyo.

14. Their position improving.
From the painful state of degradation described above the Mahārs are gradually being rescued by the levelling and liberalising tendency of British rule, which must be to these depressed classes an untold blessing. With the right of acquiring property they have begun to assert themselves, and the extension of railways more especially has a great effect in abolishing caste distinctions. The Brāhman who cannot afford a second-class fare must either not travel or take the risk of rubbing shoulders with a Mahār in a third-class carriage, and if he chooses to consider himself defiled will have to go hungry and thirsty until he gets the opportunity of bathing at his journey's end. The observance of the rules of impurity thus becomes so irksome that they are gradually falling into abeyance.

15. Occupation.
The principal occupations of the Mahārs are the weaving of coarse country cloth and general labour. They formerly spun their own yarn, and their fabrics were preferred by the cultivators for their durability. But practically all thread is now bought from the mills; and the weaving industry is also in a depressed condition. Many Mahārs have now taken to working in the mills, and earn better wages than they could at home. In Bombay a number of them are employed as police-constables.[1] They are usually the village watchmen of the Marātha Districts, and in this capacity were remunerated by contributions of grain from the tenants, the hides and flesh of animals dying in the village, and plots of rent-free land. For these have now been substituted in

[1] *Bombay Gazetteer*, vol. xi. p. 73.

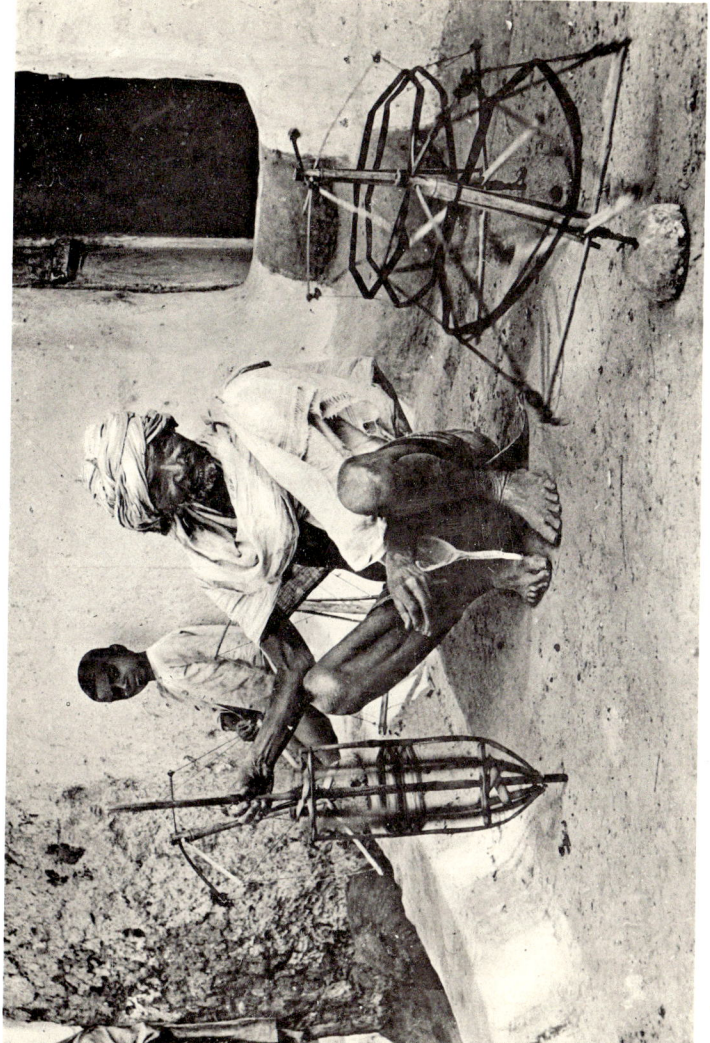

WINDING THREAD.

the Central Provinces a cash payment fixed by Government. In Berār the corresponding official is known as the Kāmdār Mahār. Mr. Kitts writes of him:[1] As fourth *balutedār* on the village establishment the Mahār holds a post of great importance to himself and convenience to the village. To the patel (headman), patwāri and big men of the village he acts often as a personal servant and errand-runner; for a smaller cultivator he will also at times carry a torch or act as escort. He had formerly to clean the horses of travellers, and was also obliged, if required, to carry their baggage.[2] For the services which he thus renders as *pāndhewār* the Mahār receives from the cultivators certain grain-dues. When the cut juāri is lying in the field the Mahārs go round and beg for a measure of the ears (*bhīk payāli*). But the regular payment is made when the grain has been threshed. Another duty performed by the Mahār is the removal of the carcases of dead animals. The flesh is eaten and the skin retained as wage for the work. The patel and his relatives, however, usually claim to have the skins of their own animals returned; and in some places where half the agriculturists of the village claim kinship with the patel the Mahārs feel and resent the loss. A third duty is the opening of grain-pits, the noxious gas from which sometimes produces asphyxia. For this the Mahārs receive the tainted grain. They also get the clothes from a corpse which is laid on the pyre, and the pieces of the burnt wood which remain when the body has been consumed. Recent observations in the Nāgpur country show that the position of the Mahārs is improving. In Nāgpur it is stated:[3] "Looked down upon as outcastes by the Hindus they are hampered by no sense of dignity or family prejudice. They are fond of drink, but are also hard workers. They turn their hands to anything and everything, but the great majority are agricultural labourers. At present the rural Mahār is in the background. If there is only one well in the village he may not use it, but has to get his water where he can. His sons are consigned to a corner in the village school, and

---

[1] *Bombay Gazetteer*, vol. xi. p. 73.
[2] Grant Duff, *History of the Marāthās*, vol. i. p. 24.
[3] *Nāgpur Settlement Report* (1899), p. 29.

the schoolmaster, if not superior to caste prejudices, discourages their attendance. Nevertheless, Mahārs will not remain for years downtrodden in this fashion, and are already pushing themselves up from this state of degradation. In some places they have combined to dig wells, and in Nāgpur have opened a school for members of their own community. Occasionally a Mahār is the most prosperous man in the village. Several of them are moneylenders in a small way, and a few are mālguzārs." Similarly in Bhandāra Mr. Napier writes that a new class of small creditors has arisen from the Mahār caste. These people have given up drinking, and lead an abstemious life, wishing to raise themselves in social estimation. Twenty or more village kotwārs were found to be carrying on moneylending transactions on a small scale, and in addition many of the Mahārs in towns were exceedingly well off.

1. Origin of the caste.

Mahli, Mahili.[1]—A small caste of labourers, palanquin-bearers and workers in bamboo belonging to Chota Nāgpur. In 1911 about 300 Mahlis were returned from the Feudatory States in this tract. They are divided into five subcastes: the Bānsphor-Mahli, who make baskets and do all kinds of bamboo-work; the Pāhar-Mahli, basket-makers and cultivators; the Sulunkhi, cultivators and labourers; the Tānti who carry litters; and the Mahli-Munda, who belong to Lohardaga. Sir H. Risley states that a comparison of the totemistic sections of the Mahlis given in the Appendix to his *Tribes and Castes* with those of the Santāls seems to warrant the conjecture that the main body of the caste are merely a branch of the Santāls. Four or five septs, Hansda a wild goose, Hemron, Murmu the nilgai, Saren or Sarihin, and perhaps Tudu or Turu are common to the two tribes. The Mahlis are also closely connected with the Mundas. Seven septs of the main body of the Mahlis, Dumriār the wild fig, Gundli a kind of grain, Kerketa a bird, Mahukal a bird (long-tail), Tirki, Tunduār and Turu are also Munda septs; and the three septs given of the Mahli-Munda sub-caste, Bhuktuār, Lāng Chenre, and Sānga are all found

---

[1] This article consists of extracts from Sir H. Risley's account of the caste in the *Tribes and Castes of Bengal.*

among the Mundas; while four septs, Hansda a wild goose, Induār a kind of eel, as well as Kerketa and Tirki, already mentioned, are common to the Mahlis and Turis, who are also recognised by Sir H. Risley as an offshoot of the Munda tribe with the same occupation as the Mahlis, of making baskets.[1] The Santāls and Mundas were no doubt originally one tribe, and it seems that the Mahlis are derived from both of them, and have become a separate caste owing to their having settled in villages more or less of the open country, and worked as labourers, palanquin-bearers and bamboo-workers much in the same manner as the Turis. Probably they work for hire for Hindus, and hence their status may have fallen lower than that of the parent tribe, who remained in their own villages in the jungles. Colonel Dalton notes[2] that the gipsy Berias use Mānjhi and Mahali as titles, and it is possible that some of the Mahlis may have joined the Beria community.

2. Social customs.

Only a very few points from Sir H. Risley's account of the caste need be recorded here, and for further details the reader may be referred to his article in the *Tribes and Castes of Bengal.* A bride-price of Rs. 5 is customary, but it varies according to the means of the parties. On the wedding day, before the usual procession starts to escort the bridegroom to the bride's house, he is formally married to a mango tree, while the bride goes through the same ceremony with a mahua. At the entrance to the bride's house the bridegroom, riding on the shoulders of some male relation and bearing on his head a vessel of water, is received by the bride's brother, equipped in similar fashion, and the two cavaliers sprinkle one another with water. At the wedding the bridegroom touches the bride's forehead five times with vermilion and presents her with an iron armlet. The remarriage of widows and divorce are permitted. When a man divorces his wife he gives her a rupee and takes away the iron armlet which was given her at her wedding. The Mahlis will admit members of any higher caste into the community. The candidate for admission must pay a small sum to the caste headman, and give a

---

[1] See lists of exogamous septs of Mahli, Sandāl, Munda and Puri in Appendix to *Tribes and Castes of Bengal.*
[2] *Ethnology of Bengal,* p. 326.

feast to the Mahlis of the neighbourhood, at which he must eat a little of the leavings of food left by each guest on his leaf-plate. After this humiliating rite he could not, of course, be taken back into his own caste, and is bound to remain a Mahli.

MAJHWĀR

LIST OF PARAGRAPHS

1. *Origin of the tribe.*
2. *The Mīrzāpur Majhwārs derived from the Gonds.*
3. *Connection with the Kawars.*
4. *Exogamy and totemism.*
5. *Marriage customs.*
6. *Birth and funeral rites.*
7. *Religious dance.*

Majhwār, Mānjhi, Mājhia.[1]—A small mixed tribe who have apparently originated from the Gonds, Mundas and Kawars. About 14,000 Majhwārs were returned in 1911 from the Raigarh, Sargūja and Udaipur States. The word Mānjhi means the headman of a tribal subdivision, being derived from the Sanskrit *madhya*, or he who is in the centre.[2] In Bengal Mānjhi has the meaning of the steersman of a boat or a ferryman, and this may have been its original application, as the steersman might well be he who sat in the centre.[3] When a tribal party makes an expedition by boat, the leader would naturally occupy the position of steersman, and hence it is easy to see how the term Mānjhi came to be applied to the leader or head of the clan and to be retained as a title for general use. Sir H. Risley gives it as a title of the Kewats or fishermen and many other castes and tribes in Bengal. But it is also the name for a village headman among the Santāls, and whether this meaning is derived from the prior signification of steersman or is of independent origin is uncertain. In Raigarh Mr. Hīra Lāl states that the Mānjhis or Mājhias are fishermen and are sometimes classed with the Kewats. They appear to be Kols who

1. Origin of the tribe.

---

[1] This article is based on papers by Mr. Hīra Lāl and Suraj Baksh Singh, Assistant Superintendent, Udaipur State, with references to Mr. Crooke's exhaustive article on the Majhwārs in his *Tribes and Castes*.

[2] Crooke, art. Majhwār, para. 1.

[3] *Tribes and Castes of Bengal*, art. Mānjhi.

have taken to fishing and, being looked down on by the other Kols on this account, took the name of Mājhia or Mānjhi, which they now derive from Machh, a fish. "The appearance of the Mājhias whom I saw and examined was typically aboriginal and their language was a curious mixture of Mundāri, Santāl and Korwa, though they stoutly repudiated connection with any of these tribes. They could count only up to three in their own language, using the Santāl words *mit, baria, pia*. Most of their terms for parts of the body were derived from Mundāri, but they also used some Santāli and Korwa words. In their own language they called themselves Hor, which means a man, and is the tribal name of the Mundas."

2. The Mīrzāpur Majhwārs derived from the Gonds.

On the other hand the Majhwārs of Mīrzāpur, of whom Mr. Crooke gives a detailed and interesting account, clearly appear to be derived from the Gonds. They have five subdivisions, which they say are descended from the five sons of their first Gond ancestor. These are Poiya, Tekām, Marai, Chika and Oiku. Four of these names are those of Gond clans, and each of the five subtribes is further divided into a number of exogamous septs, of which a large proportion bear typical Gond names, as Markām, Netām, Tekām, Mashām, Sindrām and so on. The Majhwārs of Mīrzāpur also, like the Gonds, employ Pathāris or Pardhāns as their priests, and there can thus be no doubt that they are mainly derived from the Gonds. They would appear to have come to Mīrzāpur from Sargūja and the Vindhyan and Satpūra hills, as they say that their ancestors ruled from the forts of Mandla, Garha in Jubbulpore, Sārangarh, Raigarh and other places in the Central Provinces.[1] They worship a deified Ahīr, whose legs were cut off in a fight with some Rāja, since when he has become a troublesome ghost. "He now lives on the Ahlor hill in Sargūja, where his petrified body may still be seen, and the Mānjhis go there to worship him. His wife lives on the Jhoba hill in Sargūja. Nobody but a Baiga dares to ascend the hill, and even the Rāja of Sargūja when he visits the neighbourhood sacrifices a black goat. Mānjhis believe that if these two deities are duly propitiated they can give anything they need." The story makes it

[1] Crooke, *Tribes and Castes of Bengal*, art. Mānjhi, para. 4.

probable that the ancestors of these Mānjhis dwelt in Sargūja. The Mānjhis of Mīrzāpur are not boatmen or fishermen and have no traditions of having ever been so. They are a backward tribe and practise shifting cultivation on burnt-out patches of forest. It is possible that they may have abandoned their former aquatic profession on leaving the neighbourhood of the rivers, or they may have simply adopted the name, especially since it has the meaning of a village headman and is used as a title by the Santāls and other castes and tribes. Similarly the term Munda, which at first meant the headman of a Kol village, is now the common name for the Kol tribe in Chota Nāgpur.

Again the Mānjhis appear to be connected with the Kawar tribe. Mr. Hīra Lāl states that in Raigarh they will take food with Kewats, Gonds, Kawars and Rāwats or Ahīrs, but they will not eat rice and pulse, the most important and sacred food, with any outsiders except Kawars; and this they explain by the statement that their ancestors and those of the Kawars were connected. In Mīrzāpur the Kaurai Ahīrs will take food and water from the Majhwārs, and these Ahīrs are not improbably derived from the Kawars.[1] Here the Majhwārs also hold an oath taken when touching a broadsword as most binding, and the Kawars of the Central Provinces worship a sword as one of their principal deities.[2] Not improbably the Mānjhis may include some Kewats, as this caste also use Mānjhi for a title; and Mānjhi is both a subcaste and title of the Khairwārs. The general conclusion from the above evidence appears to be that the caste is a very heterogeneous group whose most important constituents come from the Gond, Munda, Santāl and Kawar tribes. Whether the original bond of connection among the various people who call themselves Mānjhi was the common occupation of boating and fishing is a doubtful point.

3. Connection with the Kawars.

The Mānjhis of Sargūja, like those of Raigarh, appear to be of Munda and Santāl rather than of Gond origin. They have no subdivisions, but a number of totemistic septs. Those of the Bhainsa or buffalo sept are split into the Lotan and Singhan subsepts, *lotan* meaning a place where buffaloes

4. Exogamy and totemism.

---

[1] Crooke, *Tribes and Castes of Bengal*, art. Mānjhi, para. 63.
[2] *Ibidem*, para. 54.

wallow and *singh* a horn. The Lotan Bhainsa sept say that their ancestor was born in a place where a buffalo had wallowed, and the Singhan Bhainsa that their ancestor was born while his mother was holding the horn of a buffalo. These septs consider the buffalo sacred and will not yoke it to a plough or cart, though they will drink its milk. They think that if one of them killed a buffalo their clan would become extinct. The Bāghani Majhwārs, named after the *bāgh* or tiger, think that a tiger will not attack any member of their sept unless he has committed an offence entailing temporary excommunication from caste. Until this offence has been expiated his relationship with the tiger as head of his sept is in abeyance and the tiger will eat him as he would any other stranger. If a tiger meets a member of the sept who is free from sin, he will run away. When the Bāghani sept hear that any Majhwār has killed a tiger they purify their houses by washing them with cowdung and water. Members of the Khoba or peg sept will not make a peg or drive one into the ground. Those of the Dūmar[1] or fig-tree sept say that their first ancestor was born under this tree. They consider the tree to be sacred and never eat its fruit, and worship it once a year. Members of the sept named after the *shiroti* tree worship the tree every Sunday.

5. Marriage customs.

Marriage within the sept is prohibited and for three generations between persons related through females. Marriage is adult, but matches are arranged by the parents of the parties. At betrothal the elders of the caste must be regaled with *cheora* or parched rice and liquor. A bride-price of Rs. 10 is paid, but a suitor who cannot afford this may do service to his father-in-law for one or two years in lieu of it. At the wedding the bridegroom puts a copper ring on the bride's finger and marks her forehead with vermilion. The couple walk seven times round the sacred post, and seven little heaps of rice and pieces of turmeric are arranged so that they may touch one of them with their big toes at each round. The bride's mother and seven other women place some rice in the skirts of their cloths and the bridegroom throws this over his shoulder. After this he

[1] *Ficus glomerata.*

picks up the rice and distributes it to all the women present, and the bride goes through the same ceremony. The rice is no doubt an emblem of fertility, and its presentation to the women may perhaps be expected to render them fertile.

On the birth of a child the navel-string is buried in front of the house. When a man is at the point of death they place a little cooked rice and curds in his mouth so that he may not go hungry to the other world, in view of the fact that he has probably eaten very little during his illness. Some cotton and rice are also placed near the head of the corpse in the grave so that he may have food and clothing in the next world. Mourning is observed for five days, and at the end of this period the mourners should have their hair cut, but if they cannot get it done on this day, the rite may be performed on the same day in the following year.

6. Birth and funeral rites.

The tribe worship Dūlha Deo, the bridegroom god, and also make offerings to their ploughs at the time of eating the new rice and at the Holi and Dasahra festivals. They dance the *karma* dance in the months of Asārh and Kunwār or at the beginning and end of the rains. When the time has come the Gaontia headman or the Baiga priest fetches a branch of the *karma* tree from the forest and sets it up in his yard as a notice and invitation to the village. After sunset all the people, men, women and children, assemble and dance round the tree, to the accompaniment of a drum known as Māndar. The dancing continues all night, and in the morning the host plucks up the branch of the *karma* tree and consigns it to a stream, at the same time regaling the dancers with rice, pulse and a goat. This dance is a religious rite in honour of Karam Rāja, and is believed to keep sickness from the village and bring it prosperity. The tribe eat flesh, but abstain from beef and pork. Girls are tattooed on arrival at puberty with representations of the *tulsi* or basil, four arrow-heads in the form of a cross, and the foot-ornament known as *pairi*.

7. Religious dance.

Māl, Māle, Māler, Māl Pahāria.[1] — A tribe of the Rājmahal hills, who may be an isolated branch of the

---

[1] Based entirely on Colonel Dalton's account in the *Ethnology of Bengal*, and Sir H. Risley's in the *Tribes and Castes of Bengal*.

Savars. In 1911 about 1700 Māls were returned from the Chota Nāgpur Feudatory States recently transferred to the Central Provinces. The customs of the Māls resemble those of the other hill tribes of Chota Nāgpur. Sir H. Risley states that the average stature is low, the complexion dark and the figure short and sturdy. The following particulars are reproduced from Colonel Dalton's account of the tribe:

"The hill lads and lasses are represented as forming very romantic attachments, exhibiting the spectacle of real lovers 'sighing like furnaces,' and the cockney expression of 'keeping company' is peculiarly applicable to their courtship. If separated only for an hour they are miserable, but there are apparently few obstacles to the enjoyment of each other's society, as they work together, go to market together, eat together, and sleep together! But if it be found that they have overstepped the prescribed limits of billing and cooing, the elders declare them to be out of the pale, and the blood of animals must be shed at their expense to wash away the indiscretion and obtain their readmission into society.

"On the day fixed for a marriage the bridegroom with his relations proceeds to the bride's father's house, where they are seated on cots and mats, and after a repast the bride's father takes his daughter's hand and places it in that of the bridegroom, and exhorts him to be loving and kind to the girl that he thus makes over to him. The groom then with the little finger of his right hand marks the girl on the forehead with vermilion, and then, linking the same finger with the little finger of her right hand, he leads her away to his own house.

"The god of hunting is called Autga, and at the close of every successful expedition a thank-offering is made to him. This is the favourite pastime, and one of the chief occupations of the Mālers, and they have their game laws, which are strictly enforced. If a man, losing an animal which he has killed or wounded, seeks for assistance to find it, those who aid are entitled to one-half of the animal when found. Another person accidentally coming on dead or wounded game and appropriating it, is subjected to a severe fine. The Mānjhi or headman of the village is entitled to a share of all game killed by any of his people. Any one who kills a hunting dog is fined twelve rupees. Certain parts of an animal are tabooed to females as food, and if they infringe this law Autga is offended and game becomes scarce. When the hunters are unsuccessful it is often assumed that this is the cause, and the augur never fails to point out the transgressing female, who must provide a propitiatory offering. The Mālers use poisoned arrows, and when they kill game the flesh round the wound is cut off and thrown away as unfit for food. Cats are under the protection of the game laws, and a person found guilty of killing one is made to give a small quantity of salt to every child in the village.

"I nowhere find any description of the dances and songs of the Pahārias. Mr. Atkinson found the Mālers extremely reticent on the subject, and with difficulty elicited that they had a dancing-place in every village, but it is only when under the influence of God Bacchus that they indulge in the amusement. All accounts agree in ascribing to the Pahārias an immoderate devotion to strong drink, and Buchanan tells us that when they are dancing a person goes round with a pitcher of the home-brew and, without disarranging the performers, who are probably linked together by circling or entwining arms, pours into the mouth of each, male and female, a refreshing and invigorating draught. The beverage is the universal *pachwai*, that is, fermented grain. The grain, either maize, rice or *janera* (*Holcus sorghum*), is boiled and spread out on a mat to cool. It is then mixed with a ferment of vegetables called *takar*, and kept in a large earthen vessel for some days; warm water may at any time be mixed with it, and in a few hours it ferments and is ready for use."

When the attention of English officers was first drawn to them in 1770 the Māles of the Rājmahal hills were a tribe of predatory freebooters, raiding and terrorising the plain country from the foot of the hills to the Ganges. It was Mr. Augustus Cleveland, Collector of Bhāgalpur, who reduced them to order by entering into engagements with the chiefs for the prevention and punishment of offences among their own tribesmen, confirming them in their estates and jurisdiction, and enrolling a corps of Māles, which became the Bhāgalpur Hill Rangers, and was not disbanded till the Mutiny. Mr. Cleveland died at the age of 29, having successfully demonstrated the correct method of dealing with the wild forest tribes, and the Governor-General in Council erected a tomb and inscription to his memory, which was the original of that described by Mr. Kipling in *The Tomb of his Ancestors*, though the character of the first John Chinn in the story was copied from Outram.[1]

Māla.—A low Telugu caste of labourers and cotton-weavers. They numbered nearly 14,000 persons in the Central Provinces in 1911, belonging mainly to the Chānda, Nāgpur, Jubbulpore, and Yeotmāl Districts, and the Bastar State. The Marāthas commonly call them Telugu Dhers, but they themselves prefer to be known as 'Telangi Sadar Bhoi,' which sounds a more respectable designation. They are also known as Mannepuwār and Netkāni. They are the Pariahs of the Telugu country, and are regarded as impure and degraded. They may be distinguished by their manner of tying the head-cloth more or less in a square shape, and by their loin-cloths, which are worn very loose and not knotted. Those who worship Narsinghswāmi, the man-lion incarnation of Vishnu, are called Namaddār, while the followers of Mahādeo are known as Lingadārs. The former paint their foreheads with vertical lines of sandal-paste, and the latter with horizontal ones. The Mālas were formerly zealous partisans of the right-handed sect in Madras, and the description of this curious system of faction given by the Abbé Dubois more than a century ago may be reproduced :[2]

"Most castes belong either to the left-hand or right-hand faction. The former comprises the Vaishyas or trading classes, the Panchālas or artisan classes and some of the low Sūdra castes. It also contains the lowest caste, viz. the Chaklas or leather-workers, who are looked upon as its chief support. To the right-hand faction belong most of the higher castes of Sūdras. The Pariahs (Mālas) are also its

[1] See *The Khāndesh Bhīl Corps*, by Mr. A. H. A. Simcox, p. 62.
[2] *Hindu Manners, Customs and Ceremonies*, ed. 1897, pp. 25, 26.

great support, as a proof of which they glory in the title of *Valangai Maugattar* or Friends of the Right Hand. In the disputes and conflicts which so often take place between the two factions it is always the Pariahs who make the most disturbance and do the most damage. The Brāhmans, Rājas and several classes of Sūdras are content to remain neutral and take no part in these quarrels. The opposition between the two factions arises from certain exclusive privileges to which both lay claim. But as these alleged privileges are nowhere clearly defined and recognised, they result in confusion and uncertainty, and are with difficulty capable of settlement. When one faction trespasses on the so-called right of the other, tumults arise which spread gradually over large tracts of territory, afford opportunity for excesses of all kinds, and generally end in bloody conflicts. The Hindu, ordinarily so timid and gentle in all other circumstances of life, seems to change his nature completely on occasions like these. There is no danger that he will not brave in maintaining what he calls his rights, and rather than sacrifice a little of them he will expose himself without fear to the risk of losing his life. The rights and privileges for which the Hindus are ready to fight such sanguinary battles appear highly ridiculous, especially to a European. Perhaps the sole cause of the contest is the right to wear slippers or to ride through the streets in a palanquin or on horseback during marriage festivals. Sometimes it is the privilege of being escorted on certain occasions by armed retainers, sometimes that of having a trumpet sounded in front of a procession, or of being accompanied by native musicians at public ceremonies." The writer of the *Madras Census Report* of 1871 states:[1] "It is curious that the females of two of the inferior castes should take different sides to their husbands in these disputes. The wives of the agricultural labourers side with the left hand, while their husbands help in fighting the battles of the right, and the shoemakers' wives also take the side opposed to their husbands. During these festival disturbances, the ladies who hold political views opposed to those of their husbands deny to the latter all the privileges

[1] Page 130.

of the connubial state." The same writer states that the right-hand castes claimed the prerogative of riding on horseback in processions, of appearing with standards bearing certain devices, and of erecting twelve pillars to sustain their marriage booths; while the left-hand castes might not have more than eleven pillars, nor use the same standards as the right. The quarrels arising out of these small differences of opinion were so frequent and serious in the seventeenth century that in the town of Madras it was found necessary to mark the respective boundaries of the right- and left-hand castes, and to forbid the right-hand castes in their processions from occupying the streets of the left hand and vice versa. These disturbances have gradually tended to disappear under the influence of education and good government, and no instance of them is known to have occurred in the Central Provinces. The division appears to have originated among the members of the Sākta sect or the worshippers of Sakti as the female principle of life in nature. Dr. L. D. Barnett writes:[1]—" The followers of the sect are of two schools. The 'Walkers in the Right Way' (*Dakshināchārī*) pay a service of devotion to the deity in both male and female aspects, and except in their more pronounced tendency to dwell upon the horrific aspects of the deity (as Kāli, Durga, etc.), they differ little from ordinary Saivas and Vaishnavas. The 'Walkers in the Left Way' (*Vāmāchārī*), on the other hand, concentrate their thought upon the godhead in its sexually maternal aspect, and follow rites of senseless magic and—theoretically at least —promiscuous debauchery." As has been seen, the religious differences subsequently gave rise to political factions.

[1] *Hinduism*, in 'Religions Ancient and Modern' Series, p. 26.

MĀLI

LIST OF PARAGRAPHS

1. *General notice of the caste, and its social position.*
2. *Caste legend.*
3. *Flowers offered to the gods.*
4. *Custom of wearing garlands.*
5. *Subcastes.*
6. *Marriage.*
7. *Widow-marriage, divorce and polygamy.*
8. *Disposal of the dead.*
9. *Religion.*
10. *Occupation.*
11. *Traits and characters.*
12. *Other functions of the Māli.*
13. *Physical appearance.*

Māli, Marār, Marāl.[1]—The functional caste of vegetable and flower-gardeners. The terms Māli and Marār appear to be used indifferently for the same caste, the former being more common in the west of the Province and the latter in the eastern Satpūra Districts and the Chhattīsgarh plain. In the Nerbudda valley and on the Vindhyan plateau the place of both Māli and Marār is taken by the Kāchhi of Upper India.[2] Marār appears to be a Marāthi name, the original term, as pointed out by Mr. Hira Lāl, being Malāl, or one who grows garden-crops in a field; but the caste is often called Māli in the Marātha country and Marār in the Hindi Districts. The word Māli is derived from the Sanskrit *māla*, a garland. In 1911 the Mālis numbered nearly 360,000 persons in the present area of the Central Provinces, and 200,000 in Berār. A German writer remarks of the caste[3] that: "It cannot be considered to be a very ancient one. Generally speaking, it may be said that flowers have scarcely a place in the Veda. Wreaths of flowers, of

1. *General notice of the caste, and its social position.*

---

[1] This article is based principally on Mr. Low's description of the Marārs in the *Bālāghāt District Gazetteer* and on a paper by Major Sutherland, I.M.S.

[2] *C.P. Census Report* (1891), para. 180.

[3] Schröder, *Prehistoric Antiquities*, 121, quoted in Crooke's *Tribes and Castes*, art. Māli.

course, are used as decorations, but the separate flowers and their beauty are not yet appreciated. That lesson was first learned later by the Hindus when surrounded by another flora. Amongst the Homeric Greeks, too, in spite of their extensive gardening and different flowers, not a trace of horticulture is yet to be found." It seems probable that the first Mālis were not included among the regular cultivators of the village but were a lower group permitted to take up the small waste plots of land adjoining the inhabited area and fertilised by its drainage, and the sandy stretches in the beds of rivers, on which they were able to raise the flowers required for offerings and such vegetables as were known. They still hold a lower rank than the ordinary cultivator. Sir D. Ibbetson writes [1] of the gardening castes: "The group now to be discussed very generally hold an inferior position among the agricultural community and seldom if ever occupy the position of the dominant tribe in any considerable tract of country. The cultivation of vegetables is looked upon as degrading by the agricultural classes, why I know not, unless it be that night-soil is generally used for their fertilisation; and a Rājpūt would say: 'What! Do you take me for an Arāin?' if anything was proposed which he considered derogatory." But since most Mālis in the Central Provinces strenuously object to using night-soil as a manure the explanation that this practice has caused them to rank below the agricultural castes does not seem sufficient. And if the use of night-soil were the real circumstance which determined their social position, it seems certain that Brāhmans would not take water from their hands as they do. Elsewhere Sir D. Ibbetson remarks: [2] "The Mālis and Sainis, like all vegetable growers, occupy a very inferior position among the agricultural castes; but of the two the Sainis are probably the higher, as they more often own land or even whole villages, and are less generally mere market-gardeners than are the Mālis." Here is given what may perhaps be the true reason for the status of the Mālī caste as a whole. Again Sir C. Elliot wrote in the *Hoshangābād Settlement Report*: "Garden crops are considered as a kind of fancy agriculture and the true cultivator, the Kisān, looks on them with

[1] *Punjab Census Report* (1881), para. 483. [2] *Ibidem*, para. 484.

contempt as little peddling matters; what stirs his ambition is a fine large wheat-field eighty or a hundred acres in extent, as flat as a billiard-table and as black as a Gond." Similarly Mr. Low [1] states that in Bālāghāt the Panwārs, the principal agricultural caste, look down on the Marārs as growers of petty crops like *sama* and kutki. In Wardha the Dāngris, a small caste of melon and vegetable growers, are an offshoot of the Kunbis; and they will take food from the Kunbis, though these will not accept it from them, their social status being thus distinctly lower than that of the parent caste. Again the Kohlis of Bhandāra, who grow sugarcane with irrigation, are probably derived from an aboriginal tribe, the Kols, and, though they possess a number of villages, rank lower than the regular cultivating castes. It is also worth noting that they do not admit tenant-right in their villages among their own caste, and allot the sugarcane plots among the cultivators at pleasure.[2] In Nimār the Mālis rank below the Kunbis and Gūjars, the good agricultural castes, and it is said that they grow the crops which the cultivators proper do not care to grow. The Kāchhis, the gardening caste of the northern Districts, have a very low status, markedly inferior to that of the Lodhis and Kurmis and little if any better than the menial Dhīmars. Similarly, as will be seen later, the Marārs themselves have customs pointing clearly to a non-Aryan origin. The Bhoyars of Betūl, who grow sugarcane, are probably of mixed origin from Rājpūt fathers and mothers of the indigenous tribes; they eat fowls and are much addicted to liquor and rank below the cultivating castes. The explanation seems to be that the gardening castes are not considered as landholders, and have not therefore the position which attaches to the holding of land among all early agricultural peoples, and which in India consisted in the status of a constituent member of the village community. So far as ceremonial purity goes there is no difference between the Mālis and the cultivating castes, as Brāhmans will take water from both. It may be surmised that this privilege has been given to the Mālis because they grow the flowers required for offerings to the gods, and

---

[1] *Bālāghāt District Gazetteer*, para. 59.

[2] Mr. Napier's *Bhandara Settlement Report*, quoted in article on Kohli.

sometimes officiate as village priests and temple servants; and their occupation, though not on a level with regular agriculture, is still respectable. But the fact that Brāhmans will take water from them does not place the Mālis on an equality with the cultivating castes, any more than it does the Nais (barbers) and Dhīmars (watermen), the contemned menial servants of the cultivators, from whom Brāhmans will also take water from motives of convenience.

2. Caste legend.

The Mālis have a Brāhmanical legend of the usual type indicating that their hereditary calling was conferred and ratified by divine authority.[1] This is to the effect that the first Māli was a garland-maker attached to the household of Rāja Kānsa of Mathura. One day he met with Krishna, and, on being asked by him for a chaplet of flowers, at once gave it. On being told to fasten it with string, he, for want of any other, took off his sacred thread and tied it, on which Krishna most ungenerously rebuked him for his simplicity in parting with his *paīta*, and announced that for the future his caste would be ranked among the Sūdras.

The above story, combined with the derivation of Māli from *māla*, a garland, makes it a plausible hypothesis that the calling of the first Mālis was to grow flowers for the adornment of the gods, and especially for making the garlands with which their images were and still are decorated. Thus the Mālis were intimately connected with the gods and naturally became priests of the village temples, in which capacity they are often employed. Mr. Nesfield remarks of the Māli:[2] "To Hindus of all ranks, including even the Brāhmans, he acts as a priest of Mahādeo in places where no Gosain is to be found, and lays the flower offerings on the *lingam* by which the deity is symbolised. As the Māli is believed to have some influence with the god to whose temple he is attached, none objects to his appropriating the fee which is nominally presented to the god himself. In the worship of those village godlings whom the Brāhmans disdain to recognise and whom the Gosain is not permitted to honour the Māli is sometimes employed to present the offering. He

[1] *Tribes and Castes of Bengal*, art. Māli.
[2] *Brief View of the Caste System*, p. 15.

is thus the recognised hereditary priest of the lower and more ignorant classes of the population." In the Central Provinces Mālis are commonly employed in the temples of Devi because goats are offered to the goddess and hence the worship cannot be conducted by Brāhmans. They also work as servants in Jain temples under the priest. They sweep the temple, clean the utensils, and do other menial business. This service, however, does not affect their religion and they continue to be Hindus.

His services in providing flowers for the gods would be remunerated by contributions of grain from the cultivators, the acceptance of which would place the Māli below them in the rank of a village menial, though higher than most of the class owing to the purity of his occupation. His status was probably much the same as that of the Guraos or village priests of Mahādeo in the Marātha country. And though he has now become a cultivator, his position has not improved to the level of other cultivating castes for the reasons already given. It was probably the necessity of regularly watering his plants in order to obtain a longer and more constant supply of blooms which first taught the Māli the uses of irrigation.

3. Flowers offered to the gods.

Flowers are *par excellence* suited for the offerings and adornment of the gods, and many Hindus have rose or other plants in their houses whose flowers are destined to the household god. There is little reason to doubt that this was the purpose for which cultivated flowers were first grown. The marigold, lotus and champak are favourite religious flowers, while the *tulsi* or basil is itself worshipped as the consort of Vishnu; in this case, however, the scent is perhaps the more valued feature. In many Hindu households all flowers brought into the house are offered to the household god before being put to any other use. A Brāhman schoolboy to whom I had given some flowers to copy in drawing said that his mother had offered them to the god Krishna before he used them. When faded or done with they should be consigned to the sacred element, water, in any stream or river. The statues of the gods are adorned with sculptured garlands or hold them in their hands. A similar state of things prevailed in classical antiquity :

> Who are these coming to the sacrifice?
> To what green altar, O mysterious priest,
> Lead'st thou that heifer lowing at the skies,
> And all her silken flanks with garlands drest?

And,

> Fairer than these, though temple thou hast none,
> Nor altar decked with flowers,
> Nor virgin choir to make delicious moan
> Upon the midnight hours.

M. Fustel de Coulanges describes the custom of wearing crowns or garlands of flowers in ancient Rome and Greece as follows: "It is clear that the communal feasts were religious ceremonies. Each guest had a crown on the head; it was an ancient custom to crown oneself with leaves or flowers for any solemn religious act." "The more a man is adorned with flowers," they said, "the more pleasing he is to the gods; but they turn away from him who wears no crown at his sacrifice." And again, 'A crown is the auspicious herald which announces a prayer to the gods.'[1]

Among the Persians the flowers themselves are worshipped:[2] "When a pure Iranian sauntered through (the Victoria Gardens in Bombay) ... he would stand awhile and meditate over every flower in his path, and always as in a vision; and when at last the vision was fulfilled, and the ideal flower found, he would spread his mat or carpet before it, and sit before it to the going down of the sun, when he would arise and pray before it, and then refold his mat or carpet and go home; and the next night, and night after night, until that bright particular flower faded away, he would return to it, bringing his friends with him in ever-increasing numbers, and sit and sing and play the guitar or lute before it—and anon they all would arise together and pray before it; and after prayers, still sit on, sipping sherbet and talking the most hilarious and shocking scandal, late into the moonlight."

4. Custom of wearing garlands.

From the custom of placing garlands on the gods as a mark of honour has no doubt arisen that of garlanding guests. This is not confined to India but obtained in

---

[1] *La Cité antique*, 21st ed., p. 181.
[2] *The Antiquity of Oriental Carpets*, Sir G. Birdwood (Society of Arts, 6th November 1908).

Rome and probably in other countries. The word 'chaplet'[1] originally meant a garland or wreath to be worn on the head; and a garland of leaves with four flowers at equal distances. Dryden says, 'With chaplets green upon their foreheads placed.' The word *māla* originally meant a garland, and subsequently a rosary or string of beads. From this it seems a legitimate deduction that rosaries or strings of beads of a sacred wood were substituted for flower-garlands as ornaments for the gods in view of their more permanent nature. Having been thus sanctified they may have come to be worn as a mark of holiness by saints or priests in imitation of the divine images, this being a common or universal fashion of Hindu ascetics. Subsequently they were found to serve as a useful means of counting the continuous repetition of prayers, whence arose the phrase 'telling one's beads.' Like the Sanskrit *māla*, the English word rosary at first meant a garland of roses and subsequently a string of beads, probably made from rose-wood, on which prayers were counted. From this it may perhaps be concluded that the images of the deities were decorated with garlands of roses in Europe, and the development of the rosary was the same as the Indian *māla*. If the rose was a sacred flower we can more easily understand its importance as a badge in the Wars of the Roses.

5. Subcastes.

The caste has numerous endogamous groups, varying in different localities. The Phūlmālis, who derive their name from their occupation of growing and selling flowers (*phūl*), usually rank as the highest. The Ghāse Mālis are the only subcaste which will grow and prepare turmeric in Wardha; but they will not sell milk or curds, an occupation to which the Phūlmālis, though the highest subcaste, have no objection. In Chānda the Kosaria Mālis, who take their name from Kosala, the classical designation of the Chhattīsgarh country, are the sole growers of turmeric, while in Berār the Halde subcaste, named after the plant, occupy the same position. The Kosaria or Kosre subcaste abstain from liquor, and their women wear glass bangles only on one hand and silver ones on the other. The objection entertained to the cultivation of turmeric by Hindus generally is said to be based on the fact that when the roots are boiled numbers of small insects are necessarily

---

[1] The derivations of chaplet and rosary are taken from Ogilvy's *Dictionary*.

destroyed; but the other Mālis relate that one of the ancestors of the caste had a calf called Hardulia, and one day he said to his daughter, *Haldi pakā*, or 'Cook turmeric.' But the daughter thought that he said 'cook Hardulia,' so she killed and roasted the calf, and in consequence of this her father was expelled from the caste, and his descendants are the Ghāse or Halde subcaste. Ever since this happened the shape of a calf may be seen in the flower of turmeric. This legend has, however, no real value and the meaning of the superstition attaching to the plant is obscure. Though the growing of turmeric is tabooed yet it is a sacred plant, and no Hindu girl, at least in the Central Provinces, can be married without having turmeric powder rubbed on her body. Mr. Gordon remarks in *Indian Folk-Tales* : "I was once speaking to a Hindu gardener of the possibility of turmeric and garlic being stolen from his garden. These two vegetables are never stolen,' he replied, 'for we Hindus believe that he who steals turmeric and garlic will appear with six fingers in the next birth, and this deformity is always considered the birth-mark of a thief.'" The Jīre Mālis are so named because they were formerly the only subcaste who would grow cumin (*jira*), but this distinction no longer exists as other Mālis, except perhaps the Phūlmālis, now grow it. Other subcastes have territorial names, as Baone from Berār, Jaipuria, Kanaujia, and so on. The caste have also exogamous septs or *bargas*, with designations taken from villages, titles or nicknames or inanimate objects.

6. Marriage.

Marriage is forbidden between members of the same sept and between first and second cousins. Girls are generally betrothed in childhood and should be married before maturity. In the Uriya country if no suitable husband can be found for a girl she is sometimes made to go through the marriage ceremony with a peg of mahua wood driven into the ground and covered over with a cloth. She is then tied to a tree in the forest and any member of the caste may go and release her, when she becomes his wife. The Marārs of Bālāghāt and Bhandāra have the *lamjhana* form of marriage, in which the prospective husband serves for his wife; this is a Dravidian custom and shows their connection with the forest tribes. The marriage ceremony follows the standard form prevalent in

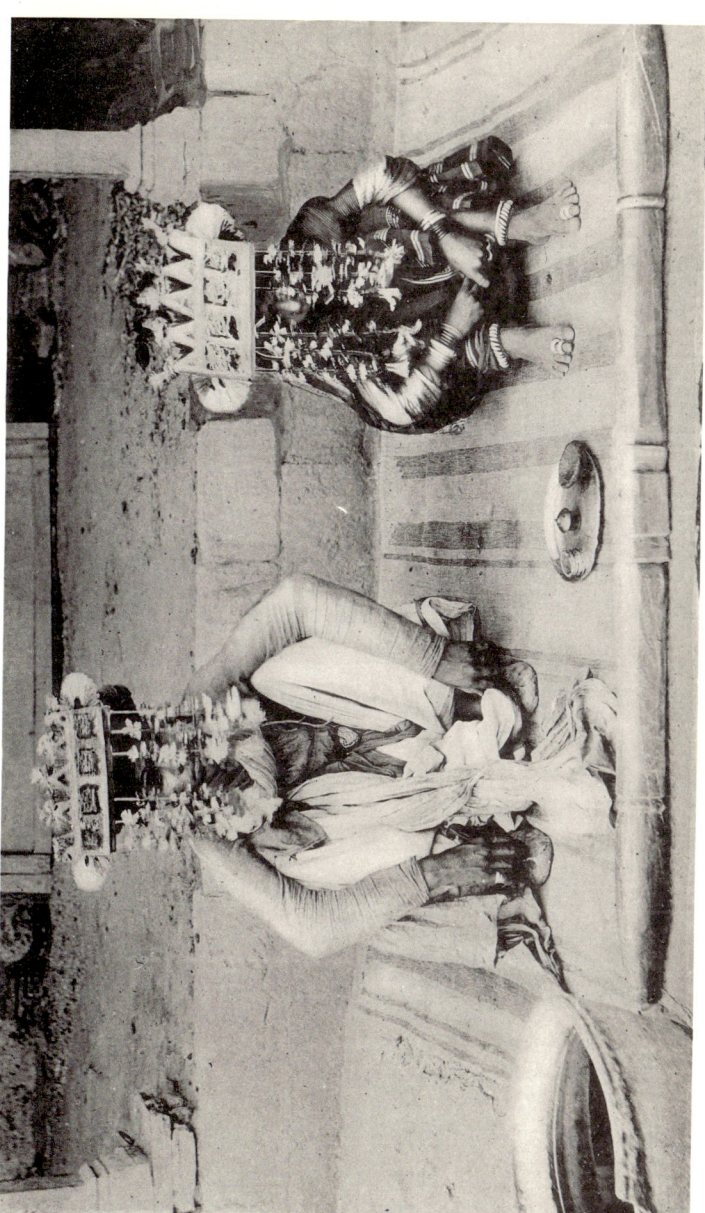

BRIDE AND BRIDEGROOM WITH MARRIAGE CROWNS.

the locality. In Betūl the couple go seven times round a slab on which a stone roller is placed, with their clothes knotted together and holding in their hands a lighted lamp. The slab and roller may be the implements used in powdering turmeric. "Among the Marārs of Bālāghāt[1] the maternal uncle of the bridegroom goes to the village of the bride and brings back with him the bridal party. The bride's party do not at once cross the boundary of the bridegroom's village, but will stay outside it for a few hours. Word is sent and the bridegroom's party will bring out cooked food, which they eat with the bride's party. This done, they go to the house of the bridegroom and the bride forthwith walks five times round a pounding-stone. Next day turmeric is applied to the couple, and the caste people are given a feast. The essential portion of the ceremony consists in the rubbing of vermilion on the foreheads of the couple under the cover of a cloth. The caste permit the practice of *ralla-palla* or exchanging sisters in marriage. They are said to have a custom at weddings known as *kondia*, according to which a young man of the bridegroom's party, called the *Sānd* or bull, is shut up in a house at night with all the women of the bride's party; he is at liberty to seize and have intercourse with any of them he can catch, while they are allowed to beat him as much as they like. It is said that he seldom has much cause to congratulate himself." But the caste have now become ashamed of this custom and it is being abandoned. In Chhattīsgarh the Marārs, like other castes, have the forms of marriage known as the *Badi Shādi* and *Chhoti Shādi* or great and small weddings. The former is an elaborate form of marriage, taking place at the house of the bride. Those who cannot afford the expense of this have a 'Small Wedding' at the house of the bridegroom, at which the rites are curtailed and the expenditure considerably reduced.

Widow-marriage is permitted. The widower, accompanied by his relatives and a horn-blower, goes to the house of the widow, and here a space is plastered with cowdung and the couple sit on two wooden boards while their clothes are knotted together. In Bālāghāt[2] the bridegroom and bride

7. Widow-marriage, divorce and polygamy.

---

[1] *Bālāghāt District Gazetteer* (C. E. Low), para. 59.
[2] *Ibidem, loc. cit.*

bathe in a tank and on emerging the widow throws away her old cloth and puts on a new one. After this they walk five times round a spear planted in the ground. Divorce is permitted and can be effected by mutual consent of the parties. Like other castes practising intensive cultivation the Mālis marry several wives when they can afford it, in order to obtain the benefit of their labour in the vegetable garden; a wife being more industrious and honest than a hired labourer. But this practice results in large families and household dissensions, leading to excessive subdivision of property, and wealthy members of the caste are rare. The standard of sexual morality is low, and if an unmarried girl goes wrong her family conceal the fact and sometimes try to procure an abortion. If these efforts are unsuccessful a feast must be given to the caste and a lock of the woman's hair is cut off by way of punishment. A young hard-working wife is never divorced, however bad her character may be, but an old woman is sometimes abandoned for very little cause.

8. Disposal of the dead.

The dead may be either buried or burnt; in the former case the corpse is laid with the feet to the north. Mourning is observed only for three days and propitiatory offerings are made to the spirits of the dead. If a man is killed by a tiger his family make a wooden image of a tiger and worship it.

9. Religion.

Devi is the principal deity of the Mālis. Weddings are celebrated before her temple and large numbers of goats are sacrificed to the favourite goddess at her festival in the month of Māgh (January). Many of the Marārs of Bālāghāt are Kabīrpanthis and wear the necklace of that sect; but they appear none the less to intermarry freely with their Hindu caste-fellows.[1] After the birth of a child it is stated that all the members of the sept to which the parents belong remain impure for five days, and no one will take food or water from them.

10. Occupation.

The Māli combines the callings of a gardener and nurseryman. "In laying out a flower-garden and in arranging beds," Mr. Sherring remarks,[2] "the Māli is exceedingly

---

[1] *Bālāghāt District Gazetteer*, para. 59.
[2] *Hindu Castes*, vol. i. p. 327.

expert. His powers in this respect are hardly surpassed by gardeners in England. He lacks of course the excellent botanical knowledge of many English gardeners, and also the peculiar skill displayed by them in grafting and crossing, and in watching the habits of plants. Yet in manipulative labour, especially when superintended by a European, he is, though much slower in execution, almost if not quite equal to gardeners at home." They are excellent and very laborious cultivators, and show much skill in intensive cultivation and the use of water. Mālis are the best sugarcane growers of Betūl and their holdings usually pay a higher rental than those of other castes. "In Bālāghāt," Mr. Low remarks,[1] "they are great growers of tobacco and sugarcane, favouring the alluvial land on the banks of rivers. They mostly irrigate by a *dhekli* or dipping lift, from temporary wells or from water-holes in rivers. The pole of the lift has a weight at one end and a kerosene tin suspended from the other. Another form of lift is a hollowed tree trunk worked on a fulcrum, but this only raises the water a foot or two. The Marārs do general cultivation as well; but as a class are not considered skilled agriculturists. The proverb about their cultivating status is:

Marār, Māli jote tāli
Tāli margayi, dhare kudāli,

or, 'The Marār yokes cows; if the cow dies he takes to the pickaxe'; implying that he is not usually rich enough to keep bullocks." The saying has also a derogatory sense, as no good Hindu would yoke a cow to the plough. Another form of lift used by the Kāchhis is the Persian wheel. In this two wheels are fixed above the well or tank and long looped ropes pass over them and down into the well, between which a line of earthen pots is secured. As the ropes move on the wheels the pots descend into the well, are filled with water, brought up, and just after they reach the apex of the wheel and turn to descend again, the water pours out to a hollow open tree-trunk, from which a channel conveys it to the field. The wheel which turns the rope is worked by a man pedalling, but he cannot do more than about three hours

---

[1] *Bālāghāt District Gazetteer, loc. cit.*

a day. The common lift for gardens is the *mot* or bag made of the hide of a bullock or buffalo. This is usually worked by a pair of bullocks moving forwards down a slope to raise the *mot* from the well and backwards up the slope to let it down when empty.

11. Traits and character.

"It is necessary," the account continues, "for the Marār's business for one member at least of his family to go to market with his vegetables ; and the Marārin is a noteworthy feature in all bazārs, sitting with her basket or garment spread on the ground, full of white onions and garlic, purple brinjals and scarlet chillies, with a few handfuls of strongly flavoured green stuff. Whether from the publicity which it entails on their women or from whatever cause, the Marārin does not bear the best of reputations for chastity ; and is usually considered rather a bold, coarse creature. The distinctive feature of her attire is the way in which she ties up her body-cloth so as to leave a tail sticking up behind ; whence the proverb shouted after her by rude little boys : ' Jump from roof to roof, Monkey. Pull the tail of the Marārin, Monkey.' She also rejoices in a very large *tikli* or spangle on her forehead and in a peculiar kind of *angia* (waistcoat). The caste are usually considered rather clannish and morose. They live in communities by themselves, and nearly always inhabit a separate hamlet of the village. The Marārs of a certain place are said to have boycotted a village carpenter who lost an axe belonging to one of their number, so that he had to leave the neighbourhood for lack of custom."

12. Other functions of the Māli.

Many Mālis live in the towns and keep vegetable- or flower-gardens just outside. They sell flowers, and the Māli girls are very good flower-sellers, Major Sutherland says, being famous for their coquetry. A saying about them is : " The crow among birds, the jackal among beasts, the barber among men and the Mālin among women ; all these are much too clever." The Māli also prepares the *maur* or marriage-crown, made from the leaves of the date-palm, both for the bride and bridegroom at marriages. In return he gets a present of a rupee, a piece of cloth and a day's food. He also makes the garlands which are used for presentation at entertainments, and supplies the daily bunches of flowers which are required as offerings for

BULLOCKS DRAWING WATER WITH MOT.

Bemrose, Collo., Derby.

Mahādeo. The Māli keeps garlands for sale in the bazār, and when a well-to-do person passes he goes up and puts a garland round his neck and expects a present of a pice or two.

"Physically," Mr. Low states, "the Marār is rather a poor-looking creature, dark and undersized; but the women are often not bad looking, and dressed up in their best at a wedding, rattling their castanets and waving light-coloured silk handkerchiefs, give a very graceful dance. The caste are not as a rule celebrated for their cleanliness. A polite way of addressing a Marār is to call him Patel."

13. Physical appearance.

Mallāh, Malha.[1]—A small caste of boatmen and fishermen in the Jubbulpore and Narsinghpur Districts, which numbered about 5000 persons in 1911. It is scarcely correct to designate the Mallāhs as a distinct caste, as in both these Districts it appears from inquiry that the term is synonymous with Kewat. Apparently, however, the Mallāhs do form a separate endogamous group, and owing to many of them having adopted the profession of growing hemp, a crop which respectable Hindu castes usually refuse to cultivate, it is probable that they would not be allowed to intermarry with the Kewats of other Districts. In the United Provinces Mr. Crooke states that the Mallāhs, though, as their Arabic name indicates, of recent origin, have matured into a definite social group, including a number of endogamous tribes. The term Mallāh has nothing to do with the Mulla or Muhammadan priest among the frontier tribes, but comes from an Arabic word meaning 'to be salt,' or, according to another derivation, 'to move the wings as a bird.'[2] The Mallāhs of the Central Provinces are also, in spite of their Arabic name, a purely Hindu caste. In Narsinghpur they say that their original ancestor was one Bali or Balirām, who was a boatman and was so strong that he could carry his boat to the river and back under his armpit. On one occasion he ferried Rāma across the Ganges in Benāres, and it is said

---

[1] This article is based on papers by Mr. Shyāmācharan, B.A., B.L., Pleader, Narsinghpur, and Pyāre Lāl Misra, Ethnographic clerk.

[2] Crooke's *Tribes and Castes of the N.W.P. and Oudh*, art. Mallāh.

that Rāma gave him a horse to show his gratitude; but Balirām was so ignorant that he placed the bridle on the horse's tail instead of the head. And from this act of Balirām's arose the custom of having the rudder of a boat at the stern instead of at the bow. The Mallāhs in the Central Provinces appear from their family names to be immigrants from Bundelkhand. Their customs resemble those of lower-class Hindus. Girls are usually married under the age of twelve years, and the remarriage of widows is permitted, while divorce may be effected in the presence of the *panchāyat* or caste committee by the husband and wife breaking a straw between them. They are scantily clothed and are generally poor. A proverb about them says:

> *Jahān bethen Malao*
> *Tahān lāge alao,*

or, 'Where Mallāhs sit, there is always a fire.' This refers to their custom of kindling fires on the river-bank to protect themselves from cold. In Narsinghpur the Mallāhs have found a profitable opening in the cultivation of hemp, a crop which other Hindu castes until recently tabooed on account probably of the dirty nature of the process of cleaning out the fibre and the pollution necessarily caused to the water-supply. They sow and cut hemp on Sundays and Wednesdays, which are regarded as auspicious days. They also grow melons, and will not enter a melon-field with their shoes on or allow a woman during her periodical impurity to approach it. The Mallāhs are poor and illiterate, but rank with Dhīmars and Kewats, and Brāhmans will take water from their hands.

Māna.[1]—A Dravidian caste of cultivators and labourers belonging to the Chānda District, from which they have spread to Nāgpur, Bhandāra and Bālāghāt. In 1911 they numbered nearly 50,000 persons, of whom 34,000 belonged to Chānda. The origin of the caste is obscure. In the *Chānda Settlement Report* of 1869 Major Lucie Smith wrote of them: "Tradition asserts that prior to the Gond

[1] This article is based on papers by Mr. Hīra Lāl and G. Padaya Naidu of the Gazetteer Office.

conquest the Mānas reigned over the country, having their strongholds at Surajgarh in Ahiri and at Mānikgarh in the Mānikgarh hills, now of Hyderābād, and that after a troubled rule of two hundred years they fell before the Gonds. In appearance they are of the Gond type, and are strongly and stoutly made; while in character they are hardy, industrious and truthful. Many warlike traditions still linger among them, and doubtless in days gone by they did their duty as good soldiers, but they have long since hung up sword and shield and now rank among the best cultivators of rice in Chānda." Another local tradition states that a line of Māna princes ruled at Wairāgarh. The names of three princes are remembered: Kurumpruhoda, the founder of the line; Surjāt Badwāik, who fortified Surjāgarh; and Gahilu, who built Mānikgarh. As regards the name Mānikgarh, it may be mentioned that the tutelary deity of the Nāgvansi kings of Bastar, who ruled there before the accession of the present Rāj-Gond dynasty in the fourteenth century, was Mānikya Devi, and it is possible that the chiefs of Wairāgarh were connected with the Bastar kings. Some of the Mānas say that they, as well as the Gowāris, are offshoots of the Gond tribe; and a local saying to the effect that 'The Gond, the Gowāri and the Māna eat boiled juāri or beans on leaf-plates' shows that they are associated together in the popular mind. Hislop states that the Ojhas, or soothsayers and minstrels of the Gonds, have a subdivision of Māna Ojhas, who lay claim to special sanctity, refusing to take food from any other caste.[1] The Gonds have a subdivision called Mannewār, and as *wār* is only a Telugu suffix for the plural, the proper name Manne closely resembles Māna. It is shown in the article on the Parja tribe that the Parjas were a class of Gonds or a tribe akin to them, who were dominant in Bastar prior to the later immigration under the ancestors of the present Bastar dynasty. And the most plausible hypothesis as to the past history of the Mānas is that they were also the rulers of some tracts of Chānda, and were displaced like the Parjas by a Gond invasion from the south.

In Bhandāra, where the Mānas hold land, it is related

[1] *Papers on the Aboriginal Tribes of the Central Provinces*, p. 6.

that in former times a gigantic kite lived on the hill of Ghurkundi, near Sākoli, and devoured the crops of the surrounding country by whole fields at a time. The king of Chānda proclaimed that whoever killed the kite would be granted the adjoining lands. A Māna shot the kite with an arrow and its remains were taken to Chānda in eight carts, and as his reward he received the grant of a zamīndāri. In appearance the Mānas, or at least some of them, are rather fine men, nor do their complexion and features show more noticeable traces of aboriginal descent than those of the local Hindus. But their neighbours in Chānda and Bastar, the Māria Gonds, are also taller and of a better physical type than the average Dravidian, so that their physical appearance need not militate against the above hypothesis. They retained their taste for fighting until within quite recent times, and in Kātol and other towns below the Satpūra hills, Mānas were regularly enlisted as a town guard for repelling the Pindāri raids. Their descendants still retain the ancestral matchlocks, and several of them make good use of these as professional *shikāris* or hunters. Many of them are employed as servants by landowners and moneylenders for the collection of debts or the protection of crops, and others are proprietors, cultivators and labourers, while a few even lend money on their own account. Mānas hold three zamīndāri estates in Bhandāra and a few villages in Chānda; here they are considered to be good cultivators, but have the reputation as a caste of being very miserly, and though possessed of plenty, living only on the poorest and coarsest food.[1] The Māna women are proverbial for the assistance which they render to their husbands in the work of cultivation.

Owing to their general adoption of Marātha customs, the Mānas are now commonly regarded as a caste and not a forest tribe, and this view may be accepted. They have two subcastes, the Badwāik Mānas, or soldiers, and the Khād Mānas, who live in the plains and are considered to be of impure descent. Badwāik or 'The Great Ones' is a titular term applied to a person carrying arms, and assumed by certain Rājpūts and also by some of the lower castes.

[1] Rev. A. Wood in *Chānda District Gazetteer*, para. 96.

A third group of Mānas are now amalgamated with the Kunbis as a regular subdivision of that caste, though they are regarded as somewhat lower than the others. They have also a number of exogamous septs of the usual titular and totemistic types, the few recognisable names being Marāthi. It is worth noticing that several pairs of these septs, as Jamāre and Gazbe, Narnari and Chudri, Wāgh and Rāwat, and others are prohibited from intermarriage. And this may be a relic of some wider scheme of division of the type common among the Australian aborigines. The social customs of the Mānas are the same as those of the other lower Marātha castes, as described in the articles on Kunbi, Kohli and Mahār. A bride-price of Rs. 12-8 is usually paid, and if the bridegroom's father has the money, he takes it with him on going to arrange for the match. Only one married woman of the bridegroom's family accompanies him to the wedding, and she throws rice over him five times. Four days in the year are appointed for the celebration of weddings, the festivals of Shivrātri and of Akhātij, and a day each in the months of Māgh (January) and Phāgun (February). This rule, however, is not universal. Brāhmans do not usually officiate at their ceremonies, but they employ a Brāhman to prepare the rice which is thrown over the couples. Marriage within the sept is forbidden, as well as the union of the children of two sisters. But the practice of marrying a brother's daughter to a sister's son is a very favourite one, being known as Māhunchār, and in this respect the Mānas resemble the Gonds. When a widow is to be remarried, she stops on the way by the bank of a stream as she is proceeding to her new husband's house, and here her clothes are taken off and buried by an exorcist with a view to laying the first husband's spirit and preventing it from troubling the new household. If a woman goes wrong with a man of another caste she is not finally cast out, but if she has a child she must first dispose of it to somebody else after it is weaned. She may then be re-admitted into caste by having her hair shaved off and giving three feasts; the first is prepared by the caste and eaten outside her house, the second is prepared by her relatives and eaten within her house, and at the third the caste reinstate her by partaking of food cooked by herself. The dead are either buried or burnt; in the former case a feast is given immediately after the burial and no further mourning is observed; in the latter the period of mourning is three days. As among the Gonds, the dead are laid with feet to the north. A woman is impure for seven days after child-birth.

The Mānas have Bhāts or genealogists of their own caste, a separate one being appointed for each sept. The Bhāt of any sept can only accept gifts from members of that sept, though he may take food from any one of the caste. The Bhāts are in the position of beggars, and the other Mānas will not take food from them. Every man must have a Bhāt for his family under penalty of being temporarily put out of caste. It is said that the Bhāts formerly had books showing the pedigrees of the different families, but that once in a spirit of arrogance they placed their shoes upon the books; and the other Mānas, not brooking this insolence, burnt the books. The gravity of such an act may be realised when it is stated that if anybody even threatens to hit a Māna with a shoe, the indignity put upon him is so great that he is temporarily excluded from caste and penalised for readmission. Since this incident the Bhāts have to address the Mānas as 'Brahma,' to show their respect, the Māna replying 'Rām, Rām.' Their women wear short loincloths, exposing part of the thigh, like the Gonds. They eat pork and drink liquor, but will take cooked food only from Brāhmans.

1. History and nature of the sect.

Mānbhao.[1]—A religious sect or order, which has now become a caste, belonging to the Marātha Districts of the Central Provinces and to Berār. Their total strength in India in 1911 was 10,000 persons, of whom the Central Provinces and Berār contained 4000. The name would appear to have some such meaning as 'The reverend brothers.' The Mānbhaos are stated to be a Vaishnavite

---

[1] This article is compiled from notes on the caste drawn up by Colonel Mackenzie and contributed to the *Pioneer* newspaper by Mrs. Horsburgh; Captain Mackintosh's *Account of the Manbhaos* (India Office Tracts); and a paper by Pyāre Lāl Misra, Ethnographic clerk.

order founded in Berār some two centuries ago.[1] They themselves say that their order is a thousand years old and that it was founded by one Arjun Bhat, who lived at Domegaon, near Ahmadnagar. He was a great Sanskrit scholar and a devotee of Krishna, and preached his doctrines to all except the impure castes. Ridhpur, in Berār, is the present headquarters of the order, and contains a monastery and three temples, dedicated to Krishna and Dattātreya,[2] the only deities recognised by the Mānbhaos. Each temple is named after a village, and is presided over by a Mahant elected from the celibate Mānbhaos. There are other Mahants, also known after the names of villages or towns in which the monasteries over which they preside are located. Among these are Sheone, from the village near Chāndur in Amraoti District; Akulne, a village near Ahmadnagar; Lāsorkar, from Lāsor, near Aurangābād; Mehkarkar, from Mehkar in Buldāna; and others. The order thus belongs to Berār and the adjoining parts of India. Colonel Mackenzie describes Ridhpur as follows: "The name is said to be derived from *ridh*, meaning blood, a Rākshas or demon having been killed there by Parasurāma, and it owes its sanctity to the fact that the god lived there. Black stones innumerable scattered about the town show where the god's footsteps became visible. At Ridhpur Krishna is represented by an ever-open, sleeplessly watching eye, and some Mānbhaos carry about a small black stone disk with an eye painted on it as an amulet." Frequently their shrines contain no images, but are simply *chabutras* or platforms built over the place where Krishna or Dattātreya left marks of their footprints. Over the platform is a small veranda, which the Mānbhaos kiss, calling upon the name of the god. Sukli, in Bhandāra, is also a headquarters of the caste, and contains many Mānbhao tombs. Here they burn camphor in honour of Dattātreya and make offerings of cocoanuts. They make pilgrimages to the different shrines at the full moons of Chait (March) and Kārtik (October). They pay reverence to no deities except Krishna and Dattātreya, and observe

---

[1] *Berār Census Report* (1881), p. 62.
[2] Dattātreya was a celebrated Sivite devotee who has been deified as an incarnation of Siva.

the festivals of Gokul Ashtami in August and Datta-Jayantri in December. They consider the month of Aghan (November) as holy, because Krishna called it so in the Bhāgavat-Gīta. This is their sacred book, and they reject the other Hindu scriptures. Their conception of Krishna is based on his description of himself to Arjun in the Bhāgavat-Gīta as follows: "'Behold things wonderful, never seen before, behold in this my body the whole world, animate and inanimate. But as thou art unable to see with these thy natural eyes, I will give thee a heavenly eye, with which behold my divine connection.'

"The son of Pandu then beheld within the body of the god of gods standing together the whole universe divided forth into its vast variety. He was overwhelmed with wonder and every hair was raised on end. 'But I am not to be seen as thou hast seen me even by the assistance of the Vedas, by mortification, by sacrifices, by charitable gifts: but I am to be seen, to be known in truth, and to be obtained by that worship which is offered up to me alone: and he goeth unto me whose works are done for me: who esteemeth me supreme: who is my servant only: who hath abandoned all consequences, and who liveth amongst all men without hatred.'"

Again: "He my servant is dear to me who is free from enmity, the friend of all nature, merciful, exempt from all pride and selfishness, the same in pain and in pleasure, patient of wrong, contented, constantly devout, of subdued passions and firm resolves, and whose mind and understanding are fixed on me alone."

2. Divisions of the order.

The Mānbhaos are now divided into three classes: the Brahmachāri; the Gharbāri; and the Bhope. The Brahmachāri are the ascetic members of the sect who subsist by begging and devote their lives to meditation, prayer and spiritual instruction. The Gharbāri are those who, while leading a mendicant life, wearing the distinctive black dress of the order and having their heads shaved, are permitted to get married with the permission of their Mahant or *guru*. The ceremony is performed in strict privacy inside a temple. A man sometimes signifies his choice of a spouse by putting his *jholi* or beggar's wallet upon hers; if she lets it remain there, the betrothal is complete. A woman may show her preference for a man by bringing a pair of garlands and placing one on his head and the other on that of the image of Krishna. The marriage is celebrated according to the custom of the Kunbis, but without feasting or music. Widows are permitted to marry again. Married women do not wear bangles nor toe-rings nor the customary necklace of beads; they put on no jewellery, and have no *choli* or bodice. The Bhope or Bhoall, the third division of the caste, are wholly secular and wear no distinctive dress, except sometimes a black head-cloth. They may engage in any occupation that pleases them, and sometimes act as servants in the temples of the caste. In Berār they are divided into thirteen *bas* or orders, named after the disciples of Arjun Bhat, who founded the various shrines. The Mānbhaos are recruited by initiation of both men and women from any except the impure castes. Young children who have been vowed by their parents to a religious life or are left without relations, are taken into the order. Women usually join it either as children or late in life. The celibate members, male or female, live separately in companies like monks and nuns. They do not travel together, and hold services in their temples at different times. A woman admitted into the order is henceforward the disciple of the woman who initiated her by whispering the *guru mantra* or sacred verse into her ear. She addresses her preceptress as mother and the other women as sisters. The Mānbhaos are intelligent and generally literate, and they lead a simple and pure life. They are respectable and are respected by the people, and a *guru* or spiritual teacher is often taken from them in place of a Brāhman or Gosain. They often act as priests or *gurus* to the Mahārs, for whom Brāhmans will not perform these services. Their honesty and humility are proverbial among the Kunbis, and are in pleasing contrast to the character of many of the Hindu mendicant orders. They consider it essential that all their converts should be able to read the Bhāgavat-Gīta or a commentary on it, and for this purpose teach them to read and write during the rainy season when they are assembled at one of their monasteries.

3. Religious observances and customs.

One of the leading tenets of the Mānbhaos is a respect for all forms of animal and even vegetable life, much on a par with that of the Jains. They strain water through a cloth before drinking it, and then delicately wipe the cloth to preserve any insects that may be upon it. They should not drink water in, and hence cannot reside in, any village where animal sacrifices are offered to a deity. They will not cut down a tree nor break off a branch, or even a blade of grass, nor pluck a fruit or an ear of corn. Some, it is said, will not even bathe in tanks for fear of destroying insect-life. For this reason also they readily accept cooked food as alms, so that they may avoid the risk of the destruction of life involved in cooking. The Mānbhaos dislike the din and noise of towns, and live generally in secluded places, coming into the towns only to beg. Except in the rains they wander about from place to place. They beg in the morning, and then return home and, after bathing and taking their food, read their religious books. They must always worship Krishna before taking food, and for this purpose when travelling they carry an image of the deity about with them. They will take food and water from the higher castes, but they must not do so from persons of low caste on pain of temporary excommunication. They neither smoke nor chew tobacco. Both men and women shave the head clean, and men also the face. This is first done on initiation by the village barber. But the *sendhi* or scalp-lock and moustaches of the novice must be cut off by his *guru*, this being the special mark of his renunciation of the world. The scalp-locks of the various candidates are preserved until a sufficient quantity of hair has been collected, when ropes are made of it, which they fasten round their loins. This may be because Hindus attach a special efficacy to the scalp-lock, perhaps as being the seat of a man's strength or power. The nuns also shave their heads, and generally eschew every kind of personal adornment. Both monks and nuns usually dress in black or ashen-grey clothes as a mark of humility, though some have discarded black in favour of the usual Hindu mendicant colour of red ochre. The black colour is in keeping with the complexion of Krishna, their chief god. They dye their cloths with lamp-black mixed with a little water and oil. They usually sleep on the ground, with the exception of those who are Mahants, and they sometimes have no metal vessels, but use bags made of strong cloth for holding food and water. Men's names have the suffix *Boa*, as Datto Boa, Kesho Boa, while those of boys end in *da*, as Manoda, Raojīda, and those of women in Bai, as Gopa Bai, Som Bai. The dead are buried, not in the common burial-grounds, but in some waste place. The corpse is laid on its side, facing the east, with head to the north and feet to the south. A piece of silk or other valuable cloth is placed on it, on which salt is sprinkled, and the earth is then filled in and the ground levelled so as to leave no trace of the grave. No memorial is erected over a Mānbhao tomb, and no mourning nor ceremony of purification is observed, nor are oblations offered to the spirits of the dead. If the dead man leaves any property, it is expended on feeding the brotherhood for ten days; and if not, the Mahant of his order usually does this in his name.

The Mānbhaos are dissenters from orthodox Hinduism, and have thus naturally incurred the hostility of the Brāhmans. Mr. Kitts remarks of them:[1] "The Brāhmans hate the Mānbhaos, who have not only thrown off the Brāhmanical yoke themselves, but do much to oppose the influence of Brāhmans among the agriculturists. The Brāhmans represent them as descended from one Krishna Bhat, a Brāhman who was outcasted for keeping a beautiful Māng woman as his mistress. His four sons were called the *Māng-bhaos* or Māng brothers." This is an excellent instance of the Brāhman talent for pressing etymology into their service as an argument, in which respect they resemble the Jesuits. By asserting that the Mānbhaos are descended from a Māng woman, one of the most despised castes, they attempt to dispose of these enemies of a Brāhman hegemony without further ado.

4. Hostility between Mānbhaos and Brāhmans.

Another story about their wearing black or ashen-coloured clothes related by Colonel Mackenzie is that Krishna Bhat's followers, refusing to believe the aspersions cast on their leader by the Brāhmans, but knowing that

[1] *Berār Census Report* (1881), p. 62.

some one among them had been guilty of the sin imputed to him, determined to decide the matter by the ordeal of fire. Having made a fire, they cast into it their own clothes and those of their *guru*, each man having previously written his name on his garments. The sacred fire made short work of all the clothes except those of Krishna Bhat, which it rejected and refused to burn, thereby forcing the unwilling disciples to believe that the finger of God pointed to their revered *guru* as the sinner. In spite of the shock of thus discovering that their idol had feet of very human clay, they still continued to regard Krishna Bhat's precepts as good and worthy of being followed, only stipulating that for all time Mānbhaos should wear clothes the colour of ashes, in memory of the sacred fire which had disclosed to them their *guru's* sin.

Captain Mackintosh also relates that "About A.D. 1780, a Brāhman named Anand Rishi, an inhabitant of Paithan on the Godāvari, maltreated a Mānbhao, who came to ask for alms at his door. This Mānbhao, after being beaten, proceeded to his friends in the vicinity, and they collected a large number of brethren and went to the Brāhman to demand satisfaction; Anand Rishi assembled a number of Gosains and his friends, and pursued and attacked the Mānbhaos, who fled and asked Ahalya Bai, Rāni of Indore, to protect them; she endeavoured to pacify Anand Rishi by telling him that the Mānbhaos were her *gurus*; he said that they were Māngs, but declared that if they agreed to his proposals he would forgive them; one of them was that they were not to go to a Brāhman's house to ask for alms, and another that if any Brāhman repeated Anand Rishi's name and drew a line across the road when a Mānbhao was advancing, the Mānbhao, without saying a word, must return the road he came. Notwithstanding this attempt to prevent their approaching a Brāhman's house, they continue to ask alms of the Brāhmans, and some Brāhmans make a point of supplying them with provisions."

This story endeavours to explain a superstition still observed by the caste. This is that when a Mānbhao is proceeding along a road, if any one draws a line across the road with a stick in front of him the Mānbhao will wait without passing the line until some one else comes up and crosses it before him. In reality this is probably a primitive superstition similar to that which makes a man stop when a snake has crossed the road in front of him and efface its track before proceeding. It is said that the members of the order also carry their sticks upside down, and a saying is repeated about them :

> *Mānbhao hokar kāle kapre dārhi mūchi mundhāta hai,*
> *Ulti lakri hāth men pakri woh kya Sāhib milta hai ;*

or, "The Mānbhao wears black clothes, shaves his face and holds his stick upside down, and thinks he will find God that way."

This saying is attributed to Kabīr.

MĀNG

LIST OF PARAGRAPHS

1. *Origin and traditions.*
2. *Subdivisions.*
3. *Marriage.*
4. *Widow-marriage.*
5. *Burial.*
6. *Occupation.*
7. *Religion and social status.*

1. Origin and traditions.

Mǎng.[1]—A low impure caste of the Marātha Districts, who act as village musicians and castrate bullocks, while their women serve as midwives. The Māngs are also sometimes known as Vājantri or musician. They numbered more than 90,000 persons in 1911, of whom 30,000 belonged to the Nāgpur and Nerbudda Divisions of the Central Provinces, and 60,000 to Berār. The real origin of the Māngs is obscure, but they probably originated from the subject tribes and became a caste through the adoption of the menial services which constitute their profession. In a Marātha book called the Shūdra Kamlākar,[2] it is stated that the Māng was the offspring of the union of a Vaideh man and an Ambashtha woman. A Vaideh was the illegitimate child of a Vaishya father and a Brāhman mother, and an Ambashtha of a Brāhman father and a Vaishya mother. The business of the Māng was to play on the flute and to make known the wishes of the Rāja to his subjects by beat of drum. He was to live in the forest or outside the village, and was not to enter it except with the Rāja's permission. He was to remove the dead bodies of strangers, to hang criminals, and to take away and appropriate the clothes and bedding of the dead. The Māngs themselves relate the following legend of their origin as given by Mr. Sāthe : Long ago before cattle were used for

---

[1] This article is based partly on a paper by Mr. Achyut Sitārām Sāthe, Extra Assistant Commissioner.
[2] P. 389.

ploughing, there was so terrible a famine upon the earth that all the grain was eaten up, and there was none left for seed. Mahādeo took pity on the few men who were left alive, and gave them some grain for sowing. In those days men used to drag the plough through the earth themselves. But when a Kunbi, to whom Mahādeo had given some seed, went to try and sow it, he and his family were so emaciated by hunger that they were unable, in spite of their united efforts, to get the plough through the ground. In this pitiable case the Kunbi besought Mahādeo to give him some further assistance, and Mahādeo then appeared, and, bringing with him the bull Nandi, upon which he rode, told the Kunbi to yoke it to the plough. This was done, and so long as Mahādeo remained present, Nandi dragged the plough peaceably and successfully. But as soon as the god disappeared, the bull became restive and refused to work any longer. The Kunbi, being helpless, again complained to Mahādeo, when the god appeared, and in his wrath at the conduct of the bull, great drops of perspiration stood upon his brow. One of these fell to the ground, and immediately a coal-black man sprang up and stood ready to do Mahādeo's bidding. He was ordered to bring the bull to reason, and he went and castrated it, after which it worked well and quietly; and since then the Kunbis have always used bullocks for ploughing, and the descendants of the man, who was the first Māng, are employed in the office for which he was created. It is further related that Nandi, the bull, cursed the Māng in his pain, saying that he and his descendants should never derive any profit from ploughing with cattle. And the Māngs say that to this day none of them prosper by taking to cultivation, and quote the following proverb: '*Keli kheti, Zhāli mati,*' or, 'If a Māng sows grain he will only reap dust.' [1]

2. Subdivisions.

The caste is divided into the following subcastes: Dakhne, Khāndeshe and Berārya, or those belonging to the Deccan, Khāndesh and Berār; Ghodke, those who tend horses; Dafle, tom-tom players; Uchle, pickpockets; Pindāri, descendants of the old freebooters; Kakarkādhe, stone-diggers; Holer, hide-curers; and Garori The Garoris [1]

[1] See also separate article Māng-Garori.

are a sept of vagrant snake-charmers and jugglers. Many are professional criminals.

3. Marriage.
The caste is divided into exogamous family groups named after animals or other objects, or of a titular nature. One or two have the names of other castes. Members of the same group may not intermarry. Those who are well-to-do marry their daughters very young for the sake of social estimation, but there is no compulsion in this matter. In families which are particularly friendly, Mr. Sāthe remarks, children may be betrothed before birth if the two mothers are with child together. Betel is distributed, and a definite contract is made, on the supposition that a boy and girl will be born. Sometimes the abdomen of each woman is marked with red vermilion. A grown-up girl should not be allowed to see her husband's face before marriage. The wedding is held at the bride's house, but if it is more convenient that it should be in the bridegroom's village, a temporary house is found for the bride's party, and the marriage-shed is built in front of it. The bride must wear a yellow bodice and cloth, yellow and red being generally considered among Hindus as the auspicious colours for weddings. When she leaves for her husband's house she puts on another or going-away dress, which should be as fine as the family can afford, and thereafter she may wear any colour except white. The distinguishing marks of a married woman are the *mangal-sūtram* or holy thread, which her husband ties on her neck at marriage; the *garsoli* or string of black beads round the neck; the silver toe-rings and glass bangles. If any one of these is lost, it must be replaced at once, or she is likely soon to be a widow. The food served at the wedding-feast consists of rice and pulse, but more essential than these is an ample provision of liquor. It is a necessary feature of a Māng wedding that the bridegroom should go to it riding on a horse. The Mahārs, another low caste of the Marātha Districts, worship the horse, and between them and the Māngs there exists a long-standing feud, so that they do not, if they can help it, drink of the same well. The sight of a Māng riding on a horse is thus gall and wormwood to the Mahārs, who consider it a terrible degradation to the noble animal, and this fact

MĀNG MUSICIANS WITH DRUMS.

inflaming their natural enmity, formerly led to riots between the castes. Under native rule the Māngs were public executioners, and it was said to be the proudest moment of a Māng's life when he could perform his office on a Mahār.

The bride proceeds to her husband's house for a short visit immediately after the marriage, and then goes home again. Thereafter, till such time as she finally goes to live with him, she makes brief visits for festivals or on other social occasions, or to help her mother-in-law, if her assistance is required. If the mother-in-law is ill and requires somebody to wait on her, or if she is a shrew and wants some one to bully, or if she has strict ideas of discipline and wishes personally to conduct the bride's training for married life, she makes the girl come more frequently and stay longer.

4. Widow-marriage.

The remarriage of widows is permitted, and a widow may marry any one except persons of her own family group or her husband's elder brother, who stands to her in the light of a father. She is permitted, but not obliged, to marry her husband's younger brother, but if he has performed the dead man's obsequies, she may not marry him, as this act has placed him in the relation of a son to her deceased husband. More usually the widow marries some one in another village, because the remarriage is always held in some slight disrepute, and she prefers to be at a distance from her first husband's family. Divorce is said to be permitted only for persistent misconduct on the part of the wife.

5. Burial.

The caste always bury the dead and observe mourning only for three days. On returning from a burial they all get drunk, and then go to the house of the deceased and chew the bitter leaves of the *nīm* tree (*Melia indica*). These they then spit out of their mouths to indicate their complete severance from the dead man.

6. Occupation.

The caste beat drums at village festivals, and castrate cattle, and they also make brooms and mats of date-palm and keep leeches for blood-letting. Some of them are village watchmen and their women act as midwives. As soon as a baby is born, the midwife blows into its mouth, ears and nose in order to clear them of any impediments. When a man is initiated by a *guru* or spiritual preceptor, the latter blows into his ear, and the Māngs therefore say that on account of this act of the midwife they are the *gurus* of all Hindus. During an eclipse the Māngs beg, because the demons Rāhu and Ketu, who are believed to swallow the sun and moon on such occasions, were both Māngs, and devout Hindus give alms to their fellow-castemen in order to appease them. Those of them who are thieves are said not to steal from the persons of a woman, a bangle-seller, a Lingāyat Māli or another Māng.[1] In Marātha villages they sometimes take the place of Chamārs, and work in leather, and one writer says of them: "The Māng is a village menial in the Marātha villages, making all leather ropes, thongs and whips, which are used by the cultivators; he frequently acts as watchman; he is by profession a thief and executioner; he readily hires himself as an assassin, and when he commits a robbery he also frequently murders." In his menial capacity he receives presents at seed-time and harvest, and it is said that the Kunbi will never send the Māng empty away, because he represents the wrath of Mahādeo, being made from the god's sweat when he was angry.

7. Religion and social status.

The caste especially venerate the goddess Devi. They apparently identify Devi with Sāraswati, the goddess of wisdom, and they have a story to the effect that once Brahma wished to ravish his daughter Sāraswati. She fled from him and went to all the gods, but none of them would protect her for fear of Brahma. At last in despair she came to a Māng's house, and the Māng stood in the door and kept off Brahma with a wooden club. In return for this Sāraswati blessed him and said that he and his descendants should never lack for food. They also revere Mahādeo, and on every Monday they worship the cow, placing vermilion on her forehead and washing her feet. The cat is regarded as a sacred animal, and a Māng's most solemn oath is sworn on a cat. A house is defiled if a cat or a dog dies or a cat has kittens in it, and all the earthen pots must be broken. If a man accidentally kills a cat or a dog a heavy penance is

[1] *Berār Census Report* (1881), p. 147.

exacted, and two feasts must be given to the caste. To kill an ass or a monkey is a sin only less heinous. A man is also put out of caste if kicked or beaten with a shoe by any one of another caste, even a Brāhman, or if he is struck with the *kathri* or mattress made of rags which the villagers put on their sleeping-cots. Mr. Gayer remarks[1] that "The Māngs show great respect for the bamboo; and at a marriage the bridal couple are made to stand in a bamboo basket. They also reverence the *nīm* tree, and the Māngs of Sholapur spread *hariāli*[2] grass and *nīm* leaves on the spot where one of their caste dies." The social status of the Māngs is of the lowest. They usually live in a separate quarter of the village and have a well for their own use. They may not enter temples. It is recorded that under native rule the Mahārs and Māngs were not allowed within the gates of Poona between 3 P.M. and 9 A.M., because before nine and after three their bodies cast too long a shadow; and whenever their shadow fell upon a Brāhman it polluted him, so that he dare not taste food or water until he had bathed and washed the impurity away. So also no low-caste man was allowed to live in a walled town; cattle and dogs could freely enter and remain but not the Mahār or Māng.[3] The caste will eat the flesh of pigs, rats, crocodiles and jackals and the leavings of others, and some of them will eat beef. Men may be distinguished by the *senai* flute which they carry and by a large ring of gold or brass worn in the lobe of the ear. A Māng's sign-manual is a representation of his *bhall-singāra* or castration-knife. Women are tattooed before marriage, with dots on the forehead, nose, cheeks and chin, and with figures of a date-palm on the forearm, a scorpion on the palm of the hand, and flies on the fingers. The caste do not bear a good character, and it is said of a cruel man, '*Māng-Nirdayi*,' or 'Hardhearted as a Māng.'

Māng-Garori.—This is a criminal subdivision of the Māng caste, residing principally in Berār. They were not

---

[1] *Lectures on the Criminal Tribes of the Central Provinces*, p. 79.
[2] *Cynodon dactylon.*
[3] Dr. Murray Mitchell's *Great Religions of India*, p. 63.

separately recorded at the census. The name Garori appears to be a corruption of Garūdi, and signifies a snake-charmer.[1] Garūda, the Brahminy kite, the bird on which Vishnu rides, was the great subduer of snakes, and hence probably snake-charmers are called Garūdi. Some of the Māng-Garoris are snake-charmers, and this may have been the original occupation of the caste, though the bulk of them now appear to live by dealing in cattle and thieving. The following notice of them is abstracted from Major Gunthorpe's *Notes on Criminal Tribes*.[2] They usually travel about with small *pāls* or tents, taking their wives, children, buffaloes and dogs with them. The men are well set up and tall. Their costume is something like that worn by professional gymnasts, consisting of light and short reddish-brown drawers (*chaddi*), a waistband with fringe at either end (*katchhe*), and a sheet thrown over the shoulders. The Nāik or headman of the camp may be recognised by his wearing some red woollen cloth about his person or a red shawl over his shoulders. The women have short *sāris* (body-cloths), usually of blue, and tied in the Telugu fashion. They are generally very violent when any attempt is made to search an encampment, especially if there is stolen property concealed in it. Instances have been known of their seizing their infants by the ankles and swinging them round their heads, declaring they would continue doing so till the children died, if the police did not leave the camp. Sometimes also the women of a gang have been known to throw off all their clothing and appear in a perfect state of nudity, declaring they would charge the police with violating their modesty. Men of this tribe are expert cattle-lifters, but confine themselves chiefly to buffaloes, which they steal while out grazing and very dexterously disguise by trimming the horns and firing, so as to avoid recognition by their rightful owners. To steal goats and sheep is also one of their favourite occupations, and they will either carry the animals off from their pens at night or kill them while out grazing, in the following manner: having marked a sheep or goat which is feeding farthest away from the flock, the thief awaits his opportunity till the shepherd's back is turned,

---

[1] From a note by Mr. Hīra Lāl. [2] Times Press, Bombay, 1882.

when the animal is quickly captured. Placing his foot on the back of the neck near the head, and seizing it under the chin with his right hand, the thief breaks the animal's neck by a sudden jerk; he then throws the body into a bush or in some dip in the ground to hide it, and walks away, watching from a distance. The shepherd, ignorant of the loss of one of his animals, goes on leisurely driving his flock before him, and when he is well out of sight the Māng-Garori removes the captured carcase to his encampment. Great care is taken that the skin, horns and hoofs should be immediately burnt so as to avoid detection. Their ostensible occupation is to trade in barren half-starved buffaloes and buffalo calves, or in country ponies. They also purchase from Gaoli herdsmen barren buffaloes, which they profess to be able to make fertile; if successful they return them for double the purchase-money, but if not, having obtained if possible some earnest-money, they abscond and sell the animals at a distance.[1] Like the Bhāmtas, the Māng-Garoris, Major Gunthorpe states, make it a rule not to give a girl in marriage until the intended husband has proved himself an efficient thief. Mr. Gayer [2] writes as follows of the caste: "I do not think Major Gunthorpe lays sufficient emphasis on the part taken by the women in crimes, for they apparently do by far the major part of the thieving. Sherring says the men never commit house-breaking and very seldom rob on the highway: he calls them 'wanderers, showmen, jugglers and conjurors,' and describes them as robbers who get their information by performing before the houses of rich bankers and others. Māng-Gārori [3] women steal in markets and other places of public resort. They wait to see somebody put down his clothes or bag of rupees and watch till his attention is attracted elsewhere, when, walking up quietly between the article and its owner, they drop their petticoat either over or by it, and manage to transfer the stolen property into their basket while picking up the petticoat. If an unfavourable omen occurs on the way when the women set out to pilfer they place a stone on the ground and dash

---

[1] Kennedy, *Criminal Classes of the Bombay Presidency*, p. 122.

[2] *Lectures on some Criminal Tribes of India.*

[3] This passage is quoted by Mr. Gayer from the Supplement to the Central Provinces Police Gazette of 24th January 1905.

another on to it saying, 'If the obstacle is removed, break'; if the stone struck is broken, they consider that the obstacle portended by the unfavourable omen is removed from their path, and proceed on their way; but if not, they return. Stolen articles are often bartered at liquor-shops for drink, and the Kalārs act as receivers of stolen property for the Māng-Gāroris."

The following are some particulars taken from an old account of the criminal Māngs:[1] Their leader or headman was called the *naik* and was elected by a majority of votes, though considerable regard was paid to heredity. The *naik's* person and property were alike inviolable; after a successful foray each of the gang contributed a quarter of his share to the *naik*, and from the fund thus made up were defrayed the expenses of preparation, religious offerings and the triumphal feast. A pair of shoes were usually given to a Brāhman and alms to the poor. To each band was attached an informer, who was also receiver of the stolen goods. These persons were usually bangle- or perfume-sellers or jewellers. In this capacity they were admitted into the women's apartments and so enabled to form a correct notion of the topography of a house and a shrewd guess as to the wealth of its inmates. Like all barbarous tribes and all persons addicted to criminal practices the Māngs were extremely superstitious. They never set out on an expedition on a Friday. After the birth of a child the mother and another woman stood on opposite sides of the cradle, and the former tossed her child to the other, commending it to the mercy of Jai Gopāl, and waited to receive it back in like manner in the name of Jai Govind. Both Gopāl and Govind are names of Krishna. The Māngs usually married young in life. If a girl happened to hang heavy on hand she was married at the age of puberty to the deity. In other words, she was attached as a prostitute to the temple of the god Khandoba or the goddess Yellama. Those belonging to the service of the latter were wont in the month of February to parade the streets in a state of utter nudity. When a bachelor wished to marry a widow

---

[1] Hutton's *Thugs, Dacoits and Gang-robbers of India* (1857), pp. 164-168, quoting an account by Captain Barr.

he was first united to a swallow-wort plant, and this was immediately dug up and transplanted, and withering away left him at liberty to marry the widow. If a lady survived the sorrow caused by the death of two or three husbands she could not again enter the holy state unless she consented to be married with a fowl under her armpit; the unfortunate bird being afterwards killed to appease the manes of her former consorts.

Manihār.[1]—A small caste of pedlars and hawkers. In northern India the Manihārs are makers of glass bangles, and correspond to the Kachera caste of the Central Provinces. Mr. Nesfield remarks[2] that the special industry of the Manihārs of the United Provinces is the making of glass bangles or bracelets. These are an indispensable adjunct to the domestic life of the Hindu woman; for the glass bangle is not worn for personal ornament, but as the badge of the matrimonial state, like the wedding-ring in Europe. But in the Central Provinces glass bangles are made by the Kacheras and the Muhammadan Turkāris or Sīsgars, and the Manihārs are petty hawkers of stationery and articles for the toilet, such as miniature looking-glasses, boxes, stockings, needles and thread, spangles, and imitation jewellery; and Hindu Jogis and others who take to this occupation are accustomed to give their caste as Manihār. In 1911 nearly 700 persons belonging to the caste were returned from the northern Districts of the Central Provinces. The Manihārs are nominally Muhammadans, but they retain many Hindu customs. At their weddings they erect a marriage-tent, anoint the couple with oil and turmeric and make them wear a *kankan* or wrist-band, to which is attached a small purse containing a little mustard-seed and a silver ring. The mustard is intended to scare away the evil spirits. When the marriage procession reaches the bride's village it is met by her people, one of whom holds a bamboo in his hands and bars the advance of the procession. The bridegroom's father thereupon makes a present of a rupee

---

[1] This article is based on papers by Rai Sāhib Nānakchand, B.A., Headmaster, Saugor High School, and Munshi Pyāre Lāl Misra of the Gazetteer office.

[2] *Brief View*, p. 30.

to the village *panchāyat*, and his people are allowed to proceed. When the bridegroom reaches the bride's house he finds her younger sister carrying a *kalās* or pot of water on her head; he drops a rupee into it and enters the house. The bride's sister then comes holding above her head a small frame like a *tāzia*[1] with a cocoanut core hanging inside. She raises the frame as high as she can to prevent the bridegroom from plucking out the cocoanut core, which, however, he succeeds in doing in the end. The girl applies powdered *mehndi* or henna to the little finger of the boy's right hand, in return for which she receives a rupee and a piece of cloth. The Kāzi then recites verses from the Korān which the bridegroom repeats after him, and the bride does the same in her turn. This is the Nikāh or marriage proper, and before it takes place the bridegroom's father must present a nose-ring to the bride. The parents also fix the Meher or dowry, which, however, is not a dowry proper, but a stipulation that if the bridegroom should put away his wife after marriage he will pay her a certain agreed sum. After the Nikāh the bridegroom is given some spices, which he grinds on a slab with a roller. He must do the grinding very slowly and gently so as to make no noise, or it is believed that the married life of the couple will be broken by quarrels. A widow is permitted to marry the younger brother of her deceased husband, but not his elder brother. The caste bury their dead with the head to the north. The corpse is first bathed and wrapped in a new white sheet, with another sheet over it, and is then laid on a cot or in a *janāza* or coffin. While it is being carried to the cemetery the bearers are changed every few steps, so that every man who accompanies the funeral may carry the corpse for a short distance. When it is lowered into the grave the sheet is taken off and given to a Fakīr or beggar. When the body is covered with earth the priest reads the funeral verses at a distance of forty steps from the grave. Feasts are given to the caste-fellows on the third, tenth, twentieth and fortieth days after the death. The Manihārs observe the Shabrāt festival by distributing to the caste-fellows

---

[1] The *tāzias* are ornamental representations of the tomb of Hussain, which the Muhammadans make at the Muharram festival.

halua or a mixture of melted butter and flour. The Shabrāt is the middle night of the month Shabān, and Muhammad declared that on this night God registers the actions which every man will perform during the following year, and all those who are fated to die and the children who are to be born. Like Hindu widows the Manihār women break their bangles when their husband's corpse is removed to the burial-ground. The Manihārs eat flesh, but not beef or pork; and they also abstain from alcoholic liquor. If a girl is seduced and made pregnant before marriage either by a man of the caste or an outsider, she remains in her father's house until her child has been born, and may then be married either to her paramour or any other man of the caste by the simple repetition of the Nikāh or marriage verses, omitting all other ceremonies. The Manihārs will admit into their community converted Hindus belonging even to the lowest castes.

Mannewār.[1]—A small tribe belonging to the south or Telugu-speaking portion of the Chānda District, where they mustered about 1600 persons in 1911. The home of the tribe is the Hyderābād State, where it numbers 22,000 persons, and the Mannewārs are said to have once been dominant over a part of that territory. The name is derived from a Telugu word *mannem*, meaning forest, while *wār* is the plural termination in Telugu, Mannewār thus signifying 'the people of the forest.' The tribe appear to be the inferior branch of the Koya Gonds, and they are commonly called Mannewār Koyas as opposed to the Koya Doras or the superior branch, Dora meaning 'lord' or master. The Koya Doras thus correspond to the Raj-Gonds of the north of the Province and the Mannewār Koyas to the Dhur or 'dust' Gonds.[2] The tribe is divided into three exogamous groups: the Nalugu Velpulu worshipping four gods, the Ayidu Velpulu worshipping five, and the Anu Velpulu six. A man must marry a woman of one of the divisions worshipping a different number of gods from his

---

[1] This article is based on a note furnished by Mr. M. Aziz, Officiating Nāib-Tahsīldār, Sironcha.

[2] From a glossary published by Mr. Gupta, Assistant Director of Ethnology for India.

own, but the Mannewārs do not appear to know the names of these gods, and consequently no veneration can be paid to them at present, and they survive solely for the purpose of regulating marriage. When a betrothal is made a day is fixed for taking an omen. In the early morning the boy who is to be married has his face washed and turmeric smeared on his feet, and is seated on a wooden seat inside the house. The elders of the village then proceed outside it towards the rising sun and watch for any omen given by an animal or bird crossing their path. If this is good the marriage is celebrated, and if bad the match is broken off. In the former case five of the elders take their food on returning from the search for the omen and immediately proceed to the bride's village. Here they are met by the Pesāmuda or village priest, and stay for three days, when the amount of the dowry is settled and a date fixed for the wedding. The marriage ceremony resembles that of the low Telugu castes. The couple are seated on a plough-yoke, and coloured rice is thrown on to their heads, and the bridegroom ties the *mangalya* or bead necklace, which is the sign of marriage, round the neck of the bride. If a girl is deformed, or has some other drawback which prevents her from being sought in marriage, she is given away with her sister to a first cousin [1] or some other near relative, the two sisters being married to him together. A widow may marry any man of the tribe except her first husband's brothers. If a man takes a widow to his house without marrying her he is fined three rupees, while for adultery with a married woman the penalty is twenty rupees. A divorce can always be obtained, but if the husband demands it he is mulcted of twenty rupees by the caste committee, while a wife who seeks a divorce must pay ten rupees. The Mannewārs make an offering of a fowl and some liquor to the ploughshare on the festival of Ganesh Chaturthi. After the picking of the flowers of the mahua [2] they worship that tree, offering to it some of the liquor distilled from the new flowers, with a fowl and a goat. This is known as the Burri festival. At the Holi feast the Mannewārs make two human figures to represent Kāmi and Rati, or the god of

[1] Generally the paternal aunt's son.   [2] *Bassia latifolia.*

love and his wife. The male figure is then thrown on to the Holi fire with a live chicken or an egg. This may be a reminiscence of a former human sacrifice, which was a common custom in many parts of the world at the spring festival. The caste usually bury the dead, but are beginning to adopt cremation. They do not employ Brāhmans for their ceremonies and eat all kinds of food, including the flesh of pigs, fowls and crocodiles, but in view of their having nominally adopted Hinduism, they abstain from beef.

MARĀTHA

LIST OF PARAGRAPHS

1. *Numerical statistics.*
2. *Double meaning of the term Marātha.*
3. *Origin and position of the caste.*
4. *Exogamous clans.*
5. *Other subdivisions.*
6. *Social customs.*
7. *Religion.*
8. *Present position of the caste.*
9. *Nature of the Marātha insurrection.*
10. *Marātha women in past times.*
11. *The Marātha horseman.*
12. *Cavalry in the field.*
13. *Military administration.*
14. *Sitting Dharna.*
15. *The infantry.*
16. *Character of the Marātha armies.*

1. Numerical statistics.
Marātha, Mahrātta.—The military caste of southern India which manned the armies of Sivaji, and of the Peshwa and other princes of the Marātha confederacy. In the Central Provinces the Marāthas numbered 34,000 persons in 1911, of whom Nāgpur contained 9000 and Wardha 8000, while the remainder were distributed over Raipur, Hoshangābād and Nimār. In Berār their strength was 60,000 persons, the total for the combined province being thus 94,000. The caste is found in large numbers in Bombay and Hyderābād, and in 1901 the India Census tables show a total of not less than five million persons belonging to it.

2. Double meaning of the term Marātha.
It is difficult to avoid confusion in the use of the term Marātha, which signifies both an inhabitant of the area in which the Marāthi language is spoken, and a member of the caste to which the general name has in view of their historical importance been specifically applied. The native name for the Marāthi-speaking country is Mahārāshtra, which has been variously interpreted as 'The great country' or 'The country of the Mahārs.'[1] A third explanation of the name

[1] Sir H. Risley's *India Census Report* (1901), Ethnographic Appendices, p. 93.

is from the Rāshtrakūta dynasty which was dominant in this area for some centuries after A.D. 750. The name Rāshtrakūta was contracted into Rattha, and with the prefix of Mahā or Great might evolve into the term Marātha. The Rāshtrakūtas have been conjecturally identified with the Rāthor Rājpūts. The *Nāsik Gazetteer*[1] states that in 246 B.C. Mahāratta is mentioned as one of the places to which Asoka sent an embassy, and Mahārashtraka is recorded in a Chālukyan inscription of A.D. 580 as including three provinces and 99,000 villages. Several other references are given in Sir J. Campbell's erudite note, and the name is therefore without doubt ancient. But the Marāthas as a people do not seem to be mentioned before the thirteenth or fourteenth century.[2] The antiquity of the name would appear to militate against the derivation from the Rāshtra-kūta dynasty, which did not become prominent till much later, and the most probable meaning of Mahārāshtra would therefore seem to be 'The country of the Mahārs.' Mahāratta and Marātha are presumably derivatives from Mahārāshtra.

3. Origin and position of the caste.

The Marāthas are a caste formed from military service, and it seems probable that they sprang mainly from the peasant population of Kunbis, though at what period they were formed into a separate caste has not yet been determined. Grant-Duff mentions several of their leading families as holding offices under the Muhammadan rulers of Bījapur and Ahmadnagar in the fifteenth and sixteenth centuries, as the Nimbhālkar, Ghārpure and Bhonsla;[3] and presumably their clansmen served in the armies of those states. But whether or no the designation of Marātha had been previously used by them, it first became prominent during the period of Sivaji's guerilla warfare against Aurāngzeb. The Marāthas claim a Rājpūt origin, and several of their clans have the names of Rājpūt tribes, as Chauhān, Panwār, Solanki and Suryavansi. In 1836 Mr. Enthoven states,[4] the Sesodia Rāna of Udaipur, the head of the purest Rājpūt house, was satisfied from inquiries conducted by an

---

[1] P. 48, footnote.
[2] *Nāsik Gazetteer, ibidem*. Elphinstone's *History*, p. 246.
[3] The proper spelling is Bhosle, but Bhonsla is adopted in deference to established usage.
[4] *Bombay Census Report* (1901), pp. 184-185.

agent that the Bhonslas and certain other families had a right to be recognised as Rājpūts. Colonel Tod states that Sivaji was descended from a Rājpūt prince Sujunsi, who was expelled from Mewār to avoid a dispute about the succession about A.D. 1300. Sivaji is shown as 13th in descent from Sujunsi. Similarly the Bhonslas of Nāgpur were said to derive their origin from one Bunbir, who was expelled from Udaipur about 1541, having attempted to usurp the kingdom.[1] As Rājpūt dynasties ruled in the Deccan for some centuries before the Muhammadan conquest, it seems reasonable to suppose that a Rājpūt aristocracy may have taken root there. This was Colonel Tod's opinion, who wrote: " These kingdoms of the south as well as the north were held by Rājpūt sovereigns, whose offspring, blending with the original population, produced that mixed race of Marāthas inheriting with the names the warlike propensities of their ancestors, but who assume the names of their abodes as titles, as the Nimalkars, the Phalkias, the Patunkars, instead of their tribes of Jādon, Tüar, Püar, etc."[2] This statement would, however, apply only to the leading houses and not to the bulk of the Marātha caste, who appear to be mainly derived from the Kunbis. In Sholāpur the Marāthas and Kunbis eat together, and the Kunbis are said to be bastard Marāthas.[3] In Satāra the Kunbis have the same division into 96 clans as the Marāthas have, and many of the same surnames.[4] The writer of the *Satāra Gazetteer* says:[5] " The census of 1851 included the Marāthas with the Kunbis, from whom they do not form a separate caste. Some Marātha families may have a larger strain of northern or Rājpūt blood than the Kunbis, but this is not always the case. The distinction between Kunbis and Marāthas is almost entirely social, the Marāthas as a rule being better off, and preferring even service as a constable or messenger to husbandry." Exactly the same state of affairs prevails in the Central Provinces and Berār, where the body of the caste are commonly known as Marātha Kunbis. In Bombay the Marāthas will take daughters from the Kunbis in marriage for their sons, though they will not give their daughters

---

[1] *Rājasthān*, i. 269. [2] *Ibidem*, ii. 420. [3] *Sholapur Gazetteer*, p. 87.
[4] *Satāra Gazetteer*, p. 64. [5] *Ibidem*, p. 75.

STATUE OF MARĀTHA LEADER, BĪMBĀJI
BHONSLA, IN ARMOUR.

in return. But a Kunbi who has got on in the world and become wealthy may by sufficient payment get his sons married into Maratha families, and even be adopted as a member of the caste.[1] In 1798 Colonel Tone, who commanded a regiment of the Peshwa's army, wrote[2] of the Marathas: "The three great tribes which compose the Maratha caste are the Kunbi or farmer, the Dhangar or shepherd, and the Goāla or cowherd; to this original cause may perhaps be ascribed that great simplicity of manner which distinguishes the Maratha people."

It seems then most probable that, as already stated, the Maratha caste was of purely military origin, constituted from the various castes of Mahārāshtra who adopted military service, though some of the leading families may have had Rājpūts for their ancestors. Sir D. Ibbetson thought that a similar relation existed in past times between the Rājpūts and Jāts, the landed aristocracy of the Jāt caste being gradually admitted to Rājpūt rank. The Khandaits or swordsmen of Orissa are a caste formed in the same manner from military service. In the *Imperial Gazetteer* Sir H. Risley suggests that the Maratha people were of Scythian origin:

"The physical type of the people of this region accords fairly well with this theory, while the arguments derived from language and religion do not seem to conflict with it. ... On this view the wide-ranging forays of the Marathas, their guerilla methods of warfare, their unscrupulous dealings with friend and foe, their genius for intrigue and their consequent failure to build up an enduring dominion, might well be regarded as inherited from their Scythian ancestors."

4. Exogamous clans.

In the Central Provinces the Marathas are divided into 96 exogamous clans, known as the Chhānava Kule, which marry with one another. During the period when the Bhonsla family were rulers of Nāgpur they constituted a sort of inner circle, consisting of seven of the leading clans, with whom alone they intermarried; these are known as the Sātghare or Seven Houses, and consist of the Bhonsla, Gūjar, Ahirrao, Mahādik, Sirke, Palke and Mohte clans.

[1] *Bombay Census Report* (1907), ibidem. [2] *Letter on the Marāthas* (India Office Tracts).

These houses at one time formed an endogamous group, marrying only among themselves, but recently the restriction has been relaxed, and they have arranged marriages with other Marātha families. It may be noted that the present representatives of the Bhonsla family are of the Gūjar clan to which the last Rāja of Nāgpur, Raghūji III., belonged prior to his adoption. Several of the clans, as already noted, have Rājpūt sept names; and some are considered to be derived from those of former ruling dynasties; as Chālke, from the Chālukya Rājpūt kings of the Deccan and Carnatic; More, who may represent a branch of the great Maurya dynasty of northern India; Sālunke, perhaps derived from the Solanki kings of Gujarāt; and Yādav, the name of the kings of Deogiri or Daulatābād.[1] Others appear to be named after animals or natural objects, as Sinde from *sindi* the date-palm tree, Ghorpade from *ghorpad* the iguana; or to be of a titular nature, as Kāle black, Pāndhre white, Bhāgore a renegade, Jagthāp renowned, and so on. The More, Nimbhālkar, Ghātge, Māne, Ghorpade, Dafle, Jādav and Bhonsla clans are the oldest, and held prominent positions in the old Muhammadan kingdoms of Bījapur and Ahmadnagar. The Nimbhālkar family were formerly Panwār Rājpūts, and took the name of Nimbhālkar from their ancestral village Nimbālik. The Ghorpade family are an offshoot of the Bhonslas, and obtained their present name from the exploit of one of their ancestors, who scaled a fort in the Konkan, previously deemed impregnable, by passing a cord round the body of a *ghorpad* or iguana.[2] A noticeable trait of these Marātha houses is the fondness with which they clung to the small estates or villages in the Deccan in which they had originally held the office of a patel or village headman as a *watan* or hereditary right, even after they had carved out for themselves principalities and states in other parts of India. The present Bhonsla Rāja takes his title from the village of Deor in the Poona country. In former times we read of the Rāja of Satāra clinging to the *watans* he had inherited from Sivaji after he had lost his crown in all but the name; Sindhia was always termed

---

[1] *Satāra Gazetteer*, p. 75.
[2] Grant-Duff, 4th edition (1878), vol. i. pp. 70-72.

patel or village headman in the revenue accounts of the villages he acquired in Nimār; while it is said that Holkar and the Panwār of Dhār fought desperately after the British conquest to recover the *pateli* rights of Deccan villages which had belonged to their ancestors.[1]

Besides the 96 clans there are now in the Central Provinces some local subcastes who occupy a lower position and do not intermarry with the Marāthas proper. Among these are the Deshkar or 'Residents of the country'; the Waindesha or those of Berār and Khāndesh; the Gangthade or those dwelling on the banks of the Godāvari and Wainganga; and the Ghātmāthe or residents of the Mahādeo plateau in Berār. It is also stated that the Marāthas are divided into the *Khāsi* or 'pure' and the *Kharchi* or the descendants of handmaids. In Bombay the latter are known as the Akarmāshes or 11 *māshas*, meaning that as twelve *māshas* make a tola, a twelfth part of them is alloy.

5. Other subdivisions.

A man must not marry in his own clan or that of his mother. A sister's son may be married to a brother's daughter, but not vice versa. Girls are commonly married between five and twelve years of age, and the ceremony resembles that of the Kunbis. The bridegroom goes to the bride's house riding on horseback and covered with a black blanket. When a girl first becomes mature, usually after marriage, the Marāthas perform the Shāntik ceremony. The girl is secluded for four days, after which she is bathed and puts on new clothes and dresses her hair and a feast is given to the caste-fellows. Sometimes the bridegroom comes and is asked whether he has visited his wife before she became mature, and if he confesses that he has done so a small fine is imposed on him. Such cases are, however, believed to be rare. The Marāthas proper forbid widow-marriage, but the lower groups allow it. If a maiden is seduced by one of the caste she may be married to him as if she were a widow, a fine being imposed on her family; but if she goes wrong with an outsider she is finally expelled. Divorce is not ostensibly allowed but may be concluded by agreement between the parties. A wife who commits adultery is cast off and expelled from the caste. The caste burn their

6. Social customs.

[1] Forsyth, *Nimār Settlement Report*.

dead when they can afford it and perform the *shrāddh* ceremony in the month of *Kunwār* (September), when oblations are offered to the dead and a feast is given to the caste-fellows. Sometimes a tomb is erected as a memorial to the dead, but without his name, and is surmounted usually by an image of Mahādeo. The caste eat the flesh of clean animals and of fowls and wild pig, and drink liquor. Their rules about food are liberal like those of the Rājpūts, a too great stringency being no doubt in both cases incompatible with the exigencies of military service. They make no difference between food cooked with or without water, and will accept either from a Brāhman, Rājpūt, Tirole Kunbi, Lingāyat Bania or Phūlmāli.

The Marāthas proper observe the *parda* system with regard to their women, and will go to the well and draw water themselves rather than permit their wives to do so. The women wear ornaments only of gold or glass and not of silver or any baser metal. They are not permitted to spin cotton as being an occupation of the lower classes. The women are tattooed in the centre of the forehead with a device resembling a trident. The men commonly wear a turban made of many folds of cloth twisted into a narrow rope and large gold rings with pearls in the upper part of the ear. Like the Rājpūts they often have their hair long and wear beards and whiskers. They assume the sacred thread and invest a boy with it when he is seven or eight years old or on his marriage. Till then they let the hair grow on the front of his head, and when the thread ceremony is performed they cut this off and let the *choti* or scalp-lock grow at the back. In appearance the men are often tall and well-built and of a light wheat-coloured complexion.

7. Religion.

The principal deity of the Marāthas is Khandoba, a warrior incarnation of Mahādeo. He is supposed to have been born in a field of millet near Poona and to have led the people against the Muhammadans in early times. He had a watch-dog who warned him of the approach of his enemies, and he is named after the *khanda* or sword which he always carried. In Bombay [1] he is represented on horseback with

[1] *Bombay Gazetteer*, vol. xviii. part i. pp. 413-414.

two women, one of the Bania caste, his wedded wife, in front of him, and another, a Dhangarin, his kept mistress, behind. He is considered the tutelary deity of the Marātha country, and his symbol is a bag of turmeric powder known as *bhandār*. The caste worship Khandoba on Sundays with rice, flowers and incense, and also on the 21st day of Māgh (January), which is called *Champa Sashthi* and is his special festival. On this day they will catch hold of any dog, and after adorning him with flowers and turmeric give him a good feed and let him go again. The Marāthas are generally kind to dogs and will not injure them. At the Dasahra festival the caste worship their horses and swords and go out into the field to see a blue-jay in memory of the fact that the Marātha marauding expeditions started on Dasahra. On coming back they distribute to each other leaves of the *shami* tree (*Bauhinia racemosa*) as a substitute for gold. It was formerly held to be fitting among the Hindus that the warrior should ride a horse (geldings being unknown) and the zamīndār or landowner a mare, as more suitable to a man of peace. The warriors celebrated their Dasahra, and worshipped their horses on the tenth day of the light fortnight of *Kunwār* (September), while the cultivators held their festival and worshipped their mares on the ninth day. It is recorded that the great Rāghuji Bhonsla, the first Rāja of Nāgpur, held his Dasahra on the ninth day, in order to proclaim the fact that he was by family an agriculturist and only incidentally a man of arms.[1]

8. Present position of the caste.

The Marāthas present the somewhat melancholy spectacle of an impoverished aristocratic class attempting to maintain some semblance of their former position, though they no longer have the means to do so. They flourished during two or three centuries of almost continuous war, and became a wealthy and powerful caste, but they find a difficulty in turning their hands to the arts of peace. Sir R. Craddock writes of them in Nāgpur:

"Among the Marāthas a large number represent connections of the Bhonsla family, related by marriage or by illegitimate descent to that house. A considerable proportion of the Government political pensioners are Marāthas.

[1] Elliott, *Hoshangābād Settlement Report*.

Many of them own villages or hold tenant land, but as a rule they are extravagant in their living; and several of the old Marātha nobility have fallen very much in the world. Pensions diminish with each generation, but the expenditure shows no corresponding decrease. The sons are brought up to no employment and the daughters are married with lavish pomp and show. The native army does not much attract them, and but few are educated well enough for the dignified posts in the civil employ of Government. It is a question whether their pride of race will give way before the necessity of earning their livelihood soon enough for them to maintain or regain some of their former position. Otherwise those with the largest landed estates may be saved by the intervention of Government, but the rest must gradually deteriorate till the dignities of their class have become a mere memory. The humbler members of the caste find their employment as petty contractors or traders, private servants, Government peons, *sowārs*, and hangers-on in the retinue of the more important families.

"What [1] little display his means afford a Marātha still tries to maintain. Though he may be clad in rags at home, he has a spare dress which he himself washes and keeps with great care and puts on when he goes to pay a visit. He will hire a boy to attend him with a lantern at night, or to take care of his shoes when he goes to a friend's house and hold them before him when he comes out. Well-to-do Marāthas have usually in their service a Brāhman clerk known as *divānji* or minister, who often takes advantage of his master's want of education to defraud him. A Marātha seldom rises early or goes out in the morning. He will get up at seven or eight o'clock, a late hour for a Hindu, and attend to business if he has any or simply idle about chewing or smoking tobacco and talking till ten o'clock. He will then bathe and dress in a freshly-washed cloth and bow before the family gods which the priest has already worshipped. He will dine, chew betel and smoke tobacco and enjoy a short midday rest. Rising at three, he will play cards, dice or chess, and in the evening will go out walking or riding or

---

[1] The following description is taken from the Ethnographic Appendices to Sir H. H. Risley's *India Census Report* of 1901.

pay a visit to a friend. He will come back at eight or nine and go to bed at ten or eleven. But Marāthas who have estates to manage lead regular, fairly busy lives."

Sir D. Ibbetson drew attention to the fact that the rising of the Marāthas against the Muhammadans was almost the only instance in Indian history of what might correctly be called a really national movement. In other cases, as that of the Sikhs, though the essential motive was perhaps of the same nature, it was obscured by the fact that its ostensible tendency was religious. The *gurus* of the Sikhs did not call on their followers to fight for their country but for a new religion. This was only in accordance with the Hindu intellect, to which the idea of nationality has hitherto been foreign, while its protests against both alien and domestic tyrannies tend to take the shape of a religious revolt. A similar tendency is observable even in the case of the Marāthas, for the rising was from its inception largely engineered by the Marātha Brāhmans, who on its success hastened to annex for themselves a leading position in the new Poona state. And it has been recorded that in calling his countrymen to arms, Sivaji did not ask them to defend their hearths and homes or wives and children, but to rally for the protection of the sacred persons of Brāhmans and cows. [9. Nature of the Marātha insurrection.]

Although the Marāthas have now in imitation of the Rājpūts and Muhammadans adopted the *parda* system, this is not a native custom, and women have played quite an important part in their history. The women of the household have also exercised a considerable influence and their opinions are treated with respect by the men. Several instances occur in which women of high rank have successfully acted as governors and administrators. In the Bhonsla family the Princess Bāka Bāi, widow of Raghūji II., is a conspicuous instance, while the famous or notorious Rāni of Jhānsi is another case of a Marātha lady who led her troops in person, and was called the best man on the native side in the Mutiny. [10. Marātha women in past times.]

This article may conclude with one or two extracts to give an idea of the way in which the Marātha soldiery took the field. Grant Duff describes the troopers as follows : [11. The Marātha horseman.]

"The Marātha horsemen are commonly dressed in a pair of light breeches covering the knee, a turban which many of them fasten by passing a fold of it under the chin, a frock of quilted cotton, and a cloth round the waist, with which they generally gird on their swords in preference to securing them with their belts. The horseman is armed with a sword and shield; a proportion in each body carry matchlocks, but the great national weapon is the spear, in the use of which and the management of their horse they evince both grace and dexterity. The spearmen have generally a sword, and sometimes a shield; but the latter is unwieldy and only carried in case the spear should be broken. The trained spearmen may always be known by their riding very long, the ball of the toe touching the stirrup; some of the matchlockmen and most of the Brāhmans ride very short and ungracefully. The bridle consists of a single headstall of cotton-rope, with a small but very severe flexible bit."

12. Cavalry in the field.

The following account of the Marātha cavalry is given in General Hislop's *Summary of the Marātha and Pindāri Campaigns* of 1817–1819:

"The Marāthas possess extraordinary skill in horsemanship, and so intimate an acquaintance with their horses, that they can make their animals do anything, even in full speed, in halting, wheeling, etc.; they likewise use the spear with remarkable dexterity, sometimes in full gallop, grasping their spears short and quickly sticking the point in the ground; still holding the handles, they turn their horse suddenly round it, thus performing on the point of a spear as on a pivot the same circle round and round again. Their horses likewise never leave the particular class or body to which they belong; so that if the rider should be knocked off, away gallops the animal after its fellows, never separating itself from the main body. Every Marātha brings his own horse and his own arms with him to the field, and possibly in the interest they possess in this private equipment we shall find their usual shyness to expose themselves or even to make a bold vigorous attack. But if armies or troops could be frightened by appearances these horses of the Marāthas would dishearten the bravest, actually darkening the plains with their numbers and clouding the horizon with dust for miles and miles around. A little fighting, however, goes a great way with them, as with most others of the native powers in India."

On this account the Marāthas were called *razāh-bazān* or lance-wielders. One Muhammadan historian says : "They so use the lance that no cavalry can cope with them. Some 20,000 or 30,000 lances are held up against their enemy so close together as not to leave a span between their heads. If horsemen try to ride them down the points of the spears are levelled at the assailants and they are unhorsed. While cavalry are charging them they strike their lances against each other and the noise so frightens the horses of the enemy that they turn round and bolt."[1] The battle-cries of the Marāthas were, '*Har, Har Mahādeo,*' and '*Gopāl, Gopāl.*'[2]

13. Military administration

An interesting description of the internal administration of the Marātha cavalry is contained in the letter on the Marāthas by Colonel Tone already quoted. But his account must refer to a period of declining efficiency and cannot represent the military system at its best :

"In the great scale of rank and eminence which is one peculiar feature of Hindu institutions the Marātha holds a very inferior situation, being just removed one degree above those castes which are considered absolutely unclean. He is happily free from the rigorous observances as regards food which fetter the actions of the higher castes. He can eat of all kinds of food with the exception of beef ; can dress his meal at all times and seasons ; can partake of all victuals dressed by any caste superior to his own ; washing and praying are not indispensable in his order and may be practised or omitted at pleasure. The three great tribes which compose the Marātha caste are the Kunbi or farmer, the Dhangar or shepherd and the Goāla or cowherd ; to this original cause may perhaps be ascribed that great simplicity of manner which distinguishes the Marātha people. Homer mentions princesses going in person to the fountain to wash their household linen. I can affirm having seen the daughters of a prince who was able to bring an army into the field much larger than the whole Greek con-

---

[1] Irvine's *Army of the Mughals,* p. 82.
[2] *Ibidem,* p. 232. Gopāl is a name of Krishna.

VOL. IV P

federacy, making bread with their own hands and otherwise employed in the ordinary business of domestic housewifery. I have seen one of the most powerful chiefs of the Empire, after a day of action, assisting in kindling a fire to keep himself warm during the night, and sitting on the ground on a spread saddle-cloth dictating to his secretaries.

"The chief military force of the Marāthas consists in their cavalry, which may be divided into four distinct classes: First the Khāsi Pagah or household forces of the prince; these are always a fine well-appointed body, the horses excellent, being the property of the Sirkār, who gives a monthly allowance to each trooper of the value of about eight rupees. The second class are the cavalry furnished by the Sillādārs,[1] who contract to supply a certain number of horse on specified terms, generally about Rs. 35 a month, including the trooper's pay. The third and most numerous description are volunteers, who join the camp bringing with them their own horse and accoutrements; their pay is generally from Rs. 40 to Rs. 50 a month in proportion to the value of their horse. There is a fourth kind of native cavalry called Pindāris, who are mere marauders, serve without any pay and subsist but by plunder, a fourth part of which they give to the Sirkār; but these are so very licentious a body that they are not employed but in one or two of the Marātha services.

"The troops collected in this manner are under no discipline whatever and engage for no specific period, but quit the army whenever they please; with the exception of furnishing a picquet while in camp, they do no duty but in the day of battle.

"The Marātha cavalry is always irregularly and badly paid; the household troops scarcely ever receive money, but are furnished with a daily allowance of coarse flour and some other ingredients from the bazār which just enable them to exist. The Sillādār is very nearly as badly

---

[1] Lit. armour-bearers. Colonel Tone writes: "I apprehend from the meaning of this term that it was formerly the custom of this nation, as was the case in Europe, to appear in armour. I have frequently seen a kind of coat-of-mail worn by the Marātha horsemen, known as a *beuta*, which resembles our ancient hauberk; it is made of chain work, interlinked throughout, fits close to the body and adapts itself to all its motions."

situated. In his arrangements with the State he has allotted to him a certain proportion of jungle where he pastures his cattle; here he and his family reside, and his sole occupation when not on actual service is increasing his Pagah or troop by breeding out of his mares, of which the Marātha cavalry almost entirely consist. There are no people in the world who understand the method of rearing and multiplying the breed of cattle equal to the Marāthas. It is by no means uncommon for a Sillādār to enter a service with one mare and in a few years be able to muster a very respectable Pagah. They have many methods of rendering the animal prolific; they back their colts much earlier than we do and they are consequently more valuable as they come sooner on the effective strength.

"When called upon for actual service the Sillādār is obliged to give muster. Upon this occasion it is always necessary that the Brāhman who takes it should have a bribe; and indeed the Hāzri, as the muster is termed, is of such a nature that it could not pass by any fair or honourable means. Not only any despicable *tattus* are substituted in the place of horses but animals are borrowed to fill up the complement. Heel-ropes and grain-bags are produced as belonging to cattle supposed to be at grass; in short every mode is practised to impose on the Sirkār, which in turn reimburses itself by irregular and bad payments; for it is always considered if the Sillādārs receive six months' arrears out of the year that they are exceedingly well paid. The Volunteers who join the camp are still worse situated, as they have no collective force, and money is very seldom given in a Marātha State without being extorted. In one word, the native cavalry are the worst-paid body of troops in the world. But there is another grand error in this mode of raising troops which is productive of the worst effects. Every man in a Marātha camp is totally independent; he is the proprietor of the horse he rides, which he is never inclined to risk, since without it he can get no service. This single circumstance destroys all enterprise and spirit in the soldier, whose sole business, instead of being desirous of distinguishing himself, is to keep out of the way of danger; for notwithstanding every horseman on entering a service has a certain value put upon his horse, yet should he lose it even in action he never receives any compensation or at least none proportioned to his loss. If at any time a Silladār is disgusted with the service he can go away without meeting any molestation even though in the face of an enemy. In fact the pay is in general so shamefully irregular that a man is justified in resorting to any measure, however apparently unbecoming, to attain it. It is also another very curious circumstance attending this service that many great Silladārs have troops in the pay of two or three chiefs at the same time, who are frequently at open war with each other.

14. Sitting Dharna.

"To recover an arrear of pay there is but one known mode which is universally adopted in all native services, the Mughal as well as the Marātha; this is called Dharna,[1] which consists in putting the debtor, be he who he will, into a state of restraint or imprisonment, until satisfaction be given or the money actually obtained. Any person in the Sirkār's service has a right to demand his pay of the Prince or his minister, and to sit in Dharna if it be not given; nor will he meet with the least hindrance in doing so; for none would obey an order that interfered with the Dharna, as it is a common cause; nor does the soldier incur the slightest charge of mutiny for his conduct, or suffer in the smallest manner in the opinion of his Chief, so universal is the custom. The Dharna is sometimes carried to very violent lengths and may either be executed on the Prince or his minister indifferently, with the same effect; as the Chief always makes it a point of honour not to eat or drink while his Diwān is in duress; sometimes the Dharna lasts for many days, during which time the party upon whom it is exercised is not suffered to eat or drink or wash or pray, or in short is not permitted to move from the spot where he sits, which is frequently bare-headed in the sun, until the money or security be given; so general is this mode of recovery that I suppose the Marātha Chiefs may be said to be nearly one-half of their time in a state of Dharna.

[1] In order to obtain redress by Dharna the creditor or injured person would sit starving himself outside his debtor's door, and if he died the latter would be held to have committed a mortal sin and would be haunted by his ghost; see also article on Bhāt. The account here given must be exaggerated.

"In the various Marātha services there are very little more than a bare majority who are Marāthas by caste, and very few instances occur of their ever entering into the infantry at all. The sepoys in the pay of the different princes are recruited in Hindustān, and principally of the Rājpūt and Pūrbia caste; these are perhaps the finest race of men in the world for figure and appearance; of lofty stature, strong, graceful and athletic; of acute feelings, high military pride, quick, apprehensive, brave, prudent and economic; at the same time it must be confessed they are impatient of discipline, and naturally inclined to mutiny. They are mere soldiers of fortune and serve only for their pay. There are also a great number of Musalmāns who serve in the different Marātha armies, some of whom have very great commands.

"The Marātha cavalry at times make very long and rapid marches, in which they do not suffer themselves to be interrupted by the monsoon or any violence of weather. In very pressing exigencies it is incredible the fatigue a Marātha horseman will endure; frequently many days pass without his enjoying one regular meal, but he depends entirely for subsistence on the different corn-fields through which the army passes: a few heads of juāri, which he chafes in his hands while on horseback, will serve him for the day; his horse subsists on the same fare, and with the addition of opium, which the Marāthas frequently administer to their cattle, is enabled to perform incredible marches."

The above analysis of the Marātha troops indicates that their real character was that of freebooting cavalry, largely of the same type as, though no doubt greatly superior in tone and discipline to the Pindāris. Like them they lived by plundering the country. "The Marāthas," Elphinstone remarked, "are excellent foragers. Every morning at daybreak long lines of men on small horses and ponies are seen issuing from their camps in all directions, who return before night loaded with fodder for the cattle, with firewood torn down from houses, and grain dug up from the pits where it had been concealed by the villagers; while other detachments go to a distance for some days and collect proportionately larger supplies of the same kind."[1] They could thus dispense with a commissariat, and being nearly all mounted were able to make extraordinarily long marches, and consequently to carry out effectively surprise attacks and when repulsed to escape injury in the retreat. Even at Pānīpat where their largest regular force took the field under Sadāsheo Rao Bhao, he had 70,000 regular and irregular cavalry and only 15,000 infantry, of whom 9000 were hired sepoys under a Muhammadan leader. The Marāthas were at their best in attacking the slow-moving and effeminate Mughal armies, while during their period of national ascendancy under the Peshwa there was no strong military power in India which could oppose their forays. When they were by the skill of their opponents at length brought to a set battle, their fighting qualities usually proved to be distinctly poor. At Pānīpat they lost the day by a sudden panic and flight after Ibrahīm Khān Gārdi had obtained for them a decided advantage; while at Argaon and Assaye their performances were contemptible. After the recovery from Pānīpat and the rise of the independent Marātha states, the assistance of European officers was invoked to discipline and train the soldiery.[2]

[1] Elphinstone's *History*, 7th ed. p. 748.   [2] *Ibidem*, p. 753.

MEHTAR

[*Bibliography*: Mr. R. Greeven's *Knights of the Broom*, *Benāres*, 1894 (pamphlet); Mr. Crooke's *Tribes and Castes*, art. Bhangi; Sir H. Risley's *Tribes and Castes*, art. Hari; Sir E. Maclagan's *Punjab Census Report*, 1891 (Sweeper Sects); Sir D. Ibbetson's *Punjab Census Report*, 1881 (art. Chuhra); *Bombay Gazetteer*, *Hindus of Gujarāt*, Mr. Bhimbhai Kirparam.]

LIST OF PARAGRAPHS

1. *Introductory notice.*
2. *Caste subdivisions.*
3. *Social organisation.*
4. *Caste punishments.*
5. *Admission of outsiders.*
6. *Marriage customs.*
7. *Disposal of the dead.*
8. *Devices for procuring children.*
9. *Divination of sex.*
10. *Childbirth.*
11. *Treatment of the mother.*
12. *Protecting the lives of children.*
13. *Infantile diseases.*
14. *Religion. Vālmīki.*
15. *Lālbeg.*
16. *Adoption of foreign religions.*
17. *Social status.*
18. *Occupation.*
19. *Occupation (continued).*

Mehtar, Bhangi, Hāri,[1] **Dom, Lālbegi.**—The caste of sweepers and scavengers. In 1911 persons returning themselves as Mehtar, Bhangi and Dom were separately classified, and the total of all three was only 30,000. In this Province they generally confine themselves to their hereditary occupation of scavenging, and are rarely met with outside the towns and large villages. In most localities the supply of sweepers does not meet the demand. The case is quite different in northern India, where the sweeper castes—the Chuhra in the Punjab, the Bhangi in the United Provinces and the Dom in Bengal—are all of them of great numerical strength. With these castes only a small proportion are employed on scavengers' work and the rest are labourers

1. Introductory notice.

---

[1] Some information has been obtained from a paper by Mr. Harbans Rai, Clerk of Court, Damoh.

like the Chamārs and Mahārs of the Central Provinces. The present sweeper caste is made up of diverse elements, and the name Mehtar, generally applied to it, is a title meaning a prince or leader. Its application to the caste, the most abject and despised in the Hindu community, is perhaps partly ironical ; but all the low castes have honorific titles, which are used as a method of address either from ordinary politeness or by those requiring some service, on the principle, as the Hindus say, that you may call an ass your uncle if you want him to do something for you. The regular caste of sweepers in northern India are the Bhangis, whose name is derived by Mr. Crooke from the Sanskrit *bhanga*, hemp, in allusion to the drunken habits of the caste. In support of this derivation he advances the Beria custom of calling their leaders Bhangi or hemp-drinker as a title of honour.[1] In Mr. Greeven's account also, Lālbeg, the patron saint of the sweepers, is described as intoxicated with the hemp drug on two occasions.[2] Mr. Bhīmbhai Kirpārām suggests[3] that Bhangia means broken, and is applied to the sweepers because they split bamboos. In Kaira, he states, the regular trade of the Bhangias is the plaiting of baskets and other articles of split bamboo, and in that part of Gujarāt if a Koli is asked to split a bamboo he will say, 'Am I to do Bhangia's work ?' The derivation from the hemp-plant is, however, the more probable. In the Punjab, sweepers are known as Chuhra, and this name has been derived from their business of collecting and sweeping up scraps (*chūra-jhārna*). Similarly, in Bombay they are known as Olganas or scrap-eaters. The Bengal name Hāri is supposed to come from *haddi*, a bone ; the Hāri is the bone-gatherer, and was familiar to early settlers of Calcutta under the quaint designation of the 'harry-wench.'[4] In the Central Provinces sections of the Ghasia, Mahār and Dom castes will do sweepers' work, and are therefore amalgamated with the Mehtars. The caste is thus of mixed constitution, and also forms a refuge for persons expelled from their own societies for social offences. But though called by different names,

---

[1] Rājendrā Lāl Mitra, quoted in art. on Beria.
[2] Greeven, *op. cit.* pp. 29, 33.
[3] *Op. cit.* p. 334.
[4] Greeven, p. 66, quoting from *Echoes of Old Calcutta*.

the sweeper community in most provinces appears to have the same stock of traditions and legends. The name of Mehtar is now generally employed, and has therefore been taken as the designation of the caste.

Mr. Greeven gives seven main subdivisions, of which the Lālbegis or the followers of Lālbeg, the patron saint of sweepers, are the most important. The Rāwats appear to be an aristocratic subdivision of the Lālbegis, their name being a corruption of the Sanskrit Rājpūtra, a prince. The Shaikh Mehtars are the only real Muhammadan branch, for though the Lālbegis worship a Musalmān saint they remain Hindus. The Hāris or bone-gatherers, as already stated, are the sweepers of Bengal. The Helas may either be those who carry baskets of sweepings, or may derive their name from *hela*, a cry; and in that case they are so called as performing the office of town-criers, a function which the Bhangi usually still discharges in northern India.[1] The other subcastes in his list are the Dhānuks or bowmen and the Bānsphors or cleavers of bamboos. In the Central Provinces the Shaikh Mehtars belong principally to Nāgpur, and another subcaste, the Makhia, is also found in the Marāthā Districts and in Berār; those branches of the Ghasia and Dom castes who consent to do scavengers' work now form separate subcastes of Mehtars in the same locality, and another group are called Narnolia, being said to take their name from a place called Narnol in the Punjab. The Lālbegis are often considered here as Muhammadans rather than Hindus, and bury their dead. In Saugor the sweepers are said to be divided into Lālbegis or Muhammadans and Doms or Hindus. The Lālbegi, Dom or Dumar and the Hela are the principal subcastes of the north of the Province, and Chuhra Mehtars are found in Chhattīsgarh. Each subcaste is divided into a number of exogamous sections named after plants and animals.

2. Caste subdivisions.

In Benāres each subdivision, Mr. Greeven states, has an elaborate and quasi-military organisation. Thus the Lālbegi sweepers have eight companies or *berhas*, consisting of the sweepers working in different localities; these are the Sadar, or those employed by private residents in canton-

3. Social organisation.

[1] Crooke, *op. cit.*

ments; the Kāli Paltan, who serve the Bengal Infantry; the Lāl Kurti, or Red-coats, who are employed by the British Infantry; the Teshan (station), or those engaged at the three railway stations of the town; the Shahar, or those of the city; the Rāmnagar, taking their name from the residence of the Mahārāja of Benāres, whom they serve; the Kothīwāl, or Bungalow men, who belong to residents in the civil lines; and lastly the Genereli, who are the descendants of sweepers employed at the military headquarters when Benāres was commanded by a General of Division. This special organisation is obviously copied from that of the garrison and is not found in other localities, but deserves mention for its own interest. All the eight companies are commanded by a Brigadier, the local head of the caste, whose office is now almost hereditary; his principal duty is to give two dinners to the whole caste on election, with sweetmeats to the value of fourteen rupees. Each company has four officers—a Jamādār or president, a Munsif or spokesman, a Chaudhari or treasurer and a Nāib or summoner. These offices are also practically hereditary, if the candidate entitled by birth can afford to give a dinner to the whole subcaste and a turban to each President of a company. All the other members of the company are designated as Sipāhis or soldiers. A caste dispute is first considered by the inferior officers of each company, who report their view to the President; he confers with the other Presidents, and when an agreement has been reached the sentence is formally confirmed by the Brigadier. When any dispute arises, the aggrieved party, depositing a process-fee of a rupee and a quarter, addresses the officers of his company. Unless the question is so trivial that it can be settled without caste punishments, the President fixes a time and place, of which notice is given to the messengers of the other companies; each of these receives a fee of one and a quarter annas and informs all the Sipāhis in his company.

4. Caste punishments.

Only worthy members of the caste, Mr. Greeven continues, are allowed to sit on the tribal matting and smoke the tribal pipe (huqqa). The proceedings begin with the outspreading (usually symbolic) of a carpet and the smoking of a water-pipe handed in turn to each clansman. For this purpose the members sit on the carpet in three lines, the officers in front and the private soldiers behind. The parties and their witnesses are heard and examined, and a decision is pronounced. The punishments imposed consist of fines, compulsory dinners and expulsion from the caste; expulsion being inflicted for failure to comply with an order of fine or entertainment. The formal method of outcasting consists in seating the culprit on the ground and drawing the tribal mat over his head, from which the turban is removed; after this the messengers of the eight companies inflict a few taps with slippers and birch brooms. It is alleged that unfaithful women were formerly tied naked to trees and flogged with birch brooms, but that owing to the fatal results that occasionally followed such punishment, as in the case of the five kicks among Chamārs (tanners) and the scourging with the clothes line which used to prevail among Dhobis (washermen), the caste has now found it expedient to abandon these practices. When an outcaste is readmitted on submission, whether by paying a fine or giving a dinner, he is seated apart from the tribal mat and does penance by holding his ears with his hands and confessing his offence. A new huqqa, which he supplies, is carried round by the messenger, and a few whiffs are taken by all the officers and Sipāhis in turn. The messenger repeats to the culprit the council's order, and informs him that should he again offend his punishment will be doubled. With this warning he hands him the water-pipe, and after smoking this the offender is admitted to the carpet and all is forgotten in a banquet at his expense.

The sweepers will freely admit outsiders into their community, and the caste forms a refuge for persons expelled from their own societies for sexual or moral offences. Various methods are employed for the initiation of a neophyte; in some places he, or more frequently she, is beaten with a broom made of wood taken from a bier, and has to give a feast to the caste; in others a slight wound is made in his body and the blood of another sweeper is allowed to flow on to it so that they mix; and a glass of sherbet and sugar, known as the cup of nectar, is prepared

5. Admission of outsiders.

by the priest and all the members of the committee put their fingers into it, after which it is given to the candidate to drink; or he has to drink water mixed with cowdung into which the caste-people have dipped their little fingers, and a lock of his hair is cut off. Or he fasts all day at the shrine of Lālbeg and in the evening drinks sherbet after burning incense at the shrine; and gives three feasts, the first on the bank of a tank, the second in his courtyard and the third in his house, representing his gradual purification for membership; at this last he puts a little water into every man's cup and receives from him a piece of bread, and so becomes a fully qualified caste-man. Owing to this reinforcement from higher castes, and perhaps also to their flesh diet, the sweepers are not infrequently taller and stronger as well as lighter in colour than the average Hindu.

6. Marriage customs.

The marriage ceremony in the Central Provinces follows the ordinary Hindu ritual. The *lagan* or paper fixing the date of the wedding is written by a Brāhman, who seats himself at some distance from the sweeper's house and composes the letter. This paper must not be seen by the bride or bridegroom, nor may its contents be read to them, as it is believed that to do so would cause them to fall ill during the ceremony. Before the bridegroom starts for the wedding his mother waves a wooden pestle five times over his head, passing it between his legs and shoulders. After this the bridegroom breaks two lamp-saucers with his right foot, steps over the rice-pounder and departs for the bride's house without looking behind him. The *sawāsas* or relatives of the parties usually officiate at the ceremony, but the well-to-do sometimes engage a Brāhman, who sits at a distance from the house and calls out his instructions. When a man wishes to marry a widow he must pay six rupees to the caste committee and give a feast to the community. Divorce is permitted for incompatibility of temper, or immorality on the part of the wife, or if the husband suffers from leprosy or impotence. Among the Lālbegis, when a man wishes to get rid of his wife he assembles the brethren and in their presence says to her, 'You are as my sister,' and she answers, 'You are as my father and brother.'[1]

[1] Crooke, *op. cit.* para. 52.

The dead are usually buried, but the well-to-do some- 7. Disposal
times cremate them. In Benāres the face or hand of the of the dead.
corpse is scorched with fire to symbolise cremation and it
is then buried. In the Punjab the ghosts of sweepers are
considered to be malevolent and are much dreaded; and
their bodies are therefore always buried or burnt face
downwards to prevent the spirit escaping; and riots have
taken place and the magistrates have been appealed to to
prevent a Chuhra from being buried face upwards.[1] In
Benāres as the body is lowered into the grave the sheet is
withdrawn for a moment from the features of the departed
to afford him one last glimpse of the heavens, while with
Muhammadans the face is turned towards Mecca. Each
clansman flings a handful of dust over the corpse, and after
the earth is filled in crumbles a little bread and sugar-cake
and sprinkles water upon the grave. A provision of bread,
sweetmeats and water is also left upon it for the soul of the
departed.[2] In the Central Provinces the body of a man is
covered with a white winding-sheet and that of a woman
with a red one. If the death occurs during the lunar
conjunction known as Panchak, four human images of flour
are made and buried with the dead man, as they think
that if this is not done four more deaths will occur in the
family.

If a woman greatly desires a child she will go to a 8. Devices
shrine and lay a stone on it which she calls the *dharna* or for procuring
deposit or pledge. Then she thinks that she has put the children.
god under an obligation to give her a child. She vows that
if she becomes pregnant within a certain period, six or nine
months, she will make an offering of a certain value. If
the pregnancy comes she goes to the temple, makes the
offering and removes the stone. If the desired result does
not happen, however, she considers that the god has broken
his obligation and ceases to worship him. If a barren
woman desires a child she should steal on a Sunday or a
Wednesday a strip from the body-cloth of a fertile woman
when it is hung out to dry; or she may steal a piece of rope
from the bed in which a woman has been delivered of a
child, or a piece of the baby's soiled swaddling clothes or a

---

[1] Ibbetson, *op. cit.* para. 227.   [2] Greeven, *op. cit.* p. 21.

piece of cloth stained with the blood of a fertile woman. This last she will take and bury in a cemetery and the others wear round her waist; then she will become fertile and the fertile woman will become barren. Another device is to obtain from the midwife a piece of the navel-string of a newborn child and swallow it. For this reason the navel-string is always carefully guarded and its disposal seen to.

9. Divination of sex.

If a pregnant woman is thin and ailing they think a boy will be born; but if fat and well that it will be a girl. In order to divine the sex of a coming child they pour a little oil on the stomach of the woman; if the oil flows straight down it is thought that a boy will be born and if crooked a girl. Similarly if the hair on the front of her body grows straight they think the child will be a boy, but if crooked a girl; and if the swelling of pregnancy is more apparent on the right side a boy is portended, but if on the left side a girl. If delivery is retarded they go to a gunmaker and obtain from him a gun which has been discharged and the soiling of the barrel left uncleaned; some water is put into the barrel and shaken up and then poured into a vessel and given to the woman to drink, and it is thought that the quality of swift movement appertaining to the bullet which soiled the barrel will be communicated to the woman and cause the swift expulsion of the child from her womb.

10. Childbirth.

When a woman is in labour she squats down with her legs apart holding to the bed in front of her, while the midwife rubs her back. If delivery is retarded the midwife gets a broom and sitting behind the woman presses it on her stomach, at the same time drawing back the upper part of her body. By this means they think the child will be forced from the womb. Or the mother of the woman in labour will take a grinding-stone and stand holding it on her head so long as the child is not born. She says to her daughter, 'Take my name,' and the daughter repeats her mother's name aloud. Here the idea is apparently that the mother takes on herself some of the pain which has to be endured by the daughter, and the repetition of her name by the daughter will cause the goddess of childbirth to hasten the period of delivery in order to terminate the unjust sufferings of the mother for which the goddess has become responsible. The mother's name exerts pressure or influence on the goddess who is at the time occupied with the daughter or perhaps sojourning in her body.

11. Treatment of the mother.

If a child is born in the morning they will give the mother a little sugar and cocoanut to eat in the evening, but if it is born in the evening they will give her nothing till next morning. Milk is given only sparingly as it is supposed to produce coughing. The main idea of treatment in childbirth is to prevent either the mother or child from taking cold or chill, this being the principal danger to which they are thought to be exposed. The door of the birth chamber is therefore kept shut and a fire is continually burning in it night and day. The woman is not bathed for several days, and the atmosphere and general insanitary conditions can better be imagined than described. With the same end of preventing cold they feed the mother on a hot liquid produced by cooking thirty-six ingredients together. Most of these are considered to have the quality of producing heat or warmth in the body, and the following are a few of them: Pepper, ginger, *azgan* (a condiment), turmeric, nutmeg, *ajwāin* (aniseed), dates, almonds, raisins, cocoanut, wild *singāra* or water-nut, cumin, *chironji*,[1] the gum of the *babūl*[2] or *khair*,[3] asafoetida, borax, saffron, clarified butter and sugar. The mixture cannot be prepared for less than two rupees and the woman is fed on it for five days beginning from the second day after birth, if the family can afford the expense.

12. Protecting the lives of children.

If the mother's milk runs dry, they use the dried bodies of the little fish caught in the shallow water of fields and tanks, and sometimes supposed to have fallen down with the rain. They are boiled in a little water and the fish and water are given to the woman to consume. Here the idea is apparently that as the fish has the quality of liquidness because it lives in water, so by eating it this will be communicated to the breasts and the milk will flow again. If a woman's children die, then the next time she is in labour they bring a goat all of one colour. When the birth of the child takes place and it falls from the womb on to the

---

[1] The fruit of the *achār* (*Buchanania latifolia*).
[2] *Acacia arabica*.   [3] *Acacia catechu*.

ground no one must touch it, but the goat, which should if possible be of the same sex as the child, is taken and passed over the child twenty-one times. Then they take the goat and the after-birth to a cemetery and here cut the goat's throat by the *halāl* rite and bury it with the after-birth. The idea is thus that the goat's life is a substitute for that of the child. By being passed over the child it takes the child's evil destiny upon itself, and the burial in a cemetery causes the goat to resemble a human being, while the after-birth communicates to it some part of the life of the child. If a mother is afraid her child will die, she sells it for a few cowries to another woman. Of course the sale is only nominal, but the woman who has purchased the child takes a special interest in it, and at the naming or other ceremony she will give it a jewel or such other present as she can afford. Thus she considers that the fictitious sale has had some effect and that she has acquired a certain interest in the child.

13. Infantile diseases.

If a baby, especially a girl, has much hair on its body, they make a cake of gram-flour and rub it with sesamum oil all over the body, and this is supposed to remove the hair.

If a child's skin dries up and it pines away, they think that an owl has taken away a cloth stained by the child when it was hung out to dry. The remedy is to obtain the liver of an owl and hang it round the child's neck.

For jaundice they get the flesh of a yellow snake which appears in the rains, and of the *rohu* fish which has yellowish scales, and hang them to its neck; or they get a verse of the Korān written out by a Maulvi or Muhammadan priest and use this as an amulet; or they catch a small frog alive, tie it up in a yellow cloth and hang it to the child's neck by a blue thread until it dies. For tetanus the jaws are branded outside and a little musk is placed on the mother's breast so that the child may drink it with the milk. When the child begins to cut its teeth they put honey on the gums and think that this will make the teeth slip out early as the honey is smooth and slippery. But as the child licks the gums when the honey is on them they fear that this may cause the teeth to grow broad and crooked like the tongue. Another device is to pass a piece of gold round the child's gums. If they want the child to have pretty teeth its maternal uncle threads a number of grains of rice on a piece of string and hangs them round its neck, so that the teeth may grow like the rice. If the child's navel is swollen, the maternal uncle will go out for a walk and on his return place his turban over the navel. For averting the evil eye the liver of the Indian badger is worn in an amulet, this badger being supposed to haunt cemeteries and feed on corpses; some hairs of a bear also form a very favourite amulet, or a tiger's claws set in silver, or the tail of a lizard enclosed in lac and made into a ring.

14. Religion. Vālmīki.

The religion of the sweepers has been described at length by Mr. Greeven and Mr. Crooke. It centres round the worship of two saints, Lālbeg or Bale Shāh and Bālnek or Bālmīk, who is really the huntsman Vālmīki, the reputed author of the Rāmāyana. Bālmīk was originally a low-caste hunter called Ratnakār, and when he could not get game he was accustomed to rob and kill travellers. But one day he met Brahma and wished to kill him; but he could not raise his club against Brahma, and the god spoke and convinced him of his sins, directing him to repeat the name of Rāma until he should be purified of them. But the hunter's heart was so evil that he could not pronounce the divine name, and instead he repeated '*Māra, Māra*' (*struck, struck*), but in the end by repetition this came to the same thing. Mr. Greeven's account continues: "As a small spark of fire burneth up a heap of cotton, so the word Rāma cleaneth a man of all his sins. So the words 'Rām, Rām,' were taught unto Ratnakār who ever repeated them for sixty thousand years at the self-same spot with a heart sincere. All his skin was eaten up by the white ants. Only the skeleton remained. Mud had been heaped over the body and grass had grown up, yet within the mound of mud the saint was still repeating the name of Rāma. After sixty thousand years Brahma returned. No man could he see, yet he heard the voice of Rām, Rām, rising from the mound of mud. Then Brahma bethought him that the saint was beneath. He besought Indra to pour down rain and to wash away the mud. Indra complied with his request and the rain washed away the mud. The saint came forth. Nought save bones remained. Brahma called aloud to the saint. When the saint beheld him he prostrated himself and spake: 'Thou hast taught me the words "Rām, Rām," which have cleansed away all my sins.' Then spake Brahma: 'Hitherto thou wast Ratnakār. From to-day thy name shall be Vālmīki (from *valmīk*, an ant-hill). Now do thou compose a Rāmāyana in seven parts, containing the deeds and exploits of Rāma.'" Vālmīki had been or afterwards became a sweeper and was known as 'cooker of dog's food' (Swapach), a name applied to sweepers,[1] who have adopted him as their eponymous ancestor and patron saint.

15. Lālbeg. Lālbeg, who is still more widely venerated, is considered to have been Ghāzi Miyān, the nephew of Sultān Muhammad of Ghazni, and a saint much worshipped in the Punjab. Many legends are told of Lālbeg, and his worship is described by Mr. Greeven as follows:[2] "The ritual of Lālbeg is conducted in the presence of the whole brotherhood, as a rule at the festival of the Diwāli and on other occasions when special business arises. The time for worship is after sunset and if possible at midnight. His shrine consists of a mud platform surrounded by steps, with four little turrets at the corners and a spire in the centre, in which is placed a lamp filled with clarified butter and containing a wick of twisted tow. Incense is thrown into the flame and offerings of cakes and sweetmeats are made. A lighted huqqa is placed before the altar and as soon as the smoke rises it is understood that a whiff has been drawn by the hero." A cock is offered to Lālbeg at the Dasahra festival. When a man is believed to have been affected by the evil eye they wave a broom in front of the sufferer muttering the name of the saint. In the Damoh District the *guru* or priest who is the successor of Lālbeg comes from the Punjab every year or two. He is richly clad and is followed by a sweeper carrying an umbrella. Other Hindus say that his teaching is that no one who is not a Lālbegi can go to heaven, but those on whom the dust raised by a Lālbegi sweeping settles acquire some modicum of virtue. Similarly Mr. Greeven

---

[1] Some writers consider that Bālmīk, the sweeper-saint, and Vālmīki, the author of the Rāmāyana, are not identical.
[2] Page 38.

remarks:[1] "Sweepers by no means endorse the humble opinion entertained with respect to them; for they allude to castes such as Kunbis and Chamārs as petty (*chhota*), while a common anecdote is related to the effect that a Lālbegi, when asked whether Muhammadans could obtain salvation, replied: 'I never heard of it, but perhaps they might slip in behind Lālbeg.'"

On the whole the religion of the Lālbegis appears to be monotheistic and of a sufficiently elevated character, resembling that of the Kabīrpanthis and other reforming sects. Its claim to the exclusive possession of the way of salvation is a method of revolt against the menial and debased position of the caste. Similarly many sweepers have become Muhammadans and Sikhs with the same end in view, as stated by Mr. Greeven:[2] "As may be readily imagined, the scavengers are merely in name the disciples of Nānak Shāh, professing in fact to be his followers just as they are prepared at a moment's notice to become Christians or Muhammadans. Their object is, of course, merely to acquire a status which may elevate them above the utter degradation of their caste. The acquaintance of most of them with the doctrines of Nānak Shāh is at zero. They know little and care less about his rules of life, habitually disregarding, for instance, the prohibitions against smoking and hair-cutting. In fact, a scavenger at Benāres no more becomes a Sikh by taking Nānak Shāh's motto than he becomes a Christian by wearing a round hat and a pair of trousers." It was probably with a similar leaning towards the more liberal religion that the Lālbegis, though themselves Hindus, adopted a Muhammadan for their tutelary saint. In the Punjab Muhammadan sweepers who have given up eating carrion and refuse to remove night-soil rank higher than the others, and are known as Musalli.[3] And in Saugor the Muhammadans allow the sweepers to come into a mosque and to stand at the back, whereas, of course, they cannot approach a Hindu temple. Again in Bengal it is stated, "The Dom is regarded with both disgust and fear by all classes of Hindus, not only on

16. Adoption of foreign religions.

---

[1] Page 8.   [2] Page 54.
[3] *Punjab Census Report* (1881), para. 599.

account of his habits being abhorrent and abominable, but also because he is believed to have no humane or kindly feelings"; and further, "It is universally believed that Doms do not bury or burn their dead, but dismember the corpse at night like the inhabitants of Thibet, placing the fragments in a pot and sinking them in the nearest river or reservoir. This horrid idea probably originated from the old Hindu law, which compelled the Doms to bury their dead at night."[1] It is not astonishing that the sweepers prefer a religion whose followers will treat them somewhat more kindly. Another Muhammadan saint revered by the sweepers of Saugor is one Zāhir Pīr. At the fasts in Chait and Kunwār (March and September) they tie cocoanuts wrapped in cloth to the top of a long bamboo, and marching to the tomb of Zāhir Pīr make offerings of cakes and sweetmeats. Before starting for his day's work the sweeper does obeisance to his basket and broom.

17. Social status.
The sweeper stands at the very bottom of the social ladder of Hinduism. He is considered to be the representative of the Chandāla of Manu,[2] who was said to be descended of a Sūdra father and a Brāhman woman. "It was ordained that the Chandāla should live without the town; his sole wealth should be dogs and asses; his clothes should consist of the cerecloths of the dead; his dishes should be broken pots and his ornaments rusty iron. No one who regarded his duties should hold intercourse with the Chandālas and they should marry only among themselves. By day they might roam about for the purposes of work, but should be distinguished by the badges of the Rāja, and should carry out the corpse of any one who died without kindred. They should always be employed to slay those who by the law were sentenced to be put to death, and they might take the clothes of the slain, their beds and their ornaments." Elsewhere the Chandāla is said to rank in impurity with the town boar, the dog, a woman during her monthly illness and a eunuch, none of whom must a Brāhman allow to see him when eating.[3] Like the Chandāla, the sweeper cannot be touched, and he

---

[1] Sir H. Risley, *l.c.*, art. Dom.
[2] *Institutes*, x. 12-29-30.
[3] *Ibidem*, iv. 239, quoted by Mr. Crooke, art. Dom.

himself acquiesces in this and walks apart. In large towns he sometimes carries a kite's wing in his turban to show his caste, or goes aloof saying *pois*, which is equivalent to a warning. When the sweeper is in company he will efface himself as far as possible behind other people. He is known by his basket and broom, and men of other castes will not carry these articles lest they should be mistaken for a sweeper. The sweeper's broom is made of bamboo, whereas the ordinary house-broom is made of date-palm leaves. The house-broom is considered sacred as the implement of Lakshhmi used in cleaning the house. No one should tread upon or touch it with his foot. The sweeper's broom is a powerful agent for curing the evil eye, and mothers get him to come and wave it up and down in front of a sick child for this purpose. Nevertheless it is lucky to see a sweeper in the morning, especially if he has his basket with him. In Gujarāt Mr. Bhīmbhai Kirpārām writes of him: "Though he is held to be lower and more unclean, the Bhangia is viewed with kindlier feelings than the Dhed (Mahār). To meet the basket-bearing Bhangia is lucky, and the Bhangia's blessing is valued. Even now if a Government officer goes into a Bhangia hamlet the men with hands raised in blessing say : 'May your rule last for ever.'" A sweeper will eat the leavings of other people, but he will not eat in their houses ; he will take the food away to his own house. It is related that on one occasion a sweeper accompanied a marriage party of Lodhis (cultivators), and the Lodhi who was the host was anxious that all should share his hospitality and asked the sweeper to eat in his house ;[1] but he repeatedly refused, until finally the Lodhi gave him a she-buffalo to induce him to eat, so that it might not be said that any one had declined to share in his feast. No other caste, of course, will accept food or water from a sweeper, and only a Chamār (tanner) will take a *chilam* or clay pipe-bowl from his hand. The sweeper will eat carrion and the flesh of almost all animals, including snakes, lizards, crocodiles and tigers, and also the leavings of food of almost any caste. Mr. Greeven remarks :[2] "Only

---

[1] Probably not within the house but in the veranda or courtyard.
[2] *Ibidem.*

Lālbegis and Rāwats eat food left by Europeans, but all eat food left either by Hindus or Muhammadans; the Sheikh Mehtars as Muhammadans alone are circumcised and reject pig's flesh. Each subcaste eats uncooked food with all the others, but cooked food alone." From Betūl it is reported that the Mehtars there will not accept food, water or tobacco from a Kāyasth, and will not allow one to enter their houses.

18. Occupation.
Sweeping and scavenging in the streets and in private houses are the traditional occupations of the caste, but they have others. In Bombay they serve as night watchmen, town-criers, drummers, trumpeters and hangmen. Formerly the office of hangman was confined to sweepers, but now many low-caste prisoners are willing to undertake it for the sake of the privilege of smoking tobacco in jail which it confers. In Mīrzāpur when a Dom hangman is tying a rope round the neck of a criminal he shouts out, '*Dohai Mahārāni, Dohai Sarkār, Dohai Judge Sāhib*,' or 'Hail Great Queen! Hail Government! Hail Judge Sahib!' in order to shelter himself under their authority and escape any guilt attaching to the death.[1] In the Central Provinces the hangman was accompanied by four or five other sweepers of the caste *panchāyat*, the idea being perhaps that his act should be condoned by their presence and approval and he should escape guilt. In order to free the executioner from blame the prisoner would also say: "*Dohai Sarkar ke, Dohai Kampani ke; jaisa maine khūn kiya waisa apne khūn ko pahunchha*," or "Hail to the Government and the Company; since I caused the death of another, now I am come to my own death"; and all the *Panches* said, '*Rām, Rām*.' The hangman received ten rupees as his fee, and of this five rupees were given to the caste for a feast and an offering to Lālbeg to expiate his sin. In Bundelkhand sweepers are employed as grooms by the Lodhis, and may put everything on to the horse except a saddle-cloth. They are also the village musicians, and some of them play on the rustic flute called *shahnai* at weddings, and receive their food all the time that the ceremony lasts. Sweepers are, as a rule, to be found only in large villages, as in small ones

---

[1] Crooke, *Tribes and Castes*, art. Dom, para. 34.

there is no work for them. The caste is none too numerous in the Central Provinces, and in villages the sweeper is often not available when wanted for cleaning the streets. The Chamārs of Bundelkhand will not remove the corpses of a cat or a dog or a squirrel, and a sweeper must be obtained for the purpose. These three animals are in a manner holy, and it is considered a sin to kill any one of them. But their corpses are unclean. A Chamār also refuses to touch the corpse of a donkey, but a Kumhār (potter) will sometimes do this; if he declines a sweeper must be fetched. When a sweeper has to enter a house in order to take out the body of an animal, it is cleaned and whitewashed after he has been in. In Hoshangābād an objection appears to be felt to the entry of a sweeper by the door, as it is stated that a ladder is placed for him, so that he presumably climbs through a window. Or where there are no windows it is possible that the ladder may protect the sacred threshold from contact with his feet. The sweeper also attends at funerals and assists to prepare the pyre; he receives the winding-sheet when this is not burnt or buried with the corpse, and the copper coins which are left on the ground as purchase-money for the site of the grave. In Bombay in rich families the winding-sheet is often a worked shawl costing from fifty to a hundred rupees.[1] When a Hindu widow breaks her bangles after her husband's death, she gives them, including one or two whole ones, to a Bhangia woman.[2] A letter announcing a death is always carried by a sweeper.[3] In Bengal a funeral could not be held without the presence of a Dom, whose functions are described by Mr. Sherring[4] as follows: "On the arrival of the dead body at the place of cremation, which in Benāres is at the basis of one of the steep stairs or *ghāts*, called the Burning-Ghāt, leading down from the streets above to the bed of the river Ganges, the Dom supplies five logs of wood, which he lays in order upon the ground, the rest of the wood being given by the family of the deceased. When the pile is ready for burning a handful of lighted straw is brought by

---

[1] *Bombay Gazetteer, l.c.*
[2] *Ibidem.*
[3] *Punjab Census Report* (1881), and *Bombay Gazetteer, l.c.*
[4] *Hindu Tribes and Castes*, quoted by Sir H. Risley, art. Dom.

the Dom, and is taken from him and applied by one of the chief members of the family to the wood. The Dom is the only person who can furnish the light for the purpose; and if for any reason no Dom is available, great delay and inconvenience are apt to arise. The Dom exacts his fee for three things, namely, first for the five logs, secondly for the bunch of straw, and thirdly for the light."

19. Occupation (continued).

During an eclipse the sweepers reap a good harvest; for it is believed that Rāhu, the demon who devours the sun and moon and thus causes an eclipse, was either a sweeper or the deity of the sweepers, and alms given to them at this time will appease him and cause him to let the luminaries go. Or, according to another account, the sun and moon are in Rāhu's debt, and he comes and duns them, and this is the eclipse; and the alms given to sweepers are a means of paying the debt. In Gujarāt as soon as the darkening sets in the Bhangis go about shouting, '*Garhandān, Vastradān, Rupādān*,' or 'Gifts for the eclipse, gifts of clothes, gifts of silver.'[1] The sweepers are no doubt derived from the primitive or Dravidian tribes, and, as has been seen, they also practise the art of making bamboo mats and baskets, being known as Bānsphor in Bombay on this account. In the Punjab the Chuhras are a very numerous caste, being exceeded only by the Jāts, Rājpūts and Brāhmans. Only a small proportion of them naturally find employment as scavengers, and the remainder are agricultural labourers, and together with the vagrants and gipsies are the hereditary workers in grass and reeds.[2] They are closely connected with the Dhānuks, a caste of hunters, fowlers and village watchmen, being of nearly the same status.[3] And Dhānuk, again, is in some localities a complimentary term for a Basor or bamboo-worker. It has been seen that Vālmīki, the patron saint of the sweepers, was a low-caste hunter, and this gives some reason for the supposition that the primary occupations of the Chūhras and Bhangis were hunting and working in grass and bamboo. In one of the legends of the sweeper saint Bālmīk or Vālmīki given by Mr. Greeven,[4] Bālmīk was the youngest of the five Pāndava brothers, and

[1] *Bombay Gazetteer, l.c.*
[2] Ibbetson, *l.c.* para. 596.
[3] *Ibidem*, para. 601.
[4] *L.c.* pp. 25, 26.

was persuaded by the others to remove the body of a calf which had died in their courtyard. But after he had done so they refused to touch him, so he went into the wilderness with the body; and when he did not know how to feed himself the carcase started into life and gave him milk until he was full grown, when it died again of its own accord. Bālmīk burst into tears, not knowing how he was to live henceforward, but a voice cried from heaven saying, " Of the sinews (of the calf's body) do thou tie winnows (*sūp*), and of the caul do thou plait sieves (*chalni*)." Bālmīk obeyed, and by his handiwork gained the name of Sūpaj or the maker of winnowing-fans. These are natural occupations of the non-Aryan forest tribes, and are now practised by the Gonds.

Meo, Mewāti.—The Muhammadan branch of the Mīna tribe belonging to the country of Mewāt in Rājputāna which is comprised in the Alwar, Bharatpur and Jaipur States and the British District of Gurgaon. A few Meos were returned from the Hoshangābād and Nimār Districts in 1911, but it is doubtful whether any are settled here, as they may be wandering criminals. The origin of the Meo is discussed in the article on the Mīna tribe, but some interesting remarks on them by Mr. Channing and Major Powlett in the *Rājputāna Gazetteer* may be reproduced here. Mr. Channing writes :[1]

" The tribe, which has been known in Hindustān according to the Kutub Tawārīkh for 850 years, was originally Hindu and became Muhammadan. Their origin is obscure. They themselves claim descent from the Rājpūt races of Jādon, Kachhwāha and Tuar, and they may possibly have some Rājpūt blood in their veins ; but they are probably, like many other similar tribes, a combination from ruling and other various stocks and sources, and there is reason to believe them very nearly allied with the Mīnas, who are certainly a tribe of the same structure and species. The Meos have twelve clans or *pāls*, the first six of which are identical in name and claim the same descent as the first six clans of the Mīnas. Intermarriage between them both was

[1] *Rājputāna Gazetteer*, vol. i. p. 165.

the rule until the time of Akbar, when owing to an affray at the marriage of a Meo with a Mīna the custom was discontinued. Finally, their mode of life is or was similar, as both tribes were once notoriously predatory. It is probable that the original Meos were supplemented by converts to Islām from other castes. It is said that the tribe were conquered and converted in the eleventh century by Māsūd, son of Amīr Sālār and grandson of Sultān Mahmūd Subaktagin on the mother's side, the general of the forces of Mahmūd of Ghazni. Māsūd is still venerated by the Meos, and they swear by his name. They have a mixture of Hindu and Muhammadan customs. They practise circumcision, *nikāh*,[1] and the burial of the dead. They make pilgrimages to the tomb of Māsūd in Bahraich in Oudh, and consider the oath taken on his banner the most binding. They also make pilgrimages to Muhammadan shrines in India, but never perform the *Haj*. Of Hindu customs they observe the Holi or Diwāli; their marriages are never arranged in the same *got* or sept; and they permit daughters to inherit. They call their children indiscriminately by both Muhammadan and Hindu names. They are almost entirely uneducated, but have bards and musicians to whom they make large presents. These sing songs known as Rātwai, which are commonly on pastoral and agricultural subjects. The Meos are given to the use of intoxicating drinks, and are very superstitious and have great faith in omens. The dress of the men and women resembles that of the Hindus. Infanticide was formerly common among them, but it is said to have entirely died out. They were also formerly robbers by avocation; and though they have improved they are still noted cattle-lifters."

In another description of them by Major Powlett it is stated that, besides worshipping Hindu gods and keeping Hindu festivals, they employ a Brāhman to write the Pīli Chhitthi or yellow note fixing the date of a marriage. They call themselves by Hindu names with the exception of Rām; and Singh is a frequent affix, though not so common as Khān. On the Amāwas or monthly conjunction of the sun and moon, Meos, in common with Hindu Ahīrs and Gūjars, cease from labour; and when they make a well the first proceeding

---

[1] A Muhammadan form of marriage.

is to erect a *chabūtra* (platform) to Bhaironji or Hanumān. However, when plunder was to be obtained they have often shown little respect for Hindu shrines and temples; and when the sanctity of a threatened place has been urged, the retort has been, ' *Tum to Deo, Ham Meo,*' or ' You may be a Deo (God), but I am a Meo.'

Meos do not marry in their *pāl* or clan, but they are lax about forming connections with women of other castes, whose children they receive into the community. As already stated, Brāhmans take part in the formalities preceding a marriage, but the ceremony itself is performed by a Kāzi. As agriculturists Meos are inferior to their Hindu neighbours. The point in which they chiefly fail is in working their wells, for which they lack patience. Their women, whom they do not confine, will, it is said, do more field-work than the men; indeed, one often finds women at work in the crops when the men are lying down. Like the women of low Hindu castes they tattoo their bodies, a practice disapproved by Musalmāns in general. Abul Fazl writes that the Meos were in his time famous runners, and one thousand of them were employed by Akbar as carriers of the post.

Mīna, Deswāli, Maina.—A well-known caste of Rājputāna which is found in the Central Provinces in the Hoshangābād, Nimār and Saugor Districts. About 8000 persons of the caste were returned in 1911. The proper name for them is Mīna, but here they are generally known as Deswāli, a term which they probably prefer, as that of Mīna is too notorious. A large part of the population of the northern Districts is recruited from Bundelkhand and Mārwār, and these tracts are therefore often known among them as ' Desh ' or native country. The term Deswāli is applied to groups of many castes coming from Bundelkhand, and has apparently been specially appropriated as an *alias* by the Mīnas. The caste are sometimes known in Hoshangābād as Maina, which Colonel Tod states to be the name of the highest division of the Mīnas. The designation of Pardeshi or ' foreigner ' is also given to them in some localities. The Deswālis came to Harda about A.D. 1750, being invited by the Marātha Amīl or governor, who gave one family a grant of three

1. The Mīnas locally termed Deswālis.

villages. They thus gained a position of some dignity, and this reaching the ears of their brothers in Jaipur they also came and settled all over the District.[1] In view of the history and character of the Mīnas, of which some account will be given, it should be first stated that under the *régime* of British law and order most of the Deswālis of Hoshangābād have settled down into steady and honest agriculturists.

2. Historical notice of the Mīna tribe.

The Mīnas were a famous robber tribe of the country of Mewāt in Rājputāna, comprised in the Alwar and Bharatpur States and the British District of Gurgaon.[2] They are also found in large numbers in Jaipur State, which was formerly held by them. The Meos and Mīnas are now considered to be branches of one tribe, the former being at least nominally Muhammadans by religion and the latter Hindus. A favourite story for recitation at their feasts is that of Darya Khān Meo and Sasibādani Mīni, a pair of lovers whose marriage led to a quarrel between the tribes to which they belonged, in the time of Akbar. This dispute caused the cessation of the practice of intermarriage between Meos and Mīnas which had formerly obtained. Both the Meos and Mīnas are divided into twelve large clans called *pāl*, the word *pāl* meaning, according to Colonel Tod, 'a defile in a valley suitable for cultivation or defence.' In a sandy desert like Rājputāna the valleys of streams might be expected to be the only favourable tracts for settlement, and the name perhaps therefore is a record of the process by which the colonies of Mīnas in these isolated patches of culturable land developed into exogamous clans marrying with each other. The Meos have similarly twelve *pāls*, and the names of six of these are identical with those of the Mīnas.[3] The names of the *pāls* are taken from those of Rājpūt clans,[4] but the recorded lists differ, and there are now many other *gots* or *septs* outside the *pāls*. The Mīnas seem originally to have been an aboriginal or pre-Aryan tribe of Rājputāna, where they

---

[1] Elliott's *Hoshangābād Settlement Report*, p. 63.

[2] Cunningham's *Archaeological Survey Reports*, xx. p. 24.

[3] *Ibidem*.

[4] General Cunningham's enumeration of the *pāls* is as follows: Five Jādon clans—Chhirkilta, Dalāt, Dermot, Nai, Pundelot; five Tuar clans—Balot, Darwār, Kalesa, Lundāvat, Rattāwat; one Kachhwāha clan—Dingāl; one Bargjūar clan—Singāl. Besides these there is one miscellaneous or half-blood clan, Palakra, making up the common total of $12\frac{1}{2}$ clans.

are still found in considerable numbers. The Rāja of Jaipur was formerly marked on the forehead with blood taken from the great toe of a Mīna on the occasion of his installation. Colonel Tod records that the Amber or Jaipur State was founded by one Dholesai in A.D. 967 after he had slaughtered large numbers of the Mīnas by treachery. And in his time the Mīnas still possessed large immunities and privileges in the Jaipur State. When the Rājpūts settled in force in Rājputāna, reducing the Mīnas to subjection, illicit connections would naturally arise on a large scale between the invaders and the women of the conquered country. For even when the Rājpūts only came as small isolated parties of adventurers, as into the Central Provinces, we find traces of such connections in the survival of castes or subcastes of mixed descent from them and the indigenous tribes. It follows therefore that where they occupied the country and settled on the soil the process would be still more common. Accordingly it is generally recognised that the Mīnas are a caste of the most mixed and impure descent, and it has sometimes been supposed that they were themselves a branch of the Rājpūts. In the Punjab when one woman accuses another of illicit intercourse she is said 'Mīna dena,' or to designate her as a Mīna.[1] Further it is stated[2] that "The Mīnas are of two classes, the Zamīndāri or agricultural and the Chaukīdāri or watchmen. These Chaukīdāri Mīnas are the famous marauders." The office of village watchman was commonly held by members of the aboriginal tribes, and these too furnished the criminal classes. Another piece of evidence of the Dravidian origin of the tribe is the fact that there exists even now a group of Dhedia or impure Mīnas who do not refuse to eat cow's flesh. The Chaukīdāri Mīnas, dispossessed of their land, resorted to the hills, and here they developed into a community of thieves and bandits recruited from all the outcastes of society. Sir A. Lyall wrote[3] of the caste as "a Cave of Adullam which has stood open for centuries. With them a captured woman is solemnly admitted by a form of adoption

---

[1] Ibbetson's *Punjab Census Report*, para. 582. Sir D. Ibbetson considered it doubtful, however, whether the expression referred to the Mīna caste.
[2] Major Powlett, *Gazetteer of Alwar*.
[3] *Asiatic Studies*, vol. i. p. 162.

into one circle of affinity, in order that she may be lawfully married into another." With the conquest of northern India by the Muhammadans, many of the Mīnas, being bound by no ties to Hinduism, might be expected to embrace the new and actively proselytising religion, while their robber bands would receive fugitive Muhammadans as recruits as well as Hindus. Thus probably arose a Musalmān branch of the community, who afterwards became separately designated as the Meos. As already seen, the Meos and Mīnas intermarried for a time, but subsequently ceased to do so. As might be expected, the form of Islām professed by the Meos is of a very bastard order, and Major Powlett's account of it is reproduced in a short separate notice of that tribe.

3. Their robberies.

The crimes and daring of the Mīnas have obtained for them a considerable place in history. A Muhammadan historian, Zia-ud-dīn Bāmi, wrote of the tribe:[1] "At night they were accustomed to come prowling into the city of Delhi, giving all kinds of trouble and depriving people of their rest, and they plundered the country houses in the neighbourhood of the city. Their daring was carried to such an extent that the western gates of the city were shut at afternoon prayer and no one dared to leave it after that hour, whether he travelled as a pilgrim or with the display of a king. At afternoon prayer they would often come to the Sarhouy, and assaulting the water-carriers and girls who were fetching water they would strip them and carry off their clothes. In turn they were treated by the Muhammadan rulers with the most merciless cruelty. Some were thrown under the feet of elephants, others were cut in halves with knives, and others again were flayed alive from head to foot." Regular campaigns against them were undertaken by the Muhammadans,[2] as in later times British forces had to be despatched to subdue the Pindāris. Bābar on his arrival at Agra described the Mewāti leader Rāja Hasan Khān as 'the chief agitator in all these confusions and insurrections'; and Firishta mentions two terrible slaughters of Mewātis in

---

[1] Quoted in Dowson's *Elliott's History of India*, iii. p. 103.
[2] Dowson's *Elliott*, iv. pp. 60, 75,

283, quoted in Crooke's *Tribes and Castes*.

A.D. 1259 and 1265. In 1857 Major Powlett records that in Alwar they assembled and burnt the State ricks and carried off cattle, though they did not succeed in plundering any towns or villages there. In British territory they sacked Firozpur and other villages, and when a British force came to restore order many were hanged. Sir D. Ibbetson wrote of them in the Punjab:[1]

"The Mīnas are the boldest of our criminal classes. Their headquarters so far as the Punjab is concerned are in the village of Shāhjahānpur, attached to the Gurgaon District but surrounded on all sides by Rājputāna territory. There they until lately defied our police and even resisted them with armed force. Their enterprises are on a large scale, and they are always prepared to use violence if necessary. In Mārwār they are armed with small bows which do considerable execution. They travel great distances in gangs of from twelve to twenty men, practising robbery and dacoity even as far as the Deccan. The gangs usually start off immediately after the Diwāli feast and often remain absent the whole year. They have agents in all the large cities of Rājputāna and the Deccan who give them information, and they are in league with the carrying castes of Mārwār. After a successful foray they offer one-tenth of the proceeds at the shrine of Kāli Devi."

Like other criminals they were very superstitious, and Colonel Tod records that the partridge and the *maloli* or wagtail were their chief birds of omen. A partridge clamouring on the left when he commenced a foray was a certain presage of success to a Mīna. Similarly, Mr. Kennedy notes that the finding of a dried goatskin, either whole or in pieces, among the effects of a suspected criminal is said to be an infallible indication of his identity as a Mīna, the flesh of the goat's tongue being indispensable in connection with the taking of omens. In Jaipur the Mīnas were employed as guards, as a method of protection against their fellows, for whose misdeeds they were held responsible. Rent-free lands were given to them, and they were always employed to escort treasure. Here they became the most faithful and trusted of the Rāja's servants. It is related

[1] *Census Report* (1881), para. 582.

that on one occasion a Mīna sentinel at the palace had received charge of a basket of oranges. A friend of the same tribe came to him and asked to be shown the palace, which he had never seen. The sentinel agreed and took him over the palace, but when his back was turned the friend stole one orange from the basket. Subsequently the sentinel counted the oranges and found one short; on this he ran after his friend and taxed him with the theft, which being admitted, the Mīna said that he had been made to betray his trust and had become dishonoured, and drawing his sword cut off his friend's head. The ancient treasure of Jaipur or Amber was, according to tradition, kept in a secret cave in the hills under a body of Mīna guards who alone knew the hiding-place, and would only permit any part of it to be withdrawn for a great emergency. Nor would they accept the orders of the Rāja alone, but required the consent of the heads of the twelve principal noble families of Amber, branches of the royal house, before they would give up any part of the treasure. The criminal Mīnas are said to inhabit a tract of country about sixty-five miles long and forty broad, stretching from Shāhpur forty miles north of Jaipur to Guraora in Gurgaon on the Rohtak border. The popular idea of the Mīna, Mr. Crooke remarks,[1] is quite in accordance with his historical character; his niggardliness is shown in the saying, 'The Meo will not give his daughter in marriage till he gets a mortar full of silver'; his pugnacity is expressed in, 'The Meo's son begins to avenge his feuds when he is twelve years old'; and his toughness in, 'Never be sure that a Meo is dead till you see the third-day funeral ceremony performed.'

4. The Deswālis of the Central Provinces.

As already stated, the Deswālis of the Central Provinces have abandoned the wild life of their ancestors and settled down as respectable cultivators. Only a few particulars about them need be recorded. Girls are usually married before they are twelve years old and boys at sixteen to twenty. A sum of Rs. 24 is commonly paid for the bride, and a higher amount up to Rs. 71 may be given, but this is the maximum, and if the father of the girl takes more he will be fined by the caste and made to refund the

[1] *Tribes and Castes of the N.W.P.* art. Meo.

balance. A triangle with some wooden models of birds is placed on the marriage-shed and the bridegroom strikes at these with a stick; formerly he fired a gun at them to indicate that he was a hunter by profession. A Brāhman is employed to celebrate the marriage. A widow is usually taken by her late husband's younger brother, but if there be none the elder brother may marry her, contrary to the general rule among Hindus. The object is to keep the woman in the family, as wives are costly. If she is unwilling to marry her brother-in-law, however, no compulsion is exercised and she may wed another man. Divorce is allowed, and in Rājputāna is very simply effected. If tempers do not assimilate or other causes prompt them to part, the husband tears a shred from his turban which he gives to his wife, and with this simple bill of divorce, placing two jars of water on her head, she takes whatever path she pleases, and the first man who chooses to ease her of her load becomes her future lord. '*Jehur nikāla*,' 'Took the jar and went forth,' is a common saying among the mountaineers of Merwara.[1]

The dead are cremated, the corpse of a man being wrapped in a white and that of a woman in a coloured cloth. They have no *shrāddh* ceremony, but mourn for the dead only on the last day of Kārtik (October), when they offer water and burn incense. Deswālis employ the Parsai or village Brāhman to officiate at their ceremonies, but owing to their mixed origin they rank below the cultivating castes, and Brāhmans will not take water from them. In Jaipur, however, Major Powlett says, their position is higher. They are, as already seen, the trusted guards of the palace and treasury, and Rājpūts will accept food and water from their hands. This concession is no doubt due to the familiarity induced by living together for a long period, and parallel instances of it can be given, as that of the Panwārs and Gonds in the Central Provinces. The Deswālis eat flesh and drink liquor, but abstain from fowls and pork. When they are invited to a feast they do not take their own brass vessels with them, but drink out of earthen pots supplied by the host, having the liquor

[1] *Rājasthān*, i. p. 589.

poured on to their hands held to the mouth to avoid actual contact with the vessel. This is a Mārwāri custom and the Jāts also have it. Before the commencement of the feast the guests wait until food has been given to as many beggars as like to attend. In Saugor the food served consists only of rice and pulse without vegetables or other dishes. It is said that a Mīna will not eat salt in the house of another man, because he considers that to do so would establish the bond of *Nimak-khai* or salt-eating between them, and he would be debarred for ever from robbing that man or breaking into his house. The guests need not sit down together as among other Hindus, but may take their food in batches; so that the necessity of awaiting the arrival of every guest before commencing the feast is avoided. The Deswālis will not kill a black-buck nor eat the flesh of one, but they assign no reason for this and do not now worship the animal. The rule is probably, however, a totemistic survival. The men may be known by their manly gait and harsh tone of voice, as well as by a peculiar method of tying the turban; the women have a special ornament called *rākhdi* on the forehead and do not wear spangles or toe-rings. They are said also to despise ornaments of the baser metals as brass and pewter. They are tattooed with dots on the face to set off the fair-coloured skin by contrast, in the same manner as patches were carried on the face in Europe in the eighteenth century. A tattoo dot on a fair face is likened by a Hindu poet to a bee sitting on a half-opened mango.

Mirāsi.—A Muhammadan caste of singers, minstrels and genealogists, of which a few members are found in the Central Provinces. General Cunningham says that they are the bards and singers of the Meos or Mewātis at all their marriages and festivals.[1] Mr. Crooke is of opinion that they are undoubtedly an offshoot of the great Dom caste who are little better than sweepers.[2] The word Mirāsi is derived from the Arabic *mirās*, inheritance, and its signification is supposed to be that the Mirāsis are the hereditary bards and singers

[1] *Archaeological Reports*, vol. xx. p. 26.

[2] *Tribes and Castes of the North-Western Provinces*, vol. iii. p. 496.

of the lower castes, as the Bhāt is of the Rājpūts. *Mirās* as a word may, however, be used of any hereditary right, as that of the village headman or Karnam, or even those of the village watchman or temple dancing-girl, all of whom may have a *mirāsi* right to fees or perquisites or plots of land held as remuneration for service.[1] The Mirāsis are also known as Pakhāwaji, from the *pakhāwaj* or timbrel which they play; as Kawwāl or one who speaks fluently, that is a professional story-teller; and as Kalāwant or one possessed of art or skill. The Mirāsis are most numerous in the Punjab, where they number a quarter of a million. Sir D. Ibbetson says of them:[2] "The social position of the Mirāsi as of all minstrel castes is exceedingly low, but he attends at weddings and similar occasions to recite genealogies. Moreover there are grades even among Mirāsis. The outcaste tribes have their Mirāsis, who though they do not eat with their clients and merely render their professional services are considered impure by the Mirāsis of the higher castes. The Mirāsi is generally a hereditary servant like the Bhāt, and is notorious for his exactions, which he makes under the threat of lampooning the ancestors of him from whom he demands fees. The Mirāsi is almost always a Muhammadan." They are said to have been converted to Islām in response to the request of the poet Amīr Khusru, who lived in the reign of Ala-ud-dīn Khilji (A.D. 1295). The Mirāsi has two functions, the men being musicians, storytellers and genealogists, while the women dance and sing, but only before the ladies of the zenāna. Mr. Nesfield[3] says that they are sometimes regularly entertained as jesters to help these ladies to kill time and reconcile them to their domestic prisons. As they do not dance before men they are reputed to be chaste, as no woman who is not a prostitute will dance in the presence of men, though singing and playing are not equally condemned. The implements of the Mirāsis are generally the small drum (*dholak*), the cymbals (*majīra*) and the gourd lute (*kingri*).[4]

---

[1] Baden Powell's *Land Systems of British India*, vol. iii. p. 116.
[2] *Punjab Ethnography*, p. 289.
[3] *Brief View*, p. 43.
[4] Crooke, *loc. cit.*

MOCHI[1]

LIST OF PARAGRAPHS

1. *General notice.*
2. *Legends of origin.*
3. *Art among the Hindus.*
4. *Antagonism of Mochis and Chamārs.*
5. *Exogamous groups.*
6. *Social customs.*
7. *Shoes.*

1. General notice.

Mochi, Muchi, Jīngar, Jirayat, Jīldgar, Chitrakār, Chitevari, Musabir.—The occupational caste of saddlers and cobblers. In 1911 about 4000 Mochis and 2000 Jīngars were returned from the Central Provinces and Berār, the former residing principally in the Hindustāni and the latter in the Marāthi-speaking Districts. The name is derived from the Sanskrit *mochika* and the Hindustāni *mojna*, to fold, and the common name *mojah* for socks and stockings is from the same root (Platts). By origin the Mochis are no doubt an offshoot of the Chamār caste, but they now generally disclaim the connection. Mr. Nesfield observes[2] that, " The industry of tanning is preparatory to and lower than that of cobblery, and hence the caste of Chamār ranks decidedly below that of Mochi. The ordinary Hindu does not consider the touch of a Mochi so impure as that of the Chamār, and there is a Hindu proverb to the effect that ' Dried or prepared hide is the same thing as cloth,' whereas the touch of the raw hide before it has been tanned by the Chamār is considered a pollution. The Mochi does not eat carrion like the Chamār nor does he eat swine's flesh ; nor does his wife ever practise the much-loathed art of midwifery." In the Central Provinces, as in northern India, the caste may be considered to

[1] This article is partly based on papers by Mr. Gopāl Parmanand, Deputy Inspector of Schools, Saugor, and Mr. Shamsuddīn, Sub-Inspector City Police, Saugor.
[2] *Brief View.*

have two branches, the lower one consisting of the Mochis who make and cobble shoes and are admittedly descended from Chamārs; while the better-class men either make saddles and harness, when they are known as Jīngar; or bind books, when they are called Jīldgar; or paint and make clay idols, when they are given the designation either of Chitrakār, Chitevari or Murtikār. In Berār some Jīngars have taken up the finer kinds of iron-work, such as mending guns, and are known as Jirāyat. All these are at great pains to dissociate themselves from the Chamār caste. They call themselves Thākur or Rājpūt and have exogamous sections the names of which are identical with those of the Rājpūt septs. The same people have assumed the name of Rishi in Bengal, and, according to a story related by Sir H. Risley, claim to be debased Brāhmans; while in the United Provinces Mr. Crooke considers them to be connected with the Srivāstab Kāyasths, with whom they intermarry and agree in manners and customs. The fact that in the three Provinces these workers in leather claim descent from three separate high castes is an interesting instance of the trouble which the lower-class Hindus will take to obtain a slight increase in social consideration; but the very diversity of the accounts given induces the belief that all Mochis were originally sprung from the Chamārs. In Bombay, again, Mr. Enthoven[1] writes that the caste prefers to style itself Arya Somavansi Kshatriya or Aryan Kshatriyas of the Moon division; while they have all the regular Brāhmanical *gotras* as Bhāradwāja, Vasishtha, Gautam and so on.

The following interesting legends as to the origin of the caste adduced by them in support of their Brāhmanical descent are related[2] by Sir H. Risley: "One of the Prajā-pati, or mind-born sons of Brahma, was in the habit of providing the flesh of cows and clarified butter as a burnt-offering (*Ahuti*) to the gods. It was then the custom to eat a portion of the sacrifice, restore the victim to life, and drive it into the forest. On one occasion the Prajā-pati failed to resuscitate the sacrificial animal, owing to his wife, who was pregnant at the time, having clandestinely made away with a portion.

2. Legends of origin.

[1] *Bombay Ethnographic Survey Draft Monograph on Jīngar.* [2] *Tribes and Castes of Bengal,* art. Mochi.

Alarmed at this he summoned all the other Prajā-patis, and they sought by divination to discover the cause of the failure. At last they ascertained what had occurred, and as a punishment the wife was cursed and expelled from their society. The child which she bore was the first Mochi or tanner, and from that time forth, mankind being deprived of the power of reanimating cattle slaughtered for food, the pious abandoned the practice of killing kine altogether. Another story is that Muchirām, the ancestor of the caste, was born from the sweat of Brahma while dancing. He chanced to offend the irritable sage Durvāsa, who sent a pretty Brāhman widow to allure him into a breach of chastity. Muchirām accosted the widow as mother, and refused to have anything to do with her; but Durvāsa used the miraculous power he had acquired by penance to render the widow pregnant so that the innocent Muchirām was made an outcaste on suspicion. From her two sons are descended the two main branches of the caste in Bengal."

3. Art among the Hindus.

In the Central Provinces the term Mochi is often used for the whole caste in the northern Districts, and Jīngar in the Marātha country; while the Chitrakārs or painters form a separate group. Though the trades of cobbler and bookbinder are now widely separated in civilised countries, the connection between them is apparent since both work in leather. It is not at first sight clear why the painter should be of the same caste, but the reason is perhaps that his brushes are made of the hair of animals, and this is also regarded as impure, as being a part of the hide. If such be the case a senseless caste rule of ceremonial impurity has prevented the art of painting from being cultivated by the Hindus; and the comparatively poor development of their music may perhaps be ascribed to the same cause, since the use of the sinews of animals for stringed instruments would also prevent the educated classes from learning to play them. Thus no stringed instruments are permitted to be used in temples, but only the gong, cymbal, horn and conch-shell. And this rule would greatly discourage the cultivation of music, which art, like all the others, has usually served in its early period as an appanage to religious services. It has been held that instruments were originally employed at temples and shrines in order to scare away evil spirits by their noise while the god was being fed or worshipped, and not for the purpose of calling the worshippers together; since noise is a recognised means of driving away spirits, probably in consequence of its effect in frightening wild animals. It is for the same end that music is essential at weddings, especially during the night when the spirits are more potent; and this is the primary object of the continuous discordant din which the Hindus consider a necessary accompaniment to a wedding.

Except for this ceremonial strictness Hinduism should have been favourable to the development of both painting and sculpture, as being a polytheistic religion. In the early stages of society religion and art are intimately connected, as is shown by the fact that images and paintings are at first nearly always of deities or sacred persons or animals, and it is only after a considerable period of development that secular subjects are treated. Similarly architecture is in its commencement found to be applied solely to sacred buildings, as temples and churches, and is only gradually diverted to secular buildings. The figures sculptured by the Mochis are usually images for temples, and those who practise this art are called Murtikar, from *murti*, an image or idol; and the pictures of the Chitrakārs were until recently all of deities or divine animals, though secular paintings may now occasionally be met with. And the uneducated believers in a polytheistic religion regularly take the image for the deity himself, at first scarcely conceiving of the one apart from the other. Thus some Bharewas or brass-workers say that they dare not make metal images of the gods, because they are afraid that the badness of their handiwork might arouse the wrath of the gods and move them to take revenge. The surmise might in fact be almost justifiable that the end to which figures of men and animals were first drawn or painted, or modelled in clay or metal was that they might be worshipped as images of the deities, the savage mind not distinguishing at all between an image of the god and the god himself. For this reason monotheistic religions would be severely antagonistic to the arts, and such is in fact the case. Thus the Muhammadan commentary, the Hadith, has a verse: " Woe to him who has painted a living creature! At the day of the last judgment the persons represented by him will come out of the tomb and join themselves to him to demand of him a soul. Then that man, unable to give life to his work, will burn in eternal flames." And in Judaism the familiar prohibition of the Second Commandment appears to be directed to the same end.

Hindu sculpture has indeed been fairly prolific, but is not generally considered to have attained to any degree of artistic merit. Since sculpture is mainly concerned with the human form it seems clear that an appreciation of the beauty of muscular strength and the symmetrical development of the limbs is an essential preliminary to success in this art; and such a feeling can only arise among a people who set much store on feats of bodily strength and agility. This has never been the character of the Hindus, whose religion encourages asceticism and mortification of the body, and points to mental self-absorption and detachment from worldly cares and exercises as the highest type of virtue.

4. Antagonism of Mochis and Chamārs.

As a natural result of the pretensions to nobility made by the Mochis, there is no love lost between them and the Chamārs; and the latter allege that the Mochis have stolen their *rāmpi*, the knife with which they cut leather. On this account the Chamārs will neither take water to drink from the Mochis nor mend their shoes, and will not even permit them to try on a new pair of shoes until they have paid the price set on them; for they say that the Mochis are half-bred Chamārs and therefore cannot be permitted to defile the shoes of a true Chamār by trying them on; but when they have been paid for, the maker has severed connection with them, and the use to which they may be put no longer affects him.

5. Exogamous groups.

In the Central Provinces the Mochis are said to have forty exogamous sections or *gotras*, of which the bulk are named after all the well-known Rājpūt clans, while two agree with those of the Chamārs. And they have also an equal number of *kheras* or groups named after villages. The limits of the two groups seem to be identical; thus members of the sept named after the Kachhwāha Rājpūts say that their *khera* or village name is Mungāvali in Gwālior; those of

IMAGE OF THE GOD VISHNU AS VITHOBA.

the Ghangere sept give Chanderi as their *khera*, the Sitāwat sept Dhāmoni in Saugor, the Didoria Chhatarpur, the Narele Narwar, and so on. The names of the village groups have now been generally forgotten and they are said to have no influence on marriage, which is regulated by the Rājpūt sept names; but it seems probable that the *kheras* were the original divisions and the Rājpūt *gotras* have been more recently adopted in support of the claims already noticed.

The Mochis have adopted the customs of the higher Hindu castes. A man may not take a wife from his own *gotra*, his mother's *gotra* or from a family into which a girl from his own family has married. They usually marry their daughters in childhood and employ Brāhmans in their ceremonies, and no degradation attaches to these latter for serving as their priests. In minor domestic ceremonies for which the Brāhman is not engaged his place is taken by a relative, who is called *sawāsa*, and is either the sister's husband, daughter's husband, or father's sister's husband, of the head of the family. They permit widow-remarriage and divorce, and in the southern Districts effect a divorce by laying a pestle between the wife and husband. They burn their dead and observe mourning for the usual period. After a death they will not again put on a coloured head-cloth until some relative sets it on their heads for the first time on the expiry of the period of mourning. They revere the ordinary Hindu deities, and like the Chamārs they have a family god, known as Mair, whose representation in the shape of a lump of clay is enshrined within the house and worshipped at marriages and deaths. In Saugor he is said to be the collective representative of the spirits of their ancestors. In some localities they eat flesh and drink liquor, but in others abstain from both. Among the Hindus the Mochis rank considerably higher than the Chamārs; their touch does not defile and they are permitted to enter temples and take part in religious ceremonies. The name of a Saugor Mochi is remembered who became a good drawer and painter and was held in much esteem at the Peshwa's court. In northern India about half the Mochis are Muhammadans, but in the Central Provinces they are all Hindus.

In view of the fact that many of the Mochis were

6. Social customs.

7. Shoes.

Muhammadans and that slippers are mainly a Muhammadan article of attire Buchanan thought it probable that they were brought into India by the invaders, the Hindus having previously been content with sandals and wooden shoes. He wrote: "Many Hindus now use leather slippers, but some adhere to the proper custom of wearing sandals, which have wooden soles, a strap of leather to pass over the instep, and a wooden or horn peg with a button on its top. The foot is passed through the strap and the peg is placed between two of the toes."[1] It is certain, however, that leather shoes and slippers were known to the Hindus from a fairly early period: "The episode related in the Rāmāyana of Bhārata placing on the vacant throne of Ajodhya a pair of Rāma's slippers, which he worshipped during the latter's protracted exile, shows that shoes were important articles of wear and worthy of attention. In Manu and the Mahābhārata slippers are also mentioned and the time and mode of putting them on pointed out. The Vishnu Purāna enjoins all who wish to protect their persons never to be without leather shoes. Manu in one place expresses great repugnance to stepping into another's shoes and peremptorily forbids it, and the Purānas recommend the use of shoes when walking out of the house, particularly in thorny places and on hot sand."[2] Thus shoes were certainly worn by the Hindus before Muhammadan times, though loose slippers may have been brought into fashion by the latter. And it seems possible that the Mochis may have adopted Islām, partly to obtain the patronage of the followers of the new religion, and also to escape from the degraded position to which their profession of leather-working was relegated by Hinduism and to dissociate themselves from the Chamārs.

Mowār.—A small caste of cultivators found in the Chhattīsgarh country, in the Raipur and Bilāspur Districts and the Raigarh State. They numbered 2500 persons in 1901. The derivation of the name is obscure, but they themselves say that it is derived from Mow or Mowagarh,

---

[1] *Eastern India*, vol. iii. p. 105.
[2] Rājendra Lāl Mitra, *Indo-Aryans*, vol. i. pp. 222, 223.

a town in the Jhānsi District of the United Provinces, and they also call themselves Mahuwār or the inhabitants of Mow. They say that the Rāja of Mowagarh, under whom they were serving, desired to marry the daughter of one of their Sirdārs (headmen), because she was extremely beautiful, but her father refused, and when the Rāja persisted in his desire they left the place in a body and came to Ratanpur in the time of Rāja Bīmbaji, in A.D. 1770. A Bilāspur writer states that the Mowārs are an offshoot from the Rajwār Rājpūts of Sargūja State. Colonel Dalton writes[1] of the Rajwār Rājpūts of Sargūja and other adjoining States that they are peaceably disposed cultivators, who declare themselves to be fallen Kshatriyas; but he remarks later that they are probably aborigines, as they do not conform to Hindu customs, and they are skilled in a dance called Chailo, which he considers to be of Dravidian origin. In another place he remarks that the Rajwārs of Bengal admit that they are derived from the miscegenation of Kurmis and Kols. The fact that the Mowārs of Sārangarh make a representation of a bow and arrow on their documents, instead of signing their names, affords some support to the theory that they are probably a branch of one of the aboriginal tribes. The name may be derived from *mowa*, a radish, as the Mowārs of Bilāspur are engaged principally in garden cultivation.

The Mowārs have no subcastes, but are divided into a number of exogamous groups, principally of a totemistic nature. Those of the Sūrajha or sun sept throw away their earthen pots on the occasion of an eclipse, and those of the Hataia or elephant sept will not ride on an elephant and worship that animal at the Dasahra festival. Members of other septs named after the cobra, the crow, the monkey and the tiger will not kill their totem animal, and when they see the dead body of one of its species they throw away their earthen cooking-pots as a sign of mourning. The marriage of persons belonging to the same sept and also that of first cousins is prohibited. If an unmarried girl is seduced by a man of the caste she becomes his wife and is not expelled, but the caste will not eat food cooked by her. But a girl going wrong with an outsider is finally cast

[1] *Ethnology of Bengal*, p. 326.

out. The marriage and other social customs resemble those of the Kurmis. The caste employ Brāhmans at their ceremonies and have a great regard for them. Their *gurus* or spiritual preceptors are Bairāgis and Gosains. They eat the flesh of clean animals and a few drink liquor, but most of them abstain from it. Their women are tattooed on the arms and hands with figures intended to represent deer, flies and other animals and insects. The caste say that they were formerly employed as soldiers under the native chiefs, but they are now all cultivators. They grow all kinds of grain and vegetables, except turmeric and onions. A few of them are landowners, and the majority tenants. Very few are constrained to labour for hire. In appearance the men are generally strong and healthy, and of a dark complexion.

1. Origin of the caste.

Murha.—A Dravidian caste of navvies and labourers found in Jubbulpore and the adjoining Districts, to the number of about 1500 persons. The name Murha has been held to show that the caste are connected with the Munda tribe. The Murhas, however, call themselves also Khare Bind Kewat and Lunia or Nunia (salt-maker), and in Jubbulpore they give these two names as subdivisions of the caste. And these names indicate that the caste are an offshoot of the large Bind tribe of Bengal and northern India, though in parts of the Central Provinces they have probably been recruited from the Kols or Mundas. Sir H. Risley[1] records a story related by the Binds to the effect that they and the Nunias were formerly one, and that the existing Nunias are descended from a Bind who consented to dig a grave for a Muhammadan king and was put out of caste for doing so. And he remarks that the Binds may be a true primitive tribe and the Nunias a functional group differentiated from them by taking to the manufacture of earth salt. This explanation of the relationship of the Binds and Nunias seems almost certainly correct. In the United Provinces the Binds are divided into the Khare and Dhusia or first and second subcastes, and the Khare Binds also call themselves Kewat.[2] And the Murhas of

---

[1] *Tribes and Castes of Bengal*, art. Bind.

[2] Crooke's *Tribes and Castes*, art. Bind.

Narsinghpur call themselves Khare Bind Kewats, though the other Kewats repudiate all connection with them. There seems thus to be no doubt that the Murhas of these Provinces are another offshoot of the Bind tribe like the Nunias, who have taken up the profession of navvies and earthworkers and thus become a separate caste. Mr. Hīra Lāl notes that the Narsinghpur District contains a village Nonia, which is inhabited solely by Murhas who call themselves Khare Bind Kewat. As the village is no doubt named Nonia or Nunia after them, we thus have an instance of all the three designations being applied to the same set of persons. The Murhas say that they came into Narsinghpur from Rewah, and they still speak the Bagheli dialect, though the current vernacular of the locality is Bundeli. The Binds themselves derive their name from the Vindhya (Bindhya) hills.[1] They relate that a traveller passing by the Vindhya hills heard a strange flute-like sound coming out of a clump of bamboos. He cut a shoot and took from it a fleshy substance, which afterwards grew into a man, the supposed ancestor of the Binds. In Mandla the Murhas say that the difference between themselves and the Nunias is that the latter make field-embankments and other earthwork, while the Murhas work in stone and build bridges. According to their own story they were brought to Mandla from their home in Eastern Oudh more than ten generations ago by a Gond king of the Garha-Mandla dynasty for the purpose of building his fort or castle. He gave them two villages for their maintenance which they have now lost. The caste has, however, probably received some local accretions and in Mandla some Murhas appear to be Kols ; members of this tribe are generally above the average in bodily strength and are in considerable request for employment on earth- and stone-work.

2. Marriage customs.

In Narsinghpur the Murhas appear to have no regular exogamous divisions. Some of them remember the names of their *kheros* or ancestral villages and do not marry with families belonging to the same *khero*, but this is not a regular rule of the caste. Generally speaking, persons descended through males from a common ancestor do not intermarry so long as they remember the relationship. In Mandla they

---

[1] *Tribes and Castes of Bengal,* loc. cit.

have five divisions, of which the highest is Pūrbia. The name Pūrbia (Eastern) is commonly applied in the Central Provinces to persons coming from Oudh, and in this case the Pūrbia Murhas are probably the latest immigrants from home and have a superior status on this account. Up till recently they practised hypergamy with the other groups, taking daughters from them in marriage, but not giving their daughters to them. This rule is now, however, breaking down on account of the difficulty they find in getting their daughters married. The children of brothers and sisters may marry in some places, but in others neither they nor their children may marry with each other. Anta Sānta or the exchange of girls between two families is permitted. The bridegroom's father has to pay from five to twenty rupees as a *chari* or bride-price to the girl's father, which sum is regarded as the remuneration of the latter for having brought up his daughter. In the case of the daughter of a headman the bride-price is sometimes as high as Rs. 150. In Damoh a curious survival of marriage by capture remains. The bridegroom's party give a ram or he-goat to the bride's party and these take it to their shed, cut its head off and hang it by the side of the *khām* or marriage-pole. The brother-in-law of the bridegroom or of his father then sallies forth to bring back the head of the animal, but is opposed by the women of the bride's party, who belabour him and his friends with sticks, brooms and rolling-pins. But in the end the head is always taken away. The binding portion of the marriage is the *bhānwar* or walking round the sacred post. When the bride is leaving for her husband's house the women of her party take seven balls of flour with burning wicks thrust into them, and place them in a winnowing-fan. They wave this round the bride's head and then throw the balls and after them the fan over the litter in which the bride is seated. The bridegroom's party must catch the fan, and if they let it fall to the ground they are much laughed at for their clumsiness. When the pair arrive at the bridegroom's house, the fan is again waved over their heads; and a cloth is spread before the house, on which seven burning wicks are placed like the previous ones. The bride walks quickly over the cloth to the house and the bridegroom must keep pace with her, picking up the burning flour balls as he goes. When the pair arrive at the house the bridegroom's sister shuts the door and will not open it until she is given a present. Divorce and the remarriage of widows are permitted.

The caste worship the ordinary Hindu deities. Well-to-do members burn their dead and the poorer ones bury them. The corpse is usually placed with the head to the south as is the custom among the primitive tribes, but in some localities the Hindu fashion of laying the head to the north has been adopted. Two pice are thrown down by the grave or burning-*ghāt* to buy the site, and these are taken by the sweeper. The ashes are collected on the third day and thrown into a river. The usual period of mourning is only three days, but it is sometimes extended to nine days when the chief mourner is unable to feed the caste-fellows on the third day, and the feast may in case of necessity be postponed to any time within six months of the death. The chief mourner puts on a new white cloth and eats nothing but rice and pulse without salt. *3. Funeral rites.*

The caste are employed on all kinds of earthwork, such as building walls, excavating trenches, and making embankments in fields. Their trade implements consist of a pickaxe, a basket, and a thin wooden hod to fill the earth into the basket. The Murha invokes these as follows: "Oh! my lord the basket, my lord the pickaxe shaped like a snake, and my lady the hod, come and eat up those who do not pay me for my work!" The Murhas are strict in their rules about food and will not accept cooked food even from a Brāhman, but notwithstanding this, their social position is so low that not even a sweeper would take food from them. The caste eat flesh and drink liquor, but abstain from fowls, pork and beef. They engage Brāhmans on the occasion of births and marriages, but not usually for funerals. The women tattoo their bodies after marriage, and the charge for this should always be paid by the maternal uncle's wife, the paternal aunt, or some other similar relation of the girl. The fact that among most Hindus a girl must be tattooed before leaving for her husband's house, and that the cost of the operation must always be paid for by her own family, seems *4. Occupation.*

to indicate that tattooing was formerly a rite of puberty for the female sex. A wife must not mention the name of her husband or of any person who stands in the relation of father, mother, uncle or aunt to him. Parents do not call their eldest son by his proper name, but by some pet name. Women are impure for five days during menstruation and are not allowed to cook for that period. The Murhas have a caste *panchāyat* or committee, the head of which is known as Patel or Mukhia, the office being hereditary. He receives a part of all fines levied for the commission of social offences. In appearance the caste are dark and short of stature, and have some resemblance to the Kols.

5. Women's song.

In conclusion, I reproduce one of the songs which the women sing as they are carrying the basketfuls of earth or stones at their work; in the original each line consists of two parts, the last words of which sometimes rhyme with each other :

Our mother Nerbudda is very kind ; blow, wind, we are hot with labour.
He said to the Maina : Go, carry my message to my love.
The red ants climb up the mango-tree ; and the daughter follows her mother's way.
I have no money to give her even lime and tobacco ; I am poor, so how can I tell her of my love.
The boat has gone down on the flood of the Nerbudda ; the fisher-woman is weeping for her husband.
She has no bangles on her arm nor necklace on her neck ; she has no beauty, but seeks her lovers throughout the village.
Bread from the girdle, curry from the *lota* ; let us go, beloved, the moon is shining.
The leaves of gram have been plucked from the plants ; I think much on Dadaria, but she does not come.
The love of a stranger is as a dream ; think not of him, beloved, he cannot be yours.
Twelve has struck and it is thirteen time (past the time of labour) ; oh, overseer, let your poor labourers go.
The betel-leaf is pressed in the mouth (and gives pleasure) ; attractive eyes delight the heart.
Catechu, areca and black cloves ; my heart's secret troubles me in my dreams.
The Nerbudda came and swept away the rubbish (from the works) ; fly away, bees, do not perch on my cloth.
The colour does not come on the wheat ; her youth is passing, but she cannot yet drape her cloth on her body.
Like the sight of rain-drops splashing on the ground ; so beautiful is she to look upon.

COOLIE WOMEN WITH BABIES SLUNG AT THE SIDE.

It rains and the hidden streams in the woodland are filled (and come to view); hide as long as you may, some day you must be seen.

The mahua flowers are falling from the trees on the hill; leave me your cloth so that I may know you will return.

He went to the bazār and brought back a cocoanut; it is green without, but insects are eating the core.

He went to the hill and cut strings of bamboo; you cannot drape your cloth, you have wound it round your body.

The coral necklace hangs on the peg; if you become the second wife of my husband I shall give you clothes.

She put on her clothes and went to the forest; she met her lover and said you are welcome to me.

He went to the bazār and bought potatoes; but if he had loved me he would have brought me liquor.

The fish in the river are on the look-out; the Brāhman's daughter is bathing with her hair down.

The arhar-stumps stand in the field; I loved one of another caste, but must give him up.

He ate betel and coloured his teeth; his beloved came from without and knew him.

The ploughmen are gone to the field; my clever writer is gone to the court-house.

The Nerbudda flows like a bent bow; a beautiful youth is standing in court.[1]

The broken areca-nuts lie in the forest; when a man comes to misfortune no one will help him.

The broken areca-nuts cannot be mended; and two hearts which are sundered cannot be joined.

Ask me for five rupees and I will give you twenty-five; but I will not give my lover for the whole world.

I will put bangles on my arm; when the other wife sees me she will die of jealousy.

Break the bangles which your husband gave you; and put others on your wrists in my name.

O my lover, give me bangles; make me armlets, for I am content with you.

My lover went to the bazār at Lakhanpur; but he has not brought me even a *choli*[2] that I liked.

I had gone to the bazār and bought fish; she is so ugly that the flies would not settle on her.

Nagasia, Naksia.—A primitive tribe found principally in the Chota Nāgpur States. They now number 16,000 persons in the Central Provinces, being returned almost entirely from Jashpur and Sargūja. The census returns are, however, liable to be inaccurate as the Nagasias frequently call themselves Kisān, a term which is also applied to the

---

[1] The clever writer referred to in the preceding line. [2] Breast-cloth.

Oraons. The Nagasias say that they are the true Kisāns whereas the Oraons are only so by occupation. The Oraons, on the other hand, call the Nagasias Kisāda. The tribe derive their name from the Nāg or cobra, and they say that somebody left an infant in the forest of Setambu and a cobra came and spread its hood over the child to protect him from the rays of the sun. Some Mundas happened to pass by and on seeing this curious sight they thought the child must be destined to greatness, so they took him home and made him their king, calling him Nagasia, and from him the tribe are descended. The episode of the snake is, of course, a stock legend related by many tribes, but the story appears to indicate that the Nagasias are an offshoot of the Mundas; and this hypothesis is strengthened by the fact that Nāgbasia is often used as an alternative name for the Mundas by their Hindu neighbours. The term Nāgbasia is supposed to mean the original settlers (*basia*) in Nāg (Chota Nāgpur).

The tribe are divided into the Telha, Dhuria and Senduria groups. The Telhas are so called because at the marriage ceremony they mark the forehead of the bride with *tel* (oil), while the Dhurias instead of oil use dust (*dhur*) taken from the sole of the bridegroom's foot, and the Sendurias like most Hindu castes employ vermilion (*sendur*) for this purpose. The Telhas and Dhurias marry with each other, but not with the Sendūrias, who consider themselves to be superior to the others and use the term Nāgbansia or 'Descendants of the Snake' as their tribal name. The Telha and Dhuria women do not wear glass bangles on their arms but only bracelets of brass, while the Sendurias wear glass bangles and also armlets above the elbow. Telha women do not wear nose-rings or tattoo their bodies, while the Sendūrias do both. The Telhas say that the tattooing needle and vermilion, which they formerly employed in their marriages, were stolen from them by Wāgdeo or the tiger god. So they hit upon sesamum oil as a substitute, which must be pressed for ceremonial purposes in a bamboo basket by unmarried boys using a plough-yoke. This is probably, Mr. Hīra Lāl remarks, merely the primitive method of extracting oil, prior to the invention of the Teli's *ghāni* or oil-press; and the practice is an instance of the common rule that articles employed in ceremonial and religious rites should be prepared by the ancient and primitive methods which for ordinary purposes have been superseded by more recent labour-saving inventions.

Nāhal, Nihāl.[1]—A forest tribe who are probably a mixture of Bhīls and Korkus. In 1911 they numbered 12,000 persons, of whom 8000 belonged to the Hoshangābād, Nimār and Betūl Districts, and nearly 4000 to Berār. They were classed at the census as a subtribe of Korkus. According to one story they are descended from a Bhīl father and a Korku mother, and the writer of the *Khāndesh Gazetteer* calls them the most savage of the Bhīls. But in the Central Provinces their family or sept names are the same as those of the Korkus, and they speak the Korku language. Mr. Kitts[2] says that the Korkus who first went to Berār found the Nāhals in possession of the Melghāt hills. Gradually the latter caste lost their power and became the village drudges of the former. He adds that the Nāhals were fast losing their language, and the younger generation spoke only Korku. The two tribes were very friendly, and the Nāhals acknowledged the superior position of the Korkus. This, if it accurately represents the state of things prevailing for a long period, and was not merely an incidental feature of their relative position at the time Mr. Kitts' observations were made, would tend to show that the Nāhals were the older tribe and had been subjected by the Korkus, just as the Korkus themselves and the Baigas have given way to the Gonds. Mr. Crosthwaite also states that the Nāhal is the drudge of the Korku and belongs to a race which is supposed to have been glorious before the Korku star arose, and which is now fast dying out. In any case there is no doubt that the Nāhals are a very mixed tribe, as they will even now admit into the community Gonds, Korkus and nearly all the Hindu castes, though in some localities they will not eat from the other tribes and the lower Hindu castes and therefore refuse to admit them. There are, moreover,

1. The tribe and its subdivisions.

---

[1] This article is mainly compiled from papers by Mr. Hīra Lāl and Bābu Gulāb Singh, Superintendent of Land Records, Betūl.
[2] *Berār Census Report* (1881), p. 158.

two subdivisions of the caste called Korku and Marāthi Nāhals respectively. The latter are more Hinduised than the former and disclaim any connection with the Korkus. The Nāhals have totemistic exogamous septs. Those of the Kāsa sept worship a tortoise and also a bell-metal plate, which is their family god. They never eat off a bell-metal plate except on one day in the month of Māgh (January), when they worship it. The members of the Nāgbel sept worship the betel-vine or 'snake-creeper,' and refrain from chewing betel-leaves, and they also worship the Nāg or cobra and do not kill it, thus having a sort of double totem. The Bhawaria sept, named after the *bhaunr* or black bee, do not eat honey, and if they see a person taking the honey-comb from a nest they will run away. The Khadia sept worship the spirits of their ancestors enshrined in a heap of stones (*khad*), or according to another account they worship a snake which sits on a heap of pebbles. The Surja sept worship Sūrya or the sun by offering him a fowl in the month of Pūs (December-January), and some members of the sept keep a fast every Sunday. The Saoner sept worship the *san* or flax plant.

2. Marriage.

Marriage is prohibited between members of the same sept, but there are no other restrictions and first cousins may marry. Both sexes usually marry when adult, and sexual license before wedlock is tolerated. A Brāhman is employed only for fixing the date of the ceremony. The principal part of the marriage is the knotting together of the bride's and bridegroom's clothes on two successive days. They also gamble with tamarind seeds, and it is considered a lucky union if the bridegroom wins. A bride-price is usually paid consisting of Rs. 1-4 to Rs. 5 in cash, some grain and a piece of cloth for the bride's mother. The remarriage of widows is allowed, and the couple go five times round a bamboo stick which is held up to represent a spear, the ceremony being called *barchhi se bhānwar phirna* or the marriage of the spear.

3. Religion.

The Nāhals worship the forest god called Jhārkhandi in the month of Chait, and until this rite has been performed they do not use the leaves or fruits of the *palās*,[1] *aonlā*[2] or

---

[1] *Butea frondosa.*   [2] *Phyllanthus emblica.*

mango trees. When the god is worshipped they collect branches and leaves of these trees and offer cooked food to them and thereafter commence using the new leaves, and the fruit and timber. They also worship the ordinary village godlings. The dead are buried, except in the case of members of the Surja or sun sept, whose corpses are burnt. Cooked food is offered at the grave for four days after the death.

4. Occupation.

The Nāhals were formerly a community of hill-robbers, 'Nāhal, Bhīl, Koli' being the phrase generally used in old documents to designate the marauding bands of the western Satpūra hills. The Rāja of Jītgarh and Mohkot in Nimār has a long account in his genealogy of a treacherous massacre of a whole tribe of Nāhals by his ancestor in Akbar's time, in recognition of which the Jītgarh pargana was granted to the family. Mr. Kitts speaks of the Nahals of Berār as having once been much addicted to cattle-lifting, and this propensity still exists in a minor degree in the Central Provinces, accentuated probably by the fact that a considerable number of Nāhals follow the occupation of graziers. Some of them are also village watchmen, and another special avocation of theirs is the collection of the oil of the marking-nut tree (*Semecarpus anacardium*). This is to some extent a dangerous trade, as the oil causes swellings on the body, besides staining the skin and leaving a peculiar odour. The workers wrap a fourfold layer of cloth round their fingers with ashes between each fold, while the rest of the body is also protected by cloth when gathering the nuts and pounding them to extract the oil. At the end of the day's work powdered tamarind and *ghī* are rubbed on the whole body. The oil is a stimulant, and is given to women after delivery and to persons suffering from rheumatism.

5. Social status.

The social status of the Nāhals is very low and they eat the flesh of almost all animals, while those who graze cattle eat beef. Cow-killing is not regarded as an offence. They are also dirty and do not bathe for weeks together. To get maggots in a wound is, however, regarded as a grave offence, and the sufferer is put out of the village and has to live alone until he recovers.

NAI

LIST OF PARAGRAPHS

1. *Structure of the caste.*
2. *Marriage and other customs.*
3. *Occupation.*
4. *Other services.*
5. *Duties at weddings.*
6. *The barber-surgeon.*
7. *A barber at the court of Oudh.*
8. *Character and position of the barber.*
9. *Beliefs about hair.*
10. *Hair of kings and priests.*
11. *The beard.*
12. *Significance of removal of the hair and shaving the head.*
13. *Shaving the head by mourners.*
14. *Hair offerings.*
15. *Keeping hair unshorn during a vow.*
16. *Disposal of cut hair and nails.*
17. *Superstitions about shaving the hair.*
18. *Reasons why the hair was considered the source of strength.*

1. Structure of the caste.

Nai, Nao, Mhāli, Hajjām, Bhandāri, Mangala.[1]—The occupational caste of barbers. The name is said to be derived from the Sanskrit *nāpita*, according to some a corruption of *snāpitri*, one who bathes. In Bundelkhand he is also known as Khawās, which was a title for the attendant on a grandee; and Birtiya, or 'He that gets his maintenance (*vritti*) from his constituents.'[2] Mhāli is the Marāthi name for the caste, Bhandāri the Uriya name and Mangala the Telugu name. The caste numbered nearly 190,000 persons in the Central Provinces in 1911, being distributed over all Districts. Various legends of the usual type are related of its origin, but, as Sir. H. Risley observes, it is no doubt wholly of a functional character. The subcastes in the Central Provinces entirely bear out this view, as they are

---

[1] This article is compiled from papers by Mr. Chatterji, retired E.A.C., Jubbulpore; Professor Sadāshiva Jairām, M.A., Hislop College, Nāgpur; and Mr. C. Shrinivās Naidu, First Assistant Master, Sironcha, Chānda; and from the Central Provinces District Gazetteers.

[2] Mr. Crooke's *Tribes and Castes*, art. Nai.

very numerous and principally of the territorial type: Telange of the Telugu country, Marāthe, Pardeshi or northerners, Jhāria or those of the forest country of the Wainganga Valley, Bandhaiya or those of Bāndhogarh, Barāde of Berār, Bundelkhandi, Mārwāri, Mathuria from Mathura, Gadhwaria from Garha near Jubbulpore, Lānjia from Lānji in Bālāghāt, Mālwi from Mālwa, Nimāri from Nimār, Deccane, Gujarāti, and so on. Twenty-six divisions in all are given. The exogamous groups are also of different types, some of them being named after Brāhman saints, as Gautam, Kashyap, Kosil, Sandil and Bhāradwāj; others after Rājpūt clans as Sūrajvansi, Jāduvansi, Solanki and Panwār; while others are titular or totemistic, as Nāik, leader; Seth, banker; Rāwat, chief; Nāgesh, cobra; Bāgh, a tiger; Bhādrawa, a fish.

2. Marriage and other customs.

The exogamous groups are known as *khero* or *kul*, and marriage between members of the same group is prohibited. Girls are usually wedded between the ages of eight and twelve and boys between fifteen and twenty. A girl who goes wrong before marriage is finally expelled from the caste. The wedding ceremony follows the ritual prevalent in the locality as described in the articles on Kurmi and Kunbi. At an ordinary wedding the expenses on the girl's side amount to about Rs. 150, and on the boy's to Rs. 200. The remarriage of widows is permitted. In the northern Districts the widow may wed the younger brother of her deceased husband, but in the Marātha country she may not be married to any of his relatives. Divorce may be effected at the instance of the husband before the caste committee, and a divorced woman is at liberty to marry again. The Nais worship all the ordinary Hindu deities. On the Dasahra and Diwāli festivals they wash and revere their implements, the razor, scissors and nail-pruners. They pay regard to omens. It is unpropitious to sneeze or hear the report of a gun when about to commence any business; and when a man is starting on a journey, if a cat, a squirrel, a hare or a snake should cross the road in front of him he will give it up and return home. The bodies of the dead are usually burnt. In Chhattīsgarh the poor throw the corpses of their dead into the Mahānadi, and the bodies of children dying under one year of age were until recently buried in the courtyard of the house. The period of mourning for adults is ten days and for children three days. The chief mourner must take only one meal a day, which he cooks himself until the ceremony of the tenth day is performed.

3. Occupation.
"The barber's trade," Mr. Crooke states,[1] "is undoubtedly of great antiquity. In the Veda we read, 'Sharpen us like the razor in the hands of the barber'; and again, 'Driven by the wind, Agni shaves the hair of the earth like the barber shaving a beard.'" In early times they must have enjoyed considerable dignity; Upali the barber was the first propounder of the law of the Buddhist church. The village barber's leather bag contains a small mirror (*ārsi*), a pair of iron pincers (*chimta*), a leather strap, a comb (*kanghi*), a piece of cloth about a yard square and some oil in a phial. He shaves the faces, heads and armpits of his customers, and cuts the nails of both their hands and feet. He uses cold water in summer and hot in winter, but no soap, though this has now been introduced in towns. For the poorer cultivators he does a rapid scrape, and this process is called '*asūdhal*' or a 'tearful shave,' because the person undergoing it is often constrained to weep. The barber acquires the knowledge of his art by practice on the more obliging of his customers, hence the proverb, 'The barber's son learns his trade on the heads of fools.' The village barber is usually paid by a contribution of grain from the cultivators, calculated in some cases according to the number of ploughs of land possessed by each, in others according to the number of adult males in the family. In Saugor he receives 20 lbs. of grain annually for each adult male or $22\frac{1}{2}$ lbs. per plough of land, besides presents of a basket of grain at seed-time and a sheaf at harvest. Cultivators are usually shaved about once a fortnight. In towns the barber's fee may vary from a pice to two annas for a shave, which is, as has been seen, a much more protracted operation with a Hindu than with a European. It is said that Berār is now so rich that even ordinary cultivators can afford to pay the barber two annas (2d.) for a single shave, or the same price as in the suburbs of London.

[1] *Tribes and Castes*, art. Nai, para. 5.

After he has shaved a client the barber pinches and rubs his arms, presses his fingers together and cracks the joints of each finger, this last action being perhaps meant to avert evil spirits. He also does massage, a very favourite method of treatment in India, and also inexpensive as compared with Europe. For one rupee a month in towns the barber will come and rub a man's legs five or ten minutes every day. Cultivators have their legs rubbed in the sowing season, when the labour is intensely hard owing to the necessity of sowing all the land in a short period. If a man is well-to-do he may have his whole head and body rubbed with scented oil. Landowners have often a barber as a family servant, the office descending from father to son. Such a man will light his master's *chilam* (pipe-bowl) or huqqa (water-pipe), clean and light lamps, prepare his bed, tell his master stories to send him to sleep, act as escort for the women of the family when they go on a journey and arrange matches for the children. The barber's wife attends on women in child-birth after the days of pollution are over, and rubs oil on the bodies of her clients, pares their nails and paints their feet with red dye at marriages and on other festival occasions.

4. Other services.

The barber has also numerous and important duties[1] in connection with marriages and other festival occasions. He acts as the Brāhman's assistant, and to the lower castes, who cannot employ a Brāhman, he is himself the matrimonial priest. The important part which he plays in marriage ceremonies has led to his becoming the matchmaker among all respectable castes. He searches for a suitable bride or bridegroom, and is often sent to inspect the other party to a match and report his or her defects to his clients. He may arrange the price or dowry, distribute the invitations and carry the presents from one house to the other. He supplies the leaf-plates and cups which are used at weddings, as the family's stock of metal vessels is usually quite inadequate for the number of guests. The price of these is about 4 annas (4d.) a hundred. He also provides the *torans* or strings of leaves which are hung over the door of

5. Duties at weddings.

---

[1] The following account is largely taken from Mr. Nesfield's *Brief View of the Caste System*, pp. 42, 43.

the house and round the marriage-shed. At the feast the barber is present to hand to the guests water, betel-leaf and pipes as they may desire. He also partakes of the food, seated at a short distance from the guests, in the intervals of his service. He lights the lamps and carries the torches during the ceremony. Hence he was known as Masālchi or torch-bearer, a name now applied by Europeans to a menial servant who lights and cleans the lamps and washes the plates after meals. The barber and his wife act as prompters to the bride and bridegroom, and guide them through the complicated ritual of the wedding ceremony, taking the couple on their knees if they are children, and otherwise sitting behind them. The barber has a prescriptive right to receive the clothes in which the bridegroom goes to the bride's house, as on the latter's arrival he is always presented with new clothes by the bride's father. As the bridegroom's clothes may be an ancestral heirloom, a compact is often made to buy them back from the barber, and he may receive as much as Rs. 50 in lieu of them. When the first son is born in a family the barber takes a long bamboo stick, wraps it round with cloth and puts an earthen pot over it and carries this round to the relatives, telling them the good news. He receives a small present from each household.

6. The barber-surgeon.

The barber also cleans the ears of his clients and cuts their nails, and is the village surgeon in a small way. He cups and bleeds his patients, applies leeches, takes out teeth and lances boils. In this capacity he is the counterpart of the barber-surgeon of mediaeval Europe. The Hindu physicians are called Baid, and are, as a rule, a class of Brāhmans. They derive their knowledge from ancient Sanskrit treatises on medicine, which are considered to have divine authority. Consequently they think it unnecessary to acquire fresh knowledge by experiment and observation, as they suppose the perfect science of medicine to be contained in their sacred books. As these books probably do not describe surgical operations, of which little or nothing was known at the time when they were written, and as surgery involves contact with blood and other impure substances, the Baids do not practise it, and the villagers are left to get on as best they can with the ministrations of the barber. It is interesting to note that a similar state of things appears to have prevailed in Europe. The monks were the early practitioners of medicine and were forbidden to practise surgery, which was thus left to the barber-chirurgeon. The status of the surgeon was thus for long much below that of the physician.[1] The mediaeval barber of Europe kept a bottle of blood in his window, to indicate that he undertook bleeding and the application of leeches, and the coloured bottles in the chemist's window may have been derived from this. It is also said that the barber's pole originally served as a support for the patient to lean on while he was being bled, and those barbers who did the work of bleeding patients painted their poles in variegated red and white stripes to show it.

Perhaps the most successful barber known to Indian history was not a Hindu at all, but a Peninsular and Oriental Company's cabin-boy, who became the barber of one of the last kings of Oudh, Nasīr-ud-Dīn, in the early part of the nineteenth century, and rose to the position of a favourite courtier. He was entrusted with the supply of every European article used at court, and by degrees became a regular guest at the royal table, and sat down to take dinner with the king as a matter of right; nor would his majesty taste a bottle of wine opened by any other hands than the barber's.[2] This was, however, a wise precaution as it turned out, since after he had finally been forced to part with the barber the king was poisoned by his own relatives. The barber was also made keeper of the royal menagerie, for which he supplied the animals and their food, and made enormous profits. The following is an account of the presentation of the barber's monthly bill of expenses:[3] "It was after tiffin, or lunch, when we usually retired from the palace until dinner-time at nine o'clock, that the favourite entered with a roll of paper in his hand. In India, long documents, legal and commercial, are usually written, not in books or on successive sheets, but on a long roll, strip

7. A barber at the court of Oudh.

---

[1] *Eighteenth Century Middle-Class Life*, by C. S. Torres, in the *Nineteenth Century and After*, Sept. 1910.

[2] *Private Life of an Eastern King*, p. 17.

[3] *Ibidem*, p. 107.

being joined to strip for that purpose, and the whole rolled up like a map.

"'Ha, Khan!' said the king, observing him; 'the monthly bill, is it?'

"'It is, your majesty,' was the smiling reply.

"'Come, out with it; let us see the extent. Unrol it, Khan.'

"The king was in a playful humour; and the barber was always in the same mood as the king. He held the end of the roll in his hand, and threw the rest along the floor, allowing it to unrol itself as it retreated. It reached to the other side of the long apartment—a goodly array of items and figures, closely written too. The king wanted it measured. A measure was brought and the bill was found to be four yards and a half long. I glanced at the amount; it was upwards of Rs. 90,000, or £9000!"

The barber, however, encouraged the king in every form of dissipation and excess, until the state of the Oudh court became such a scandal that the king was forced by the British Government to dismiss him.[1] He retired, it was said, with a fortune of £240,000.

8. Character and position of the barber.

The barber is also, Mr. Low writes,[2] the scandal-bearer and gossip-monger of the village. His cunning is proverbial, and he is known as *Chhattīsa* from the saying—

*Nai hai chhattīsa
Khai an ka pīsa,*

or 'A barber has thirty-six talents by which he eats at the expense of others.' His loquacity is shown in the proverb, 'As the crow among birds so the barber among men.' The barber and the professional Brāhman are considered to be jealous of their perquisites and unwilling to share with their caste-fellows, and this is exemplified in the proverb, "The barber, the dog and the Brāhman, these three snarl at meeting one of their own kind." The joint association of the Brāhman priest and the barber with marriages and other ceremonies has led to the saying, "As there are

---

[1] *Private Life of an Eastern King,* p. 330.

[2] In the *Balāghāt District Gazetteer.*

always reeds in a river so there is always a barber with a Brāhman." The barber's astuteness is alluded to in the saying, 'Nine barbers are equal to seventy-two tailors.' The fact that it is the barber's duty to carry the lights in marriage processions has led to the proverb, " At the barber's wedding all are gentlemen and it is awkward to have to ask somebody to carry the torch." The point of this is clear, though no English equivalent occurs to the mind. And a similar idea is expressed by 'The barber washes the feet of others but is ashamed to wash his own.' It would appear from these proverbs that the Nai is considered to enjoy a social position somewhat above his deserts. Owing to the nature of his duties, which make him a familiar inmate of the household and bring him into contact with the persons of his high-caste clients, the caste of the Nai is necessarily considered to be a pure one and Brāhmans will take water from his hands. But, on the other hand, his calling is that of a village menial and has also some elements of impurity, as in cupping which involves contact with blood, and in cutting the nails and hair of the corpse before cremation. He is thus looked down upon as a menial and also considered as to some extent impure. No member of a cultivating caste would salute a barber first or look upon him as an equal, though Brāhmans put them on the same level of ceremonial purity by taking water from both. The barber's loquacity and assurance have been made famous by the *Arabian Nights*, but they have perhaps been affected by the more strenuous character of life, and his conversation does not flow so freely as it did. Often he now confines himself to approving and adding emphasis to any remarks of the patron and greeting any of his little witticisms with bursts of obsequious laughter. In Madras, Mr. Pandiān states, the village barber, like the washerman, is known as the son of the village. If a customer does not pay him his dues, he lies low, and when he has begun to shave the defaulter engages him in a dispute and says something to excite his anger. The latter will then become abusive to the barber, whom he regards as a menial, and perhaps strike him, and this gives the barber an opportunity to stop shaving him and rush off to lay a complaint at the village court-house, leaving his enemy to proceed home with half his head shaved and thus exposed to general ridicule.[1]

9. Beliefs about hair.

Numerous customs appear to indicate that the hair was regarded as the special seat of bodily strength. The Rājpūt warriors formerly wore their hair long and never cut it, but trained it in locks over their shoulders. Similarly the Marātha soldiers wore their hair long. The Hatkars, a class of Marātha spearmen, might never cut their hair while engaged on military service. A Sikh writer states of Guru Govind, the founder of the militant Sikh confederacy: "He appeared as the tenth Avatār (incarnation of Vishnu). He established the Khālsa, his own sect, and by exhibiting singular energy, leaving the hair on his head, and seizing the scimitar, he smote every wicked person."[2] As is well known, no Sikh may cut his hair, and one of the five marks of the Sikh is the *kanga* or comb, which he must always carry in order to keep his hair in proper order. A proverb states that 'The origin of a Sikh is in his hair.'[3] The following story, related by Sir J. Malcolm, shows the vital importance attached by the Sikh to his hair and beard: "Three inferior agents of Sikh chiefs were one day in my tent. I was laughing and joking with one of them, a Khālsa Sikh, who said he had been ordered to attend me to Calcutta. Among other subjects of our mirth I rallied him on trusting himself so much in my power. 'Why, what is the worst,' he said, 'that you can do to me?' I passed my hand across my chin, imitating the act of shaving. The man's face was in an instant distorted with rage and his sword half-drawn. 'You are ignorant,' he said to me, 'of the offence you have given; I cannot strike you who are above me, and the friend of my master and the state; but no power,' he added, indicating the Khālsa Sikhs, 'shall save these fellows who dared to smile at your action.' It was with the greatest difficulty and only by the good offices of some Sikh Chiefs that I was able to pacify his wounded honour."[4] These instances appear to show

---

[1] D. B. Pandiān, *Indian Village Life*, under Barber.
[2] Quoted in Malcolm's *Sketch of the Sikhs*, Asiatic Researches, vol. xi., 1810, p. 289.
[3] Quoted in Sir D. Ibbetson's account of the Sikhs in *Punjab Census Report* (1881).
[4] *Sketch of the Sikhs*, ibidem, pp. 284, 285.

clearly that the Sikhs considered their hair of vital importance; and as fighting was their object in life, it seems most probable that they thought their strength in war was bound up in it. Similarly when the ancient Spartans were on a military expedition purple garments were worn and their hair was carefully decked with wreaths, a thing which was never done at home.[1] And when Leonidas and his three hundred were holding the pass of Thermopylae, and Xerxes sent scouts to ascertain what the Greeks were doing in their camp, the report was that some of them were engaged in gymnastics and warlike exercises, while others were merely sitting and combing their long hair. If the hypothesis already suggested is correct, the Spartan youths so engaged were perhaps not merely adorning themselves for death, but, as they thought, obtaining their full strength for battle. "The custom of keeping the hair unshorn during a dangerous expedition appears to have been observed, at least occasionally, by the Romans. Achilles kept unshorn his yellow hair, because his father had vowed to offer it to the river Sperchius if ever his son came home from the wars beyond the sea."[2]

When the Bhīls turned out to fight they let down their long hair prior to beginning the conflict with their bows and arrows.[3] The pirates of Surat, before boarding a ship, drank *bhāng* and hemp-liquor, and when they wore their long hair loose they gave no quarter.[4] The Mundas appear to have formerly worn their hair long and some still do. Those who are converted to Christianity must cut their hair, but a non-Christian Munda must always keep the *chundi* or pigtail. If the *chundi* is very long it is sometimes tied up in a knot.[5] Similarly the Oraons wore their hair long like women, gathered in a knot behind, with a wooden or iron comb in it. Those who are Christians can be recognised by the fact that they have cut off their pigtails. A man of the low Pārdhi caste of hunters must never have his hair touched by a razor after he has once killed a deer. As already seen, every orthodox Hindu wore till recently a

---

[1] Professor Blümners, *Home Life of the Ancient Greeks*, translation, p. 455.
[2] *Golden Bough*, 2nd ed. vol. iii. p. 370.
[3] Hendley, *Account of the Bhīls*, *J.A.S.B.* vol. xxxiv., 1875, p. 360.
[4] *Bombay Gazetteer, Hindus of Gujarāt*, p. 528.
[5] S. C. Roy, *The Mundas and their Country*, p. 369.

choti or scalp-lock, which should theoretically be as long as a cow's tail. Perhaps the idea was that for those who were not warriors it was sufficient to retain this and have the rest of the head shaved. The *choti* was never shaved off in mourning for any one but a father. The lower castes of Muhammadans, if they have lost several children, will allow the scalp-lock to grow on the heads of those subsequently born, dedicating it to one of their Muhammadan saints. The Kanjars relate of their heroic ancestor Māna that after he had plunged a bow so deeply into the ground that no one could withdraw it, he was set by the Emperor of Delhi to wrestle against the two most famous Imperial wrestlers. These could not overcome him fairly, so they made a stratagem, and while one provoked him in front the other secretly took hold of his *choti* behind. When Māna started forward his *choti* was thus left in the wrestler's hands, and though he conquered the other wrestler, showing him the sky as it is said, the loss of his *choti* deprived him for ever after of his virtue as a Hindu and in no small degree of his renown as an ancestor.[1] Thus it seems clear that a special virtue attaches to the *choti*. Before every warlike expedition the people of Minahassa in Celebes used to take the locks of hair of a slain foe and dabble them in boiling water to extract the courage; this infusion of bravery was then drunk by the warriors.[2] In a modern Greek folk-tale a man's strength lies in three golden hairs on his head. When his mother plucks them out, he grows weak and timid and is slain by his enemies.[3] The Red Indian custom of taking the scalp of a slain enemy and sometimes wearing the scalps at the waist-belt may be due to the same relief.

In Ceram the hair might not be cut because it was the seat of a man's strength; and the Gaboon negroes for the same reason would not allow any of their hair to pass into the possession of a stranger.[4]

10. Hair of kings and priests.

If the hair was considered to be the special source of strength and hence frequently of life, that of the kings and priests, in whose existence the primitive tribe believed its

---

[1] W. Kirkpatrick in *J.A.S.B.*, July 1911, p. 438.
[2] *Golden Bough*, 3rd ed. vol. viii. p. 153.
[3] *G. B.*, 3rd ed., *Balder the Beautiful*, vol. ii. p. 103.
[4] Dr. Jevons, *Introduction to the History of Religion*, p. 45.

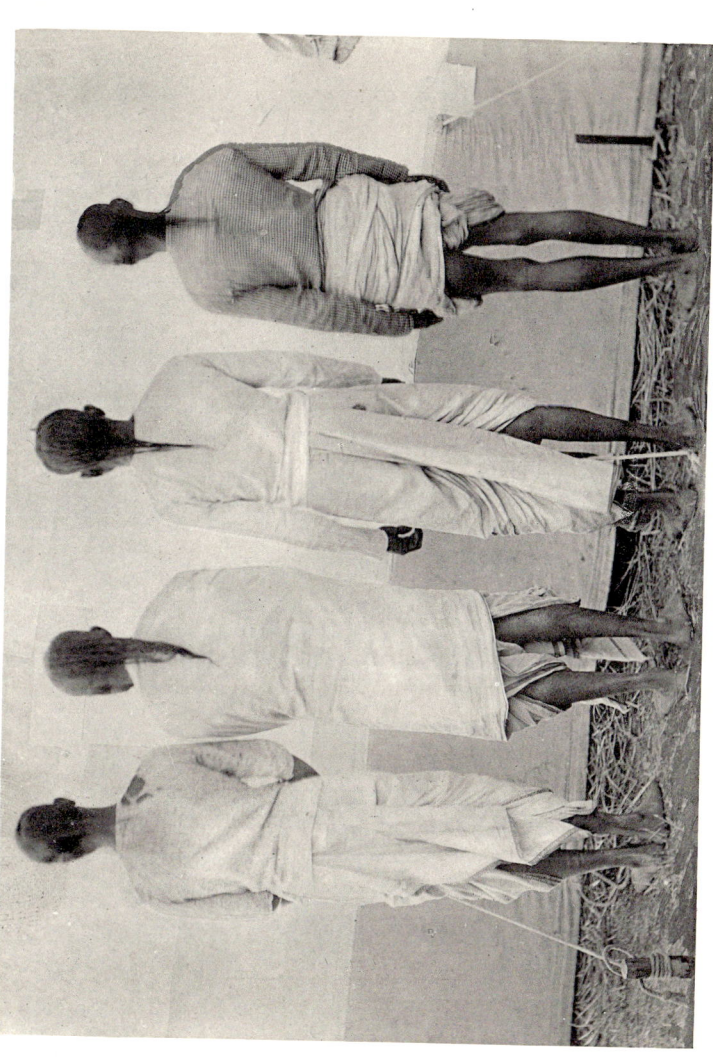

HINDU MEN SHOWING THE *CHOTI* OR SCALP-LOCK.

own communal life to be bound up, would naturally be a matter of peculiar concern. That it was so has been shown in the *Golden Bough*. Two hundred years ago the hair and nails of the Mikādo of Japan could only be cut when he was asleep.[1] The hair of the Flamen Dialis at Rome could be cut only by a freeman and with a bronze knife, and his hair and nails when cut had to be buried under a lucky tree.[2] The Frankish kings were never allowed to crop their hair; from their childhood upwards they had to keep it unshorn. The hair of the Aztec priests hung down to their hams so that the weight of it became very troublesome; for they might never crop it so long as they lived, or at least till they had been relieved from their office on the score of old age.[3] In the Māle Pahāria tribe from the time that any one devoted himself to the profession of priest and augur his hair was allowed to grow like that of a Nazarite; his power of divination entirely disappeared if he cut it.[4] Among the Bawarias of India the Bhuva or priest of Devi may not cut or shave his hair under penalty of a fine of Rs. 10. A Parsi priest or Mobed must never be bare-headed and never shave his head or face.[5] Professor Robertson Smith states: "As a diadem is in its origin nothing more than a fillet to confine hair that is worn long, I apprehend that in old times the hair of Hebrew princes like that of a Maori chief, was taboo, and that Absalom's long locks (2 Sam. xiv. 26) were the mark of his political pretensions and not of his vanity. When the hair of a Maori chief was cut, it was collected and buried in a sacred place or hung on a tree; and it is noteworthy that Absalom's hair was cut annually at the end of the year, in the sacred season of pilgrimage, and that it was collected and weighed."[6]

The importance attached by other races to the hair of the head seems among the Muhammadans to have been concentrated specially in the beard. The veneration displayed for the beard in this community is well known. The Prophet ordained that the minimum length of the beard should be

11. The beard.

---

[1] *Golden Bough*, 2nd ed. vol. i. p. 234.
[2] *Ibidem*, vol. i. p. 242.
[3] *Ibidem*, vol. i. pp. 368, 369.
[4] Dalton, *Ethnology of Bengal*, p. 270.
[5] *Bombay Gazetteer*, Parsis of Gujarāt, p. 226.
[6] *Religion of the Semites*, note i. pp. 483, 484.

VOL. IV T

the breadth of five fingers. When the beard is turning grey they usually dye it with henna and sometimes with indigo ; it may be thought that a grey beard is a sign of weakness. The Prophet said, 'Change the whiteness of your hair, but not with anything black.' It is not clear why black was prohibited. It is said that the first Caliph Abu Bakar was accustomed to dye his beard red with henna, and hence this practice has been adopted by Muhammadans.[1] The custom of shaving the chin is now being adopted by young Muhammadans, but as they get older they still let the beard grow. A very favourite Muhammadan oath is, 'By the beard of the Prophet'; and in Persia if a man thinks another is mocking him he says, 'Do you laugh at my beard?' Neither Hindus nor Muhammadans have any objection to becoming bald, as the head is always covered by the turban in society. But when a man wishes to grow a beard it is a serious drawback if he is unable to do it; and he will then sometimes pluck the young wheat-ears and rub the juice over his cheeks and chin so that he may grow bearded like the wheat. Among the Hindus, Rājpūts and Marāthas, as well as the Sikhs, commonly wore beards, all of these being military castes. Both the beard and hair were considered to impart an aspect of ferocity to the countenance, and when the Rājpūts and Muhammadans were going into battle they combed the hair and trained the beard to project sideways from the face. When a Muhammadan wears a beard he must have hair in the centre of his chin, whereas a Hindu shaves this part. A Muhammadan must have his moustache short so that it may not touch and defile food entering the mouth. It is related that a certain Kāzi had a small head and a very long beard ; and he had a dream that a man with a small head and a long beard must be a fool. When he woke up he thought this was applicable to himself. As he could not make his head larger he decided to make his beard smaller, and looked for scissors to cut part of it off. But he could not find any scissors, and being in a hurry to shorten his beard he decided to burn away part of it, and set it alight. But the fire consumed the whole of his beard before he could put it out, and he then realised the truth of the dream.

---

[1] *Bombay Gazetteer, Muhammadans of Gujarāt*, p. 52.

If the hair was considered to be the source of a man's strength and vigour, the removal of it would involve the loss of this and might be considered especially to debar him from fighting or governing. The instances given from the *Golden Bough* have shown the fear felt by many people of the consequences of the removal of their hair. The custom of shaving the head might also betoken the renunciation of the world and of the pursuit of arms. This may be the reason why monks shaved the head, a practice which was followed by Buddhist as well as Christian monks. A very clear case is also given by Sir James Frazer: "When the wicked brothers Clotaire and Childebert coveted the kingdom of their dead brother Clodomir, they inveigled into their power their little nephews, the two sons of Clodomir; and having done so, they sent a messenger bearing scissors and a naked sword to the children's grandmother, Queen Clotilde, at Paris. The envoy showed the scissors and the sword to Clotilde, and bade her choose whether the children should be shorn and live, or remain unshorn and die. The proud queen replied that if her grandchildren were not to come to the throne she would rather see them dead than shorn. And murdered they were by their ruthless uncle Clotaire with his own hand."[1] In this case it appears that if their hair was shorn the children could not come to the throne but would be destined to become monks. Similarly, in speaking of the Georgians, Marco Polo remarks that they cut their hair short like churchmen.[2] When a member of the religious order of the Mānbhaos is initiated his head is shaved clean by the village barber, and the scalp-lock and moustache must be cut off by his *guru* or preceptor, this being perhaps the special mark of his renunciation of the world. The scalp-locks are preserved and made into ropes which some of them fasten round their loins. Members of the Hindu orders generally shave their scalp-locks and the head on initiation, probably for the same reason as the Mānbhaos. But afterwards they often let the whole of their hair grow long. These men imagine that by the force of their austerities they will obtain divine power, so

12. Significance of removal of the hair and shaving the head.

---

[1] *Golden Bough*, 2nd ed. vol. i. p. 368.
[2] Yule's ed. i. 50, quoted in *Bombay Gazetteer, Hindus of Gujarāt*, p. 470.

their religious character appears to be of a different order from monasticism. Perhaps, therefore, they wear their hair long in order to increase their spiritual potency. They themselves now say that they do it in imitation of the god Siva and the ancient ascetics who had long matted locks. The common Hindu practice of shaving the heads of widows may thus be interpreted as a symbol of their complete renunciation of the world and of any idea of remarriage. It was accompanied by numerous other rules designed to make a widow's life a continual penance. This barbarous custom was formerly fairly general, at least among the higher castes, but is rapidly being abandoned except by one or two of the stricter sections of Brāhmans. Shaving the head might also be imposed as a punishment. Thus in the time of the reign of the Emperor Chandraguptra Maurya in the fourth century B.C. it is stated that ordinary wounding by mutilation was punished by the corresponding mutilation of the offender, in addition to the amputation of his hand. The crime of giving false evidence was visited with mutilation of the extremities; and in certain unspecified cases, serious offences were punished by the shaving of the offender's hair, a penalty regarded as specially infamous.[1] The cutting off of some or all of the hair is at the present time a common punishment for caste offences. Among the Korkus a man and woman caught in adultery have each a lock of hair cut off. If a Chamār man and woman are detected in the same offence, the heads of both are shaved clean of hair. A Dhīmar girl who goes wrong before marriage has a lock of her hair cut off as a penalty, the same being done in several other castes.

13. Shaving the head by mourners.

The exact significance which is to be attached to the removal by mourners of their hair after a death is perhaps doubtful. Sir James Frazer shows that the Australian aborigines are accustomed to let their own blood flow on to the corpse of a dead kinsman and to place their cut hair on the corpse. He suggests that in both cases the object is to strengthen the feeble spirit within the corpse and sustain its life, in order that it may be born again. As a development

[1] Mr. V. A. Smith, *Early History of India*, 2nd ed. p. 128.

of such a rite the hair might have become an offering to the dead, and later still its removal might become a sacrifice and indication of grief. In this manner the common custom of tearing the hair in token of grief and mourning for the dead would be accounted for. Whether the Hindu custom of shaving the heads of mourners was also originally a sacrifice and offering appears to be uncertain. Professor Robertson Smith considered [1] that in this case the hair is shaved off as a means of removing impurity, and quotes instances from the Bible where lepers and persons defiled by contact with the dead are purified by shaving the hair.[2] As the father of a child is also shaved after its birth, and the shaving must here apparently be a rite of purification, it probably has the same significance in the case of mourners; it is not clear whether any element of sacrifice is also involved. The degree to which the Hindu mourner parts with his hair varies to some extent with the nearness of the relationship, and for females or distant relatives they do not always shave. The mourners are shaved on the last day of the impurity, when presents are given to the Mahā-Brāhman, and the latter, representing the dead man, is also shaved with them. When a Hindu is at the point of death, before he makes the gifts for the good of his soul the head is shaved with the exception of his *choti* or scalp-lock, the chin and upper lip. Often the corpse is also shaved after death.

Another case of the hair offering is that made in fulfilment of a vow or at a temple. In this case the hair appears to be a gift-offering which is made to the god as representing the life and strength of the donor; owing to the importance attached to the hair as the source of life and strength, it was a very precious sacrifice. Sir James Frazer also suggests that the hair so given would impart life and strength to the god, of which he stood in need, just as he needed food to nourish him. Among the Hindus it is a common practice to take a child to some well-known temple to have its hair cut for the first time, and to offer the clippings of hair to the deity. If they cannot go to the temple to have the hair cut they have it cut at home,

14. Hair offerings.

---

[1] *Religion of the Semites*, p. 33.   [2] Lev. xiv. 9 and Deut. xxi. 12.

and either preserve the whole hair or a lock of it, until an opportunity occurs to offer it at the temple. In some castes a Brāhman is invited at the first cutting of a child's hair, and he repeats texts and blesses the child; the first lock of hair is then cut by the child's maternal uncle, and its head is shaved by the barber. A child's hair is cut in the first, third or fifth year after birth, but not in the second or fourth year. Among the Muhammadans when a child's hair is cut for the first time, or at least on one occasion in its life, the hair should be weighed against silver or gold and the amount distributed in charity. In these cases also it would appear that the hair as a valuable part of the child is offered to the god to obtain his protection for the life of the child. If a woman has no child and desires one, or if she has had children and lost them, she will vow her next child's hair to some god or temple. A small patch known as *chench* is then left unshorn on the child's head until it can be taken to the temple.

15. Keeping hair unshorn during a vow.

It was also the custom to keep the hair unshorn during the performance of a vow. "While his vow lasted a Nazarite might not have his hair cut: 'All the days of the vow of his separation there shall no razor come upon his head.'[1] The Egyptians on a journey kept their hair uncut till they returned home.[2] Among the Chatti tribe of the ancient Germans the young warriors never clipped their hair or their beard till they had slain an enemy. Six thousand Saxons once swore that they would not clip their hair nor shave their beards until they had taken vengeance on their enemies."[3] Similarly, Hindu religious mendicants keep their hair long while they are journeying on a pilgrimage, and when they arrive at the temple which is their goal they shave it all off and offer it to the god. In this case, as the hair is vowed as an offering, it clearly cannot be cut during the performance of the vow, but must be preserved intact. When the task to be accomplished for the fulfilment of a vow is a journey or the slaying of enemies, the retention of the hair is probably also

---

[1] *Golden Bough*, 2nd ed. vol. i. p. 371.
[2] *Ibidem*, 2nd ed. vol. i. p. 370.
[3] *Ibidem*, 2nd ed. vol. i. p. 371.

meant to support and increase the wearer's strength for the accomplishment of his purpose.

16. Disposal of cut hair and nails.

If the hair contained a part of the wearer's life and strength its disposal would be a matter of great importance, because, according to primitive belief, these qualities would remain in it after it had been severed. Hence, if an enemy obtained it, by destroying the hair or some analogous action he might injure or destroy the life and strength of the person to whom it belonged. The Hindus usually wrap up a child's first hair in a ball of dough and throw it into a running stream, with the cuttings of his nails. Well-to-do people also place a rupee in the ball, so that it is now regarded as an offering. The same course is sometimes followed with the hair and nails cut ceremoniously at a wedding, and possibly on one or two other occasions, such as the investiture with the sacred thread; but the belief is decaying, and ordinarily no care is taken of the shorn hair. In Berār when the Hindus cut a child's hair for the first time they sometimes bury it under a water-pot where the ground is damp, perhaps with the idea that the child's hair will grow thickly and plentifully like grass in a damp place. It is a common belief that if a barren woman gets hold of a child's first hair and wears it round her waist the fertility of the child's mother will be transferred to her. The Sarwaria Brāhmans shave a child's hair in its third year. A small silver razor is made specially for the occasion, costing a rupee and a quarter, and the barber first touches the child's hair with this and then shaves it ceremoniously with his own razor.[1] The Halbas think that the severed clippings of hair are of no use for magic, but if a witch can cut a lock of hair from a man's head she can use it to work magic on him. In making an image of a person with intent to injure or destroy him, it was customary to put a little of his hair into the image, by which means his life and strength were conveyed to it. A few years ago a London newspaper mentioned the case of an Essex man entering a hairdresser's and requesting the barber to procure for him a piece of a certain customer's hair. When asked the reason for this curious demand, he

---

[1] Mr. Crooke's *Tribes and Castes*, art. Sarwaria.

stated that the customer had injured him and he wished to
'work a spell' against him.¹ In the Pārsi Zend-Avesta
it is stated that if the clippings of hair or nails are allowed
to fall in the ground or ditches, evil spirits spring up from
them and devour grain and clothing in the house. It was
therefore ordained for the Pārsis through their prophet
Zarathustra that the cuttings of hair or nails should be buried
in a deep hole ten paces from a dwelling, twenty paces
from fire, and fifty paces from the sacred bundles called
baresmān. Texts should be said over them and the hole
filled in. Many Pārsis still bury their cut hair and nails
four inches under ground, and an extracted tooth is disposed
of in the same manner.² Some Hindus think that the nail-
parings should always be thrown into a frequented place,
where they will be destroyed by the traffic. If they are
thrown on to damp earth they will grow into a plant which
will ruin the person from whose body they came. It is
said that about twenty years ago a man in Nāgpur was
ruined by the growth of a piece of finger-nail, which
had accidentally dropped into a flower-pot in his house.
Apparently in this case the nail is supposed to contain
a portion of the life and strength of the person to whom it
belonged, and if the nail grows it gradually absorbs more
and more of his life and strength, and he consequently
becomes weaker and weaker through being deprived of it.
The Hindu superstition against shaving the head appears to
find a parallel regarding the nails in the old English saying:

> Cut no horn
> On the Sabbath morn.

Among some Hindus it is said that the toe-nails should not
be cut at all until a child is married, when they are cut
ceremoniously by the barber.

17. Superstitions about shaving the hair. Since the removal of the hair is held to involve a certain
loss of strength and power, it should only be effected at
certain seasons and not on auspicious days. A man who
has male children should not have his head shaved on
Monday, as this may cause his children to die. On the

---

¹ *Occult Review,* October 1909. *Gazetteer, Pārsis of Gujarāt,* p.
² *Orphéus,* p. 99, and *Bombay* 220.

other hand, a man who has no children will fast on Sunday in the hope of getting them, and therefore he will neither shave his head nor visit his wife on that day. A Hindu must not be shaved on Thursday, because this is the day of the planet Jupiter, which is also known as Guru, and his act would be disrespectful to his own *guru* or preceptor. Tuesday is Devi's day, and a man will not get shaved on that day ; nor on Saturday, because it is Hanumān's day.[1] On Sundays, Wednesdays and Fridays he may be shaved, but not if the day happens to be the new moon, full moon, or the Ashtami or Ekadashi, that is the eighth or eleventh day of the fortnight. He should not shave on the day that he is going on a journey. If all these rules were strictly observed there would be very few days on which one could get shaved but many of them are necessarily more honoured in the breach. Wednesdays and Fridays are the best days for shaving, and by shaving on these days a man will see old age. Debtors are shaved on Wednesdays, as they think that this will help them to pay off their debts. Some Brāhmans are not shaved during the month of Shrāwan (July), when the crops are growing, nor during the nine days of the months of Kunwār (September) and Chait (March), when a fast is observed and the *jawaras*[2] are sown. After they have been shaved high-caste Hindus consider themselves impure till they have bathed. They touch no person or thing in the house, and sometimes have the water thrown on them by a servant so as to avoid contact with the vessels. They will also neither eat, drink nor smoke until they have bathed. Sometimes they throw so much water over the head in order to purify themselves as to catch a bad cold. In this case, apparently, the impurity accrues from the loss of the hair, and the man feels that virtue has gone out of him. Women never shave their hair with a razor, as they think that to do so would make the body so heavy after death that it could not be carried to the place of cremation. They carefully pluck out the hair under the armpits and the pubic hair with a pair of pincers. A

---

[1] Hanumān is worshipped on this day in order to counteract the evil influence of the planet Saturn, whose day it really is.

[2] Pots in which wheat-stalks are sown and tended for nine days, corresponding to the Gardens of Adonis.

girl's hair may be cut with scissors, but not after she is ten years old or is married. Sometimes a girl's hair is not cut at all, but her father will take a pearl and entwine it into her hair, where it is left until she is married. It is considered very auspicious to give away a girl in marriage with hair which has never been cut, and a pearl in it. After marriage she will take out the pearl and wear it in an ornament.

18. Reasons why the hair was considered the source of strength.

The above evidence appears to indicate that the belief of a man's strength and vigour being contained in his hair is by no means confined to the legend of Samson, but is spread all over the world. This has been pointed out by Professor Robertson Smith,[1] Professor Wilken and others. Sir J. G. Frazer also adduces several instances in the *Golden Bough* to show that the life or soul was believed to be contained in the hair. This may well have been the case, but the hair was also specialised, so to speak, as the seat of bodily vigour and strength. The same idea appears to have applied in a minor measure to the nails and teeth. The rules for disposing of the cut hair usually apply to the parings of nails, and the first teeth are also deposited in a rat's hole or on the roof of the house. As suggested by Professor Robertson Smith it seems likely that the strength and vigour of the body was believed to be located in the hair, and also to a less extent in the nails and teeth, because they grew more visibly and quickly than the body and continued to do so after it had attained to maturity. The hair and nails continue to grow all through life, and though the teeth do not grow when fully formed, the second teeth appear when the body is considerably developed and the wisdom teeth after it is fully developed. The hair grows much more palpably and vigorously than the nails and teeth, and hence might be considered especially the source of strength. Other considerations which might confirm the idea are that men have more hair on their bodies than women, and strongly built men often have a large quantity of hair. Some of the stronger wild animals have long hair, as the lion, bear and wild boar; and the horse, often considered the embodiment of strength, has a

[1] *Religion of the Semites*, p. 324.

long mane. And when anger is excited the hair sometimes appears to rise, as it were, from the skin. The nails and teeth were formerly used on occasion as weapons of offence, and hence might be considered to contain part of the strength and vigour of the body.

Finally, it may be suggested as a possibility that the Roundheads cut their hair short as a protest against the superstition that a soldier's hair must be long, which originated in the idea that strength is located in the hair and may have still been current in their time. We know that the Puritans strove vainly against the veneration of the Maypole as the spirit of the new vegetation,[1] and against the old nature-rites observed at Christmas, the veneration of fire as the preserver of life against cold, and the veneration of the evergreen plants, the fir tree, the holly, and the mistletoe, which retained their foliage through the long night of the northern winter, and were thus a pledge to man of the return of warmth and the renewal of vegetation in the spring. And it therefore seems not altogether improbable that the Puritans may have similarly contended against the superstition as to the wearing of long hair.

Naoda.[2]—A small caste found in the Nimār District and in Central India. The name means a rower and is derived from *nao*, a boat. The caste are closely connected with the Mallāhs or Kewats, but have a slightly distinctive position, as they are employed to row pilgrims over the Nerbudda at the great fair held at Siva's temple on the island of Mandhāta. They say that their ancestors were Rājpūts, and some of their family names, as Solanki, Rāwat and Mori, are derived from those of Rājpūt septs. But these have probably been adopted in imitation of their Kshatriya overlords. The caste is an occupational one. They have a tradition that in former times a Naoda boatman recovered the corpse of a king's daughter, who had drowned

---

[1] *Golden Bough*, 2nd ed. vol. i. p. 203.
[2] In 1911 the Naodas numbered 700 persons in the Central Provinces. About 1000 were returned in Central India in 1891, but in 1901 they were amalgamated with the Mallāhs or Kewats. This article is based on a paper by Mr. P. R. Kaipitia, Forest Ranger.

herself in the river wearing costly jewels, and the king as a reward granted them the right of ferrying pilgrims at Mandhāta, which they still continue to enjoy, keeping their earnings for themselves. They have a division of impure blood called the Gāte or bastard Naodas, who marry among themselves, and any girl who reaches the age of puberty without being married is relegated to this. In the case of a caste whose numbers are so small, irregular connections with outsiders must probably be not infrequent. Another report states that adult unmarried girls are not expelled but are married to a pīpal tree. But girls are sought after, and it is customary to pay a bride-price, the average amount of which is Rs. 25. Before the bridegroom starts for his wedding his mother takes and passes in front of him, successively from his head to his feet, a pestle, some stalks of *rūsa* grass, a churning rod and a winnowing-fan. This is done with the object of keeping off evil spirits, and it is said that by her action she threatens to pound the spirits with the pestle, to tie them up with the grass, to churn and mash them with the churning-rod, and to scatter them to the winds with the winnowing-fan. When a man wishes to divorce his wife he simply turns her out of the house in the presence of four or five respectable men of the caste. The marriage of a widow is celebrated on a Sunday or Tuesday, the clothes of the couple being tied together by another widow at night. The following day they spend together in a garden, and in the evening are escorted home by their relatives with torches and music. Next morning the woman goes to the well and draws water, and her husband, accompanying her, helps her to lift the water-pots on to her shoulder.

The caste worship the ordinary Hindu deities and especially Bhairon, the guardian of the gate of Mahādeo's temple. They have a nail driven into the bow of their boat which is called 'Bhairon's nail,' and at the Dasahra festival they offer to this a white pumpkin with cocoanuts, vermilion, incense and liquor. The caste hold in special reverence the cow, the dog and the tamarind tree. The dog is sacred as being the animal on which Bhairava rides, and their most solemn oaths are sworn by a dog or a cow.

They will on no account cut or burn the tamarind tree, and the women veil their faces before it. They cannot explain this sentiment, which is probably due to some forgotten belief of the nature of totemism. To kill a cow or a cat intentionally involves permanent exclusion from the caste, while the slaughter of a squirrel, dog, horse, buffalo or monkey is punished by temporary exclusion, it being equally sinful to allow any of these animals to die with a rope round its neck. The Naodas eat the flesh of pigs and fowls, but they occupy a fairly good social position and Brāhmans will take water from their hands.

NAT

LIST OF PARAGRAPHS

1. *The Nats not a proper caste.*
2. *Muhammadan Nats.*
3. *Social customs of the Nats. Their low status.*
4. *Acrobatic performances.*
5. *Sliding or walking on ropes as a charm for the crops.*
6. *Snake-charmers.*

1. The Nats not a proper caste.

Nat,[1] Bādi, Dang-Charha, Karnati, Bāzigar, Sapera.—The term Nat (Sanskrit Nata—a dancer) appears to be applied indefinitely to a number of groups of vagrant acrobats and showmen, especially those who make it their business to do feats on the tight-rope or with poles, and those who train and exhibit snakes. Bādi and Bāzigar mean a rope-walker, Dang-Charha a rope-climber, and Sapera a snake-charmer. In the Central Provinces the Garūdis or snake-charmers, and the Kolhātis, a class of gipsy acrobats akin to the Berias, are also known as Nat, and these are treated in separate articles. It is almost certain that a considerable section, if not the majority, of the Nats really belong to the Kanjar or Beria gipsy castes, who themselves may be sprung from the Doms.[2] Sir D. Ibbetson says: "They wander about with their families, settling for a few days or weeks at a time in the vicinity of large villages or towns, and constructing temporary shelters of grass. In addition to practising acrobatic feats and conjuring of a low class, they make articles of grass, straw and reeds for sale; and in the centre of the Punjab are said to act as Mirāsis, though this is perhaps doubtful. They often practise surgery and physic in a small way and

---

[1] This article is partly compiled from notes furnished by Mr. Adurām Chaudhri and Mr. Jagannāth Prasad, Naib-Tahsīldārs. [2] See art. Kanjar.

are not free from suspicion of sorcery."[1] This account would just as well apply to the Kanjar gipsies, and the Nat women sometimes do tattooing like Kanjar or Beria women. In Jubbulpore also the caste is known as Nat Beria, indicating that the Nats there are probably derived from the Beria caste. Similarly Sir H. Risley gives Bāzigar and Kabūtari as groups of the Berias of Bengal, and states that these are closely akin to the Nats and Kanjars of Hindustān.[2] An old account of the Nats or Bāzigars[3] would equally well apply to the Kanjars; and in Mr. Crooke's detailed article on the Nats several connecting links are noticed. The Nat women are sometimes known as Kabūtari or pigeon, either because their acrobatic feats are like the flight of the tumbler pigeon, or on account of the flirting manner with which they attract their male customers.[4] In the Central Provinces the women of the small Gopāl caste of acrobats are called Kabūtari, and this further supports the hypothesis that Nat is rather an occupational term than the name of a distinct caste, though it is quite likely that there may be Nats who have no other caste. The Bādi or rope-dancer group again is an offshoot of the Gond tribe, at least in the tracts adjoining the Central Provinces. They have Gond septs as Marai, Netām, Wīka,[5] and they have the *damru* or drum used by the Gaurias or snake-charmers and jugglers of Chhattīsgarh, who are also derived from the Gonds. The Chhattīsgarhi Dang-Charhas are Gonds who say they formerly belonged to Panna State and were supported by Rāja Amān Singh of Panna, a great patron of their art. They sing a song lamenting his death in the flower of his youth. The Karnatis or Karnataks are a class of Nats who are supposed to have come from the Carnatic. Mr. Crooke notes that they will eat the leavings of all high castes, and are hence known as Khushhāliya or 'Those in prosperous circumstances.'[6]

One division of the Nats are Muhammadans and seem to

2. Muhammadan Nats.

[1] *Punjab Census Report* (1881), para. 588.

[2] *Tribes and Castes of Bengal*, art. Beria.

[3] *Asiatic Researches*, vol. vii., 1803, by Captain Richardson.

[4] *Tribes and Castes*, art. Nat.

[5] Crooke, *l.c.*, art. Nat.

[6] *Ibidem*.

be to some extent a distinctive group. They have seven *gotras*—Chicharia, Damaria, Dhalbalki, Pūrbia, Dhondabalki, Karimki and Kalasia. They worship two Birs or spirits, Halaila Bir and Sheikh Saddu, to whom they sacrifice fowls in the months of Bhādon (August) and Baisākh (April). Hindus of any caste are freely admitted into their community, and they can marry Hindu girls.

3. Social customs of the Nats. Their low status.

Generally the customs of the Nats show them to be the dregs of the population. There is no offence which entails permanent expulsion from caste. They will eat any kind of food including snakes, crocodiles and rats, and also take food from the hands of any caste, even it is said from sweepers. It is not reported that they prostitute their women, but there is little doubt that this is the case; in the Punjab[1] when a Nat woman marries, the first child is either given to the grandmother as compensation for the loss of the mother's gains as a prostitute, or is redeemed by a payment of Rs. 30. Among the Chhattīsgarhi Dang-Charhas a bride-price of Rs. 40 is paid, of which the girl's father only keeps ten, and the remaining sum of Rs. 30 is expended on a feast to the caste. Some of the Nats have taken to cultivation and become much more respectable, eschewing the flesh of unclean animals. Another group of the caste keep trained dogs and hunt the wild pig with spears like the Kolhātis of Berār. The villagers readily pay for their services in order to get the pig destroyed, and they sell the flesh to the Gonds and lower castes of Hindus. Others hunt jackals with dogs in the same manner. They eat the flesh of the jackals and dispose of any surplus to the Gonds, who also eat it. The Nats worship Devi and also Hanumān, the monkey god, on account of the acrobatic powers of monkeys. But in Bombay they say that their favourite and only living gods are their bread-winners and averters of hunger, the drum, the rope and the balancing-pole.[2]

4. Acrobatic performances.

The tight-rope is stretched between two pairs of bamboos, each pair being fixed obliquely in the ground and crossing each other at the top so as to form a socket over which the

---

[1] Ibbetson, *Punjab Census Report* (1886), para. 588.

[2] *Bombay Gazetteer*, vol. xx. p. 186, quoted in Mr. Crooke's article.

rope passes. The ends of the rope are taken over the crossed bamboos and firmly secured to the ground by heavy pegs. The performer takes another balancing-pole in his hands and walks along the rope between the poles which are about 12 feet high. Another man beats a drum, and a third stands under the rope singing the performer's praises and giving him encouragement. After this the performer ties two sets of cow or buffalo horns to his feet, which are secured to the back of the skulls so that the flat front between the horns rests on the rope, and with these he walks over the rope, holding the balancing-rod in his hands and descends again. Finally he takes a brass plate and a cloth and again ascends the rope. He places the plate on the rope and folds the cloth over it to make a pad. He then stands on his head on the pad with his feet in the air and holds the balancing-rod in his hands; two strings are tied to the end of this rod and the other ends of the strings are held by the man underneath. With the assistance of the balancing-rod the performer then jerks the plate along the rope with his head, his feet being in the air, until he arrives at the end and finally descends again. This usually concludes the performance, which demands a high degree of skill. Women occasionally, though rarely, do the same feats. Another class of Nats walk on high stilts and the women show their confidence by dancing and singing under them. A saying about the Nats is: *Nat ka bachcha to kalābazi hi karega*; or 'The rope-dancer's son is always turning somersaults.'[1]

5. Sliding or walking on ropes as a charm for the crops.

The feats of the Nats as tight-rope walkers used apparently to make a considerable impression on the minds of the people, as it is not uncommon to find a deified Nat, called Nat Bāba or Father Nat, as a village god. A Natni or Nat woman is also sometimes worshipped, and where two sharp peaks of hills are situated close to each other, it is related that in former times there was a Natni, very skilful on the tight-rope, who performed before the king; and he promised her that if she would stretch a rope from the peak of one hill to that of the other and walk across it he would marry her and make her wealthy. Accordingly the rope was stretched, but the queen from jealousy went and cut it

[1] Temple and Fallon's *Hindustāni Proverbs*, p. 171.

half through in the night, and when the Natni started to walk the rope broke and she fell down and was killed. She was therefore deified and worshipped. It is probable that this legend recalls some rite in which the Nat was employed to walk on a tight-rope for the benefit of the crops, and, if he failed, was killed as a sacrifice; for the following passage taken from Traill's account of Kumaon [1] seems clearly to refer to some such rite:

"Drought, want of fertility in the soil, murrain in cattle, and other calamities incident to husbandry are here invariably ascribed to the wrath of particular gods, to appease which recourse is had to various ceremonies. In the Kumaon District offerings and singing and dancing are resorted to on such occasions. In Garhwāl the measures pursued with the same view are of a peculiar nature, deserving of more particular notice. In villages dedicated to the protection of Mahādeva propitiatory festivals are held in his honour. At these Bādis or rope-dancers are engaged to perform on the tight-rope, and slide down an inclined rope stretched from the summit of a cliff to the valley beneath and made fast to posts driven into the ground. The Bādi sits astride on a wooden saddle, to which he is tied by thongs; the saddle is similarly secured to the *bast* or sliding cable, along which it runs, by means of a deep groove; sandbags are tied to the Bādi's feet sufficient to secure his balance, and he is then, after various ceremonies and the sacrifice of a kid, started off; the velocity of his descent is very great, and the saddle, however well greased, emits a volume of smoke throughout the greater part of his progress. The length and inclination of the *bast* necessarily vary with the nature of the cliff, but as the Bādi is remunerated at the rate of a rupee for every hundred cubits, hence termed a tola, a correct measurement always takes place; the longest *bast* which has fallen within my observation has been twenty-one tolas, or 2100 cubits in length. From the precautions taken as above mentioned the only danger to be apprehended by the Bādi is from breaking of the rope, to provide against which the latter, commonly from one and a half to two inches in diameter, is made wholly by his own hand; the material used is the

[1] *As. Res.* vol. xvi., 1828, p. 213.

bhābar grass. Formerly, if a Bādi fell to the ground in his course, he was immediately despatched with a sword by the surrounding spectators, but this practice is now, of course, prohibited. No fatal accident has occurred from the performance of this ceremony since 1815, though it is probably celebrated at not less than fifty villages in each year. After the completion of the sliding, the *bast* or rope is cut up and distributed among the inhabitants of the village, who hang the pieces as charms on the eaves of their houses. The hair of the Bādi is also taken and preserved as possessing similar virtues. He being thus made the organ to obtain fertility for the lands of others, the Bādi is supposed to entail sterility on his own; and it is firmly believed that no grain sown with his hand can ever vegetate. Each District has its hereditary Bādi, who is supported by annual contributions of grain from the inhabitants." It is not improbable that the performance of the Nat is a reminiscence of a period when human victims were sacrificed for the crops, this being a common practice among primitive peoples, as shown by Sir J. G. Frazer in *Attis, Adonis, Osiris*. Similarly the spirits of Nats which are revered in the Central Provinces may really be those of victims killed during the performance of some charm for the good of the crops, akin to that still prevalent in the Himalayas. The custom of making the Nat slide down a rope is of the same character as that of swinging a man in the air by a hook secured in his flesh, which was formerly common in these Provinces. But in both cases the meaning of the rite is obscure.

6. Snake-charmers. The groups who practise snake-charming are known as Sapera or Garūdi and in the Marātha Districts as Madāri. Another name for them is Nāg-Nathi, or one who seizes a cobra. They keep cobras, pythons, scorpions, and the iguana or large lizard, which they consider to be poisonous. Some of them when engaged with their snakes wear two pieces of tiger-skin on their back and chest, and a cap of tiger-skin in which they fix the eyes of various birds. They have a hollow gourd on which they produce a kind of music and this is supposed to charm the snakes. When catching a cobra they pin its head to the ground with a stick and then seize it in a cleft bamboo and prick out the poison-

fangs with a large needle. They think that the teeth of the iguana are also poisonous and they knock them out with a stick, and if fresh teeth afterwards grow they believe them not to contain poison. The python is called Ajgar, which is said to mean eater of goats. In captivity the pythons will not eat of themselves, and the snake-charmers chop up pieces of meat and fowls and placing the food in the reptile's mouth massage it down the body. They feed the pythons only once in four or five days. They have antidotes for snake-bite, the root of a creeper called *kalipār* and the bark of the *karheya* tree. When a patient is brought to them they give him a little pepper, and if he tastes the pungent flavour they think that he has not been affected by snake-poison, but if it seems tasteless that he has been bitten. Then they give him small pieces of the two antidotes already mentioned with tobacco and $2\frac{1}{2}$ leaves of the *nīm* tree [1] which is sacred to Devi. On the festival of Nāg-Panchmi (Cobra's Fifth) they worship their cobras and give them milk to drink and then take them round the town or village and the people also worship and feed the snakes and give a present of a few annas to the Sapera. In towns much frequented by cobras, a special adoration is paid to them. Thus in Hatta in the Damoh District a stone image of a snake, known as Nāg-Bāba or Father Cobra is worshipped for a month before the festival of Nāg-Panchmi. During this period one man from every house in the village must go to Nāg-Bāba's shrine outside and take food there and come back. And on Nāg-Panchmi the whole town goes out in a body to pay him reverence, and it is thought that if any one is absent the cobras will harass him for the whole year. But others say that cobras will only bite men of low caste. The Saperas will not kill a snake as a rule, but occasionally it is said that they kill one and cut off the head and eat the body, this being possibly an instance of eating the divine animal at a sacrificial meal. The following is an old account of the performances of snake-charmers in Bengal : [2]

"Hence, on many occasions throughout the year, the

---

[1] *Melia indica*.
[2] *Bengali Festivals and Holidays*, by the Rev. Bihāri Lāl De, *Calcutta Review*, vol. v. pp. 59, 60.

SNAKE-CHARMER WITH COBRAS.

dread Manasa Devi, the queen of snakes, is propitiated by presents, vows and religious rites. In the month of Shrābana the worship of the snake goddess is celebrated with great éclat. An image of the goddess, seated on a water-lily, encircled with serpents, or a branch of the snake-tree (a species of Euphorbia), or a pot of water, with images of serpents made of clay, forms the object of worship. Men, women and children, all offer presents to avert from themselves the wrath of the terrific deity. The Māls or snake-catchers signalise themselves on this occasion. Temporary scaffolds of bamboo work are set up in the presence of the goddess. Vessels filled with all sorts of snakes are brought in. The Māls, often reeling with intoxication, mount the scaffolds, take out serpents from the vessels, and allow them to bite their arms. Bite after bite succeeds; the arms run with blood; and the Māls go on with their pranks, amid the deafening plaudits of the spectators. Now and then they fall off from the scaffold and pretend to feel the effects of poison, and cure themselves by their incantations. But all is mere pretence. The serpents displayed on the occasion and challenged to do their worst, have passed through a preparatory state. Their fangs have been carefully extracted from their jaws. But most of the vulgar spectators easily persuade themselves to believe that the Māls are the chosen servants of Siva and the favourites of Manasa. Although their supernatural pretensions are ridiculous, yet it must be confessed that the Māls have made snakes the subject of their peculiar study. They are thoroughly acquainted with their qualities, their dispositions, and their habits. They will run down a snake into its hole, and bring it out thence by main force. Even the terrible cobra is cowed down by the controlling influence of a Māl. When in the act of bringing out snakes from their subterranean holes, the Māls are in the habit of muttering charms, in which the names of Manasa and Mahādeva frequently occur; superstition alone can clothe these unmeaning words with supernatural potency. But it is not inconsistent with the soundest philosophy to suppose that there may be some plants whose roots are disagreeable to serpents, and from which they instinctively turn away. All snake-catchers of Bengal are provided with a bundle of the roots of some plant which they carefully carry along with them, when they set out on their serpent-hunting expeditions. When a serpent, disturbed in its hole, comes out furiously hissing with rage, with its body coiled, and its head lifted up, the Māl has only to present before it the bundle of roots above alluded to, at the sight of which it becomes spiritless as an eel. This we have ourselves witnessed more than once."

These Māls appear to have been members of the aboriginal Māle or Māle Pahāria tribe of Bengal.

Nunia, Lunia.[1]—A mixed occupational caste of salt-makers and earth-workers, made up of recruits from the different non-Aryan tribes of northern India. The word *non* means salt, and is a corruption of the Sanskrit *lavana*, 'the moist,' which first occurs as a name for sea-salt in the Atharva Veda.[2] In the oldest prose writings salt is known as Saindhava or 'that which is brought from the Indus,' this perhaps being Punjab rock-salt. The Nunias are a fairly large caste in Bengal and northern India, numbering 800,000 persons, but the Central Provinces and Berār contain only 3000, who are immigrants from Upper India. Here they are navvies and masons, a calling which they have generally adopted since the Government monopoly has interfered with their proper business of salt-refining. The mixed origin of the caste is shown by the list of their subdivisions in the United Provinces, which includes the names Mallāh, Kewat, Kūchbandhia, Bind, Musahār, Bhuinhār and Lodha, all of which are distinct castes, besides a number of territorial subcastes. A list of nearly thirty subcastes is given by Mr. Crooke, and this is an instance of the tendency of migratory castes to split up into small groups for the purpose of arranging marriages, owing to the difficulty of ascertaining the status and respectability of each other's families, and the unwillingness to contract alliances with those whose social position may turn out to be not wholly satisfactory. "The internal structure of the caste," Mr. Crooke remarks, "is far from clear; it would appear that

---

[1] Based on papers by Munshi Kanhya Lāl of the Gazetteer Office, and Mr. Mīr Patcha, Tahsīldār, Bilāspur.

[2] Mr. Crooke's *Tribes and Castes*, art. Lunia.

they are still in a state of transition, and the different endogamous subcastes are not as yet fully recognised." In Bilāspur the Nunias have three local subcastes, the Bandhaiya, the Ratanpuria and the Kharodhia. The two last, deriving their names from the towns of Ratanpur and Kharod in Bilāspur, are said to have been employed in former times in the construction of the temples and other buildings which abound in these localities, and have thus acquired a considerable degree of professional skill in masonry work; while the Bandhaiya, who take their name from Bāndhogarh, confine themselves to the excavation of tanks and wells. The exogamous divisions of the caste are also by no means clearly defined; in Mīrzāpur they have a system of local subdivisions called *dīh*, each subdivision being named after the village which is supposed to be its home. The word *dīh* itself means a site or village. Those who have a common *dīh* do not intermarry.[1] This fact is interesting as being an instance of the direct derivation of the exogamous clan from residence in a parent village and not from any heroic or supposititious ancestor.

The caste have a legend which shows their mixed origin. Some centuries ago, they say, a marriage procession consisting of Brāhmans, Rājpūts, Banias and Gosains went to a place near Ajodhya. After the ceremony was over the bride, on being taken to the bridegroom's lodging, scraped up a little earth with her fingers and put it in her mouth. She found it had a saltish taste, and spat it out on the ground, and this enraged the tutelary goddess of the village, who considered herself insulted, and swore that all the bride's descendants should excavate salt in atonement; and thus the caste arose.

In Bilāspur the caste permit a girl to be married to a boy younger than herself. A price of five rupees has to be paid for the bride, unless her family give a girl in exchange. The bridegroom is taken to the wedding in a palanquin borne by Mahārs. After its conclusion the couple are carried back in the litter for some distance, after which the bridegroom gets out and walks or rides. When he goes to fetch his wife on her coming of age the bridegroom wears

[1] Mr. Crooke's *Tribes and Castes*, art. Lunia.

white clothes, which is rather peculiar, as white is not a lucky colour among the Hindus. The Nunias employ Brāhmans at their ceremonies, and they have a caste *panchāyat* or committee, whose headman is known as Kurha. The Bilāspur section of the caste has two Kurhas. Here Brāhmans take water from them, but not in all places. They consider their traditional occupation to have been the extraction of salt and saltpetre from saline earth. At present they are generally employed in the excavation of tanks and the embankment of fields, and they also sink wells, build and erect houses, and undertake all kinds of agricultural labour.

Ojha.—The community of soothsayers and minstrels of the Gonds. The Ojhas may now be considered a distinct subtribe, as they are looked down upon by the Gonds and marry among themselves. They derive their name from the word *ojh*, meaning 'entrail,' their original duty having been, like that of the Roman augurs, to examine the entrails of the victim immediately after it had been slain as an offering to the gods. In 1911 the Ojhas numbered about 5000 persons distributed over all Districts of the Central Provinces. At present the bulk of the community subsist by beggary. The word Ojha is of Sanskrit and not of Gond origin and is applied by the Hindus to the seers or magicians of several of the primitive tribes, while there is also a class of Ojha Brāhmans who practise magic and divination. The Gond Ojhas, who are the subject of this article, originally served the Gonds and begged from them alone, but in some parts of the western Satpūras they are also the minstrels of the Korkus. Those who beg from the Korkus play on a kind of drum called *dhānk*, while the Gond Ojhas use the *kingri* or lyre. Some of them also catch birds and are therefore known as Moghia. Mr. Hislop[1] remarks of them: "The Ojhas follow the two occupations of bard and fowler. They lead a wandering life and when passing through villages they sing from house to house the praises of their heroes, dancing with castanets in their hands, bells at their ankles and long feathers of jungle birds in their turbans. They sell live

---

[1] *Papers relating to the Aboriginal Tribes of the C.P.*, p. 6.

quails and the skins of a species of Buceros named Dhanchīria; these are used for making caps and for hanging up in houses in order to secure wealth (*dhan*), while the thighbones of the same bird when fastened round the waists of children are deemed an infallible preservative against the assaults of devils and other such calamities. Their wives tattoo the arms of Hindu and Gond women. Among them there is a subdivision known as the Māna Ojhas, who rank higher than the others. Laying claim to unusual sanctity, they refuse to eat with any one, Gonds, Rājpūts or even Brāhmans, and devote themselves to the manufacture of rings and bells which are in request among their own race, and even of *lingas* (phallic emblems) and *nandis* (bull images), which they sell to all ranks of the Hindu community. Their wives are distinguished by wearing the cloth of the upper part of the body over the right shoulder, whereas those of the common Ojhas and of all the other Gonds wear it over the left."

Mr. Tawney wrote of the Ojhas as follows:[1] "The Ojha women do not dance. It is only men who do so, and when thus engaged they put on special attire and wear anklets with bells. The Ojhas like the Gonds are divided into six or seven god *gots* (classes or septs), and those with the same number of gods cannot intermarry. They worship at the same Deokhala (god's threshing-floor) as the Gonds, but being regarded as an inferior caste they are not allowed so near the sacred presence. Like the Gonds they incorporate the spirits of the dead with the gods, but their manner of doing so is somewhat different, as they make an image of brass to represent the soul of the deceased and keep this with the household gods. As with the Gonds, if a household god makes himself too objectionable he is quietly buried to keep him out of mischief and a new god is introduced into the family. The latter should properly bear the same name as his degraded predecessor, but very often does not. The Ojhas are too poor to indulge in the luxury of burning their deceased friends and therefore invariably bury them."

The customs of the Ojhas resemble those of the Gonds.

---

[1] Note by Mr. Tawney as Deputy Commissioner of Chhindwāra, quoted in *Central Provinces Census Report* of 1881 (Mr. Drysdale).

They take the bride to the bridegroom's house to be married, and a widow among them is expected, though not obliged, to wed her late husband's younger brother. They eat the flesh of fowls, pigs, and even oxen, but abstain from that of monkeys, crocodiles and jackals. They will not touch an ass, a cat or a dog, and consider it sinful to kill animals which bark or bray.

They will take food from the hands of all except the most impure castes, and will admit into the community any man who has taken an Ojha woman to live with him, even though he be a sweeper, provided that he will submit to the prescribed test of begging from the houses of five Gonds and eating the leavings of food of the other Ojhas. They will pardon the transgression of one of their women with an outsider of any caste whatever, if she is able and willing to provide the usual penalty feast. They have no *sūtak* or period of impurity after a death, but merely take a mouthful of liquor and consider themselves clean. In physical appearance the Ojhas resemble the Gonds but are less robust. They rank below the Gonds and are considered as impure by the Hindu castes. In 1865, an Ojha held a village in Hoshangābād District which he had obtained as follows:[1] "He was singing and dancing before Rāja Rāghuji, when the Rāja said he would give a rent-free village to any one who would pick up and chew a quid of betel-leaf which he (the Rāja) had had in his mouth and had spat out. The Ojha did this and got the village."

The Maithil or Tirhūt Brāhmans who are especially learned in Tāntric magic are also sometimes known as Ojha, and a family bearing this title were formerly in the service of the Gond kings of Mandla. They do not now admit that they acted as augurs or soothsayers, but state that their business was to pray continuously for the king's success when he was engaged in any battle, and to sit outside the rooms of sick persons repeating the sacred Gāyatri verse for their recovery. This is often repeated ten times, counting by a special method on the joints of the fingers and is then known as *Jap*. When it is repeated a larger number of times, as 54 or 108, a rosary is used.

[1] Sir C. A. Elliott's *Hoshangābād Settlement Report*, p. 70.

ORAON

[*Authorities*: The most complete account of the Oraons is a monograph entitled, *The Religion and Customs of the Oraons*, by the late Rev. Father P. Dehon, published in 1906 in the *Memoirs of the Asiatic Society of Bengal*, vol. i. No. 9. The tribe is also described at length by Colonel Dalton in *The Ethnography of Bengal*, and an article on it is included in Mr. (Sir H.) Risley's *Tribes and Castes of Bengal*. References to the Oraons are contained in Mr. Bradley Birt's *Chota Nāgpur*, and Mr. Ball's *Jungle Life in India*. The Kurukh language is treated by Dr. Grierson in the volume of the Linguistic Survey on *Munda and Dravidian Languages*. The following article is principally made up of extracts from the accounts of Father Dehon and Colonel Dalton. Papers have also been received from Mr. Hīra Lāl, Mr. Balārām Nand, Deputy Inspector of Schools, Sambalpur, Mr. Jeorākhan Lāl, Deputy Inspector of Schools, Bilāspur, and Munshi Kanhya Lāl of the Gazetteer Office.]

LIST OF PARAGRAPHS

1. *General notice.*
2. *Settlement in Chota Nāgpur.*
3. *Subdivisions.*
4. *Pre-nuptial licence.*
5. *Betrothal.*
6. *Marriage ceremony.*
7. *Special customs.*
8. *Widow-remarriage and divorce.*
9. *Customs at birth.*
10. *Naming a child.*
11. *Branding and tattooing.*
12. *Dormitory discipline.*
13. *Disposal of the dead.*
14. *Worship of ancestors.*
15. *Religion. The supreme deity.*
16. *Minor godlings.*
17. *Human sacrifice.*
18. *Christianity.*
19. *Festivals. The Karma or May-day.*
20. *The Sāl flower festival.*
21. *The harvest festival.*
22. *Fast for the crops.*
23. *Physical appearance and costume of the Oraons.*
24. *Dress of women.*
25. *Dances.*
26. *Social customs.*
27. *Social rules.*
28. *Character.*
29. *Language.*

Oraon, Uraon, Kurukh, Dhangar, Kūda, Kisān.— 1. General notice. The Oraons are an important Dravidian tribe of the Chota Nāgpur plateau, numbering altogether about 750,000 persons, of whom 85,000 now belong to the Central Provinces, being residents of the Jashpur and Sargūja States and the neighbouring tracts. They are commonly known in the Central Provinces as Dhāngar or Dhāngar-Oraon. In Chota Nāgpur the word Dhāngar means a farmservant engaged according to a special customary contract, and it has come to be applied to the Oraons, who are commonly employed in this capacity. Kūda means a digger or navvy in Uriya, and enquiries made by Mr. B. C. Mazumdar and Mr. Hīra Lāl have demonstrated that the 18,000 persons returned under this designation from Raigarh and Sambalpur in 1901 were really Oraons. The same remark applies to 33,000 persons returned from Sambalpur as Kisān or cultivator, these also being members of the tribe. The name by which the Oraons know themselves is Kurukh or Kurunkh, and the designation of Oraon or Orao has been applied to them by outsiders. The meaning of both names is obscure. Dr. Halm[1] was of opinion that the word *kurukh* might be identified with the Kolarian *horo*, man, and explained the term Oraon as the totem of one of the septs into which the Kurukhs were divided. According to him Oraon was a name coined by the Hindus, its base being *orgorān*, hawk or cunny bird, used as the name of a totemistic sept. Sir G. Grierson, however, suggested a connection with the Kaikāri, *urūpai*, man ; Burgandi *urāpo*, man ; *urāng*, men. The Kaikāris are a Telugu caste, and as the Oraons are believed to have come from the south of India, this derivation sounds plausible. In a similar way Sir. G. Grierson states, Kurukh may be connected with Tamil *kurūgu*, an eagle, and be the name of a totemistic clan. Compare also names, such as Korava, Kurru, a dialect of Tamil, and Kudāgu. In the Nerbudda valley the farmservant who pours the seed through the tube of the sowing-plough is known as Oraya ; this word is probably derived from the verb *ūrna* to pour, and means 'one who pours.' Since the principal characteristic of the Oraons among the Hindus is their universal employment as farmservants and labourers, it may be suggested that the name is derived from this term. Of the other names by which they are known to outsiders Dhāngar means a farmservant, Kūda a digger, and Kisān a cultivator. The name Oraon and its variant Orao is very close to Oraya, which, as already seen, means a farmservant. The nasal seems to

---

[1] *Linguistic Survey*, vol. iv. p. 406.

be often added or omitted in this part of the country, as Kurukh or Kurunkh.

2. Settlement in Chota Nāgpur.

According to their own traditions, Mr. Gait writes,[1] "The Kurukh tribe originally lived in the Carnatic, whence they went up the Nerbudda river and settled in Bihār on the banks of the Son. Driven out by the Muhammadans, the tribe split into two divisions, one of which followed the course of the Ganges and finally settled in the Rājmahāl hills: while the other went up the Son and occupied the north-western portion of the Chota Nāgpur plateau, where many of the villages they occupy are still known by Mundāri names. The latter were the ancestors of the Oraons or Kurukhs, while the former were the progenitors of the Māle or Saonria as they often call themselves." Towards Lohardaga the Oraons found themselves among the Mundas or Kols, who probably retired by degrees and left them in possession of the country. "The Oraons," Father Dehon states, "are an exceedingly prolific tribe and soon become the preponderant element, while the Mundas, being conservative and averse to living among strangers, emigrate towards another jungle. The Mundas hate zamīndārs, and whenever they can do so, prefer to live in a retired corner in full possession of their small holding; and it is not at all improbable that, as the zamīndārs took possession of the newly-formed villages, they retired towards the east, while the Oraons, being good beasts of burden and more accustomed to subjection, remained." In view of the fine physique and martial character of the Larka or Fighting Kols or Mundas, Dalton was sceptical of the theory that they could ever have retired before the Oraons; but in addition to the fact that many villages in which Oraons now live have Mundāri names, it may be noted that the headman of an Oraon village is termed Munda and is considered to be descended from its founder, while for the Pāhan or priest of the village gods, the Oraons always employ a Munda if available, and it is one of the Pāhan's duties to point out the boundary of the village in cases of dispute; this is a function regularly assigned to the earliest residents, and seems to be strong evidence that

[1] *Bengal Census Report* (1901).

the Oraons found the Mundas settled in Chota Nāgpur when they arrived there. It is not necessary to suppose that any conquest or forcible expropriation took place; and it is probable that, as the country was opened up, the Mundas by preference retired to the wilder forest tracts, just as in the Central Provinces the Korkus and Baigas gave way to the Gonds, and the Gonds themselves relinquished the open country to the Hindus. None of the writers quoted notice the name Munda as applied to the headman of an Oraon village, but it can hardly be doubted that it is connected with that of the tribe; and it would be interesting also to know whether the Pāhan or village priest takes his name from the Pāns or Gandas. Dalton says that the Pāns are domesticated as essential constituents of every Ho or Kol village community, but does not allude to their presence among the Oraons. The custom in the Central Provinces, by which in Gond villages the village priest is always known as Baiga, because in some localities members of the Baiga tribe are commonly employed in the office, suggests the hypothesis of a similar usage here. In villages first settled by Oraons, the population, Father Dehon states, is divided into three *khūnts* or branches, named after the Munda, Pāhan and Mahto, the founders of the three branches being held to have been sons of the first settler. Members of each branch belong therefore to the same sept or *got*. Each *khūnt* has a share of the village lands.

3. Subdivisions. The Oraons have no proper subcastes in the Central Provinces, but the Kudas and Kisāns, having a distinctive name and occupation, sometimes regard themselves as separate bodies and decline intermarriage with other Oraons. In Bengal Sir H. Risley gives five divisions, Barga, Dhānka, Kharia, Khendro and Munda; of these Kharia and Munda are the names of other tribes, and Dhānka may be a variant for Dhāngar. The names show that as usual with the tribes of this part of the country the law of endogamy is by no means strict. The tribe have also a large number of exogamous septs of the totemistic type, named after plants and animals. Members of any sept commonly abstain from killing or eating their sept totem. A man must not marry a member of his own sept nor a first cousin on the mother's side.

Marriage is adult and pre-nuptial unchastity appears to be tacitly recognised. Oraon villages have the institution of the Dhūmkuria or Bachelors' dormitory, which Dalton describes as follows:[1] "In all the older Oraon villages when there is any conservation of ancient customs, there is a house called the Dhūmkuria in which all the bachelors of the village must sleep under penalty of a fine. The huts of the Oraons have insufficient accommodation for a family, so that separate quarters for the young men are a necessity. The same remark applies to the young unmarried women, and it is a fact that they do not sleep in the house with their parents. They are generally frank enough when questioned about their habits, but on this subject there is always a certain amount of reticence, and I have seen girls quietly withdraw when it was mooted. I am told that in some villages a separate building is provided for them like the Dhūmkuria, in which they consort under the guardianship of an elderly duenna, but I believe the more common practice is to distribute them among the houses of the widows, and this is what the girls themselves assert, if they answer at all when the question is asked; but however billeted, it is well known that they often find their way to the bachelors' hall, and in some villages actually sleep there. I not long ago saw a Dhūmkuria in a Sargūja village in which the boys and girls all slept every night." Colonel Dalton considered it uncertain that the practice led to actual immorality, but the fact can hardly be doubted. Sexual intercourse before marriage, Sir H. Risley says, is tacitly recognised, and is so generally practised that in the opinion of the best observers no Oraon girl is a virgin at the time of her marriage. "To call this state of things immoral is to apply a modern conception to primitive habits of life. Within the tribe, indeed, the idea of sexual morality seems hardly to exist, and the unmarried Oraons are not far removed from the condition of modified promiscuity which prevails among many of the Australian tribes. Provided that the exogamous circle defined by the totem is respected, an unmarried woman may bestow her favours on whom she will. If, however, she becomes pregnant, arrangements are made to get her married without delay,

4. Pre-nuptial licence.

[1] *Ethnography*, p. 248.

and she is then expected to lead a virtuous life."[1] According to Dalton, however, *liaisons* between boys and girls of the same village seldom end in marriage, as it is considered more respectable to bring home a bride from a distance. This appears to arise from the primitive rule of exogamy that marriage should not be allowed between those who have been brought up together. The young men can choose for themselves, and at dances, festivals and other social gatherings they freely woo their sweethearts, giving them flowers for the hair and presents of grilled field-mice, which the Oraons consider to be the most delicate of food. Father Dehon, however, states that matches are arranged by the parents, and the bride and bridegroom have nothing to say in the matter. Boys are usually married at sixteen and girls at fourteen or fifteen. The girls thus have only about two years of preliminary flirtation or Dhūmkuria life before they are settled.

5. Betrothal.

The first ceremony for a marriage is known as *pān bandhi* or the settling of the price; for which the boy's father, accompanied by some men of his village to represent the *panch* or elders, goes to the girl's house. Father Dehon states that the bride-price is five rupees and four maunds of grain. When this has been settled the rejoicings begin. "All the people of the village are invited; two boys come and anoint the visitors with oil. From every house of the village that can afford it a *handia* or pot of rice-beer is brought, and they drink together and make merry. All this time the girl has been kept inside, but now she suddenly sallies forth carrying a *handia* on her head. A murmur of admiration greets her when stepping through the crowd she comes and stands in front of her future father-in-law, who at once takes the *handia* from her head, embraces her, and gives her one rupee. From that time during the whole of the feast the girl remains sitting at the feet of her father-in-law. The whole party meanwhile continue drinking and talking; and voices rise so high that they cannot hear one another. As a diversion the old women of the village all come tumbling in, very drunk and wearing fantastic hats made of leaves, gesticulating like devils and carrying a straw manikin representing the

[1] *Tribes and Castes*, vol. ii. p. 141.

bridegroom. They all look like old witches, and in their drunken state are very mischievous."

The marriage takes place after about two years, visits being exchanged twice a year in the meantime. When the day comes the bridegroom proceeds with a large party of his friends, male and female, to the bride's house. Most of the males have warlike weapons, real or sham, and as they approach the village of the bride's family the young men from thence emerge, also armed, as if to repel the invasion, and a mimic fight ensues, which like a dissolving view blends pleasantly into a dance. In this the bride and bridegroom join, each riding on the hips of one of their friends. After this they have a feast till late in the night. Next morning bread cooked by the bride's mother is taken to the *dari* or village spring, where all the women partake of it. When they have finished they bring a vessel of water with some leaves of the mango tree in it. Meanwhile the bride and bridegroom are in the house, being anointed with oil and turmeric by their respective sisters. When everybody has gathered under the marriage-bower the boy and girl are brought out of the house and a heap is made of a plough-yoke, a bundle of thatching-grass and a curry-stone. The bride and bridegroom are made to stand on the curry-stone, the boy touching the heels of the bride with his toes, and a long piece of cloth is put round them to screen them from the public. Only their heads and feet can be seen. A goblet full of vermilion is presented to the boy, who dips his finger in it and makes three lines on the forehead of the girl; and the girl does the same to the boy, but as she has to reach him over her shoulder and cannot see him, the boy gets it anywhere on his face, which never fails to provoke hearty bursts of laughter. "When this is complete," Dalton states, "a gun is fired and then by some arrangement vessels full of water, placed over the bower, are upset, and the young couple and those near them receive a drenching shower-bath, the women shouting, 'The marriage is done, the marriage is done.' They now retire into an apartment prepared for them, ostensibly to change their clothes, but they do not emerge for some time, and when they do appear they are saluted as man and wife."

6. Marriage ceremony.

7. Special customs.

Meanwhile the guests sit round drinking *handias* or earthen pots full of rice-beer. The bride and bridegroom come out and retire a second time and are called out for the following rite. A vessel of beer is brought and the bride carries a cupful of it to the bridegroom's brother, but instead of giving it into his hand she deposits it on the ground in front of him. This is to seal a kind of tacit agreement that from that time the bridegroom's brother will not touch his sister-in-law, and was probably instituted to mark the abolition of the former system of fraternal polyandry, customs of an analogous nature being found among the Khonds and Korkus. "Then," Father Dehon continues, "comes the last ceremony, which is called *khirītengna handia* or the *handia* of the story, and is considered by the Oraons to be the true form of marriage which has been handed down to them by their forefathers. The boy and girl sit together before the people, and one of the elder men present rises and addressing the boy says: 'If your wife goes to fetch *sāg* and falls from a tree and breaks her leg, do not say that she is disfigured or crippled. You will have to keep and feed her.' Then turning to the girl: 'When your husband goes hunting, if his arm or leg is broken, do not say, "He is a cripple, I won't live with him." Do not say that, for you have to remain with him. If you prepare meat, give two shares to him and keep only one for yourself. If you prepare vegetables, give him two parts and keep only one part for yourself. If he gets sick and cannot go out, do not say that he is dirty, but clean his mat and wash him.' A feast follows, and at night the girl is brought to the boy by her mother, who says to him, 'Now this my child is yours; I do not give her for a few days but for ever; take care of her and love her well.' A companion of the bridegroom's then seizes the girl in his arms and carries her inside the house."

8. Widow-remarriage and divorce.

It is uncommon for a man to have two wives. Divorce is permitted, and is usually effected by the boy or girl running away to the Duārs or Assam. Widow-remarriage is a regular practice. The first time a widow marries again, Father Dehon states, the bridegroom must pay Rs. 3-8 for her; if successive husbands die her price goes down by a rupee on each fresh marriage, so that a fifth husband would pay only eight annas. Cases of adultery are comparatively rare. When offenders are caught a heavy fine is imposed if they are well-to-do, and if they are not, a smaller fine and a beating.

"The Oraons," Father Dehon continues, "are a very prolific race, and whenever they are allowed to live without being too much oppressed they increase prodigiously. What strikes you when you come to an Oraon village is the number of small dirty children playing everywhere, while you can scarcely meet a woman that does not carry a baby on her back. The women seem, to a great extent, to have been exempted from the curse of our first mother: 'Thou shalt bring forth, etc.' They seem to give birth to their children with the greatest ease. There is no period of uncleanness, and the very day after giving birth to a child, you will see the mother with her baby tied up in a cloth on her back and a pitcher on her head going, as if nothing had happened, to the village spring." This practice, it may be remarked in parenthesis, may arise from the former observance of the Couvade, the peculiar custom prevailing among several primitive races, by which, when a child is born, the father lies in the house and pretends to be ill, while the mother gets up immediately and goes about her work. The custom has been reported as existing among the Oraons by one observer from Bilāspur,[1] but so far without confirmation.

"A child is named eight or ten days after birth, and on this day some men of the village and the members of the family assemble at the parents' house. Two leaf-cups are brought, one full of water and the other of rice. After a preliminary formula grains of rice are let fall into the cup, first in the name of the child and then successively in those of his ancestors in the following order: paternal grandfather, paternal great-grandfather, father, paternal uncle, maternal grandfather, other relatives. When the grain dropped in the name of any relative meets the first one dropped to represent the child, he is given the name of that relative and is probably considered to be a reincarnation of him."

[1] Panna Lāl, Revenue Inspector.

11. Branding and tattooing.

"When a boy is six or seven years old it is time for him to become a member of the Dhūmkuria or common dormitory. The eldest boys catch hold of his left arm and, with burning cloth, burn out five deep marks on the lower part of his arm. This is done so that he may be recognised as an Oraon at his death when he goes into the other world." The ceremony was probably the initiation to manhood on arrival at puberty, and resembled those prevalent among the Australian tribes. With this exception men are not tattooed, but this decoration is profusely resorted to by women. They have three parallel vertical lines on the forehead which form a distinctive mark, and other patterns on the arms, chest, knees and ankles. These usually consist of lines vertical and horizontal as shown below:

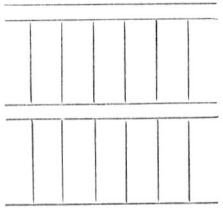

The marks on the knees are considered to be steps by which the wearer will ascend to heaven after her death. If a baby cries much it is also tattooed on the nose and chin.

12. Dormitory discipline.

The Dhūmkuria fraternity, Colonel Dalton remarks, are, under the severest penalties, bound down to secrecy in regard to all that takes place in their dormitory; and even girls are punished if they dare to tell tales. They are not allowed to join in the dances till the offence is condoned. They have a regular system of fagging in this curious institution. The small boys serve those of larger growth, shampoo their limbs, comb their hair, and so on, and they are sometimes subjected to severe discipline to make men of them.

13. Disposal of the dead.

The Oraons either bury or burn the dead. As the corpse is carried to the grave, beginning from the first cross-roads, they sprinkle a line of rice as far as the grave or pyre.

This is done so that the soul of the deceased may find its way back to the house. Before the burial or cremation cooked food and some small pieces of money are placed in the mouth of the corpse. They are subsequently, however, removed or recovered from the ashes and taken by the musicians as their fee. Some clothes belonging to the deceased and a vessel with some rice are either burnt with the corpse or placed in the grave. As the grave is being filled in they place a stalk of *orai*[1] grass vertically on the head of the corpse and gradually draw it upwards as the earth is piled on the grave. They say that this is done in order to leave a passage for the air to pass to the nostrils of the deceased. This is the grass from which reed pens are made, and the stalk is hard and hollow. Afterwards they plant a root of the same grass where the stalk is standing over the head of the corpse. On the tenth day they sacrifice a pig and fowl and bury the legs, tail, ears and nose of the pig in a hole with seven balls of iron dross. They then proceed to the grave scattering a little parched rice all the way along the path. Cooked rice is offered at the grave. If the corpse has been burnt they pick up the bones and place them in a pot, which is brought home and hung up behind the dead man's house. At night-time a relative sits inside the house watching a burning lamp, while some friends go outside the village and make a miniature hut with sticks and grass and set fire to it. They then call out to the dead man, 'Come, your house is being burnt,' and walk home striking a mattock and sickle together. On coming to the house they kick down the matting which covers the doorway; the man inside says, 'Who are you?' and they answer, 'It is we.' They watch the lamp and when the flame wavers they believe it to show that the spirit of the deceased has followed them and has also entered the house. Next day the bones are thrown into a river and the earthen pot broken against a stone.

14. Worship of ancestors.

The *pitras* or ancestors are worshipped at every festival, and when the new rice is reaped a hen is offered to them. They pray to their dead parents to accept the offering and then place a few grains of rice before the hen. If she eats them, it is a sign that the ancestors have accepted

[1] *Sorghum halepense.*

the offering and a man kills the hen by crushing its head with his closed fist. This is probably, as remarked by Father Dehon, in recollection of the method employed before the introduction of knives, and the same explanation may be given of the barbaric method of the Baigas of crushing a pig to death by a beam of wood used as a see-saw across its body, and of the Gond bride and bridegroom killing a fowl by treading on it when they first enter their house after the wedding.

15. Religion. The supreme deity.

The following account of the tribal religion is abridged from Father Dehon's full and interesting description:

"The Oraons worship a supreme god who is known as Dharmes; him they invoke in their greatest difficulties when recourse to the village priests and magicians has proved useless. Then they turn to Dharmes and say, 'Now we have tried everything, but we have still you who can help us.' They sacrifice to him a white cock. They think that god is too good to punish them, and that they are not answerable to him in any way for their conduct; they believe that everybody will be treated in the same way in the other world. There is no hell for them or place of punishment, but everybody will go to *merkha* or heaven. The Red Indians speak of the happy hunting-grounds and the Oraons imagine something like the happy ploughing-grounds, where everybody will have plenty of land, plenty of bullocks to plough it with, and plenty of rice-beer to drink after his labour. They look on god as a big zamīndār or landowner, who does nothing himself, but keeps a *chaprāsi* as an agent or debt-collector; and they conceive the latter as having all the defects so common to his profession. Baranda, the *chaprāsi*, exacts tribute from them mercilessly, not exactly out of zeal for the service of his master, but out of greed for his *talbāna* or perquisites. When making a sacrifice to Dharmes they pray: 'O god, from to-day do not send any more your *chaprāsi* to punish us. You see we have paid our respects to you, and we are going to give him his *dastūri* (tip).'

16. Minor godlings.

"But in the concerns of this world, to obtain good crops and freedom from sickness, a host of minor deities have to be propitiated. These consist of *bhūts* or spirits of the household, the sept, the village, and common deities, such as the earth and sun. Chola Pācho or the lady of the grove lives in the *sarna* or sacred grove, which has been left standing when the forest was cleared. She is credited with the power of giving rain and consequently good crops. Churel is the shade of a woman who has died while pregnant or in childbirth. She hovers over her burial-place and is an object of horror and fright to every passer-by. It is her nature to look out for a companion, and she is said always to choose that member of a family whom she liked best during her lifetime. She will then come at night and embrace him and tickle him under the arms, making him laugh till he dies. Bhūla or the wanderers are the shades of persons who have died an unnatural death, either having been murdered, hanged, or killed by a tiger. 'They all keep the scars of their respective wounds and one can imagine what a weird-looking lot they are. They are always on the move, and are, as it were, the mendicant portion of the invisible community. They are not very powerful and are responsible only for small ailments, like nightmares and slight indispositions. When an Ojha or spirit-raiser discovers that a Bhūla has appeared in the light of his lamp he shows a disappointed face, and says: 'Pshaw, only Bhūla!' No sacrifice is offered to him, but the Ojha then and there takes a few grains of rice, rubs them in charcoal and throws them at the flame of his lamp, saying, 'Take this, Bhūla, and go away.' Mūrkuri is the thumping *bhūt*. Europeans to show their kindness and familiarity thump people on the back. If this is followed by fever or any kind of sickness it will be ascribed to the passing of Mūrkuri from the body of the European into the body of the native.

"*Chordewa* is a witch rather than a *bhūt*. It is believed that some women have the power to change their soul into a black cat, who then goes about in the houses where there are sick people. Such a cat has a peculiar way of mewing, quite different from its brethren, and is easily recognised. It steals quietly into the house, licks the lips of the sick man and eats the food which has been prepared for him. The sick man soon gets worse and dies. They say it is very difficult to catch the cat, as it has all the nimbleness of its nature and the cleverness of a *bhūt*. However, they sometimes succeed, and then something wonderful happens. The woman out of whom the cat has come remains insensible, as it were in a state of temporary death, until the cat re-enters her body. Any wound inflicted on the cat will be inflicted on her; if they cut its ears or break its legs or put out its eyes the woman will suffer the same mutilation. The Oraons say that formerly they used to burn any woman who was suspected of being a *Chordewa*.

17. Human sacrifice.

"There is also Anna Kuāri or Mahādhani, who is in our estimation the most cruel and repulsive deity of all, as she requires human sacrifice. Those savage people, who put good crops above everything, look upon her in a different light. She can give good crops and make a man rich, and this covers a multitude of sins. People may be sceptical about it and say that it is impossible that in any part of India under the British Government there should still be human sacrifices. Well, in spite of all the vigilance of the authorities, there are still human sacrifices in Chota Nāgpur. As the vigilance of the authorities increases, so also does the carefulness of the Urkas or Otongas increase. They choose for their victims poor waifs or strangers, whose disappearance no one will notice. April and May are the months in which the Urkas are at work. Doīsa, Panāri, Kūkra and Sargūja have a very bad reputation. During these months no strangers will go about the country alone and during that time nowhere will boys and girls be allowed to go to the jungle and graze the cattle for fear of the Urkas. When an Urka has found a victim he cuts his throat and carries away the upper part of the ring finger and the nose. Anna Kuāri finds votaries not only among the Oraons, but especially among the big zamīndārs and Rājas of the Native States. When a man has offered a sacrifice to Anna Kuāri she goes and lives in his house in the form of a small child. From that time his fields yield double harvest, and when he brings in his paddy he takes Anna Kuāri and rolls her over the heap to double its size. But she soon becomes restless and is only pacified by new human sacrifices. At last after some years she cannot bear remaining in the same house any more and kills every one."

In Jashpur State where the Oraons number 47,000 about half the total number have become Christians. The non-Christians call themselves Sansār, and the principal difference between them is that the Christians have cut off the pigtail, while the Sansār retain it. In some families the father may be a Sansār and the son a Kiristān, and they live together without any distinction. The Christians belong to the Roman Catholic and Lutheran Missions, but though they all know their Church, they naturally have little or no idea of the distinctions of doctrine.

18. Christianity.

The principal festivals are the Sārhūl, celebrated when the *sāl* tree[1] flowers, the Karma or May-day when the rice is ready for planting out, and the Kanihāri or harvest celebration.

19. Festivals. The Karma or May-day.

"At the Karma festival a party of young people of both sexes," says Colonel Dalton, "proceed to the forest and cut a young *karma* tree (*Nauclea parvifolia*) or the branch of one; they bear this home in triumph and plant it in the centre of the Akhāra or wrestling ground. Next morning all may be seen at an early hour in holiday array, the elders in groups under the fine old tamarind trees that surround the Akhāra, and the youth of both sexes, arm-linked in a huge circle, dancing round the *karma* tree, which, festooned with garlands, decorated with strips of coloured cloth and sham bracelets and necklets of plaited straw, and with the bright faces and merry laughter of the young people encircling it, reminds one of the gift-bearing tree so often introduced at our own great festival." The tree, however, probably corresponds to the English Maypole, and the festival celebrates the renewal of vegetation.

At the Sārhūl festival the marriage of the sun-god and earth-mother is celebrated, and this cannot be done till the *sāl* tree gives the flowers for the ceremony. It takes place about the beginning of April on any day when the tree is in flower. A white cock is taken to represent the sun and a black hen the earth; their marriage is celebrated by marking them with vermilion, and they are sacrificed. The villagers then accompany the Pāhan or Baiga, the village priest, to the *sarna* or sacred grove, a remnant of the old *sāl* forest in

20. The sāl flower festival.

---

[1] *Shorea robusta.*

which is located Sarna Burhi or 'The old women of the grove.' "To this dryad," writes Colonel Dalton, "who is supposed to have great influence over the rain (a superstition not improbably founded on the importance of trees as cloud-compellers), the party offer five fowls, which are afterwards eaten, and the remainder of the day is spent in feasting. They return laden with the flowers of the *sāl* tree, and next morning with the Baiga pay a visit to every house, carrying the flowers. The women of the village all stand on the threshold of their houses, each holding two leaf-cups; one empty to receive the holy water; the other with rice-beer for the Baiga. His reverence stops at each house, and places flowers over it and in the hair of the women. He sprinkles the holy water on the seeds that have been kept for the new year and showers blessings on every house, saying, 'May your rooms and granary be filled with paddy that the Baiga's name may be great.' When this is accomplished the woman throws a vessel of water over his venerable person, heartily dousing the man whom the moment before they were treating with such profound respect. This is no doubt a rain-charm, and is a familiar process. The Baiga is prevented from catching cold by being given the cup of rice-beer and is generally gloriously drunk before he completes his round. There is now a general feast, and afterwards the youth of both sexes, gaily decked with the *sāl* blossoms, the pale cream-white flowers of which make the most becoming of ornaments against their dusky skins and coal-black hair, proceed to the Akhāra and dance all night."

21. The harvest festival.

The Kanihāri, as described by Father Dehon, is held previous to the threshing of the rice, and none is allowed to prepare his threshing-floor until it has been celebrated. It can only take place on a Tuesday. A fowl is sacrificed and its blood sprinkled on the new rice. In the evening a common feast is held at which the Baiga presides, and when this is over they go to the place where Mahādeo is worshipped and the Baiga pours milk over the stone that represents him. The people then dance. Plenty of rice-beer is brought, and a scene of debauchery takes place in which all restraint is put aside. They sing the most obscene songs and give vent to all their passions. On that day no one is responsible for any breach of morality.

Like other primitive races, and the Hindus generally, the Oraons observe the Lenten fast, as explained by Sir J. G. Frazer, after sowing their crops. Having committed his seed with every propitiatory rite to the bosom of Mother Earth, the savage waits with anxious expectation to see whether she will once again perform on his behalf the yearly miracle of the renewal of vegetation, and the growth of the corn-plants from the seed which the Greeks typified by the descent of Proserpine into Hades for a season of the year and her triumphant re-emergence to the upper air. Meanwhile he fasts and atones for any sin or shortcoming of his which may possibly have offended the goddess and cause her to hold her hand. From the beginning of *Asārh* (June) the Oraons cease to shave, abstain from eating turmeric, and make no leaf-plates for their food, but eat it straight from the cooking-vessel. This they now say is to prevent the field-mice from consuming the seeds of the rice.

22. Fast for the crops.

"The colour of most Oraons," Sir H. Risley states, "is the darkest brown approaching to black; the hair being jet-black, coarse and rather inclined to be frizzy. Projecting jaws and teeth, thick lips, low narrow foreheads, and broad flat noses are the features characteristic of the tribe. The eyes are often bright and full, and no obliquity is observable in the opening of the eyelids."

23. Physical appearance and costume of the Oraons.

"The Oraon youths," Dalton states, "though with features very far from being in accordance with the statutes of beauty, are of a singularly pleasing class, their faces beaming with animation and good humour. They are a small race, averaging 4 feet 5 inches, but there is perfect proportion in all parts of their form, and their supple, pliant, lithe figures are often models of symmetry. There is about the young Oraon a jaunty air and mirthful expression that distinguishes him from the Munda or Ho, who has more of the dignified gravity that is said to characterise the North American Indian. The Oraon is particular about his personal appearance only so long as he is unmarried, but he is in no hurry to withdraw from the Dhūmkuria community, and generally his first youth is passed before he resigns his decorative propensities.

"He wears his hair long like a woman, gathered in a knot behind, supporting, when he is in gala costume, a red or white turban. In the knot are wooden combs and other instruments useful and ornamental, with numerous ornaments of brass.[1] At the very extremity of the roll of hair gleams a small circular mirror set in brass, from which, and also from his ears, bright brass chains with spiky pendants dangle, and as he moves with the springy elastic step of youth and tosses his head like a high-mettled steed in the buoyancy of his animal spirits, he sets all his glittering ornaments in motion and displays as he laughs a row of teeth, round, white and regular, that give light and animation to his dusky features. He wears nothing in the form of a coat; his decorated neck and chest are undraped, displaying how the latter tapers to the waist, which the young dandies compress within the smallest compass. In addition to the cloth, there is always round the waist a girdle of cords made of tasar-silk or of cane. This is now a superfluity, but it is no doubt the remnant of a more primitive costume, perhaps the support of the antique fig-leaves.

"Out of the age of ornamentation nothing can be more untidy or more unprepossessing than the appearance of the Oraon. The ornaments are nearly all discarded, hair utterly neglected, and for raiment any rags are used. This applies both to males and females of middle age.

24. Dress of women.

"The dress of the women consists of one cloth, six yards long, gracefully adjusted so as to form a shawl and a petticoat. The upper end is thrown over the left shoulder and falls with its fringe and ornamented border prettily over the back of the figure. Vast quantities of red beads and a large, heavy brass ornament shaped like a *torque* are worn round the neck. On the left hand are rings of copper, as many as can be induced on each finger up to the first joint, on the right hand a smaller quantity; rings on the second toe only of brass or bell-metal, and anklets and bracelets of the same material are also worn." The women wear only

---

[1] In Bilāspur the men have an iron comb in the hair with a circular end and two prongs like a fork. Women do not wear this.

metal and not glass bangles, and this with the three vertical tattoo-marks on the forehead and the fact that the head and right arm are uncovered enables them to be easily recognised. "The hair is made tolerably smooth and amenable by much lubrication, and false hair or some other substance is used to give size to the mass into which it is gathered not immediately behind, but more or less on one side, so that it lies on the neck just behind and touching the right ear; and flowers are arranged in a receptacle made for them between the roll of hair and the head." Rings are worn in the lobes of the ear, but not other ornaments. "When in dancing costume on grand occasions they add to their head-dress plumes of heron feathers, and a gay bordered scarf is tightly bound round the upper part of the body."

"The tribe I am treating of are seen to best advantage at the great national dance meetings called Jātras, which are held once a year at convenient centres, generally large mango groves in the vicinity of old villages. As a signal to the country round, the flags of each village are brought out on the day fixed and set upon the road that leads to the place of meeting. This incites the young men and maidens to hurry through their morning's work and look up their *jātra* dresses, which are by no means ordinary attire. Those who have some miles to go put up their finery in a bundle to keep it fresh and clean, and proceed to some tank or stream in the vicinity of the tryst grove; and about two o'clock in the afternoon may be seen all around groups of girls laughingly making their toilets in the open air, and young men in separate parties similarly employed. When they are ready the drums are beaten, huge horns are blown, and thus summoned the group from each village forms its procession. In front are young men with swords and shields or other weapons, the village standard-bearers with their flags, and boys waving yaks' tails or bearing poles with fantastic arrangements of garlands and wreaths intended to represent umbrellas of dignity. Sometimes a man riding on a wooden horse is carried, horse and all, by his friends as the Rāja, and others assume the form of or paint themselves up to represent certain beasts of prey. Behind this motley group the main body

25. Dances.

form compactly together as a close column of dancers in alternate ranks of boys and girls, and thus they enter the grove, where the meeting is held in a cheery dashing style, wheeling and countermarching and forming lines, circles and columns with grace and precision. The dance with these movements is called *kharia*, and it is considered to be an Oraon rather than a Munda dance, though Munda girls join in it. When they enter the grove the different groups join and dance the *kharia* together, forming one vast procession and then a monstrous circle. The drums and musical instruments are laid aside, and it is by the voices alone that the time is given; but as many hundreds, nay, thousands, join, the effect is imposing. In serried ranks, so closed up that they appear jammed, they circle round in file, all keeping perfect step, but at regular intervals the strain is terminated by a *hurūru*, which reminds one of Paddy's 'huroosh' as he 'welts the floor,' and at the same moment they all face inwards and simultaneously jumping up come down on the ground with a resounding stamp that makes the finale of the movements, but only for a momentary pause. One voice with a startling yell takes up the strain again, a fresh start is made, and after gyrating thus till they tire of it the ring breaks up, and separating into village groups they perform other dances independently till near sunset, and then go dancing home."

26. Social customs.

But more often they go on all night. Mr. Ball mentions their dance as follows:[1] "The Oraon dance was distinct from any I had seen by the Santāls or other races. The girls, carefully arranged in lines by sizes, with the tallest at one end and the smallest at the other, firmly grasp one another's hands, and the whole movements are so perfectly in concert that they spring about with as much agility as could a single individual." Father Dehon gives the following interesting notice of their social customs: "The Oraons are very sociable beings, and like to enjoy life together. They are paying visits or *pahis* to one another nearly the whole year round. In these the *handia* (beer-jar) always plays a great part. Any man who would presume to receive visitors without offering them a *handia* would be

[1] *Jungle Life in India*, p. 134.

hooted and insulted by his guests, who would find a sympathising echo from all the people of the village. One may say that from the time of the new rice at the end of September to the end of the marriage feast or till March there is a continual coming and going of visitors. For a marriage feast forty *handias* are prepared by the groom's father, and all the people of the village who can afford it supply one also. Each *handia* gives about three gallons of rice-beer, so that in one day and a half, in a village of thirty houses, about 200 gallons of rice-beer are despatched. The Oraons are famous for their dances. They delight in spending the whole night from sunset till morning in this most exciting amusement, and in the dancing season they go from village to village. They get, as it were, intoxicated with the music, and there is never any slackening of the pace. On the contrary, the evolutions seem to increase till very early in the morning, and it sometimes happens that one of the dancers shoots off rapidly from the gyrating group, and speeds away like a spent top, and, whirlwind-like, disappears through paddy-fields and ditches till he falls entirely exhausted. Of course it is the devil who has taken possession of him. One can well imagine in what state the dancers are at the first crow of the cock, and when ' *L'aurore avec ses doigts de rose entr'ouvre les portes de l'orient,*' she finds the girls straggling home one by one, dishevelled, *traînant l'aile*, too tired even to enjoy the company of the boys, who remain behind in small groups, still sounding their tom-toms at intervals as if sorry that the performance was so soon over. And, wonderful to say and incredible to witness, they will go straight to the stalls, yoke their bullocks, and work the whole morning with the same spirit and cheerfulness as if they had spent the whole night in refreshing sleep. At eleven o'clock they come home, eat their meal, and stretched out in the verandah sleep like logs until two, when poked and kicked about unmercifully by the people of the house, they reluctantly get up with heavy eyes and weary limbs to resume their work."

The Oraons do not now admit outsiders into the tribe. There is no offence for which a man is permanently put out of caste, but a woman living with any man other than an

27. Social rules.

Oraon is so expelled. Temporary expulsion is awarded for the usual offences. The head of the caste *panchāyat* is called Panua, and when an offender is reinstated, the Panua first drinks water from his hand, and takes upon himself the burden of the erring one's transgression. For this he usually receives a fee of five rupees, and in some States the appointment is in the hands of the Rāja, who exacts a fine of a hundred rupees or more from a new candidate. The Oraons eat almost all kinds of food, including pork, fowls and crocodiles, but abstain from beef. Their status is very low among the Hindus; they are usually made to live in a separate corner of the village, and are sometimes not allowed to draw water from the village well. As already stated, the dress of the men consists only of a narrow wisp of cloth round the loins. Some of them say, like the Gonds, that they are descended from the subjects of Rāwan, the demon king of Ceylon; this ancestry having no doubt in the first instance been imputed to them by the Hindus. And they explain that when Hanumān in the shape of a giant monkey came to the assistance of Rāma, their king Rāwan tried to destroy Hanumān by taking all the loin-cloths of his subjects and tying them soaked in oil to the monkey's tail with a view to setting them on fire and burning him to death. The device was unsuccessful and Hanumān escaped, but since then the subjects of Rāwan and their descendants have never had a sufficient allowance of cloth to cover them properly.

28. Character.

"The Oraons," Colonel Dalton says, "if not the most virtuous, are the most cheerful of the human race. Their lot is not a particularly happy one. They submit to be told that they are especially created as a labouring class, and they have had this so often dinned into their ears that they believe and admit it. I believe they relish work if the taskmaster be not over-exacting. Oraons sentenced to imprisonment without labour, as sometimes happens, for offences against the excise laws, insist on joining the working gangs, and wherever employed, if kindly treated, they work as if they felt an interest in their task. In cold weather or hot, rain or sun, they go cheerfully about it, and after some nine or ten hours of toil (seasoned with a little play and chaff among themselves) they return blithely home in flower-decked groups holding each other by the hand or round the waist and singing."

The Kurukh language, Dr. Grierson states, has no written character, but the gospels have been printed in it in the Devanāgri type. The translation is due to the Rev. F. Halm, who has also published a Biblical history, a catechism and other small books in Kurukh. More than five-sixths of the Oraons are still returned as speaking their own language.

29. Language.

Pāik.—A small caste of the Uriya country formed from military service, the term *pāik* meaning 'a foot-soldier.' In 1901 the Pāiks numbered 19,000 persons in the Kālāhandi and Patna States and the Raipur District, but since the transfer of the Uriya States to Bengal less than 3000 remain in the Central Provinces. In Kālāhandi, where the bulk of them reside, they are called Nalia Sipāhis from the fact that they were formerly armed with *nalis* or matchlocks by the State. After the Khond rising of 1882 in Kālāhandi these were confiscated and bows and arrows given in lieu of them. The Pāiks say that they were the followers of two warriors, Kālmīr and Jaimīr, who conquered the Kālāhandi and Jaipur States from the Khonds about a thousand years ago. There is no doubt that they formed the rough militia of the Uriya Rājas, a sort of rabble half military and half police, like the Khandaits. But the Khandaits were probably the leaders and officers, and, as a consequence, though originally only a mixed occupational group, have acquired a higher status than the Pāiks and in Orissa rank next to the Rājpūts. The Pāiks were the rank and file, mainly recruited from the forest tribes, and they are counted as a comparatively low caste, though to strangers they profess to be Rājpūts. In Sambalpur it is said that Rājpūts, Sudhs, Bhuiyas and Gonds are called Pāiks. In Kālāhandi they wear the sacred thread, being invested with it by a Brāhman at the time of their marriage, and they say that this privilege was conferred on them by the Rāja. It is reported, however, that social distinctions may be purchased in some of the Uriya States for comparatively small sums. A Bhatra or member of a forest tribe was observed wearing the sacred thread, and, on being questioned, stated that his grandfather had purchased the right from the Rāja for Rs. 50. The privileges of wearing gold ear ornaments, carrying an umbrella, and riding on horseback were obtainable in a similar manner. It is also related that when one Rāja imported the first pair of boots seen in his State, the local landholders were allowed to wear them in turn for a few minutes on payment of five rupees each, as a token of their right thereafter to procure and wear boots of their own. In Damoh and Jubbulpore another set of Pāiks is to be found who also claim to be Rājpūts, and are commonly so called, though true Rājpūts will not eat or intermarry with them. These are quite distinct from the Sambalpur Pāiks, but have probably been formed into a caste in exactly the same manner. The sept or family names of the Uriya Pāiks sufficiently indicate their mixed descent. Some of them are as follows: Dube (a Brāhman title), Chālak Bansi (of the Chalukya royal family), Chhit Karan (belonging to the Karans or Uriya Kāyasths), Sahāni (a sais or groom), Sudh (the name of an Uriya caste), Benet Uriya (a subdivision of the Uriya or Od mason caste), and so on. It is clear that members of different castes who became Pāiks founded separate families, which in time developed into exogamous septs. Some of the septs will not eat food cooked with water in company with the rest of the caste, though they do not object to intermarrying with them. After her marriage a girl may not take food cooked by her parents nor will they accept it from her. And at a marriage party each guest is supplied with grain and cooks it himself, but everybody will eat with the bride and bridegroom as a special concession to their position. Besides the exogamous clans the Pāiks have totemistic *gots* or groups named after plants and animals, as Harin (a deer), Kadamb (a tree), and so on. But these have no bearing on marriage, and the bulk of the caste have the Nāgesh or cobra as their sept name. It is said that anybody who does not know his sept considers himself to be a Nāgesh, and if he does not know his clan, he calls himself a Mahanti. Each family among the Pāiks has also a Sainga or title, of a high-sounding nature, as Nāik (lord), Pujāri (worshipper), Baidya (physician), Raut (noble), and so on. Marriages are generally celebrated in early youth, but no penalty is incurred for a breach of this rule. If the signs of adolescence appear in a girl for the first time on a Tuesday, Saturday or Sunday, it is considered a bad omen, and she is sometimes married to a tree to avert the consequences. Widow-marriage and divorce are freely permitted. The caste burn their dead and perform the *shrāddh* ceremony. The women are tattooed, and men sometimes tattoo their arms with figures of the sun and moon in the belief that this will protect them from snake-bite. The Pāiks eat flesh and fish, but abstain from fowls and other unclean animals and from liquor. Brāhmans will not take water from them, but other castes generally do so. Some of them are still employed as armed retainers and are remunerated by free grants of land.

PANKA

LIST OF PARAGRAPHS

1. *Origin of the caste.*
2. *Caste subdivisions.*
3. *Endogamous divisions.*
4. *Marriage.*
5. *Religion.*
6. *Other customs.*
7. *Occupation.*

1. Origin of the caste.

Panka.[1]—A Dravidian caste of weavers and labourers found in Mandla, Raipur and Bilāspur, and numbering 215,000 persons in 1911. The name is a variant on that of the Pān tribe of Orissa and Chota Nāgpur, who are also known as Panika, Chīk, Gānda and by various other designations. In the Central Provinces it has, however, a peculiar application; for while the Pān tribe proper is called Gānda in Chhattīsgarh and the Uriya country, the Pankas form a separate division of the Gāndas, consisting of those who have become members of the Kabīrpanthi sect. In this way the name has been found very convenient, for since Kabīr, the founder of the sect, was discovered by a weaver woman lying on the lotus leaves of a tank, like Moses in the bulrushes, and as a newly initiated convert is purified with water, so the Pankas hold that their name is *pāni ka* or 'from water.' As far as possible then they disown their connection with the Gāndas, one of the most despised castes, and say that they are a separate caste consisting of the disciples of Kabīr. This has given rise to the following doggerel rhyme about them :

Pāni se Panka bhae, bundan rāche sharīr,
Age age Panka bhae, pāchhe Dās Kabīr.

Which may be rendered, 'The Panka indeed is born of

[1] This article is compiled from papers by Pyāre Lāl Misra, Ethnographic clerk, and Hazāri Lāl, Manager, Court of Wards, Chānda.

water, and his body is made of drops of water, but there were Pankas before Kabīr.' Or another rendering of the second line is, 'First he was a Panka, and afterwards he became a disciple of Kabīr.' Nevertheless the Pankas have been successful in obtaining a somewhat higher position than the Gāndas, in that their touch is not considered to convey impurity. This is therefore an instance of a body of persons from a low caste embracing a new religion and thereby forming themselves into a separate caste and obtaining an advance in social position.

2. Caste subdivisions.

Of the whole caste 84 per cent are Kabīrpanthis and these form one subcaste; but there are a few others. The Mānikpuria say that their ancestors came from Mānikpur in Darbhanga State about three centuries ago; the Saktaha are those who profess to belong to the Sākta sect, which simply means that they eat flesh and drink liquor, being unwilling to submit to the restrictions imposed on Kabīrpanthis; the Bajania are those who play on musical instruments, an occupation which tends to lower them in Hindu eyes; and the Dom Pankas are probably a section of the Dom or sweeper caste who have somehow managed to become Pankas. The main distinction is however between the Kabirha, who have abjured flesh and liquor, and the Saktaha, who indulge in them; and the Saktaha group is naturally recruited from backsliding Kabīrpanthis. Properly the Kabirha and Saktaha do not intermarry, but if a girl from either section goes to a man of the other she will be admitted into the community and recognised as his wife, though the regular ceremony is not performed. The Saktaha worship all the ordinary village deities, but some of the Kabirha at any rate entirely refrain from doing so, and have no religious rites except when a priest of their sect comes round, when he gives them a discourse and they sing religious songs.

3. Endogamous divisions.

The caste have a number of exogamous septs, many of which are named after plants and animals: as Tandia an earthen pot, Chhura a razor, Neora the mongoose, Parewa the wild pigeon, and others. Other septs are Panaria the bringer of betel-leaf, Kuldīp the lamp-lighter, Pandwār the washer of feet, Ghughua one who eats the leavings of the assembly, and Khetgarhia, one who watches the fields during religious worship. The Sonwānia or 'Gold-water' sept has among the Pankas, as with several of the primitive tribes, the duty of readmitting persons temporarily put out of caste; while the Naurang or nine-coloured sept may be the offspring of some illegitimate unions. The Sati sept apparently commemorate by their name an ancestress who distinguished herself by self-immolation, naturally a very rare occurrence in so low a caste as the Pankas. Each sept has its own Bhāt or genealogist who begs only from members of the sept and takes food from them.

4. Marriage.

Marriage is prohibited between members of the same sept and also between first cousins, and a second sister may not be married during the lifetime of the first. Girls are usually wedded under twelve years of age. In Mandla the father of the boy and his relatives go to discuss the match, and if this is arranged each of them kisses the girl and gives her a piece of small silver. When a Saktaha is going to look for a wife he makes a fire offering to Dūlha Deo, the young bridegroom god, whose shrine is in the cook-room, and prays to him saying, 'I am going to such and such a village to ask for a wife; give me good fortune.' The father of the girl at first refuses his consent as a matter of etiquette, but finally agrees to let the marriage take place within a year. The boy pays Rs. 9, which is spent on the feast, and makes a present of clothes and jewels to the bride. In Chānda a *chauka* or consecrated space spread with cow-dung with a pattern of lines of flour is prepared and the fathers of the parties stand inside this, while a member of the Pandwār sept cries out the names of the *gotras* of the bride and bridegroom and says that the everlasting knot is to be tied between them with the consent of five caste-people and the sun and moon as witnesses. Before the wedding the betrothed couple worship Mahādeo and Pārvati under the direction of a Brāhman, who also fixes the date of the wedding. This is the only purpose for which a Brāhman is employed by the caste. Between this date and that of the marriage neither the boy nor girl should be allowed to go to a tank or cross a river, as it is considered dangerous to their lives. The superstition has apparently some connection with the belief that the Pankas are sprung from water, but its exact meaning cannot be determined. If a girl goes wrong before marriage with a man of the caste, she is given to him to wife without any ceremony. Before the marriage seven small pitchers full of water are placed in a bamboo basket and shaken over the bride's head so that the water may fall on her. The principal ceremony consists in walking round the sacred pole called *magrohan*, the skirts of the pair being knotted together. In some localities this is done twice, a first set of perambulations being called the Kunwāri (maiden) Bhānwar, and the second one of seven, the Byāhi (married) Bhānwar. After the wedding the bride and her relations return with the bridegroom to his house, their party being known as Chauthia. The couple are taken to a river and throw their tinsel wedding ornaments into the water. The bride then returns home if she is a minor, and when she subsequently goes to live with her husband the *gauna* ceremony is performed. Widow-marriage is permitted, and divorce may be effected for bad conduct on the part of the wife, the husband giving a sort of funeral feast, called *Marti jīti ka bhāt*, to the caste-fellows. Usually a man gives several warnings to his wife to amend her bad conduct before he finally casts her off.

5. Religion.

The Pankas worship only Kabīr. They prepare a *chauka* and, sitting in it, sing songs in his praise, and a cocoanut is afterwards broken and distributed to those who are present. The assembly is presided over by a Mahant or priest and the *chauka* is prepared by his subordinate called the Dīwān. The offices of Mahant and Dīwān are hereditary, and they officiate for a collection of ten or fifteen villages. Otherwise the caste perform no special worship, but observe the full moon days of Māgh (January), Phāgun (February) and Kārtik (October) as fasts in honour of Kabīr. Some of the Kabirhas observe the Hindu festivals, and the Saktahas, as already stated, have the same religious practices as other Hindus. They admit into the community members of most castes except the impure ones. In Chhattīsgarh a new convert is shaved and the other Pankas wash their feet over him in order to purify him. He then breaks a stick in token of having given up his former caste and is invested with a necklace of *tulsi*[1] beads. A woman of any such caste who has gone wrong with a man of the Panka caste may be admitted after she has lived with him for a certain period on probation, during which her conduct must be satisfactory, her paramour also being put out of caste for the same time. Both are then shaved and invested with the necklaces of *tulsi* beads. In Mandla a new convert must clean and whitewash his house and then vacate it with his family while the Panch or caste committee come and stay there for some time in order to purify it. While they are there neither the owner nor any member of his family may enter the house. The Panch then proceed to the riverside and cook food, after driving the new convert across the river by pelting him with cowdung. Here he changes his clothes and puts on new ones, and coming back again across the stream is made to stand in the *chauk* and sip the urine of a calf. The *chauk* is then washed out and a fresh one made with lines of flour, and standing in this the convert receives to drink the *dal*, that is, water in which a little betel, raw sugar and black pepper have been mixed and a piece of gold dipped. In the evening the Panch again take their food in the convert's house, while he eats outside it at a distance. Then he again sips the *dal*, and the Mahant or priest takes him on his lap and a cloth is put over them both; the Mahant whispers the *mantra* or sacred verse into his ear, and he is finally considered to have become a full Kabirha Panka and admitted to eat with the Panch.

6. Other customs. The Pankas are strict vegetarians and do not drink liquor. A Kabirha Panka is put out of caste for eating flesh meat. Both men and women generally wear white clothes, and men have the garland of beads round the neck. The dead are buried, being laid on the back with the head pointing to the north. After a funeral the mourners bathe and then break a cocoanut over the grave and distribute it among themselves. On the tenth day they go again and break a cocoanut and each man buries a little piece of it in the earth over the grave. A little cup made of flour containing a lamp is placed on the grave for three days afterwards, and some food and water are put in a leaf cup outside

[1] The basil plant.

the house for the same period. During these days the family do not cook for themselves but are supplied with food by their friends. After childbirth a mother is supposed not to eat food during the time that the midwife attends on her, on account of the impurity caused by this woman's presence in the room.

The caste are generally weavers, producing coarse country cloth, and a number of them serve as village watchmen, while others are cultivators and labourers. They will not grow *sān*-hemp nor breed tasar silk cocoons. They are somewhat poorly esteemed by their neighbours, who say of them, 'Where a Panka can get a little boiled rice and a pumpkin, he will stay for ever,' meaning that he is satisfied with this and will not work to get more. Another saying is, 'The Panka felt brave and thought he would go to war; but he set out to fight a frog and was beaten'; and another, 'Every man tells one lie a day; but the Ahīr tells sixteen, the Chamār twenty, and the lies of the Panka cannot be counted.' Such gibes, however, do not really mean much. Owing to the abstinence of the Pankas from flesh and liquor they rank above the Gāndas and other impure castes. In Bilāspur they are generally held to be quiet and industrious.[1] In Chhattīsgarh the Pankas are considered above the average in intelligence and sometimes act as spokesmen for the village people and as advisers to zamīndārs and village proprietors. Some of them become religious mendicants and act as *gurus* or preceptors to Kabīrpanthis.[2]

7. Occupation.

---

[1] *Bilaspur Settlement Report* (1868), p. 49.

[2] From a note by Mr. Gauri Shankar, Manager, Court of Wards, Drūg.

PANWĀR RĀJPŪT

LIST OF PARAGRAPHS

1. *Historical notice. The Agnikula clans and the slaughter of the Kshatriyas by Parasurāma.*
2. *The legend of Parasurāma.*
3. *The Panwār dynasty of Dhār and Ujjain.*
4. *Diffusion of the Panwārs over India.*
5. *The Nāgpur Panwārs.*
6. *Subdivisions.*
7. *Marriage customs.*
8. *Widow-marriage.*
9. *Religion.*
10. *Worship of the spirits of those dying a violent death.*
11. *Funeral rites.*
12. *Caste discipline.*
13. *Social customs.*

1. Historical notice. The Agnikula clans and the slaughter of the Kshatriyas by Parasurāma.

Panwār,[1] **Puar, Ponwār, Prāmara Rājpūt.** — The Panwār or Pramāra is one of the most ancient and famous of the Rājpūt clans. It was the first of the four Agnikulas, who were created from the fire-pit on the summit of Mount Abu after the Kshatriyas had been exterminated by Parasurāma the Brāhman. "The fire-fountain was lustrated with the waters of the Ganges;[2] expiatory rites were performed, and after a protracted debate among the gods it was resolved that Indra should initiate the work of recreation. Having formed an image of *dūba* grass he sprinkled it with the water of life and threw it into the fire-fountain. Thence on pronouncing the *sajīvan mantra* (incantation to give life) a figure slowly emerged from the flame, bearing in the right hand a mace and exclaiming, '*Mār, Mār!*' (Slay, slay). He was called Pramār; and Abu, Dhār and Ujjain were assigned to him as a territory."

The four clans known as Agnikula, or born from the fire-pit, were the Panwār, the Chauhān, the Parihār and

---

[1] With the exception of the historical notice, this article is principally based on a paper by Mr. Muhammad Yusuf, reader to Mr. C. E. Low, Deputy Commissioner of Bālāghāt.

[2] Tod's *Rājasthān*, ii. p. 407.

the Chalukya or Solanki. Mr. D. R. Bhandarkar adduces evidence in support of the opinion that all these were of foreign origin, derived from the Gūjars or other Scythian or Hun tribes.[1] And it seems therefore not unlikely that the legend of the fire-pit may commemorate the reconstitution of the Kshatriya aristocracy by the admission of these tribes to Hinduism after its partial extinction during their wars of invasion; the latter event having perhaps been euphemised into the slaughter of the Kshatriyas by Parasurāma the Brāhman. A great number of Indian castes date their origin from the traditional massacre of the Kshatriyas by Parasurāma, saying that their ancestors were Rājpūts who escaped and took to various occupations; and it would appear that an event which bulks so largely in popular tradition must have some historical basis. It is noticeable also that Buddhism, which for some five centuries since the time of Asoka Maurya had been the official and principal religion of northern India, had recently entered on its decline. "The restoration of the Brāhmanical religion to popular favour and the associated revival of the Sanskrit language first became noticeable in the second century, were fostered by the satraps of Gujarāt and Surāshtra during the third, and made a success by the Gupta emperors in the fourth century.[2] The decline of Buddhism and the diffusion of Sanskrit proceeded side by side with the result that by the end of the Gupta period the force of Buddhism on Indian soil had been nearly spent; and India with certain local exceptions had again become the land of the Brāhman.[3] The Gupta dynasty as an important power ended about A.D. 490 and was overthrown by the Huns, whose leader Toramāna was established at Mālwa in Central India prior to A.D. 500."[4] The revival of Brāhmanism and the Hun supremacy were therefore nearly contemporaneous. Moreover one of the Hun leaders, Mihiragula, was a strong supporter of Brāhmanism and an opponent of the Buddhists. Mr. V. A. Smith writes: "The savage invader, who worshipped as his patron deity Siva, the god of destruction, exhibited ferocious hostility

[1] Foreign elements in the Hindu population, *Ind. Ant.* (January 1911), vol. xl.
[2] *Early History of India* (Oxford, Clarendon Press), 3rd ed., p. 303.
[3] *Ibidem*, 2nd ed., p. 288.
[4] *Ibidem*, p. 316.

against the peaceful Buddhist cult, and remorselessly overthrew the *stūpas* and monasteries, which he plundered of their treasures."[1] This warrior might therefore well be venerated by the Brāhmans as the great restorer of their faith and would easily obtain divine honours. The Huns also subdued Rājputāna and Central India and were dominant here for a time until their extreme cruelty and oppression led to a concerted rising of the Indian princes by whom they were defeated. The discovery of the Hun or Scythian origin of several of the existing Rājpūt clans fits in well with the legend. The stories told by many Indian castes of their first ancestors having been Rājpūts who escaped from the massacre of Parasurāma would then have some historical value as indicating that the existing occupational grouping of castes dates from the period of the revival of the Brāhman cult after a long interval of Buddhist supremacy. It is however an objection to the identification of Parasurāma with the Huns that he is the sixth incarnation of Vishnu, coming before Rāma and being mentioned in the Mahābhārata, and thus if he was in any way historical his proper date should be long before their time. As to this it may be said that he might have been interpolated or put back in date, as the Brāhmans had a strong interest in demonstrating the continuity of the Kshatriya caste from Vedic times and suppressing the Hun episode, which indeed they have succeeded in doing so well that the foreign origin of several of the most prominent Rājpūt clans has only been established quite recently by modern historical and archaeological research. The name Parasurāma signifies ' Rāma with the axe ' and seems to indicate that this hero came after the original Rāma. And the list of the incarnations of Vishnu is not always the same, as in one list the incarnations are nearly all of the animal type and neither Parasurāma, Rāma nor Krishna appear.

2. The legend of Parasurāma.

The legend of Parasurāma is not altogether opposed to this view in itself.[2] He was the son of a Brāhman Muni or hermit, named Jamadagni, by a lady, Renuka, of the Kshatriya caste. He is therefore not held to have been a Brāhman and neither was he a true Kshatriya. This might

---

[1] *Early History of India* (Oxford, Clarendon Press), 3rd ed., p. 319.

[2] *Garrett's Classical Dictionary of Hinduism*, s.v. Jamadagni and Rāma.

portray the foreign origin of the Huns. Jamadagni found his wife Renuka to be harbouring thoughts of conjugal infidelity, and commanded his sons, one by one, to slay her. The four elder ones successively refused, and being cursed by Jamadagni lost all understanding and became as idiots; but the youngest, Parasurāma, at his father's bidding, struck off his mother's head with a blow of his axe. Jamadagni thereupon was very pleased and promised to give Parasurāma whatever he might desire. On which Parasurāma begged first for the restoration of his mother to life, with forgetfulness of his having slain her and purification from all defilement; secondly, the return of his brothers to sanity and understanding; and for himself that he should live long and be invincible in battle; and all these boons his father bestowed. Here the hermit Jamadagni might represent the Brāhman priesthood, and his wife Renuka might be India, unfaithful to the Brāhmans and turning towards the Buddhist heresy. The four elder sons would typify the princes of India refusing to respond to the exhortations of the Brāhmans for the suppression of Buddhism, and hence themselves made blind to the true faith and their understandings darkened with Buddhist falsehood. But Parasurāma, the youngest, killed his mother, that is, the Huns devastated India and slaughtered the Buddhists; in reward for this he was made invincible as the Huns were, and his mother, India, and his brothers, the indigenous princes, regained life and understanding, that is, returned to the true Brāhman faith. Afterwards, the legend proceeds, the king Kārrtavīrya, the head of the Haihaya tribe of Kshatriyas, stole the calf of the sacred cow Kamdhenu from Jamadagni's hermitage and cut down the trees surrounding it. When Parasurāma returned, his father told him what had happened, and he followed Kārrtavīrya and killed him in battle. But in revenge for this the sons of the king, when Parasurāma was away, returned to the hermitage and slew the pious and unresisting sage Jamadagni, who called fruitlessly for succour on his valiant son. When Parasurāma returned and found his father dead he vowed to extirpate the whole Kshatriya race. 'Thrice times seven did he clear the earth of the Kshatriya caste,' says the Mahābhārata. If the first part of the story refers to the Hun conquest of northern

India and the overthrow of the Gupta dynasty, the second may similarly portray their invasion of Rājputāna. The theft of the cow and desecration of Jamadagni's hermitage by the Haihaya Rājpūts would represent the apostasy of the Rājpūt princes to Buddhist monotheism, the consequent abandonment of the veneration of the cow and the spoliation of the Brāhman shrines; while the Hun invasions of Rājputāna and the accompanying slaughter of Rājpūts would be Parasurāma's terrible revenge.

3. The Panwār dynasty of Dhār and Ujjain.

The Kings of Mālwa or Ujjain who reigned at Dhār and flourished from the ninth to the twelfth centuries were of the Panwār clan. The seventh and ninth kings of this dynasty rendered it famous.[1] "Rāja Munja, the seventh king (974-995), renowned for his learning and eloquence, was not only a patron of poets, but was himself a poet of no small reputation, the anthologies including various works from his pen. He penetrated in a career of conquest as far as the Godāvari, but was finally defeated and executed there by the Chalukya king. His nephew, the famous Bhoja, ascended the throne of Dhāra about A.D. 1018 and reigned gloriously for more than forty years. Like his uncle he cultivated with equal assiduity the arts of peace and war. Though his fights with neighbouring powers, including one of the Muhammadan armies of Mahmūd of Ghaznī, are now forgotten, his fame as an enlightened patron of learning and a skilled author remains undimmed, and his name has become proverbial as that of the model king according to the Hindu standard. Works on astronomy, architecture, the art of poetry and other subjects are attributed to him. About A.D. 1060 Bhoja was attacked and defeated by the confederate kings of Gujarāt and Chedi, and the Panwār kingdom was reduced to a petty local dynasty until the thirteenth century. It was finally superseded by the chiefs of the Tomara and Chauhān clans, who in their turn succumbed to the Muhammadans in 1401." The city of Ujjain was at this time a centre of Indian intellectual life. Some celebrated astronomers made it

---

[1] The following extract is taken from Mr. V. A. Smith's *Early History of India*, 3rd ed., pp. 395, 396. The passage has been somewhat abridged in reproduction.

their home, and it was adopted as the basis of the Hindu meridional system like Greenwich in England. The capital of the state was changed from Ujjain to Dhār or Dhāranāgra by the Rāja Bhoja already mentioned;[1] and the name of Dhār is better remembered in connection with the Panwārs than Ujjain.

A saying about it quoted by Colonel Tod was:

> *Jahān Puār tahān Dhār hai;*
> *Aur Dhār jahān Puār;*
> *Dhār bina Puār nahin;*
> *Aur nahin Puār bina Dhār:*

or, "Where the Panwār is there is Dhār, and Dhār is where the Panwār is; without the Panwārs Dhār cannot stand, nor the Panwārs without Dhār." It is related that in consequence of one of his merchants having been held to ransom by the ruler of Dhār, the Bhatti Rāja of Jaisalmer made a vow to subdue the town. But as he found the undertaking too great for him, in order to fulfil his vow he had a model of the city made in clay and was about to break it up. But there were Panwārs in his army, and they stood out to defend their mock capital, repeating as their reason the above lines; and in resisting the Rāja were cut to pieces to the number of a hundred and twenty.[2] There is little reason to doubt that the incident, if historical, was produced by the belief in sympathetic magic; the Panwārs really thought that by destroying its image the Rāja could effect injury to the capital itself,[3] just as many primitive races believe that if they make a doll as a model of an enemy and stick pins into or otherwise injure it, the man himself is similarly affected. A kindred belief prevails concerning certain mythical old kings of the Golden Age of India, of whom it is said that to destroy their opponents all they had to do was to collect a bundle of juāri stalks and

---

[1] Malcolm, i. p. 26.

[2] *Rājasthān*, ii. p. 215.

[3] A similar instance in Europe is related by Colonel Tod, concerning the origin of the Madrid Restaurant in the Bois de Boulogne at Paris. After Francis I. had been captured by the Spaniards he was allowed to return to his capital, on pledging his parole that he would go back to Madrid. But the delights of liberty and Paris were too much for honour; and while he wavered a hint was thrown out similar to that of destroying the clay city. A mock Madrid arose in the Bois de Boulogne, to which Francis retired. (*Rājasthān*, ii. p. 428.)

cut off the heads, when the heads of their enemies flew off in unison.

The Panwārs were held to have ruled from nine castles over the Marusthali or 'Region of death,' the name given to the great desert of Rājputāna, which extends from Sind to the Aravalli mountains and from the great salt lake to the flat skirting the Garah. The principal of these castles were Abu, Nundore, Umarkot, Arore, and Lodorva.[1] And, 'The world is the Prāmara's,' was another saying expressive of the resplendent position of Dhāranāgra or Ujjain at this epoch. The siege and capture of the town by the Muhammadans and consequent expulsion of the Panwārs are still a well-remembered tradition, and certain castes of the Central Provinces, as the Bhoyars and Korkus, say that their ancestors formed part of the garrison and fled to the Satpūra hills after the fall of Dhāranāgra. Mr. Crooke[2] states that the expulsion of the Panwārs from Ujjain under their leader Mitra Sen is ascribed to the attack of the Muhammadans under Shāhab-ud-dīn Ghori about A.D. 1190.

4. Diffusion of the Panwārs over India.

After this they spread to various places in northern India, and to the Central Provinces and Bombay. The modern state of Dhār is or was recently still held by a Panwār family, who had attained high rank under the Marāthas and received it as a grant from the Peshwa. Malcolm considered them to be the descendants of Rājpūt emigrants to the Deccan. He wrote of them:[3] "In the early period of Marātha history the family of Puār appears to have been one of the most distinguished. They were of the Rājpūt tribe, numbers of which had been settled in Mālwa at a remote era; from whence this branch had migrated to the Deccan. Sivaji Puār, the first of the family that can be traced in the latter country, was a landholder; and his grandsons, Sambaji and Kāloji, were military commanders in the service of the celebrated Sivaji. Anand Rao Puār was vested with authority to collect the Marātha share of the revenue of Mālwa and Gujarāt in 1734, and he soon afterwards settled at Dhār, which province,

---

[1] *Rājasthān*, ii. pp. 264, 265.   [2] *Tribes and Castes*, art. Panwār.
[3] *Memoir of Central India*, i. 96.

with the adjoining districts and the tributes of some neighbouring Rājpūt chiefs, was assigned for the support of himself and his adherents. It is a curious coincidence that the success of the Marāthas should, by making Dhār the capital of Anand Rāo and his descendants, restore the sovereignty of a race who had seven centuries before been expelled from the government of that city and territory. But the present family, though of the same tribe (Puār), claim no descent from the ancient Hindu princes of Mālwa. They have, like all the Kshatriya tribes who became incorporated with the Marāthas, adopted even in their modes of thinking the habits of that people. The heads of the family, with feelings more suited to chiefs of that nation than Rājpūt princes, have purchased the office of patel or headman in some villages in the Deccan; and their descendants continue to attach value to their ancient, though humble, rights of village officers in that quarter. Notwithstanding that these usages and the connections they formed have amalgamated this family with the Marāthas, they still claim, both on account of their high birth and of being officers of the Rāja of Satāra (not of the Peshwa), rank and precedence over the houses of Sindhia and Holkar; and these claims, even when their fortunes were at the lowest ebb, were always admitted as far as related to points of form and ceremony." The great Marātha house of Nimbhālkar is believed to have originated from ancestors of the Panwār Rājpūt clan. While one branch of the Panwārs went to the Deccan after the fall of Dhār and marrying with the people there became a leading military family of the Marāthas, the destiny of another group who migrated to northern India was less distinguished. Here they split into two, and the inferior section is described by Mr. Crooke as follows:[1] "The Khidmatia, Barwār or Chobdār are said to be an inferior branch of the Panwārs, descended from a low-caste woman. No high-caste Hindu eats food or drinks water touched by them." According to the Ain-i-Akbari[2] a thousand men of the sept guarded the environs of the palace of Akbar, and Abul Fazl says of them: "The caste to which they

---

[1] *Tribes and Castes*, art. Panwār.
[2] Blockmann, i. 252, quoted by Crooke.

belong was notorious for highway robbery, and former rulers were not able to keep them in check. The effective orders of His Majesty have led them to honesty; they are now famous for their trustworthiness. They were formerly called *Māwis*. Their chief has received the title of Khidmat Rao. Being near the person of His Majesty he lives in affluence. His men are called Khidmatias." Thus another body of Panwārs went north and sold their swords to the Mughal Emperor, who formed them into a bodyguard. Their case is exactly analogous to that of the Scotch and Swiss Guards of the French kings. In both cases the monarch preferred to entrust the care of his person to foreigners, on whose fidelity he could the better rely, as their only means of support and advancement lay in his personal favour, and they had no local sympathies which could be used as a lever to undermine their loyalty. Buchanan states that a Panwār dynasty ruled for a considerable period over the territory of Shāhabād in Bengal. And Jagdeo Panwār was the trusted minister of Sidhrāj, the great Solanki Rāja of Gujarāt. The story of the adventures of Jagdeo and his wife when they set out together to seek their fortune is an interesting episode in the Rāsmāla. In the Punjab the Panwārs are found settled up the whole course of the Sutlej and along the lower Indus, and have also spread up the Biās into Jalandhar and Gurdāspur.[1]

5. The Nāgpur Panwārs.

While the above extracts have been given to show how the Panwārs migrated from Dhār to different parts of India in search of fortune, this article is mainly concerned with a branch of the clan who came to Nāgpur, and subsequently settled in the rice country of the Wainganga Valley. At the end of the eleventh century Nāgpur appears to have been held by a Panwār ruler as an appanage of the kingdom of Mālwa.[2] It has already been seen how the kings of Mālwa penetrated to Berār and the Godāvari, and Nāgpur may well also have fallen to them. Mr. Muhammad Yūsuf quotes an inscription as existing at Bhāndak in Chānda of the year A.D. 1326, in which it is mentioned that the Panwār of Dhār

---

[1] Ibbetson, P. C. R., para. 448.
[2] His name, Lakshma Deva, is given in a stone inscription dated A.D. 1104-1105.

repaired a statue of Jag Nārāyan in that place.[1] Nothing more is heard of them in Nāgpur, and their rule probably came to an end with the subversion of the kingdom of Mālwa in the thirteenth century. But there remain in Nāgpur and in the districts of Bhandāra, Bālāghāt and Seoni to the north and east of it a large number of Panwārs, who have now developed into an agricultural caste. It may be surmised that the ancestors of these people settled in the country at the time when Nāgpur was held by their clan, and a second influx may have taken place after the fall of Dhār. According to their own account, they first came to Nagardhan, an older town than Nāgpur, and once the headquarters of the locality. One of their legends is that the men who first came had no wives, and were therefore allowed to take widows of other castes into their houses. It seems reasonable to suppose that something of this kind happened, though they probably did not restrict themselves to widows. The existing family names of the caste show that it is of mixed ancestry, but the original Rājpūt strain is still perfectly apparent in their fair complexions, high foreheads and in many cases grey eyes. The Panwārs have still the habit of keeping women of lower castes to a greater degree than the ordinary, and this has been found to be a trait of other castes of mixed origin, and they are sometimes known as Dhākar, a name having the sense of illegitimacy. Though they have lived for centuries among a Marāthi-speaking people, the Panwārs retain a dialect of their own, the basis of which is Bagheli or eastern Hindi. When the Marāthas established themselves at Nāgpur in the eighteenth century some of the Panwārs took military service under them and accompanied a general of the Bhonsla ruling family on an expedition to Cuttack. In return for this they were rewarded with grants of the waste and forest lands in the valley of the Wainganga river, and here they developed great skill in the construction

---

[1] The inscription is said to be in one of the temples in Winj Bāsini, near Bhāndak, in the Devanāgri character in Marāthi, and to run as follows: "Consecration of Jagnārāyan (the serpent of the world). Dajíanashnaku, the son of Chogneka, he it was who consecrated the god. The Panwār, the ruler of Dhār, was the third repairer of the statue. The image was carved by Gopināth Pandit, inhabitant of Lonār Mehkar. Let this shrine be the pride of all the citizens, and let this religious act be notified to the chief and other officers."

of tanks and the irrigation of rice land, and are the best agricultural caste in this part of the country. Their customs have many points of interest, and, as is natural, they have abandoned many of the caste observances of the Rājpūts. It is to this group of Panwārs[1] settled in the Marātha rice country of the Wainganga Valley that the remainder of this article is devoted.

6. Subdivisions.

They number about 150,000 persons, and include many village proprietors and substantial cultivators. The quotations already given have shown how this virile clan of Rājpūts travelled to the north, south and east from their own country in search of a livelihood. Everywhere they made their mark so that they live in history, but they paid no regard to the purity of their Rājpūt blood and took to themselves wives from the women of the country as they could get them. The Panwārs of the Wainganga Valley have developed into a caste marrying among themselves. They have no subcastes but thirty-six exogamous sections. Some of these have the names of Rājpūt clans, while others are derived from villages, titles or names of offices, or from other castes. Among the titular names are Chaudhri (headman), Patlia (patel or chief officer of a village) and Sonwānia (one who purifies offenders among the Gonds and other tribes). Among the names of other castes are Bopcha or Korku, Bhoyar (a caste of cultivators), Pārdhi (hunter), Kohli (a local cultivating caste) and Sahria (from the Saonr tribe). These names indicate how freely they have intermarried. It is noticeable that the Bhoyars and Korkus of Betūl both say that their ancestors were Panwārs of Dhār, and the occurrence of both names among the Panwārs of Bālāghāt may indicate that these castes also have some Panwār blood. Three names, Rahmat (kind), Turukh or Turk, and Farīd (a well-known saint), are of Muhammadan origin, and indicate intermarriage in that quarter.

7. Marriage customs.

Girls are usually, but not necessarily, wedded before adolescence. Occasionally a Panwār boy who cannot afford a regular marriage will enter his prospective father-in-law's

---

[1] A few Panwār Rājpūts are found in the Saugor District, but they are quite distinct from those of the Marātha country, and marry with the Bundelas. They are mentioned in the article on that clan.

TRANSPLANTING RICE.

house and serve him for a year or more, when he will obtain a daughter in marriage. And sometimes a girl will contract a liking for some man or boy of the caste and will go to his house, leaving her home. In such cases the parents accept the accomplished fact, and the couple are married. If the boy's parents refuse their consent they are temporarily put out of caste, and subsequently the neighbours will not pay them the customary visits on the occasions of family joys and griefs. Even if a girl has lived with a man of another caste, as long as she has not borne a child, she may be re-admitted to the community on payment of such penalty as the elders may determine. If her own parents will not take her back, a man of the same *gotra* or section is appointed as her guardian and she can be married from his house.

The ceremonies of a Panwār marriage are elaborate. Marriage-sheds are erected at the houses both of the bride and bridegroom in accordance with the usual practice, and just before the marriage, parties are given at both houses; the village watchman brings the *toran* or string of mango-leaves, which is hung round the marriage-shed in the manner of a triumphal arch, and in the evening the party assembles, the men sitting at one side of the shed and the women at the other. Presents of clothes are made to the child who is to be married, and the following song is sung:

The mother of the bride grew angry and went away to the mango grove.
Come soon, come quickly, Mother, it is the time for giving clothes.
The father of the bridegroom has sent the bride a fold of cloth from his house,
The fold of it is like the curve of the winnowing-fan, and there is a bodice decked with coral and pearls.

Before the actual wedding the father of the bridegroom goes to the bride's house and gives her clothes and other presents, and the following is a specimen given by Mr. Muhammad Yūsuf of the songs sung on this occasion:

Five years old to-day is Bāja Bai the bride;
Send word to the mother of the bridegroom;
Her dress is too short, send for the Koshta, Husband;
The Koshta came and wove a border to the dress.

Afterwards the girl's father goes and makes similar presents to the bridegroom. After many preliminary ceremonies the marriage procession proper sets forth, consisting of men only. Before the boy starts his mother places her breast in his mouth; the maid-servants stand before him with vessels of water, and he puts a pice in each. During the journey songs are sung, of which the following is a specimen:

> The linseed and gram are in flower in Chait.[1]
> O! the boy bridegroom is going to another country;
> O Mother! how may he go to another country?
> Make payment before he enters another country;
> O Mother! how may he cross the border of another country?
> Make payment before he crosses the border of another country;
> O Mother! how may he touch another's bower?
> Make payment before he touches another's bower;
> O Mother! how shall he bathe with strange water?
> Make payment before he bathes with strange water;
> O Mother! how may he eat another's *banwat*?[2]
> Make payment before he eats another's *banwat*;
> O Mother! how shall he marry another woman?
> He shall wed her holding the little finger of her left hand.

The bridegroom's party are always driven to the wedding in bullock-carts, and when they approach the bride's village her people also come to meet them in carts. All the party then turn and race to the village, and the winner obtains much distinction. The cartmen afterwards go to the bridegroom's father and he has to make them a present of from one to forty rupees. On arriving at the village the bridegroom is carried to Devi's shrine in a man's arms, while four other men hold a canopy over him, and from there to the marriage-shed. He touches a bamboo of this, and a man seated on the top pours turmeric and water over his head. Five men of the groom's party go to the bride's house carrying salt, and here their feet are washed and the *tīka* or mark of anointing is made on their foreheads. Afterwards they carry rice in the same manner and with this is the wedding-rice, coloured yellow with turmeric and known as the Lagun-gāth. Before sunset the bridegroom goes to the bride's house for the wedding. Two baskets are hung before Dulha Deo's shrine inside the house, and the couple are seated in these with a cloth between them. The ends of their clothes are knotted,

---

[1] March.   [2] Rice boiled with milk and sugar.

each places the right foot on the left foot of the other and holds the other's ear with the hand. Meanwhile a Brāhman has climbed on to the roof of the house, and after saying the names of the bride and bridegroom shouts loudly, '*Rām nawara, Sīta nawari, Saodhān*,' or 'Rām, the Bridegroom, and Sīta, the Bride, pay heed.' The people inside the house repeat these words and someone beats on a brass plate; the wedding-rice is poured over the heads of the couple, and a quid of betel is placed first in the mouth of one and then of the other. The bridegroom's party dance in the marriage-shed and their feet are washed. Two plough-yokes are brought in and a cloth spread over them, and the couple are seated on them face to face. A string of twisted grass is drawn round their necks and a thread is tied round their marriage crowns. The bride's dowry is given and her relatives make presents to her. This property is known as *khamora*, and is retained by a wife for her own use, her husband having no control over it. It is customary also in the caste for the parents to supply clothes to a married daughter as long as they live, and during this period a wife will not accept any clothes from her husband. On the following day the maid-servants bring a present of *gulāl* or red powder to the fathers of the bride and bridegroom, who sprinkle it over each other. The bridegroom's father makes them a present of from one to twenty rupees according to his means, and also gives suitable fees to the barber, the washerman, the Barai or betel-leaf seller and the Bhāt or bard. The maid-servants then bring vessels of water and throw it over each other in sport. After the evening meal, the party go back, the bride and bridegroom riding in the same cart. As they start the women sing:

> Let us go to the basket-maker
> And buy a costly pair of fans;
> Fans worth a lot of money;
> Let us praise the mother of the bride.

8. Widow-marriage.

After a few days at her husband's house the bride returns home, and though she pays short visits to his family from time to time, she does not go to live with her husband until she is adolescent, when the usual *pathoni* or going-away ceremony is performed to celebrate the event. The people repeat a set of verses containing advice which the bride's mother is supposed to give her on this occasion, in which the desire imputed to the caste to make money out of their daughters is satirised. They are no doubt libellous as being a gross exaggeration, but may contain some substratum of truth. The gist of them is as follows: "Girl, if you are my daughter, heed what I say. I will make you many sweetmeats and speak words of wisdom. Always treat your husband better than his parents. Increase your private money (*khamora*) by selling rice and sugar; abuse your sisters-in-law to your husband's mother and become her favourite. Get influence over your husband and make him come with you to live with us. If you cannot persuade him, abandon your modesty and make quarrels in the household. Do not fear the village officers, but go to the houses of the patel[1] and Pāndia[2] and ask them to arrange your quarrel."

It is not intended to imply that Panwār women behave in this manner, but the passage is interesting as a sidelight on the joint family system. It concludes by advising the girl, if she cannot detach her husband from his family, to poison him and return as a widow. This last counsel is a gibe at the custom which the caste have of taking large sums of money for a widow on her second marriage. As such a woman is usually adult, and able at once to perform the duties of a wife and to work in the fields, she is highly valued, and her price ranges from Rs. 25 to Rs. 1000. In former times, it is stated, the disposal of widows did not rest with their parents but with the Sendia or headman of the caste. The last of them was Karūn Panwār of Tumsar, who was empowered by the Bhonsla Rāja of Nāgpur to act in this manner, and was accustomed to receive an average sum of Rs. 25 for each widow or divorced woman whom he gave away in marriage. His power extended even to the reinstatement of women expelled from the caste, whom he could subsequently make over to any one who would pay for them. At the end of his life he lost his authority among the people by keeping a Dhīmar woman as a mistress, and he had no successor. A Panwār widow must not marry again

---

[1] Village headman.   [2] Patwāri or village accountant.

until the expiry of six months after her husband's death. The stool on which a widow sits for her second marriage is afterwards stolen by her husband's friends. After the wedding when she reaches the boundary of his village the axle of her cart is removed, and a new one made of *tendu* wood is substituted for it. The discarded axle and the shoes worn by the husband at the ceremony are thrown away, and the stolen stool is buried in a field. These things, Mr. Hīra Lāl points out, are regarded as defiled, because they have been accessories in an unlucky ceremony, that of the marriage of a widow. On this point Dr. Jevons writes [1] that the peculiar characteristic of taboo is this transmissibility of its infection or contagion. In ancient Greece the offerings used for the purification of the murderer became themselves polluted during the process and had to be buried. A similar reasoning applies to the articles employed in the marriage of a widow. The wood of the *tendu* or ebony tree [2] is chosen for the substituted axle, because it has the valuable property of keeping off spirits and ghosts. When a child is born a plank of this wood is laid along the door of the room to keep the spirits from troubling the mother and the newborn infant. In the same way, no doubt, this wood keeps the ghost of the first husband from entering with the widow into her second husband's village. The reason for the ebony-wood being a spirit-scarer seems to lie in its property of giving out sparks when burnt. "The burning wood gives out showers of sparks, and it is a common amusement to put pieces in a camp fire in order to see the column of sparks ascend." [3] The sparks would have a powerful effect on the primitive mind and probably impart a sacred character to the tree, and as they would scare away wild animals, the property of averting spirits might come to attach to the wood. The Panwārs seldom resort to divorce, except in the case of open and flagrant immorality on the part of a wife. "They are not strict," Mr. Low writes,[4] "in the matter of sexual offences within the caste, though they bitterly resent and if able heavily avenge any attempt on the virtue of their women by an outsider. The men of the caste are on the

---

[1] *Introduction to the History of Religion*, p. 59.
[2] *Diospyros tomentosa.*
[3] Gamble, *Manual of Indian Timbers*, p. 461.
[4] *Balāghāt District Gazetteer.*

other hand somewhat notorious for the freedom with which they enter into relations with the women of other castes." They not infrequently have Gond and Ahīr girls from the families of their farmservants as members of their households.

9. Religion. The caste worship the ordinary Hindu divinities, and their household god is Dūlha Deo, the deified bridegroom. He is represented by a nut and a date, which are wrapped in a cloth and hung on a peg in the wall of the house above the platform erected to him. Every year, or at the time of a marriage or the birth of a first child, a goat is offered to Dūlha Deo. The animal is brought to the platform and given some rice to eat. A dedicatory mark of red ochre is made on its forehead and water is poured over the body, and as soon as it shivers it is killed. The shivering is considered to be an indication from the deity that the sacrifice is acceptable. The flesh is cooked and eaten by the family inside the house, and the skin and bones are buried below the floor. Nārāyan Deo or Vishnu or the Sun is represented by a bunch of peacock's feathers. He is generally kept in the house of a Mahār, and when his worship is to be celebrated he is brought thence in a gourd to the Panwār's house, and a black goat, rice and cakes are offered to him by the head of the household. While the offering is being made the Mahār sings and dances, and when the flesh of the goat is eaten he is permitted to sit inside the Panwār's house and begin the feast, the Panwārs eating after him. On ordinary occasions a Mahār is not allowed to come inside the house, and any Panwār who took food with him would be put out of caste; and this rite is no doubt a recognition of the position of the Mahārs as the earlier residents of the country before the Panwārs came to it. The Turukh or Turk sept of Panwārs pay a similar worship to Bāba Farīd, the Muhammadan saint of Girar. He is also represented by a bundle of peacock's feathers, and when a goat is sacrificed to him a Muhammadan kills it and is the first to partake of its flesh.

10. Worship of the spirits of those dying a violent death. When a man has been killed by a tiger (*bāgh*) he is deified and worshipped as Bāgh Deo. A hut is made in the yard of the house, and an image of a tiger is placed inside and worshipped on the anniversary of the man's death.

The members of the household will not afterwards kill a tiger, as they think the animal has become a member of the family. A man who is bitten by a cobra (*nāg*) and dies is similarly worshipped as Nāg Deo. The image of a snake made of silver or iron is venerated, and the family will not kill a snake. If a man is killed by some other animal, or by drowning or a fall from a tree, his spirit is worshipped as Ban Deo or the forest god with similar rites, being represented by a little lump of rice and red lead. In all these cases it is supposed, as pointed out by Sir James Frazer, that the ghost of the man who has come to such an untimely end is especially malignant, and will bring trouble upon the survivors unless appeased with sacrifices and offerings. A good instance of the same belief is given by him in *Psyche's Task*[1] as found among the Karens of Burma: "They put red, yellow and white rice in a basket and leave it in the forest, saying: Ghosts of such as died by falling from a tree, ghosts of such as died of hunger or thirst, ghosts of such as died by the tiger's tooth or the serpent's fang, ghosts of the murdered dead, ghosts of such as died by smallpox or cholera, ghosts of dead lepers, oh ill-treat us not, seize not upon our persons, do us no harm! Oh stay here in this wood! We will bring hither red rice, yellow rice, and white rice for your subsistence."

That the same superstition is generally prevalent in the Central Provinces appears to be shown by the fact that among castes who practise cremation, the bodies of men who come to a violent end or die of smallpox or leprosy are buried, though whether burial is considered as more likely to prevent the ghost from walking than cremation, is not clear. Possibly, however, it may be considered that the bodies are too impure to be committed to the sacred fire.

Cremation of the dead is the rule, but the bodies of those who have not died a natural death are buried, as also of persons who are believed to have been possessed of the goddess Devi in their lifetime. The bodies of small children are buried when the Khīr Chatai ceremony has not

---

[1] P. 62, quoting from Bringand, *Missions Catholiques*, xx. (1888), *Les Karens de la Birmanie, Les* p. 208.

been performed. This takes place when a child is about two years old: he is invited to the house of some member of the same section on the Diwāli day and given to eat some Khīr or a mess of new rice with milk and sugar, and thus apparently is held to become a proper member of the caste, as boys do in other castes on having their ears pierced. When a corpse is to be burnt a heap of cowdung cakes is made, on which it is laid, while others are spread over it, together with butter, sugar and linseed. The fire with which the pyre is kindled is carried by the son or other chief mourner in an earthen pot at the head of the corpse. After the cremation the ashes of the body are thrown into water, but the bones are kept by the chief mourner; his head and face are then shaved by the barber, and the hair is thrown into the water with most of the bones; he may retain a few to carry them to the Nerbudda at a convenient season, burying them meanwhile under a mango or pīpal tree. A present of a rupee or a cow may be made to the barber. After the removal of a dead body the house is swept, and the rubbish with the broom and dustpan are thrown away outside the village. Before the body is taken away the widow of the dead man places her hands on his breast and forehead, and her bangles are broken by another widow. The *shrāddh* ceremony is performed every year in the month of Kunwār (September) on the same day of the fortnight as that on which the death took place. On the day before the ceremony the head of the household goes to the houses of those whom he wishes to invite, and sticks some grains of rice on their foreheads. The guests must then fast up to the ceremony. On the following day, when they arrive at noon, the host, wearing a sacred thread of twisted grass, washes their feet with water in which the sacred *kusa* grass has been mixed, and marks their foreheads with sandal-paste and rice. The leaf-plates of the guests are set out inside the house, and a very small quantity of cooked rice is placed in each. The host then gathers up all this rice and throws it on to the roof of the house while his wife throws up some water, calling aloud the name of the dead man whose *shrāddh* ceremony is being performed, and after this the whole party take their dinner.

As has been shown, the Panwārs have abandoned most of the distinctive Rājpūt customs. They do not wear the sacred thread and they permit the remarriage of widows. They eat the flesh of goats, fowls, wild pig, game-birds and fish, but abstain from liquor except on such ceremonial occasions as the worship of Nārāyan Deo, when every one must partake of it. Mr. Low states that the injurious habit of smoking *madak* (a preparation of opium) is growing in the caste. They will take water to drink from a Gond's hand and in some localities even cooked food. This is the outcome of their close association in agriculture, the Gonds having been commonly employed as farmservants by Panwār cultivators. A Brāhman usually officiates at their ceremonies, but his presence is not essential and his duties may be performed by a member of the caste. Every Panwār male or female has a *guru* or spiritual preceptor, who is either a Brāhman, a Gosain or a Bairāgi. From time to time the *guru* comes to visit his *chela* or disciple, and on such occasions the *chauk* or sacred place is prepared with lines of wheat-flour. Two wooden stools are set within it and the *guru* and his *chela* take their seats on these. Their heads are covered with a new piece of cloth and the *guru* whispers some text into the ear of the disciple. Sweetmeats and other delicacies are then offered to the *guru*, and the disciple makes him a present of one to five rupees. When a Panwār is put out of caste two feasts have to be given on reinstatement, known as the Maili and Chokhi Roti (impure and pure food). The former is held in the morning on the bank of a tank or river and is attended by men only. A goat is killed and served with rice to the caste-fellows, and in serious cases the offender's head and face are shaved, and he prays, 'God forgive me the sin, it will never be repeated.' The Chokhi Roti is held in the evening at the offender's house, the elders and women as well as men of the caste being present. The Sendia or leader of the caste eats first, and he will not begin his meal unless he finds a *douceur* of from one to five rupees deposited beneath his leaf-plate. The whole cost of the ceremony of readmission is from fifteen to fifty rupees.

The Panwār women wear their clothes tied in the

12. Caste discipline.

13. Social customs.

Hindustāni and not in the Marātha fashion. They are tattooed on the legs, hands and face, the face being usually decorated with single dots which are supposed to enhance its beauty, much after the same fashion as patches in England. Padmākar, the Saugor poet, Mr. Hīra Lāl remarks, compared the dot on a woman's chin to a black bee buried in a half-ripe mango. The women, Mr. Low says, are addicted to dances, plays and charades, the first being especially graceful performances. They are skilful with their fingers and make pretty grass mats and screens for the house, and are also very good cooks and appreciate variety in food. The Panwārs do not eat off the ground, but place their dishes on little iron stands, sitting themselves on low wooden stools. The housewife is a very important person, and the husband will not give anything to eat or drink out of the house without her concurrence. Mr. Low writes on the character and abilities of the Panwārs as follows: "The Panwār is to Bālāghāt what the Kunbi is to Berār or the Gūjar to Hoshangābād, but at the same time he is less entirely attached to the soil and its cultivation, and much more intelligent and cosmopolitan than either. One of the most intelligent officials in the Agricultural Department is a Panwār, and several members of the caste have made large sums as forest and railway contractors in this District; Panwār *shikāris* are also not uncommon. They are generally averse to sedentary occupations, and though quite ready to avail themselves of the advantages of primary education, they do not, as a rule, care to carry their studies to a point that would ensure their admission to the higher ranks of Government service. Very few of them are to be found as patwāris, constables or peons. They are a handsome race, with intelligent faces, unusually fair, with high foreheads, and often grey eyes. They are not, as a rule, above middle height, but they are active and hard-working and by no means deficient in courage and animal spirits, or a sense of humour. They are clannish in the extreme, and to elucidate a criminal case in which no one but Panwārs are concerned, and in a Panwār village, is usually a harder task than the average local police officer can tackle. At times they are apt to affect, in conversation with Government officials, a whining and unpleasant tone, especially when pleading their claim to some concession or other; and they are by no means lacking in astuteness and are good hands at a bargain. But they are a pleasant, intelligent and plucky race, not easily cast down by misfortune and always ready to attempt new enterprises in almost any direction save those indicated by the Agricultural Department.

"In the art of rice cultivation they are past masters. They are skilled tank-builders, though perhaps hardly equal to the Kohlis of Chānda. But they excel especially in the mending and levelling of their fields, in neat transplantation, and in the choice and adaptation of the different varieties of rice to land of varying qualities. They are by no means specially efficient as labourers, though they and their wives do their fair share of field work; but they are well able to control the labour of others, especially of aborigines, through whom most of their tank and other works are executed."

PARDHĀN

LIST OF PARAGRAPHS

1. *General notice.*
2. *Tribal subdivisions.*
3. *Marriage.*
4. *Religion.*
5. *Social customs.*
6. *Methods of cheating among Pathāris.*
7. *Musicians and priests.*

1. General notice.

Pardhān, Pathāri, Panāl.—An inferior branch of the Gond tribe whose occupation is to act as the priests and minstrels of the Gonds. In 1911 the Pardhāns numbered nearly 120,000 persons in the Central Provinces and Berār. The only other locality where they are found is Hyderābād, which returned 8000. The name Pardhān is of Sanskrit origin and signifies a minister or agent. It is the regular designation of the principal minister of a Rājpūt State, who often fulfils the functions of a Mayor of the Palace. That it was applied to the tribe in this sense is shown by the fact that they are also known as Diwān, which has the same meaning. There is a tradition that the Gond kings employed Pardhāns as their ministers, and as the Pardhāns acted as genealogists they may have been more intelligent than the Gonds, though they are in no degree less illiterate. To themselves and their Gond relations the Pardhāns are frequently not known by that name, which has been given to them by the Hindus, but as Panāl. Other names for the tribe are Parganiha, Desai and Pathāri. Parganiha is a title signifying the head of a *pargana*, and is now applied by courtesy to some families in Chhattīsgarh. Desai has the same signification, being a variant of Deshmukh or the Marātha revenue officer in charge of a circle of villages. Pathāri means a bard or genealogist, or according to another derivation a hillman. On the Satpūra plateau and

GROUP OF PARDHĀNS.

in Chhattīsgarh the tribe is known as Pardhān Pathāria. In Bālāghāt they are also called Mokāsi. The Gonds themselves look down on the Pardhāns and say that the word Pathāria means inferior, and they relate that Bura Deo, their god, had seven sons. These were talking together one day as they dined and they said that every caste had an inferior branch to do it homage, but they had none ; and they therefore agreed that the youngest brother and his descendants should be inferior to the others and make obeisance to them, while the others promised to treat him almost as their equal and give him a share in all the offerings to the dead. The Pardhāns or Pathārias are the descendants of the youngest brother and they accost the Gonds with the greeting 'Bābu Johār,' or 'Good luck, sir.' The Gonds return the greeting by saying 'Pathāri Johār,' or 'How do you do, Pathāri.' Curiously enough Johār is also the salutation sent by a Rājpūt chief to an inferior landholder,[1] and the custom must apparently have been imitated by the Gonds. A variant of the story is that one day the seven Gond brothers were worshipping their god, but he did not make his appearance ; so the youngest of them made a musical instrument out of a string and a piece of wood and played on it. The god was pleased with the music and came down to be worshipped, and hence the Pardhāns as the descendants of the youngest brother continue to play on the *kingri* or lyre, which is their distinctive instrument. The above stories have been invented to account for the social inferiority of the Pardhāns to the Gonds, but their position merely accords with the general rule that the bards and genealogists of any caste are a degraded section. The fact is somewhat contrary to preconceived ideas, but the explanation given of it is that such persons make their living by begging from the remainder of the caste and hence are naturally looked down upon by them ; and further, that in pursuit of their calling they wander about to attend at wedding feasts all over the country, and consequently take food with many people of doubtful social position. This seems a reasonable interpretation of the rule of the in-

---

[1] *Tod's Rājasthān*, i. p. 165. But Johār is a common term of salutation among the Hindus.

feriority of the bard, which at any rate obtains generally among the Hindu castes.

2. Tribal sub-divisions.

The tribe have several endogamous divisions, of which the principal are the Rāj Pardhāns, the Gānda Pardhāns and the Thothia Pardhāns. The Rāj Pardhāns appear to be the descendants of alliances between Rāj Gonds and Pardhān women. They say that formerly the priests of Bura Deo lived a celibate life, and both men and women attended to worship the god; but on one occasion the priests ran away with some women and after this the Gonds did not know who should be appointed to serve the deity. While they were thus perplexed, a *kingri* (or rude wooden lyre) fell from heaven on to the lap of one of them, and, in accordance with this plain indication of the divine will, he became the priest, and was the ancestor of the Rāj Pardhāns; and since this *contretemps* the priests are permitted to marry, while women are no longer allowed to attend the worship of Bura Deo. The Thothia subtribe are said to be the descendants of illicit unions, the word Thothia meaning 'maimed'; while the Gāndas are the offspring of intermarriages between the Pardhāns and members of that degraded caste. Other groups are the Mādes or those of the Mād country in Chānda and Bastar, the Khalotias or those of the Chhattīsgarh plain, and the Deogarhias of Deogarh in Chhindwāra; and there are also some occupational divisions, as the Kandres or bamboo-workers, the Gaitas who act as priests in Chhattīsgarh, and the Arakhs who engage in service and sell old clothes. A curious grouping is found in Chānda, where the tribe are divided into the Gond Pathāris and Chor or 'Thief' Pathāris. The latter have obtained their name from their criminal propensities, but they are said to be proud of it and to refuse to intermarry with any families not having the designation of Chor Pathāri. In Raipur the Pathāris are said to be the offspring of Gonds by women of other castes, and the descendants of such unions. The exogamous divisions of the Pardhāns are the same as those of the Gonds, and like them they are split up into groups worshipping different numbers of gods whose members may not marry with one another.

A Pardhān wedding is usually held in the bridegroom's

village in some public place, such as the market or cross-roads. The boy wears a blanket and carries a dagger in his hand. The couple walk five times round in a circle, after which the boy catches hold of the girl's hand. He tries to open her fist which she keeps closed, and when he succeeds in this he places an iron ring on her little finger and puts his right toe over that of the girl's. The officiating priest then ties the ends of their clothes together and five chickens are killed. The customary bride-price is Rs. 12, but it varies in different localities. A widower taking a girl bride has, as a rule, to pay a double price. A widow is usually taken in marriage by her deceased husband's younger brother.

3. Marriage.

As the priests of the Gonds, the Pardhāns are employed to conduct the ceremonial worship of their great god Bura Deo, which takes place on the third day of the bright fortnight of Baisākh (April). Many goats or pigs are then offered to him with liquor, cocoanuts, betel-leaves, flowers, lemons and rice. Bura Deo is always enshrined under a tree outside the village, either of the mahua or *sāj* (*Terminalia tomentosa*) varieties. In Chhattīsgarh the Gonds say that the origin of Bura Deo was from a child born of an illicit union between a Gond and a Rāwat woman. The father murdered the child by strangling it, and its spirit then began to haunt and annoy the man and all his relations, and gradually extended its attentions to all the Gonds of the surrounding country. It finally consented to be appeased by a promise of adoration from the whole tribe, and since then has been installed as the principal deity of the Gonds. The story is interesting as showing how completely devoid of any supernatural majesty or power is the Gond conception of their principal deity.

4. Religion.

Like the Gonds, the Pardhāns will eat almost any kind of food, including beef, pork and the flesh of rats and mice, but they will not eat the leavings of others. They will take food from the hands of Gonds, but the Gonds do not return the compliment. Among the Hindus generally the Pardhāns are much despised, and their touch conveys impurity while that of a Gond does not. Every Pardhān has tattooed on his left arm near the inside of the elbow a dotted figure which represents his totem or the animal, plant or other

5. Social customs.

natural object after which his sept is named. Many of them have a better type of countenance than the Gonds, which is perhaps due to an infusion of Hindu blood. They are also generally more intelligent and cunning. They have criminal propensities, and the Pathārias of Chhattīsgarh are especially noted for cattle-lifting and thieving. Writing forty years ago Captain Thomson[1] described the Pardhāns of Seoni as bearing the very worst of characters, many of them being regular cattle-lifters and gang robbers. In some parts of Seoni they had become the terror of the village proprietors, whose houses and granaries they fired if they were in any way reported on or molested. Since that time the Pardhāns have become quite peaceable, but they still have a bad reputation for petty thieving.

6. Methods of cheating among Pathāris.

In Chhattīsgarh one subdivision is said to be known as Sonthaga (*sona*, gold, and *thag*, a cheat), because they cheat people by passing counterfeit gold. Their methods were described as follows in 1872 by Captain McNeill, District Superintendent of Police:[2] "They procure a quantity of the dry bark of the pīpal,[3] mahua,[4] tamarind or *gular*[5] trees and set it on fire; when it has become red-hot it is raked into a small hole and a piece of well-polished brass is deposited among the glowing embers. It is constantly moved and turned about and in ten or fifteen minutes has taken a deep orange colour resembling gold. It is then placed in a small heap of wood-ashes and after a few minutes taken out again and carefully wrapped in cotton-wool. The peculiar orange colour results from the sulphur and resin in the bark being rendered volatile. They then proceed to dispose of the gold, sometimes going to a fair and buying cattle. On concluding a bargain they suddenly find they have no money, and after some hesitation reluctantly produce the gold, and say they are willing to part with it at a disadvantage, thereby usually inducing the belief that it has been stolen. The cupidity of the owner of the cattle is aroused, and he accepts the gold at a rate which would be very advantageous if it were genuine.

[1] *Seoni Settlement Report* (1867), p. 43.
[2] From a collection of notes on Pathāris by various police officers. The passage is somewhat abridged in reproduction.
[3] *Ficus R.*
[4] *Bassia latifolia.*
[5] *Ficus glomerata.*

At other times they join a party of pilgrims, to which some of their confederates have already obtained admission in disguise, and offer to sell their gold as being in great want of money. A piece is first sold to the confederates on very cheap terms and the other pilgrims eagerly participate." It would appear that the Pathāris have not much to learn from the owners of buried treasure or the confidence or three-card trick performers of London, and their methods are in striking contrast to the guileless simplicity usually supposed to be a characteristic of the primitive tribes. Mr. White states that "All the property acquired is taken back to the village and there distributed by a *panchāyat* or committee, whose head is known as Mokāsi. The Mokāsi is elected by the community and may also be deposed by it, though he usually holds office for life ; to be a successful candidate for the position of Mokāsi one should have wealth and experience and it is not a disadvantage to have been in jail. The Mokāsi superintends the internal affairs of the community and maintains good relations with the proprietor and village watchman by means of gifts."

7. Musicians and priests.

The Pardhāns and Pathāris are also, as already stated, village musicians, and their distinctive instrument the *kingri* or *kingadi* is described by Mr. White as consisting of a stick passed through a gourd. A string or wire is stretched over this and the instrument is played with the fingers. Another kind possesses three strings of woven horse-hair and is played with the help of a bow. The women of the Gānda Pardhān subtribe act as midwives. Mr. Tawney' wrote of the Pardhāns of Chhindwāra :[1] " The Rāj-Pardhāns are the bards of the Gonds and they can also officiate as priests, but the Bhumka generally acts in the latter capacity and the Pardhāns confine themselves to singing the praises of the god. At every public worship in the Deo-khalla or dwelling-place of the gods, there should, if possible, be a Pardhān, and great men use them on less important occasions. They cannot even worship their household gods or be married without the Pardhāns. The Rāj-Pardhāns are looked down on by the Gonds, and considered as somewhat inferior, seeing that they take the

[1] Note already quoted.

offerings at religious ceremonies and the clothes of the dear departed at funerals. This has never been the business of a true Gond, who seems never happier than when wandering in the jungle, and who above all things loves his axe, and next to that a tree to chop at. There is nothing in the ceremonies or religion of the Pardhāns to distinguish them from the Gonds."

PĀRDHI

LIST OF PARAGRAPHS

1. *General notice of the caste.*
2. *Subdivisions.*
3. *Marriage and funeral customs.*
4. *Religion.*
5. *Dress, food and social customs.*
6. *Ordeals.*
7. *Methods of catching birds.*
8. *Hunting with leopards.*
9. *Decoy stags.*
10. *Hawks.*
11. *Crocodile fishing.*
12. *Other occupations and criminal practices.*

Pārdhi,[1] **Bahelia, Mīrshikār, Moghia, Shikāri, Tākankar.**—A low caste of wandering fowlers and hunters. They numbered about 15,000 persons in the Central Provinces and Berār in 1911, and are found scattered over several Districts. These figures include about 2000 Bahelias. The word Pārdhi is derived from the Marāthi *paradh*, hunting. Shikāri, the common term for a native hunter, is an alternative name for the caste, but particularly applied to those who use firearms, which most Pārdhis refuse to do. Moghia is the Hindustāni word for fowler, and Tākankar is the name of a small occupational offshoot of the Pārdhis in Berār, who travel from village to village and roughen the household grinding-mills when they have worn smooth. The word is derived from *tākna*, to tap or chisel. The caste appears to be a mixed group made up of Bāwarias or other Rājpūt outcastes, Gonds and social derelicts from all sources. The Pārdhis perhaps belong more especially to the Marātha country, as they are numerous in Khāndesh, and many of them talk a dialect of Gujarāti. In the

1. *General notice of the caste.*

---

[1] This article is partly compiled from papers by Mr. Adurām Chaudhri and Pandit Pyāre Lāl Misra of the Gazetteer Office, and extracts from Mr. Kitts' *Berār Census Report* (1881), and Mr. Sewell's note on the caste quoted in Mr. Gayer's *Lectures on the Criminal Tribes of the Central Provinces.*

northern Districts their speech is a mixture of Mārwāri and Hindi, while they often know Marāthi or Urdu as well. The name for the similar class of people in northern India is Bahelia, and in the Central Provinces the Bahelias and Pārdhis merge into one another and are not recognisable as distinct groups. The caste is recruited from the most diverse elements, and women of any except the impure castes can be admitted into the community; and on this account their customs differ greatly in different localities. According to their own legends the first ancestor of the Pārdhis was a Gond, to whom Mahādeo taught the art of snaring game so that he might avoid the sin of shooting it; and hence the ordinary Pārdhis never use a gun.

2. Subdivisions.

Like other wandering castes the Pārdhis have a large number of endogamous groups, varying lists being often given in different areas. The principal subcastes appear to be the Shikāri or Bhīl Pārdhis, who use firearms; the Phānse Pārdhis, who hunt with traps and snares; the Langoti Pārdhis, so called because they wear only a narrow strip of cloth round the loins; and the Tākankars. Both the Tākankars and Langotis have strong criminal tendencies. Several other groups are recorded in different Districts, as the Chitewāle, who hunt with a tame leopard; the Gāyake, who stalk their prey behind a bullock; the Gosain Pārdhis, who dress like religious mendicants in ochre-coloured clothes and do not kill deer, but only hares, jackals and foxes; the Shīshi ke Telwāle, who sell crocodile's oil; and the Bandarwāle who go about with performing monkeys. The Bahelias have a subcaste known as Kārijāt, the members of which only kill birds of a black colour. Their exogamous groups are nearly all those of Rājpūt tribes, as Sesodia, Panwār, Solanki, Chauhān, Rāthor, and so on; it is probable that these have been adopted through imitation by vagrant Bāwarias and others sojourning in Rājputāna. There are also a few groups with titular or other names, and it is stated that members of clans bearing Rājpūt names will take daughters from the others in marriage, but will not give their daughters to them.

Girls appear to be somewhat scarce in the caste and a bride-price is usually paid, which is given as Rs. 9 in

Chānda, Rs. 35 in Bilāspur, and Rs. 60 or more in Hoshangābād and Saugor. If a girl should be seduced by a man of the caste she would be united to him by the ceremony of a widow's marriage : but her family will require a bride from her husband's family in exchange for the girl whose value he has destroyed. Even if led astray by an outsider a girl may be readmitted into the caste ; and in the extreme case of her being debauched by her brother, she may still be married to one of the community, but no one will take food from her hands during her lifetime, though her children will be recognised as proper Pārdhis. A special fine of Rs. 100 is imposed on a brother who commits this crime. The ceremony of marriage varies according to the locality in which they reside ; usually the couple walk seven times round a *tānda* or collection of their small mat tents. In Berār a cloth is held up by four poles as a canopy over them and they are preceded by a married woman carrying five pitchers of water. Divorce and the marriage of widows are freely permitted. The caste commonly bury their dead, placing the head to the north. They do not shave their heads in token of mourning.

3. Marriage and funeral customs.

In Berār their principal deity is the goddess Devi, who is known by different names. Every family of Langoti Pārdhis has, Mr. Gayer states,[1] its image in silver of the goddess, and because of this no Langoti Pārdhi woman will wear silver below the waist or hang her *sāri* on a peg, as it must never be put on the same level as the goddess. They also sometimes refuse to wear red or coloured clothes, one explanation for this being that the image of the goddess is placed on a bed of red cloth. In Hoshangābād their principal deity is called Guraiya Deo, and his image, consisting of a human figure embossed in silver, is kept in a leather bag on the west side of their tents ; and for this reason women going out of the encampment for a necessary purpose always proceed to the east. They also sleep with their feet to the east. Goats are offered to Guraiya Deo and their horns are placed in his leather bag. In Hoshangābād they sacrifice a fowl to the ropes of their tents at the Dasahra and Diwāli festivals, and on the former

4. Religion.

[1] *Lectures on Criminal Tribes of the C.P.*, p. 19.

occasion clean their hunting implements and make offerings to them of turmeric and rice. They are reported to believe that the sun and moon die and are reborn daily. The hunter's calling is one largely dependent on luck or chance, and, as might be expected, the Pārdhis are firm believers in omens, and observe various rules by which they think their fortune will be affected. A favourite omen is the simple device of taking some rice or juāri in the hand and counting the grains. Contrary to the usual rule, even numbers are considered lucky and odd ones unlucky. If the first result is unsatisfactory a second or third trial may be made. If a winnowing basket or millstone be let fall and drop to the right hand it is a lucky omen, and similarly if a flower from Devi's garland should fall to the right side. The bellowing of cows, the mewing of a cat, the howling of a jackal and sneezing are other unlucky omens. If a snake passes from left to right it is a bad omen and if from right to left a good one. A man must not sleep with his head on the threshold of a house or in the doorway of a tent under penalty of a fine of Rs. 2-8; the only explanation given of this rule is that such a position is unlucky because a corpse is carried out across the threshold. A similar penalty is imposed if he falls down before his wife even by accident. A Pārdhi, with the exception of members of the Sesodia clan, must never sleep on a cot, a fine of five rupees being imposed for a breach of this rule. A man who has once caught a deer must not again have the hair of his head touched by a razor, and thus the Pārdhis may be recognised by their long and unkempt locks. A breach of this rule is punished with a fine of fifteen rupees, but it is not observed everywhere. A woman must never step across the rope or peg of a tent, nor upon the place where the blood of a deer has flowed on to the ground. During her monthly period of impurity a woman must not cross a river nor sit in a boat. A Pārdhi will never kill or sell a dog and they will not hunt wild dogs even if money is offered to them. This is probably because they look upon the wild dog as a fellow-hunter, and consider that to do him injury would bring ill-luck upon themselves. A Pārdhi has also theoretically a care for the preservation of game. When he has caught a number of birds in his trap, he will let a pair of them loose so that they may go on breeding. Women are not permitted to take any part in the work of hunting, but are confined strictly to their household duties. A woman who kicks her husband's stick is fined Rs. 2-8. The butt end of the stick is employed for mixing vegetables and other purposes, but the meaning of the rule is not clear unless one of its uses is for the enforcement of conjugal discipline. A Pārdhi may not swear by a dog, a cat or a squirrel. Their most solemn oath is in the name of their deity Guraiya Deo, and it is believed that any one who falsely takes this oath will become a leper. The Phāns Pārdhis may not travel in a railway train, and some of them are forbidden even to use a cart or other conveyance.

5. Dress, food and social customs.

In dress and appearance the Pārdhis are disreputable and dirty. Their features are dark and their hair matted and unkempt. They never wear shoes and say that they are protected by a special promise of the goddess Devi to their first ancestor that no insect or reptile in the forests should injure them. The truth is, no doubt, that shoes would make it impossible for them to approach their game without disturbing it, and from long practice the soles of their feet become impervious to thorns and minor injuries. Similarly the Langoti Pārdhis are so called because they wear only a narrow strip of cloth round the loins, the reason probably being that a long one would impede them by flapping and catching in the brushwood. But the explanation which they themselves give,[1] a somewhat curious one in view of their appearance, is that an ordinary *dhoti* or loin-cloth if worn might become soiled and therefore unlucky. Their women do not have their noses pierced and never wear spangles or other marks on the forehead. The Pārdhis still obtain fire by igniting a piece of cotton with flint and iron. Mr. Sewell notes that their women eat at the same time as the men, instead of after them as among most Hindus. They explain this custom by saying that on one occasion a woman tried to poison her husband and it was therefore adopted as a precaution against similar attempts; but no doubt it has always prevailed, and the more orthodox

[1] *Berār Census Report* (1881), p. 135.

practice would be almost incompatible with their gipsy life. Similar reasons of convenience account for their custom of celebrating marriages all the year round and neglecting the Hindu close season of the four months of the rains. They travel about with little huts made of matting, which can be rolled up and carried off in a few minutes. If rain comes on they seek shelter in the nearest village.[1] In some localities the caste eat no food cooked with butter or oil. They are usually considered as an impure caste, whose touch is a defilement to Hindus. Brāhmans do not officiate at their ceremonies, though the Pārdhis resort to the village Joshi or astrologer to have a propitious date indicated for marriages. They have to pay for such services in money, as Brāhmans usually refuse to accept even uncooked grain from them. After childbirth women are held to be impure and forbidden to cook for their families for a period varying from six weeks to six months. During their periodical impurity they are secluded for four, six or eight days, the Pārdhis observing very strict rules in these matters, as is not infrequently the case with the lowest castes. Their caste meetings, Mr. Sewell states, are known as Deokāria or 'An act performed in honour of God'; at these meetings arrangements for expeditions are discussed and caste disputes decided. The penalty for social offences is a fine of a specified quantity of liquor, the liquor provided by male and female delinquents being drunk by the men and women respectively. The punishment for adultery in either sex consists in cutting off a piece of the left ear with a razor, and a man guilty of intercourse with a prostitute is punished as if he had committed adultery. The Pārdhi women are said to be virtuous.

6. Ordeals. The Pārdhis still preserve the primitive method of trial by ordeal. If a woman is suspected of misconduct she is made to pick a pice coin out of boiling oil; or a pīpal leaf is placed on her hand and a red-hot axe laid over it, and if her hand is burnt or she refuses to stand the test she is pronounced guilty. Or, in the case of a man, the accused is made to dive into water; and as he dives an arrow is shot

[1] *Bombay Ethnographic Survey*, art. Pārdhi.

from a bow. A swift runner fetches and brings back the arrow, and if the diver can remain under water until the runner has returned he is held to be innocent. In Nimār, if an unmarried girl becomes pregnant, two cakes of dough are prepared, a piece of silver being placed in one and a lump of coal in the other. The girl takes one of the cakes, and if it is found to contain the coal she is expelled from the community, while if she chooses the piece of silver, she is pardoned and made over to one of the caste. The idea of the ordeal is apparently to decide the question whether her condition was caused by a Pārdhi or an outsider.

The Phāns Pārdhis hunt all kinds of birds and the smaller animals with the *phānda* or snare. Mr. Ball describes their procedure as follows:[1] "For peacock, sāras crane and bustard they have a long series of nooses, each provided with a wooden peg and all connected with a long string. The tension necessary to keep the nooses open is afforded by a slender slip of antelope's horn (very much resembling whalebone), which forms the core of the loop. Provided with several sets of these nooses, a trained bullock and a shield-like cloth screen dyed buff and pierced with eye-holes, the bird-catcher sets out for the jungle, and on seeing a flock of pea-fowl circles round them under cover of the screen and the bullock, which he guides by a nose-string. The birds feed on undisturbed, and the man rapidly pegs out his long strings of nooses, and when all are properly disposed, moves round to the opposite side of the birds and shows himself; when they of course run off, and one or more getting their feet in the nooses fall forwards and flap on the ground; the man immediately captures them, knowing that if the strain is relaxed the nooses will open and permit of the bird's escape. Very cruel practices are in vogue with these people with reference to the captured birds, in order to keep them alive until a purchaser is found. The peacocks have a feather passed through the eyelids, by which means they are effectually blinded, while in the case of smaller birds both the legs and wings are broken." Deer, hares and even pig are also caught by a strong rope with running nooses. For smaller birds the

7. Methods of catching birds.

[1] *Jungle Life in India*, pp. 586-587.

appliance is a little rack about four inches high with uprights a few inches apart, between each of which is hung a noose. Another appliance mentioned by Mr. Ball is a set of long conical bag nets, which are kept open by hooks and provided with a pair of folding doors. The Pārdhi has also a whistle made of deer-horn, with which he can imitate the call of the birds. Tree birds are caught with bird-lime as described by Sir G. Grierson.[1] The Bahelia has several long shafts of bamboos called *nāl* or *nār*, which are tied together like a fishing rod, the endmost one being covered with bird-lime. Concealing himself behind his bamboo screen the Bahelia approaches the bird and when near enough strikes and secures it with his rod; or he may spread some grain out at a short distance, and as the birds are hopping about over it he introduces the pole, giving it a zig-zag movement and imitating as far as possible the progress of a snake. Having brought the point near one of the birds, which is fascinated by its stealthy approach, he suddenly jerks it into its breast and then drawing it to him, releases the poor palpitating creature, putting it away in his bag, and recommences the same operation. This method does not require the use of bird-lime.

8. Hunting with leopards.

The manner in which the Chita Pārdhis use the hunting leopard (*Felis jubata*) for catching deer has often been described.[2] The leopard is caught full-grown by a noose in the manner related above. Its neck is first clasped in a wooden vice until it is half-strangled, and its feet are then bound with ropes and a cap slipped over its head. It is partially starved for a time, and being always fed by the same man, after a month or so it becomes tame and learns to know its master. It is then led through villages held by ropes on each side to accustom it to the presence of human beings. On a hunting party the leopard is carried on a cart, hooded, and, being approached from down wind, the deer allow the cart to get fairly close to them. The Indian antelope or black-buck are the usual quarry, and as these frequent cultivated land, they regard country carts without suspicion. The hood is then taken off and the leopard

---

[1] *Peasant Life in Bihār*, p. 80.

[2] See Jerdon's *Mammals of India*, p. 97. The account there given is quoted in the *Chhindwāra District Gazetteer*, pp. 16-17.

springs forward at the game with extreme velocity, perhaps exceeding that which any other quadruped possesses. The accounts given by Jerdon say that for the moment its speed is greater than that of a race-horse. It cannot maintain this for more than three or four hundred yards, however, and if in that distance the animal has not seized its prey, it relinquishes the pursuit and stalks about in a towering passion. The Pārdhis say that when it misses the game the leopard is as sulky as a human being and sometimes refuses food for a couple of days. If successful in the pursuit, it seizes the antelope by the throat; the kepeer then comes up, and cutting the animal's throat collects some of the blood in the wooden ladle with which the leopard is always fed; this is offered to him, and dropping his hold he laps it up eagerly, when the hood is cleverly slipped on again.

The conducting of the cheetah from its cage to the chase is by no means an easy matter. The keeper leads him along, as he would a large dog, with a chain; and for a time as they scamper over the country the leopard goes willingly enough; but if anything arrests his attention, some noise from the forest, some scented trail upon the ground, he moves more slowly, throws his head aloft and peers savagely round. A few more minutes perhaps and he would be unmanageable. The keeper, however, is prepared for the emergency. He holds in his left hand a cocoanut shell, sprinkled on the inside with salt; and by means of a handle affixed to the shell he puts it at once over the nose of the cheetah. The animal licks the salt, loses the scent, forgets the object which arrested his attention, and is led quietly along again.[1]

9. Decoy stags.

For hunting stags, tame stags were formerly used as decoys according to the method described as follows: " We had about a dozen trained stags, all males, with us. These, well acquainted with the object for which they were sent forward, advanced at a gentle trot over the open ground towards the skirt of the wood. They were observed at once by the watchers of the herd, and the boldest of the wild animals advanced to meet them. Whether the intention was to welcome them peacefully or to do battle for their

[1] *Private Life of an Eastern King*, p. 75.

pasturage I cannot tell; but in a few minutes the two parties were engaged in a furious contest. Head to head, antlers to antlers, the tame deer and the wild fought with great fury. Each of the tame animals, every one of them large and formidable, was closely engaged in contest with a wild adversary, standing chiefly on the defensive, not in any feigned battle or mimicry of war but in a hard-fought combat. We now made our appearance in the open ground on horseback, advancing towards the scene of conflict. The deer on the skirts of the wood, seeing us, took to flight; but those actually engaged maintained their ground and continued the contest. In the meantime a party of native huntsmen, sent for the purpose, gradually drew near to the wild stags, getting in between them and the forest. What their object was we were not at the time aware; in truth it was not one that we could have approved or encouraged. They made their way into the rear of the wild stags, which were still combating too fiercely to mind them; they approached the animals, and with a skilful cut of their long knives the poor warriors fell hamstrung. We felt pity for the noble animals as we saw them fall helplessly on the ground, unable longer to continue the contest and pushed down of course by the decoy-stags. Once down, they were unable to rise again."[1]

10. Hawks.   Hawks were also used in a very ingenious fashion to prevent duck from flying away when put upon water: "The trained hawks were now brought into requisition, and marvellous it was to see the instinct with which they seconded the efforts of their trainers. The ordinary hawking of the heron we had at a later period of this expedition; but the use now made of the animal was altogether different, and displayed infinitely more sagacity than one would suppose likely to be possessed by such an animal. These were trained especially for the purpose for which they were now employed. A flight of ducks—thousands of birds—were enticed upon the water as before by scattering corn over it. The hawks were then let fly, four or five of them. We made our appearance openly upon the bank, guns in hand, and the living swarm of birds rose at once into the air. The hawks circled above them, however, in a rapid revolving

[1] *Private Life of an Eastern King*, pp. 69, 71.

flight and they dared not ascend high. Thus was our prey retained fluttering in mid-air, until hundreds had paid the penalty with their lives. Only picture in your mind's eye the circling hawks above gyrating monotonously, the fluttering captives in mid-air, darting now here, now there to escape, and still coward-like huddling together; and the motley group of sportsmen on the bank and you have the whole scene before you at once." [1]

For catching crocodile, a method by which as already stated one group of the Pārdhis earn their livelihood, a large double hook is used, baited with a piece of putrid deer's flesh and attached to a hempen rope 70 or 80 feet long. When the crocodile has swallowed the hook, twenty or thirty persons drag the animal out of the water and it is despatched with axes. Crocodiles are hunted only in the months of Pūs (December), Māgh (January) and Chait (March), when they are generally fat and yield plenty of oil. The flesh is cut into pieces and stewed over a slow fire, when it exudes a watery oil. This is strained and sold in bottles at a rupee a seer (2 lbs.). It is used as an embrocation for rheumatism and for neck galls of cattle. The Pārdhis do not eat crocodile's flesh.

11. Crocodile fishing.

A body of Pārdhis are sometimes employed by all the cultivators of a village jointly for the purpose of watching the spring crops during the day and keeping black-buck out of them. They do this perhaps for two or three months and receive a fixed quantity of grain. The Tākankars are regularly employed as village servants in Berār and travel about roughening the stones of the household grinding-mills when their surfaces have worn smooth. For this they receive an annual contribution of grain from each household. The caste generally have criminal tendencies and Mr. Sewell states, that "The Langoti Pārdhis and Tākankars are the worst offenders. Ordinarily when committing dacoity they are armed with sticks and stones only. In digging through a wall they generally leave a thin strip at which the leader carefully listens before finally bursting through. Then when the hole has been made large enough, he strikes a match and holding it in front of him so that his features are shielded

12. Other occupations and criminal practices.

[1] *Private Life of an Eastern King*, pp. 39-40.

has a good survey of the room before entering. . . . As a rule, they do not divide the property on or near the scene of the crime, but take it home. Generally it is carried by one of the gang well behind the rest so as to enable it to be hidden if the party is challenged." In Bombay they openly rob the standing crops, and the landlords stand in such awe of them that they secure their goodwill by submitting to a regular system of blackmail.[1]

[1] *Bombay Ethnographic Survey, ibidem.*

PARJA

LIST OF PARAGRAPHS

1. *General notice of the tribe.*
2. *Exogamous septs.*
3. *Kinship and marriage.*
4. *Marriage dance.*
5. *Nuptial ceremony.*
6. *Widow-marriage and divorce.*
7. *Religion and festivals.*
8. *Disposal of the dead.*
9. *Occupation and social customs.*

Parja.—A small tribe,[1] originally an offshoot of the Gonds, who reside in the centre and east of the Bastar State and the adjoining Jaipur zamīndāri of Madras. They number about 13,000 persons in the Central Provinces and 92,000 in Madras, where they are also known as Poroja. The name Parja appears to be derived from the Sanskrit Parja, a subject. The following notice of it is taken from the *Madras Census Report*[2] of 1871 : " The term Parja is, as Mr. Carmichael has pointed out, merely a corruption of a Sanskrit term signifying a subject ; and it is understood as such by the people themselves, who use it in contradistinction to a free hillman. Formerly, says a tradition that runs through the whole tribe, Rājas and Parjas were brothers, but the Rājas took to riding horses or, as the Barenja Parjas put it, sitting still, and we became carriers of burdens and Parjas. It is quite certain in fact that the term Parja is not a tribal denomination, but a class denomination ; and it may be fitly rendered by the familiar epithet of ryot. There is no doubt, however, that by far the greater number of these Parjas are akin to the Khonds of the Ganjam Maliāhs. They are thrifty, hardworking cultivators, undisturbed by the intestinal broils which their cousins in the north engage in,

1. General notice of the tribe.

---

[1] This article is based on papers by Mr. Panda Baijnāth and other officers of the Bastar State. [2] By Dr. Cornish.

and they bear in their breasts an inalienable reverence for their soil, the value of which they are rapidly becoming acquainted with. Their ancient rights to these lands are acknowledged by colonists from among the Aryans, and when a dispute arises about the boundaries of a field possessed by recent arrivals a Parja is usually called in to point out the ancient landmarks. Gadbas are also represented as indigenous from the long lapse of years that they have been in the country, but they are by no means of the patriarchal type that characterises the Parjas."

In Bastar the caste are also known as Dhurwa, which may be derived from Dhur, the name applied to the body of Gonds as opposed to the Rāj-Gonds. In Bastar, Dhurwa now conveys the sense of a headman of a village. The tribe have three divisions, Thakara or Tagara, Peng and Mudara, of which only the first is found in Bastar. Thakara appears to be a corruption of Thākur, a lord, and the two names point to the conclusion that the Parjas were formerly dominant in this tract. They themselves have a story, somewhat resembling the one quoted above from Madras, to the effect that their ancestor was the elder brother of the first Rāja of Bastar when he lived in Madras, to the south of Warangal. From there he had to flee on account of an invasion of the Muhammadans, and was accompanied by the goddess Dānteshwari, the tutelary deity of the Rājas of Bastar. In accordance with the command of the goddess the younger brother was considered as the Rāja and rode on a horse, while the elder went before him carrying their baggage. At Bhadrachallam they met the Bhatras, and further on the Halbas. The goddess followed them, guiding their steps, but she strictly enjoined on the Rāja not to look behind him so as to see her. But when they came to the sands of the rivers Sankani and Dankani, the tinkle of the anklets of the goddess could not be heard for the sand. The Rāja therefore looked behind him to see if she was following, on which she said that she could go no more with him, but he was to march as far as he could and then settle down. The two brothers settled in Bastar, where the descendants of the younger became the ruling clan, and those of the elder were their servants, the Parjas. The story indicates, perhaps, that the Parjas were the original Gond inhabitants and rulers of the country, and were supplanted by a later immigration of the same tribe, who reduced them to subjection, and became Rāj-Gonds. Possibly the first transfer of power was effected by the marriage of an immigrant into a Parja Rāja's family, as so often happened with these old dynasties. The Parjas still talk about the Rāni of Bastar as their *Bohu* or 'younger brother's wife,' and the custom is probably based on some such legend. The Madras account of them as the arbiters of boundary disputes points to the same conclusion, as this function is invariably assigned to the oldest residents in any locality. The Parjas appear to be Gonds and not Khonds. Their sept names are Gondi words, and their language is a form of Gondi, called after them Parji. Parji has hitherto been considered a form of Bhatri, but Sir G. Grierson [1] has now classified the latter as a dialect of the Uriya language, while Parji remains 'A local and very corrupt variation of Gondi, considerably mixed with Hindi forms.' While then the Parjas, in Bastar at any rate, must be held to be a branch of the Gonds, they may have a considerable admixture of the Khonds, or other tribes in different localities, as the rules of marriage are very loose in this part of the country.[2]

2. Exogamous septs.

The tribe have exogamous totemistic septs, as Bāgh a tiger, Kachhim a tortoise, Bokda a goat, Netām a dog, Gohi a big lizard, Pandki a dove and so on. If a man kills accidentally the animal after which his sept is named, the earthen cooking-pots of his household are thrown away, the clothes are washed, and the house is purified with water in which the bark of the mango or *jāmun* [3] tree has been steeped. This is in sign of mourning, as it is thought that such an act will bring misfortune. If a man of the snake sept kills a snake accidentally, he places a piece of new yarn on his head, praying for forgiveness, and deposits the body on an anthill, where snakes are supposed to live. If a man of the goat sept eats goat's flesh, it is thought that he will

---

[1] *Linguistic Survey*, vol. ix. p. 554; vol. ii. part ii. pp. 434 ff.
[2] In the article on Gond it is suggested that the Gonds and Khonds were originally one tribe, and the fact that the Parjas have affinities with both of them appears to support this view.
[3] *Eugenia jambolana*.

become blind at once. A Parja will not touch the body of his totem-animal when dead, and if he sees any one killing or teasing it when alive, he will go away out of sight. It is said that a man of the Kachhim sept once found a tortoise while on a journey, and leaving it undisturbed, passed on. When the tortoise died it was reborn in the man's belly and troubled him greatly, and since then every Parja is liable to be afflicted in the same way in the side of the abdomen, the disease which is produced being in fact enlarged spleen. The tortoise told the man that as he had left it lying by the road, and had not devoted it to any useful purpose, he was afflicted in this way. Consequently, when a man of the Kachhim sept finds a tortoise nowadays, he gives it to somebody else who can cut it up. The story is interesting as a legend of the origin of spleen, but has apparently been invented as an excuse for killing the sacred animal.

3. Kinship and marriage.

Marriage is prohibited in theory between members of the same sept. But as the number of septs is rather small, the rule is not adhered to, and members of the same sept are permitted to marry so long as they do not come from the same village; the original rule of exogamy being perhaps thus exemplified. The proposal for a match is made by the boy's father, who first offers a cup of liquor to the girl's father in the bazār, and subsequently explains his errand. If the girl's father, after consulting with his family, disapproves of the match, he returns an equal quantity of liquor to the boy's father in token of his decision. The girl is usually consulted, and asked if she would like to marry her suitor, but not much regard is had to her opinion. If she dislikes him, however, she usually runs away from him after a short interlude of married life. If a girl becomes pregnant with a caste-fellow before marriage, he is required to take her, and give to the family the presents which he would make to them on a regular marriage. The man can subsequently be properly married to some other woman, but the girl cannot be married at all. If a girl is seduced by a man outside the caste, she is made over to him. It is essential for a man to be properly married at least once, and an old bachelor will sometimes go through the form of being wedded to his maternal uncle's daughter, even though she may be an infant. If no proposal for marriage is made for a girl, she is sometimes handed over informally to any man who likes to take her, and who is willing to give as much for her as the parents would receive for a regular marriage. A short time before the wedding, the boy's father sends a considerable quantity of rice to the girl's father, and on the day before he sends a calf, a pot of liquor, fifteen annas worth of copper coin, and a new cloth. The bridegroom's expenses are about Rs. 50, and the bride's about Rs. 10.

At weddings the tribe have a dance called Surcha, for which the men wear a particular dress consisting of a long coat, a turban and two or three scarves thrown loosely over the shoulders. Strings of little bells are tied about the feet, and garlands of beads round the neck; sometimes men and women dance separately, and sometimes both sexes together in a long line or a circle. Music is provided by bamboo flutes, drums and an iron instrument something like a flute. As they dance, songs are sung in the form of question and answer between the lines of men and women, usually of a somewhat indecent character. The following short specimen may be given:—

4. Marriage dance.

Man. If you are willing to go with me we will both follow the officer's elephant. If I go back without you my heart can have no rest.

Woman. Who dare take me away from my husband while the Company is reigning. My husband will beat me and who will pay him the compensation?

Man. You had better make up your mind to go with me. I will ask the Treasurer for some money and pay it to your husband as compensation.

Woman. Very well, I will make ready some food, and will run away with you in the next bright fortnight.

These dialogues often, it is said, lead to quarrels between husband and wife, as the husband cannot rebuke his wife in the assembly. Sometimes the women fall in love with men in the dance, and afterwards run away with them.

The marriage takes place at the boy's house, where two marriage-sheds are made. It is noticeable that the bride on going to the bridegroom's house to be married is accompanied only by her female relatives, no man of her family being allowed to be with her. This is probably a reminis-

5. Nuptial ceremony.

cence of the old custom of marriage by capture, as in former times she was carried off by force, the opposition of her male relatives having been quelled. In memory of this the men still do not countenance the wedding procession by their presence. The bridal couple are made to sit down together on a mat, and from three to seven pots of cold water are poured over them. About a week after the wedding the couple go to a market with their friends, and after walking round it they all sit down and drink liquor.

6. Widow-marriage and divorce.

The remarriage of widows is permitted, and a widow is practically compelled to marry her late husband's younger brother, if he has one. If she persistently refuses to do so, in spite of the strongest pressure, her parents turn her out of their house. In order to be married the woman goes to the man's house with some friends; they sit together on the ground, and the friends apply the *tīka* or sign by touching their foreheads with dry rice. A man can divorce his wife if she is of bad character, or if she is supposed to be under an unfavourable star, or if her children die in infancy. A divorced woman can marry again as if she were a widow.

7. Religion and festivals.

The Parjas worship the class of divinities of the hills and forests usually revered among primitive tribes, as well as Dānteshwari, the tutelary goddess of Bastar. On the day that sowing begins they offer a fowl to the field, first placing some grains of rice before it. If the fowl eats the rice they prognosticate a good harvest, and if not the reverse. A few members of the tribe belong to the Rāmānandi sect, and on this account a little extra attention is paid to them. If such a one is invited to a feast he is given a wooden seat, while others sit on the ground. It is said that a few years ago a man became a Kabīrpanthi, but he subsequently went blind and his son died, and since this event the sect is absolutely without adherents. Most villages have a Sirha or man who is possessed by the deity, and his advice is taken in religious matters, such as the detection of witches. Another official is called Medha Gantia or 'The Counter of posts.' He appoints the days for weddings, calculating them by counting on his fingers, and also fixes auspicious days for the construction of a house or for the commencement of sowing. It is probable that in former times he kept count of the days by numbering posts or trees. When rain is wanted the people fix a piece of wood into the ground, calling it Bhīmsen Deo or King of the Clouds. They pour water over it and pray to it, asking for rain. Every year, after the crops are harvested, they worship the rivers or streams in the village. A snake, a jackal, a hare and a dog wagging its ears are unlucky objects to see when starting on a journey, and also a dust devil blowing along in front. They do not kill wild dogs, because they say that tigers avoid the forests where these reside, and some of them hold that a tiger on meeting a wild dog climbs a tree to get out of his way. Wednesday and Thursday are lucky days for starting on a journey, and the operations of sowing, reaping and threshing should be commenced and completed on one of these days. When a man intends to build a house he places a number of sets of three grains of rice, one resting on the other two, on the ground in different places. Each set is covered by a leaf-cup with some earth to hold it down. Next morning the grains are inspected, and if the top one has fallen down the site is considered to be lucky, as indicating that the earth is wishful to bear the burden of a house in this place. A house should face to the east or west, and not to the north or south. Similarly, the roads leading out of the village should run east or west from the starting-point. The principal festivals of the Parjas are the Hareli[1] or feast of the new vegetation in July, the Nawākhāni[2] or feast of the new rice crop in August or September, and the Am Nawākhāni or that of the new mango crop in April or May. At the feasts the new season's crop should be eaten, but if no fresh rice has ripened, they touch some of the old grain with a blade of a growing rice-plant, and consider that it has become the new crop. On these occasions ancestors are worshipped by members of the family only inside the house, and offerings of the new crops are made to them.

8. Disposal of the dead.

The dead are invariably buried, the corpse being laid in the ground with head to the east and feet to the west. This is probably the most primitive burial, it being supposed that the region of the dead is towards the west, as the setting

---

[1] Hareli, *lit.* 'the season of greenness.'
[2] Nawākhāni, *lit.* 'the new eating.'

sun disappears in that direction. The corpse is therefore laid in the grave with the feet to the west ready to start on its journey. Members of the tribe who have imbibed Hindu ideas now occasionally lay the corpse with the head to the north in the direction of the Ganges. Rice-gruel, water and a tooth-stick are placed on the grave nightly for some days after death. As an interesting parallel instance, near home, of the belief that the soul starts on a long journey after death, the following passage may be quoted from Mr. Gomme's Folklore: "Among the superstitions of Lancashire is one which tells us of a lingering belief in a long journey after death, when food is necessary to support the soul. A man having died of apoplexy at a public dinner near Manchester, one of the company was heard to remark, 'Well, poor Joe, God rest his soul! He has at least gone to his long rest wi' a belly full o' good meat, and that's some consolation!' And perhaps a still more remarkable instance is that of the woman buried in Curton Church, near Rochester, who directed by her will that the coffin was to have a lock and key, the key being placed in her dead hand, so that she might be able to release herself at pleasure."[1]

After the burial a dead fish is brought on a leaf-plate to the mourners, who touch it, and are partly purified. The meaning of this rite, if there be any, is not known. After the period of mourning, which varies from three to nine days, is over, the mourners and their relatives must attend the next weekly bazār, and there offer liquor and sweets in the name of the dead man, who upon this becomes ranked among the ancestors.

9. Occupation and social customs.

The Parjas are cultivators, and grow rice and other crops in the ordinary manner. Many of them are village headmen, and to these the term Dhurwa is more particularly applied. The tribe will eat fowls, pig, monkeys, the large lizard, field-rats, and bison and wild buffalo, but they do not eat carnivorous animals, crocodiles, snakes or jackals. Some of them eat beef while others have abjured it, and they will not accept the leavings of others. They are not considered to be an impure caste. If any man or woman belonging to a higher caste has a *liaison* with a Parja, and is on that

[1] *Folklore as a Historical Science* (G. L. Gomme), pp. 191, 192.

account expelled from their own caste, he or she can be admitted as a Parja. In their other customs and dress and ornaments the tribe resemble the Gonds of Bastar. Women are tattooed on the chest and arms with patterns of dots. The young men sometimes wear their hair long, and tie it in a bunch behind, secured by a strip of cloth.

PĀSI

LIST OF PARAGRAPHS

1. *The nature and origin of the caste.*
2. *Brahmanical legends.*
3. *Its mixed composition.*
4. *Marriage and other customs.*
5. *Religion, superstitions and social customs.*
6. *Occupation.*
7. *Criminal tendencies.*

1. The nature and origin of the caste.

Pāsi, Passi.[1]—A Dravidian occupational caste of northern India, whose hereditary employment is the tapping of the palmyra, date and other palm trees for their sap. The name is derived from the Sanskrit *pāshika*, 'One who uses a noose,' and the Hindi *pās* or *pāsa*, a noose. It is a curious fact that when the first immigrant Parsis from Persia landed in Gujarāt they took to the occupation of tapping palm trees, and the poorer of them still follow it. The resemblance in the name, however, can presumably be nothing more than a coincidence. The total strength of the Pāsis in India is about a million and a half persons, nearly all of whom belong to the United Provinces and Bihār. In the Central Provinces they number 3500, and reside principally in the Jubbulpore and Hoshangābād Districts. The caste is now largely occupational, and is connected with the Bhars, Arakhs, Khatīks and other Dravidian groups of low status. But in the past they seem to have been of some importance in Oudh. "All through Oudh," Mr. Crooke states, "they have traditions that they were lords of the country, and that their kings reigned in the Districts of Kheri, Hardoi and Unao. Rāmkot, where the town of Bāngarmau in Unao now stands, is said to have been one of their chief strongholds. The last of the Pāsi lords of

[1] Based principally on Mr. Crooke's article on the caste in his *Tribes and Castes of the North-Western Provinces and Oudh.*

Rāmkot, Rāja Santhar, threw off his allegiance to Kanauj and refused to pay tribute. On this Rāja Jaichand gave his country to the Banāphar heroes Alha and Udal, and they attacked and destroyed Rāmkot, leaving it the shapeless mass of ruins which it now is." Similar traditions prevail in other parts of Oudh. It is also recorded that the Rājpāsis, the highest division of the caste, claim descent from Tilokchand, the eponymous hero of the Bais Rājpūts. It would appear then that the Pāsis were a Dravidian tribe who held a part of Oudh before it was conquered by the Rājpūts. As the designation of Pāsi is an occupational term and is derived from the Sanskrit, it would seem that the tribe must formerly have had some other name, or they may be an occupational offshoot of the Bhars. In favour of this suggestion it may be noted that the Bhars also have strong traditions of their former dominance in Oudh. Thus Sir C. Elliott states in his *Chronicles of Unao*[1] that after the close of the heroic age, when Ajodhya was held by the Sūrajvansi Rājpūts under the great Rāma, we find after an interval of historic darkness that Ajodhya has been destroyed, the Sūrajvansis utterly banished, and a large extent of country is being ruled over by aborigines called Cheros in the far east, Bhars in the centre and Rājpāsis in the west. Again, in Kheri the Pāsis always claim kindred with the Bhars,[2] and in Mīrzāpur[3] the local Pāsis represent the Bhars as merely a subcaste of their own tribe, though this is denied by the Bhars themselves. It seems therefore a not improbable hypothesis that the Pāsis and perhaps also the kindred tribe of Arakhs are functional groups formed from the Bhar tribe. For a discussion of the early history of this important tribe the reader must be referred to Mr. Crooke's excellent article.

The following tradition is related by the Pāsis themselves in Mīrzāpur and the Central Provinces: One day a man was going to kill a number of cows. Parasurāma was at that time practising austerities in the jungles. Hearing the cries of the sacred animals he rushed to their assistance, but the cow-killer was aided by his friends. So

2. Brāhmanical legends.

---

[1] Quoted in Mr. Crooke's *Tribes and Castes*, art. Bhar.
[2] Art. Pāsi, para. 3. [3] Art. Bhar, para. 4.

Parasurāma made five men out of *kusha* grass and brought them to life by letting drops of his perspiration fall upon them. Hence arose the name Pāsi, from the Hindi *pasīna*, sweat. The men thus created rescued the cows. Then they returned to Parasurāma and asked him to provide them with a wife. Just at that moment a Kāyasth girl was passing by, and her Parasurāma seized and made over to the Pāsis. From them sprang the Kaithwās subcaste. Another legend related by Mr. Crooke tells that during the time Parasurāma was incarnate there was an austere devotee called Kuphal who was asked by Brahma to demand of him a boon, whereupon he requested that he might be perfected in the art of thieving. His request was granted, and there is a well-known verse regarding the devotions of Kuphal, the pith of which is that the mention of the name of Kuphal, who received a boon from Brahma, removes all fear of thieves; and the mention of his three wives—Māya (illusion), Nidra (sleep), and Mohani (enchantment)—deprives thieves of success in their attempts against the property of those who repeat these names. Kuphal is apparently the progenitor of the caste, and the legend is intended to show how the position of the Pāsis in the Hindu cosmos or order of society according to the caste system has been divinely ordained and sanctioned, even to the recognition of theft as their hereditary pursuit.

3. Its mixed composition.

Whatever their origin may have been the composition of the caste is now of a very mixed nature. Several names of other castes, as Gūjar, Guāl or Ahīr, Arakh, Khatīk, Bahelia, Bhīl and Bania, are returned as divisions of the Pāsis in the United Provinces. Like all migratory castes they are split into a number of small groups, whose constitution is probably not very definite. The principal subcastes in the Central Provinces are the Rājpāsis or highest class, who probably were at one time landowners; the Kaithwās or Kaithmās, supposed to be descended from a Kāyasth, as already related; the Tirsulia, who take their name from the *trisūla* or three-bladed knife used to pierce the stem of the palm tree; the Bahelia or hunters, and Chiriyamār or fowlers; the Ghudchadha or those who ride on ponies, these being probably saises or horse-keepers; the Khatīk or butchers and Gūjar or graziers; and the Māngta or beggars, these being the bards and genealogists of the caste, who beg from their clients and take food from their hands; they are looked down on by the other Pāsis.

In the Central Provinces the tribe have now no exogamous groups; they avoid marriage with blood relations as far back as their memory carries them. At their weddings the couple walk round the *srāwan* or heavy log of wood, which is dragged over the fields before sowing to break up the larger clods of earth. In the absence of this an ordinary plough or harrow will serve as a substitute, though why the Pāsis should impart a distinctively agricultural implement into their marriage ceremony is not clear. Like the Gonds, the Pāsis celebrate their weddings at the bridegroom's house and not at the bride's. Before the wedding the bridegroom's mother goes and sits over a well, taking with her seven *urad* cakes[1] and stalks of the plant. The bridegroom walks seven times round the well, and at each turn the parapet is marked with red and white clay and his mother throws one of the cakes and stalks into the well. Finally, the mother threatens to throw herself into the well, and the bridegroom begs her not to do so, promising that he will serve and support her. Divorce and the remarriage of widows are freely permitted. Conjugal morality is somewhat lax, and Mr. Crooke quotes a report from Pertābgarh to the effect that if a woman of a tribe become pregnant by a stranger and the child be born in the house of her father or husband, it will be accepted as a Pāsi of pure blood and admitted to all tribal privileges. The bodies of adults may be buried or burnt as convenient, but those of children or of persons dying from smallpox, cholera or snake-bite are always buried. Mourning is observed during ten days for a man and nine days for a woman, while children who die unmarried are not mourned at all.

4. Marriage and other customs.

The Pāsis worship all the ordinary Hindu deities. All classes of Brāhmans will officiate at their marriages and other ceremonies, and do anything for them which does not involve touching them or any article in their houses. In Bengal, Sir H. Risley writes, the employment of Brāhmans

5. Religion, superstitions and social customs.

[1] A pulse of a black colour (*Phaseolus radiatus*).

for the performance of ceremonies appears to be a very recent reform for, as a rule, in sacrifices and funeral ceremonies, the worshipper's sister's son performs the functions of a priest. "Among the Pāsis of Monghyr this ancient custom, which admits of being plausibly interpreted as a survival of female kinship, still prevails generally." The social status of the Pāsis is low, but they are not regarded as impure. At their marriage festivals, Mr. Gayer notes, boys are dressed up as girls and made to dance in public, but they do not use drums or other musical instruments. They breed pigs and cure the bacon obtained from them. Marriage questions are decided by the tribal council, which is presided over by a chairman (*Chaudhri*) selected at each meeting from among the most influential adult males present. The council deals especially with cases of immorality and pollution caused by journeys across the black water (*kāla pāni*), which the criminal pursuits of the tribe occasionally necessitate.

6. Occupation.

The traditional occupation of the Pāsis, as already stated, is the extraction of the sap of palm trees. But some of them are hunters and fowlers like the Pārdhis, and like them also they make and mend grindstones, while others are agriculturists; and the caste has also strong criminal propensities, and includes a number of professional thieves. Some are employed in the Nāgpur mills and others have taken small building contracts. Pāsis are generally illiterate and in poor circumstances, and are much addicted to drink. In climbing[1] palm trees to tap them for their juice the worker uses a heel-rope, by which his feet are tied closely together. At the same time he has a stout rope passing round the tree and his body. He leans back against this rope and presses the soles of his feet, thus tied together, against the tree. He then climbs up the tree by a series of hitches or jerks of his back and feet alternately. The juice of the palmyra palm (*tār*) and the date palm (*khajūr*) is extracted by the Pāsi. The *tār* trees, Sir H. Risley states,[2] are tapped from March to May, and the date palm in the cold season. The juice of the former, known as *tāri* or

---

[1] These sentences are taken from Dr. Grierson's *Peasant Life in Behār*, p. 79.
[2] *Tribes and Castes of Bengal*, art. Pāsi.

toddy, is used in the manufacture of bread, and an intoxicating liquor is obtained from it by adding sugar and grains of rice. Hindustāni drunkards often mix *dhatūra* with the toddy to increase its intoxicating properties. The quantity of juice extracted from one tree varies from five to ten pounds. Date palm *tāri* is less commonly drunk, being popularly believed to cause rheumatism, but is extensively used in preparing sugar.

Eighty years ago, when General Sleeman wrote, the Pāsis were noted thieves. In his *Journey through Oudh* [1] he states that in Oudh there were then supposed to be one hundred thousand families of Pāsis, who were skilful thieves and robbers by profession, and were formerly Thugs and poisoners as well. They generally formed the worst part of the gangs maintained by refractory landowners, "who keep Pāsis to fight for them, as they pay themselves out of the plunder and cost little to their employers. They are all armed with bows and are very formidable at night. They and their refractory employés keep the country in a perpetual state of disorder." Mr. Gayer notes [2] that the criminally disposed members of the caste take contracts for the watch and sale of mangoes in groves distant from habitations, so that their movements will not be seen by prying eyes. They also seek employment as roof-thatchers, in which capacity they are enabled to ascertain which houses contain articles worth stealing. They show considerable cunning in disposing of their stolen property. The men will go openly in the daytime to the receiver and acquaint him with the fact that they have property to dispose of; the receiver goes to the bazār, and the women come to him with grass for sale. They sell the grass to the receiver, and then accompany him home with it and the stolen property, which is artfully concealed in it.

7. Criminal tendencies.

Patwa, Patwi, Patra, Ilākeband.—The occupational caste of weavers of fancy silk braid and thread. In 1911 the Patwas numbered nearly 6000 persons in the Central

---

[1] The following passage is taken from Mr. Crooke's article on Pāsi, and includes quotations from the *Sitāpur* and *Hardoi Settlement Reports*.
[2] *Lectures on Criminal Tribes of the Central Provinces.*

Provinces, being returned principally from the Narsinghpur, Raipur, Saugor, Jubbulpore and Hoshangābād Districts. About 800 were resident in Berār. The name is derived from the Sanskrit *pata*, woven cloth, or Hindi *pāt*, silk. The principal subcastes of the Patwas are the Naraina; the Kanaujia, also known as Chhipi, because they sew marriage robes; the Deobansi or 'descendants of a god,' who sell lac and glass bangles; the Lakhera, who prepare lac bangles; the Kachera, who make glass bangles; and others. Three of the above groups are thus functional in character. They have also Rājpūt and Kāyastha subcastes, who may consist of refugees from those castes received into the Patwa community. In the Central Provinces the Patwas and Lakheras are in many localities considered to be the same caste, as they both deal in lac and sell articles made of it; and the account of the occupations of the Lakhera caste also applies largely to the Patwas. The exogamous groups of the caste are named after villages, or titles or nicknames borne by the reputed founder of the group. They indicate that the Patwas of the Central Provinces are generally descended from immigrants from northern India. The Patwa usually purchases silk and colours it himself. He makes silk strings for pyjamas and coats, armlets and other articles. Among these are the silk threads called *rākhis*, used on the Rakshābandhan festival,[1] when the Brāhmans go round in the morning tying them on to the wrists of all Hindus as a protection against evil spirits. For this the Brāhman receives a present of one or two pice. The *rākhi* is made of pieces of raw silk fibre twisted together, with a knot at one end and a loop at the other. It goes round the wrist, and the knot is passed through the loop. Sisters also tie it round their brothers' wrists and are given a present. The Patwas make the *phundri* threads for tying up the hair of women, whether of silk or cotton, and various threads used as amulets, such as the *janjīra*, worn by men round the neck, and the *ganda* or wizard's thread, which is tied round the arm after incantations have been said over it; and the

---

[1] The word Rakshābandhan is said to mean literally, 'the bond of protection.' Another suggested derivation, 'binding the devil,' is perhaps incorrect.

necklets of silk or cotton thread bound with thin silver wire which the Hindus wear at Anant Chaudas, a sort of All Saints' Day, when all the gods are worshipped. In this various knots are made by the Brāhmans, and in each a number of deities are tied up to exert their beneficent influence for the wearer of the thread. These are the bands which Hindus commonly wear on their necks. The Patwas thread necklaces of gold and jewels on silk thread, and also make the strings of cowries, slung on pack-thread, which are tied round the necks of bullocks when they race on the Pola day, and on ponies, probably as a charm. After a child is born in the family of one of their clients, the Patwas make tassels of cotton and hemp thread coloured red, green and yellow, and hang them to the centre-beam of the house and the top of the child's cradle, and for this they get a present, which from a rich man may be as much as ten rupees. The sacred thread proper is usually made by Brāhmans in the Central Provinces. Some of the Patwas wander about hawking their wares from village to village. Besides the silk threads they sell the *tiklis* or large spangles which women wear on their foreheads, lac bangles and balls of henna, and the large necklaces of lac beads covered with tinsel of various colours which are worn in Chhattīsgarh. A Patwa must not rear the tasar silkworm nor boil the cocoons on pain of expulsion from caste.

PINDĀRI

LIST OF PARAGRAPHS

1. *Origin of the name.*
2. *Rise of the Pindāris.*
3. *Their strength and sphere of operations.*
4. *Pindāri expeditions and methods.*
5. *Return from an expedition.*
6. *Suppression of the Pindāris. Death of Chītu.*
7. *Character of the Pindāris.*
8. *The existing Pindāris.*
9. *Attractions of a Pindāri's life.*

1. Origin of the name.

Pindāri, Pindāra, Pendhāri.[1]—The well-known professional class of freebooters, whose descendants now form a small cultivating caste. In the Central Provinces they numbered about 150 persons in 1911, while there are about 10,000 in India. They are mainly Muhammadans but include some Hindus. The Pindāris of the Central Provinces are for the most part the descendants of Gonds, Korkus and Bhīls whose children were carried off in the course of raids, circumcised, and brought up to follow the profession of a Pindāri. When the bands were dispersed many of them returned to their native villages and settled down. Malcolm considered that the name Pindāri was derived from *pinda*, an intoxicating drink, and was given to them on account of their dissolute habits. He adds that Karīm Khān, a famous Pindāri leader, had never heard of any other reason for the name, and Major Henley had the etymology confirmed by the most intelligent of the Pindāris of whom he inquired.[2] In support of this may be adduced the name of Bhangi, given to the sweeper caste on account of their drinking *bhang* or hemp. Wilson

---

[1] The historical account of the Pindāris is compiled from Malcolm's *Memoir of Central India*, Grant-Duff's *History of the Marāthas*, and Prinsep's *Transactions in India* (1825). Some notes on the modern Pindāris have been furnished by Mr. Hīra Lāl, and Mr. Waman Rustom Mandloi, Naib-Tahsildār, Harda.

[2] *Memoir of Central India*, i. p. 433.

again held the most probable derivation to be from the Marāthi *pendha*, in the sense of a bundle of rice-straw, and *hara* one who takes, because the name was originally applied to horsemen who hung on to an army and were employed in collecting forage. The fact that the existing Pindāris are herdsmen and tenders of buffaloes and thus might well have been employed for the collection of forage may be considered somewhat to favour the above view; but the authors of *Hobson-Jobson*, after citing these derivations, continue : " We cannot think any of the etymologies very satisfactory. We venture another as a plausible suggestion merely. Both *pind-parna* in Hindi and *pindas-basnen* in Marāthi signify ' to follow,' the latter being defined as 'to stick closely ; to follow to the death ; used of the adherence of a disagreeable fellow.' Such phrases could apply to these hangers-on of an army in the field looking out for prey." Mr. W. Irvine [1] has suggested that the word comes from a place or region called Pandhār, which is referred to by native historians and seems to have been situated between Burhānpur and Handia on the Nerbudda ; and states that there is good evidence to prove that a large number of Pindāris were settled in this part of the country. Mr. D. Chisholm reports from Nimār that "Pandhār or Pāndhar is the name given to a stream which rises in the Gularghāt hills of the Asīr range and flows after a very circuitous course into the Masak river by Mandeva. The name signifies five, as it is joined by four other small streams. The Asīr hills were the haunts of the Pindāris, and the country about these, especially by the banks of the Pandhār, is very wild ; but it is not commonly known that the Pindāris derived their name from this stream." And as the Pindāris are first heard of as hangers-on of the Marātha armies in the Deccan prior to A.D. 1700, it seems unlikely also that their name can be taken from a place in the Nimār District, where it is not recorded that they were settled before 1794. Nor does the Pandhār itself seem sufficiently important to have given a name to the whole body of freebooters. Malcolm's or Wilson's derivations are perhaps on the whole the most probable. Prinsep writes : " Pindāra seems to have the same

[1] *Indian Antiquary*, 1900.

reference to Pandour that Kuzāk has to Cossack. The latter word is of Turkish origin but is commonly used to express a mounted robber in Hindustān." Though the Pandours were the predatory light cavalry of the Austrian army, and had considerable resemblance to the Pindāris, it does not seem possible to suppose that there is any connection between the two words. The Pendra zamīndāri in Bilāspur is named after the Pindāris, the dense forests of the Rewah plateau which includes Pendra having been one of their favourite asylums of refuge.

2. Rise of the Pindāris.

The Pindāri bands appear to have come into existence during the wars of the late Muhammadan dynasties in the Deccan, and in the latter part of the seventeenth century they attached themselves to the Marāthas in their revolt against Aurāngzeb. The first mention of the name occurs at this time. During and after the Marātha wars many of the Pindāri leaders obtained grants in Central India from Sindhia and Holkar, and were divided into two parties owing a nominal allegiance to these princes and designated as the Sindhia Shāhi and Holkar Shāhi. In the period of chaos which reigned at this time outside British territories their raids in all directions attended by the most savage atrocities became more and more intolerable. These outrages extended from Bundelkhand to Cuddapah south of Madras and from Orissa to Gujarāt.

When attached to the Marātha armies, Malcolm states, the Pindāris always camped separately and were not permitted to plunder in the Marātha territories; they were given an allowance averaging four annas each a day, and further supported themselves by employing their small horses and bullocks in carrying grain, forage and wood, for which articles the Pindāri bazār was the great mart. When let loose to pillage, which was always the case some days before the army entered an enemy's country, all allowances stopped; no restraint whatever was put upon these freebooters till the campaign was over, when the Marātha commander, if he had the power, generally seized the Pindāri chiefs or surrounded their camps and forced them to yield up the greater part of their booty. A knowledge of this practice led the Pindāris to redouble their excesses, that they might be able to satisfy without ruin the expected rapacity of their employers.

In 1794, Grant-Duff writes, Sindhia assigned some lands to the Pindāris near the banks of the Nerbudda, which they soon extended by conquests from the Grassias or original independent landholders in their neighbourhood. Their principal leaders at that time were two brothers named Hiru and Burun, who are said to have been put to death for their aggressions on the territory of Sindhia and of Rāghuji Bhonsla. The sons of Hiru and Burun became Pindāri chiefs; but Karīm Khān, a Pindāra who had acquired great booty at the plunder of the Nizām's troops after the battle of Hurdla, and was distinguished by superior cunning and enterprise, was the principal leader of this refuse of the Marātha armies. Karīm got the district of Shujahalpur from Umar Khān which, with some additions, was afterwards confirmed to him by Sindhia. During the war of 1803 and the subsequent disturbed state of the country Karīm contrived to obtain possession of several districts in Mālwa belonging to Sindhia's jāgirdārs; and his land revenue at one time is said to have amounted to fifteen lakhs of rupees a year. He also wrested some territory from the Nawāb of Bhopāl on which he built a fort as a place of security for his family and of deposit for his plunder. Karīm was originally a Sindhia Shāhi, but like most of the Pindāris, except about 5000 of the Holkar Shāhis who remained faithful, he changed sides or plundered his master whenever it suited his convenience, which was as often as he found an opportunity. Sindhia, jealous of his encroachments, on pretence of lending him some gems inveigled him to an interview, made him prisoner, plundered his camp, recovered the usurped districts and lodged Karīm in the fort of Gwalior.

A number of leaders started up after the confinement of Karīm, of whom Chitu, Dost Muhammad, Namdār Khān and Sheikh Dullah became the most conspicuous. They associated themselves with Amīr Khān in 1809 during his expedition to Berār; and in 1810, when Karīm Khān purchased his release from Gwalior, they assembled under that leader a body of 25,000 horse and some battalions of newly raised infantry with which they again proposed to invade Berār; but Chitu, always jealous of Karīm's ascendency, was detached by Rāghuji Bhonsla from the alliance, and afterwards co-operated with Sindhia in attacking him; Karīm was in consequence driven to seek an asylum with his old patron Amīr Khān, but by the influence of Sindhia Amīr Khān kept him in a state of confinement until 1816.

When the Marāthas ceased to spread themselves over India, the Pindāris who had attended their armies were obliged to plunder the territories of their former protectors for subsistence. To the unemployed soldiery of India, particularly to the Muhammadans, the life of a Pindāra had many allurements; but the Marātha horsemen who possessed hereditary rights or had any pretensions to respectability did not readily join them. One of the above leaders, Sheikh Dullah or Abdullah, apparently became a dacoit after the Pindāris had been dispersed, and he is still remembered in Hoshangābād and Nimār in the following saying:

> *Niche zamīn aur upar Allah,*
> *Aur bīch men phiren Sheikh Dullah,*

or 'God is above and the earth beneath, and Sheikh Dullah ranges at his will between.'

3. Their strength and sphere of operations.

In 1814, Prinsep states,[1] the actual military force at the disposal of the Pindāris amounted to 40,000 horse, inclusive of the Pathāns, who though more orderly and better disciplined than the Pindāris of the Nerbudda, possessed the same character and were similarly circumstanced in every respect, supporting themselves entirely by depredations whenever they could practise them. Their number would be doubled were we to add the remainder of Holkar's troops of the irregular kind, which were daily deserting the service of a falling house in order to engage in the more profitable career of predatory enterprise; and the loose cavalry establishments of Sindhia and the Bhonsla, which were bound by no ties but those of present entertainment, and were always in great arrears of pay. The presence of this force in the centre of India and able to threaten each of the three Presidencies imposed the most extensive annual precautions for defence, in spite of which the territories of our allies were continually overrun. On two occasions, once

---

[1] *Transactions in India*, 1813-23, by H. T. Prinsep.

when they entered Gujarāt in 1808–9 and again in 1812 when the Bengal provinces of Mīrzāpur and Shahābād were devastated, they penetrated into our immediate territories. Grant-Duff records that in one raid on the coast from Masulipatam northward they in ten days plundered 339 villages, burning many, killing and wounding 682 persons, torturing 3600 and carrying off or destroying property to the amount of two lakhs and a half. Indeed their reputation was such that the mere rumour of an incursion caused a regular panic at Madras in 1816, of which General Hislop gives an amusing account:[1] " In the middle of this year the troops composing the garrison of Fort St. George were moved out and encamped on the island outside Black Town wall. This imprudent step was taken, as was affirmed, to be in readiness to meet the Pindāris, who were reported to be on their road to Madras, although it was well known that not half a dozen of them were at that time within 200 miles of the place. The native inhabitants of all classes throughout Madras and its vicinity were in the utmost alarm, and looked for places of retreat and security for their property. It brought on Madras all the distresses in imagination of Hyder Ali's invasion. It was about this period that an idle rumour reached Madras of the arrival of the Pindāris at the Mount; all was uproar, flight and despair to the walls of Madras. This alarm originated in a few Dhobis and grass-cutters of the artillery having mounted their *tattus* and, in mock imitation of the Pindāris, galloped about and played with long bamboos in their hands in the vicinity of the Mount. The effect was such, however, that many of the civil servants and inhabitants of the Mount Road packed up and moved to the Fort for protection. Troopers, messengers, etc., were seen galloping to the Government House and thence to the different public authorities. Such was the alarm in the Government House that on the afternoon of that day an old officer, anxious to offer some advice to the Governor, rode smartly to the Government gardens, and on reaching the entrance observed the younger son of the Governor running with all possible speed into the house; who having got to a place of security ventured to

[1] *Marātha and Pindāri Campaigns.*

look back and then discovered in the old officer a face which he had before seen; when turning back again he exclaimed, 'Upon my word, sir, I was so frightened I took you for a Pindārī.'"

4. Pindārī expeditions and methods.

A Pindārī expedition[1] usually started at the close of the rains, as soon as the rivers became fordable after the Dasahra festival in October. Their horses were then shod, having previously been carefully trained to prepare them for long marches and hard work. A leader of tried courage having been chosen as Luhbaria, all who were so inclined set forth on a foray, or Luhbar as it was called in the Pindārī nomenclature, the strength of the party often amounting to several thousands. In every thousand Pindārīs about 400 were tolerably well mounted and armed; of this number about every fifteenth man carried a matchlock, but their favourite weapon was the ordinary bamboo spear of the Marāthas, from 12 to 18 feet long. Of the remaining 600 two-thirds were usually common Lootais or plunderers, indifferently mounted and armed with every variety of weapon; and the rest slaves, attendants and camp-followers, mounted on *tattus* or wild ponies and keeping up with the Luhbar in the best manner they could. They were encumbered neither by tents nor baggage; each horseman carried a few cakes of bread for his own subsistence and some feeds of grain for his horse. They advanced at the rapid rate of forty or fifty miles a day, neither turning to the right nor to the left till they arrived at their place of destination. They then divided, and made a sweep of all the cattle and property they could find; committing at the same time the most horrid atrocities and destroying what they could not carry away. They trusted to the secrecy and suddenness of the irruption for avoiding those who guarded the frontiers of the countries they invaded; and before a force could be brought against them they were on their return. Their chief strength lay in their being intangible. If pursued they made marches of extraordinary length, sometimes upwards of sixty miles, by roads almost impracticable for regular troops. If overtaken they dispersed and reassembled at an appointed rendezvous; if followed to

[1] The above is compiled from the accounts given by Prinsep and Malcolm.

the country from which they issued they broke into small parties. The cruelties they perpetrated were beyond belief. As it was impossible for them to remain more than a few hours on the same spot the utmost despatch was necessary in rifling any towns or villages into which they could force an entrance; every one whose appearance indicated the probability of his possessing money was immediately put to the most horrid torture till he either pointed out his hoard or died under the infliction. Nothing was safe from the pursuit of Pindāri lust or avarice; it was their common practice to burn and destroy what they could not carry away; and in the wantonness of barbarity to ravish and murder women and children under the eyes of their husbands and parents. The ordinary modes of torture inflicted by these miscreants were to apply red-hot irons to the soles of the feet; or to throw the victim on the ground and place a plank or beam across his chest on which two men pressed with their whole weight; and to throw oil on the clothes and set fire to them, or tie wisps of rag soaked in oil to the ends of all the victim's fingers and set fire to these. Another favourite method was to put hot ashes into a horse-bag, which they tied over a man's mouth and nostrils and thumped him on the back until he inhaled the ashes. The effect on the lungs of the sufferer was such that few long survived the operation.

The return of the Pindāris from an expedition presented at one view their character and habits. When they recrossed the Nerbudda and reached their homes their camp became like a fair. After the claims of the chief of the territory (whose right was a fourth part of the booty, but who generally compounded for one or two valuable articles) had been satisfied, the usual share paid to their Luhbaria, or chosen leader for the expedition, and all debts to merchants and others who had made advances discharged, the plunder of each man was exposed for sale; traders from every part came to make cheap bargains; and while the women were busy in disposing of their husbands' property, the men, who were on such occasions certain of visits from all their friends, were engaged in hearing music, seeing dancers and drolls, and in drinking. This life of debauchery and excess lasted

5. Return from an expedition.

till their money was gone; they were then compelled to look for new scenes of rapine, or, if the season was favourable, were supported by their chiefs, or by loans at high interest from merchants who lived in their camps, many of whom amassed large fortunes. This worst part of the late population of Central India is, as a separate community, now extinct.[1]

6. Suppression of the Pindāris. Death of Chitu.

The result of the Pindāri raids was that Central India was being rapidly reduced to the condition of a desert, and the peasants, unable to support themselves on the land, had no option but to join the robber bands or starve. It was not until 1817 that Lord Hastings obtained authority from home to take regular measures for their repression; and at the same time he also forced or persuaded the principal chiefs of Central India to act vigorously in concert with him. When these were put into operation and the principal routes from Central India occupied by British detachments, the Pindāris were completely broken up and scattered in the course of a single campaign. They made no stand against regular troops, and their bands, unable to escape from the ring of forces drawn round them, were rapidly dispersed over the country. The people eagerly plundered and seized them in revenge for the wrongs long suffered at their hands, and the Bhīl Grassias or border landholders gladly carried out the instructions to hunt them down. On one occasion a native havildar with only thirty-four men attacked and put a large body of them to flight. The principal chiefs, reduced to the condition of hunted outlaws in the jungles, soon accepted the promise of their lives, and on surrendering were either settled on a grant of land or kept in confinement. The well-known leader Chitu joined Apa Sāhib, who had then escaped from Nāgpur and was in hiding in the Pachmarhi hills. Being expelled from there in February 1819 he proceeded to the fort of Asīrgarh in Nimār, but was refused admittance by Sindhia's commandant. He sought shelter in the neighbouring jungle, and on horseback and alone attempted to penetrate a thick cover known to be infested with tigers. He was missed for some days afterwards and no one knew what had become of him.

---

[1] That is when Malcolm wrote his *Memoir*.

His horse was at last discovered grazing near the margin of the forest, saddled and bridled, and exactly in the state in which it was when Chitu had last been seen upon it. Upon search a bag of Rs. 250 was found in the saddle; and several seal rings with some letters of Apa Sāhib, promising future reward, served more completely to fix the identity of the horse's late master. These circumstances, combined with the known resort of tigers to the spot, induced a search for the body, when at no great distance some clothes clotted with blood, and farther on fragments of bones, and at last the Pindāri's head entire with features in a state to be recognised, were successively discovered. The chief's mangled remains were given over to his son for interment, and the miserable fate of one who so shortly before had ridden at the head of twenty thousand horse gave an awful lesson of the uncertainty of fortune and drew pity even from those who had been victims of his barbarity when living.[1]

7. Character of the Pindāris.

The Pindāris, as might be expected, were recruited from all classes and castes, and though many became Muhammadans the Hindus preserved the usages of their respective castes. Most of the Hindu men belonged to the Ladul or grass-cutter class, and their occupation was to bring grass and firewood to the camps. "Those born in the Durrahs or camps," Malcolm states,[2] "appear to have been ignorant in a degree almost beyond belief and were in the same ratio superstitious. The women of almost all the Muhammadan Pindāris dressed like Hindus and worshipped Hindu deities. From accompanying their husbands in most of their excursions they became hardy and masculine; they were usually mounted on small horses or camels, and were more dreaded by the villagers than the men, whom they exceeded in cruelty and rapacity." Colonel Tod notes that the Pindāris, like other Indian robbers, were devout in the observance of their religion:

"A short distance to the west of the Regent's (Kotāh) camp is the Pindāri-ka-chhaoni, where the sons of Karīm Khān, the chief leader of those hordes, resided; for in

---

[1] This account is copied from Prinsep's *Transactions*.
[2] *Memoir*, ii. p. 177.

those days of strife the old Regent would have allied himself with Satan, if he had led a horde of plunderers. I was greatly amused to see in this camp the commencement of an Id-Gāh or place of prayer; for the villains, while they robbed and murdered even defenceless women, prayed five times a day!"[1]

8. The existing Pindāris.

While the freebooting Pindāris had no regular caste organisation, their descendants have now become more or less of a caste in accordance with the usual tendency of a distinctive occupation, producing a difference in status, to form a fresh caste. The existing Pindāris in the Central Provinces are both Muhammadans and Hindus, the Muhammadans, as already stated, having been originally the children of Hindus who were kidnapped and converted. It is one of the very few merits of the Pindāris that they did not sell their captives to slavery. Their numerous prisoners of all ages and both sexes were employed as servants, made over to the chiefs or held to ransom from their relatives, but the Pindāris did not carry on like the Banjāras a traffic in slaves.[2] The Muhammadan Pindāris were said some time ago to have no religion, but with the diffusion of knowledge they have now adopted the rites of Islam and observe its rules and restrictions. In Bhandāra the Hindu Pindāris are Garoris or Gowāris. They say that the ancestors of the Pindāris and Gowāris were two brothers, the business of the Pindāri brother being to tend buffaloes and that of the Gowāri brother to herd cows. These Pindāris will beg from the owners of buffaloes for the above reason. They revere the dog and will not kill it, and also worship snakes and tigers, believing that these animals never do them injury. They carry their dead to the grave in a sitting posture, seated in a *jholi* or wallet, and bury them in the same position. They wear their beards and do not shave. Some of these Pindāris are personal servants, others cultivators and labourers, and others snake-charmers and jugglers.

9. Attractions of a Pindāri's life.

The freebooting life of the Pindāris, unmitigated scoundrels though they were, no doubt had great charms, and must often have been recalled with regret by those who

[1] *Rājasthān*, ii. p. 674.   [2] Malcolm, ii. p. 177.

settled down to the quiet humdrum existence of a cultivator. This feeling has been admirably depicted in Sir Alfred Lyall's well-known poem, of which it will be permissible to quote a short extract:

When I rode a Dekhani charger with the saddle-cloth gold-laced,
And a Persian sword and a twelve-foot spear and a pistol at my waist.
It's many a year gone by now; and yet I often dream
Of a long dark march to the Jumna, of splashing across the stream,
Of the waning moon on the water and the spears in the dim starlight
As I rode in front of my mother [1] and wondered at all the sight.
Then the streak of the pearly dawn—the flash of a sentinel's gun,
The gallop and glint of horsemen who wheeled in the level sun,
The shots in the clear still morning, the white smoke's eddying wreath,
Is this the same land that I live in, the dull dank air that I breathe?
And if I were forty years younger, with my life before me to choose,
I wouldn't be lectured by Kafirs or bullied by fat Hindoos;
But I'd go to some far-off country where Musalmāns still are men,
Or take to the jungle like Chetoo, and die in the tiger's den.

Prabhu, Parbhu.—The Marātha caste of clerks, accountants and patwāris corresponding to the Kāyasths. They numbered about 1400 persons in the southern Districts of the Central Provinces and Berār in 1911. The Prabhus, like the Kāyasths, claim to be descendants of a child of Chandra Sena, a Kshatriya king and himself a son of Arjun, one of the five Pāndava brothers. Chandra Sena was slain by Parasurāma, the Brāhman destroyer of the Kshatriyas, but the child was saved by a Rishi, who promised that he should be brought up as a clerk. The boy was named Somrāj and was married to the daughter of Chitra Gupta, the recorder of the dead. The caste thus claim Kshatriya origin. The name Prabhu signifies 'lord,' but the Brāhmans pretend that the real name of the caste was Parbhu, meaning one of irregular birth. The Prabhus say that Parbhu is a colloquial corruption used by the uneducated. The *gotras* of the Prabhus are eponymous, the names being the same as those of Brāhmans. In the Central Provinces many of them have the surname of Chitnavīs or Secretary. Child-marriage is in vogue and widow-remarriage is forbidden. The wedding ceremony resembles that of the Brāhmans.

1. Historical notice.

[1] The Pindāri's childhood is recalled here, *vide* poem.

In his *Description of a Prabhu marriage*[1] Rai Bahādur B. A. Gupte shows how the old customs are being broken through among the educated classes under the influence of modern ideas. Marriages are no longer arranged without regard to the wishes of the couple, which are thus ascertained: "The next step[2] is to find out the inclination of the hero of the tale. His friends and equals do that easily enough. They begin talking of the family and the girl, and are soon able to fathom his mind. They leave on his desk all the photographs of the girls offered and watch his movements. If he is sensible he quietly drops or returns all the likenesses except the one he prefers, and keeps this in his drawer. He dare not display it, for it is immodest to do so. The news of the approval by the boy soon reaches the parents of the girl." Similarly in her case: "The girl has no direct voice, but her likes and dislikes are carefully fathomed through her girl friends. If she says, 'Why is papa in such a hurry to get rid of me,' or turns her face and goes away as soon as the proposed family is mentioned, a sensible father drops the case and turns his attention to some other boy. This is the direct result of higher education under British rule, but among the masses the girl has absolutely no voice, and the boy has very little unless he revolts and disobediently declines to accept a girl already selected." Similarly the educated Prabhus are beginning to dispense with the astrologer's calculations showing the agreement of the horoscopes of the couple, which are too often made a cloak for the extortion of large presents. "It very often happens that everything is amicably settled except the greed of the priest, and he manages to find out some disagreement between the horoscopes of the marriageable parties to vent his anger. This trick has been sufficiently exposed, and the educated portion of this ultra-literary caste have in most cases discarded horoscopes and planetary conjunctions altogether. Under these restrictions the only thing the council of astrologers have to do is to draw up two documents giving diagrams based on the names of the parties—for names are presumably selected

---

[1] Pamphlet published in connection with the Ethnographic Survey.
[2] *A Prabhu Marriage*, p. 3 *et seq.*

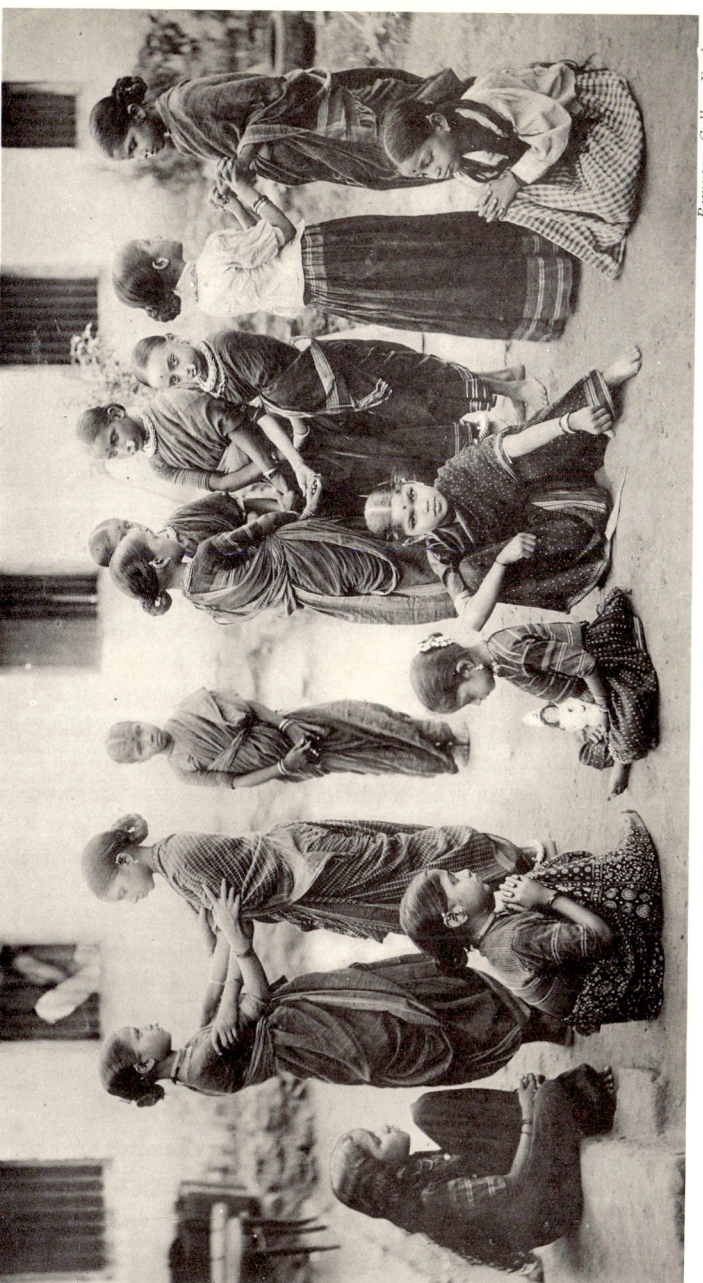

LITTLE GIRLS PLAYING.

according to the conjunctions of the stars at birth. But they are often not, and depend on the liking of the father for a family god, a mythological hero, a patron or a celebrated ancestor in the case of the boy. In that of the girl the favourite deity or a character in the most recent fable or drama the father has just read."

According to custom the bridegroom should go to the bride's house to be married, but if it is more convenient to have the wedding at the bridegroom's town, the bride goes there to a temporary house taken by her father, and then the bridegroom proceeds to a temple with his party and is welcomed as if he had arrived on completion of a journey. Mr. Gupte thus describes the reception of the bride when she has come to be married: "But there comes an urgent telegram. The bride and her mother are expected and information is given to the bridegroom's father. In all haste preparations are made to give her a grand and suitable reception. Oh, the flutter among the girls assembled in the house of the bridegroom from all quarters. Every one is dressed in her best and is trying to be the foremost in welcoming the new bride, the Goddess Lakshmi. The numerous maidservants of the house want to prostrate themselves before their future queen on the Sūna or borderland of the city, which is of course the railway station. Musicians have been already despatched and the platform is full of gaily dressed girls. The train arrives, the party assemble at the waiting-room, a maidservant waves rice and water to 'take off' the effects of evil eyes and they start amid admiring eyes of the passengers and onlookers. As soon as the bride reaches her father's temporary residence another girl waves rice and water and throws it away. The girls of the bridegroom's house run home and come back again with a Kalash (water-pot) full of water, with its mouth covered with mango-leaves and topped over with a cocoanut and a large tray of sugar. This is called *Sakhar pāni*, sugar and water, the first to wash the mouth with and the second to sweeten it. The girls have by this time all gathered round the bride and are busy cheering her up with encouraging remarks: 'Oh, she is a Rati, the goddess of beauty,' says one, and another, 'How delicate,' 'What a fine nose' from a third, and 'Look at her eyes' from a fourth. All complimentary and comforting. 'We are glad it is our house you are coming to,' says a sister-in-law in prospect. 'We are happy you are going to be our *mālikin* (mistress),' adds a maidservant. As soon as the elder ladies have completed their courteous inquiries *pān-supāri* and *attar* are distributed and the party returns home. But on arrival the girls gather round the bridegroom to tease him. 'Oh, you Sudhārak (reformer),' 'Oh, you Sāhib (European), *you* have selected your bride.' 'You have seen her *before* marriage. You have broken the rule of the society. You ought to be excommunicated.' 'But,' says another, 'he will now have no time to speak to us. His Rati (goddess of beauty) and he! The Sāhib and the Memsāhib! We shall all be forgotten now. Who cares for sisters and cousins in these days of civilisation?' But all these little jokes of the little girls are meant as congratulations to him for having secured a good girl." At a wedding among the highest families such as is described here, the bridegroom is presented with drinking cups and plates, trays for holding sandalwood paste, betel-leaf and an incense-burner, all in solid silver to the value of about Rs. 1000; water-pots and cooking vessels and a small bath in German silver costing Rs. 300 to Rs. 400; and a set of brass vessels.[1]

2. General customs.

The Prabhus wear the sacred thread. In Bombay boys receive it a short time before their marriage without the ceremonies which form part of the regular Brāhman investiture. On the fifth day after the birth of a child, the sword and also pens, paper and ink are worshipped, the sword being the symbol of their Kshatriya origin and the pens, paper and ink of their present occupation of clerks.[2] The funeral ceremonies, Mr. Enthoven writes, are performed during the first thirteen days after death. Oblations of rice are offered every day, in consequence of which the soul of the dead attains a spiritual body, limb by limb, till on the thirteenth day it is enabled to start on its journey. In twelve months the journey ends, and a *shrāddh* ceremony is performed on an extensive scale on the anniversary of

---

[1] *A Prabhu Marriage*, pp. 26-27.
[2] *Bombay Ethnographic Survey*, art. Prabhu.

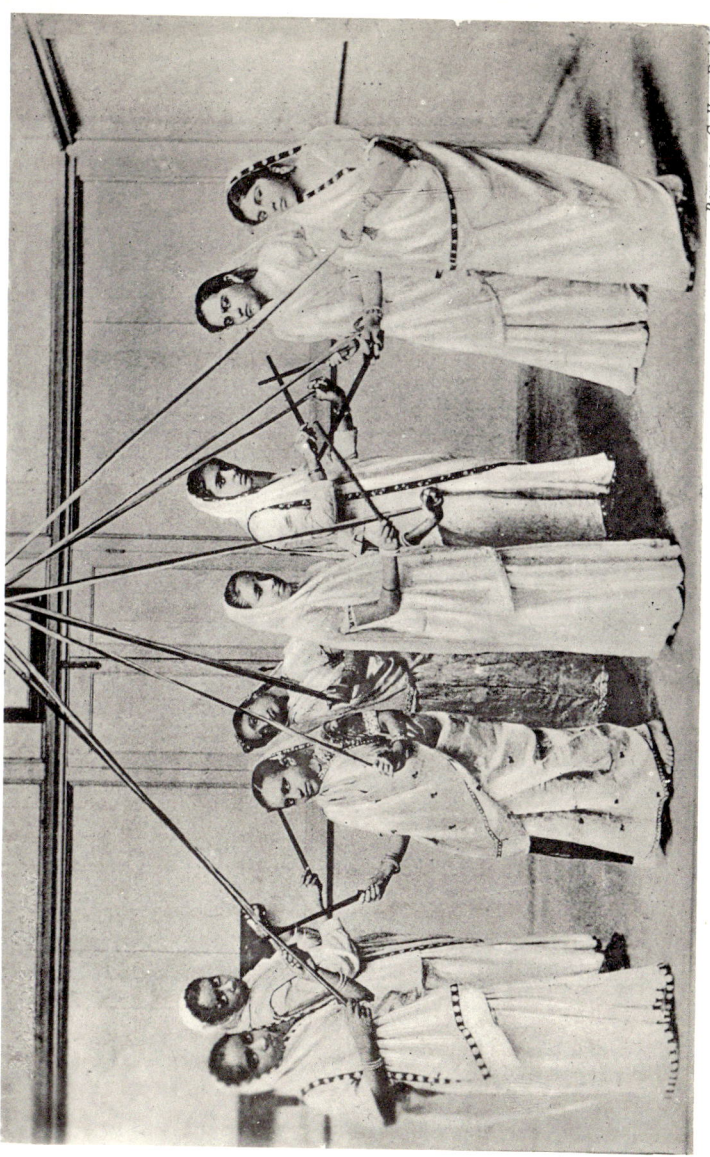

GUJARĀTI GIRLS DOING FIGURES WITH STRINGS AND STICKS.

the death. Most of the Prabhus are in Government service and others are landowners. In the Bombay Presidency[1] they had at first almost a monopoly of Government service as English writers, and the term Prabhu was commonly employed to denote a clerk of any caste who could write English. Both men and women of the caste are generally of a fair complexion, resembling the Marātha Brāhmans. The taste of the women in dress is proverbial, and when a Sunār, Sutār or Kasār woman has dressed herself in her best for some family festival, she will ask her friends, '*Prabhuin disto*,' or 'Do I look like a Prabhu?'

Rāghuvansi, Rāghvi.—A class of Rājpūts of impure descent, who have now developed in the Central Provinces into a caste of cultivators, marrying among themselves. Their first settlement here was in the Nerbudda Valley, and Sir C. Elliott wrote of them:[2] "They are a queer class, all professing to be Rājpūts from Ajodhia, though on cross-examination they are obliged to confess that they did not come here straight from Ajodhia, but stopped in Bundelkhand and the Gwalior territory by the way. They are obviously of impure blood as they marry only among themselves; but when they get wealthy and influential they assume the sacred thread, stop all familiarity with Gūjars and Kirārs (with whom they are accustomed to smoke the huqqa and to take water) and profess to be very high-caste Rājpūts indeed." From Hoshangābād they have spread to Betūl, Chhindwāra and Nāgpur and now number 24,000 persons in all in the Central Provinces. Chhindwāra, on the Satpūra plateau, is supposed to have been founded by one Ratan Rāghuvansi, who built the first house on the site, burying a goat alive under the foundations. The goat is still worshipped as the tutelary deity of the town. The name Rāghuvansi is derived from Rāja Rāghu, king of Ajodhia and ancestor of the great Rāma, the hero of the Rāmāyana. In Nāgpur the name has been shortened to Rāghvi, and the branch of the caste settled here is somewhat looked down upon by their fellows in Hoshangābād.

1. Historical notice.

---

[1] *Bombay Gazetteer*, ix. p. 68, footnotes.
[2] *Hoshangābād Settlement Report* (1807), p. 60.

Sir R. Craddock[1] states that their religion is unorthodox and they have *gurus* or priests of their own caste, discarding Brāhmans. Their names end in Deo. Their origin, however, is still plainly discernible in their height, strength of body and fair complexion. The notice continues : 'Whatever may happen to other classes the Rāghvi will never give way to the moneylender. Though he is fond of comfort he combines a good deal of thrift with it, and the clannish spirit of the caste would prevent any oppression of Rāghvi tenants by a landlord or moneylender of their own body." In Chhindwāra, Mr. Montgomerie states,[2] they rank among the best cultivators, and formerly lived in clans, holding villages on *bhaiachāri* or communal tenure. As mālguzārs or village proprietors, they are very prone to absorb tenant land into their home-farms.

2. Social customs.

The Rāghuvansis have now a set of exogamous groups of the usual low-caste type, designated after titles, nicknames or natural objects. They sometimes invest their sons with the sacred thread at the time of marriage instead of performing the proper thread ceremony. Some discard the cord after the wedding is over. At a marriage the Rāghuvansis of Chhindwāra and Nāgpur combine the Hindustāni custom of walking round the sacred pole with the Marātha one of throwing coloured rice on the bridal couple. Sometimes they have what is known as a *gānkar* wedding. At this, flour, sugar and *ghī*[3] are the only kinds of food permissible, large cakes of flour and sugar being boiled in pitchers full of *ghī*, and everybody being given as much of this as he can eat. The guests generally over-eat themselves, and as weddings are celebrated in the hot weather, one or two may occasionally die of repletion. The neighbours of Rāghuvansis say that the host considers such an occurrence as evidence of the complete success of his party, but this is probably a libel. Such a wedding feast may cost two or three thousand rupees. After the wedding the women of the bride's party attack those of the bridegroom's with bamboo sticks, while these retaliate by throwing red powder on them. The remarriage of widows is freely permitted, but

---

[1] *Nāgpur Settlement Report.*   [2] *Settlement Report.*
[3] Preserved butter.

a widow must be taken from the house of her own parents or relatives, and not from that of her first husband or his parents. In fact, if any members of the dead husband's family meet the second husband on the night of the wedding they will attack him and a serious affray may follow. On reaching her new house the woman enters it by a back door, after bathing and changing all her clothes. The old clothes are given away to a barber or washerman, and the presentation of new clothes by the second husband is the only essential ceremony. No wife will look on a widow's face on the night of her second marriage, for fear lest by doing so she should come to the same position. The majority of the caste abstain from liquor, and they eat flesh in some localities, but not in others. The men commonly wear beards divided by a shaven patch in the centre of the chin; and the women have two body-cloths, one worn like a skirt according to the northern custom. Mr. Crooke states[1] that "in northern India a tradition exists among them that the cultivation of sugar is fatal to the farmer, and that the tiling of a house brings down divine displeasure upon the owner; hence to this day no sugar is grown and not a tiled house is to be seen in their estates." These superstitions do not appear to be known at all in the Central Provinces.

Rājjhar, Rājbhar, Lajjhar.—A caste of farmservants found in the northern Districts. In 1911 they numbered about 8000 persons in the Central Provinces, being returned principally from the Districts of the Satpūra plateau. The names Rājjhar and Rājbhar appear to be applied indiscriminately to the same caste, who are an offshoot of the great Bhar tribe of northern India. The original name appears to have been Rāj Bhar, which signifies a landowning Bhar, like Rāj-Gond, Rāj-Korku and so on. In Mandla all the members of the caste were shown as Rājbhar in 1891, and Rājjhar in 1901, and the two names seem to be used interchangeably in other Districts in the same manner. Some section or family names, such as Bamhania, Patela, Barhele and others, are common to people calling themselves Rājjhar and Rājbhar. But, though practically the same

1. General notice.

[1] *Tribes and Castes*, art. Raghūvansi.

caste, the Rājjhars seem, in some localities, to be more backward and primitive than the Rājbhars. This is also the case in Berār, where they are commonly known as Lajjhar and are said to be akin to the Gonds. A Gond will there take food from a Lajjhar, but not a Lajjhar from a Gond. They are more Hinduised than the Gonds and have prohibited the killing or injuring of cows by some caste penalties.[1]

2. Origin and subdivisions.

The caste appears to be in part of mixed origin arising from the unions of Hindu fathers with women of the Bhar tribe. Several of their family names are derived from those of other castes, as Bamhania (from Brāhman), Sunārya (from Sunār), Baksaria (a Rājpūt sept), Ahīriya (an Ahīr or cowherd), and Bisātia from Bisāti (a hawker). Other names are after plants or animals, as Baslya from the *bāns* or bamboo, Mohanya from the *mohin* tree, Chhitkaria from the *sītaphal* or custard-apple tree, Hardaya from the banyan tree, Rīchhya from the bear, and Dukhania from the buffalo. Members of this last sept will not drink buffalo's milk or wear black cloth, because this is the colour of their totem animal. Members of septs named after other castes have also adopted some natural object as a sept totem; thus those of the Sunārya sept worship gold as being the metal with which the Sunār is associated. Those of the Bamhania sept revere the banyan and pipal trees, as these are held sacred by Brāhmans. The Bakraria or Bagsaria sept believe their name to be derived from that of the *bāgh* or tiger, and they worship this animal's footprints by tying a thread round them.

3. Marriage.

The marriage of members of the same sept, and also that of first cousins, is forbidden. The caste do not employ Brāhmans at their marriage and other ceremonies, and they account for this somewhat quaintly by saying that their ancestors were at one time accustomed to rely on the calculations of Brāhman priests; but many marriages which the Brāhman foretold as auspicious turned out very much the reverse; and on this account they have discarded the Brāhman, and now determine the suitability or otherwise of a projected union by the common primitive custom of

[1] Kitts' *Berār Census Report* (1881), p. 157.

throwing two grains of rice into a vessel of water and seeing whether they will meet. The truth is probably that they are too backward ever to have had recourse to the Brāhman priest, but now, though they still apparently have no desire for his services, they recognise the fact to be somewhat discreditable to themselves, and desire to explain it away by the story already given. In Hoshangābād the bride still goes to the bridegroom's house to be married as among the Gonds. A bride-price is paid, which consists of four rupees, a *khandi*[1] of juāri or wheat, and two pieces of cloth. This is received by the bride's father, who, however, has in turn to pay seven rupees eight annas and a goat to the caste *panchāyat* or committee for the arrangement and sanction of the match. This last payment is known as *Sharāb-ka-rupaya* or liquor-money, and with the goat furnishes the wherewithal for a sumptuous feast to the caste. The marriage-shed must be made of freshly-cut timber, which should not be allowed to fall to the ground, but must be supported and carried off on men's shoulders as it is cut. When the bridegroom arrives at the marriage-shed he is met by the bride's mother and conducted by her to an inner room of the house, where he finds the bride standing. He seizes her fist, which she holds clenched, and opens her fingers by force. The couple then walk five times round the *chauk* or sacred space made with lines of flour on the floor, the bridegroom holding the bride by her little finger. They are preceded by some relative of the bride, who walks round the post carrying a pot of water, with seven holes in it; the water spouts from these holes on to the ground, and the couple must tread in it as they go round the post. This forms the essential and binding portion of the marriage. That night the couple sleep in the same room with a woman lying between them. Next day they return to the bridegroom's house, and on arriving at his door the boy's mother meets him and touches his head, breast and knees with a churning-stick, a winnowing-fan and a pestle, with the object of exorcising any evil spirits who may be accompanying the bridal couple. As the pair enter the marriage-shed erected before the bridegroom's house they are drenched with water

---

[1] About 400 lbs.

by a man sitting on the roof, and when they come to the door of the house the bridegroom's younger brother, or some other boy, sits across it with his legs stretched out to prevent the bride from entering. The girl pushes his legs aside and goes into the house, where she stays for three months with her husband, and then returns to her parents for a year. After this she is sent to her husband with a basket of fried cakes and a piece of cloth, and takes up her residence with him. When a widow is to be married, the couple pour turmeric and water over each other, and then walk seven times round in a circle in an empty space, holding each other by the hand. A widow commonly marries her deceased husband's younger brother, but is not compelled to do so. Divorce is permitted for adultery on the part of the wife.

4. Social customs. The caste bury their dead with the head pointing to the west. This practice is peculiar, and is also followed, Colonel Dalton states, by the hill Bhuiyas of Bengal, who in so doing honour the quarter of the setting sun. When a burial takes place, all the mourners who accompany the corpse throw a little earth into the grave. On the same day some food and liquor are taken to the grave and offered to the dead man's spirit, and a feast is given to the caste-fellows. This concludes the ceremonies of mourning, and the next day the relatives go about their business. The caste are usually petty cultivators and labourers, while they also collect grass and fuel for sale, and propagate the lac insect. In Seoni they have a special relation with the Ahīrs, from whom they will take cooked food, while they say that the Ahīrs will also eat from their hands. In Narsinghpur a similar connection has been observed between the Rājjhars and the Lodhi caste. This probably arises from the fact that the former have worked for several generations as the farm-servants of Lodhi or Ahīr employers, and have been accustomed to live in their houses and partake of their meals, so that caste rules have been abandoned for the sake of convenience. A similar intimacy has been observed between the Panwārs and Gonds, and other castes who stand in this relation to each other. The Rājjhars will also eat *katcha* food (cooked with water) from Kunbis and Kahārs. But in

Hoshangābād some of them will not take food from any caste, even from Brāhmans. Their women wear glass bangles only on the right hand, and a brass ornament known as *māthi* on the left wrist. They wear no ornaments in the nose or ears, and have no breast-cloth. They are tattooed with dots on the face and patterns of animals on the right arm, but not on the left arm or legs. A *liaison* between a youth and maiden of the caste is considered a trifling matter, being punished only with a fine of two to four annas or pence. A married woman detected in an intrigue is mulcted in a sum of four or five rupees, and if her partner be a man of another caste a lock of her hair is cut off. The caste are generally ignorant and dirty, and are not much better than the Gonds and other forest tribes.

RĀJPŪT

[The following article is based mainly on Colonel Tod's classical *Annals and Antiquities of Rājasthān*, 2nd ed., Madras, Higginbotham, 1873, and Mr. Crooke's articles on the Rājpūt clans in his *Tribes and Castes of the North-Western Provinces and Oudh*. Much information as to the origin of the Rājpūt clans has been obtained from inscriptions and worked up mainly by the late Mr. A. M. T. Jackson and Messrs. B. G. and D. R. Bhandarkar; this has been set out with additions and suggestions in Mr. V. A. Smith's *Early History of India*, 3rd ed., and has been reproduced in the subordinate articles on the different clans. Though many of the leading clans are very weakly represented in the Central Provinces, some notice of them is really essential in an article treating generally of the Rājpūt caste, on however limited a scale, and has therefore been included. In four cases, Panwār, Jādum, Rāghuvansi and Daharia, the original Rājpūt clans have now developed into separate cultivating castes, ranking well below the Rājpūts; separate articles have been written on these as for independent castes.]

LIST OF PARAGRAPHS

1. *Introductory notice.*
2. *The thirty-six royal races.*
3. *The origin of the Rājpūts.*
4. *Subdivisions of the clans.*
5. *Marriage customs.*
6. *Funeral rites.*
7. *Religion.*
8. *Food.*
9. *Opium.*
10. *Improved training of Rājpūt chiefs.*
11. *Dress.*
12. *Social customs.*
13. *Seclusion of women.*
14. *Traditional character of the Rājpūts.*
15. *Occupation.*

LIST OF SUBORDINATE ARTICLES

1. Baghel.
2. Bāgri.
3. Bais.
4. Baksaria.
5. Banāphar.
6. Bhadauria.
7. Bisen.
8. Bundela.
9. Chandel.
10. Chauhān.
11. Dhākar.
12. Gaharwār, Gherwāl.
13. Gaur, Chamār-Gaur.
14. Haihaya, Haihaivansi, Kālachuri.
15. Hūna, Hoon.
16. Kachhwāha, Cutchwāha.
17. Nāgvansi.
18. Nikumbh.
19. Pāik.
20. Parihār.
21. Rāthor, Rāthaur.

22. Sesodia, Gahlot, Ahāria.
23. Solankhi, Solanki, Chalukya.
24. Somvansi, Chandravansi.
25. Sūrajvansi.
26. Tomara, Tuar, Tunwar.
27. Yādu, Yādava, Yādu-Bhatti, Jādon.

Rājpūt, Kshatriya, Chhatri, Thākur.—The Rājpūts are the representatives of the old Kshatriya or warrior class, the second of the four main castes or orders of classical Hinduism, and were supposed to have been made originally from the arms of Brahma. The old name of Kshatriya is still commonly used in the Hindi form Chhatri, but the designation Rājpūt, or son of a king, has now superseded it as the standard name of the caste. Thākur, or lord, is the common Rājpūt title, and that by which they are generally addressed. The total number of persons returned as Rājpūts in the Province in 1911 was about 440,000. India has about nine million Rājpūts in all, and they are most numerous in the Punjab, the United Provinces, and Bihār and Orissa, Rājputāna returning under 700,000 and Central India about 800,000.

1. Introductory notice.

The bulk of the Rājpūts in the Central Provinces are of very impure blood. Several groups, such as the Panwārs of the Wainganga Valley, the Rāghuvansis of Chhindwāra and Nāgpur, the Jādams of Hoshangābād and the Daharias of Chhattīsgarh, have developed into separate castes and marry among themselves, though a true Rājpūt must not marry in his own clan. Some of them have abandoned the sacred thread and now rank with the good cultivating castes below Banias. Reference may be made to the separate articles on these castes. Similarly the Sūrajvansi, Gaur or Gorai, Chauhān, and Bāgri clans marry among themselves in the Central Provinces, and it is probable that detailed research would establish the same of many clans or parts of clans bearing the name of Rājpūt in all parts of India. If the definition of a proper Rājpūt were taken, as it should be correctly, as one whose family intermarried with clans of good standing, the caste would be reduced to comparatively small dimensions. The name Dhākar, also shown as a Rājpūt clan, is applied to a person of illegitimate birth, like Vidūr. Over 100,000 persons, or nearly a quarter of the total, did not return the name of any clan in 1911, and these are all of mixed or illegitimate descent. They are numerous in Nimār, and are there known as *chhoti-tur* or low-class Rājpūts. The Bāgri Rājpūts of Seoni and the Sūrajvansis of Betal marry among themselves, while the Bundelas of Saugor intermarry with two other local groups, the Panwār and Dhundhele, all the three being of impure blood. In Jubbulpore a small clan of persons known as Pāik or foot-soldier return themselves as Rājpūts, but are no doubt a mixed low-caste group. Again, some landholding sections of the primitive tribes have assumed the names of Rājpūt clans. Thus the zamīndārs of Bilāspur, who originally belonged to the Kawar tribe, call themselves Tuar or Tomara Rājpūts, and the landholding section of the Mundas in Chota Nāgpur say that they are of the Nāgvansi clan. Other names are returned which are not those of Rājpūt clans or their offshoots at all. If these subdivisions, which cannot be considered as proper Rājpūts, and all those who have returned no clan be deducted, there remain not more than 100,000 who might be admitted to be pure Rājpūts in Rājputāna. But a close local scrutiny even of these would no doubt result in the detection of many persons who have assumed and returned the names of good clans without being entitled to them. And many more would come away as being the descendants of remarried widows. A Rājpūt of really pure family and descent is in fact a person of some consideration in most parts of the Central Provinces.

2. The thirty-six royal races.

Traditionally the Rājpūts are divided into thirty-six great clans or races, of which Colonel Tod gives a list compiled from different authorities as follows (alternative names by which the clan or important branches of it are known are shown in brackets):

1. Ikshwaka or Sūrajvansi.
2. Indu, Somvansi or Chandravansi.
3. Gahlot or Sesodia (Rāghuvansi).
4. Yādu (Bhatti, Jareja, Jādon, Banāphar).
5. Tuar or Tomara.
6. Rāthor.
7. Kachhwāha (Cutchwāha).
8. Prāmara or Panwār (Mori).
9. Chauhān (Hāra, Khichi, Nikumbh, Bhadauria).
10. Chalukya or Solankhi (Baghel).
11. Parihār.
12. Chawara or Chaura.
13. Tāk or Takshac (Nāgvansi, Mori).

14. Jit or Gete.
15. Hūna.
16. Kāthi.
17. Balla.
18. Jhalla.
19. Jaitwa or Kamari.
20. Gohil.
21. Sarweya.
22. Silar.
23. Dhābi.
24. Gaur.
25. Doda or Dor.
26. Gherwāl or Gaharwār (Bundela).
27. Badgūjar.
28. Sengar.
29. Sikarwāl.
30. Bais.
31. Dahia.
32. Johia.
33. Mohil.
34. Nikumbh.
35. Rājpali.
36. Dahima.

And two extra, Hul and Daharia.

Several of the above races are extinct or nearly so, and on the other hand some very important modern clans, as the Gautam, Dikhit and Bisen, and such historically important ones as the Chandel and Haihaya, are not included in the thirty-six royal races at all. Practically all the clans should belong either to the solar and lunar branch, that is, should be descended from the sun or moon, but the division, if it ever existed, is not fully given by Colonel Tod. Two special clans, the Sūrajvansi and Chandra or Somvansi, are named after the sun and moon respectively; and a few others, as the Sesodia, Kachhwāha, Gohil, Bais and Badgūjar, are recorded as being of the solar race, descended from Vishnu through his incarnation as Rāma. The Rāthors also claimed solar lineage, but this was not wholly conceded by the Bhāts, and the Dikhits are assigned to the solar branch by their legends. The great clan of the Yādavas, of whom the present Jādon or Jādum and Bhatti Rājpūts are representatives, was of the lunar race, tracing their descent from Krishna, though, as a matter of fact, Krishna was also an incarnation of Vishnu or the sun; and the Tuar or Tomara, as well as the Jit or Gete, the Rājpūt section of the modern Jāts, who were considered to be branches of the Yādavas, would also be of the moon division. The Gautam and Bisen clans, who are not included in the thirty-six royal races, now claim lunar descent. Four clans, the Panwār, Chauhān, Chalukya or Solankhi, and Parihār, had a different origin, being held to have been born through the agency of the gods from a fire-pit on the summit of Mount Abu. They are hence known as Agnikula or the fire races. Several clans, such as the

Tāk or Takshac, the Hūna and the Chaura, were considered by Colonel Tod to be the representatives of the Huns or Scythians, that is, the nomad invading tribes from Central Asia, whose principal incursions took place during the first five centuries of the Christian era.

At least six of the thirty-six royal races, the Sarweya, Silar, Doda or Dor, Dahia, Johia and Mohil, were extinct in Colonel Tod's time, and others were represented only by small settlements in Rājputāna and Surat. On the other hand, there are now a large number of new clans, whose connection with the thirty-six is doubtful, though in many cases they are probably branches of the old clans who have obtained a new name on settling in a different locality.

3. The origin of the Rājpūts.

It was for long the custom to regard the Rājpūts as the direct descendants and representatives of the old Kshatriya or warrior class of the Indian Aryans, as described in the Vedas and the great epics. Even Colonel Tod by no means held this view in its entirety, and modern epigraphic research has caused its partial or complete abandonment. Mr. V. A. Smith indeed says:[1] " The main points to remember are that the Kshatriya or Rājpūt caste is essentially an occupational caste, composed of all clans following the Hindu ritual who actually undertook the act of government; that consequently people of most diverse races were and are lumped together as Rājpūts, and that most of the great clans now in existence are descended either from foreign immigrants of the fifth or sixth century A.D. or from indigenous races such as the Gonds and Bhars." Colonel Tod held three clans, the Tāk or Takshac, the Hūna and the Chaura, to be descended from Scythian or nomad Central Asian immigrants, and the same origin has been given for the Haihaya. The Hūna clan actually retains the name of the White Huns, from whose conquests in the fifth century it probably dates its existence. The principal clan of the lunar race, the Yādavas, are said to have first settled in Delhi and at Dwārka in Gujarāt. But on the death of Krishna, who was their prince, they were expelled from

[1] *Early History of India* (Oxford, Clarendon Press), 3rd edition, p. 414.

these places, and retired across the Indus, settling in Afghānistan. Again, for some reason which the account does not clearly explain, they came at a later period to India and settled first in the Punjab and afterwards in Rājputāna. The Jit or Jāt and the Tomara clans were branches of the Yādavas, and it is supposed that the Jits or Jāts were also descended from the nomad invading tribes, possibly from the Yueh-chi tribe who conquered and occupied the Punjab during the first and second centuries.[1] The legend of the Yādavas, who lived in Gujarāt with their chief Krishna, but after his defeat and death retired to Central Asia, and at a later date returned to India, would appear to correspond fairly well with the Sāka invasion of the second century B.C. which penetrated to Kāthiāwār and founded a dynasty there. In A.D. 124 the second Sāka king was defeated by the Andhra king Vilivāyakura II. and his kingdom destroyed.[2] But at about the same period, the close of the first century, a fresh horde of the Sākas came to Gujarāt from Central Asia and founded another kingdom, which lasted until it was subverted by Chandragupta Vikramaditya about A.D. 390.[3] The historical facts about the Sākas, as given on the authority of Mr. V. A. Smith, thus correspond fairly closely with the Yādava legend. And the later Yueh-chi immigrants might well be connected by the Bhāts with the Sāka hordes who had come at an earlier date from the same direction, and so the Jāts[4] might be held to be an offshoot of the Yādavas. This connection of the Yādava and Jāt legends with the facts of the immigration of the Sākas and Yueh-chi appears a plausible one, but may be contradicted by historical arguments of which the writer is ignorant. If it were correct we should be justified in identifying the lunar clans of Rājpūts with the early Scythian immigrants of the first and second centuries. Another point is that Buddha is said to be the progenitor

---

[1] *Early History of India*, pp. 252, 254.
[2] *Ibidem*, p. 210.
[3] *Ibidem*, p. 227.
[4] Colonel Tod states that the proper name of the caste was Jit or Jat, and was changed to Jāt by a section of them who also adopted Muhammadanism. Colonel Tod also identifies the Jats or Jits with the Yueh-chi as suggested in the text (*Rājasthān*, i. p. 97).

of the whole Indu or lunar race.[1] It is obvious that Buddha had no real connection with these Central Asian tribes, as he died some centuries before their appearance in India. But the Yueh-chi or Kushān kings of the Punjab in the first and second centuries A.D. were fervent Buddhists and established that religion in the Punjab. Hence we can easily understand how, if the Yādus or Jāts and other lunar clans were descended from the Sāka and Yueh-chi immigrants, the legend of their descent from Buddha, who was himself a Kshatriya, might be devised for them by their bards when they were subsequently converted from Buddhism to Hinduism. The Sākas of western India, on the other hand, who it is suggested may be represented by the Yādavas, were not Buddhists in the beginning, whether or not they became so afterwards. But as has been seen, though Buddha was their first progenitor, Krishna was also their king while they were in Gujarāt, so that at this time they must have been supposed to be Hindus. The legend of descent from Buddha arising with the Yueh-chi or Kushāns might have been extended to them. Again, the four Agnikula or fire-born clans, the Parihār, Chalukya or Solankhi, Panwār and Chauhān, are considered to be the descendants of the White Hun and Gūjar invaders of the fifth and sixth centuries. These clans were said to have been created by the gods from a firepit on the summit of Mount Abu for the re-birth of the Kshatriya caste after it had been exterminated by the slaughter of Parasurāma the Brāhman. And it has been suggested that this legend refers to the cruel massacres of the Huns, by which the bulk of the old aristocracy, then mainly Buddhist, was wiped out; while the Huns and Gūjars, one at least of whose leaders was a fervent adherent of Brāhmanism and slaughtered the Buddhists of the Punjab, became the new fire-born clans on being absorbed into Hinduism.[2] The name of the Huns is still retained in the Hūna clan, now almost extinct. There remain the clans descended from the sun through Rāma, and it would be

---

[1] *Rājasthān*, i. p. 42. Mr. Crooke points out that the Buddha here referred to is probably the planet Mercury. But it is possible that he may have been identified with the religious reformer as the names seem to have a common origin.

[2] See also separate articles on Panwār, Rājpūt and Gūjar.

tempting to suppose that these are the representatives of the old Aryan Kshatriyas. But Mr. Bhandarkar has shown [1] that the Sesodias, the premier clan of the solar race and of all Rājpūts, are probably sprung from Nāgar Brāhmans of Gujarāt, and hence from the Gūjar tribes; and it must therefore be supposed that the story of solar origin and divine ancestry was devised because they were once Brāhmans, and hence, in the view of the bards, of more honourable origin than the other clans. Similarly the Badgūjar clan, also of solar descent, is shown by its name of *bara* or great Gūjar to have been simply an aristocratic section of the Gūjars; while the pedigree of the Rāthors, another solar clan, and one of those who have shed most lustre on the Rājpūt name, was held to be somewhat doubtful by the Bhāts, and their solar origin was not fully admitted. Mr. Smith gives two great clans as very probably of aboriginal or Dravidian origin, the Gaharwār or Gherwāl, from whom the Bundelas are derived, and the Chandel, who ruled Bundelkhand from the ninth to the twelfth centuries, and built the fine temples at Mahoba, Kālanjar and Khajarāho as well as making many great tanks. This corresponds with Colonel Tod's account, which gives no place to the Chandels among the thirty-six royal races, and states that the Gherwāl Rājpūt is scarcely known to his brethren in Rājasthān, who will not admit his contaminated blood to mix with theirs, though as a brave warrior he is entitled to their fellowship.[2] Similarly the Kāthi clan may be derived from the indigenous Kāthi tribe who gave their name to Kāthiāwār. And the Sūrajvansi, Somvansi and Nāgvansi clans, or descendants of the sun, moon and snake, which are scarcely known in Rājputāna, may represent landholding sections of lower castes or non-Aryan tribes who have been admitted to Rājpūt rank. But even though it be found that the majority of the Rājpūt clans cannot boast a pedigree dating farther back than the first five centuries of our era, this is at any rate an antiquity to which few if any of the greatest European houses can lay claim.

Many of the great clans are now split up into a number

---

[1] *J.A.S.B.*, 1909, p. 167, *Guhilots*. See also annexed article on Rājpūt Sesodia.
[2] *Ibidem*, i. p. 105.

4. Subdivisions of the clans.

of branches. The most important of these were according to locality, the different *sachae* or branches being groups settled in separate areas. Thus the Chalukya or Solankhi had sixteen branches, of which the Baghels of Rewah or Baghelkhand were the most important. The Panwārs had thirty-five branches, of which the Mori and the Dhunda, now perhaps the Dhundele of Saugor, are the best known. The Gahlot had twenty-four branches, of which one, the Sesodia, became so important that it has given its name to the whole clan. The Chamār-Gaur section of the Gaur clan now claim a higher rank than the other Gaurs, though the name would apparently indicate the appearance of a Chamār in their family tree; while the Tilokchandi Bais form an aristocratic section of the Bais clan, named after a well-known king, Tilokchand, who reigned in upper India about the twelfth century and is presumably claimed by them as an ancestor. Besides this the Rājpūts have *gotras*, named after eponymous saints exactly like the Brāhman *gotras*, and probably adopted in imitation of the Brāhmans. Since, theoretically, marriage is prohibited in the whole clan, the *gotra* divisions would appear to be useless, but Sir H. Risley states that persons of the same clan but with different *gotras* have begun to intermarry. Similarly it would appear that the different branches of the great clans mentioned above must intermarry in some cases; while in the Central Provinces, as already stated, several clans have become regular castes and form endogamous and not exogamous groups. In northern India, however, Mr. Crooke's accounts of the different clans indicate that marriage within the clan is as a rule not permitted. The clans themselves and their branches have different degrees of rank for purposes of marriage, according to the purity of their descent, while in each clan or subclan there is an inferior section formed of the descendants of remarried widows, or even the offspring of women of another caste, who have probably in the course of generations not infrequently got back into their father's clan. Thus many groups of varying status arise, and one of the principal rules of a Rājpūt's life was that he must marry his daughter, sometimes into a clan of equal, or sometimes into one of higher rank than his own. Hence arose great difficulty in arranging the marriages of girls and sometimes the payment of a price to the bridegroom; while in order to retain the favour of the Bhāts and avoid their sarcasm, lavish expenditure had to be incurred by the bride's father on presents to these rapacious mendicants.[1] Thus a daughter became in a Rājpūt's eyes a long step on the road to ruin, and female infanticide was extensively practised. This crime has never been at all common in the Central Provinces, where the rule of marrying a daughter into an equal or higher clan has not been enforced with the same strictness as in northern India. But occasional instances formerly occurred in which the child's neck was placed under one leg of its mother's cot, or it was poisoned with opium or by placing the juice of the *ākra* or swallow-wort plant on the mother's nipple.

Properly the proposal for a Rājpūt marriage should emanate from the bride's side, and the customary method of making it was to send a cocoanut to the bridegroom. 'The cocoanut came,' was the phrase used to intimate that a proposal of marriage had been made.[2] It is possible that the bride's initiative was a relic of the Swayamwāra or maiden's choice, when a king's daughter placed a garland on the neck of the youth she preferred among the competitors in a tournament, and among some Rājpūts the Jāyamāla or garland of victory is still hung round the bridegroom's neck in memory of this custom; but it may also have been due to the fact that the bride had to pay the dowry. One tenth of this was paid as earnest when the match had been arranged, and the boy's party could not then recede from it. At the entrance of the marriage-shed was hung the *toran*, a triangle of three wooden bars, having the apex crowned with the effigy of a peacock. The bridegroom on horseback, lance in hand, proceeded to break the *toran*, which was defended by the damsels of the bride. They assailed him with missiles of various kinds, and especially with red powder made from the flowers of the *palās*[3] tree, at the same time singing songs full of immoral allusions. At length the

5. Marriage customs.

---

[1] See also article Bhāt.

[2] *Rājasthān*, i. pp. 231, 232.

[3] *Butea frondosa*. This powder is also used at the Holi festival and has some sexual significance.

toran was broken amid the shouts of the retainers, and the fair defenders retired. If the bridegroom could not attend in person his sword was sent to represent him, and was carried round the marriage-post with the bride, this being considered a proper and valid marriage. At the rite of *hātleva* or joining the hands of the couple it was customary that any request made by the bridegroom to the bride's father should meet with compliance, and this usage has led to many fatal results in history. Another now obsolete custom was that the bride's father should present an elephant to his son-in-law as part of the dowry, but when a man could not afford a real elephant a small golden image of the animal might be substituted. In noble families the bride was often accompanied to her husband's house by a number of maidens belonging to the servant and menial castes. These were called Devadhari or lamp-bearers, and became inmates of the harem, their offspring being *golas* or slaves. In time of famine many of the poor had also perforce to sell themselves as slaves in order to obtain subsistence, and a chief's household would thus contain a large number of them. They were still adorned in Mewār, Colonel Tod states, like the Saxon slaves of old, with a silver ring round the left ankle instead of the neck. They were well treated, and were often among the best of the military retainers; they took rank among themselves according to the quality of the mothers, and often held confidential places about the ruler's person. A former chief of Deogarh would appear at court with three hundred *golas* or slaves on horseback in his train, men whose lives were his own.[1] These special customs have now generally been abandoned by the Rājpūts of the Central Provinces, and their weddings conform to the usual Hindu type as described in the article on Kurmi. The remarriage of widows is now recognised in the southern Districts, though not in the north; but even here widows frequently do marry and their offspring are received into the caste, though with a lower status than those who do not permit this custom. Among the Baghels a full Rājpūt will allow a relative born of a remarried widow to cook his food for him, but not to add the salt nor to eat it with him.

[1] *Rājasthān*, i. p. 159.

Those who permit the second marriage of widows also allow a divorced woman to remain in the caste and to marry again. But among proper Rājpūts, as with Brāhmans, a wife who goes wrong is simply put away and expelled from the society. Polygamy is permitted and was formerly common among the chiefs. Each wife was maintained in a separate suite of rooms, and the chief dined and spent the evening alternately with each of them in her own quarters. The lady with her attendants would prepare dinner for him and wait upon him while he ate it, waving the punkah or fan behind him and entertaining him with her remarks, which, according to report, frequently constituted a pretty severe curtain lecture.

6. Funeral rites.

The dead are burnt, except infants, whose bodies are buried. Mourning is observed for thirteen days for a man, nine days for a woman, and three days for a child. The *shrāddh* ceremony or offering of sacrificial cakes to the spirit is performed either during the usual period in the month of Kunwār (September), or on the anniversary day of the death. It was formerly held that if a Kshatriya died on the battlefield it was unnecessary to perform his funeral rites because his spirit went straight to heaven, and thus the end to which the ceremonies were directed was already attained without them. It was also said that the wife of a man dying such a death should not regard herself as a widow nor undergo the privations imposed on widowhood. But this did not apply so far as self-immolation was concerned, since the wives of warriors dying in battle very frequently became *sati*. In the case of chiefs also it was sometimes the custom, probably for political reasons, that the heir should not observe mourning ; because if he did so he would be incapable of appearing in an assembly for thirteen days, or of taking the public action which might be requisite to safeguard his succession. The body of the late chief would be carried out by the back door of the house, and as soon as it left his successor would take his seat on the *gaddi* or cushion and begin to discharge the public business of government.

7. Religion.

The principal deity of the Rājpūts is the goddess Devi or Durga in her more terrible form as the goddess of war. Their swords were sacred to her, and at the Dasahra festival they worshipped their swords and other weapons of war and their horses. The dreadful goddess also protected the virtue of the Rājpūt women and caused to be enacted the terrible holocausts, not infrequent in Rājpūt history, when some stronghold was besieged and could hold out no longer. A great furnace was then kindled in the citadel and into this the women, young and old, threw themselves, or else died by their husbands' swords, while the men, drunk with *bhāng* and wearing saffron-coloured robes, sallied out to sell their lives to the enemy as dearly as possible. It is related that on one occasion Akbar desired to attempt the virtue of a queen of the Sesodia clan, and for that purpose caused her to lose herself in one of the mazes of his palace. The emperor appeared before her suddenly as she was alone, but the lady, drawing a dagger, threatened to plunge it into her breast if he did not respect her, and at the same time the goddess of her house appeared riding on a tiger. The baffled emperor gave way and retired, and her life and virtue were saved.

The Rājpūts also worship the sun, whom many of them look upon as their first ancestor. They revere the animals and trees sacred to the Hindus, and some clans show special veneration to a particular tree, never cutting or breaking the branches or leaves. In this manner the Bundelas revere the *kadamb* tree, the Panwārs the *nīm*[1] tree, the Rāthors the pīpal[2] tree, and so on. This seems to be a relic of totemistic usage. In former times each clan had also a tribal god, who was its protector and leader and watched over the destinies of the clan. Sometimes it accompanied the clan into battle. "Every royal house has its palladium, which is frequently borne to battle at the saddle-bow of the prince. Rao Bhima Hāra of Kotah lost his life and protecting deity together. The celebrated Khīchi (Chauhān) leader Jai Singh never took the field without the god before him. 'Victory to Bujrung' was his signal for the charge so dreaded by the Marātha, and often has the deity been sprinkled with his blood and that of the foe."[3] It is said that a Rājpūt should always kill a snake if he sees one, because the snake, though a prince among Rājpūts, is an enemy,

---

[1] *Melia indica.*   [2] *Ficus R.*
[3] *Rājasthān*, i. p. 123.

and he should not let it live. If he does not kill it, the snake will curse him and bring ill-luck upon him. The same rule applies, though with less binding force, to a tiger.

The Rājpūts eat the flesh of clean animals, but not pigs or fowls. They are, however, fond of the sport of pig-sticking, and many clans, as the Bundelas and others, will eat the flesh of the wild pig. This custom was perhaps formerly universal. Some of them eat of male animals only and not of females, either because they fear that the latter would render them effeminate or that they consider the sin to be less. Some only eat animals killed by the method of *jatka* or severing the head with one stroke of the sword or knife. They will not eat animals killed in the Muhammadan fashion by cutting the throat. They abstain from the flesh of the *nīlgai* or blue bull as being an animal of the cow tribe. Among the Brāhmans and Rājpūts food cooked with water must not be placed in bamboo baskets, nor must anything made of bamboo be brought into the *rasoya* or cooking-place, or the *chauka*, the space cleaned and marked out for meals. A special brush of date-palm fibre is kept solely for sweeping these parts of the house. At a Rājpūt banquet it was the custom for the prince to send a little food from his own plate or from the dish before him to any guest whom he especially wished to honour, and to receive this was considered a very high distinction. In Mewār the test of legitimacy in a prince of the royal house was the permission to eat from the chief's plate. The grant of this privilege conferred a recognised position, while its denial excluded the member in question from the right to the succession.[1] This custom indicates the importance attached to the taking of food together as a covenant or sacrament.

8. Food.

The Rājpūts abstain from alcoholic liquor, though some of the lower class, as the Bundelas, drink it. In classical times there is no doubt that they drank freely, but have had to conform to the prohibition of liquor imposed by the Brāhmans on high-caste Hindus. In lieu of liquor they became much addicted to the noxious drugs, opium and gānja or Indian hemp, drinking the latter in the form of the intoxicating liquid known as *bhāng*, which is prepared

9. Opium.

[1] *Rājasthān*, i. pp. 267, 268.

from its leaves. *Bhāng* was as a rule drunk by the Rājpūts before battle, and especially as a preparation for those last sallies from a besieged fortress in which the defenders threw away their lives. There is little reason to doubt that they considered the frenzy and carelessness of death produced by the liquor as a form of divine possession. Opium has contributed much to the degeneration of the Rājpūts, and their relapse to an idle, sensuous life when their energies were no longer maintained by the need of continuous fighting for the protection of their country. The following account by Forbes of a Rājpūt's daily life well illustrates the slothful effeminacy caused by the drug:[1] "In times of peace and ease the Rājpūt leads an indolent and monotonous life. It is usually some time after sunrise before he bestirs himself and begins to call for his hookah; after smoking he enjoys the luxury of tea or coffee, and commences his toilet and ablutions, which dispose of a considerable part of the morning. It is soon breakfast-time, and after breakfast the hookah is again in requisition, with but few intervals of conversation until noon. The time has now arrived for a siesta, which lasts till about three in the afternoon. At this hour the chief gets up again, washes his hands and face, and prepares for the great business of the day, the distribution of the red cup, *kusumba* or opium. He calls together his friends into the public hall, or perhaps retires with them to a garden-house. Opium is produced, which is pounded in a brass vessel and mixed with water; it is then strained into a dish with a spout, from which it is poured into the chief's hand. One after the other the guests now come up, each protesting that *kusumba* is wholly repugnant to his taste and very injurious to his health, but after a little pressing first one and then another touches the chief's hand in two or three places, muttering the names of Deos (gods), friends or others, and drains the draught. Each after drinking washes the chief's hand in a dish of water which a servant offers, and after wiping it dry with his own scarf makes way for his neighbour. After this refreshment the chief and his guests sit down in the public hall, and amuse themselves with chess, draughts or games of chance, or perhaps dancing-girls are called in to

[1] *Rāsmāla*, ii. p. 261.

exhibit their monotonous measures, or musicians and singers, or the never-failing favourites, the Bhāts and Chārans. At sunset the torch-bearers appear and supply the chamber with light, upon which all those who are seated therein rise and make obeisance towards the chief's cushion. They resume their seats, and playing, singing, dancing, story-telling go on as before. At about eight the chief rises to retire to his dinner and his hookah, and the party is broken up." There is little reason to doubt that the Rājpūts ascribed a divine character to opium and the mental exaltation produced by it, as suggested in the article on Kalār in reference to the Hindus generally. Opium was commonly offered at the shrines of deified Rājpūt heroes. Colonel Tod states: "*Umul lār khāna*, to eat opium together, is the most inviolable pledge, and an agreement ratified by this ceremony is stronger than any adjuration."[1] The account given by Forbes of the manner in which the drug was distributed by the chief from his own hand to all his clansmen indicates that the drinking of it was the renewal of a kind of pledge or covenant between them, analogous to the custom of pledging one another with wine, and a substitute for the covenant made by taking food together, which originated from the sacrificial meal. It has already been seen that the Rājpūts attached the most solemn meaning and virtue to the act of partaking of the chief's food, and it is legitimate to infer that they regarded the drinking of a sacred drug like opium from his hand in the same light. The following account[2] of the drinking of healths in a Highland clan had, it may be suggested, originally the same significance as the distribution of opium by the Rājpūt chief: "Lord Lovat was wont in the hall before dinner to have a kind of herald proclaiming his pedigree, which reached almost up to Noah, and showed each man present to be a cadet of his family, whilst after dinner he drank to every one of his cousins by name, each of them in return pledging him—the better sort in French claret, the lower class in husky (whisky)." Here also the drinking of wine together perhaps implied the renewal of a pledge of fealty and protection between the chief and his clansmen,

---

[1] *Rājasthān*, i. p. 553.
[2] *Reminiscences of Lady Dorothy Nevill*, Nelson's edition, p. 367.

all of whom were held to be of his kin. The belief in the kinship of the whole clan existed among the Rājpūts exactly as in the Scotch clans. In speaking of the Rāthors Colonel Tod states that they brought into the field fifty thousand men, *Ek bāp ka beta*, the sons of one father, to combat with the emperor of Delhi; and remarks: "What a sensation does it not excite when we know that a sentiment of kindred pervades every individual of this immense affiliated body, who can point out in the great tree the branch of his origin, of which not one is too remote from the main stem to forget his pristine connection with it."[1]

The taking of opium and wine together, as already described, thus appear to be ceremonies of the same character, both symbolising the renewal of a covenant between kinsmen.

10. Improved training of Rājpūt chiefs.

The temptations to a life of idleness and debauchery to which Rājpūt gentlemen were exposed by the cessation of war have happily been largely met and overcome by the careful education and training which their sons now receive in the different chiefs' colleges and schools, and by the fostering of their taste for polo and other games. There is every reason to hope that a Rājpūt prince's life will now be much like that of an English country gentleman, spent largely in public business and the service of his country, with sport and games as relaxation. Nor are the Rājpūts slow to avail themselves of the opportunities for the harder calling of arms afforded by the wars of the British Empire, in which they are usually the first to proffer their single-hearted and unselfish assistance.

11. Dress.

The most distinctive feature of a Rājpūt's dress was formerly his turban; the more voluminous and heavy this was, the greater distinction attached to the bearer. The cloth was wound in many folds above the head, or cocked over one ear as a special mark of pride. An English gentleman once remarked to the minister of the Rao of Cutch on the size and weight of his turban, when the latter replied, 'Oh, this is nothing, it only weighs fifteen pounds.'[2] A considerable reverence attached to the turban, probably because it was the covering of the head, the seat of life, and

---

[1] *Rājasthān*, ii. p. 3.   [2] Mrs. Postans, *Cutch*, p. 35.

the exchanging of turbans was the mark of the closest friendship. On one occasion Shāh Jahān, before he came to the throne of Delhi, changed turbans with the Rāna of Mewār as a mark of amity. Shāh Jahān's turban was still preserved at Udaipur, and seen there by Colonel Tod in 1820. They also wore the beard and moustaches very long and full, the moustache either drooping far below the chin, or being twisted out stiffly on each side to impart an aspect of fierceness. Many Rājpūts considered it a disgrace to have grey beards or moustaches, and these were accustomed to dye them with a preparation of indigo. Thus dyed, however, after a few days the beard and moustache assumed a purple tint, and finally faded to a pale plum colour, far from being either deceptive or ornamental. The process of dyeing was said to be tedious, and the artist compelled his patient to sit many hours under the indigo treatment with his head wrapped up in plantain leaves.[1] During the Muhammadan wars, however, the Rājpūts gave up their custom of wearing beards in order to be distinguished from Moslems, and now, as a rule, do not retain them, while most of them have also discarded the long moustaches and large turbans. In battle, especially when they expected to die, the Rājpūts wore saffron-coloured robes as at a wedding. At the same time their wives frequently performed *sati*, and the idea was perhaps that they looked on their deaths as the occasion of a fresh bridal in the warrior's Valhalla. Women wear skirts and shoulder-cloths, and in Rājputāna they have bangles of ivory or bone instead of the ordinary glass, sometimes covering the arm from the shoulders to the wrist. Their other ornaments should be of gold if possible, but the rule is not strictly observed, and silver and baser metals are worn.

The Rājpūts wear the sacred thread, but many of them have abandoned the proper *upanayana* or thread ceremony, and simply invest boys with it at their marriage. In former times, when a boy became fit to bear arms, the ceremony of *kharg bandai*, or binding on of the sword, was performed, and considered to mark his attainment of manhood. The king himself had his sword thus bound on by the first of his vassals. The Rājpūts take food cooked with water (*katchi*)

12. Social customs.

[1] Mrs. Postans, *Cutch*, p. 138.

only from Brāhmans, and that cooked without water (*pakki*) from Banias, and sometimes from Lodhis and Dhīmars. Brāhmans will take *pakki* food from Rājpūts, and Nais and Dhīmars *katchi* food. When a man is ill, however, he may take food from members of such castes as Kurmi and Lodhi as a matter of convenience without incurring caste penalties. The large turbans and long moustaches and beards no longer characterise their appearance, and the only point which distinguishes a Rājpūt is that his name ends with Singh (lion). But this suffix has also been adopted by others, especially the Sikhs, and by such castes as the Lodhis and Rāj-Gonds who aspire to rank as Rājpūts. A Rājpūt is usually addressed as Thākur or lord, a title which properly applies only to a Rājpūt landholder, but has now come into general use. The head of a state has the designation of Rāja or Rāna, and those of the leading states of Mahārāja or Mahārāna, that is, great king. Mahārāna, which appears to be a Gujarāti form, is used by the Sesodia family of Udaipur. The sons of a Rāja are called Kunwar or prince. The title Rao appears to be a Marāthi form of Rāj or Rāja; it is retained by one or two chiefs, but has now been generally adopted as an honorific suffix by Marātha Brāhmans. Rawat appears to have been originally equivalent to Rājpūt, being simply a diminutive of Rājpūtra, the Sanskrit form of the latter. It is the name of a clan of Rājpūts in the Punjab, and is used as an honorific designation by Ahīrs, Saonrs, Kols and others.

13. Seclusion of women.

Women are strictly secluded by the Rājpūts, especially in Upper India, but this practice does not appear to have been customary in ancient times, and it would be interesting to know whether it has been copied from the Muhammadans. It is said that a good Rājpūt in the Central Provinces must not drive the plough, his wife must not use the *rehnta* or spinning-wheel, and his household may not have the *kathri* or *gudri*, the mattress made of old pieces of cloth or rag sewn one on top of the other, which is common in the poorer Hindu households.

The Rājpūts as depicted by Colonel Tod resembled the knights of the age of chivalry. Courage, strength and endurance were the virtues most highly prized. One of the

Rājpūt trials of strength, it is recorded, was to gallop at full speed under the horizontal branch of a tree and cling to it while the horse passed on. This feat appears to have been a common amusement, and it is related in the annals of Mewār that the chief of Bunera broke his spine in the attempt; and there were few who came off without bruises and falls, in which consisted the sport. Of their martial spirit Colonel Tod writes: "The Rājpūt mother claims her full share in the glory of her son, who imbibes at the maternal fount his first rudiments of chivalry; and the importance of this parental instruction cannot be better illustrated than in the ever-recurring simile, 'Make thy mother's milk resplendent.' One need not reason on the intensity of sentiment thus implanted in the infant Rājpūt, of whom we may say without metaphor the shield is his cradle and daggers his playthings, and with whom the first commandment is, 'Avenge thy father's feud.'[1] A Rājpūt yet loves to talk of the days of chivalry, when three things alone occupied him, his horse, his lance and his mistress; for she is but third in his estimation after all, and to the first two he owed her."[2] And of their desire for fame: "This sacrifice (of the Johar) accomplished, their sole thought was to secure a niche in that immortal temple of fame, which the Rājpūt bard as well as the great minstrel of the West peoples 'with youths who died to be by poets sung.' For this the Rājpūt's anxiety has in all ages been so great as often to defeat even the purpose of revenge, his object being to die gloriously rather than to inflict death; assured that his name would never perish, but, preserved in immortal rhyme by the bard, would serve as the incentive to similar deeds."[3] He sums up their character in the following terms: "High courage, patriotism, loyalty, honour, hospitality and simplicity are qualities which must at once be conceded to them; and if we cannot vindicate them from charges to which human nature in every clime is obnoxious; if we are compelled to admit the deterioration of moral dignity from continual inroads of, and their consequent collision with rapacious conquerors; we must yet admire the quantum of virtue

---

[1] *Rājasthān*, i. pp. 543, 544.   [2] *Ibidem*, i. p. 125.
[3] *Ibidem*, ii. p. 52.

which even oppression and bad example have failed to banish. The meaner vices of deceit and falsehood, which the delineators of national character attach to the Asiatic without distinction, I deny to be universal with the Rājpūts, though some tribes may have been obliged from position to use these shields of the weak against continuous oppression."[1] The women prized martial courage no less than the men: they would hear with equanimity of the death of their sons or husbands in the battlefield, while they heaped scorn and contumely on those who returned after defeat. They were constantly ready to sacrifice themselves to the flames rather than fall into the hands of a conqueror; and the Johar, the final act of a besieged garrison, when the women threw themselves into the furnace, while the men sallied forth to die in battle against the enemy, is recorded again and again in Rājpūt annals. Three times was this tragedy enacted at the fall of Chitor, formerly the capital fortress of the Sesodia clan; and the following vivid account is given by Colonel Tod of a similar deed at Jaisalmer, when the town fell to the Muhammadans:[2] "The chiefs were assembled; all were unanimous to make Jaisalmer resplendent by their deeds and preserve the honour of the Yādu race. Muhāj thus addressed them: 'You are of a warlike race and strong are your arms in the cause of your prince; what heroes excel you who thus tread in the Chhatri's path? For the maintenance of my honour the sword is in your hands; let Jaisalmer be illumined by its blows upon the foe.' Having thus inspired the chiefs and men, Muhāj and Ratan repaired to the palace of their queens. They told them to take the *sohāg*[3] and prepare to meet in heaven, while they gave up their lives in defence of their honour and their faith. Smiling the Rāni replied, 'This night we shall prepare, and by the morning's light we shall be inhabitants of heaven'; and thus it was with all the chiefs and their wives. The night was passed together for the last time in preparation for the awful morn. It came; ablutions and prayers were finished and at the royal gate were convened children, wives and

---

[1] *Rājasthān*, i. p. 552.
[2] Vol. ii. p. 227.
[3] A ceremony of smearing vermilion on the bride before a wedding, which is believed to bring good fortune.

mothers. They bade a last farewell to all their kin; the Johar commenced, and twenty-four thousand females, from infancy to old age, surrendered their lives, some by the sword, others in the volcano of fire. Blood flowed in torrents, while the smoke of the pyre ascended to the heavens: not one feared to die, and every valuable was consumed with them, so that not the worth of a straw was preserved for the foe. The work done, the brothers looked upon the spectacle with horror. Life was now a burden and they prepared to quit it. They purified themselves with water, paid adoration to the divinity, made gifts to the poor, placed a branch of the *tulsi*[1] in their casques, the *sāligrām*[2] round their neck; and having cased themselves in armour and put on the saffron robe, they bound the marriage crown around their heads and embraced each other for the last time. Thus they awaited the hour of battle. Three thousand eight hundred warriors, their faces red with wrath, prepared to die with their chiefs." In this account the preparation for the Johar as if for a wedding is clearly brought out, and it seems likely that husbands and wives looked on it as a bridal preparatory to the resumption of their life together in heaven.

Colonel Tod gives the following account of a Rājpūt's arms:[3] "No prince or chief is without his *silla-khāna* or armoury, where he passes hours in viewing and arranging his arms. Every favourite weapon, whether sword, dagger, spear, matchlock or bow, has a distinctive epithet. The keeper of the armoury is one of the most confidential officers about the person of the prince. These arms are beautiful and costly. The *sirohi* or slightly curved blade is formed like that of Damascus, and is the greatest favourite of all the variety of weapons throughout Rājputāna. The long cut-and-thrust sword is not uncommon, and also the *khanda* or double-edged sword. The matchlocks, both of Lahore and the country, are often highly finished and inlaid with mother-of-pearl and gold; those of Boondi are the best. The shield of the rhinoceros-hide offers the best resistance, and is often ornamented with animals beautifully painted

---

[1] The basil plant, sacred to Vishnu.
[2] A round black stone, considered to be a form of Vishnu.
[3] *Rājasthān*, i. p. 555.

and enamelled in gold and silver. The bow is of buffalo-horn, and the arrows of reed, which are barbed in a variety of fashions, as the crescent, the trident, the snake's tongue, and other fanciful forms." It is probable that the forms were in reality by no means fanciful, but were copied from sacred or divine objects; and similarly the animals painted on the shields may have been originally the totem animals of the clan.

15. Occupation. The traditional occupation of a Rājpūt was that of a warrior and landholder. Their high-flown titles, Bhupāl (Protector of the earth), Bhupati (Lord of the earth), Bhusur (God of the earth), Bahuja (Born from the arms), indicate, Sir H. Risley says,[1] the exalted claims of the tribe. The notion that the trade of arms was their proper vocation clung to them for a very long time, and has retarded their education, so that they have perhaps lost status relatively to other castes under British supremacy. The rule that a Rājpūt must not touch the plough was until recently very strictly observed in the more conservative centres, and the poorer Rājpūts were reduced by it to pathetic straits for a livelihood, as is excellently shown by Mr. Barnes in the *Kāngra Settlement Report*:[2] "A Miān or well-known Rājpūt, to preserve his name and honour unsullied, must scrupulously observe four fundamental maxims: first, he must never drive the plough; second, he must never give his daughter in marriage to an inferior nor marry himself much below his rank; thirdly, he must never accept money in exchange for the betrothal of his daughter; and lastly, his female household must observe strict seclusion. The prejudice against the plough is perhaps the most inveterate of all; that step can never be recalled; the offender at once loses the privileged salutation; he is reduced to the second grade of Rājpūts; no man will marry his daughter, and he must go a step lower in the social scale to get a wife for himself. In every occupation of life he is made to feel his degraded position. In meetings of the tribe and at marriages the Rājpūts undefiled by the plough will refuse to sit at meals with the Hal Bāh or plough-driver as he is

---

[1] *Tribes and Castes of Bengal*, art. Rājpūt.

[2] Quoted in Sir D. Ibbetson's *Punjab Census Report* (1881), para. 456.

contemptuously styled; and many to avoid the indignity of exclusion never appear at public assemblies. . . . It is melancholy to see with what devoted tenacity the Rājpūt clings to these deep-rooted prejudices. Their emaciated looks and coarse clothes attest the vicissitudes they have undergone to maintain their fancied purity. In the quantity of waste land which abounds in the hills, a ready livelihood is offered to those who will cultivate the soil for their daily bread; but this alternative involves a forfeiture of their dearest rights, and they would rather follow any precarious pursuit than submit to the disgrace. Some lounge away their time on the tops of the mountains, spreading nets for the capture of hawks; many a day they watch in vain, subsisting on berries and on game accidentally entangled in their nets; at last, when fortune grants them success, they despatch the prize to their friends below, who tame and instruct the bird for the purpose of sale. Others will stay at home and pass their time in sporting, either with a hawk or, if they can afford it, with a gun; one Rājpūt beats the bushes and the other carries the hawk ready to be sprung after any quarry that rises to the view. At the close of the day if they have been successful they exchange the game for a little meal and thus prolong existence over another span. The marksman armed with a gun will sit up for wild pig returning from the fields, and in the same manner barter their flesh for other necessaries of life. However, the prospect of starvation has already driven many to take the plough, and the number of seceders daily increases. Our administration, though just and liberal, has a levelling tendency; service is no longer to be procured, and to many the stern alternative has arrived of taking to agriculture and securing comparative comfort, or enduring the pangs of hunger and death. So long as any resource remains the fatal step will be postponed, but it is easy to foresee that the struggle cannot be long protracted; necessity is a hard task-master, and sooner or later the pressure of want will overcome the scruples of the most bigoted." The objection to ploughing appears happily to have been quite overcome in the Central Provinces, as at the last census nine-tenths of the whole caste were shown as employed in pasture and agriculture, one-tenth of the Rājpūts being landholders, three-fifths actual cultivators, and one-fifth labourers and woodcutters. The bulk of the remaining tenth are probably in the police or other branches of Government service.

Rājpūt, Baghel.—The Baghel Rājpūts, who have given their name to Baghelkhand or Rewah, the eastern part of Central India, are a branch of the Chalukya or Solankhi clan, one of the four Agnikulas or those born from the fire-pit on Mount Abu. The chiefs of Rewah are Baghel Rājpūts, and the late Mahārāja Rāghurāj Singh has written a traditional history of the sept in a book called the *Bhakt Māla*.[1] He derives their origin from a child, having the form of a tiger (*bāgh*), who was born to the Solankhi Rāja of Gujarāt at the intercession of the famous saint Kabīr. One of the headquarters of the Kabīrpanthi sect are at Kawardha, which is close to Rewah, and the ruling family are members of the sect; hence probably the association of the Prophet with their origin. The *Bombay Gazetteer*[2] states that the founder of the clan was one Anoka, a nephew of the Solankhi king of Gujarāt, Kumarpāl (A.D. 1143–1174). He obtained a grant of the village Vaghela, the tiger's lair, about ten miles from Anhilvāda, the capital of the Solankhi dynasty, and the Baghel clan takes its name from this village. Subsequently the Baghels extended their power over the whole of Gujarāt, but in A.D. 1304 the last king, Karnadeva, was driven out by the Muhammadans, and one of his most beautiful wives was captured and sent to the emperor's harem. Karnadeva and his daughter fled and hid themselves near Nāsik, but the daughter was subsequently also taken, while it is not stated what became of Karnadeva. Mr. Hīra Lāl suggests that he fled towards Rewah, and that he is the Karnadeva of the list of Rewah Rājas, who married a daughter of the Gond-Rājpūt dynasty of Garha-Mandla.[3] At any rate the Baghel branch of the Solankhis apparently migrated to Rewah from Gujarāt and founded that State

---

[1] Mr. Crooke's *Tribes and Castes*, art. Baghel.
[2] Vol. i. part i. p. 198.
[3] See also a history of the Baghels, called *Pratāp Vinod*, written by Khān Bahādur Rahmat Ali Khān, and translated by Thākur Pratāp Singh, Revenue Commissioner of Rewah.

about the fourteenth century, as in the fifteenth they became prominent. According to Captain Forsyth, the Baghels claim descent from a tiger, and protect it when they can; and, probably, as suggested by Mr. Crooke,[1] the name is really totemistic, or is derived from some ancestor of the clan who obtained the name of the tiger as a title or nickname, like the American Red Indians. The Baghels are found in the Hoshangābād District, and in Mandla and Chhattīsgarh which are close to Rewah. Amarkantak, at the source of the Nerbudda, is the sepulchre of the Mahārājas of Rewah, and was ceded to them with the Sohāgpur tahsīl of Mandla after the Mutiny, in consideration of their loyalty and services during that period.

Rājpūt, Bāgri.—This clan is found in small numbers in the Hoshangābād and Seoni Districts. The name Bāgri, Malcolm says,[2] is derived from that large tract of plain called Bāgar or 'hedge of thorns,' the Bāgar being surrounded by ridges of wooded hills on all sides as if by a hedge. The Bāgar is the plain country of the Bikaner State, and any Jāt or Rājpūt coming from this tract is called Bāgri.[3] The Rājpūts of Bikaner are Rāthors, but they are not numerous, and the great bulk of the people are Jāts. Hence it is probable that the Bāgris of the Central Provinces were originally Jāts. In Seoni they say that they are Baghel Rājpūts, but this claim is unsupported by any tradition or evidence. In Central India the Bāgris are professed robbers and thieves, but these seem to be a separate group, a section of the Badhak or Bāwaria dacoits, and derived from the aboriginal population of Central India. The Bāgris of Seoni are respectable cultivators and own a number of villages. They rank higher than the local Panwārs and wear the sacred thread, but will remove dead cattle with their own hands. They marry among themselves.

Rājpūt, Bais.[4]—The Bais are one of the thirty-six royal

---

[1] Article Baghel, quoting Forsyth's *Highlands of Central India*.

[2] *Memoir of Central India*, vol. ii. p. 479.

[3] *Punjab Census Report* (1881), para. 445.

[4] This article consists entirely of extracts from Mr. Crooke's article on the Bais Rājpūts.

races. Colonel Tod considered them a branch of the Sūrajvansi, but according to their own account their eponymous ancestor was Sālivāhana, the mythic son of a snake, who conquered the great Rāja Vikramaditya of Ujjain and fixed his own era in A.D. 55. This is the Sāka era, and Sālivāhana was the leader of the Sāka nomads who invaded Gujarāt on two occasions, before and shortly after the beginning of the Christian era. It is suggested in the article on Rājpūt that the Yādava lunar clan are the representatives of these Sākas, and if this were correct the Bais would be a branch of the lunar race. The fact that they are snake-worshippers is in favour of their connection with the Yādavas and other clans, who are supposed to represent the Scythian invaders of the first and subsequent centuries, and had the legend of being descended from a snake. The Bais, Mr. Crooke says, believe that no snake has destroyed, or ever can destroy, one of the clan. They seem to take no precautions against the bite except hanging a vessel of water at the head of the sufferer, with a small tube at the bottom, from which the water is poured on his head as long as he can bear it. The cobra is, in fact, the tribal god. The name is derived by Mr. Crooke from the Sanskrit Vaishya, one who occupies the soil. The principal hero of the Bais was Tilokchand, who is supposed to have come from the Central Provinces. He lived about A.D. 1400, and was the premier Rāja of Oudh. He extended his dominions over all the tract known as Baiswāra, which comprises the bulk of the Rai Bareli and Unao Districts, and is the home of the Bais Rājpūts. The descendants of Tilokchand form a separate subdivision known as Tilokchandi Bais, who rank higher than the ordinary Bais, and will not eat with them. The Bais Rājpūts are found all over the United Provinces. In the Central Provinces they have settled in small numbers in the northern and eastern Districts.

Rājpūt, Baksaria.—A small clan found principally in the Bilāspur District, who derive their name from Baxār in Bengal. They were accustomed to send a litter, that is to say, a girl of their clan, to the harem of each Mughal Emperor, and this has degraded them. They allow widow-marriage, and do not wear the sacred thread. It is probable that they marry among themselves, as other Rājpūts do not intermarry with them, and they are no doubt an impure group with little pretension to be Rājpūts. The name Baksaria is found in the United Provinces as a territorial subcaste of several castes.

Rājpūt, Banāphar.—Mr. Crooke states that this sept is a branch of the Yādavas, and hence it is of the lunar race. The sept is famous on account of the exploits of the heroes Alha and Udal who belonged to it, and who fought for the Chandel kings of Mahoba and Khajurāha in their wars against Prithwi Rāj Chauhān, the king of Delhi. The exploits of Alha and Udal form the theme of poems still well known and popular in Bundelkhand, to which the sept belongs. The Banāphars have only a moderately respectable rank among Rājpūts.[1]

Rājpūt, Bhadauria.—An important clan who take their name from the village of Bhadāwar near Ater, south of the Jumna. They are probably a branch of the Chauhāns, being given as such by Colonel Tod and Sir H. M. Elliot.[2] Mr. Crooke remarks[3] that the Chauhāns are disposed to deny this relationship, now that from motives of convenience the two tribes have begun to intermarry. If they are, as supposed, an offshoot of the Chauhāns, this is an instance of the subdivision of a large clan leading to intermarriage between two sections, which has probably occurred in other instances also. This clan is returned from the Hoshangābād District.

Rājpūt, Bisen.—This clan belongs to the United Provinces and Oudh. They do not appear in history before the time of Akbar, and claim descent from a well-known Brāhman saint and a woman of the Sūrajvansi Rājpūts whom he married. The Bisens occupy a respectable position among Rājpūts, and intermarry with other good clans.

[1] Mr. Crooke's *Tribes and Castes*, art. Banāphar.
[2] *Rājasthān*, i. p. 88, and *Supplementary Glossary, s.v.*
[3] *Tribes and Castes, s.v.*

Rājpūt, Bundela.—A well-known clan of Rājpūts of somewhat inferior position, who have given their name to Bundelkhand, or the tract comprised principally in the Districts of Saugor, Damoh, Jhānsi, Hamīrpur and Bānda, and the Panna, Orchha, Datia and other States. The Bundelas are held to be derived from the Gaharwār or Gherwāl Rājpūts, and there is some reason for supposing that these latter were originally an aristocratic section of the Bhar tribe with some infusion of Rājpūt blood. But the Gaharwārs now rank almost with the highest clans. According to tradition one of the Gaharwār Rājas offered a sacrifice of his own head to the Vindhya-basini Devi or the goddess of the Vindhya hills, and out of the drops (*bund*) of blood which fell on the altar a boy was born. He returned to Panna and founded the clan which bears the name Bundela, from *bund*, a drop.[1] It is probable that, as suggested by Captain Luard, the name is really a corruption of Vindhya or Vindhyela, a dweller in the Vindhya hills, where, according to their own tradition, the clan had its birth. The Bundelas became prominent in the thirteenth or fourteenth century, after the fall of the Chandels. "Orchha became the chief of the numerous Bundela principalities; but its founder drew upon himself everlasting infamy, by putting to death the wise Abul Fazl, the historian and friend of the magnanimous Akbar, and the encomiast and advocate of the Hindu race. From the period of Akbar the Bundelas bore a distinguished part in all the grand conflicts, to the very close of the monarchy."[2]

The Bundelas held the country up to the Nerbudda in the Central Provinces, and, raiding continually into the Gond territories south of the Nerbudda on the pretence of protecting the sacred cow which the Gonds used for ploughing, they destroyed the castle on Chauragarh in Narsinghpur on a crest of the Satpūras, and reduced the Nerbudda valley to subjection. The most successful chieftain of the tribe was Chhatarsāl, the Rāja of Panna, in the eighteenth century, who was virtually ruler of all Bundelkhand; his dominions extending from Bānda in the north to Jubbulpore in the

---

[1] Mr. Crooke's *Tribes and Castes*, art. Bundela.
[2] *Rājasthān*, i. p. 106.

south, and from Rewah in the east to the Betwa River in the west. But he had to call in the help of the Peshwa to repel an invasion of the Mughal armies, and left a third of his territory by will to the Marāthas. Chhatarsāl left twenty-two legitimate and thirty illegitimate sons, and their descendants now hold several small Bundela States, while the territories left to the Peshwa subsequently became British. The chiefs of Panna, Orchha, Datia, Chhatarpur and numerous other small states in the Bundelkhand agency are Bundela Rājpūts.[1] The Bundelas of Saugor do not intermarry with the good Rājpūt clans, but with an inferior group of Panwārs and another clan called Dhundhele, perhaps an offshoot of the Panwārs, who are also residents of Saugor. Their character, as disclosed in a number of proverbial sayings and stories current regarding them, somewhat resembles that of the Scotch highlanders as depicted by Stevenson. They are proud and penurious to the last degree, and quick to resent the smallest slight. They make good *shikāris* or sportsmen, but are so impatient of discipline that they have never found a vocation by enlisting in the Indian Army. Their characteristics are thus described in a doggerel verse: "The Bundelas salute each other from miles apart, their *pagris* are cocked on the side of the head till they touch the shoulders. A Bundela would dive into a well for the sake of a cowrie, but would fight with the Sardārs of Government." No Bania could go past a Bundela's house riding on a pony or holding up an umbrella; and all low-caste persons who passed his house must salute it with the words, *Diwān ji ko Rām Rām*. Women must take their shoes off to pass by. It is related that a few years ago a Bundela was brought up before the Assistant Commissioner, charged with assaulting a tahsīl process-server, and threatening him with his sword. The Bundela, who was very poor and wearing rags, was asked by the magistrate whether he had threatened the man with his sword. He replied "Certainly not; the sword is for gentlemen like you and me of equal position. To him, if I had wished to beat him I would have taken my shoe." Another story is that there was once a very overbearing Tahsīldār, who had a

---

[1] *Imperial Gazetteer*, articles Bundelkhand and Panna.

shoe $2\frac{1}{2}$ feet long with which he used to collect the land revenue. One day a Bundela mālguzār appeared before him on some business. The Tahsīldār kept his seat. The Bundela walked quietly up to the table and said, "Will the Sirkār step aside with me for a moment, as I have something private to say." The Tahsīldār got up and walked aside with him, on which the Bundela said, 'That is sufficient, I only wished to tell you that you should rise to receive me.' When the Bundelas are collected at a feast they sit with their hands folded across their stomachs and their eyes turned up, and remain impassive while food is being put on their plates, and never say, 'Enough,' because they think that they would show themselves to be feeble men if they refused to eat as much as was put before them. Much of the food is thus ultimately wasted, and given to the sweepers, and this leads to great extravagance at marriages and other ceremonial occasions. The Bundelas were much feared and were not popular landlords, but they are now losing their old characteristics and settling down into respectable cultivators.

Rājpūt, Chandel.—An important clan of Rājpūts, of which a small number reside in the northern Districts of Saugor, Damoh and Jubbulpore, and also in Chhattīsgarh. The name is derived by Mr. Crooke from the Sanskrit *chandra*, the moon. The Chandel are not included in the thirty-six royal races, and are supposed to have been a section of one of the indigenous tribes which rose to power. Mr. V. A. Smith states that the Chandels, like several other dynasties, first came into history early in the ninth century, when Nannuka Chandel about A.D. 831 overthrew a Parihār chieftain and became lord of the southern parts of Jejāka-bhukti or Bundelkhand. Their chief towns were Mahoba and Kālanjar in Bundelkhand, and they gradually advanced northwards till the Jumna became the frontier between their dominions and those of Kanauj. They fought with the Gūjar-Parihār kings of Kanauj and the Kālachuris of Chedi, who had their capital at Tewar in Jubbulpore, and joined in resisting the incursions of the Muhammadans. In A.D. 1182 Parmāl, the Chandel king, was defeated by Prithwi Rāja, the

Chauhān king of Delhi, after the latter had abducted the Chandel's daughter. This was the war in which Alha and Udal, the famous Banāphar heroes, fought for the Chandels, and it is commemorated in the Chand-Raisa, a poem still well known to the people of Bundelkhand. In A.D. 1203 Kālanjar was taken by the Muhammadan Kutb-ud-Dīn Ibak, and the importance of the Chandel rulers came to an end, though they lingered on as purely local chiefs until the sixteenth century. The Chandel princes were great builders, and beautified their chief towns, Mahoba, Kālanjar and Khajurāho with many magnificent temples and lovely lakes, formed by throwing massive dams across the openings between the hills.[1] Among these were great irrigation works in the Hamīrpur District, the forts of Kālanjar and Ajaighar, and the noble temples at Khajurāho and Mahoba.[2] Even now the ruins of old forts and temples in the Saugor and Damoh Districts are attributed by the people to the Chandels, though many were in fact probably constructed by the Kālachuris of Chedi.

Mr. Smith derives the Chandels either from the Gonds or Bhars, but inclines to the view that they were Gonds. The following considerations tend, I venture to think, to favour the hypothesis of their origin from the Bhars. According to the best traditions, the Gonds came from the south, and practically did not penetrate to Bundelkhand. Though Saugor and Damoh contain a fair number of Gonds they have never been of importance there, and this is almost their farthest limit to the north-west. The Gond States in the Central Provinces did not come into existence for several centuries after the commencement of the Chandel dynasty, and while there are authentic records of all these states, the Gonds have no tradition of their dominance in Bundelkhand. The Gonds have nowhere else built such temples as are attributed to the Chandels at Khajurāho, whilst the Bhars were famous builders. " In Mīrzāpur traces of the Bhars abound on all sides in the shape of old tanks and village forts. The bricks found in the Bhar-dīhs or forts are of enormous dimensions, and frequently measure 19 by 11 inches, and

---

[1] *Early History of India*, 3rd edition, pp. 390-394.

[2] Mr. Crooke's *Tribes and Castes*, art. Chandel.

are $2\frac{1}{4}$ inches thick. In quality and size they are similar to bricks often seen in ancient Buddhist buildings. The old capital of the Bhars, five miles from Mīrzāpur, is said to have had 150 temples."[1] Elliot remarks[2] that "common tradition assigns to the Bhars the possession of the whole tract from Gorakhpur to Bundelkhand and Saugor, and many old stone forts, embankments and subterranean caverns in Gorakhpur, Azamgarh, Jaunpur, Mīrzāpur and Allahābād, which are ascribed to them, would seem to indicate no inconsiderable advance in civilisation." Though there are few or no Bhars now in Bundelkhand, there are a large number of Pāsis in Allahābād which partly belongs to it, and small numbers in Bundelkhand; and the Pāsi caste is mainly derived from the Bhars;[3] while a Gaharwār dynasty, which is held to be derived from the Bhars, was dominant in Bundelkhand and Central India before the rise of the Chandels. According to one legend, the ancestor of the Chandels was born with the moon as a father from the daughter of the high priest of the Gaharwār Rāja Indrajīt of Benāres or of Indrajīt himself.[4] As will be seen, the Gaharwārs were an aristocratic section of the Bhars. Another legend states that the first Chandel was the offspring of the moon by the daughter of a Brāhman Pandit of Kalanjar.[5] In his *Notes on the Bhars of Bundelkhand*[6] Mr. Smith argues that the Bhars adopted the Jain religion, and also states that several of the temples at Khajurāho and Mahoba, erected in the eleventh century, are Jain. These were presumably erected by the Chandels, but I have never seen it suggested that the Gonds were Jains or were capable of building Jain temples in the eleventh century. Mr. Smith also states that Maniya Deo, to whom a temple exists at Mahoba, was the tutelary deity of the Chandels; and that the only other shrine of Maniya Deo discovered by him in the Hamīrpur District was in a village reputed formerly to have been held by the Bhars.[7] Two instances of intercourse between the Chandels and Gonds are given, but

[1] Sherring's *Castes and Tribes*, i. pp. 359, 360.
[2] *Supplemental Glossary*, art. Bhar.
[3] See art. Pāsi.
[4] Crooke's *Tribes and Castes*, art. Chandel.
[5] *Ibidem*.
[6] *J.A.S.B.* vol. xlvi. (1877), p. 232.
[7] *Ibidem*, p. 233.

the second of them, that the Rāni Dūrgavati of Mandla was a Chandel princess, belongs to the sixteenth century, and has no bearing on the origin of the Chandels. The first instance, that of the Chandel Rāja Kīrat Singh hunting at Maniagarh with the Gond Rāja of Garha-Mandla, cannot either be said to furnish any real evidence in favour of a Gond origin for the Chandels; it may be doubted whether there was any Gond Rāja of Garha-Mandla till after the fall of the Kālachuri dynasty of Tewar, which is quite close to Garha-Mandla, in the twelfth century; and a reference so late as this would not affect the question.[1] Finally, the Chandels are numerous in Mīrzāpur, which was formerly the chief seat of the Bhars, while the Gonds have never been either numerous or important in Mīrzāpur. These considerations seem to point to the possibility of the derivation of the Chandels from the Bhars rather than from the Gonds; and the point is perhaps of some interest in view of the suggestion in the article on Kol that the Gonds did not arrive in the Central Provinces for some centuries after the rise of the Chandel dynasty of Khajurāho and Mahoba. The Chandels may have simply been a local branch of the Gaharwārs, who obtained a territorial designation from Chanderi, or in some other manner, as has continually happened in the case of other clans. The Gaharwārs were probably derived from the Bhars. The Chandels now rank as a good Rājpūt clan, and intermarry with the other leading clans.

Rājpūt, Chauhān.—The Chauhān was the last of the Agnikula or fire-born clans. According to the legend: "Again Vasishtha seated on the lotus prepared incantations; again he called the gods to aid; and as he poured forth the libation a figure arose, lofty in stature, of elevated front, hair like jet, eyes rolling, breast expanded, fierce, terrific, clad in armour with quiver filled, a bow in one hand and a brand in the other, quadriform (Chaturanga), whence his name was given as Chauhān." This account makes the Chauhān the most important of the fire-born clans, and Colonel Tod says that he was the most valiant of the Agnikulas, and it may be asserted not of them only but of

[1] *J.A.S.B.* vol. xlvi. (1877), p. 233.

the whole Rājpūt race ; and though the swords of the Rāhtors would be ready to contest the point, impartial decision must assign to the Chauhān the van in the long career of arms.[1] General Cunningham shows that even so late as the time of Prithwi Rāj in the twelfth century the Chauhāns had no claim to be sprung from fire, but were content to be considered descendants of a Brāhman sage Bhrigu.[2] Like the other Agnikula clans the Chauhāns are now considered to have sprung from the Gurjara or White Hun invaders of the fifth and sixth centuries, but I do not know whether this is held to be definitely proved in their case. Sāmbhar and Ajmer in Rājputāna appear to have been the first home of the clan, and inscriptions record a long line of thirty-nine kings as reigning there from Anhul, the first created Chauhān. The last but one of them, Vigraha Rāja or Bisāl Deo, in the middle of the twelfth century extended the ancestral dominions considerably, and conquered Delhi from a chief of the Tomara clan. At this time the Chauhāns, according to their own bards, held the line of the Nerbudda from Garha-Mandla to Maheshwar and also Asīrgarh, while their dominions extended north to Hissar and south to the Aravalli hills.[3] The nephew of Bisāl Deo was Prithwi Rāj, the most famous Chauhān hero, who ruled at Sāmbhar, Ajmer and Delhi. His first exploit was the abduction of the daughter of Jaichand, the Gaharwār Rāja of Kanauj, in about A.D. 1175. The king of Kanauj had claimed the title of universal sovereign and determined to celebrate the Ashwa-Medha or horse-sacrifice, at which all the offices should be performed by vassal kings. Prithwi Rāj alone declined to attend as a subordinate, and Jaichand therefore made a wooden image of him and set it up at the gate in the part of doorkeeper. But when his daughter after the tournament took the garland of flowers to bestow it on the chief whom she chose for her husband, she passed by all the assembled nobles and threw the garland on the neck of the wooden image. At this moment Prithwi Rāj dashed in with a few companions, and catching her up, escaped with

---

[1] *Rājasthān*, i. pp. 86, 87.
[2] *Archaeological Reports*, ii. 255, quoted in Mr. Crooke's art. Chauhān.
[3] *Imperial Gazetteer, India*, vol. ii. p. 312.

her from her father's court.¹ Afterwards, in 1182, Prithwi Rāj defeated the Chandel Rāja Parmāl and captured Mahoba. In 1191 Prithwi Rāj was the head of a confederacy of Hindu princes in combating the invasion of Muhammad Ghori. He repelled the Muhammadans at Tarāin about two miles north of Delhi, but in the following year was completely defeated and killed at Thaneswar, and soon afterwards Delhi and Ajmer fell to the Muhammadans. The Chauhān kingdom was broken up, but scattered parts of it remained, and about A.D. 1307 Asīrgarh in Nimār, which continued to be held by the Chauhāns, was taken by Ala-ud-Dīn Khilji and the whole garrison put to the sword except one boy. This boy, Raisi Chauhān, escaped to Rājputāna, and according to the bardic chronicle his descendants formed the Hāra branch of the Chauhāns and conquered from the Mīnas the tract known as Hāravati, from which they perhaps took their name.² This is now comprised in the Kotah and Bundi states, ruled by Hāra chiefs. Another well-known offshoot from the Chauhāns are the Khīchi clan, who belong to the Sind-Sāgar Doāb; and the Nikumbh and Bhadauria clans are also derived from them. The Chauhāns are numerous in the Punjab and United Provinces and rank as one of the highest Rājpūt clans. In the Central Provinces they are found principally in the Narsinghpur and Hoshangābād Districts, and also in Mandla. The Chauhān Rājpūts of Mandla marry among themselves, with other Chauhāns of Mandla, Seoni and Bālāghāt. They have exogamous sections with names apparently derived from villages like an ordinary caste. The remarriage of widows is forbidden, but those widows who desire to do so go and live with a man and are put out of caste. This, however, is said not to happen frequently. A widow's hair is not shaved, but her glass bangles are broken, she is dressed in white, made to sleep on the ground, and can wear no ornaments. Owing to the renown of the clan their name has been adopted by numerous classes of inferior Rājpūts and low Hindu castes who have no right to it. Thus in the Punjab a large subcaste of Chamārs call themselves Chauhān, and in the Bilāspur District a low caste

---

¹ *Early History of India* and *Imperial Gazetteer, loc. cit.*
² *Rājasthān*, ii. p. 419.

of village watchmen go by this name. These latter may be descendants of the illegitimate offspring of Chauhān Rājpūts by low-caste women.

Rājpūt, Dhākar.—In the Central Provinces this term has the meaning of one of illegitimate descent, and it is often used by the Kirārs, who are probably of mixed descent from Rājpūts. In northern India, however, the Dhākars are a clan of Rājpūts, who claim Sūrajvansi origin; but this is not generally admitted. Mr. Crooke states that some are said to be emigrants from the banks of the Nerbudda; but the main body say they came from Ajmer in the sixteenth century. They were notorious in the eighteenth century for their lawlessness, and gave the imperial Mughal officers much trouble in the neighbourhood of Agra, rendering the communications between that city and Etāwah insecure. In the Mutiny they broke out again, and are generally a turbulent, ill-conducted sept, always ready for petty acts of violence and cattle-stealing. They are, however, recognised as Rājpūts of good position and intermarry with the best clans.[1]

In the Central Provinces the Dhākars are found principally in Hoshangābād, and it is doubtful if they are proper Rājpūts.

Rājpūt, Gaharwār, Gherwāl.— This is an old clan. Mr. V. A. Smith states that they had been dominant in Central India about Nowgong and Chhatarpur before the Parihārs in the eighth century. The Parihār kings were subsequently overthrown by the Chandels of Mahoba. In their practice of building embankments and constructing lakes the Chandels were imitators of the Gaharwārs, who are credited with the formation of some of the most charming lakes in Bundelkhand.[2] And in A.D. 1090 a Rāja of the Gaharwār clan called Chandradeva seized Kanauj (on the Ganges north-west of Lucknow), and established his

---

[1] The above particulars are taken from Mr. Crooke's article Dhākara in his *Tribes and Castes*.

[2] *Early History of India*, 3rd edition, p. 391.

authority certainly over Benāres and Ajodhia, and perhaps over the Delhi territory. Govindachandra, grandson of Chandradeva, enjoyed a long reign, which included the years A.D. 1114 and 1154. His numerous land grants and widely distributed coins prove that he succeeded to a large extent in restoring the glories of Kanauj, and in making himself a power of considerable importance. The grandson of Govindachandra was Jayachandra, renowned in the popular Hindu poems and tales of northern India as Rāja Jaichand, whose daughter was carried off by the gallant Rai Pithora or Prithwi Rāj of Ajmer. Kanauj was finally captured and destroyed by Shihāb-ud-Dīn in 1193, when Jaichand retired towards Benāres but was overtaken and slain.[1] His grandson, Mr. Crooke says,[2] afterwards fled to Kantit in the Mīrzāpur District and, overcoming the Bhar Rāja of that place, founded the family of the Gaharwār Rājas of Kantit Bijaypur, which was recently still in existence. All the other Gaharwārs trace their lineage to Benāres or Bijaypur. The predecessors of the Gaharwārs in Kantit and in a large tract of country lying contiguous to it were the Bhars, an indigenous race of great enterprise, who, though not highly civilised, were far removed from barbarism. According to Sherring they have left numerous evidences of their energy and skill in earthworks, forts, dams and the like.[3] Similarly Elliot says of the Bhars: "Common tradition assigns to them the possession of the whole tract from Gorakhpur to Bundelkhand and Saugor, and the large pargana of Bhadoi or Bhardai in Benāres is called after their name. Many old stone forts, embankments and subterranean caverns in Gorakhpur, Azamgarh, Jaunpur, Mīrzāpur and Allahābād, which are ascribed to them, would seem to indicate no inconsiderable advance in civilisation."[4] Colonel Tod says of the Gaharwārs: "The Gherwāl Rājpūt is scarcely known to his brethren in Rājasthān, who will not admit his contaminated blood to mix with theirs, though as a brave warrior he is entitled to their fellowship."[5] It is thus curious that the Gaharwārs, who are one of the oldest clans

---

[1] *Early History of India*, 3rd edition, p. 385.
[2] *Tribes and Castes*, art. Gaharwār.
[3] *Tribes and Castes*, i. p. 75.
[4] *Supplementary Glossary*, p. 33.
[5] *Rājasthān*, i. p. 105.

to appear in authentic history, if they ruled Central India in the eighth century before the Parihārs, should be considered to be of very impure origin. And as they are subsequently found in Mīrzāpur, a backward forest tract which is also the home of the Bhars, and both the Gaharwārs and Bhars have a reputation as builders of tanks and forts, it seems likely that the Gaharwārs were really, as suggested by Mr. V. A. Smith, the aristocratic branch of the Bhars, probably with a considerable mixture of Rājpūt blood. Elliot states that the Bhars formerly occupied the whole of Azamgarh, the pargana of Bara in Allahābād and Khariagarh in the Kanauj tract. This widespread dominance corresponds with what has been already stated as regards the Gaharwārs, who, according to Mr. V. A. Smith, ruled in Central India, Kanauj, Oudh, Benāres and Mīrzāpur. And the name Gaharwār, according to Dr. Hoernle, is connected with the Sanskrit root *gah*, and has the sense of 'dwellers in caves or deep jungle.'[1] The origin of the Gaharwārs is of interest in the Central Provinces, because it is from them that the Bundela clan of Saugor and Bundelkhand is probably descended.[2]

The Gaharwārs, Mr. Crooke states, now hold a high rank among Rājpūt septs; they give daughters to the Baghel, Chandel and Bisen, and take brides of the Bais, Gautam, Chauhān, Parihār and other clans. The Gaharwārs are found in small numbers in the Central Provinces, chiefly in the Chhattīsgarh Districts and Feudatory States.

Rājpūt, Gaur, Chamar Gaur.—Colonel Tod remarks of this tribe: "The Gaur tribe was once respected in Rājasthān, though it never there attained to any considerable eminence. The ancient kings of Bengal were of this race, and gave their name to the capital, Lakhnauti." This town in Bengal, and the kingdom of which it was the capital, were known as Gauda, and it has been conjectured that the Gaur Brāhmans and Rājpūts were named after it. Sir H. M. Elliot and Mr. Crooke, however, point out that the home of the Gaur Brāhmans and Rājpūts and a cultivating caste,

---

[1] Quoted in Mr. Crooke's article on Gaharwār.
[2] See art. Rājpūt, Bundela.

the Gaur Tāgas, is in the centre and west of the United Provinces, far removed from Bengal; the Gaur Brāhmans now reside principally in the Meerut Division, and between them and Bengal is the home of the Kanaujia Brāhmans. General Cunningham suggests that the country comprised in the present Gonda District round the old town of Srāvāsti, was formerly known as Gauda, and was hence the origin of the caste name.[1] The derivation from Gaur in Bengal is perhaps, however, more probable, as the name was best known in connection with this tract. The Gaur Rājpūts do not make much figure in history. "Repeated mention of them is found in the wars of Prithwi Rāj as leaders of considerable renown, one of whom founded a small state in the centre of India. This survived through seven centuries of Mogul domination, till it at length fell a prey indirectly to the successes of the British over the Marāthas, when Sindhia in 1809 annihilated the power of the Gaur and took possession of his capital, Supur."[2]

In the United Provinces the Gaur Rājpūts are divided into three groups, the Bāhman, or Brāhman, the Bhāt, and the Chamār Gaur. Of these the Chamār Gaur, curiously enough appear to rank the highest, which is accounted for by the following story: When trouble fell upon the Gaur family, one of their ladies, far advanced in pregnancy, took refuge in a Chamār's house, and was so grateful to him for his disinterested protection that she promised to call her child by his name. The Bhāts and Brāhmans, to whom the others fled, do not appear to have shown a like chivalry, and hence, strange as it may appear, the subdivisions called after their name rank below the Chamār Gaur.[3] The names of the subsepts indicate that this clan of Rājpūts is probably of mixed origin. If the Brāhman subsept is descended from Brāhmans, it would be only one of several probable cases of Rājpūt clans originating from this caste. As regards the Bhāt subcaste, the Chārans or Bhāts of Rājputāna are admittedly Rājpūts, and there is therefore nothing curious in finding a Bhāt subsection in a Rājpūt clan. What the real origin of the Chamār Gaurs was is difficult to surmise.

---

[1] Quoted in Mr. Crooke's article Gaur Brāhman.
[2] *Rajasthān*, i. p. 105.
[3] *Supplemental Glossary*, s.v.

The Chamār Gaur is now a separate clan, and its members intermarry with the other Gaur Rājpūts, affording an instance of the subdivision of clans. In the Central Provinces the greater number of the persons returned as Gaur Rājpūts really belong to a group known as Gorai, who are considered to be the descendants of widows or kept women in the Gaur clan, and marry among themselves. They should really therefore be considered a separate caste, and not members of the Rājpūt caste proper. In the United Provinces the Gaurs rank with the good Rājpūt clans. In the Central Provinces the Gaur and Chamār-Gaur clans are returned from most Districts of the Jubbulpore and Nerbudda divisions, and also in considerable numbers from Bhandāra.

Rājpūt, Haihaya, Haihaivansi, Kālachuri.—This well-known historical clan of the Central Provinces is not included among the thirty-six royal races, and Colonel Tod gives no information about them. The name Haihaya is stated to be a corruption of Ahihaya, which means snake-horse, the legend being that the first ancestor of the clan was the issue of a snake and a mare. Haihaivansi signifies descendants of the horse. Colonel Tod states that the first capital of the Indu or lunar race was at Mahesvati on the Nerbudda, still existing as Maheshwar, and was founded by Sahasra Arjuna of the Haihaya tribe.[1] This Arjuna of the thousand arms was one of the Pāndava brothers, and it may be noted that the Ratanpur Haihaivansis still have a story of their first ancestor stealing a horse from Arjuna, and a consequent visit of Arjuna and Krishna to Ratanpur for its recovery. Since the Haihayas also claim descent from a snake and are of the lunar race, it seems not unlikely that they may have belonged to one of the Scythian or Tartar tribes, the Sākas or Yueh-chi, who invaded India shortly after the commencement of the Christian era, as it has been conjectured that the other lunar Rājpūt clans worshipping or claiming descent from a snake originated from these tribes. The Haihaivansis or Kālachuris became dominant in the Nerbudda valley about the sixth century, their earliest

[1] *Rajasthān*, i. p. 36.

inscription being dated A.D. 580. Their capital was moved to Tripura or Tewar near Jubbulpore about A.D. 900, and from here they appear to have governed an extensive territory for about 300 years, and were frequently engaged in war with the adjoining kingdoms, the Chandels of Mahoba, the Panwārs of Mālwa, and the Chalukyas of the south. One king, Gangeyadeva, appears even to have aspired to become the paramount power in northern India, and his sovereignty was recognised in distant Tirhūt. Gangeyadeva was fond of residing at the foot of the holy fig-tree of Prayāga (Allahābād), and eventually found salvation there with his hundred wives. From about A.D. 1100 the power of the Kālachuri or Haihaya princes began to decline, and their last inscription is dated A.D. 1196. It is probable that they were subverted by the Gond kings of Garha-Mandla, the first of whom, Jadurai, appears to have been in the service of the Kālachuri king, and subsequently with the aid of a dismissed minister to have supplanted his former master.[1] The kingdom of the Kālachuri or Haihaya kings was known as Chedi, and, according to Mr. V. A. Smith, corresponded more or less roughly to the present area of the Central Provinces.[2]

In about the tenth century a member of the reigning family of Tripura was appointed viceroy of some territories in Chhattīsgarh, and two or three generations afterwards his family became practically independent of the parent house, and established their own capital at Ratanpur in Bilāspur District (A.D. 1050). This state was known as Dakshin or southern Kosāla. During the twelfth century its importance rapidly increased, partly no doubt on the ruins of the Jubbulpore kingdom, until the influence of the Ratanpur princes, Ratnadeva II. and Prithwideva II., may be said to have extended from Amarkantak to beyond the Godāvari, and from the confines of Berār in the west to

---

[1] The above notice of the Kālachuri or Haihaya dynasty of Tripura is taken from the detailed account in the *Jubbulpore District Gazetteer*, pp. 42-47, compiled by Mr. A. E. Nelson, C.S., and Rai Bahādur Hīra Lāl.

[2] *Early History of India*, 3rd edition, p. 390. This, however, does not only refer to the Jubbulpore branch, whose territories did not probably include the south and east of the present Central Provinces, but includes also the country over which the Ratanpur kings subsequently extended their separate jurisdiction.

the boundaries of Orissa in the east.¹ The Ratanpur kingdom of Chedi or Dakshin Kosāla was the only one of the Rājpūt states in the Central Provinces which escaped subversion by the Gonds, and it enjoyed a comparatively tranquil existence till A.D. 1740, when Ratanpur fell to the Marāthas almost without striking a blow. "The only surviving representative of the Haihayas of Ratanpur," Mr. Wills states,² "is a quite simple-minded Rājpūt who lives at Bargaon in Raipur District. He represents the junior or Raipur branch of the family, and holds five villages which were given him revenue-free by the Marāthas for his maintenance. The mālguzār of Senduras claims descent from the Ratanpur family, but his pretensions are doubtful. He enjoys no privileges such as those of the Bargaon Thākur, to whom presents are still made when he visits the chiefs who were once subordinate to his ancient house." In the Ballia District of the United Provinces³ are some Hayobans Rājpūts who claim descent from the Ratanpur kings. Chandra Got, a cadet of this house, is said to have migrated northwards in A.D. 850⁴ and settled in the Sāran District on the Ganges, where he waged successful war with the aboriginal Cheros. Subsequently one of his descendants violated a Brāhman woman called Maheni of the house of his Purohit or family priest, who burnt herself to death, and is still locally worshipped. After this tragedy the Hayobans Rājpūts left Sāran and settled in Ballia. Colonel Tod states that, "A small branch of these ancient Haihayas yet exist in the country of the Nerbudda, near the very top of the valley, at Sohāgpur in Baghelkhand, aware of their ancient lineage, and, though few in number, are still celebrated for their valour."⁵ This Sohāgpur must apparently be the Sohāgpur tahsīl of Rewah, ceded from Mandla after the Mutiny.

Rājpūt, Hūna, Hoon.—This clan retains the name and

---

¹ *Bilāspur District Gazetteer*, chap. ii., in which a full and interesting account of the Ratanpur kingdom is given by Mr. C. U. Wills, C.S.
² *Ibidem*, p. 49.
³ Mr. Crooke's *Tribes and Castes*, art. Hayobans.
⁴ The date is too early, as is usual in these traditions. Though the Haihaivansis only founded Ratanpur about A.D. 1050, their own legends put it ten centuries earlier.
⁵ *Rajasthān*, i. p. 36.

memory of the Hun barbarian hordes, who invaded India at or near the epoch of their incursions into Europe. It is practically extinct; but in his *Western India* Colonel Tod records the discovery of a few families of Hūnas in Baroda State: "At a small village opposite Ometa I discovered a few huts of Huns, still existing under the ancient name of Hoon, by which they are known to Hindu history. There are said to be three or four families of them at the village of Trisavi, three *kos* from Baroda, and although neither feature nor complexion indicate much relation to the Tartar-visaged Hun, we may ascribe the change to climate and admixture of blood, as there is little doubt that they are descended from these invaders, who established a sovereignty on the Indus in the second and sixth centuries of the Christian era, and became so incorporated with the Rājpūt population as to obtain a place among the thirty-six royal races of India, together with the Gete, the Kāthi, and other tribes of the Sacae from Central Asia, whose descendants still occupy the land of the sun-worshipping Saura or Chaura, no doubt one of the same race."

Rājpūt, Kachhwāha, Cutchwāha.—A celebrated clan of Rājpūts included among the thirty-six royal races, to which the Mahārājas of the important states of Amber or Jaipur and Alwar belong. They are of the solar race and claim descent from Kash, the second son of the great king Rāma of Ajodhia, the incarnation of Vishnu. Their original seat, according to tradition, was Rohtās on the Son river, and another of their famous progenitors was Rāja Nal, who migrated from Rohtās and founded Narwar.[1] The town of Damoh in the Central Provinces is supposed to be named after Damyanti, Rāja Nal's wife. According to General Cunningham the name Kachhwāha is an abbreviation of Kachhaha-ghāta or tortoise-killer. The earliest appearance of the Kachhwāha Rājpūts in authentic history is in the tenth century, when a chief of the clan captured Gwalior from the Parihār-Gūjar kings of Kanauj and established himself there. His dynasty had an independent existence till A.D. 1128, when it became tributary

[1] *Rajasthān*, ii. p. 319.

to the Chandel kings of Mahoba.[1] The last prince of Gwalior was Tejkaran, called Dūlha Rai or the bridegroom prince, and he received from his father-in-law the district of Daora in the present Jaipur State, where he settled. In 1150 one of his successors wrested Amber from the Mīnas and made it his capital. The Amber State from the first acknowledged the supremacy of the Mughal emperors, and the chief of the period gave his daughter in marriage to Akbar. This chief's son, Bhagwān Dās, is said to have saved Akbar's life at the battle of Sarnāl. Bhagwān Dās gave a daughter to Jahāngīr, and his adopted son, Mān Singh, the next chief, was one of the most conspicuous of the Mughal Generals, and at different periods was governor of Kābul, Bengal, Bihār and the Deccan. The next chief of note, Jai Singh I., appears in all the wars of Aurāngzeb in the Deccan. He was commander of 6000 horse, and captured Sivaji, the celebrated founder of the Marātha power. The present city of Jaipur was founded by a subsequent chief, Jai Singh II., in 1728. During the Mutiny the Mahārāja of Jaipur placed all his military power at the disposal of the Political Agent, and in every way assisted the British Government. At the Durbar of 1877 his salute was raised to 21 guns. Jaipur, one of the largest states in Rājputāna, has an area of nearly 16,000 square miles, and a population of 2½ million persons. The Alwar State was founded about 1776 by Pratāp Singh, a descendant of a prince of the Jaipur house, who had separated from it three centuries before. It has an area of 3000 square miles and a population of nearly a million.[2] In Colonel Tod's time the Kachhwāha chiefs in memory of their descent from Rāma, the incarnation of the sun, celebrated with great solemnity the annual feast of the sun. On this occasion a stately car called the chariot of the sun was brought from Rāma's temple, and the Mahārāja ascending into it perambulated his capital. The images of Rāma and Siva were carried with the army both in Alwar and Jaipur. The banner of Amber was always called the *Pānchranga*

---

[1] *Early History of India*, 3rd edition, p. 381.
[2] The above information is taken from the new *Imperial Gazetteer*, articles Jaipur and Alwar States.

or five-coloured flag, and is frequently mentioned in the traditions of the Rājpūt bards. But it does not seem to be stated what the five colours were. Some of the finest soldiers in the old Sepoy army were Kachhwāha Rājpūts. The Kachhwāhas are fairly numerous in the United Provinces and rank with the highest Rājpūt clans.[1] In the Central Provinces they are found principally in the Saugor, Hoshangābād and Nimār Districts.

Rājpūt, Nāgvansi.—This clan are considered to be the descendants of the Tāk or Takshac, which is one of the thirty-six royal races, and was considered by Colonel Tod to be of Scythian origin. The Takshac were also snake-worshippers. "Nāga and Takshac are synonymous appellations in Sanskrit for the snake, and the Takshac is the celebrated Nāgvansa of the early heroic history of India. The Mahābhārat describes in its usual allegorical style the war between the Pāndus of Indraprestha and the Takshacs of the north. Parikhīta, a prince on the Pāndu side, was assassinated by the Takshac, and his son and successor, Janamejaya, avenged his death and made a bonfire of 20,000 snakes."[2] This allegory is supposed to have represented the warfare of the Aryan races against the Sākas or Scythians. The Tāk or Takshac would be one of the clans held to be derived from the earlier invading tribes from Central Asia, and of the lunar race. The Tāk are scarcely known in authentic history, but the poet Chand mentions the Tāk from Aser or Asīrgarh as one of the princes who assembled at the summons of Prithwi Rāj of Delhi to fight against the Muhammadans. In another place he is called Chatto the Tāk. Nothing more is known of the Tāk clan unless the cultivating Tāga caste of northern India is derived from them. But the Nāgvansi clan of Rājpūts, who profess to be descended from them, is fairly numerous. Most of the Nāgvansis, however, are probably in reality descended from landholders of the indigenous tribes who have adopted the name of this clan, when they wished to claim rank as Rājpūts. The change is rendered more easy by

---

[1] Mr. Crooke's *Tribes and Castes*, art. Kachhwāha.

[2] *Rājasthān*, i. p. 94 ; Elliot's *Supplemental Glossary*, art. Gaur Tāga.

the fact that many of these tribes have legends of their own, showing the descent of their ruling families from snakes, the snake and tiger, owing to their deadly character, being the two animals most commonly worshipped. Thus the landholding section of the Kols or Mundas of Chota Nāgpur have a long legend[1] of their descent from a princess who married a snake in human form, and hence call themselves Nāgvansi Rājpūts; and Dr. Buchanan states that the Nāgvansi clan of Gorakhpur is similarly derived from the Chero tribe.[2] In the Central Provinces the Nāgvansi Rājpūts number about 400 persons, nearly all of whom are found in the Chhattīsgarh Districts and Feudatory States, and are probably descendants of Kol or Munda landholding families.

Rājpūt, Nikumbh.—The Nikumbh is given as one of the thirty-six royal races, but it is also the name of a branch of the Chauhāns, and it seems that, as suggested by Sherring,[3] it may be an offshoot from the great Chauhān clan. The Nikumbh are said to have been given the title of Sirnet by an emperor of Delhi, because they would not bow their heads on entering his presence, and when he fixed a sword at the door some of them allowed their necks to be cut through by the sword rather than bend the head. The term Sirnet is supposed to mean headless. A Chauhān column with an inscription of Rāja Bisal Deo was erected at Nigumbode, a place of pilgrimage on the Jumna, a few miles below Delhi, and it seems a possible conjecture that the Nikumbhs may have obtained their name from this place.[4] Mr. Crooke, however, takes the Nikumbh to be a separate clan. The foundation of most of the old forts and cities in Alwar and northern Jaipur is ascribed to them, and two of their inscriptions of the twelfth and thirteenth centuries have been discovered in Khāndesh. In northern India some of them are now known as Rāghuvansi.[5] They are chiefly found in the Hoshangābād and Nimār Districts, and may be connected with the Rāghuvansi or Rāghwi caste of these Provinces.

[1] See article on Kol.
[2] *Eastern India*, ii. 461, quoted in Mr. Crooke's art. Nāgvansi.
[3] *Tribes and Castes*, vol. i. art. Nikumbh.
[4] *Rājasthān*, ii. p. 417.
[5] Mr. Crooke's *Tribes and Castes*, art. Nikumbh.

Rājpūt, Pāik.—This term means a foot-soldier, and is returned from the northern Districts. It belongs to a class of men formerly maintained as a militia by zamīndārs and landholders for the purpose of collecting their revenue and maintaining order. They were probably employed in much the same manner in the Central Provinces as in Bengal, where Buchanan thus describes them:[1] "In order to protect the money of landowners and convey it from place to place, and also, as it is alleged, to enforce orders, two kinds of guards are kept. One body called Burkandāz, commanded by Duffadārs and Jemādārs, seems to be a more recent establishment. The other called Pāik, commanded by Mīrdhas and Sirdārs, are the remains of the militia of the Bengal kingdom. Both seem to have constituted the foot-soldiers whose number makes such a formidable appearance in the Ain-i-Akbari. These unwieldy establishments seem to have been formed when the Government collected rent immediately from the farmer and cultivator, and when the same persons managed not only the collections but the police and a great part of the judicial department. This vast number of armed men, more especially the latter, formed the infantry of the Mughal Government, and were continued under the zamīndārs, who were anxious to have as many armed men as possible to support them in their depredations. And these establishments formed no charge, as they lived on lands which the zamīndār did not bring to account." The Pāiks are thus a small caste formed from military service like the Khandaits or swordsmen of Orissa, and are no doubt recruited from all sections of the population. They have no claim to be considered as Rājpūts.

Rājpūt, Parihār.—This clan was one of the four Agnikulas or fire-born. Their founder was the first to issue from the fire-fountain, but he had not a warrior's mien. The Brāhmans placed him as guardian of the gate, and hence his name, *Prithi-ha-dwāra*, of which Parihār is supposed to be a corruption.[2] Like the Chauhāns and Solankis the Parihār clan is held to have originated from the Gurjara or Gūjar invaders who came with the white Huns in the

---

[1] *Eastern India*, ii. p. 919.   [2] *Rājasthān*, i. p. 86.

fifth and sixth centuries, and they were one of the first of the Gūjar Rājpūt clans to emerge into prominence. They were dominant in Bundelkhand before the Chandels, their last chieftain having been overthrown by a Chandel prince in A.D. 831.[1] A Parihār-Gūjar chieftain, whose capital was at Bhinmāl in Rājputāna, conquered the king of Kanauj, the ruler of what remained of the dominions of the great Harsha Vārdhana, and established himself there about A.D. 816.[2] Kanauj was then held by Gūjar-Parihār kings till about 1090, when it was seized by Chandradeva of the Gaharwār Rājpūt clan. The Parihār rulers were thus subverted by the Gaharwārs and Chandels, both of whom are thought to be derived from the Bhars or other aboriginal tribes, and these events appear to have been in the nature of a rising of the aristocratic section of the indigenous residents against the Gūjar rulers, by whom they had been conquered and perhaps taught the trade of arms. After this period the Parihārs are of little importance. They appear to have retired to Rājputāna, as Colonel Tod states that Mundore, five miles north of Jodhpur, was their headquarters until it was taken by the Rāhtors. The walls of the ruined fortress of Mundore are built of enormous square masses of stone without cement, and attest both its antiquity and its former strength.[3] The Parihārs are scattered over Rājputāna, and a colony of them on the Chambal was characterised as the most notorious body of thieves in the annals of Thug history.[4] Similarly in Etāwah they are said to be a peculiarly lawless and desperate community.[5] The Parihār Rājpūts rank with the leading clans and intermarry with them. In the Central Provinces they are found principally in Saugor, Damoh and Jubbulpore.

Rājpūt, Rāthor, Rāthaur.—The Rāthor of Jodhpur or Mārwār is one of the most famous clans of Rājpūts, and that which is most widely dominant at the present time, including as it does the Rājas of Jodhpur, Bikaner, Ratlām, Kishengarh and Idar, as well as several smaller states. The

[1] *Early History of India*, 3rd edition, p. 390.
[2] *Ibidem*, pp. 378, 379.
[3] *Rājasthān*, i. p. 91.
[4] *Ibidem*.
[5] Mr. Crooke's *Tribes and Castes*, art. Parihār.

origin of the Rāthor clan is uncertain. Colonel Tod states that they claim to be of the solar race, but by the bards of the race are denied this honour; and though descended from Kash, the second son of Rāma, are held to be the offspring of one of his progeny, Kashyap, by the daughter of a Dait (Titan). The view was formerly held that the dynasty which wrested Kanauj from the descendants of Harsha Vārdhana, and held it from A.D. 810 to 1090, until subverted by the Gaharwārs, were Rāthors, but proof has now been obtained that they were really Parihār-Gūjars. Mr. Smith suggests that after the destruction of Kanauj by the Muhammadans under Shihāb-ud-Dīn Ghori in A.D. 1193 the Gaharwār clan, whose kings had conquered it in 1090 and reigned there for a century, migrated to the deserts of Mārwār in Rājputāna, where they settled and became known as Rāthors.[1] It has also been generally held that the Rāshtrakūta dynasty of Nāsik and Mālkhed in the Deccan which reigned from A.D. 753 to 973, and built the Kailāsa temples at Ellora were Rāthors, but Mr. Smith states that there is no evidence of any social connection between the Rāshtrakūtas and Rāthors.[2] At any rate Siāhji, the grandson or nephew of Jai Chand, the last king of Kanauj, who had been drowned in the Ganges while attempting to escape, accomplished with about 200 followers—the wreck of his vassalage—the pilgrimage to Dwārka in Gujarāt. He then sought in the sands and deserts of Rājputāna a second line of defence against the advancing wave of Muhammadan invasion, and planted the standard of the Rāthors among the sandhills of the Luni in 1212. This, however, was not the first settlement of the Rāthors in Rājputāna, for an inscription, dated A.D. 997, among the ruins of the ancient city of Hathūndi or Hastikūndi, near Bāli in Jodhpur State, tells of five Rāthor Rājas who ruled there early in the tenth century, and this fact shows that the name Rāthor is really much older than the date of the fall of Kanauj.[3]

In 1381 Siāhji's tenth successor, Rao Chonda, took Mundore from a Parihār chief, and made his possession secure by marrying the latter's daughter. A subsequent

---

[1] *Early History of India*, 3rd edition, p. 389.   [2] *Ibidem*, p. 413.
[3] *Imperial Gazetteer*, art. Bali.

chief, Rao Jodha, laid the foundation of Jodhpur in 1459, and transferred thither the seat of government. The site of Jodhpur was selected on a peak known as Joda-gīr, or the hill of strife, four miles distant from Mundore on a crest of the range overlooking the expanse of the desert plains of Mārwār. The position for the new city was chosen at the bidding of a forest ascetic, and was excellently adapted for defence, but had no good water-supply.[1] Joda had fourteen sons, of whom the sixth, Bīka, was the founder of the Bikaner state. Rāja Sur Singh (1595–1620) was one of Akbar's greatest generals, and the emperor Jahāngīr buckled the sword on to his son Gaj Singh with his own hands. Gaj Singh, the next Rāja (1620–1635), was appointed viceroy of the Deccan, as was his successor, Jaswant Singh, under Aurāngzeb. The Mughal Emperors, Colonel Tod remarks, were indebted for half their conquests to the Lākh Tulwār Rāhtorān, the hundred thousand swords which the Rāhtors boasted that they could muster.[2] On another occasion, when Jahāngīr successfully appealed to the Rājpūts for support against his rebel son Khusru, he was so pleased with the zeal of the Rāthor prince, Rāja Gaj Singh, that he not only took the latter's hand, but kissed it,[3] perhaps an unprecedented honour. But the constant absence from his home on service in distant parts of the empire was so distasteful to Rāja Sur Singh that, when dying in the Deccan, he ordered a pillar to be erected on his grave containing his curse upon any of his race who should cross the Nerbudda. The pomp of imperial greatness or the sunshine of court favour was as nothing with the Rāthor chiefs, Colonel Tod says, when weighed against the exercise of their influence within their own cherished patrimony. The simple fare of the desert was dearer to the Rāthor than all the luxuries of the imperial banquet, which he turned from in disgust to the recollection of the green pulse of Mundore, or his favourite *rabi* or maize porridge, the prime dish of the Rāthor.[4] The Rāthor princes have been not less ready in placing themselves and the forces of their States at the disposal of the British Government, and the latest and perhaps most

---

[1] *Rajasthān*, ii. pp. 16, 17.
[2] *Ibidem*, i. p. 81.
[3] *Ibidem*, ii. p. 37.
[4] *Ibidem*, ii. p. 35.

brilliant example of their loyalty occurred during 1914, when the veteran Sir Partāp Singh of Idar insisted on proceeding to the front against Germany, though over seventy years of age, and was accompanied by his nephew, a boy of sixteen.

The Ratlām State was founded by Ratan Singh, a grandson of Rāja Udai Singh of Jodhpur, who was born about 1618, and obtained it as a grant for good service against the Usbegs at Kandahār and the Persians in Khorasān about 1651—52. Kishangarh was founded by Kishan Singh, a son of the same Rāja Udai Singh, who obtained a grant of territory from Akbar about 1611. Idar State in Gujarāt has, according to its traditions, been held by Rāthor princes from a very early period. Jodhpur State is the largest in Rājputāna, with an area of 35,000 square miles, and a population of two million. The Mahārāja is entitled to a salute of twenty-one guns. A great part of the State is a sandy desert, and its older name of Mārwār is, according to Colonel Tod, a corruption of Mārusthān, or the region of death. In the Central Provinces the Rāthor Rājpūts number about 6000 persons, and are found mainly in the Saugor, Jubbulpore, Narsinghpur and Hoshangābād Districts. The census statistics include about 5000 persons enumerated in Mandla and Bilāspur, nearly all of whom are really Rāthor Telis.

Rājpūt, Sesodia, Gahlot, Ahāria. — The Gahlot or Sesodia is generally admitted to be the premier Rājpūt clan. Their chief is described by the bards as " The Sūryavānsi Rāna, of royal race, Lord of Chitor, the ornament of the thirty-six royal races." The Sesodias claim descent from the sun, through Loh, the eldest son of the divine Rāma of Ajodhia. In token of their ancestry the royal banner of Mewār consisted of a golden sun on a crimson field. Loh is supposed to have founded Lahore. His descendants migrated to Saurāshtra or Kāthiāwār, where they settled at Vidurbha or Balabhi, the capital of the Valabhi dynasty. The last king of Valabhi was Silāditya, who was killed by an invasion of barbarians, and his posthumous son, Gohā-ditya, ruled in Idar and the hilly country in the south-west of Mewār. From him the clan took its name of Gohelot or Gahlot. Mr. D. R. Bhandarkar, however, from a detailed examination of the inscriptions relating to the Sesodias, arrives at the conclusion that the founders of the line were Nāgar Brāhmans from Vadnagar in Gujarāt, the first of the line being one Guhadatta, from which the clan takes its name of Gahlot.[1] The family were also connected with the ruling princes of Valabhi. Mr. Bhandarkar thinks that the Valabhi princes, and also the Nāgar Brāhmans, belonged to the Maitraka tribe, who, like the Gūjars, were allied to the Huns, and entered India in the fifth or sixth century. Mr. Bhandarkar's account really agrees quite closely with the traditions of the Sesodia bards themselves, except that he considers Guhadatta to have been a Nāgar Brāhman of Valabhi, and descended from the Maitrakas, a race allied to the Huns, while the bards say that he was a descendant of the Aryan Kshatriyas of Ajodhia, who migrated to Surat and established the Valabhi kingdom. The earliest prince of the Gahlot dynasty for whom a date has been obtained is Sīla, A.D. 646, and he was fifth in descent from Guhadatta, who may therefore be placed in the first part of the sixth century. Bāpa, the founder of the Gahlot clan in Mewār, was, according to tradition, sixth in descent from Gohāditya, and he had his capital at Nāgda, a few miles to the north of Udaipur city.[2] A tradition quoted by Mr. Bhandarkar states that Bāpa was the son of Grahadāta. He succeeded in propitiating the god Siva. One day the king of Chitor died and left no heir to his throne. It was decided that whoever would be garlanded by a certain elephant would be placed on the throne. Bāpa was present on the occasion, and the elephant put the garland round his neck not only once, but thrice. Bāpa was thus seated on the throne. One day he was suffering from some eye-disease. A physician mixed a certain medicine in alcoholic liquor and applied it to his eyes, which were speedily cured. Bāpa afterwards inquired what the medicine was, and learnt the truth. He trembled like a reed and said, "I am a Brāhman, and you have given me medicine mixed in liquor. I have lost my caste." So saying he drank molten lead (*sīsa*), and forthwith

[1] *J.A.S.B.* (1909), vol. v. p. 167.   [2] *Imperial Gazetteer*, loc. cit.

died, and hence arose the family name Sesodia.[1] This story, current in Rājputāna, supports Mr. Bhandarkar's view of the Brāhman origin of the clan. According to tradition Bāpa went to Chitor, then held by the Mori or Prāmara Rājpūts, to seek his fortune, and was appointed to lead the Chitor forces against the Muhammadans on their first invasion of India.[2] After defeating and expelling them he ousted the Mori ruler and established himself at Chitor, which has since been the capital of the Sesodias. The name Sesodia is really derived from Sesoda, the residence of a subsequent chief Rāhup, who captured Mundore and was the first to bear the title of Rāna of Mewār. Similarly Ahāria is another local name from Ahār, a place in Mewār, which was given to the clan. They were also known as Rāghuvansi, or of the race of king Rāghu, the ancestor of the divine Rāma. The Rāghuvansis of the Central Provinces, an impure caste of Rājpūt origin, are treated in a separate article, but it is not known whether they were derived from the Sesodias. From the fourteenth century the chronicles of the Sesodias contain many instances of Rājpūt courage and devotion. Chitor was sacked three times before the capital was removed to Udaipur, first by Ala-ul-Din Khilji in 1303, next by Bahādur Shāh, the Muhammadan king of Gujarāt in 1534, and lastly by Akbar in 1567. These events were known as Sāka or massacres of the clan. On each occasion the women of the garrison performed the Johar or general immolation by fire, while the men sallied forth, clad in their saffron-coloured robes and inspired by *bhāng*, to die sword in hand against the foe. At the first sack the goddess of the clan appeared in a dream to the Rāna and demanded the lives of twelve of its chiefs as a condition of its preservation. His eleven sons were in their turn crowned as chief, each ruling for three days, while on the fourth he sallied out and fell in battle.[3] Lastly, the Rāna devoted himself in order that his favourite son Ajeysi might be spared and might perpetuate the clan. At the second sack 32,000 were slain, and at the third 30,000. Finally Aurāngzeb destroyed the

---

[1] Bhandarkar, *loc. cit.* p. 180.
[2] The following extracts from the history of the clan are mainly taken from the article on Udaipur State in the *Imperial Gazetteer*.
[3] *Rājasthān*, i. pp. 222, 223.

temples and idols at Chitor, and only its ruins remain. Udaipur city was founded in 1559. The Sesodias resisted the Muhammadans for long, and several times defeated them. Udai Singh, the founder of Udaipur, abandoned his capital and fled to the hills, whence he caused his own territory to be laid waste, with the object of impeding the imperial forces. Of this period it is recorded that the Rānas were from father to son in outlawry against the emperor, and that sovereign had carried away the doors of the gate of Chitor, and had set them up in Delhi. Fifty-two rājas and chiefs had perished in the struggle, and the Rāna in his trouble lay at nights on a counterpane spread on the ground, and neither slept in his bed nor shaved his hair; and if he perchance broke his fast, had nothing better with which to satisfy it than beans baked in an earthen pot. For this reason it is that certain practices are to this day observed at Udaipur. A counterpane is spread below the Rāna's bed, and his head remains unshaven and baked beans are daily laid upon his plate.[1] A custom of perhaps somewhat similar origin is that in this clan man and wife take food together, and the wife does not wait till her husband has finished. It is said that the Sesodia Rājpūts are the only caste in India among whom this rule prevails, and it may have been due to the fact that they had to eat together in haste when occasion offered during this period of guerilla warfare.

In 1614 Rāna Amar Singh, recognising that further opposition was hopeless, made his submission to the emperor, on the condition that he should never have to present himself in person but might send his two sons in his place. This stipulation being accepted, the heir-apparent Karan Singh proceeded to Ajmer where he was magnanimously treated by Jahāngīr and shortly afterwards the imperial troops were withdrawn from Chitor. It is the pride of the Udaipur house that it never gave a daughter in marriage to any of the Musalmān emperors, and for many years ceased to intermarry with other Rājpūt families who had formed such alliances. But Amar Singh II. (1698–1710) made a league with the Mahārājas of Jodhpur and Jaipur for mutual protection against the Muhammadans; and it

---

[1] Forbes, *Rāsmala*, i. p. 400.

was one of the conditions of the compact that the latter chiefs should regain the privilege of marriage with the Udaipur family which had been suspended since they had given daughters in marriage to the emperors. But the Rāna unfortunately added a proviso that the son of an Udaipur princess should succeed to the Jodhpur or Jaipur States in preference to any elder son by another mother. The quarrels to which this stipulation gave rise led to the conquest of the country by the Marāthas, at whose hands Mewār suffered more cruel devastation than it had ever been subjected to by the Muhammadans. Ruinous war also ensued between Jodhpur and Jaipur for the hand of the famous Udaipur princess Kishen Kumāri at the time when Rājputāna was being devastated by the Marāthas and Pindāris; and the quarrel was only settled by the voluntary death of the object of contention, who, after the kinsman sent to slay her had recoiled before her young beauty and innocence, willingly drank the draught of opium four times administered before the fatal result could be produced.[1]

The Mahārāna of Udaipur is entitled to a salute of nineteen guns. The Udaipur State has an area of nearly 13,000 square miles and a population of about a million persons. Besides Udaipur three minor states, Partābgarh, Dungarpur and Banswāra, are held by members of the Sesodia clan. In the Central Provinces the Sesodias numbered nearly 2000 persons in 1911, being mainly found in the districts of the Nerbudda Division.

Rājpūt, Solankhi, Solanki, Chalukya.—This clan was one of the Agnikula or fire-born, and are hence considered to have probably been Gurjaras or Gūjars. Their original name is said to have been Chaluka, because they were formed in the palm (*chalu*) of the hand. They were not much known in Rājputāna, but were very prominent in the Deccan. Here they were generally called Chalukya, though in northern India the name Solankhi is more common. As early as A.D. 350 Pulakesin I. made himself master of the town

---

[1] *Rajasthān* i. pp. 398, 399. The death of the young princess was mainly the work of Amīr Khān Pindāri who brought pressure on the Rāna to consent to it in order to save his state.

of Vātāpi, the modern Bādāmi in the Bijāpur District, and founded a dynasty, which developed into the most powerful kingdom south of the Nerbudda, and lasted for two centuries, when it was overthrown by the Rāshtrakūtas.[1] Pulākesin II. of this Chalukya dynasty successfully resisted an inroad of the great emperor Harsha Vardhana of Kanauj, who aspired to the conquest of the whole of India. The Rāshtrakūta kings governed for two centuries, and in A.D. 973 Taila or Tailapa II., a scion of the old Chalukya stock, restored the family of his ancestors to its former glory, and founded the dynasty known as that of the Chalukyas of Kalyān, which lasted like that which it superseded for nearly two centuries and a quarter, up to about A.D. 1190. In the tenth century apparently another branch of the clan migrated from Rājputāna into Gujarāt and established a new dynasty there, owing to which Gujarāt, which had formerly been known as Lāta, obtained its present name.[2] The principal king of this line was Sidh Rāj Solankhi, who is well known to tradition. From these Chalukya or Solankhi rulers the Baghel clan arose, which afterwards migrated to Rewah. The Solankhis are found in the United Provinces, and a small number are returned from the Central Provinces, belonging mainly to Hoshangābād and Nimār.

Rājpūt, Somvansi, Chandravansi.—These two are returned as separate septs, though both names mean 'Descendants of the moon.' Colonel Tod considers Sūrajvansi and Somvansi, or the descendants of the sun and moon as the first two of the thirty-six royal clans, from which all the others were evolved. But he gives no account of them, nor does it appear that they were regularly recognised clans in Rājputāna. It is probable that both Somvansi and Chandravansi, as well as Sūrajvansi and perhaps Nāgvansi (Descendants of the snake) have served as convenient designations for Rājpūts of illegitimate birth, or for

---

[1] If the Chalukyas were in the Deccan in the fourth century they could not have originated from the Hun and Gūjar invaders of the fifth and sixth centuries, but must have belonged to an earlier horde.

[2] *Some Problems of Ancient Indian History*, by Dr. Rudolf Hoernle, *J.R.A.S.* (1905), pp. 1-14.

landholding sections of the cultivating castes and indigenous tribes when they aspired to become Rājpūts. Thus the Sūrajvansis, and Somvansis of different parts of the country might be quite different sets of people. There seems some reason for supposing that the Somvansis of the United Provinces as described by Mr. Crooke are derived from the Bhar tribe;[1] in the Central Provinces a number of Somvansis and Chandravansis are returned from the Feudatory States, and are probably landholders who originally belonged to one of the forest tribes residing in them. I have heard the name Somvansi applied to a boy who belonged to the Baghel clan of Rājpūts, but he was of inferior status on account of his mother being a remarried widow, or something of the kind.

Rājpūt, Sūrajvansi.—The Sūrajvansi (Descendants of the Sun) is recorded as the first of the thirty-six royal clans, but Colonel Tod gives no account of it, and it does not seem to be known to history as a separate clan. Mr. Crooke mentions an early tradition that the Sūrajvansis migrated from Ajodhia to Gujarāt in A.D. 224, but this is scarcely likely to be authentic in view of the late dates now assigned for the origin of the important Rājpūt clans. Sūrajvansi should properly be a generic term denoting any Rājpūt belonging to a clan of the solar race, and it seems likely that it may at different times have been adopted by Rājpūts who were no longer recognised in their own clan, or by families of the cultivating castes or indigenous tribes who aspired to become Rājpūts. Thus Mr. Crooke notes that a large section of the Soiris (Savaras or Saonrs) have entirely abandoned their own tribal name and call themselves Sūrajvansi Rājpūts;[2] and the same thing has probably happened in other cases. In the Central Provinces the Sūrajvansis belong mainly to Hoshangābād, and here they form a separate caste, marrying among themselves and not with other Rājpūt clans. Hence they would not be recognised as proper Rājpūts, and are probably a promoted group of some cultivating caste.

---

[1] *Tribes and Castes*, s.v.   [2] *Ibidem*, art. Soiri.

Rājpūt, Tomara, Tuar, Tunwar.—This clan is an ancient one, supposed by Colonel Tod to be derived from the Yādavas or lunar race. The name is said to come from *tomar*, a club.[1] The Tomara clan was considered to be a very ancient one, and the great king Vikramāditya, whose reign was the Hindu Golden Age, was held to have been sprung from it. These traditions are, however, now discredited, as well as that of Delhi having been built by a Tomara king, Anang Pāl I., in A.D. 733. Mr. V. A. Smith states that Delhi was founded in 993–994, and Anangapāla, a Tomara king, built the Red Fort about 1050. In 1052 he removed the celebrated iron pillar, on which the eulogy of Chandragupta Vikramāditya is incised, from its original position, probably at Mathura, and set it up in Delhi as an adjunct to a group of temples from which the Muhammadans afterwards constructed the great mosque.[2] This act apparently led to the tradition that Vikramāditya had been a Tomara, and also to a much longer historical antiquity being ascribed to the clan than it really possessed. The Tomara rule at Delhi only lasted about 150 years, and in the middle of the twelfth century the town was taken by Bisāl Deo, the Chauhān chieftain of Ajmer, whose successor, Prithwi Rāj, reigned at Delhi, but was defeated and killed by the Muhammadans in A.D. 1192. Subsequently, perhaps in the reign of Ala-ud-Dīn Khilji, a Tomara dynasty established itself at Gwalior, and one of their kings, Dungara Singh (1425–1454), had executed the celebrated rock-sculptures of Gwalior.[3] In 1518 Gwalior was taken by the Muhammadans, and the last Tomara king reduced to the status of an ordinary jāgīrdār. The Tomara clan is numerous in the Punjab country near Delhi, where it still possesses high rank, but in the United Provinces it is not so much esteemed.[4] No ruling chief now belongs to this clan. In the Central Provinces the Tomaras or Tunwars belong principally to the Hoshangābād District. The zamīndārs of Bilāspur, who were originally of the Tawar subcaste of the Kawar tribe, now also claim to be Tomara Rājpūts on the strength of the similarity of the name.

[1] Mr. Crooke's *Tribes and Castes*, art. Tomara.
[2] *Early History of India*, 3rd edition, p. 386.
[3] Elliot, *Supplemental Glossary, s.v.*
[4] Mr. Crooke's *Tribes and Castes*, art. Tomara.

Rājpūt, Yādu, Yādava, Yādu-Bhatti, Jādon.[1]—The Yādus are a well-known historical clan. Colonel Tod says that the Yādu was the most illustrious of all the tribes of Ind, and became the patronymic of the descendants of Buddha, progenitor of the lunar (Indu) race. It is not clear, even according to legendary tradition, what, if any, connection the Yādus had with Buddha, but Krishna is held to have been a prince of this tribe and founded Dwārka in Gujarāt with them, in which locality he is afterwards supposed to have been killed. Colonel Tod states that the Yādu after the death of Krishna, and their expulsion from Dwārka and Delhi, the last stronghold of their power, retired by Multān across the Indus, founded Ghazni in Afghānistān, and peopled these countries even to Samārcand. Again driven back on the Indus they obtained possession of the Punjab and founded Salbhānpur. Thence expelled they retired across the Sutlej and Gāra into the Indian deserts, where they founded Tannote, Derawāl and Jaisalmer, the last in A.D. 1157. It has been suggested in the main article on Rājpūt that the Yādus might have been the Sākas, who invaded India in the second century A.D. This is only a speculation. At a later date a Yādava kingdom existed in the Deccan, with its capital at Deogiri or Daulatābād and its territory lying between that place and Nāsik.[2] Mr. Smith states that these Yādava kings were descendants of feudatory nobles of the Chalukya kingdom, which embraced parts of western India and also Gujarāt. The Yādu clan can scarcely, however, be a more recent one than the Chalukya, as in that case it would not probably have been credited with having had Krishna as its member. The Yādava dynasty only lasted from A.D. 1150 to 1318, when the last prince of the line, Harāpala, stirred up a revolt against the Muhammadans to whom the king, his father-in-law, had submitted, and being defeated, was flayed alive and decapitated. It is noticeable that the Yādu-Bhatti Rājpūts of Jaisalmer claim descent from Sālivāhana, who founded the Sāka era in A.D. 78, and it is believed that this era belonged to the Sāka dynasty of Gujarāt, where, according

---

[1] See also article Jādum for a separate account of the local caste in the Central Provinces.

[2] *Early History of India*, 3rd edition, p. 434.

to the tradition given above, the Yādus also settled. This point is not important, but so far as it goes would favour the identification of the Sākas with the Yādavas.

The Bhatti branch of the Yādus claim descent from Bhāti, the grandson of Sālivāhana. They have no legend of having come from Gujarāt, but they had the title of Rāwal, which is used in Gujarāt, and also by the Sesodia clan who came from there. The Bhattis are said to have arrived in Jaisalmer about the middle of the eighth century, Jaisalmer city being founded much later in A.D. 1183. Jaisalmer State, the third in Rājputāna, has an area of 16,000 square miles, most of which is desert, and a population of about 100,000 persons. The chief has the title of Mahārāwal and receives a salute of fifteen guns. The Jareja Rājpūts of Sind and Cutch are another branch of the Yādus who have largely intermarried with Muhammadans. They now claim descent from Jāmshīd, the Persian hero, and on this account, Colonel Tod states, the title of their rulers is Jām. They were formerly much addicted to female infanticide. The name Yādu has in other parts of India been corrupted into Jādon, and the class of Jādon Rājpūts is fairly numerous in the United Provinces, and in some places is said to have become a caste, its members marrying among themselves. This is also the case in the Central Provinces, where they are known as Jādum, and have been treated under that name in a separate article. The small State of Karauli in Rājputāna is held by a Jādon chief.

Rajwār.[1]—A low cultivating caste of Bihār and Chota Nāgpur, who are probably an offshoot of the Bhuiyas. In 1911 a total of 25,000 Rajwārs were returned in the Central Provinces, of whom 22,000 belong to the Sargūja State recently transferred from Bengal. Another 2000 persons are shown in Bilāspur, but these are Mowārs, an offshoot of the Rajwārs, who have taken to the profession of gardening and have changed their name. They probably rank a little higher than the bulk of the Rajwārs. " Traditionally," Colonel Dalton states, " the Rajwārs appear

---

[1] Based on the accounts of Sir H. Risley and Colonel Dalton and a paper by Pandit G. L. Pāthak, Superintendent, Korea State.

to connect themselves with the Bhuiyas; but this is only in Bihār. The Rajwārs in Sargūja and the adjoining States are peaceably disposed cultivators, who declare themselves to be fallen Kshatriyas; they do not, however, conform to Hindu customs, and they are skilled in a dance called Chailo, which I believe to be of Dravidian origin. The Rajwārs of Bengal admit that they are the descendants of mixed unions between Kurmis and Kols. They are looked upon as very impure by the Hindus, who will not take water from their hands." The Rajwārs of Bihār told Buchanan that their ancestor was a certain Rishi, who had two sons. From the elder were descended the Rajwārs, who became soldiers and obtained their noble title; and from the younger the Musāhars, who were so called from their practice of eating rats, which the Rajwārs rejected. The Musāhars, as shown by Sir H. Risley, are probably Bhuiyas degraded to servitude in Hindu villages, and this story confirms the Bhuiya origin of the Rajwārs. In the Central Provinces the Bhuiyas have a subcaste called Rajwār, which further supports this hypothesis, and in the absence of evidence to the contrary it is reasonable to suppose that the Rajwārs are an offshoot of the Bhuiyas, as they themselves say, in Bihār. The substitution of Kols for Bhuiyas in Bengal need not cause much concern in view of the great admixture of blood and confused nomenclature of all the Chota Nāgpur tribes. In Bengal, where the Bhuiyas have settled in Hindu villages, and according to the usual lot of the forest tribes who entered the Hindu system have been degraded into the servile and impure caste of Musāhars, the Rajwārs have shared their fate, and are also looked upon as impure. But in Chota Nāgpur the Bhuiyas have their own villages and live apart from the Hindus, and here the Rajwārs, like the landholding branches of other forest tribes, claim to be an inferior class of Rājpūts.

In Sargūja the caste have largely adopted Hindu customs. They abstain from liquor, employ low-class Brāhmans as priests, and worship the Hindu deities. When a man wishes to arrange a match for his son he takes a basket of wheat-cakes and proceeding to the house of the girl's father sets them down outside. If the match is acceptable the girl's mother comes and takes the cakes into the house and the betrothal is then considered to be ratified. At the wedding the bridegroom smears vermilion seven times on the parting of the bride's hair, and the bride's younger sister then wipes a little of it off with the end of the cloth. For this service she is paid a rupee by the bridegroom. Divorce and the remarriage of widows are permitted. After the birth of a child the mother is given neither food nor water for two whole days; on the third day she gets only boiled water to drink and on the fourth day receives some food. The period of impurity after a birth extends to twelve days. When the navel-string drops it is carefully put away until the next Dasahra, together with the child's hair, which is cut on the sixth day. On the Dasahra festival all the women of the village take them to a tank, where a lotus plant is worshipped and anointed with oil and vermilion, and the hair and navel-string are then buried at its roots. The dead are burned, and the more pious keep the bones with a view to carrying them to the Ganges or some other sacred river. Pending this, the bones are deposited in the cow-house, and a lamp is kept burning in it every night so long as they are there. The Rajwārs believe that every man has a soul or Prān, and they think that the soul leaves the body, not only at death, but whenever he is asleep or becomes unconscious owing to injury or illness. Dreams are the adventures of the soul while wandering over the world apart from the body. They think it very unlucky for a man to see his own reflection in water and carefully avoid doing so.

1. General notice.

Rāmosi, Rāmoshi.—A criminal tribe of the Bombay Presidency, of which about 150 persons were returned from the Central Provinces and Berār in 1911. They belong to the western tract of the Satpūras adjoining Khāndesh. The name is supposed to be a corruption of Rāmvansi, meaning 'The descendants of Rāma.' They say[1] that when Rāma, the hero of the Rāmāyana, was driven from his kingdom by his step-mother Kaikeyi, he went to the forest land south

---

[1] *B. G. Poona*, Part I., p. 409.

of the Nerbudda. His brother Bharat, who had been raised to the throne, could not bear to part with Rāma, so he followed him to the forest, began to do penance, and made friends with a rough but kindly forest tribe. After Rāma's restoration Bharat took two foresters with him to Ajodhia (Oudh) and brought them to the notice of Rāma, who appointed them village watchmen and allowed them to take his name. If this is the correct derivation it may be compared with the name of Rāwanvansi or Children of Rāwan, the opponent of Rāma, which is applied to the Gonds of the Central Provinces. The Rāmosis appear to be a Hinduised caste derived from the Bhīls or Kolis or a mixture of the two tribes. They were formerly a well-known class of robbers and dacoits. The principal scenes of their depredations were the western Ghāts, and an interesting description of their methods is given by Captain Mackintosh in his account of the tribe.[1] Some extracts from this are here reproduced.

2. Methods of robbery.

They armed themselves chiefly with swords, taking one, two or three matchlocks, or more should they judge it necessary. Several also carried their shields and a few had merely sticks, which were in general shod with small bars of iron from eight to twelve inches in length, strongly secured by means of rings and somewhat resembling the ancient mace. One of the party carried a small copper or earthen pot or a cocoanut-shell with a supply of *ghī* or clarified butter in it, to moisten their torches with before they commenced their operations. The Rāmosis endeavoured as much as possible to avoid being seen by anybody either when they were proceeding to the object of their attack or returning afterwards to their houses. They therefore travelled during the night-time; and before daylight in the morning they concealed themselves in a jungle or ravine near some water, and slept all day, proceeding in this way for a long distance till they reached the vicinity of the village to be attacked. When they were pursued and much pressed, at times they would throw themselves into a bush or under a prickly pear

[1] *An Account of the Origin and Present Condition of the Tribe of Rāmosis* (Bombay, 1833; India Office Tracts. Also published in the *Madras Journal of Literature and Science*.)

plant, coiling themselves up so carefully that the chances were their pursuers would pass them unnoticed. If they intended to attack a treasure party they would wait at some convenient spot on the road and sally out when it came abreast of them, first girding up their loins and twisting a cloth tightly round their faces, to prevent the features from being recognised. Before entering the village where their dacoity or *durrowa* was to be perpetrated, torches were made from the turban of one of the party, which was torn into three, five or seven pieces, but never into more, the pieces being then soaked with butter. The same man always supplied the turban and received in exchange the best one taken in the robbery. Those who were unarmed collected bags of stones, and these were thrown at any people who tried to interfere with them during the dacoity. They carried firearms, but avoided using them if possible, as their discharge might summon defenders from a distance. They seldom killed or mutilated their victims, except in a fight, but occasionally travellers were killed after being robbed as a measure of precaution. They retreated with their spoils as rapidly as possible to the nearest forest or hill, and from there, after distributing the booty into bags to make it portable, they marched off in a different direction from that in which they had come. Before reaching their homes one of the party was deputed with an offering of one, two or five rupees to be presented as an offering to their god Khandoba or the goddess Bhawāni in fulfilment of a vow. All the spoil was then deposited before their Nāik or headman, who divided it into equal shares for members of the gang, keeping a double share for himself.

3. Rāmosis employed as village watchmen.

In order to protect themselves from the depredations of these gangs the villagers adopted a system of hiring a Rāmosi as a surety to be responsible for their property, and this man gradually became a Rakhwāldār or village watchman. He received a grant of land rent-free and other perquisites, and also a fee from all travellers and gangs of traders who halted in the village in return for his protection during the night. If a theft or house-breaking occurred in a village, the Rāmosi was held responsible to the owner for the value of the property, unless a large gang had been engaged. If he failed to discover the thief he engaged to make the lost property good to the owner within fifteen days or a month unless its value was considerable. If a gang had been engaged, the Rāmosi, accompanied by the patel and other village officials and cultivators, proceeded to track them by their footprints. Obtaining a stick he cut it to the exact length of the footprint, or several such if a number of prints could be discovered, and followed the tracks, measuring the footprints, to the boundary of the village. The inhabitants of the adjoining village were then called and were responsible for carrying on the trail through their village. The measures of footprints were handed over to them, and after satisfying themselves that the marks came from outside and extended into their land they took up the trail accompanied by the Rāmosi. In this way the gang was tracked from village to village, and if it was run to earth the residents of the villages to which it belonged had to make good the loss. If the tracks were lost owing to the robbers having waded along a stream or got on to rocky ground or into a public road, then the residents of the village in whose borders the line failed were considered responsible for the stolen property. Usually, however, a compromise was made, and they paid half, while the other half was raised from the village in which the theft occurred. If the Rāmosi failed to track the thieves out of the village he had to make good the value of the theft, but he was usually assisted by the village officer. Often, too, the owner had to be contented with half or a quarter of the amount lost as compensation. In the early part of the century the Rāmosis of Poona became very troublesome and constantly committed robberies in the houses of Europeans. As a consequence a custom grew up of employing a Rāmosi as chaukidār or watchman for guarding the bungalow at night on a salary of seven rupees a month, and soon became general. It was the business of the Rāmosi watchman to prevent other Rāmosis from robbing the house. Apparently this was the common motive for the custom, prevalent up to recent years, of paying a man solely for the purpose of watching the house at night, and it originated, as in

4. Social customs.

Poona, as a form of insurance and an application of the proverb of setting a thief to catch a thief. The selection of village watchmen from among the low criminal castes appears to have been made on the same principle.

The principal deity of the Rāmosis is Khandoba, the Marātha god of war.[1] He is the deified sword, the name being *khanda-aba* or sword-father. An oath taken on the Bhandar or little bag of turmeric dedicated to Khandoba is held by them most sacred and no Rāmosi will break this oath. Every Rāmosi has a family god known as Devak, and persons having the same Devak cannot intermarry. The Devak is usually a tree or a bunch of the leaves of several trees. No one may eat the fruit of or otherwise use the tree which is his Devak. At their weddings the branches of several trees are consecrated as Devaks or guardians of the wedding. A Gurao cuts the leafy branches of the mango, *umar*,[2] *jāmun*[3] and of the *rui*[4] and *shami*[5] shrubs and a few stalks of grass and sets them in Hanumān's temple. From here the bridegroom's parents, after worshipping Hanumān with a betel-leaf and five areca-nuts, take them home and fasten them to the front post of the marriage-shed. When the bridegroom is taken before the family gods of the bride, he steals one of them in token of his profession, but afterwards restores it in return for a payment of money. In social position the Rāmosis rank a little above the Mahārs and Māngs, not being impure. They speak Marāthi but have also a separate thieves' jargon of their own, of which a vocabulary is given in the account of Captain Mackintosh. When a Rāmosi child is seven or eight years old he must steal something. If he is caught and goes to prison the people are delighted, fall at his feet when he comes out and try to obtain him as a husband for their daughters.[6] It is doubtful whether these practices obtain in the Central Provinces, and as the Rāmosis are not usually reckoned here among the notorious criminal tribes they may probably have taken to more honest pursuits.

---

[1] This paragraph is mainly compiled from the *Nāsik* and *Poona* volumes of the *Bombay Gazetteer*.
[2] *Ficus glomerata*.
[3] *Eugenia jambolana*.
[4] *Calotropis gigantea*.
[5] *Bauhinia racemosa*.
[6] *Poona Gazetteer*, part i. p. 425.

Rangrez.—The Muhammadan caste of dyers. The caste is found generally in the northern Districts, and in 1901 its members were included with the Chhīpas, from whom, however, they should be distinguished as having a different religion and also because they practise a separate branch of the dyeing industry. The strength of the caste in the Central Provinces does not exceed a few hundred persons. The Rangrez is nominally a Muhammadan of the Sunni sect, but the community forms an endogamous group after the Hindu fashion, marrying only among themselves. Good-class Muhammadans will neither intermarry with nor even take food from members of the Rangrez community. In Sohāgpur town of Hoshangābād this is divided into two branches, the Kherālawālas or immigrants from Kherāla in Mālwa and the local Rangrezes. These two groups will take food together but will not intermarry. Kherālawāla women commonly wear a skirt like Hindu women and not Muhammadan pyjamas. In Jubbulpore the Rangrez community employ Brāhmans to conduct their marriage and other ceremonies. Long association with Hindus has as usual caused the Rangrez to conform to their religious practices and the caste might almost be described as a Hindu community with Muhammadan customs. The bulk of them no doubt were originally converted Hindus, but as their ancestors probably immigrated from northern India their present leaning to that religion would perhaps be not so much an obstinate retention of pre-Islamic ritual as a subsequent lapse following on another change of environment. In northern India Mr. Crooke records them as being governed mainly by Muhammadan rules. There [1] they hold themselves to be the descendants of one Khwāja Bali, a very pious man, about whom the following verse is current:

Khwāja Bali Rangrez
Range Khuda ki sez :

'Khwāja Bali dyes the bed of God.' The name is derived from *rang*, colour, and *rez, rekhtān,* to pour. In Bihār, Sir G. Grierson states [2] the word Rangrez is often con-

---
[1] *Tribes and Castes,* art. Rangrez.
[2] *Peasant Life in Bihār,* p. 101, footnote.

founded with 'Angrezi' or 'English'; and the English are sometimes nicknamed facetiously Rangrez or 'dyers.' The saying, 'Were I a dyer I would dye my own beard first,' in reference to the Muhammadan custom of dyeing the beard, has the meaning of 'Charity begins at home.'[1]

The art of the Rangrez differs considerably from that of the Chhīpa or Rangāri, the Hindu dyer, and he produces a much greater variety of colours. His principal agents were formerly the safflower (*Carthamus tinctorius*), turmeric and myrobalans. The fact that the brilliant red dye of safflower was as a rule only used by Muhammadan dyers, gives some ground for the supposition that it may have been introduced by them to India. This would account for the existence of a separate caste of Muhammadan dyers, and in support of it may be adduced the fact that the variety of colours is much greater in the dress of the residents of northern India and Rājputāna than in those of the Marātha Districts. The former patronise many different shades, more especially for head-cloths, while the latter as a rule do not travel beyond red, black or blue. The Rangrez obtains his red shades from safflower, yellow from *haldi* or turmeric, green from a mixture of indigo and turmeric, purple from indigo and safflower, *khāki* or dust-colour from myrobalans and iron filings, orange from turmeric and safflower, and *badāmi* or almond-colour from turmeric and two wild plants *kachora* and *nāgarmothi*, the former of which gives a scent. Cloths dyed in the *badāmi* shades are affected, when they can afford it, by Gosains and other religious mendicants, who thus dwell literally in the odour of sanctity. Muhammadans generally patronise the shades of green or purple, the latter being often used as a lining for white coats. Fakīrs or Muhammadan beggars wear light green. Mārwāri Banias and others from Rājputāna like the light yellow, pink or orange shades. A green or black head-cloth is with them a sign of mourning. Cloths dyed in yellow or scarlet are bought by Brāhmans and other castes of Hindus for their marriages. Blue is not a lucky colour among the Hindus and is considered as on a level with black. It may be worn on ordinary occasions, but not at festivals or at auspicious

[1] Temple and Fallon's *Hindustani Proverbs*.

periods. Muhammadans rather affect black and do not consider it an unlucky colour. I have seen a Rangrez dye a piece of cloth in about twenty colours in the course of two or three hours, but several of these dyes are fugitive and will not stand washing. The trade of the Rangrez is being undermined by the competition of cheap chemical dyes imported from Germany and sold in the form of powders; the process of dyeing with these is absolutely simple and can be carried out by any one. They are far cheaper than safflower, and this agent has consequently been almost driven from the market. People buy a little dyeing powder from the bazār and dye their own cloths. But men will only wear cloths dyed in this manner, and known as *katcha kapra*, on their heads and not on their bodies; women sometimes wear them also on their bodies. The decay in the indigenous art of dyeing must be a matter for regret.

Rautia.[1]—A cultivating caste of the Chota Nāgpur plateau. In 1911 about 12,000 Rautias were enumerated in the Province, nearly all of whom belong to the Jashpur State with a few in Sargūja. These states lie outside the scope of the Ethnographic Survey and hence no regular inquiry has been made on the Rautias. The following brief notice is mainly taken from the account of the caste in Sir H. Risley's *Tribes and Castes of Bengal*. He describes the caste as, "refined in features and complexion by a large infusion of Aryan blood. Their chief men hold estates on quit-rent from the Mahārāja of Chota Nāgpur, and the bulk of the remainder are tenants with occupancy right and often paying only a low quit-rent or half the normal assessment." These favourable tenures may probably be explained by the fact that they were held in former times on condition of military service, and were analogous to the feudal fiefs of Europe. The Rautias themselves say that this was their original occupation in Chota Nāgpur. The name Rautia is a form of Rāwat, and this latter word signifies a prince and is a title borne by relatives of a Rāja. It may be noticed

1. Origin of the tribe.

---

[1] Based on Sir H. Risley's account of the tribe in the *Tribes and Castes of Bengal*, and on notes taken by Mr. Hīra Lāl at Raigarh.

that Rāwat is the ordinary name by which the Ahīr caste is known in Chhattīsgarh, the neighbouring country to Chota Nāgpur in the Central Provinces; and further that the Rautias will take food from a Chhattīsgarhi Rāwat. This fact, coupled with the identity of the name, appears to demonstrate a relationship of the two castes. The Rautias will not take food from any other Hindu caste, but they will eat with the Kawar and Gond tribes, at least in Raigarh. The Kawars have a subtribe called Rautia as also have the Kols. In Sir H. Risley's list of the sept-names of the Rautias[1] we find two names, Aind the eel, and Rukhi a squirrel, which are also the names of Munda septs, and one, Karsāyal or deer, which is the name of a Kawar sept. They have also a name Sanwāni, which is probably Sonwāni or 'gold-water,' and is common to many of the primitive tribes. The most plausible hypothesis of the origin of the Rautias on the above facts seems to be that they were a tribal militia in Chota Nāgpur, the leaders being Ahīrs or Rāwats with possibly a sprinkling of the local Rājpūts, while the main body were recruited from the Kawar and Kol tribes. The Khandaits or swordsmen of Orissa furnish an exact parallel to the Rautias, being a tribal militia, who have now become a caste, and are constituted mainly from the Bhuiya tribe with a proportion of Chasas or cultivators and Rājpūts. They also have obtained possession of the land, and in Orissa the Sresta or good Khandaits rank next to the Rājpūts. The history and position of the Rautias appears to be similar to that of the Khandaits. The Halbas of Bastar are probably another nearly analogous instance. They were Gonds, who apparently formed the tribal militia of the Rājas of Bastar and got grants of land and consequently a certain rise in status though not to the same level as the Khandaits and Rautias. It does not seem that the Rautias have any special connection with the Gonds, and their acceptance of food from Gonds may perhaps, as suggested by Mr. Hīra Lāl, be due to the fact that they served a Gond Rāja.

2. Subdivisions.

The Rautias had formerly three subdivisions, the Barki, Majhli and Chhotki Bhīr or Gorhi, or the high, middle and low class Rautias. But it is related that the Barki group

[1] *Tribes and Castes of Bengal*, vol. ii. App. I.

found that they could not obtain girls in marriage for their sons, so they extended the privileges of the *connubium* to the Majhli group after taking a caste feast. Possibly the Barki Rautias formerly practised hypergamy with the Majhli, taking daughters in marriage but not giving daughters, and in course of time this has led to the obliteration of the distinction between them. The different status of the three groups was based on their purity of descent. The Majhli and Chhotki were the descendants of Rautia fathers and mothers of other castes; the offspring going to the Majhli group if the mother was a Gond or Kawar or of respectable caste, while the children of impure Gānda and Ghasia women by Rautia fathers were admitted into the Chhotki group. These divisions confirm the hypothesis previously given of the genesis of the Rautia caste; and it is further worth noting that the Khandaits have also Bar and Chhot Gohir divisions or those of pure and mixed blood, and the Halbas of Bastar are similarly divided into the Purāit or pure Halbas, and the Surāit or descendants of Halba fathers by women of other castes. In a military society, where the men were frequently on the move or stationed in outlying forts and posts, temporary unions and illegitimate children would naturally be of common occurrence. And the mixed nature of the three castes affords some support to the hypothesis of their common origin from military service.

The tribe have totemistic septs, and retain some veneration for their totems. Those of the Bāgh or tiger sept throw away their earthen pots on hearing of the death of a tiger. Those of the Sānd or bull sept will not castrate bullocks themselves, and must have this operation performed on their plough-bullocks by others. Those of the Kānsi sept formerly, according to their own account, would not root up the *kāns* grass[1] growing in their fields, but now they no longer object to do so. Other septs are Tithi a bird, Bīra a hawk, Barwan a wild dog, and so on.

Marriage is forbidden within the sept, but is permitted between the children of a brother and a sister or of two sisters. Matches are arranged at the caste feasts and the

3. Marriage.

[1] *Saccharum spontaneum.*

usual bride-price is four rupees with six or seven pieces of cloth and some grain. When the procession arrives at the bride's village her party go out to meet it, and the Gāndas or musicians on each side try to break each other's drums, but are stopped by their employers. At the wedding two wooden images of the bridegroom and bride are made and placed in the centre of the marriage-shed. A goat is led round these and killed, and the bride and bridegroom walk round them seven times. They rub vermilion on the wooden images and then on each other's foreheads. It is probable that the wooden images are made and set up in the centre of the shed to attract the evil eye and divert it from the real bride and bridegroom, and the goat may be a substituted sacrifice on their behalf. Divorce and the remarriage of widows are permitted.

4. Funeral rites.

In the forest tracts the tribe bury the dead, placing the corpse with the feet to the south. Before being placed in the grave the corpse is rubbed with oil and turmeric and carried seven times round the grave according to the ritual of a wedding. This is called the *Chhed vivāh* or marriage to the grave. The Kabīrpanthi Rautias are placed standing in the grave with the face turned to the north. Well-to-do members of the caste burn their dead and employ Brāhmans to perform the *shrāddh* ceremony.

5. Inheritance.

The tribe have some special rules of inheritance. In Bengal[1] the eldest son of the legitimate wife inherits the whole of the father's property, subject to the obligation of making grants for the maintenance of his younger brothers. These grants decrease according to the standing of the brothers, the elder ones getting more and the younger less. Sons of a wife married by the ceremony used for widows receive smaller grants. But the widow of an elder brother counts as the regular wife of a younger brother and her sons have full rights of succession. In the Central Provinces the eldest son does not succeed to the whole property but obtains a share half as large again as the other sons. And if the father divides the property in his lifetime and participates in it he himself takes only the share of a younger son.

[1] *Tribes and Castes of Bengal*, art. Rautia.

Sanaurhia, Chandravedi.[1]

—A small but well-known community of criminals in Bundelkhand. They claim to be derived from the Sanādhya Brāhmans, and it seems possible that this may in fact have been their origin; but at present they are a confraternity recruited by the initiation of promising boys from all castes except sweepers and Chamārs;[2] and a census taken of them in northern India in 1872 showed that they included members of the following castes: Brāhman, Rājpūt, Teli, Kurmi, Ahīr, Kanjar, Nai, Dhobi, Dhīmar, Sunār and Lodhi. It is said, however, that they do not form a caste or intermarry, members of each caste continuing their relations with their own community. Their regular method of stealing is through the agency of a boy, and no doubt they pick up a likely urchin whenever they get the chance, as only selected boys would be clever enough for the work. Their trade is said to possess much fascination, and Mr. Crooke quotes a saying, 'Once a Sanaurhia always a Sanaurhia'; so that unless the increased efficiency of the police has caused the dangers of their calling to outweigh its pleasures they should have no difficulty in obtaining recruits.

1. A band of criminals.

Mr. Seagrim[3] states that their home is in the Datia State of Bundelkhand, and some of them live in the adjoining Alamgarh tract of Indore State. Formerly they also resided in the Orchha and Chanderi States of Bundelkhand, having six or eight villages in each state[4] in their sole occupation, with colonies in other villages. In 1857 it was estimated that the Tehri State contained 4000 Sanaurhias, Bānpur 300 and Datia 300. They occupied twelve villages in Tehri, and an officer of the state presided over the community and acted as umpire in the division of the spoils. The office of Mukhia or leader was hereditary in the caste, and in default of male issue descended to females. If among the booty there happened to be any object of peculiar elegance or value, it was ceremoniously presented to the chief of the state. They say that their ancestors were two Sanādhya Brāhmans

2. Traditions of origin.

---

[1] This article is based principally on an account of the Sanaurhias written by Mr. C. M. Seagrim, Inspector-General of Police, Indore, and included in Mr. Kennedy's *Criminal Classes of Bombay* (1908).

[2] Crooke's *Tribes and Castes*, art. Sanaurhia.

[3] *Criminal Classes of Bombay Presidency*, pp. 296, 297.

[4] Sleeman's *Reports on the Badhaks*, p. 327.

of the village of Rāmra in Datia State. They were both highly accomplished men, and one had the gift of prophecy, while the other could understand the language of birds. One day they met at a river a rich merchant and his wife, who were on a pilgrimage to Jagannāth. As they were drinking water a crow sitting on a tree commenced cawing, and the Sanādhya heard him say that whoever got hold of the merchant's walking-stick would be rich. The two Brāhmans then accompanied the merchant until they obtained an opportunity of making off with his stick; and they found it to be full of gold mohurs, the traveller having adopted this device as a precaution against being robbed. The Brāhmans were so pleased at their success that they took up stealing as a profession, and opened a school where they taught small boys of all castes the art of stealing property in the daytime. Prior to admission the boys were made to swear by the moon that they would never commit theft at night, and on this account they are known as Chandravedi or 'Those who observe the moon.' In Bombay and Central India this name is more commonly used than Sanaurhia. Another name for them is Uthaigīra or 'A picker-up of that which has fallen,' corresponding to the nickname of Uchla or 'Lifter' applied to the Bhāmtas. Mr. Seagrim described them as going about in small gangs of ten to twenty persons without women, under a leader who has the title of Mukhia or Nālband. The other men are called Upardār, and each of these has with him one or two boys of between eight and twelve years old, who are known as *Chauwa* (chicks) and do the actual stealing. The Nālband or leader trains these boys to their work, and also teaches them a code vocabulary (*Pārsi*) and a set of signals (*teni*) by which the Upardār can convey to them his instructions while business is proceeding. The whole gang set out at the end of the rains and, arriving at some distant place, break up into small parties; the Nālband remains at a temporary headquarters, where he receives and disposes of the spoil, and arranges for the defence of any member of the gang who is arrested, and for the support of his wife and children if he is condemned to imprisonment.

3. Methods of stealing. The methods of the Sanaurhias as described by Mr. Seagrim show considerable ingenuity. When they desire to

steal something from a stall in a crowded market two of the gang pretend to have a violent quarrel, on which all the people in the vicinity collect to watch, including probably the owner of the stall. In this case the *Chauwa* or boy, who has posted himself in a position of vantage, will quickly abstract the article agreed upon and make off. Or if there are several purchasers at a shop, the man will wait until one of them lays down his bundle while he makes payment, and then pushing up against him signal to the *Chauwa*, who snatches up the bundle and bolts. If he is caught, the Sanaurhia will come up as an innocent member of the crowd and plead for mercy on the score of his youth; and the boy will often be let off with a few slaps. Sometimes three or four Sanaurhias will proceed to some place of resort for pilgrims to bathe, and two or three of them entering the water will divert the attention of the bather by pointing out some strange object or starting a discussion. In the meantime the *Chauwas* or chicks, under the direction of another on the bank, will steal any valuable article left by the bather. The attention of any one left on shore to watch the property is diverted by a similar device. If they see a man with expensive clothes the *Chauwa* will accidentally brush against him and smear him with dirt or something that causes pollution; the victim will proceed to bathe, and one of the usual stratagems is adopted. Or the Sanaurhia will engage the man in conversation and the *Chauwa* will come running along and collide with them; on being abused by the Sanaurhia for his clumsiness he asks to be pardoned, explaining that he is only a poor sweeper and meant no harm; and on hearing this the victim, being polluted, must go off and bathe.[1] Colonel Sleeman relates the following case of such a theft:[2] "While at Saugor I got a note one morning from an officer in command of a treasure escort just arrived from Narsinghpur stating that the old Sūbahdār of his company had that morning been robbed of his gold necklace valued at Rs. 150, and requesting that I would assist him in recovering it. The old Sūbahdār brought the note, and stated that he had undressed at the brook near the

---

[1] Mr. Gayer's *Lectures on some Criminal Tribes.*

[2] *Report on the Badhak or Bāgri Dacoits* (1849), p. 328.

cantonments, and placed the necklace with his clothes, about twenty yards from the place where he bathed; that on returning to his clothes he could not find the necklace, and the only person he saw near the place was a young lad who was sauntering in the mango grove close by. This lad he had taken and brought with him, and I found after a few questions that he belonged to the Sanaurhia Brāhmans of Bundelkhand. As the old Sūbahdār had not seen the boy take the necklace or even approach the clothes, I told him that we could do nothing, and he must take the boy back to camp and question him in his own way. The boy, as I expected, became alarmed, and told me that if I would not send him back with the angry old Sūbahdār he would do anything I pleased. I bade him tell me how he had managed to secure the necklace; and he told me that while the Sūbahdār turned his back upon his clothes in prayer, he had taken it up and made it over to one of the men of his party; and that it must have been taken to their bivouac, which was in a grove about three miles from the cantonments. I sent off a few policemen, who secured the whole party, but could not find anything upon them. Seeing some signs of a hole having been freshly made under one of the trees they dug up the fresh earth and discovered the necklace, which the old man was delighted to recover so easily." Another device which they have is to beat the *Chauwa* severely in the sight of a rich stranger. The boy runs crying and clings to the stranger asking him for help, and in the meantime picks his pocket. When the Sanaurhias are convicted in Native States and put into jail they refuse to eat, pleading that they are poor Brāhmans, and pretend to starve themselves to death, and thus often get out of jail. In reply to a letter inquiring about these people from the Superintendent of Chanderi about 1851, the Rāja of Bānpur wrote:

"I have to state that from former times these people following their profession have resided in my territory and in the states of other native princes; and they have always followed this calling, but no former kings or princes or authority have ever forbidden the practice. In consequence of these people stealing by day only, and that they do not take life or distress any person by personal ill-usage, and that they do not break into houses by digging walls or breaking door-locks, but simply by their smartness manage to abstract property ; owing to such trifling thefts I looked upon their proceedings as a petty matter and have not interfered with them."[1] This recalls another famous excuse.

[1] J. Hutton, *A Popular Account of the Thugs and Dacoits and Gang-robbers of India* (London, 1857).

SĀNSIA

LIST OF PARAGRAPHS

1. *Historical notice of the caste.*
2. *Social customs.*
3. *Taboos of relationship.*
4. *Organisation for dacoity.*
5. *Description of a dacoity.*
6. *Omens.*
7. *Ordeals.*
8. *Sānsias at the present time.*

1. Historical notice of the caste.

Sānsia.[1]—A small caste of wandering criminals of northern India, who live by begging and dealing in cattle. They also steal and commit dacoities, house-breaking and thefts on railway trains. The name Sānsia is borne as well by the Uriya or Od masons of the Uriya country, but these are believed to be quite a distinct group from the criminal Sānsias of Central India and are noticed in another short article. Separate statistics of the two groups were not obtained at the census. The Sānsias are closely connected with the Berias, and say that their ancestors were two brothers Sains Mūl and Sānsi, and that the Berias are descended from the former and the Sānsias from the latter. They were the bards of the Jāt caste, and it was their custom to chronicle the names of the Jāts and their ancestors, and when they begged from Jāt families to recite their praises. The Sānsias, Colonel Sleeman states, had particular families (of the Jāts) allotted to them, from whom they had not only the privilege of begging, but received certain dues; some had fifty, some a hundred houses appointed to them, and they received yearly from the head of each house one rupee and a quarter and one day's food. When the Jāts celebrated their marriages they were

[1] This article is based almost entirely on a description of the Sānsias contained in Colonel Sleeman's *Report on the Badhak or Bāgri Dacoits* (1849). Most of the material belongs to a report drawn up at Nāgpur by Mr. C. Ramsay, Assistant Resident, in 1845.

accustomed to invite the Sānsias, who as their minstrels recited the praises of the ancestors of the Jāts, tracing them up to the time of Punya Jāt; and for this they received presents, according to the means of the parties, of cows, ponies or buffaloes. Should any Jāt demur to paying the customary dues the Sānsias would dress up a cloth figure of his father and parade with it before the house, when the sum demanded was generally given; for if the figure were fastened on a bamboo and placed over the house the family would lose caste and no one would smoke or drink water with them.[1]

The Sānsias say that their ancestors have always resided in Mārwār and Ajmer. About twenty-four miles distant from Ajmer are two towns, Pīsangān and Sagun; on their eastern side is a large tank, and the bones of all persons of the Sānsia tribe who died in any part of the country were formerly buried there, being covered by a wooden platform with four pillars.[2] On one occasion a quarrel had arisen over a Sānsia woman, and a large number of the caste were killed in this place. So they left Mārwār, and some of them came to the Deccan, where they took to house-breaking and dacoity; and so successful were they that the other Sānsias followed them and gave up all their former customs, even those of reciting the praises of and begging from the Jāts.

The Sānsias are divided into two groups, Kalkar and Malha; and these two are further subdivided into eight and twelve sections respectively. No one belonging to the Kalkar group may marry another person of that group, but he may marry anybody belonging to any section of the Malha group. Thus the two groups being exogamous the sections do not serve any purpose, but it is possible that the rules are really more complicated. In the Punjab their marriage ceremony is peculiar, the bride being covered by a basket, on which the bridegroom sits while the nuptial rites are being performed.[3] According to Colonel Sleeman, after the arrangement of a match the caste committee assemble to determine the price to be paid to the father of the girl,

2. Social customs.

---

[1] Sleeman's *Report on the Badhaks*, p. 253.
[2] *Ibidem*, p. 254.
[3] Sir D. Ibbetson, *Punjab Census Report* (1881), para. 577.

which may amount to as much as Rs. 2000. When this is settled some liquor is spilt on the ground in the name of Bhagwān or Vishnu, and an elder pronounces that the two have become man and wife; a feast is given to the caste, and the ceremony is concluded. After child-birth a woman cannot wash herself for five days, but on the sixth she may go to a stream and wash. Even on ordinary occasions a woman must never wash herself inside the house, but must always go to a stream, which rule does not apply to men. When the hair of a child begins to grow it is all shaved except the scalp-lock, which is dedicated to Bhagwān; and at ten or twelve years of age this lock is also shaved off and a dinner is given to members of the caste. The last ceremony is of the nature of a puberty-rite, and if children die prior to its performance their bodies are buried, whereas after it they have a right to cremation. After a body has been burnt the bones are buried on the spot in an earthen vessel, over the mouth of which a large stone is placed. Some pig's flesh is cooked and sweet cakes prepared, portions of which are placed upon the stone; and the deceased is then called upon, by reason of the usual ceremonies having been performed at his death, to watch over his surviving relatives. If any Sānsia happened to commit a murder when engaged in a dacoity he was afterwards obliged to make an offering for forgiveness, and to spend a rupee and a quarter in liquor for the caste-fellows. If a dacoit had himself been killed and his body abandoned, his clothes, with some new clothes, were put upon a sleeping-cot, and his companions of the same caste carried it to a convenient spot, where it was either burnt or buried in the ground.

3. Taboos of relationship.

Colonel Sleeman records some curious taboos among relations.[1] A man cannot go into the hut of his mother-in-law or of his son's wife; for if their petticoat should touch him he would be turned out of his caste and would not be admitted into it until he had paid a large sum. "If we quarrel with a woman," said a Sānsia, "and she strikes us with her petticoat we lose our caste; we should be allowed to eat and drink with our tribe, but not to perform worship

[1] P. 259.

with them nor to assist in burial rites. If a woman piles up a heap of stones and puts her petticoat upon it and throws filth upon it and says to any other, 'This disgrace fell upon your ancestors for seven generations back,' both are immediately expelled from our caste, and cannot return to it until they have paid a large sum of money."

As in the case of the Badhaks the arrangements for a dacoity were carefully organised. Each band had a Jemādār or leader, while the others were called Sipāhis or soldiers. A tenth of all the booty taken was given to the Jemādār in return for the provision of the spears, torches and other articles, and of the remainder the Jemādār received two shares and the Sipāhis one each. But no novice was permitted to share in the booty or carry a spear until he had participated in two or three successful dacoities; and inasmuch as outsiders, with the exception of the impure Dhers and Māngs, were freely admitted to the Sānsia community in return for a small money payment, some such apprenticeship as this was no doubt necessary. If a Sipāhi was killed in a dacoity his wife was entitled to a sum of Rs. 350 and half an ordinary share in future dacoities as long as she remained with the gang. The Sānsias never pitched their camp in the vicinity of the place in which they contemplated an enterprise, but despatched their scouts to it, themselves remaining some twenty miles distant.

4. Organisation for dacoity.

The scouts,[1] having prospected the town and determined the house to be exploited, usually that of the leading banker, would then proceed to it in the early morning before business began and ask to purchase some ornaments or change some money; by this request they often induced the banker to bring out his cash chest from the place of security where he was accustomed to deposit it at night, and learnt where it should be looked for. Having picked up as much information as possible, the scouts would purchase some spear-heads, bury them in a neighbouring ravine, and rejoin the main body. The party would arrive at the rendezvous in the evening, and having fitted their spears to bamboo shafts, would enter the town carrying them concealed in a bundle

5. Description of a dacoity.

---

[1] The description of a dacoity is combined from two accounts given at pp. 257, 273 of Colonel Sleeman's *Report*.

of *karbi* or the long thick stalks of the large millet, juāri.[1] One man was appointed to carry the torch,[2] and the oil to be poured on this had always to be purchased in the town or village where the dacoity was to take place, the use of any other oil being considered most unlucky. The vessel containing the oil was not allowed to touch the earth until its contents had been poured upon the torch, when it was dashed upon the ground. From this time until the completion of the dacoity no one might spit or drink water or relieve himself under penalty of putting a stop to the enterprise. The Jemādār invoked Khandoba, an incarnation of Mahādeo, and said that if by his assistance the box of money was broken at the first or second stroke of the axe, a chain of gold weighing one and a quarter tolas would be made over to him. The party then approached the shop, the roads surrounding it being picketed to guard against a rescue, and the Jemādār, accompanied by four or five men and the torch-bearer, rushed into the shop crying Dīn, Dīn. The doors usually gave way under a few heavy blows with the axe, which they wielded with great expertness, and the scout pointed out the location of the money and valuables. Once in possession of the property the torch was extinguished and the whole party made off as rapidly as possible. During their retreat they tried to avoid spearing people who pursued them, first calling out to them to go away. If any member of the party was killed or so desperately wounded that he could not be removed, the others cut off his head and carried it off so as to prevent recognition; a man who was slightly wounded would be carried off by his companions, but if the pursuit became hot and he had to be left, they cut off his head also and took it with them, escaping by this drastic method the risk of his turning approver with the consequent danger of conviction for the rest of the gang. About a mile from the place of the dacoity they stopped and mustered their party, and the Jemādār called out to the god Bhagwān to direct any pursuers in the wrong direction and enable them to reach their families. If any dacoit had ever been killed at this particular town they also called upon his spirit to assist them,

---

[1] *Sorghum vulgare*.
[2] Made of the bark of the date-palm tied with strips of cloth round some inflammable wood.

promising to offer him a goat or some liquor; and so, throwing down a rupee or two at any temple or stream which they might pass on their way, they came to their families. When about a mile away from the camp they called out 'Cuckoo' to ascertain if any misfortune had occurred during their absence; if they thought all was well they went nearer and imitated the call of the partridge; and finally when close to the encampment made a hissing noise like a snake. On arrival at the camp they at once mounted their ponies and started off, marching fifty or sixty miles a day, for two or three days.

6. Omens.

The Sānsias never committed a dacoity on moonlight nights, but had five appointed days during the dark half of the month, the seventh, ninth, eleventh, thirteenth and the night of the day on which the new moon was first seen. If they did not meet with a favourable omen on any of these nights, no dacoity was committed that month. The following is a list of omens given by one of the caste:[1] "If we see a cat when we are near the place where we intend to commit a dacoity, or we hear the relations of a dead person lamenting, or hear a person sneeze while cooking his meal, or see a dog run away with a portion of any person's food, or a kite screams while sitting on a tree, or a woman breaks the earthen vessel in which she may have been drawing water, we consider the omens unfavourable. If a person drops his turban or we meet a corpse, or the Jemādār has forgotten to put some bread into his waistbelt, or any dacoit forgets his axe or spear or sees a snake whether dead or alive; these omens are also considered unfavourable and we do not commit the dacoity. Should we see a wolf and any one of us have on a red turban, we take this and tear it into seven pieces and hang each piece upon a separate tree. We then purchase a rupee's worth of liquor and kill a goat, which is cut up into four pieces. Four men pretend that they are wolves and rushing on the four quarters of the meat seize them, imitating the howl of these animals, while the rest of the dacoits pelt them with the entrails; the meat is afterwards cooked and eaten in the name of Bhagwān."

It would appear that the explanation of this curious

[1] Sleeman, p. 263.

ceremony must be that the Sānsias thought the appearance of the wolf to be an omen that one of them would furnish a meal for him. The turban is venerated on account of its close association with the head, a sacred part of the body among Hindus, and in this case it probably served as a substituted offering for the head, while its red colour represented blood; and the mimic rite of the goat being devoured by men pretending to be wolves fulfilled the omen which portended that the wolves would be provided with a meal, and hence averted the necessity of one of the band being really devoured. In somewhat analogous fashion the Gonds and Baigas placate or drive away a tiger who has killed a man in order to prevent him from obtaining further victims. Some similar idea apparently underlay the omen of the dog running away with food. Perhaps the portent of hearing the kite scream on a tree also meant that he looked on them with a prescient eye as a future meal. On the other hand, meeting a corpse and seeing a snake are commonly considered to be lucky omens, and their inclusion in this list is curious.[1] The passage continues: "Among our favourable omens are meeting a woman selling milk; or a person carrying a basket of grain or a bag of money; or if we see a calf sucking its mother, or meet a person with a vessel of water, or a marriage procession; or if any person finds a rupee that he has lost; or we meet a bearer carrying fish or a pig or a blue-jay; if any of these occur near our camp on the day we contemplate a dacoity, we proceed forthwith to commit it and consider that these signs assure us a good booty. If a Fakīr begs from us while we are on our way to the place of dacoity we cannot give him anything." Another Sānsia said: "We think it very favourable if, when on the way to commit a dacoity, we hear or see the jackal; it is as good as gold and silver to us; also if we hear the bray of the ass in a village we consider it to be lucky."

7. Ordeals.   The following is a description given by a Sānsia of their ordeals:[2] If a Jemādār suspects a Sipāhi of secreting plunder a *panchāyat* is assembled,[3] the members of which

---

[1] But it is unlucky for a snake to cross one's path in front.
[2] Sleeman, pp. 261, 262.
[3] Committee of five persons.

receive five rupees from both parties. Seven pīpal[1] leaves are laid upon his hand and bound round with thread, and upon these a heated iron *tawa* or plate is set; he is then ordered to walk seven paces and put the plate down upon seven thorns; should he be able to do so he is pronounced innocent, but if he is burnt by the plate and throws it down he is considered guilty. Another ordeal is by fixing arrows, two of which are shot off at once from one bow, one in the name of Bhagwān (god), and the other in the name of the *panchāyat*; the place being on the bank of the river. The arrow that flies the farthest is stuck upright into the ground; upon which a man carrying a long bamboo walks up to his breast in the water and the suspected person is desired to join him. One of the *panchāyat* then claps his hands seven times and runs off to pick up the arrow; at this instant the suspected person is obliged to put his head under water, and if he can hold his breath until the other returns to the bank with the arrow and has again clapped his hands seven times he is pronounced innocent. If he cannot do so he is declared guilty and punished. A third form of ordeal was as follows: The Jemādār and the gang assemble under a pīpal tree, and after knocking off the neck of an earthen pitcher they kill a goat and collect its blood in the pitcher, and put some glass bangles in it. Four lines are drawn on the pitcher with vermilion (representing blood), and it is placed under a tree and $1\frac{1}{4}$ seers[2] of *gur* (sugar) are tied up in a piece of cloth $1\frac{1}{4}$ cubits in length and hung on to a branch of the tree. The Jemādār then says, "I will forgive any person who has not secreted more than fifteen or twenty rupees, but whoever has stolen more than that sum shall be punished." The Jemādār dips his finger in the pitcher of blood, and afterwards touches the sugar and calls out loudly, 'If I have embezzled any money may Bhagwān punish me'; and each dacoit in turn pronounces the same sentence. No one who is guilty will do this but at once makes his confession. The oath pronounced on $1\frac{1}{4}$ seers of sugar tied up in $1\frac{1}{4}$ cubits of cloth was considered the most solemn and binding which a Sānsia could take.

[1] *Ficus religiosa.* [2] The seer = 2 lbs.

8. Sānsias at the present time.

At present, Mr. Kennedy states,[1] the Sānsias travel about in gangs of varying strength with their families, bullocks, sheep, goats and dogs. The last mentioned of these animals are usually small mongrels with a terrier strain, mostly stolen or bred from types dishonestly obtained during their peregrinations. Dacoity is still the crime which they most affect, and they also break into houses and steal cattle. Men usually have a necklace of red coral and gold beads round the neck, from which is suspended a square piece of silver or gold bearing an effigy of a man on horseback. This represents either the deity Rāmdeo Pīr or one of the wearer's ancestors, and is venerated as a charm. They are very quarrelsome, and their drinking-bouts in camp usually end in a free fight, in which they also beat their women, and the affray not infrequently results in the death of one of the combatants. When this happens the slayer makes restitution to the relatives by defraying the expenses of a fresh drinking-bout.[2] During the daytime men are seldom to be found in the encampment, as they are in the habit of hiding in the ditches and jungle, where the women take them their food; at night they return to their tents, but are off again at dawn.

1. The caste and its subdivisions.

Sānsia, Uria.[3]—A caste of masons and navvies of the Uriya country. The Sānsias are really a branch of the great migratory Ud or Odde caste of earth-workers, whose name has been corrupted into various forms.[4] Thus in Chānda they are known as Wadewār or Waddar. The term Uria is here a corruption of Odde, and it is the one by which the caste prefer to be known, but they are generally called Sānsia by outsiders. The caste sometimes class the Sānsias as a subcaste of Urias, the others being Benātia Urias and Khandait Urias. Since the Uriya tract has been transferred to Bengal, and subsequently to Bihār and Orissa, there remain only about 1000 Sānsias in the Chhattīsgarh Districts and States. Although it is possible that the name

---

[1] *Criminal Classes in the Bombay Presidency*; Sānsias and Berias.
[2] Mr. Gayer, *Central Provinces Police Lectures*, p. 68.
[3] This article is mainly based on a paper by Mr. Rāma Prasād Bohidār, Assistant Master, Sambalpur High School.
[4] See article Beldār for a notice of the different groups of earth-workers.

of the caste may have been derived from some past connection, the Sānsias of the Uriya country have at present no affinities with the outcaste and criminal tribe of Sānsis or Sānsias of northern India. They enjoy a fairly high position in Sambalpur, and Brāhmans will take water from them.

They are divided into two subcastes, the Benetia and Khandait. The Benetia are the higher and look down on the Khandaits, because, it is said, these latter have accepted service as foot-soldiers, and this is considered a menial occupation. Perhaps in the households of the Uriya Rājas the tribal militia had also to perform personal services, and this may have been considered derogatory. In Orissa, on the other hand, the Khandaits have become landholders and occupy a high position next to Rājpūts. The Benetia Sānsias practise hypergamy with the Khandait Sānsias, taking their daughters in marriage, but not giving daughters to them. When a Benetia is marrying a Khandait girl his party will not take food with the bride's relatives, but only partake of some sugar and curds and depart with the bride. The Sānsias have totemistic exogamous septs, usually derived from the names of sacred objects, as Kachhap, tortoise, Sankh, the conch-shell, Tulsi, basil, and so on.

2. Marriage customs.

Girls are married between seven and ten, and after she is twelve years old a girl cannot go through the proper ceremony, but can only be wedded by a simple rite used for widows, in which vermilion is rubbed on her forehead and some grains of rice stuck on it. The marriage procession, as described by Mr. Rāma Prasād Bohidār, is a gorgeous affair: "The drummers, all drunk, head the procession, beating their drums to the tune set by the piper. Next in order are placed dancing-boys between two rows of lights carried on poles adorned with festoons of paper flowers. Rockets and fireworks have their proper share in the procession, and last of all comes the bridegroom in his wedding apparel, mounted on a horse. His person is studded with various kinds of gold necklaces borrowed for the occasion, and the fingers of his right hand are covered with rings. Bangles and chains of silver shine on his wrists and arms. His forehead is beautifully painted with ground sandalwood divided in the centre by a streak of vermilion.

His head carries a crown of palm-leaves overlaid with bright paper of various colours. A network of *malti* flowers hangs loosely from the head over the back and covers a portion of the loins of the steed. The eyes are painted with collyrium and the feet with red dye. The lips and teeth are also reddened by the betel-leaf, which the bridegroom chews in profusion. A silk cloth does the work of a belt, in which is fixed a dagger on the right side." Here the red colour which predominates in the bridegroom's decorations is lucky for the reasons given in the article on Lakhera; the blacking of the eyes is also considered to keep off evil spirits; betel-leaf is itself a powerful agent of magic and averter of spirits, and to the same end the bridegroom carries iron in the shape of the dagger. The ceremony is of the customary Uriya type. On the seventh day of the wedding the husband and wife go to the river and bathe, throwing away the sacred threads worn at the time of marriage, and also those which have been tied round their wrists. On returning home the wife piles up seven brass vessels and seven stools one above the other and the husband kicks them over, this being repeated seven times. The husband then washes his teeth with water brought from the river, breaks the vessel containing the water in the bride's house, and runs away, while the women of her family throw pailfuls of coloured water over him. On the ninth day the bride comes and smears a mixture of curds and sugar on the forehead of each member of the bridegroom's family, probably as a sign of her admission to their clan, and returns home. Divorce and the remarriage of widows are permitted.

3. Religion and worship of ancestors.

The caste worship Viswakarma, the celestial architect, and on four principal festivals they revere their trade-implements and the book on architecture, by which they work. At Dasahra a pumpkin is offered to these articles in lieu of a goat. They observe the *shrāddh* ceremony, and first make two offerings to the spirits of ancestors who have died a violent death or have committed suicide, and to those of relatives who died unmarried, for fear lest these unclean and malignant spirits should seize and defile the offerings to the beneficent ancestors. Thereafter *pindas* or sacrificial cakes are offered to three male and three female ancestors both on the father's and mother's side, twelve cakes being offered in all. The Sānsias eat the flesh of clean animals, but the consumption of liquor is strictly forbidden, on pain, it is said, of permanent exclusion from caste.

In Sambalpur the caste are usually stone-workers, making cups, mortars, images of idols and other articles. They also build tanks and wander from place to place for this purpose in large companies. It is related that on one occasion they came to dig a tank in Drūg, and the Rāja of that place, while watching their work, took a fancy to one of the Odnis, as their women were called, and wanted her to marry him. But as she was already married, and was a virtuous woman, she refused. The Rāja persisted in his demand, on which the whole body of Sānsias from Chhattīsgarh, numbering, it is said, nine lakhs of persons, left their work and proceeded to Warārbāndh, near Rāj-Nāndgaon. Here they dug the great tank of Warārbāndh[1] in one night to obtain a supply of water for themselves. But the Rāja followed them, and as they could not resist him by force, the woman whom he was pursuing burnt herself alive, and thus earned undying fame in the caste. This legend is perpetuated in the Odni Gīt, a popular folk-song in Chhattīsgarh. But it is a traditional story of the Sānsias in connection with large tanks, and in another version the scene is laid in Gujarāt.[2]

4. Occupation.

---

[1] Said to be derived from their name Waddar.

[2] Story of Jasma Odni in Sati Charita Sangrah.

SAVAR

LIST OF PARAGRAPHS

1. Distribution and historical notices.
2. Tribal legends.
3. Tribal subdivisions.
4. Marriage.
5. Death ceremonies.
6. Religion.
7. Occupation.

1. Distribution and historical notices.

Savar,[1] **Sawara, Savara, Saonr, Sahra** (and several other variations. In Bundelkhand the Savars, there called Saonrs, are frequently known by the honorific title of Rāwat).—A primitive tribe numbering about 70,000 persons in the Central Provinces in 1911, and principally found in the Chhattīsgarh Districts and those of Saugor and Damoh. The eastern branch of the tribe belongs chiefly to the Uriya country. The Savars are found in large numbers in the Madras Districts of Ganjām and Vizagapatam and in Orissa. They also live in the Bundelkhand Districts of the United Provinces. The total number of Savars enumerated in India in 1911 was 600,000, of which the Bundelkhand Districts contained about 100,000 and the Uriya country the remainder. The two branches of the tribe are thus separated by a wide expanse of territory. As regards this peculiarity of distribution General Cunningham says: " Indeed there seems good reason to believe that the Savaras were formerly the dominant branch of the great Kolarian family, and that their power lasted down to a comparatively late period, when they were pushed aside by other Kolarian tribes in the north and east, and by the Gonds in the south. In the Saugor District

---

[1] This article is principally based on papers by Munshi Gopīnāth, Naib-Tahsīldār, Sonpur, Mr. Kālūrām Pachorē, Assistant Settlement Officer, Sambalpur, and Mr. Hīra Lāl, Assistant Gazetteer Superintendent.

I was informed that the Savaras had formerly fought with the Gonds and that the latter had conquered them by treacherously making them drunk." [1] Similarly Cunningham notices that the zamīndār of Suarmār in Raipur, which name is derived from Savar, is a Gond. A difference of opinion has existed as to whether the Savars were Kolarian or Dravidian so far as their language was concerned, Colonel Dalton adopting the latter view and other authorities the former and correct one. In the Central Provinces the Savars have lost their own language and speak the Aryan Hindi or Uriya vernacular current around them. But in Madras they still retain their original speech, which is classified by Sir G. Grierson as Mundāri or Kolarian. He says: "The most southerly forms of Munda speech are those spoken by the Savars and Gadabas of the northeast of Madras. The former have been identified with the Suari of Pliny and the Sabarae of Ptolemy. A wild tribe of the same name is mentioned in Sanskrit literature, even so far back as in late Vedic times, as inhabiting the Deccan, so that the name at least can boast great antiquity." [2] As to the origin of the name Savar, General Cunningham says that it must be sought for outside the language of the Aryans. "In Sanskrit '*savara*' simply means 'a corpse.' From Herodotus, however, we learn that the Scythian word for an axe was *sagaris*, and as 'g' and 'v' are interchangeable letters *savar* is the same word as *sagar*. It seems therefore not unreasonable to infer that the tribe who were so called took their name from their habit of carrying axes. Now it is one of the striking peculiarities of the Savars that they are rarely seen without an axe in their hands. The peculiarity has been frequently noticed by all who have seen them." [3] The above opinion of Cunningham, which is of course highly speculative, is disputed by Mr. Crooke, who says that "The word Savara, if it be, as some believe, derived from *sava* a corpse, comes from the root *sav* 'to cause to decay,' and need not necessarily therefore be of non-Aryan origin, while on the other hand no distinct

---

[1] *Archæological Reports*, vol. xvii. pp. 120, 122.
[2] *India Census Report* (1901), p. 283.
[3] *Archæological Reports*, vol. xvii. p. 113.

inference can be drawn from the use of the axe by the Savars, when it is equally used by various other Dravidian jungle tribes such as the Korwas, Bhuiyas and the like."[1] In the classical stories of their origin the first ancestor of the Savars is sometimes described as a Bhīl. The word Savar is mentioned in several Sanskrit works written between 800 B.C. and A.D. 1200, and it seems probable that they are a Munda tribe who occupied the tracts of country which they live in prior to the arrival of the Gonds. The classical name Savar has been corrupted into various forms. Thus in the Bundeli dialect '*ava*' changes into '*au*' and a nasal is sometimes interpolated. *Savar* has here become Saunr or Saonr. The addition of 'a' at the end of the word sometimes expresses contempt, and Savar becomes Savara as Chamār is corrupted into *Chamra*. In the Uriya country 'v' is changed into 'b' and an aspirate is interpolated, and thus Savara became Sabra or Sahara, as Gaur has become Gahra. The word Sahara, Mr. Crooke remarks,[2] has excited speculation as to its derivation from Arabic, in which Sahara means a wilderness; and the name of the Savars has accordingly been deduced from the same source as the great Sahara desert. This is of course incorrect.

2. Tribal legends.

Various stories of the origin of the Savars are given in Sanskrit literature. In the Aitareya Brāhmana they are spoken of as the descendants of Vishwāmitra, while in the Mahābhārat they are said to have been created by Kāmdhenu, Vasishtha's wonder-working cow, in order to repel the aggression of Vishwāmitra. Local tradition traces their origin to the celebrated Seori of the Rāmāyana, who is supposed to have lived somewhere near the present Seorīnārāyan in the Bilāspur District and to have given her name to this place. Rāmchandra in his wanderings met her there, ate the plums which she had gathered for him after tasting each one herself, and out of regard for her devotion permitted her name to precede his own of Nārāyan in that given to the locality. Another story makes one Jara Savar their original ancestor, who was said to have shot

[1] Crooke's *Tribes and Castes of N.W.P.*, art. Savara.
[2] *Tribes and Castes of N.W.P.*, art. Savara.

Krishna in the form of a deer. Another states that they were created for carrying stones for the construction of the great temple at Puri and for dragging the car of Jagannāth, which they still do at the present time. Yet another connecting them with the temple of Jagannāth states that their ancestor was an old Bhīl hermit called Sawar, who lived in Karod, two miles from Seorīnārāyan. The god Jagannāth had at this time appeared in Seorīnārāyan and the old Sawar used to worship him. The king of Orissa had built the great temple at Puri and wished to install Jagannāth in it, and he sent a Brāhman to fetch him from Seorīnārāyan, but nobody knew where he was except the old hermit Sawar. The Brāhman besought him in vain to be allowed to see the god and even went so far as to marry his daughter, and finally the old man consented to take him blindfold to the place. The Brāhman, however, tied some mustard seeds in a corner of his cloth and made a hole in it so that they dropped out one by one on the way. After some time they grew up and served to guide him to the spot. This story of the mustard seeds of course finds a place in the folklore of many nations. The Brāhman then went to Seorīnārāyan alone and begged the god to go to Puri. Jagannāth consented, and assuming the form of a log of wood floated down the Mahānadi to Puri, where he was taken out and placed in the temple. A carpenter agreed to carve the god's image out of the log of wood on condition that the temple should be shut up for six months while the work was going on. But some curious people opened the door before the time and the work could not proceed, and thus the image of the god is only half carved out of the wood up to the present day. As a consolation to the old man the god ordained that the place should bear the hermit's name before his own as Seorīnārāyan. Lastly the Saonrs of Bundelkhand have the following tradition. In the beginning of creation Mahādeo wished to teach the people how to cultivate the ground, and so he made a plough and took out his bull Nandi to yoke to it. But there was dense forest on the earth, so he created a being whom he called Savar and gave him an axe to clear the forest. In the meantime Mahādeo went away to get another bullock. The Savar after clearing the forest felt very hungry, and finding nothing else to eat killed Nandi and ate his flesh on a teak leaf. And for this reason the young teak leaves when rubbed give out sap which is the colour of blood to the present day. After some time Mahādeo returned, and finding the forest well cleared was pleased with the Savar, and as a reward endowed him with the knowledge of all edible and medicinal roots and fruits of the forest. But on looking round for Nandi he found him lying dead with some of his flesh cut off. The Savar pleaded ignorance, but Mahādeo sprinkled a little nectar on Nandi, who came to life again and told what had happened. Then Mahādeo was enraged with the Savar and said, 'You shall remain a barbarian and dwell for ever in poverty in the jungles without enough to eat.' And accordingly this has always been the condition of the Savar's descendants.

Other old authors speak of the Parna or leaf-clad Savars; and a Savar messenger is described as carrying a bow in his hand "with his hair tied up in a knot behind with a creeper, black himself, and wearing a loin-cloth of *bhilawān* leaves";[1] an excellent example of 'a leaf-fringed legend.'

3. Tribal sub-divisions.

The Bundelkhand Savars have been so long separated from the others that they have sometimes forgotten their identity and consider themselves as a subtribe of Gonds, though the better informed repudiate this. They may be regarded as a separate endogamous group. The eastern branch have two main divisions called Laria and Uriya, or those belonging to Chhattīsgarh and Sambalpur respectively. A third division known as the Kālāpithia or 'Black Backs' are found in Orissa, and are employed to drag the car of Jagannāth. These on account of their sacred occupation consider themselves superior to the others, abstain from fowls and liquor, and sometimes wear the sacred thread. The Larias are the lowest subdivision. Marriage is regulated by exogamous septs or *bargas*. The northern Savars say that they have 52 of these, 52 being a number frequently adopted to express the highest possible magnitude, as if no more could be imagined. The

[1] *Tribes and Castes of Bengal*, art. Savar.

Uriya Savars say they have 80 *bargas*. Besides the prohibition of marriage within the same *barga*, the union of first cousins is sometimes forbidden. Among the Uriya Savars each *barga* has the two further divisions of Joria and Khuntia, the Jorias being those who bury or burn their dead near a *jor* or brook, and the Khuntias those who bury or burn them near a *khunt* or old tree. Jorias and Khuntias of the same *barga* cannot intermarry, but in the case of some other subdivisions of the *barga*, as between those who eat rice at one festival in the year and those eating it at two, marriage is allowed between members of the two subdivisions, thus splitting the exogamous group into two. The names of the *bargas* are usually totemistic, and the following are some examples: Badaiya, the carpenter bird; Bāgh, the tiger; Bagula, the heron; Bahra, a cook; Bhatia, a *brinjal* or egg-plant; Bīsi, the scorpion; Basantia, the trunk of the cotton tree; Hathia, an elephant; Jancher, a tree (this *barga* is divided into Bada and Kachcha, the Bada worshipping the tree and the Kachcha a branch of it, and marriage between the two subdivisions is allowed); Jharia (this *barga* keeps a lock of a child's hair unshaved for four or five years after its birth); Juādi, a gambler; Karsa, a deer; Khairaiya, the *khair* or catechu tree; Lodhi, born from the caste of that name (in Saugor); Markām, the name of a Gond sept; Rājhans, a swan; Suriya Bansia, from the sun (members of this *barga* feed the caste-fellows on the occasion of a solar eclipse and throw away their earthen pots); Silgainya from *sil*, a slate; and Tiparia from *tipari*, a basket (these two septs are divided into Kachcha and Pakka groups which can marry with each other); Sona, gold (a member of this sept does not wear gold ornaments until he has given a feast and a caste-fellow has placed one on his person).

4. Marriage.

Marriage is usually adult, but in places where the Savars live near Hindus they have adopted early marriage. A reason for preferring the latter custom is found in the marriage ceremony, when the bride and bridegroom must be carried on the shoulders of their relatives from the bride's house to the bridegroom's. If they are grown up, this part of the ceremony entails no inconsiderable labour on the relatives. In the Uriya country, while the Khuntia subdivision of each *barga* see nothing wrong in marrying a girl after adolescence, the Jorias consider it a great sin, to avoid which they sometimes marry a girl to an arrow before she attains puberty. An arrow is tied to her hand, and she goes seven times round a mahua branch stuck on an improvised altar, and drinks *ghī* and oil, thus creating the fiction of a marriage. The arrow is then thrown into a river to imply that her husband is dead, and she is afterwards disposed of by the ceremony of widow-marriage. If this mock ceremony has not been performed before the girl becomes adult, she is taken to the forest by a relative and there tied to a tree, to which she is considered to be married. She is not taken back to her father's house but to that of some relative, such as her brother-in-law or grandfather, who is permitted to talk to her in an obscene and jesting manner, and is subsequently disposed of as a widow. Or in Sambalpur she may be nominally married to an old man and then again married as a widow. The Savars follow generally the local Hindu form of the marriage ceremony. On the return of the bridal pair seven lines are drawn in front of the entrance to the bridegroom's house. Some relative takes rice and throws it at the persons returning with the marriage procession, and then pushes the pair hastily across the lines and into the house. They are thus freed from the evil spirits who might have accompanied them home and who are kept back by the rice and the seven lines. A price of Rs. 5 is sometimes paid for the bride. In Saugor if the bride's family cannot afford a wedding feast they distribute small pieces of bread to the guests, who place them in their head-cloths to show their acceptance of this substitute. To those guests to whom it is necessary to make presents five cowries are given. Widow-marriage is allowed, and in some places the widow is bound to marry her late husband's younger brother unless he declines to take her. If she marries somebody else the new husband pays a sum by way of compensation either to her father or to the late husband's family. Divorce is permitted on the husband's initiative for adultery or serious disagreement. If the wife wishes for a divorce she simply runs away from her husband. The Laria Savars must give a *mārti-jīti kā bhāt* or death-feast on the occasion of a divorce. The Uriyas simply pay a rupee to the headman of the caste.

5. Death ceremonies.

The Savars both burn and bury their dead, placing the corpse on the pyre with its head to the north, in the belief that heaven lies in that direction. On the eleventh day after the death in Sambalpur those members of the caste who can afford it present a goat to the mourners. The Savars believe that the souls of those who die become ghosts, and in Bundelkhand they used formerly to bury the dead near their fields in the belief that the spirits would watch over and protect the crops. If a man has died a violent death they raise a small platform of earth under a teak or *sāj* tree, in which the ghost of the dead man is believed to take up its residence, and nobody thereafter may cut down that tree. The Uriya Savars take no special measures unless the ghost appears to somebody in a dream and asks to be worshipped as Baghiapāt (tiger-eaten) or Masān (serpent-bitten). In such cases a *gunia* or sorcerer is consulted, and such measures as he prescribes are taken to appease the dead man's soul. If a person dies without a child a hole is made in a stone, and his soul is induced to enter it by the *gunia*. A few grains of rice are placed in the hole, and it is then closed with melted lead to imprison the ghost, and the stone is thrown into a stream so that it may never be able to get out and trouble the family. Savars offer water to the dead. A second wife usually wears a metal impression of the first wife by way of propitiation to her.

6. Religion.

The Savars worship Bhawāni under various names and also Dūlha Deo, the young bridegroom who was killed by a tiger. He is located in the kitchen of every house in some localities, and this has given rise to the proverb, '*Jai chūlha, tai Dūlha*,' or 'There is a Dūlha Deo to every hearth.' The Savars are considered to be great sorcerers. '*Sawara ke pānge, Rāwat ke bāndhe*,' or "The man bewitched by a Savar and the bullock tied up by a Rāwat (grazier) cannot escape"; and again, 'Verily the Saonr is a cup of poison.' Their charms, called Sabari *mantras*, are especially intended to appease the spirits of persons who have died a violent death. If one of their family was seriously ill they were accustomed formerly to set fire to the forest, so that by burning the small animals and insects which could not escape they might propitiate the angry gods.

7. Occupation.
The dress of the Savars is of the scantiest. The women wear *khilwān* or pith ornaments in the ear, and abstain from wearing nose-rings, a traditional method of deference to the higher castes. The proverb has it, 'The ornaments of the Sawara are *gumchi* seeds.' These are the red and black seeds of *Abrus precatorius* which are used in weighing gold and silver and are called *rati*. Women are tattooed and sometimes men also to avoid being pierced with a red-hot iron by the god of death. Tattooing is further said to allay the sexual passion of women, which is eight times more intense than that of men. Their occupations are the collection of jungle produce and cultivation. They are very clever in taking honeycombs: 'It is the Savar who can drive the black bees from their hive.' The eastern branch of the caste is more civilised than the Saonras of Bundelkhand, who still sow juāri with a pointed stick, saying that it was the implement given to them by Mahādeo for this purpose. In Saugor and Damoh they employ Brāhmans for marriage ceremonies if they can afford it, but on other occasions their own caste priests. In some places they will take food from most castes but in others from nobody who is not a Savar. Sometimes they admit outsiders and in others the children only of irregular unions; thus a Gond woman kept by a Savar would not be recognised as a member of the caste herself but her children would be Savars. A woman going wrong with an outsider of low caste is permanently excommunicated.

SONJHARA

LIST OF PARAGRAPHS

1. *Origin and constitution of the caste.*
2. *Totemism.*
3. *Marriage.*
4. *Customs at birth.*
5. *Funeral rites.*
6. *Religion.*
7. *Social customs.*
8. *Occupation.*

Sonjhara, Jhara, Jhora, Jhira.—A small occupational caste who wash for gold in river-beds, belonging to the Sambalpur, Mandla, Bālāghāt and Chānda Districts and the Chota Nāgpur Feudatory States. In 1911 they numbered about 1500 persons. The name probably comes from *sona*, gold, and *jhārna*, to sweep or wash, though, when the term Jhara only is used, some derive it from *jhori*, a streamlet. Colonel Dalton surmised that the Sonjharas were an offshoot of the Gonds, and this appears to be demonstrated by the fact that the names of their exogamous septs are identical with Gond names as Marābi, Tekām, Netām, Dhurwa and Madao. The Sonjharas of Bilāspur say that their ancestors were Gonds who dwelt at Lānji in Bālāghāt. The caste relate the tradition that they were condemned by Mahādeo to perpetual poverty because their first ancestor stole a little gold from Pārvati's crown when it fell into the river Jamuna (in Chota Nāgpur) and he was sent to fetch it out. The metal which is found in the river sands they hold to be the remains of a shower of gold which fell for two and a half days while the Banāphar heroes Alha and Udal were fighting their great battle with Prithvi Rāj, king of Delhi. The caste is partly occupational, and recruited from different sources. This is shown by the fact that in Chānda members of different septs

1. Origin and constitution of the caste.

will not eat together, though they are obliged to intermarry. In Sambalpur the Behra, Pātar, Nāik and Padhān septs eat together and intermarry. Two other septs, the Kanar and Peltrai who eat fowls and drink liquor, occupy a lower position, and members of the first four will not take food from them nor give daughters to them in marriage, though they will take daughters from these lower groups for their sons. Here they have three subcastes, the Laria or residents of Chhattīsgarh, the Uriya belonging to the Uriya country, and the Bhuinhār, who may be an offshoot from the Bhuiya tribe.

2. Totemism.

They have one recorded instance of totemism, which is of some interest. Members of the sept named after a tree called *kausa* revere the tree and explain it by saying that their ancestor, when flying from some danger, sought protection from this tree, which thereupon opened and enfolded him in its trunk. No member of the sept will touch the tree without first bathing, and on auspicious occasions, such as births and weddings, they will dig up a little earth from the roots of the tree and taking this home worship it in the house. If any member of the sept finds that he has cut off a branch or other part of this tree unwittingly he will take and consign it to a stream, observing ceremonies of mourning. Women of the Nāg or cobra sept will not mention the name of this snake aloud, just as they refrain from speaking the names of male relatives.

3. Marriage.

Marriage within the sept is forbidden, and they permit the intermarriage of the children of a brother and sister, but not of those of two sisters, though their husbands may be of different septs. Marriage is usually adult except in Sambalpur, where a girl must be provided with a husband before reaching maturity in accordance with the general rule among the Uriya castes. In Chhindwāra it is said that the Sonjharas revere the crocodile and that the presence of this animal is essential at their weddings. They do not, however, kill and eat it at a sacrificial feast as the Singrore Dhīmars are reported to do, but catch and keep it alive, and when the ceremony is concluded take it back again and deposit it in a river. After a girl has been married neither her father nor any of her own near relatives will ever take food again in the house of her husband's family, saying that they would rather starve. Each married couple also becomes a separate commensal group and will not eat with the parents of either of them. This is a common custom among low castes of mixed origin where every man is doubtful of his neighbour's parentage. Divorce and the remarriage of widows are permitted, and a woman may be divorced merely on the ground of incompetence in household management or because she does not please her husband's parents.

At child-birth they make a little separate hut for the mother near the river where they are encamped, and she remains in it for two days and a half. During this time her husband does no work; he stays a few paces distant from his wife's hut and prepares her food but does not go to the hut or touch her, and he kindles a fire between them. During the first two days the woman gets three handfuls of rice boiled thin in water, and on the third day she receives nothing until the evening, when the Sendia or head of the sept takes a little cowdung, gold and silver in his hand, and pouring water over this gives her of it to drink as many times as the number of gods worshipped by her family up to seven. Then she is pure. On this day the father sacrifices a chicken and gives a meal with liquor to the caste and names the child, calling it after one of his ancestors who is dead. Then an old woman beats on a brass plate and calls out the name which has been given in a loud voice to the whole camp so that they may all know the child's name. In Bilāspur the Sonjharas observe the custom of the Couvade, and for six days after the birth of a child the husband lies prone in his house, while the wife gets up and goes to work, coming home to give suck to the child when necessary. The man takes no food for three days and on the fourth is given ginger and raw sugar, thus undergoing the ordinary treatment of a woman after childbirth. This is supposed by them to be a sort of compensation for the labours sustained by the woman in bearing the child. The custom obtains among some other primitive races, but is now rapidly being abandoned by the Sonjharas.

4. Customs at birth.

5. Funeral rites.

The bodies of the old are cremated as a special honour, and those of other persons are buried. No one other than a member of the dead man's family may touch his corpse under a penalty of five rupees. A relative will remove the body and bury it with the feet pointing to the river or burn it by the water's edge. They mourn a child for one day and an adult for four days, and at the end the mourner is shaved and provides liquor for the community. If there be no relative, since no other man can touch the corpse, they fire the hut over it and burn it as it is lying or bury hut and body under a high mound of sand.

6. Religion.

Their principal deities are Dūlha Deo, the boy bridegroom, Nira his servant, and Kauria a form of Devi. Nira lives under an *ūmar*[1] tree and he and Dūlha Deo his master are worshipped every third year in the month of Māgh (January). Kauria is also worshipped once in three years on a Sunday in the month of Māgh with an offering of a cocoanut, and in her honour they never sit on a cot nor sleep on a stool because they think that the goddess has her seat on these articles. The real reason, however, is probably that the Sonjharas consider the use of such furniture an indication of a settled life and permanent residence, and therefore abjure it as being wanderers. Some analogous customs have been recorded of the Banjāras. They also revere the spirit of one of their female ancestors who became a Sati. They sacrifice a goat to the *genius loci* or spirit haunting the spot where they decide to start work; and they will leave it for fear of angering this spirit, which is said to appear in the form of a tiger, should they make a particularly good find.[2] They never keep dogs, and it is said that they are defiled by the touch of a dog and will throw away their food if one comes near them during their meal. The same rule applies to a cat, and they will throw away an earthen vessel touched by either of these animals. On the Diwāli day they wash their implements, and setting them up near the huts worship them with offerings of a cocoanut and vermilion.

7. Social customs.

Their rule is always to camp outside a village at a

---

[1] *F. glomerata.*
[2] *Bālāghāt Gazetteer*, C. E. Low, p. 207.

distance of not less than a mile. In the rains they make huts with a roof of bamboos sloping from a central ridge and walls of matting. The huts are built in one line and do not touch each other, at least a cubit's distance being left between each. Each hut has one door facing the east. As a rule they avoid the water of village wells and tanks, though it is not absolutely forbidden. Each man digs a shallow well in the sand behind his hut and drinks the water from it, and no man may drink the water of his neighbour's well; if he should do so or if any water from his well gets into his neighbour's, the latter is abandoned and a fresh one made. If the ground is too swampy for wells they collect the water in their wooden washing-tray and fill their vessels from it. In the cold weather they make little leaf-huts on the sand or simply camp out in the open, but they must never sleep under a tree. When living in the open each family makes two fires and sleeps together between them. Some of them have their stomachs burned and blackened from sleeping too near the fire. The Sonjharas will not take cooked food from the hands of any other caste, but their social status is very low, about equivalent to that of the parent Gond tribe. They have no fear of wild animals, not even the children. Perhaps they think that as fellow-denizens of the jungle these animals are kin to them and will not injure them.

8. Occupation.

The traditional occupation of the caste is to wash gold from the sandy beds of streams, while they formerly also washed for diamonds at Hirākud on the Mahānadi near Sambalpur and at Wairāgarh in Chānda. The industry is decaying, and in 1901 only a quarter of the total number of Sonjharas were still employed in it. Some have become cultivators and fishermen, while others earn their livelihood by sweeping up the refuse dirt of the workshops of goldsmiths and brass-workers; they wash out the particles of metal from this and sell it back to the Sunārs. The Mahānadi and Jonk rivers in Sambalpur, the Banjar in Mandla, the Son and other rivers in Bālāghāt, and the Wainganga and the eastern streams of Chānda contain minute particles of gold. The washers earn a miserable and uncertain livelihood, and indeed appear not to desire anything beyond a bare subsistence. In Bhandāra[1] it is said that they avoid any spot where they have previously been lucky, while in Chānda they have a superstition that a person making a good find of gold will be childless, and hence many dread the search.[2] When they set out to look for gold they wash three small trayfuls at three places about five cubits apart. If they find no appreciable quantity of gold they go on for one or two hundred yards and wash three more trayfuls, and proceed thus until they find a profitable place where they will halt for two or three days. A spot[3] in the dry river-bed is usually selected at the outside of a bend, where the finer sediment is likely to be found; after removing the stones and pebbles from above, the sand below is washed several times in circular wooden cradles, shaped like the top of an umbrella, of diminishing sizes, until all the clay is removed and fine particles of sand mixed with gold are visible. A large wooden spoon is used to stir up the sediment, which is washed and rubbed by hand to separate the gold more completely from the sand, and a blackish residue is left, containing particles of gold and mercury coloured black with oxide of iron. Mercury is used to pick up the gold with which it forms an amalgam. This is evaporated in a clay cupel called a *ghariya* by which the mercury is got rid of and the gold left behind.

Sudh,[4] **Sudha, Sudho, Suda.**—A cultivating caste in the Uriya country. Since the transfer of Sambalpur to Bengal only a few Sudhs remain in the Central Provinces. They are divided into four subcastes—the Bada or high Sudhs, the Dehri or worshippers, the Kabāt-konia or those holding the corners of the gate, and the Butka. These last are the most primitive and think that Rairākhol is their first home. They relate that they were born of the Pāndava hero Bhīmsen and the female demon Hedembiki, and were originally occupied in supplying leaves for the funeral ceremonies

---

[1] *Bhandāra Settlement Report* (A. J. Lawrence), p. 49.

[2] Major Lucie Smith's *Chānda Settlement Report* (1869), p. 105.

[3] The following account of the process of gold-washing is taken from Mr. Low's *Bālāghāt Gazetteer*, p. 201.

[4] This article is compiled from a paper by Mr. Bhāgirath Patnāik, Diwān of Rairākhol, and from notes taken by Mr. Hīra Lāl at Rairākhol.

of the Pāndava brothers, from which business they obtained their name of Butka or 'one who brings leaves.' They are practically a forest tribe and carry on shifting cultivation like the Khonds. According to their own story the ancestors of the Butka Sudhs once ruled in Rairākhol and reclaimed the land from the forest, that is so far as it has been reclaimed. The following story connects them with the ruling family of Rairākhol. In former times there was constant war between Bāmra and Rairākhol, and on one occasion the whole of the Rairākhol royal family was destroyed with the exception of one boy who was hidden by a Butka Sudh woman. She placed him in a cradle supported on four uprights, and when the Bāmra Rāja's soldiers came to seek for him the Sudhs swore, "If we have kept him either in heaven or earth may our god destroy us." The Bāmra people were satisfied with this reply and the child was saved, and on coming to manhood he won back his kingdom. He received the name of Janāmani or 'Jewel among men,' which the family still bear. In consequence of this incident, the Butka Sudhs are considered by the Rairākhol house as relations on their mother's side; they have several villages allotted to them and perform sacrifices for the ruling family. In some of these villages nobody may sleep on a cot or sit on a high chair, so as to be between heaven and earth in the position in which the child was saved. The Bada Sudhs are the most numerous subdivision and have generally adopted Hindu customs, so that the higher castes will take water from their hands. They neither drink liquor nor eat fowls, but the other subcastes do both. The Sudhs have totemistic *gotras* as Bhallūka (bear), Bāgh (tiger), Ullūka (owl), and others. They also have *bargas* or family names as Thākur (lord), Dānaik, Amāyat and Bīshi. The Thākur clan say that they used to hold the Baud kings in their lap for their coronation, and the Dānaik used to tie the king's turban. The Bīshi were so named because of their skill in arms, and the Amāyat collected materials for the worship of the Pānch Khanda or five swords. The *bargas* are much more numerous than the totemistic septs, and marriage either within the *barga* or within the sept is forbidden. Girls must be married before adolescence; and in the absence of a suitable husband, the girl is married to an old man who divorces her immediately afterwards, and she may then take a second husband at any time by the form for widow-remarriage. A betrothal is sealed by tying an areca-nut in a knot made from the clothes of a relative of each party and pounding it seven times with a pestle. After the marriage a silver ring is placed in a pot of water, over the mouth of which a leaf-plate is bound. The bridegroom pierces the leaf-plate with a knife, and the bride then thrusts her hand through the hole, picks out the ring and puts it on. The couple then go inside the house and sit down to a meal. The bridegroom, after eating part of his food, throws the leavings on to the bride's plate. She stops eating in displeasure, whereupon the bridegroom promises her some ornaments, and she relents and eats his leavings. It is customary for a Hindu wife to eat the leavings of food of her husband as a mark of her veneration for him. Divorce and the remarriage of widows are permitted. The Sudhs worship the Pānch Khanda or five swords, and in the Central Provinces they say that these are a representation of the five Pāndava brothers, in whose service their first ancestors were engaged. Their tutelary goddess is Khambeshwari, represented by a wooden peg (*khamba*). She dwells in the wilds of the Baud State and is supposed to fulfil all the desires of the Sudhs. Liquor, goats, buffaloes, vermilion and swallow-wort flowers are offered to her, the last two being in representation of blood. The Dehri Sudhs worship a goddess called Kandrāpat who dwells always on the summits of hills. It is believed that whenever worship is concluded the roar of her tiger is heard, and the worshippers then leave the place and allow the tiger to come and take the offerings. The goddess would therefore appear to be the deified tiger. The Bada Sudhs rank with the cultivating castes of Sambalpur, but the other three subcastes have a lower position.

SUNĀR

LIST OF PARAGRAPHS

1. *General notice of the caste.*
2. *Internal structure.*
3. *Marriage and other customs.*
4. *Religion.*
5. *Social position.*
6. *Manufacture of ornaments.*
7. *The sanctity of gold.*
8. *Ornaments. The marriage ornaments.*
9. *Beads and other ornaments.*
10. *Ear-piercing.*
11. *Origin of ear-piercing.*
12. *Ornaments worn as amulets.*
13. *Audhia Sunārs.*
14. *The Sunār as money-changer.*
15. *Malpractices of lower-class Sunārs.*

Sunār,[1] **Sonār, Soni, Hon-Potdār, Sarāf.**—The occupational caste of goldsmiths and silversmiths. The name is derived from the Sanskrit *Suvarna kār*, a worker in gold. In 1911 the Sunārs numbered 96,000 persons in the Central Provinces and 30,000 in Berār. They live all over the Province and are most numerous in the large towns. The caste appears to be a functional one of comparatively recent formation, and there is nothing on record as to its origin, except a collection of Brāhmanical legends of the usual type. The most interesting of these as related by Sir H. Risley is as follows:[2]

1. General notice of the caste.

"In the beginning of time, when the goddess Devi was busy with the construction of mankind, a giant called Sonwa-Daitya, whose body consisted entirely of gold, devoured her creations as fast as she made them. To baffle this monster the goddess created a goldsmith, furnished him with the tools of his art, and instructed him how to proceed.

---

[1] This article is partly based on an article by Mr. Raghunāth Prasād, E.A.C., formerly Deputy Superintendent of Census, with extracts from the late Mr. Nunn's Monograph on the Gold and Silver Industries, and on information furnished by Krishna Rao, Revenue Inspector, Mandla.

[2] *Tribes and Castes of Bengal*, art. Sunār.

When the giant proposed to eat him, the goldsmith suggested to him that if his body were polished his appearance would be vastly improved, and asked to be allowed to undertake the job. With the characteristic stupidity of his tribe the giant fell into the trap, and having had one finger polished was so pleased with the result that he agreed to be polished all over. For this purpose, like Aetes in the Greek legend of Medea, he had to be melted down, and the goldsmith, who was to get the body as his perquisite, giving the head only to Devi, took care not to put him together again. The goldsmith, however, overreached himself. Not content with his legitimate earnings, he must needs steal a part of the head, and being detected in this by Devi, he and his descendants were condemned to be for ever poor." The Sunārs also have a story that they are the descendants of one of two Rājpūt brothers, who were saved as boys by a Sāraswat Brāhman from the wrath of Parasurāma when he was destroying the Kshatriyas. The descendants of the other brother were the Khatris. This is the same story as is told by the Khatris of their own origin, but they do not acknowledge the connection with Sunārs, nor can the Sunārs allege that Sāraswat Brāhmans eat with them as they do with Khatris. In Gujarāt they have a similar legend connecting them with Banias. In Bombay they also claim to be Brāhmans, and in the Central Provinces a caste of goldsmiths akin to the Sunārs call themselves Vishwa Brāhmans. On the other hand, before and during the time of the Peshwas, Sunārs were not allowed to wear the sacred thread, and they were forbidden to hold their marriages in public, as it was considered unlucky to see a Sunār bridegroom. Sunār bridegrooms were not allowed to see the state umbrella or to ride in a palanquin, and had to be married at night and in secluded places, being subject to restrictions and annoyances from which even Mahārs were free.[1] Their *raison d'être* may possibly be found in the fact that the Brāhmans, all-powerful in the Poona state, were jealous of the pretensions of the Sunārs, and devised these rules as a means of suppressing them. It may be suggested that the Sunārs, being workers at an important urban

---

[1] *Bombay Gazetteer*, vol. xvii. p. 134.

industry, profitable in itself and sanctified by its association with the sacred metal gold, aspired to rank above the other artisans, and put forward the pretensions already mentioned, because they felt that their position was not commensurate with their deserts. But the Sunār is included in Grant-Duff's list of the twenty-four village menials of a Marātha village, and consequently he would in past times have ranked below the cultivators, from whom he must have accepted the annual presents of grain.

The caste have a number of subdivisions, nearly all of which are of the territorial class and indicate the various localities from which it has been recruited in these Provinces. The most important subcastes are the Audhia from Ajodhia or Oudh; the Purānia or old settlers; the Bundelkhandi from Bundelkhand; the Mālwi from Mālwa; the Lād from Lāt, the old name for the southern portion of Gujarāt; and the Mair, who appear to have been the first immigrants from Upper India and are named after Mair, the original ancestor, who melted down the golden demon. Other small groups are the Pātkars, so called because they allow *pāt* or widow-marriage, though, as a matter of fact, it is permitted by the great majority of the caste; the Pāndhare or 'White Sunārs'; and the Ahīr Sunārs, whose ancestors must presumably have belonged to the caste whose name they bear. The caste have also numerous *bainks* or exogamous septs, which differ entirely from the long lists given for Bengal and the United Provinces, and show, as Mr. Crooke remarks, the extreme fertility with which sections of this kind spring up. In the Central Provinces the names are of a titular or territorial nature. Examples of the former kind, that is, a title or nickname supposed to have been borne by the sept's founder, are: Dantele, one who has projecting teeth; Kāle, black; Munde, bald; Kolhīmāre, a killer of jackals; and Ladaiya, a jackal or a quarrelsome person. Among the territorial names are Narwaria from Narwar; Bhilsainyān from Bhilsa; Kanaujia from Kanauj; Dillīwāl from Delhi; Kālpiwāl from Kālpi. Besides the *bainks* or septs by which marriage is regulated, they have adopted the Brāhmanical eponymous *gotra*-names as Kashyap, Garg, Sāndilya, and so on. These are employed on ceremonial occasions as when a gift is made

2. Internal structure.

for the purpose of obtaining religious merit, and the *gotra*-name of the owner is recorded, but they do not influence marriage. The use of them is a harmless vanity analogous to the assumption of distinguished surnames by people who were not born to them.

3. Marriage and other customs.

Marriage is forbidden within the sept. In some localities persons descended from a common ancestor may not intermarry for five generations, but in others a brother's daughter may be wedded to a sister's son. A man is forbidden to marry two sisters while both are alive, and after his wife's death he may espouse her younger sister, but not her elder one. Girls are usually wedded at a tender age, but some Sunārs have hitherto had a rule that neither a girl nor a boy should be married until they had had smallpox, the idea being that there can be no satisfactory basis for a contract of marriage while either party is still exposed to such a danger to life and personal appearance ; just as it might be considered more prudent not to buy a young dog until it had had distemper. But with the spread of vaccination the Sunārs are giving up this custom. The marriage ceremony follows the Hindustāni or Marātha ritual according to locality.[1] In Betūl the mother of the bride ties the mother of the bridegroom to a pole with the ropes used for tethering buffaloes and beats her with a piece of twisted cloth, until the bridegroom's mother gives her a present of money or cloth and is released. The ceremony may be designed to express the annoyance of the bride's mother at being deprived of her daughter. Polygamy is permitted, but people will not give their daughter to a married man if they can find a bachelor husband for her. Well-to-do Sunārs who desire increased social distinction prohibit the marriage of widows, but the caste generally allow it.

4. Religion.

The caste venerate the ordinary Hindu deities, and many of them have sects and return themselves as Vaishnavas, Saivas or Sāktas. In some places they are said to make a daily offering to their melting-furnace so that it may bring them in a profit. When a child has been born they make a sacrifice of a goat to Dūlha Deo, the marriage-god, on the following Dasahra festival, and the body of this must be

---

[1] See articles on Kunbi and Kurmi.

eaten by the family only, no outsider being allowed to participate. In Hoshangābād it is stated that on the night before the Dasahra festival all the Sunārs assemble beside a river and hold a feast. Each of them is then believed to take an oath that he will not during the coming year disclose the amount of the alloy which a fellow-craftsman may mix with the precious metals. Any Sunār who violates this agreement is put out of caste. On the 15th day of Jeth (May) the village Sunār stops work for five days and worships his implements after washing them. He draws pictures of the goddess Devi on a piece of paper and goes round the village to affix them to the doors of his clients, receiving in return a small present.

The caste usually burn their dead and take the ashes to the Nerbudda or Ganges; those living to the south of the Nerbudda always stop at this river, because they think that if they crossed it to go to the Ganges, the Nerbudda would be offended at their not considering it good enough. If a man meets with a violent death and his body is lost, they construct a small image of him and burn this with all the proper ceremonies. Mourning is observed for ten or thirteen days, and the *shrāddh* ceremony is performed on the anniversary of a death, while the usual oblations are offered to the ancestors during the fortnight of Pitr Paksh in Kunwār (September).

5. Social position.

The more ambitious members of the caste abjure all flesh and liquor, and wear the sacred thread. These will not take cooked food even from a Brāhman. Others do not observe these restrictions. Brāhmans will usually take water from Sunārs, especially from those who wear the sacred thread. Owing to their association with the sacred metal gold, and the fact that they generally live in towns or large villages, and many of their members are well-to-do, the Sunārs occupy a fairly high position, ranking equal with, or above the cultivating castes. But, as already stated, the goldsmith was a village menial in the Marātha villages, and Sir D. Ibbetson thinks that the Jat really considers the Sunār to be distinctly inferior to himself.

6. Manufacture of ornaments.

The Sunār makes all kinds of ornaments of gold and silver, being usually supplied with the metal by his customers. He is paid according to the weight of metal used, the rate varying from four annas to two rupees with an average of a rupee per tola weight of metal for gold, and from one to two annas per tola weight of silver.[1] The lowness of these rates is astonishing when compared with those charged by European jewellers, being less than 10 per cent on the value of the metal for quite delicate ornaments. The reason is partly that ornaments are widely regarded as a means for the safe keeping of money, and to spend a large sum on the goldsmith's labour would defeat this end, as it would be lost on the reconversion of the ornaments into cash. Articles of elaborate workmanship are also easily injured when worn by women who have to labour in the fields or at home. These considerations have probably retarded the development of the goldsmith's art, except in a few isolated localities where it may have had the patronage of native courts, and they account for the often clumsy form and workmanship of his ornaments. The value set on the products of skilled artisans in early times is nevertheless shown by the statement in M'Crindle's *Ancient India* that any one who caused an artisan to lose the use of an eye or a hand was put to death.[2] In England the jeweller's profit on his wares is from 33 to 50 per cent or more, in which, of course, allowance is made for the large amount of capital locked up in them and the time they may remain on his hands. But the difference in rates is nevertheless striking, and allowance must be made for it in considering the bad reputation which the Sunār has for mixing alloy with the metal. Gold ornaments are simply hammered or punched into shape or rudely engraved, and are practically never cast or moulded. They are often made hollow from thin plate or leaf, the interior being filled up with lac. Silver ones are commonly cast in Saugor and Jubbulpore, but rarely elsewhere. The Sunār's trade appears now to be fairly prosperous, but during the famines it was greatly depressed and many members of the caste took to other occupations. Many Sunārs make small articles of brass, such as chains, bells and little boxes. Others have become cultivators and drive the

---

[1] Monograph on the Gold and Silverware of the Central Provinces (Mr. H. Nunn, I.C.S.), 1904. The tola is a rupee's weight, or two-fifths of an ounce.
[2] *Journal of Indian Art*, July 1909, p. 172.

plough themselves, a practice which has the effect of spoiling their hands, and also prevents them from giving their sons a proper training. To be a good Sunār the hands must be trained from early youth to acquire the necessary delicacy of touch. The Sunār's son sits all day with his father watching him work and handling the ornaments. Formerly the Sunār never touched a plough. Like the Pekin ivory painter—

> From early dawn he works;
> And all day long, and when night comes the lamp
> Lights up his studious forehead and thin hands.

As already stated, the Sunār obtains some social distinction from working in gold, which is a very sacred metal with the Hindus. Gold ornaments must not on this account be worn below the waist, as to do so would be considered an indignity to the holy material. Marātha and Khedāwāl Brāhman women will not have ornaments for the head and arms of any baser metal than gold. If they cannot afford gold bracelets they wear only glass ones. Other castes should, if they can afford it, wear only gold on the head. And at any rate the nose-ring and small earrings in the upper ear should be of gold if worn at all. When a man is at the point of death, a little gold, Ganges water, and a leaf of the *tulsi* or basil plant are placed in his mouth, so that these sacred articles may accompany him to the other world. So valuable as a means of securing a pure death is the presence of gold in the mouth that some castes have small pieces inserted into a couple of their upper teeth, in order that wherever and whenever they may die, the gold may be present to purify them.[1] A similar idea was prevalent in Europe. *Aurum potabile*[2] or drinkable gold was a favourite nostrum of the Middle Ages, because gold being perfect should produce perfect health; and patients when *in extremis* were commonly given water in which gold had been washed. And the belief is referred to by Shakespeare:

7. The sanctity of gold.

> Therefore, thou best of gold art worst of gold:
> Other, less fine in carat, is more precious,
> Preserving life in medicine potable.[3]

---

[1] From a monograph on rural customs in Saugor, by Major W. D. Sutherland, I.M.S.
[2] Lang, *Myth, Ritual and Religion*, i. p. 98.
[3] *2 King Henry IV*. Act IV. Sc. 4.

The metals which are used for currency, gold, silver and copper, are all held sacred by the Hindus, and this is easily explained on the grounds of their intrinsic value and their potency when employed as coin. It may be noted that when the nickel anna coinage was introduced, it was held in some localities that the coins could not be presented at temples as this metal was not sacred.

8. Ornaments. The marriage ornaments.

It can scarcely also be doubted in view of this feeling that the wearing of both gold and silver in ornaments is considered to have a protective magical effect, like that attributed to charms and amulets. And the suggestion has been made that this was the object with which all ornaments were originally worn. Professor Robertson Smith remarks :[1] " Jewels, too, such as women wore in the sanctuary, had a sacred character ; the Syriac word for an earring is *c' dāsha*, 'the holy thing,' and generally speaking, jewels serve as amulets. As such they are mainly worn to protect the chief organs of action (the hands and feet), but especially the orifices of the body, as earrings ; nose-rings hanging over the mouth ; jewels on the forehead hanging down and protecting the eyes." The precious metals, as has been seen, are usually sacred among primitive people, and when made into ornaments they have the same sanctity and protective virtue as jewels. The subject has been treated [2] with great fullness of detail by Sir J. Campbell, and the different ornaments worn by Hindu women of the Central Provinces point to the same conclusion. The *bindia* or head ornament of a Marātha Brāhman woman consists of two chains of silver or gold and in the centre an image of a cobra erect. This is Shesh-Nāg, the sacred snake, who spreads his hood over all the *lingas* of Mahādeo and is placed on the woman's head to guard her in the same way. The Kurmis and other castes do not have Shesh-Nāg, but instead the centre of the *bindia* consists of an ornament known as *bīja*, which represents the custard-apple, the sacred fruit of Sīta. The *nathni* or nose-ring, which was formerly confined to high-caste women, represents the sun and moon. The large hoop circle is the sun, and underneath in the part below

---

[1] *Religion of the Semites*, note B., p. 453.

[2] *Bombay Gazetteer, Poona*, App. D., Ornaments.

LIST OF ORNAMENTS, FROM LEFT TO RIGHT.

Three bracelets on top of board, from left to right:—
    1.—Anklet with links like coils of a snake.
    2.—*Tora*, or solid anklet.
    3.—*Naugrihi*, or wristlet of nine planets.

Second row, from left to right:—
    4.—Large *nathni*, or nose-ring.
    5.—Another *naugrihi*.
    6.—*Bīja*, or custard apple worn on head above *bindia*.
    7.—*Bindia*, or ornament worn on head.
    8.—*Hamel*, or necklace of rupees with betel-leaf pendant.

Third row, from left to right:—
    9.—Small *nathni*, or nose-ring.
    10.—*Bora*, or waistband with beads like smallpox postules.
    11.—*Kantha*, or gold necklace.
    12.—*Bohta*, or circlet for upper arm.
    13.—*Hasli*, or necklet like collar-bone.

Fourth row, from left to right:—
    14.—*Karanphūl*, or earring like marigold.
    15.—*Paijan*, or hollow tinkling anklet.
    16.—*Dhara*, or earring like shield.
    17.—Another anklet.
    18.—Another armlet, called "*koparbela*."

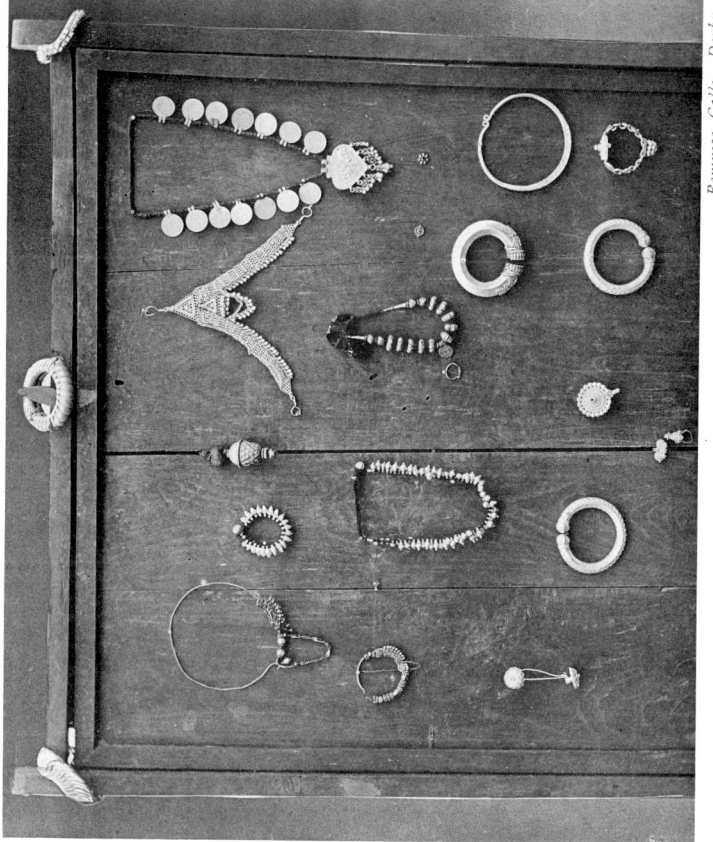

ORNAMENTS.

the nose is a small segment, which is the crescent moon and is hidden when the ornament is in wear. On the front side of this are red stones, representing the sun, and on the underside white ones for the moon. The *nathni* has some mysterious connection with a woman's virtue, and to take off her nose-ring—*nathni utārna*—signifies to dishonour a woman (Platts). In northern India women wear the nose-ring very large and sometimes cover it with a piece of cloth to guard it from view or keep it in *parda*. It is possible that the practice of Hindu husbands of cutting off the nose of a wife detected in adultery has some similar association, and is partly intended to prevent her from again wearing a nose-ring. The toe ornament of a high-caste woman is called *bichhia* and it represents a scorpion (*bichhu*). A ring on the big toe stands for the scorpion's head, a silver chain across the foot ending in another ring on the little toe is his body, and three rings with high projecting knobs on the middle toes are the joints of his tail folded back. It is of course supposed that the ornament protects the feet from scorpion bites. These three ornaments, the *bindia*, the *nathni* and the *bichhia*, must form part of the Sohāg or wedding dowry of every high-caste Hindu girl in the northern Districts, and she cannot be married without them. But if the family is poor a *laong* or gold stud to be worn in the nose may be substituted for the nose-ring. This stud, as its name indicates, is in the form of a clove, which is sacred food and is eaten on fast-days. Burning cloves are often used to brand children for cold; a fresh one being employed for each mark. A widow may not wear any of these ornaments; she is always impure, being perpetually haunted by the ghost of her dead husband, and they could thus be of no advantage to her; while, on the other hand, her wearing them would probably be considered a kind of sacrilege or pollution of the holy ornaments.

In the Marātha Districts an essential feature of a wedding is the hanging of the *mangal-sūtram* or necklace of black beads round the bride's neck. All beads which shine and reflect the light are considered to be efficacious in averting the evil eye, and a peculiar virtue, Sir J. Campbell states, attaches to black beads. A woman wears the *mangal-*

9. Beads and other ornaments.

sūtram or marriage string of beads all her life, and considers that her husband's life is to some extent bound up in it. If she breaks the thread she will not say 'my thread is broken,' but 'my thread has increased'; and she will not let her husband see her until she has got a new thread, as she thinks that to do so would cause his death. The many necklaces of beads worn by the primitive tribes and the strings of blue beads tied round the necks of oxen and ponies have the same end in view. A similar belief was probably partly responsible for the value set on precious stones as ornaments, and especially on diamonds, which sparkle most of all. The pearl is very sacred among the Hindus, and Madrāsis put a pearl into the mouth at the time of death instead of gold. Partly at least for this purpose pearls are worn set in a ring of gold in the ear, so that they may be available at need. Coral is also highly esteemed as an amulet, largely because it is supposed to change colour. The coral given to babies to suck may have been intended to render the soft and swollen gums at teething hard like the hard red stone. Another favourite shape for beads of gold is that of grains of rice, rice being a sacred grain. The gold ornament called *kantha* worn on the neck has carvings of the flowers of the *singāra* or water-nut. This is a holy plant, the eating of which on fast-days gives purity. Hence women think that water thrown over the carved flowers of the ornament when bathing will have greater virtue to purify their bodies. Another favourite ornament is the *hamel* or necklace of rupees. The sanctity of coined metal would probably be increased by the royal image and superscription and also by its virtue as currency. Mr. Nunn states that gold mohur coins are still made solely for the purpose of ornament, being commonly engraved with the formula of belief of Islām and worn by Muhammadans as a charm. Suspended to the *hamel* or necklace of rupees in front is a silver pendant in the shape of a betel-leaf, this leaf being very efficacious in magic; and on this is carved either the image of Hanumān, the god of strength, or a peacock's feather as a symbol of Kārtikeya, the god of war. The silver bar necklet known as *hasli* is intended to resemble the collar-bone. Children carried in their mother's cloth are liable to be jarred and shaken against her body, so that the collar-bone is bruised and becomes painful. It is thought that the wearing of a silver collar-bone will prevent this, just as silver eyes are offered in smallpox to protect the sufferer's eyes and a silver wire to save his throat from being choked. Little children sometimes have round the waist a band of silver beads which is called *bora*; these beads are meant to resemble the smallpox pustules and the *bora* protects the wearer from smallpox. There are usually 84 beads, this number being lucky among the Hindus. At her wedding a Hindu bride must wear a wristlet of nine little cones of silver like the *kalas* or pinnacle of a temple. This is called *nau-graha* or *nau-giri* and represents the nine planets which are worshipped at weddings—that is, the sun, moon and the five planets, Mars, Mercury, Jupiter, Venus and Saturn, which were known to the ancients and gave their names to the days of the week in many of the Aryan languages; while the remaining two are said to have been Rahu and Ketu, the nodes of the moon and the demons which cause eclipses. The *bonhta* or *bānkra*, the rigid circular bangle on the upper arm, is supposed to make a woman's arm stronger by the pressure exercised on the veins and muscles. Circular ornaments worn on the legs similarly strengthen them and prevent a woman from getting stiffness or pins and needles in her legs after long squatting on the ground. The *chutka*, a large silver ring worn by men on the big toe, is believed to attract to itself the ends of all the veins and ligaments from the navel downwards, and hold them all braced in their proper position, thus preventing rupture.

On their feet children and young girls wear the *paijan* or hollow anklet with tinkling balls inside. But when a married woman has had two or three children she leaves off the *paijan* and wears a solid anklet like the *tora* or *kasa*. It is now said that the reason why girls wear sounding anklets is that their whereabouts may be known and they may be prevented from getting into mischief in dark corners. But the real reason was probably that they served as spirit scarers, which they would do in effect by frightening away snakes, scorpions and noxious insects; for it is clear that the bites of such reptiles and insects, which often escape unseen, must be largely responsible for the vast imaginative fabric of the belief in evil spirits, just as Professor Robertson Smith demonstrates that the *jins* or *genii* of Arabia were really wild animals.[1] In India, owing to the early age of marriage and the superstitious maltreatment of women at child-birth, the mortality among girls at this period is very high; and the Hindus, ignorant of the true causes, probably consider them especially susceptible to the attacks of evil spirits.

10. Ear-piercing.

Before treating of ear-ornaments it will be convenient to mention briefly the custom of ear-piercing. This is universal among Hindus and Muhammadans, both male and female, and the operation is often performed by the Sunār. The lower Hindu castes and the Gonds consider piercing the ears to be the mark of admission to the caste community. It is done when the child is four or five years old, and till then he or she is not considered to be a member of the caste and may consequently take food from anybody. The Rāj-Gonds will not have the ears of their children pierced by any one but a Sunār; and for this they give him *sīdha* or a seer[2] of wheat, a seer of rice and an anna. Hindus employ a Sunār when one is available, but if not, an old man of the family may act. After the piercing a peacock's feather or some stalks of grass or straw are put in to keep the hole open and enlarge it. A Hindu girl has her ear pierced in five places, three being in the upper ear, one in the lobe and one in the small flap over the orifice. Muhammadans make a large number of holes all down the ear and in each of these they place a gold or silver ring, so that the ears are dragged down by the weight. Similarly their women will have ten or fifteen bangles on the legs. The Hindus also have this custom in Bhopāl, but if they do it in the Central Provinces they are chaffed with having become Muhammadans. In the upper ear Hindu women have an ornament in the shape of the *genda* or marigold, a sacred flower which is offered to all the deities. The holes in the upper and middle ear are only large enough to contain a small ring, but that in the lobe

---

[1] *Religion of the Semites*, Lecture III.   [2] 2 lbs.

is greatly distended among the lower castes. The *tarkhi* or Gond ear-ornament consists of a glass plate fixed on to a stem of *ambāri* fibre nearly an inch thick, which passes through the lobe. As a consequence the lower rim is a thin pendulous strip of flesh, very liable to get torn. But to have the hole torn open is one of the worst social mishaps which can happen to a woman. She is immediately put out of caste for a long period, and only readmitted after severe penalties, equivalent to those inflicted for getting vermin in a wound. When a woman gets her ear torn she sits weeping in her house and refuses to be comforted. At the ceremony of readmission a Sunār is sometimes called in who stitches up the ear with silver thread.[1] Low-caste Hindu and Gond women often wear a large circular embossed silver ornament over the ear which is known as *dhāra* or shield and is in the shape of an Indian shield. This is secured by chains to the hair and apparently affords some support to the lower part of the ear, which it also covers. Its object seems to be to shield and protect the lobe, which is so vulnerable in a woman, and hence the name. A similar ornament worn in Bengal is known as *dhenri* and consists of a shield-shaped disk of gold, worn on the lobe of the ear, sometimes with and sometimes without a pendant.[2]

11. Origin of ear-piercing.

The character of the special significance which apparently attaches to the custom of ear-piercing is obscure. Dr. Jevons considers that it is merely a relic of the practice of shedding the blood of different parts of the body as an offering to the deity, and analogous to the various methods of self-mutilation, flagellation and gashing of the flesh, whose common origin is ascribed to the same custom. "To commend themselves and their prayers the Quiches pierced their ears and gashed their arms and offered the sacrifice of their blood to their gods. The practice of drawing blood from the ears is said by Bastian to be common in the Orient; and Lippert conjectures that the marks left in the ears were valued as visible and permanent indications that

---

[1] From a paper on Caste Panchāyats, by the Rev. Failbus, C.M.S. Mission, Mandla.

[2] Rājendra Lāl Mitra, *Indo-Aryans*, vol. i. p. 231.

the person possessing them was under the protection of the god with whom the worshipper had united himself by his blood offering. In that case earrings were originally designed, not for ornament, but to keep open and therefore permanently visible the marks of former worship. The marks or scars left on legs or arms from which blood had been drawn were probably the origin of tattooing, as has occurred to various anthropologists."[1] This explanation, while it may account for the general custom of ear-piercing, does not explain the special guilt imputed by the Hindus to getting the lobe of the ear torn. Apparently the penalty is not imposed for the tearing of the upper part of the ear, and it is not known whether men are held liable as well as women; but as large holes are not made in the upper ear at all, nor by men in the lobe, such cases would very seldom occur. The suggestion may be made as a speculation that the continuous distension of the lobe of the ear by women and the large hole produced is supposed to have some sympathetic effect in opening the womb and making child-birth more easy. The tearing of the ear might then be considered to render the women incapable of bearing a child, and the penalties attached to it would be sufficiently explained.

12. Ornaments worn as amulets.

The above account of the ornaments of a Hindu woman is sufficient to show that her profuse display of them is not to be attributed, as is often supposed, to the mere desire for adornment. Each ornament originally played its part in protecting some limb or feature from various dangers of the seen or unseen world. And though the reasons which led to their adoption have now been to a large extent forgotten and the ornaments are valued for themselves, the shape and character remain to show their real significance. Women as being weaker and less accustomed to mix in society are naturally more superstitious and fearful of the machinations of spirits. And the same argument applies in greater degree to children. The Hindus have probably recognised that children are very delicate and succumb easily to disease, and they could scarcely fail to have done so when statistics show that about a quarter of all the babies born in India die in the first year of age. But they do not

[1] *Introduction to the History of Religion*, 3rd ed. p. 172.

attribute the mortality to its real causes of congenital weakness arising from the immaturity of the parents, insanitary treatment at and after birth, unsuitable food, and the general frailty of the undeveloped organism. They ascribe the loss of their offspring solely to the machinations of jealous deities and evil spirits, and the envy and admiration of other people, especially childless women and witches, who cast the evil eye upon them. And in order to guard against these dangers their bodies are decorated with amulets and ornaments as a means of protection. But the result is quite other than that intended, and the ornaments which are meant to protect the children from the imaginary terrors of the evil eye, in reality merely serve as a whet to illicit cupidity, and expose them a rich, defenceless prey to the violence of the murderer and the thief.

13. Audhia Sunārs.

The Audhia Sunārs usually work in bell-metal, an alloy of copper or tin and pewter. When used for ornaments the proportion of tin or pewter is increased so as to make them of a light colour, resembling silver as far as may be. Women of the higher castes may wear bell-metal ornaments only on their ankles and feet, and Marātha and Khedāwāl Brāhmans may not wear them at all. In consequence of having adopted this derogatory occupation, as it is considered, the Audhia Sunārs are looked down on by the rest of the caste. They travel about to the different village markets carrying their wares on ponies; among these, perhaps, the favourite ornament is the *kara* or curved bar anklets, which the Audhia works on to the purchaser's feet for her, forcing them over the heels with a piece of iron like a shoe-horn. The process takes time and is often painful, the skin being rasped by the iron. The woman is supported by a friend as her foot is held up behind, and is sometimes reduced to cries and tears. High-caste women do not much affect the *kara* as they object to having their foot grasped by the Sunār. They wear instead a chain anklet which they can work on themselves. The Sunārs set precious stones in ornaments, and this is also done by a class of persons called Jadia, who do not appear to be a caste. Another body of persons accessory to the trade are the Niārias, who take the ashes and sweepings from the goldsmith's shop, paying a sum of ten or twenty rupees annually for them.[1] They wash away the refuse and separate the grains of gold and silver, which they sell back to the Sunārs. Niāria also appears to be an occupational term, and not a caste.

14. The Sunār as money-changer. Formerly Sunārs were employed for counting and testing money in the public treasuries, and in this capacity they were designated as Potdār and Sarāf or Shroff. Before the introduction of the standard English coinage the money-changer's business was important and profitable, as the rupee varied over different parts of the country exactly as grain measures do now. Thus the Pondicherry rupee was worth 26 annas, while the Gujarāt rupee would not fetch $12\frac{1}{2}$ annas in the bazār. In Bengal,[2] at the beginning of the nineteenth century, people who wished to make purchases had first to exchange their rupees for cowries. The Potdār carried his cowries to market in the morning on a bullock, and gave 5760 cowries for a new *kaldār* or English rupee, while he took 5920 cowries in exchange for a rupee when his customers wanted silver back in the evening to take away with them. The profit on the *kaldār* rupee was thus one thirty-sixth on the two transactions, while all old rupees, and every kind of rupee but the *kaldār*, paid various rates of exchange or *batta*, according to the will of the money-changers, who made a higher profit on all other kinds of money than the *kaldār*. They therefore resisted the general introduction of these rupees as long as possible, and when this failed they hit on a device of marking the rupees with a stamp, under pretext of ascertaining whether they were true or false; after which the rupee was not exchangeable without paying an additional *batta*, and became as valuable to the money-changers as if it were foreign coin. As justification for their action they pretended to the people that the marks would enable those who had received the rupees to have them changed should any other dealer refuse them, and the necessities of the poor compelled them to agree to any *batta* or exchange rather than suffer delay. This was apparently the origin of the 'Shroff-marked rupees,' familiar to readers of the *Treasury Manual*; and the line in a Bhāt song, 'The

---

[1] Monograph, *loc. cit.*
[2] This account is taken from Buchanan's *Eastern India*, vol. ii. p. 100.

English have made current the *kaldār* (milled) rupee,' is thus seen to be no empty praise.

As the bulk of the capital of the poorer classes is hoarded in the shape of gold and silver ornaments, these are regularly pledged when ready money is needed, and the Sunār often acts as a pawnbroker. In this capacity he too often degenerates into a receiver of stolen property, and Mr. Nunn suggested that his proceedings should be supervised by license. Generally, the Sunār is suspected of making an illicit profit by mixing alloy with the metal entrusted to him by his customers, and some bitter sayings are current about him. One of his customs is to filch a little gold from his mother and sister on the last day of Shrāwan (July) and make it into a luck-penny.[1] This has given rise to the saying, 'The Sunār will not respect even his mother's gold'; but the implication appears to be unjust. Another saying is: '*Sona Sunār kā, abharan sansār ka,*' or, 'The ornament is the customer's, but the gold remains with the Sunār.'[2] Gold is usually melted in the employer's presence, who, to guard against fraud, keeps a small piece of the metal called *chāsni* or *māslo*, that is a sample, and when the ornament is ready sends it with the sample to an assayer or *Chokshi* who, by rubbing them on a touchstone, tells whether the gold in the sample and the ornament is of the same quality. Further, the employer either himself sits near the Sunār while the ornament is being made or sends one of his family to watch. In spite of these precautions the Sunār seldom fails to filch some of the gold while the spy's attention is distracted by the prattling of the parrot, by the coquetting of a handsomely dressed young woman of the family or by some organised mishap in the inner rooms among the women of the house.[3] One of his favourite practices is to substitute copper for gold in the interior, and this he has the best chance of doing with the marriage ornaments, as many people consider it unlucky to weigh or test the quality of these.[4] The account must, however, be taken to apply only to the small artisans,

15. Malpractices of lower-class Sunārs.

---

[1] *Bombay Gazetteer*, vol. xii. p. 71.

[2] Temple and Fallon's *Hindustāni Proverbs.*

[3] *Bombay Gazetteer, Hindus of Gujarāt*, pp. 199, 200.

[4] Pandian's *Indian Village Folk*, p. 41.

and well-to-do reputable Sunārs would be above such practices.

The goldsmith's industry has hitherto not been affected to any serious extent by the competition of imported goods, and except during periods of agricultural depression the Sunār continues to prosper.

A Persian couplet said by a lover to his mistress is, 'Gold has no scent and in the scent of flowers there is no gold ; but thou both art gold and hast scent.'

Sundi, Sundhi, Sunri or **Sondhi.**[1]—The liquor-distilling caste of the Uriya country. The transfer of Sambalpur and the Uriya States to Bihār and Orissa has reduced their strength in the Central Provinces to about 5000, found in the Raipur District and the Bastar and Chota Nāgpur Feudatory States. The caste is an important one in Bengal, numbering more than six lakhs of persons and being found in western Bengal and Bihār as well as in Orissa. The word Sundi is derived from the Sanskrit Shaundik, a spirit-seller. The caste has various genealogies of differing degrees of respectability, tracing their origin to cross unions between other castes born of Brāhmans, Kshatriyas, and Vaishyas. The following story is told of them in Madras.[2] In ancient times a certain Brāhman was famous for his magical attainments. The king of the country sent for him one day and asked him to cause the water in a tank to burn. The Brāhman saw no way of doing this, and returned homewards uneasy in his mind. On the way he met a distiller who asked him to explain what troubled him. When the Brāhman told his story the distiller promised to cause the water to burn on condition that the Brāhman gave him his daughter in marriage. This the Brāhman agreed to do, and the distiller, after surreptitiously pouring large quantities of liquor into the tank, set fire to it in the presence of the king. In accordance with the agreement he married the daughter of the Brāhman and the pair became the ancestors of the Sundi caste. In confirmation of the story it is alleged that up to the present day the women of the caste maintain the

---

[1] This article is compiled from a paper by Mr. D. Mitra, pleader, Sambalpur.
[2] *Madras Census Report*, 1891, p. 301.

recollection of their Brāhman ancestors by refusing to eat fowls or the remains of their husbands' meals. Nor will they take food from the hands of any other caste. Sir H. Risley relates the following stories current about the caste in Bengal, where its status is very low: "According to Hindu ideas, distillers and sellers of strong drink rank among the most degraded castes, and a curious story in the Vaivarta Purāna keeps alive the memory of their degradation. It is said that when Sani, the Hindu Saturn, failed to adapt an elephant's head to the mutilated trunk of Ganesh who had been accidentally slain by Siva, Viswākarma, the celestial artificer, was sent for, and by careful dissection and manipulation he fitted the incongruous parts together, and made a man called Kedāra Sena from the slices cut off in fashioning his work. This Kedāra Sena was ordered to fetch a drink of water for Bhagavati, weary and athirst. Finding on the river's bank a shell full of water he presented it to her, without noticing that a few grains of rice left in it by a parrot had fermented and formed an intoxicating liquid. Bhagavati, as soon as she had drunk, became aware of the fact, and in her anger condemned the offender to the vile and servile occupation of making spirituous liquors for mankind." Like other castes in Sambalpur the Sundis have two subcastes, the Jhārua and the Utkal or Uriya, of whom the Jhāruas probably immigrated from Orissa at an earlier period and adopted some of the customs of the indigenous tribes; for this reason they are looked down on by the more orthodox Utkalis. The caste say that they belong to the Nāgas or snake gotra, because they consider themselves to be descended from Bāsuki, the serpent with a thousand heads who formed a canopy for Vishnu. They also have *bargas* or family titles, but these at present exercise no influence on marriage. The Sundis have in fact outgrown the system of exogamy and regulate their marriages by a table of prohibited degrees in the ordinary manner, the unions of *sapindas* or persons who observe mourning together at a death being prohibited. The prohibition does not extend to cognatic relationship, but a man must not marry into the family of his paternal aunt. The fact that the old *bargas* or exogamous groups are still in existence is interesting, and an intermediate step in the process of their abandonment may be recognised in the fact that some of them are subdivided. Thus the Sāhu (lord) group has split into the Gaj Sāhu (lord of the elephant), Dhavila Sāhu (white lord), and Amila Sāhu sub-groups, and it need not be doubted that this was a convenient method adopted for splitting up the Sāhu group when it became so large as to include persons so distantly connected with each other that the prohibition of marriage between them was obviously ridiculous. As the number of Sundis in the Central Provinces is now insignificant no detailed description of their customs need be given, but one or two interesting points may be noted. Their method of observing the *pitripaksh* or worship of ancestors is as follows: A human figure is made of *kusha* grass and placed under a miniature straw hut. A lamp is kept burning before it for ten days, and every day a twig for cleaning the teeth is placed before it, and it is supplied with fried rice in the morning and rice, pulse and vegetables in the evening. On the tenth day the priest comes, and after bathing the figure seven times, places boiled rice before it for the last meal, and then sets fire to the hut and burns it, while repeating sacred verses. On the eleventh day after a death, when presents for the use of the deceased are made to a priest as his representative, the priest lies down in the new bed which is given to him, and the members of the family rub his feet and attend on him as if he were the dead man. He is also given a present sufficient to purchase food for him for a year. The Sundis worship Surādevi or the goddess of wine, whom they consider as their mother, and they refuse to drink liquor, saying that this would be to enjoy their own mother. They worship the still and all articles used in distillation at the rice-harvest and when the new mango crop appears. Large numbers of them have taken to cultivation.

1. The Tamera and Kasār.

Tamera, Tambatkar.[1]—The professional caste of coppersmiths, the name being derived from *tāmba*, copper. The

---

[1] This article is based on information contributed by Nand Kishore, Nāzir of the Deputy Commissioner's Office, Damoh; Mr. Tārāchand Dube, Municipal Member, Bilāspur; and Mr. Adurām Chaudhri of the Gazetteer Office.

Tameras, however, like the Kasārs or brass-workers, use copper, brass and bell-metal indifferently, and in the northern Districts the castes are not really distinguished, Tamera and Kasār being almost interchangeable terms. In the Marātha country, however, and other localities they are considered as distinct castes. Copper is a sacred metal, and the coppersmith's calling would be considered somewhat more respectable than that of the worker in brass or bell-metal, just as the Sunār or goldsmith ranks above both; and probably, therefore, the Tameras may consider themselves a little better than the Kasārs. As brass is an alloy made from copper and zinc, it seems likely that vessels were made from copper before they were made from brass. But copper being a comparatively rare and expensive metal, utensils made from it could scarcely have ever been generally used, and it is therefore not necessary to suppose that either the Tamera or Kasār caste came into being before the adoption of brass as a convenient material for the household pots and pans.

2. Social traditions and customs.

In 1911 the Tameras numbered about 5000 persons in the Central Provinces and Berār. They tell the same story of their origin which has already been related in the article on the Kasār caste, and trace their descent from the Haihaya Rājpūt dynasty of Ratanpur. They say that when the king Dharampāl, the first ancestor of the caste, was married, a bevy of 119 girls were sent with his bride in accordance with the practice still occasionally obtaining among royal Hindu families, and these, as usual, became the concubines of the husband or, as the Tameras say, his wives: and from the bride and her companions the 120 exogamous sections of the caste are sprung. As a fact, however, many of the sections are named after villages or natural objects. A man is not permitted to marry any one belonging to his own section or that of his mother, the union of first cousins being thus prohibited. The caste also do not favour *Anta sānta* or the practice of exchanging girls between families, the reason alleged being that after the bride's father has acknowledged the superiority of the bridegroom's father by washing his feet, it is absurd to require the latter to do the same, that is, to wash the feet of his inferior. So they may not take a girl from a family to which they have given one of their own. The real reason for the rule lies possibly in an extension of the principle of exogamy, whether based on a real fear of carrying too far the practice of intermarriage between families or an unfounded superstition that intermarriage between families already connected may have the same evil results on the offspring as the union of blood-relations. When the wedding procession is about to start, after the bridegroom has been bathed and before he puts on the *kankan* or iron wristlet which is to protect him from evil spirits, he is seated on a stool while all the male members of the household come up with their *choti* or scalp-lock untied and rub it against that of the bridegroom. Again, after the wedding ceremonies are over and the bridegroom has, according to rule, untied one of the fastenings of the marriage-shed, he also turns over a tile of the roof of the house. The meaning of the latter ceremony is not clear; the significance attaching to the *choti* has been discussed in the article on Nai.

3. Disposal of the dead.

The caste burn their dead except children, who can be buried, and observe mourning for ten days in the case of an adult and for three days for a child. A cake of flour containing two pice (farthings) is buried or burnt with the corpse. When a death takes place among the community all the members of it stop making vessels for that day, though they will transact retail sales. When mourning is over, a feast is given to the caste-fellows and to seven members of the menial and serving castes. These are known as the 'Sāttiho Jāt' or Seven Castes, and it may be conjectured that in former times they were the menials of the village and were given a meal in much the same spirit as prompts an English landlord to give his tenants a dinner on occasions of ceremony. Instances of a similar custom are noted among the Kunbis and other castes. Before food is served to the guests a leaf-plate containing a portion for the deceased is placed outside the house with a pot of water, and a burning lamp to guide his spirit to the food.

4. Religion.

The caste worship the goddess Singhbāhani or Devi riding on a tiger. They make an image of her in the most expensive metal they can afford, and worship it daily. They will on no account swear by this goddess. They worship their trade implements on the day of the new moon in Chait (March) and Bhādon (August). A trident, as a symbol of Devi, is then drawn with powdered rice and vermilion on the furnace for casting metal. A lamp is waved over the furnace and a cocoanut is broken and distributed to the caste-fellows, no outsider being allowed to be present. They quench their furnace on the new moon day of every month, the Rāmnaomi and Durgapūja or nine days' fasts in the months of Chait and Kunwār, and for the two days following the Diwāli and Holi festivals. On these days they will not prepare any new vessels, but will sell those which they have ready. The Tameras have Kanaujia Brāhmans for their priests, and the Brāhmans will take food from them which has been cooked without water and salt. On this account other Kanaujia Brāhmans require a heavy payment before they will marry with the priests of the Tameras. The caste abstain from liquor, and some of them have abjured all flesh food while others partake of it. They usually wear the sacred thread. Brāhmans will take water from their hands, and the menial castes will eat food which they have touched. They work in brass, copper and bell-metal in exactly the same manner as the Kasārs, and have an equivalent social position.

Taonla.—A small non-Aryan caste of the Uriya States. They reside principally in Bāmra and Sonpur, and numbered about 2000 persons in 1901, but since the transfer of these States to Bengal are not found in the Central Provinces. The name is said to be derived from Tālmūl, a village in the Angul District of Orissa, and they came to Bāmra and Sonpur during the Orissa famine of 1866. The Taonlas appear to be a low occupational caste of mixed origin, but derived principally from the Khond tribe. Formerly their profession was military service, and it is probable that like the Khandaits and Pāiks they formed the levies of some of the Uriya Rājas, and gradually became a caste. They have three subdivisions, of which the first consists of the Taonlas whose ancestors were soldiers. These consider themselves superior to the others, and their family names as Nāik (leader), Padhān (chief), Khandait (swordsman), and Behra (master of the kitchen) indicate their ancestral profession. The other subcastes are called Dāngua and Khond; the Dānguas, who are hill-dwellers, are more primitive than the military Taonlas, and the Khonds are apparently members of that tribe of comparatively pure descent who marry among themselves and not with other Taonlas. In Orissa Dr. Hunter says that the Taonlas are allied to the Savaras, and that they will admit a member of any caste, from whose hands they can take water, into the community. This is also the case in Bāmra. The candidate has simply to worship Kālapāt, the god of the Taonlas, and after drinking some water in which basil leaves have been dipped, to touch the food prepared for a caste feast, and his initiation is complete. As usual among the mixed castes, female morality is very lax, and a Taonla woman may have a *liaison* with a man of her own or any other caste from whom a Taonla can take water without incurring any penalty whatsoever. A man committing a similar offence must give a feast to the caste. In Sonpur the Taonlas admit a close connection with Chasas, and say that some of their families are descended from the union of Chasa men and Taonla women. They will eat the leavings of Chasas. The custom may be accounted for by the fact that the Taonlas are now generally farmservants and field-labourers, and the Chasas, as cultivators, would be their employers. A similar close connection is observable among other castes standing in the same position towards each other as the Panwārs and Gonds and the Rājbhars and Lodhis.

The Taonlas have no exogamous divisions as they all belong to the same *gotra*, that of the Nāg or cobra. Their marriages are therefore regulated by relationship in the ordinary manner. If two families find that they have no common ancestor up to the third generation they consider it lawful to intermarry. The marriage ritual is of the usual Uriya form. After the marriage the bride and the bridegroom have a ceremony of throwing a mahua branch into a river together. Divorce and widow remarriage are permitted. When a woman is divorced she returns her bangles to her husband, and receives from him a *chhor-chitthi* or letter severing connection. Then she goes before the caste *panchāyat* and pronounces her husband's name aloud. This shows that she is no longer his wife, since so long as she continued to be so, she would never mention his name.

The tutelary deity of the caste is Kālapāt, who resides at Tālmūl in Angul District. They offer him a goat at the festival of Nawākhai when the new rice is first eaten. On this day they also worship a cattle-goad as the symbol of their vocation. They revere the cobra, and will not wear wooden sandals because they think that the marks on a cobra's head are in the form of a sandal. They believe in re-birth, and when a child is born they proceed to ascertain what ancestor has become reincarnate by dropping rice grains coloured with turmeric into a pot of water. As each one is dropped they repeat the name of an ancestor, and when the first grain floats conclude that the one named has been born again. The dead are both buried and burnt. At the head of a grave they plant a bough of the *jāmun* tree (*Eugenia jambolāna*) so that the departed spirit may dwell under this cool and shady tree in the other world or in his next birth. They have also a ceremony for bringing back the soul. An earthen pot is placed upside down on four legs outside the village, and on the eleventh day after a death they proceed to the place, ringing a bell suspended to an iron rod. A cloth is spread before the spot on which the spirit of the deceased is supposed to be sitting, and they wait till an insect alights on it. This is taken to be the soul of the dead person, and it is carefully wrapped up in the cloth and carried to the house. There the cloth is unfolded and the insect allowed to go, while they proceed to inspect some rice-flour which has been spread on the ground under another pot in the house. If any mark is found on the surface of the flour they think that the dead man's spirit has returned to the house. The carrying back of the insect is thus an act calculated to assist their belief, by the simple performance of which they are able to suppose more easily that the invisible spirit has returned to the house. As already stated, the Taonlas are now generally farmservants and labourers, and their social position is low, though they rank above the impure castes and the forest tribes.

TELI

LIST OF PARAGRAPHS

1. Strength and distribution of the caste.
2. Origin and traditions.
3. Endogamous subcastes.
4. Exogamous divisions.
5. Marriage customs.
6. Widow-remarriage.
7. Religion. Caste deities.
8. Driving out evil.
9. Customs at birth and death.
10. Social status.
11. Social customs and caste penalties.
12. The Rāthor Telis.
13. Gujarāti Telis of Nimār.
14. The Teli an unlucky caste.
15. Occupation. Oil-pressing.
16. Trade and agriculture.
17. Teli beneficence.

1. Strength and distribution of the caste.

Teli.[1]—The occupational caste of oil-pressers and sellers. The Telis numbered nearly 900,000 persons in 1911, being the fifth caste in the Province in point of population. They are numerous in the Chhattīsgarh and Nāgpur Divisions, nearly 400,000 belonging to the former and 200,000 to the latter tract; while in Berār and the north of the Province they are sparsely represented. The reason for such a distribution of the caste is somewhat obscure. Vegetable oil is more largely used for food in the south and east than in the north, but while this custom might explain the preponderance of Telis in Nāgpur and Chhattīsgarh it gives no reason to account for their small numbers in Berār. In Chhattīsgarh again nearly all the Telis are cultivators, and it may be supposed that, like the Chamārs, they have found opportunity here to get possession of the land owing to its not being already taken up by the cultivating castes proper; but in the Nāgpur Division, with the exception of part of Wardha, the Telis have had no such opening and are not

[1] This article is based on papers by Mr. Prem Nārāyan, Extra Assistant Commissioner, Chānda; Mr. Mīr Pācha, Tahsīldār, Seoni; Mr. Chintāman Rao, Tahsīldār, Chānda; and Mr. K. G. Vaidya, Chānda.

large landholders. Their distribution thus remains a somewhat curious problem. But all over the Province the Telis have generally abandoned their hereditary trade of pressing oil, and have taken to trade and agriculture, the number of those returned as oil-pressers being only about seven per cent of the total strength of the caste. The name comes from the Sanskrit *tailika* or *taila*, oil, and this word is derived from the *tilli* or sesamum plant.

2. Origin and traditions.

The caste have few traditions of origin. Their usual story is that during Siva's absence the goddess Pārvati felt nervous because she had no doorkeeper to her palace, and therefore she made the god Ganesh from the sweat of her body and set him to guard the southern gate. But when Siva returned Ganesh did not know him and refused to let him enter; on which Siva was so enraged that he cut off the head of Ganesh with a stroke of his sword. He then entered the palace, and Pārvati, observing the blood on his sword, asked him what had happened, and reproached him bitterly for having slain her son. Siva was distressed, but said that he could not replace the head as it was already reduced to ashes. But he said that if any animal could be found looking towards the south he could put its head on Ganesh and bring him to life. As it happened a trader was then resting outside the palace and had with him an elephant, which was seated with its head to the south. So Siva quickly struck off the head of the elephant and placed it on the body of Ganesh and brought him to life again, and thus Ganesh got his elephant's head. But the trader made loud lamentation about the loss of his elephant, so to pacify him Siva made a pestle and mortar, utensils till then unknown, and showed him how to pound oil-seeds in them and express the oil, and enjoined him to earn a livelihood in future by this calling, and his descendants after him; and so the merchant became the first Teli. And the pestle was considered to be Siva and the mortar Pārvati. This last statement affords some support to Mr. Marten's suggestion [1] that a certain veneration attaching to the pestle and mortar and their use in marriage ceremonies may be due to the idea of their

[1] *C. P. Census Report* (1911), p. 147, referring to Professor Karl Pearson's *Chances of Death*.

typifying the male and female organs. The fact that Ganesh was set to guard the southern gate, and that the animal whose head could be placed on his body must be looking to the south, probably hinges in some way on the south being the abode of Yama, the god of death, but the connection has been forgotten by the teller of the story; it may also be noted that if the palace was in the Himalayas, the site of Kailās or Siva's heaven, the whole of India would be to the south. Another story related by Mr. Crooke [1] from Mīrzāpur is that a certain man had three sons and owned fifty-two mahua [2] trees. When he became aged and infirm he told his sons to divide the trees, but after some discussion they decided to divide not the trees themselves but their produce. One of them fell to picking up the leaves, and he was the ancestor of the Bharbhūnjas or grain-parchers, who still use leaves in their ovens; the second collected the flowers and corollas, and having distilled liquor from them became a Kalār; while the third took the kernels or fruit and crushed the oil out of them, and was the founder of the Teli caste. The country spirit generally drunk is distilled from the flowers of the mahua tree, and a cheap vegetable oil in common use is obtained from its seeds. The Telis and Kalārs are also castes of about the same status and have other points of resemblance; and the legend connecting them is therefore of some interest. Some groups of Telis who have become landed proprietors or prospered in trade have stories giving them a more exalted origin. Thus the landholding Rāthor Telis of Mandla say that they were Rāthor Rājpūts who fled from the Muhammadans and threw away their swords and sacred threads; and the Telis of Nimār, several of whom are wealthy merchants, give out that their ancestors were Modh Banias from Gujarāt who had to take to oil-pressing for a livelihood under Muhammadan rule. But these legends may perhaps be considered a natural result of their rise in the world.

3. Endogamous subcastes.

The caste has a large number of subdivisions. The principal groups in Chhattīsgarh are the Halia, Jharia and Ekbahia Telis. The Halias, who perhaps take their name from *hal*, a plough, are considered to be the best cultivators, and are said to have immigrated from Mandla some genera-

---

[1] *Tribes and Castes*, art. Teli.　　[2] *Bassia latifolia.*

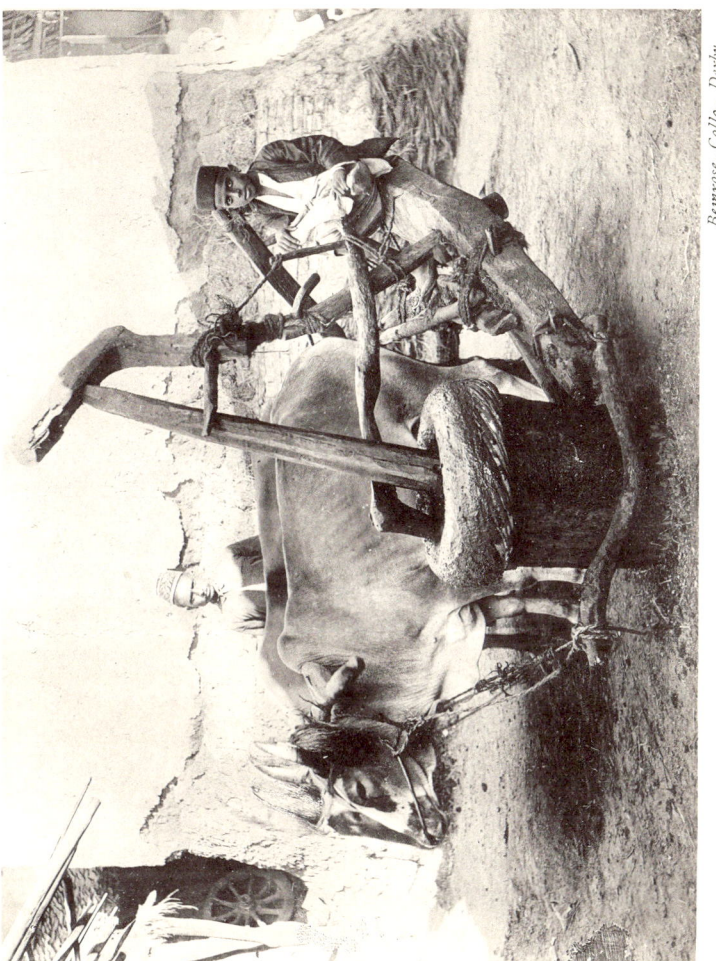

TELI'S OIL-PRESS.

tions ago. Probably the bulk of the Hindu population of Chhattīsgarh came from this direction. The name Jharia means jungly or savage, and is commonly applied to the oldest residents, but the Jharia Telis are the highest local subcaste. They require the presence of a Brāhman at their weddings, and abstain generally from liquor, fowls and pork, to which the Halias are not averse. They also bathe the corpse before it is burnt or buried, an observance omitted by the Halias. The Jharias yoke only one bullock to the oil-press, and the Halias two, a distinction which is elsewhere sufficient of itself to produce separate subcastes. The Ekbahia (one-armed) Telis are so called because their women wear glass bangles only on the right hand and metal ones on the left. This is a custom of several castes whose women do manual labour, and the reason appears to be one of convenience, as glass bangles on the working arm would be continually getting broken. Among the Ekbahia Telis it is said that a woman considers it a point of honour to have these metal bangles as numerous and heavy as her arm can bear; and at a wedding a present of three bracelets from the bridegroom to the bride is held to be indispensable. The Madpotwa are a small subcaste living near the hills, who in former times distilled liquor; they keep pigs and poultry, and rank below the others. Other groups are the Kosarias, who are called after Kosala, the old name of Chhattīsgarh, and the Chhote or Little Telis, who are of illegitimate descent. Children born out of wedlock are relegated to this group.

In the Nāgpur country the principal subdivisions are the Ekbaile and Dobaile, so called because they yoke one and two bullocks respectively to the oil-press; the distinction is still maintained, the Dobaile being also known as Tarāne. This seems a trivial reason for barring intermarriage, but it must be remembered that the yoking of the bullock to the oil-press, coupled as it is with the necessity of blindfolding the animal, is considered a great sin on the Teli's part and a degrading incident of his profession; the Teli's worst fear is that after death his soul will pass into one of his own bullocks. The Yerande Telis are so called because they formerly pressed only the *erandi* or castor-oil seed, but the rule is no longer maintained. The Yerande women leave off wearing the *choli* or breast-cloth after they have had one child, and have nothing under the *sāri* or body-cloth, but they wear this folded double. The Ruthia group are said to be so called from the noise *rut, rut* made by the oil-mill in turning. They say they are descended from the Nāg or cobra. They salute the snake when they see it and refrain from killing it, and they will not make any drawing or sign having the semblance of a snake or use any article which may be supposed to be like it. The Sao Telis are the highest group in Wardha, and have eschewed the pressing of oil. The word Sao or Sāhu is the title of a moneylender, but they are usually cultivators or village proprietors. A Brāhman will enter a Sao Teli's house, but not the houses of any other subcaste. Their women wear silver bangles on the right hand and glass ones on the left. The Batri subcaste are said to be so called from their growing the *batar*, a kind of pea, and the Hardia from raising the *haldi* or turmeric. The Teli-Kalārs appear to be a mixed group of Kalārs who have taken to the oilman's profession, and the Teli-Banias are Telis who have become shopkeepers, and may be expected in the course of time to develop either into a plebeian group of Banias or an aristocratic one of Telis. In Nimār the Gujarāti Telis, who have now grown wealthy and prosperous, claim, as already seen, to be Modh Banias, and the same pretension is put forward by their fellow-castemen in Gujarāt itself. "The large class of oilmen known in Gujarāt as Modh-Ghanelis were originally Modh Banias, who by taking to making and selling oil lost their position as Banias";[1] it seems doubtful, however, whether the reverse process has not really taken place. The Umre Telis also have the name of a subcaste of Banias. The landholding Rāthor Telis of Mandla, who now claim to be Rāthor Rājpūts, will be more fully noticed later. There are also several local subcastes, as the Mattha or Marātha Telis, who say they came from Pātan in Gujarāt, the Sirwas from the ancient city of Srāvasti in Gonda District, and the Kanaujia from Oudh.

4. Exogamous divisions.

Each subcaste is divided into a number of exogamous groups for the regulation of marriages. The names of the

[1] *Hindus of Gujarāt*, p. 72.

groups appear to be taken either from villages or titles or nicknames. Most of them cannot be recognised, but the following are a few: Bāghmāre, a tiger-killer; Deshmukh, a village officer; Vaidya, a physician; Bāwankule, the fifty-two septs; Badwāik, the great ones; Satpute, seven sons; Bhājikhāya, an eater of vegetables; Satapaise, seven pice; Ghoremādia, a horse-killer; Chaudhri, a caste headman; Ardona, a kind of gram; Malghāti, a valley; Chandan-malāgar, one who presented sandalwood; and Sanichara, born on Saturday. Three septs, Dhurwa, Besrām, a hawk, and Sonwāni, goldwater, belong to the Gonds or other tribes. The clans of the Rāthor Telis of Mandla are said to be named after villages in Jubbulpore and Maihar State.

5. Marriage customs.

The marriage of persons of the same sept and of first cousins is usually forbidden. A man may marry his wife's younger sister while she herself is alive, but never her elder sister. An unmarried girl becoming pregnant by a man of the caste is married to him by the ceremony used for a widow, and she may be readmitted even after a *liaison* with an outsider among most Telis. In Chānda the parents of a girl who is not married before puberty are fined. The proposal comes from the boy's side and a bride-price is usually paid, though not of large amount. The Halia Telis of Chhattīsgarh, like other agricultural castes, sometimes betroth their children when they are five or six months old, but as a rule no penalty attaches to the breaking of the betrothal. The betrothal is celebrated by the distribution of one or two rupees' worth of liquor to the neighbours of the caste. As among other low castes, on the day before the wedding procession starts, the bridegroom goes round to all the houses in the village and his sister dances round him with her head bent, and all the people give him presents. This is known as the Binaiki or Farewell, and the bride does the same in her village. Among the Jharia Telis the women go and worship the marriage-post at the carpenter's house while it is being made. In this subcaste the bridegroom goes to the wedding in a cart and not on horseback or in a litter as among some castes. The rule may perhaps be a recognition of their humble station. The Halia subcaste can dispense with the presence of a Brāhman at the wedding, but not the

Jharias. In Wardha the bridegroom's head is covered with a blanket, over which is placed the marriage-crown. On the arrival of the bridegroom's party they are regaled with *sherbet* or sugar and water by the bride's relatives, and sometimes red pepper is mixed with this by way of a joke. At a wedding of the Gujarāti Telis in Nimār the caste-priest carries the tutelary goddess Kāli in procession, and in front of her a pot filled with burning cotton-seeds and oil. A cloth is held over the pot, and it is believed that the power of the goddess prevents the cloth from taking fire. If this should happen some great calamity would be portended. Rāthor Teli girls, whether married or unmarried, go with their heads bare, and a woman draws her cloth over her head for the first time when she begins to live in her husband's house.

6. Widow-remarriage.

Divorce and widow-marriage are permitted. In Chhattīsgarh a widow is always kept in the family if possible, and if her late husband's brother be only a boy she is sometimes induced to put on the bangles and wait for him. If a *barandi* widow, that is one who has been married but has not lived with her husband, desires to marry again out of his family, the second husband must repay to them the amount spent on her first marriage. In Chānda, on the other hand, some Telis do not permit a widow to marry her late husband's younger brother at all, and others only when he is a bachelor or a widower. Here the minimum period for which a widow must remain single after her husband's death is one month. The engagement with a widow is arranged by the suitor's female relatives, and they pay her a rupee as earnest money. On the day fixed she goes with one or two other widows to the bridegroom's house, and from there to the bazār, where she buys two pairs of bell-metal rings, to be worn on the second toe of each foot, and some glass bangles. She remains sitting in the bazār till well after dark, when some widow goes to fetch her on behalf of her suitor. They bring her to his house, where the couple sit together, and red powder is applied to their foreheads. They then bathe and present their clothes to the washerman, putting on new clothes. The idea in all this is clearly to sever the widow as completely as possible from her old home and prevent her from being accompanied to the new one by the first husband's spirit. In some localities when a Teli widow remarries it is considered most unlucky for any one to see the face of the bride or bridegroom for twenty-four hours, or as some say for three days after the wedding. The ceremony is therefore held at night, and for this period the couple either remain shut up in the house or retire to the jungle.

The caste especially revere Mahādeo or Siva, who gave them the oil-mill. In the Nāgpur country they do not work the mill on Monday, because it is Mahādeo's day, he having the moon on his forehead. They revere the oil-mill, and when the trunk is brought to be set up in the house, if there is difficulty in moving it they make offerings to it of a goat or wheat-cakes or cocoanuts, after which it moves easily. When a Teli first sets the trunk-socket of the oil-press in the ground he buries beneath it five pieces of turmeric, some cowries and an areca-nut. In the northern Districts the Telis worship Masān Bāba, who is supposed to be the ghost of a Teli boy. He is a boy about three feet in height, black-coloured, with a long black scalp-lock. Some Telis have Masān Bāba in their possession, and when they are turning the oil-press they set him on top of it, and he makes the bullocks keep on working, so that the master can go away and leave the press. But in order to prevent him from getting into mischief a cake of flour mixed with human hair must be placed in front of the press; he will eat this, but will first pick out all the hairs one by one, and this will occupy him the whole night; but if no cake is put for him he will eat all the food in the house. A Teli who has not got Māsan must go to one who has and hire him for Rs. 1-4 a night. They then both go to the owner's oil-press, and the hirer says, 'I have hired you to-night,' and the owner says, 'Yes, I have let you for to-night'; and then the hirer goes away, and Masān Bāba follows him and will turn the oil-mill all night. A Teli who has not got Masān Bāba puts a stone on the oil-mill, and then the bullock thinks that his master Masān is sitting on it, and will go on turning the press; but this is not so good as having Masān Bāba.

7. Religion: Caste deities.

Some say that he will repay his hirer the sum of Rs. 1-4 by stealing something during the year and giving it to him. Masān may perhaps be considered as a divine personification of the oil-press, and as being the Teli's explanation of the fact that the bullock goes on turning the press without being driven, which he does not attribute simply to the animal's docility. In Chhattīsgarh Dūlha Deo is the household god of the caste, and he is said not to have any visible image or symbol, but is considered to reside in a cupboard in the house. When any member of the family falls ill it is thought that Dūlha Deo is angry, and a goat is offered to appease him. Like the other low castes the Telis of the Nāgpur country make the sacrifice of a pig to Nārāyan Deo or the Sun at intervals.

8. Driving out evil.

Here on the third day after the Pola festival in the rains the women of the caste bring the branches of a thorny creeper, with very small leaves, and call it Mārbod, and sweep out the whole house with it, saying:

'*Ira, pīra, khātka, khatkīra,*
Khānsi, kokhala, rai, rog,
Murkuto gheunja ga Mārbod,'

or, 'Oh Mārbod! sweep away all diseases, pains, coughs, bugs, flies and mosquitoes.' And then they take the pot of sweepings and throw it outside the village. Mārbod is the deity represented by the branch of the creeper. This rite takes place in the middle of the rainy season, when all kinds of insects infest the house, and colds and fever are prevalent. Mr. H. R. Crosthwaite sends the following explanation given by a Teli cultivator of an eclipse of the sun: "The Sun is indebted to a sweeper. The sweeper has gone to collect the debt and the Sun has refused to pay. The sweeper is in need of the money and is sitting *dharna* at the Sun's door; you can see his shadow across the Sun's threshold. Presently the debt will be paid and the sweeper will go away." The Telis of Nimār observe various Muhammadan practices. They fast during the month of Ramazān, taking their food in the morning before sunrise; and at Id they eat the vermicelli and dates which the Muhammadans eat in memory of the time when their forefathers lived on this food in the

Arabian desert. Such customs are a relic of the long period of Muhammadan dominance in Nimār, when the Hindus conformed partly to the religion of their masters. Many Telis are also members of the Swāmi-Nārāyan reforming sect, which may have attracted them by its disregard of the distinctions of caste and of the low status which attaches to them under Hinduism.

In Patna State a pregnant woman must not cross a river nor eat any fruit or vegetables of red colour, nor wear any black cloth. These taboos preserve her health and that of her unborn child. After the birth of a child a woman is impure for seven or nine days in Chhattīsgarh, and is then permitted to cook. The dead are either buried or burnt, cremation being an honour reserved for the old. The body is placed in both cases with the head to the north and face downwards or upwards for a male or female respectively. 9. Customs at birth and death.

The social status of the Telis is low, in the group of castes from which Brāhmans will not take water, and below such menials as the blacksmith and carpenter. Manu classes them with butchers and liquor-vendors : " From a king not born in the military class let a Brāhman accept no gift nor from such as keep a slaughter-house, or an oil-press, or put out a vintner's flag or subsist by the gains of prostitutes." This is much about the position which the Telis have occupied till recently. Brāhmans will not usually enter their houses, though they have begun to do so in the case of the land-holding subcastes. It is noticeable that the Teli has a much better position in Bengal than elsewhere. Sir H. Risley says : " Their original profession was probably oil-pressing, and the caste may be regarded as a functional group recruited from the respectable middle class of Hindu society. Oil is used by all Hindus for domestic and ceremonial purposes, and its manufacture could only be carried on by men whose social purity was beyond dispute." This is, however, quite exceptional, and Mr. Crooke, Mr. Nesfield and Sir D. Ibbetson are agreed as to his inferior, if not partly impure, status. This is only one of several instances, such as those of the barber, the potter and the weaver, of menial castes which in Bengal have now obtained a position above the agricultural castes. It may be suggested in explanation that the old fabric of 10. Social status.

Hindu society, that is the village community, has long decayed in Bengal owing to Muhammadan dominance, the concentration of estates in the hands of large proprietors and the weakening or lapse of the customary rights of tenants. Coupled with this has been the growth of an important urban population, in which the castes mentioned have raised themselves from their menial position in the villages and attained wealth and influence, just as the Gujarāti Telis are now doing in Burhānpur, while the agricultural castes of Bengal have been comparatively depressed. Hence the urban industrial castes have obtained a great rise in status. Sir H. Risley's emphasis of the importance of oil in Hindu domestic ceremonial is no doubt quite true, though it is perhaps little used in sacrifices, butter being generally preferred as a product of the sacred cow. But the inference does not seem necessarily to follow that the producer of any article shares exactly in the estimation attaching to the thing itself. Turmeric, for instance, is a sacred plant and indispensable at every wedding; but those who grow turmeric always incur a certain stigma and loss in social position. The reason for the impurity of the Teli's calling seems somewhat doubtful. That generally given is his sinful conduct in harnessing the sacred ox and blindfolding the animal's eyes to make it work continuously on the tread-mill. The labour is said to be very severe, and the bullocks often die after two or three years. As already seen, the Teli fears that after death his soul may pass into one of his own bullocks in retribution for his treatment of them during life. Another reason which may be suggested is that the crushing of oil-seeds must involve a destruction of insect life, many of the seeds being at times infested with insects. The Teli's occupation would naturally rank with the other village industries, that is below agriculture; and prior to the introduction of cash coinage he must have received contributions of grain from the tenants for supplying them with oil like the other village menials. He still takes his oil to the fields at harvest-time and gets his sheaf of grain from each holding.

11. Social customs and caste penalties.

The Telis will take cooked food from Kurmis and Kunbis, and in some localities from a Lohār or Barhai. Dhīmars are the highest caste which will take food from them. In Mandla if a man does not attend the meeting of the *panchāyat* when summoned for some special purpose, he is fined. In Chānda a Teli beaten with a shoe by any other caste has to have his head shaved and pay a rupee or two to the priest. In Mandla the Telis have made it a rule that not less than four *puris* or wheat-cakes fried in butter[1] must be given to each guest at a caste-feast, besides rice and pulse. But if an offender is poor only four or five men go to his feast, while if he is rich the whole caste go.

The Rāthor Telis of Mandla hold a number of villages. They now call themselves Rāthor, and entirely disown the name of Teli. They say that they came from the Maihar State near Panna, and that the title of Mahto, from *mahat*, great, which is borne by the leading men of the caste, was conferred on them by the Rāja of Maihar. Another story is that, as already related, they are debased Rāthor Rājpūts. Recently they have given up eating fowls and drinking liquor. They are good cultivators, borrowing among themselves at low interest and avoiding debt, and their villages are generally prosperous.

12. The Rāthor Telis.

Again, as has been seen, the Gujarāti Telis of Burhānpur have taken to trade, and some of them have become wealthy merchants and capitalists from their dealings in cotton. The position of Telis in Burhānpur was apparently one of peculiar degradation under Muhammadan rule. According to local tradition they had to remove the corpses of dead elephants, which no other caste would consent to do, and also to dig the graves of Muhammadans. It is also said that even now a Hindu becomes impure by passing under the eaves of a Teli's house, and that no dancing-girl may dance before a Teli, and if she does so will incur a penalty of Rs. 50 to her caste. The Telis, on the other hand, vigorously repudiate these allegations, which no doubt are due partly to jealousy of their present prosperity and consequent attempts to better their status. The Telis allege that they were Modh Banias in Gujarāt and when they came to Burhānpur adopted the occupation of oil-pressing, which is also countenanced by the Shāstras for a Vaishya. They say that formerly they did not permit widow-marriage, but when living under Muham-

13. Gujarāti Telis of Nimār.

---

[1] Weighing 2 oz. each.

madan rule they were constrained to get their widows married in the caste, or the Muhammadans would have taken them. The Muhammadan practices already noticed as prevalent among them are being severely repressed, and they are believed to have made a caste rule that any Teli who goes to the house of a Muhammadan will have his hair and beard shaved and be fined Rs. 50. They are also supposed to have made offers to Brāhmans of sums of Rs. 500 to Rs. 1000 to come and take their food in the verandas of the Telis' houses, but hitherto these have not been accepted.

14. The Teli an unlucky caste.

The Teli is considered a caste of bad omen. The proverb says, 'God protect me from a Teli, a Chamār and a Dhobi'; and the Teli is considered the most unlucky of the three. He is also talkative: 'Where there is a Teli there is sure to be contention.' The Teli is thought to be very close-fisted, but occasionally his cunning overreaches itself: 'The Teli counts every drop of oil as it issues from the press, but sometimes he upsets the whole pot.' The reason given for his being unlucky is his practice of harnessing and blindfolding bullocks already mentioned, and also that he presses *urad*,[1] a black-coloured pulse, the oil from which is offered to the unlucky planet Saturn on Saturdays. ' *Teli ka bail*,' or ' A Teli's bullock,' is a proverbial expression for a man who has to slave very hard for small pay.[2] The Teli is believed to have magical powers. A good magician in search of an attendant spirit will, it is said, prefer to raise the corpse of a Teli who died on a Tuesday. He proceeds to the burning-*ghāt* with chickens, eggs, some vermilion and red cloth. He seats himself near to where the corpse was burnt, and after repeating some spells offers up the chickens and eggs and breaks the cocoanut. Then it is believed that the corpse will gradually rise and take shape and be at the magician's service so long as the latter may desire. The following prescription is given for a love-charm: take the skull of a Teli's wife and cook some rice in it under a *babūl*[3] tree on a Sunday. This if given to a girl to eat will make her fall in love with him who gives it to her.

---

[1] *Phaseolus radiatas.*
[2] Mr. Crooke's *Tribes and Castes*, art. Teli.
[3] *Acacta arabica.*

OCCUPATION: OIL-PRESSING

15. Occupation. Oil-pressing.

The Teli's oil-press is a very primitive affair. It consists of a hollowed tree-trunk in which a post is placed with rounded lower end. The top of this projects perhaps three feet above the hollow trunk and is secured by two pieces of wood to a horizontal bar, one end of which presses against the trunk, while the bullock is harnessed to the outer end. The yoke-bar hangs about a foot from the ground, the inner end resting in a groove of the trunk, while the outer is supported by the poles connecting it with the churning-post. From the top of this latter a rope is also tied to the bullock's horn to keep the animal in position. The press is usually set up inside a shed, and it is said that if the bullock were not blindfolded it would quickly become too giddy to work. The bullock drags the yoke-bar round the trunk and this gives a circular movement to the top of the churning-post, causing the lower end of the latter to move as on a pivot inside the trunk. The friction thus produced crushes the oil-seed, and the oil trickles out through a hole in the lower part of the trunk. The oil of *ramtilli* or *jagni* is commonly burnt for lighting in villages, and also that of the mahua-seed. Linseed-oil is generally exported, but if used at home it is mainly as an illuminant. It is mixed with food by the Marātha castes but not in northern India. All the vegetable oils are rapidly being supplanted by kerosene, even in villages; but the inferior quality generally purchased, burnt as it is in small open saucers, gives out a great deal of smoke and is said to be very injurious to the eyesight, and students especially sustain permanent injury to the sight by working with these lamps. This want is, however, being met, and cheap lamp-burners can be bought in Bombay for about twelve annas. Owing to their having until recently supplied the only means of illumination the Telis sometimes call themselves *Dīpabans*, or 'Sons of the lamp.' Tilli or sesamum is called sweet oil; it is much eaten by Brāhmans and others in the Marātha country, and is always used for rubbing on the hair and body. On the festivals of Diwāli and Til Sankrānt all Hindus rub sesamum oil on their bodies; otherwise they put it on their hair once or twice a week, and on their bodies if they get a chill, or as a protective against cold twice or thrice a month in the winter. The Uriya castes rub oil on the body if they can afford it every day after bathing and say that it keeps off malaria. Castor-oil is used as a medicine, and by some people even as ordinary food. It is also a good lubricant, being applied to cart-wheels and machinery. Other oils mentioned by Mr. Crooke are poppy-seed, mustard, cocoanut and safflower, and those prepared from almond and the berries of the *nīm*[1] tree. The Teli's occupation is a dirty one, his house being filled with the refuse of oil and oil-seed, and Mr. Gordon notes that leprosy is very prevalent in the caste.[2]

16. Trade and agriculture.

The Telis are a very enterprising caste, and the great bulk of them have abandoned their traditional occupation and taken to others which are more profitable and respectable. In their trade, like that of the Kalār, cash payment by barter must have been substituted for customary annual contributions at an early period, and hence they learnt to keep accounts when their customers were ignorant of this accomplishment. The knowledge has stood them in good stead. Many of them have become moneylenders in a small way, and by this means have acquired villages. In the Raipur and Bilāspur Districts they own more than 200 villages and 700 in the Central Provinces as a whole. They are also shopkeepers and petty traders, travelling about with pack-bullocks like the Banjāras. Mr. A. K. Smith notes that formerly the Teli hired Banjāras to carry his goods through the jungle, as he would have been killed by them if he had ventured to do so himself. But now he travels with his own bullocks. Even in Mughal times Mr. Smith states Telis occasionally rose to important positions; Kāwaji Teli was sutler to the Imperial army, and obtained from the Emperor Jahāngīr a grant of Ashti in Wardha and an order that no one should plant betel-vine gardens in Ashti without his permission. This rule is still observed and any one wishing to have a betel-vine garden makes a present to the patel. Krishna Kānta Nandi or Kānta Bābu, the Banyan of Warren Hastings, was a Teli by caste and did much to raise their position among the Hindus.[3]

Colonel Tod gives instances in Udaipur of works of

[1] *Melia indica.*   [2] *Indian Folk Tales,* p. 10.
[3] *Tribes and Castes of Bengal,* art. Teli.

beneficence executed by Telis. "The *Teli-ki-Sarai* or oilman's caravanserai is not conspicuous for magnitude; but it is remarkable not merely for its utility but even for its elegance of design. The *Teli-ka-Pūl* or Oilman's Bridge at Nūrabād is a magnificent memorial of the trade and deserves preservation. These Telis perambulate the country with skins of oil on a bullock and from hard-earned pence erect the structures which bear their name."[1] Similarly the temple of Vishnu at Rājim is said to be named after one Rājan Telin, who discovered the image lying abandoned by the roadside. She placed her skin of oil on it to rest herself and on that day her oil never decreased, and when she had finished selling in the market she had all her oil as well as the money. Her husband suspected her of evil practices, but, when next day her mother-in-law laid a skinful of oil on the image and the same thing happened, it was seen that the god had made himself manifest to her, and a temple was built and named after her and the image enshrined in it. Similarly the image of Mahādeo at Pīthampur in Bilāspur was seen buried by a Teli in a dream, and he dug it up and made a shrine to it and was cured of dysentery. So an annual fair is held and many people go there to be healed of their diseases.

17. Teli beneficence.

[1] *Rājasthān*, vol. ii. pp. 678, 679.

THUG

[This article is based almost entirely on Colonel (Sir William) Sleeman's *Rāmaseeāna or Vocabulary of the Thugs* (1835). A small work, Hutton's *Thugs and Dacoits*, has been quoted for convenience, but it is compiled entirely from Colonel Sleeman's Reports. Another book by Colonel Sleeman, *Reports on the Depredations of the Thug Gangs*, is mainly a series of accounts of the journeys of different gangs and contains only a very brief general notice.]

LIST OF PARAGRAPHS

1. Historical notice.
2. Thuggee depicted in the caves of Ellora.
3. Origin of the Thugs.
4. Methods of assassination.
5. Account of certain murders.
6. Special incidents (continued).
7. Disguises of the Thugs.
8. Secrecy of their operations.
9. Support of landholders and villagers.
10. Murder of sepoys.
11. Callous nature of the Thugs.
12. Belief in divine support.
13. Theory of Thuggee as a religious sect.
14. Worship of Kāli.
15. The sacred pickaxe.
16. The sacred gur (sugar).
17. Worship of ancestors.
18. Fasting.
19. Initiation of a novice.
20. Prohibition of murder of women.
21. Other classes of persons not killed.
22. Belief in omens.
23. Omens and taboos.
24. Nature of the belief in omens.
25. Suppression of Thuggee.

1. Historical notice. **Thug, Phānsigar.**—The famous community of murderers who were accustomed to infest the high-roads and strangle travellers for their property. The Thugs are, of course, now extinct, having been finally suppressed by measures taken under the direction of Colonel Sleeman between 1825 and 1850. The only existing traces of them are a small number of persons known as Goranda or Goyanda in Jubbulpore, the descendants of Thugs employed in the school of industry which was established at that town. These work honestly for their living and are believed to

have no marked criminal tendencies. In the course of his inquiries, however, Colonel Sleeman collected a considerable mass of information about the Thugs, some of which is of ethnological interest, and as the works in which this is contained are out of print and not easily accessible, it seems desirable to record a portion of it here. The word Thug signifies generically a cheat or robber, while Phānsigar, which was the name used in southern India, is derived from *phānsi*, a noose, and means a strangler. The form of robbery and murder practised by these people was probably of considerable antiquity, and is referred to as follows by a French traveller, Thevenot, in the sixteenth century:

"Though the road I have been speaking of from Delhi to Agra be tolerable yet it hath many inconveniences. One may meet with tigers, panthers and lions upon it, and one can also best have a care of robbers, and above all things not to suffer anybody to come near one upon the road. The cunningest robbers in the world are in that country. They use a certain slip with a running noose which they can cast with so much sleight about a man's neck, when they are within reach of him, that they never fail, so that they can strangle him in a trice. They have another cunning trick also to catch travellers with. They send out a handsome woman upon the road, who with her hair dishevelled seems to be all in tears, sighing and complaining of some misfortune which she pretends has befallen her. Now, as she takes the same way that the traveller goes he falls easily into conversation with her, and finding her beautiful, offers her his assistance, which she accepts; but he hath no sooner taken her up behind him on horseback, but she throws the snare about his neck and strangles him, or at least stuns him until the robbers who lie hid come running to her assistance and complete what she hath begun. But besides that, there are men in those quarters so skilful in casting the snare, that they succeed as well at a distance as near at hand; and if an ox or any other beast belonging to a caravan run away, as sometimes it happens, they fail not to catch it by the neck."[1]

This passage seems to demonstrate an antiquity of

---

[1] Thevenot's *Travels*, Part III. p. 41, quoted in Dr. Sherwood's account, *Rāmaseeāna*, p. 359.

three centuries for the Thugs down to 1850. But during the period over which Sir William Sleeman's inquiries extended women never accompanied them on their expeditions, and were frequently even, as a measure of precaution, left in ignorance of the profession of their husbands.

<small>2. Thuggee depicted in the caves of Ellora.</small>

The Thugs themselves believed that the operations of their trade were depicted in the carvings of the Ellora caves, and a noted leader, Feringia, and other Thugs spoke of these carvings as follows: "Every one of the operations is to be seen there: in one place you see men strangling; in another burying the bodies; in another carrying them off to the graves. Whenever we passed near we used to go and see these caves. Every man will there find his trade described and they were all made in one night.

"Everybody there can see the secret operations of his trade; but he does not tell others of them; and no other person can understand what they mean. They are the works of God. No human hands were employed on them. That everybody admits."

Another Thug: "I have seen there the Sotha (inveigler) sitting upon the same carpet as the traveller, and in close conversation with him, just as we are when we worm out their secrets. In another place the strangler has got his *rūmāl* (handkerchief) over his neck and is strangling him; while another, the Chamochi, is holding him by the legs." I do not think there is any reason to suppose that these carvings really have anything to do with the Thugs.

<small>3. Origin of the Thugs.</small>

The Thugs did not apparently ever constitute a distinct caste like the Badhaks, but were recruited from different classes of the population. In northern and southern India three-fourths or more, and in Central India about a half, were Muhammadans, whether genuine or the descendants of converted Hindus. The Muhammadan Thugs consisted of seven clans, Bhais, Barsote, Kachuni, Hattar, Garru, Tandel and Rāthur: "And these, by the common consent of all Thugs throughout India, whether Hindus or Muhammadans, are admitted to be the most ancient and the great original trunk upon which all the others have at different times and in different places been grafted."[1] These names,

---

[1] Sleeman, p. 11.

however, are of Hindu and not of Muhammadan origin; and it seems probable that many of the Thugs were originally Banjāras or cattle-dealers and Kanjars or gipsies. One of the Muhammadan Thugs told Colonel Sleeman that, " The Arcot gangs will never intermarry with our families, saying that we once drove bullocks and were itinerant tradesmen, and consequently of lower caste."[1] Another man said[2] that at their marriages an old matron would sometimes repeat as she threw down the *tulsi* or basil, " Here's to the spirits of those who once led bears and monkeys; to those who drove bullocks and marked with the *godini* (tattooing-needle); and those who made baskets for the head." These are the regular occupations of the Kanjars and Berias, the gipsy castes who are probably derived from the Doms. And it seems not unlikely that these people may have been the true progenitors of the Thugs. There is at present a large section of Muhammadan Kanjars who are recognised as members of the caste by the Hindu section. Colonel Sleeman was of opinion that the Kanjars also practised murder by strangling, but not as a regular profession; for this would have been too dangerous, as they were accustomed to wander about with their wives and all their belongings, and the disappearance of many travellers in the locality of their camps would naturally excite suspicion. Whereas the true Thugs resided in villages and towns and many of them had other ostensible occupations, their periodical excursions for robbery and murder being veiled under the pretence of some necessary journey. But the Kanjars may have changed their mode of life on taking to this profession, and their adroitness in other forms of crime, such as killing and carrying off cattle, would make them likely persons to have discovered the advantages of a system of murder of travellers by strangulation. The existing descendants of the Thugs at Jubbulpore appear to be mainly Kanjars and Berias. For such a life it is clear that the profession of the Muhammadan religion would be of much assistance in maintaining the disguise; for it set a man free from many caste obligations and ties and also from a host of irksome restrictions as to eating and drinking with others. We

[1] P. 144. [2] P. 162.

may therefore conjecture, though without certain knowledge, that many of the Thugs may originally have become Muhammadans for convenience; and this is supported by the well-known fact that the principal deity of all of them was the Hindu goddess Kālī. Many bodies of Thugs were also recruited from other Hindu castes, of whom the Lodhas or Lodhis were perhaps the most numerous; others of the fraternity were Rājpūts, Brāhmans, Tāntis or weavers, Goālas or cowherds, Multānis or Muhammadan Banjāras, as well as the Sānsias and Kanjars or criminal vagrants and gipsies. These seem to have observed their caste rules and to have intermarried among themselves; sometimes they obtained wives from other families who had no connection with Thuggee and kept their wives in ignorance of their nefarious trade; occasionally a girl would be spared from a murdered party and married to a son of one of the Thugs; while boys were more frequently saved and brought up to the business. The Thugs said[1] that the fidelity of their wives was proverbial and they were not less loving and dutiful than those of other men, while several instances are recorded of the strong affection borne by fathers to their children.

4. Methods of assassination.

As is well known the method of the Thugs was to attach themselves to travellers, either single men or small parties, and at a convenient opportunity to strangle them, bury the bodies and make off with the property found on them. The gangs of Thugs usually contained from ten to fifty men and were sometimes much larger; on one occasion as many as three hundred and sixty Thugs accomplished the murder of a party of forty persons in Bilāspur.[2] They pretended to be traders, soldiers or cultivators and usually went without weapons in order to disarm suspicion; and this practice also furnished them with an excuse for seeking for permission to accompany parties travelling with arms. There was nothing to excite alarm or suspicion in the appearance of these murderers; but on the contrary they are described as being mild and benevolent of aspect, and peculiarly courteous, gentle and obliging. In their palmy days the leader of the gang often travelled on horseback

[1] P. 147.   [2] P. 205.

with a tent and passed for a person of consequence or a wealthy merchant. They were accustomed to get into conversation with travellers by doing them some service or asking permission to unite their parties as a measure of precaution. They would then journey on together, and strive to win the confidence of their victims by a demeanour of warm friendship and feigned interest in their affairs. Sometimes days would elapse before a favourable opportunity occurred for the murder; an instance is mentioned of a gang having accompanied a family of eleven persons for twenty days during which they had traversed upwards of 200 miles and then murdered the whole of them; and another gang accomplished 160 miles in twelve days in company with a party of sixty men, women and children, before they found a propitious occasion.[1] Their favourite time for the murder was in the evening when the whole party would be seated in the open, the Thugs mingled with their victims, talking, smoking and singing. If their numbers were sufficient three Thugs would be allotted to every victim, so that on the signal being given two of them could lay hold of his hands and feet, while the Bhurtot or strangler passed the *rūmāl* over his head and tightened it round his neck, forcing the victim backwards and not relaxing his hold till life was extinct. The *rūmāl* or 'handkerchief,' always employed for throttling victims, was really a loin-cloth or turban, in which a loop was made with a slip-knot. The Thugs called it their *sikka* or 'ensign,' but it was not held sacred like the pickaxe. When the leader of the gang cleared his throat violently it was a sign to prepare for action, and he afterwards gave the *jhirni* or signal for the murder, by saying either '*Tamākhu khā lo*,' 'Begin chewing tobacco'; '*Bhānja ko pān do*,' 'Give betel to my nephew'; or '*Ayi ho to ghiri chalo*,' 'If you are come, pray descend.' Their adroitness was such that their victims seldom or never escaped nor even had a chance of making a fight for their lives. But if several persons were to be killed some men were detached to surround the camp and cut down any one who tried to escape. The Thugs do not therefore appear to have had any religious objection to the shedding

[1] Hutton's *Thugs and Dacoits*.

of blood, but they preferred murder by strangling as being safer. After the murder the bodies were at once buried, being first cut about to prevent them from swelling on decomposition, as this might raise the surface of the earth over the grave and so attract attention. If the ground was too hard they were thrown into a ravine or down one of the shallow irrigation wells which abound in north India; and it was stated that the discovery of a body in one of these wells was so common an occurrence that the cultivators took no notice of it. If there were people in the vicinity so that it was dangerous to dig the graves in the open air, the Thugs did not scruple to inter the bodies of victims inside their own tents and to eat their food sitting on the soil above. For the attack of a horseman three men were always detailed, if practicable, so that one could seize the bridle and the other two pull him out of the saddle and strangle him; but if, as happened occasionally, a single Thug managed to kill a man on horseback, he obtained a great reputation, which even descended to his children. On the other hand, if a strangler was unlucky or clumsy, so that the cloth fell on the victim's head or face, or he got blood on his clothes or other suspicious signs, and these accidents recurred, he was known as Bisul, and was excluded from the office of strangler on account of presumed unfitness for the duty. When it was necessary for some reason to murder a party on the march, some *belhas* or scouts were sent on ahead to choose a *beil* or suitable place for the business, and see that no one was coming in the opposite direction; and when the leader said, 'Wash the cup,' it was a signal for the scouts to go forward for this purpose. If a traveller had a dog with him the dog was also killed, lest he might stay beside his master's grave and call attention to it. Another device in case of difficulty was for one of the Thugs to feign sickness. The Garru or man who did this fell down on a sudden and pretended to be taken violently ill. Some of his friends raised and supported him, while others brought water and felt his pulse; and at last one of them pretended that a charm would restore him. All were then requested to sit down, the pot of water being in the centre; all were desired to take off their belts, if they had any, and uncover their necks, and lastly to look up and see if they could count a certain number of stars. While they were thus occupied intently gazing at the sky to carry out the charm for the recovery of the sick man, the cloths were passed round their necks and they were strangled.

The secrecy and adroitness with which the Thugs conducted their murders are well illustrated by the narrative of the assassination of a native official or pleader at Lakhnādon in Seoni as given by one of the gang:[1] "We fell in with the Munshi and his family at Chhapāra between Nāgpur and Jubbulpore; and they came on with us to Lakhnādon, where we found that some companies of a native regiment under European officers were expected the next morning. It was determined to put them all to death that evening as the Munshi seemed likely to join the soldiers. The encampment was near the village and the Munshi's tent was pitched close to us. In the afternoon some of the officers' tents came on in advance and were pitched on the other side, leaving us between them and the village. The *khalāsis* were all busily occupied in pitching them. Nūr Khān and his son Sādi Khān and a few others went as soon as it became dark to the Munshi's tent, and began to play and sing upon a *sitār* as they had been accustomed to do. During this time some of them took up the Munshi's sword on pretence of wishing to look at it. His wife and children were inside listening to the music The *jhirni* or signal was given, but at this moment the Munshi saw his danger, called out murder, and attempted to rush through, but was seized and strangled. His wife hearing him ran out with the infant in her arms, but was seized by Ghabbu Khān, who strangled her and took the infant. The other daughter was strangled in the tent. The *saises* (grooms) were at the time cleaning their horses, and one of them seeing his danger ran under the belly of his horse and called murder; but he was soon seized and strangled as well as all the rest. In order to prevent the party pitching the officers' tents from hearing the disturbance, as soon as the signal was given those of the gang who were idle began

5. Account of certain murders.

[1] Sleeman, p. 170.

to play and sing as loud as they could; and two vicious horses were let loose, and many ran after them calling out as loud as they could; so that the calls of the Munshi and his party were drowned." They thought at first of keeping the infant, but decided that it was too risky, and threw it alive into the grave in which the other bodies had been placed. It is surprising to realise that in the above case about half a dozen people, awake and conscious, were killed forcibly in broad daylight within a few paces of a number of men occupied in pitching tents, without their noticing anything of the matter; and this may certainly be characterised as an instance of murder as a fine art. To show the absolute callousness of the Thugs towards their victims and the complete absence of any feelings of compassion, the story of the following murder by the same gang may be recorded.[1] The Thugs were travelling from Nāgpur toward Jubbulpore with a party consisting of Newal Singh, a Jemādār (petty officer) in the Nizām's army, his brother, his two daughters, one thirteen and the other eleven years old, his son about seven years old, two young men who were to marry the daughters, and four servants. At Dhūma the house in which the Thugs lodged took fire, and the greater number of them were seized by the police, but were released at the urgent request of Newal Singh and his two daughters, who had taken a great fancy to Khimoli, the principal leader of the gang, and some of the others. Newal Singh was related to a native officer of the British detachment at Seoni and obtained his assistance for the release of the Thugs. At this time the gang had with them two bags of silk, the property of three carriers whom they had murdered in the great temple of Kamptee, and if they had been searched by the police these must have been discovered. On reaching Jubbulpore the Thugs found a lodging in the town with Newal Singh and his family. But the merchants who were expecting the silk from Nāgpur and found that it had not arrived, induced the Kotwāl to search the lodging of the Thugs. Hearing of the approach of the police, the leader Khimoli again availed himself of the attachment of Newal Singh and his daughters,

[1] Sleeman, p. 168.

and the girls were made to sit each upon one of the two bags of silk while the police searched the place. Nothing was found and the party again set out; and five days afterwards Newal Singh and his whole family were murdered at Biseni by the Thugs whom they had twice preserved from arrest.

These murderers looked on all travellers as their legitimate prey, as sportsmen regard game. On one occasion the noted Thug, Feringia,[1] with his gang were cooking their dinners under some trees on the road when five travellers came by, but could not be persuaded to stop and partake of the meal, saying they wished to sleep at a place called Hirora that night, and had yet eight miles to go. The Thugs afterwards followed, but found no traces of the travellers at Hirora. Feringia therefore concluded that they must have fallen into the hands of another gang, and suddenly recollected having passed an encampment of Banjāras (pack-carriers) not far from the town. On the following morning he accordingly went back with a few of his comrades, and at once recognised a horse and pony which he had observed in the possession of the travellers. So he asked the Banjāras, "What have you done with the five travellers, my good friends? You have taken from us our *banij* (merchandise)." They apologised for what they had done, pleading ignorance of the lien of the other Thugs, and offered to share the booty; but Feringia declined, as none of his party had been present at the '*loading*.' They were accustomed to distinguish their most important exploits by the number of persons who were killed. Thus one murder in the Jubbulpore District was known as the 'Sāthrup,' or 'Sixty soul affair,' and another in Bilāspur as the 'Chālisrup,' or 'Murder of forty.' At this time (1807) the road between northern and southern India through the Nerbudda valley had been rendered so unsafe by the incursions of the Pindāris that travellers preferred to go through Chhattīsgarh and Sambalpur to the Ganges. This route, passing for long distances through dense forest, offered great advantages to the Thugs, and was soon infested

6. Special incidents (continued).

---

[1] He was called Feringia because he was born while his mother was fleeing from an attack on her village by troops under European officers (Feringis).

by them. In 1806, owing to the success[1] of previous expeditions, it was determined that all the Thugs of northern India should work on this road; accordingly after the Dasahra festival six hundred of them, under forty Jemādārs or leaders of note, set out from their homes, and having worshipped in the temple of Devi at Bindhyāchal, met at Ratanpur in Bilāspur. The gangs split up, and after several murders sixty of them came to Lānji in Bālāghāt, and here in two days' time fell in with a party of thirty-one men, seven women and two girls on their way to the Ganges. The Jemādārs soon became intimate with the principal men of the party, pretended to be going to the same part of India and won their confidence; and next day they all set out and in four days reached Ratanpur, where they met 160 Thugs returning from the murder of a wealthy widow and her escort. Shortly afterwards another 200 men who had heard of the travellers near Nāgpur also came up, but all the different bodies pretended to be strangers to each other. They detached sixty men to return to Nāgpur, leaving 360 to deal with the forty travellers. From Ratanpur they all journeyed to Chura (Chhuri?), and here scouts were sent on to select a proper place for the murder. This was chosen in a long stretch of forest, and two men were despatched to the village of Sutranja, farther on the road, to see that no one was coming in the opposite direction, while another picket remained behind to prevent interruption from the rear. By the time they reached the appointed place, the Bhurtots (stranglers) and Shamsias (holders) had all on some pretext or other got close to the side of the persons whom they were appointed to kill; and on reaching the spot the signal was given in several places at the same time, and thirty-eight out of forty were immediately seized and strangled. One of the girls was a very handsome young woman, and Pancham, a Jemādār, wished to preserve her as a wife for his son. But when she saw her father and mother strangled she screamed and beat her head against the ground and tried to kill herself. Pancham tried in vain to quiet her, and promised to take great care of her and marry her to his own son, who would be a great chief; but

---

[1] Sleeman, p. 205.

all to no effect. She continued to scream, and at last Pancham put the *rūmāl* (handkerchief) round her neck and strangled her. One little girl of three years old was preserved by another Jemādār and married to his son, and when she grew up often heard the story of the affair narrated. The bodies were buried in a ravine and the booty amounted to Rs. 17,000. The Thugs then decided to return home, and arrived without mishap, except that the Jemādār, Pancham, died on the way.

They were not particular, however, to ascertain that their victims carried valuable property before disposing of them. Eight annas (8d.), one of them said,[1] was sufficient remuneration for murdering a man. On another occasion two river Thugs killed two old men and obtained only a rupee's worth of coppers, two brass vessels and their body-cloths. But as a rule the gains were much larger. It sometimes happened that the Thugs themselves were robbed at night by ordinary thieves, though they usually set a watch. On one occasion a band of more than a hundred Thugs fell in with a party of twenty-seven dacoits who had with them stolen property of Rs. 13,000 in cash, with gold ornaments, gems and shawls. The Thugs asked to be allowed to travel under their protection, and the dacoits carelessly assenting were shortly afterwards all murdered.[2] As already stated, the Thugs were accustomed to live in towns or villages and many of them ostensibly followed respectable callings. The following instance of this is given by Sir W. Sleeman:[3] "The first party of Thug approvers whom I sent into the Deccan to aid Captain Reynolds recognised in the person of one of the most respectable linen-drapers of the cantonment of Hingoli, Hari Singh, the adopted son of Jawāhir Sukul, Sūbahdār of Thugs, who had been executed twenty years before. On hearing that the Hari Singh of the list sent to him of noted Thugs at large in the Deccan was the Hari Singh of the Sadar Bazār, Captain Reynolds was quite astounded ; so correct had he been in his deportment and all his dealings that he had won the esteem of all the gentlemen of the station, who used to assist him in procuring passports for his goods on their way from Bombay ; and

7. Disguises of the Thugs.

---

[1] Hutton, p. 70.   [2] *Ibidem*, p. 71.   [3] Pp. 34, 35.

yet he had, as he has since himself shown, been carrying on his trade of murder up to the very day of his arrest with gangs of Hindustān and the Deccan on all the roads around and close to the cantonments of Hingoli; and leading out his band of assassins while he pretended to be on his way to Bombay for a supply of fresh linen and broad-cloth." Another case is quoted by Mr. Oman from Taylor's *Thirty-eight Years in India*.[1] "Dr. Cheek had a child's bearer who had charge of his children. The man was a special favourite, remarkable for his kind and tender ways with his little charges, gentle in manner and unexceptionable in all his conduct. Every year he obtained leave from his master and mistress, as he said, for the filial purpose of visiting his aged mother for one month; and returning after the expiry of that time, with the utmost punctuality, resumed with the accustomed affection and tenderness the charge of his little darlings. This mild and exemplary being was the missing Thug; kind, gentle, conscientious and regular at his post for eleven months in the year he devoted the twelfth to strangulation."

8. Secrecy of their operations.

Again, as regards the secrecy with which murders were perpetrated and all traces of them hidden, Sir W. Sleeman writes:[2] "While I was in civil charge of the District of Narsinghpur, in the valley of the Nerbudda, in the years 1822–1824, no ordinary robbery or theft could be committed without my becoming aware of it, nor was there a robber or thief of the ordinary kind in the District with whose character I had not become acquainted in the discharge of my duties as magistrate; and if any man had then told me that a gang of assassins by profession resided in the village of Kandeli,[3] not four hundred yards from my court, and that the extensive groves of the village of Mundesur, only one stage from me on the road to Saugor and Bhopāl, were one of the greatest *beles* or places of murder in all India, and that large gangs from Hindustān and the Deccan used to *rendezvous* in these groves, remain in them for many days every year, and carry on their dreadful trade along all the lines of road that

---

[1] See *Cults, Customs and Superstitions of India*, p. 249.
[2] Pp. 32, 33.
[3] Kandeli adjoins the headquarters station of Narsinghpur, the two towns being divided only by a stream.

pass by and branch off from them, with the knowledge and connivance of the two landholders by whose ancestors these groves had been planted, I should have thought him a fool or a madman; and yet nothing could have been more true. The bodies of a hundred travellers lie buried in and around the groves of Mundesur; and a gang of assassins lived in and about the village of Kandeli while I was magistrate of the District, and extended their depredations to the cities of Poona and Hyderābād."

9. Support of landholders and villagers

The system of Thuggee reached its zenith during the anarchic period of the decline of the Mughal Empire, when only the strongest and most influential could obtain any assistance from the State in recovering property or exacting reparation for the deaths of murdered friends and relatives. Nevertheless, the Thugs could hardly have escaped considerable loss even from private vengeance had they been compelled to rely on themselves for protection. But this was not the case, for, like the Badhaks and other robbers, they enjoyed the countenance and support of landholders and ruling chiefs in return for presenting them with the choicest of their booty and taking holdings of land at very high rents. Sir W. Sleeman wrote[1] that, "The zamīndārs and landholders of every description have everywhere been found ready to receive these people under their protection from the desire to share in the fruits of their expeditions, and without the slightest feeling of religious or moral responsibility for the murders which they know must be perpetrated to secure these fruits. All that they require from them is a promise that they will not commit murders within their estates and thereby involve them in trouble." Sometimes the police could also be conciliated by bribes, and on one occasion when a body of Thugs who had killed twenty-five persons were being pursued by the Thākur of Powai[2] they retired upon the village of Tigura, and even the villagers came out to their support and defended them against his attack. Another officer wrote:[3] "To conclude, there seems no doubt but that this horrid crime has been fostered by all classes in the community — the landholders, the native

---

[1] P. 23.
[2] Near Bilehri in Jubbulpore.
[3] Captain Lowis in Sleeman's *Report on the Thug Gangs* (1840).

officers of our courts, the police and village authorities—all, I think, have been more or less guilty ; my meaning is not, of course, that every member of these classes, but that individuals varying in number in each class were concerned. The subordinate police officials have in many cases been *practising Thugs*, and the *chaukīdārs* or village watchmen frequently so."

10. Murder of sepoys.

A favourite class of victims were sepoys proceeding to their homes on furlough and carrying their small savings ; such men would not be quickly missed, as their relatives would think they had not started, and the regimental authorities would ascribe their failure to return to desertion. So many of these disappeared that a special Army Order was issued warning them not to travel alone, and arranging for the transmission of their money through the Government treasuries.[1] In this order it is stated that the Thugs were accustomed first to stupefy their victim by surreptitiously administering the common narcotic *dhatūra*, still a familiar method of highway robbery.

11. Callous nature of the Thugs.

Like the Badhaks and other Indian robbers and the Italian banditti the Thugs were of a very religious or superstitious turn of mind. There was not one among them, Colonel Sleeman wrote,[2] who doubted the divine origin of Thuggee : " Not one who doubts that he and all who have followed the trade of murder, with the prescribed rites and observance, were acting under the immediate orders and auspices of the goddess, Devi, Durga, Kāli or Bhawāni, as she is indifferently called, and consequently there is not one who feels the slightest remorse for the murders which he may have perpetrated or abetted in the course of his vocation. A Thug considers the persons murdered precisely in the light of victims offered up to the goddess ; and he remembers them as a priest of Jupiter remembered the oxen and a priest of Saturn the children sacrificed upon their altars. He meditates his murders without any misgivings, he perpetrates them without any emotions of pity, and he recalls them without any feeling of remorse. They trouble not his dreams, nor does their recollection ever cause him inquietude in darkness, in solitude or in the hour of death."

[1] Pp. 15, 16.   [2] P. 7.

And again: "The most extraordinary trait in the characters of these people is not this that they can look back upon all the murders they have perpetrated without any feelings of remorse, but that they can look forward indifferently to their children, whom they love as tenderly as any man in the world, following the same trade of murder or being united in marriage to men who follow the trade. When I have asked them how they could cherish these children through infancy and childhood under the determination to make them murderers or marry them to murderers, the only observation they have ever made was that formerly there was no danger of their ever being hung or transported, but that now they would rather that their children should learn some less dangerous trade.

12. Belief in divine support.

They considered that all their victims were killed by the agency of God and that they were merely irresponsible agents, appointed to live by killing travellers as tigers by feeding on deer. If a man committed a real murder they held that his family must become extinct, and adduced the fact that this fate had not befallen them as proof that their acts of killing were justifiable. Nay, they even held that those who oppressed them were punished by the goddess:[1] "Was not Nanha, the Rāja of Jālon," said one of them, "made leprous by Devi for putting to death Budhu and his brother Khumoli, two of the most noted Thugs of their day? He had them trampled under the feet of elephants, but the leprosy broke out on his body the very next day. When Mūdhaji Sindhia caused seventy Thugs to be executed at Mathura was he not warned in a dream by Devi that he should release them? And did he not the very day after their execution begin to spit blood? And did he not die within three months?" Their subsequent misfortunes and the success of the British officers against them they attributed to their disobedience of the ordinances of Devi in slaying women and other classes of prohibited persons and their disregard of her omens. They also held that the spirits of all their victims went straight to Paradise, and this was the reason why the Thugs were not troubled by them as other murderers were.

[1] P. 150.

13. Theory of Thuggee as a religious sect.

The fact that the Thugs considered themselves to be directed by the deity, reinforced by their numerous superstitious beliefs and observances, has led to the suggestion by one writer that they were originally a religious sect, whose principal tenet was the prohibition of the shedding of blood. There is, however, no evidence in support of this view in the accounts of Colonel Sleeman, incomparably the best authority. Their method of strangulation was, as has been seen, simply the safest and most convenient means of murder: it enabled them to dispense with arms, by the sight of which the apprehensions of their victims would have been aroused, and left no traces on the site of the crime to be observed by other travellers. On occasion also they did not scruple to employ weapons; as in the murder of seven treasure-bearers near Hindoria in Damoh, who would not probably have allowed the Thugs to approach them, and in consequence were openly attacked and killed with swords.[1] Other instances are given in Colonel Sleeman's narrative, and they were also accustomed to cut and slash about the bodies of their victims after death. The belief that they were guided by the divine will may probably have arisen as a means of excusing their own misdeeds to themselves and allaying their fear of such retribution as being haunted by the ghosts of their victims. Similar instances of religious beliefs and practices are given in the accounts of other criminals, such as the Badhaks and Sānsias. And the more strict and serious observances of the Thugs may be accounted for by the more atrocious character of their crimes and the more urgent necessity of finding some palliative.

The veneration paid to the pickaxe, which will shortly be described, merely arises from the common animistic belief that tools and implements generally achieve the results obtained from them by their inherent virtue and of their own volition, and not from the human hand which guides them and the human brain which fashioned them to serve their ends. Members of practically all castes worship the implements of their profession and thus afford evidence of the same belief, the most familiar instance of which is perhaps, 'The pestilence that walketh in the darkness and

---

[1] Sleeman's *Report on the Thug Gangs*, Introduction, p. vi.

THE GODDESS KĀLI.

the arrow that flieth by noonday'; where the writer intended no metaphor but actually thought that the pestilence walked and the arrow flew of their own volition.

14. Worship of Kāli.

Kāli or Bhawāni was the principal deity of the Thugs, as of most of the criminal and lower castes; and those who were Muhammadans got over the difficulty of her being a Hindu goddess by pretending that Fātima, the daughter of the Prophet, was an incarnation of her. In former times they held that the goddess was accustomed to relieve them of the trouble of destroying the dead bodies by devouring them herself; but in order that they might not see her doing this she had strictly enjoined on them never to look back on leaving the site of a murder. On one occasion a novice of the fraternity disobeyed this rule and, unguardedly looking behind him, saw the goddess in the act of feasting upon a body with the half of it hanging out of her mouth. Upon this she declared that she would no longer devour those whom the Thugs slaughtered; but she agreed to present them with one of her teeth for a pickaxe, a rib for a knife and the hem of her lower garment for a noose, and ordered them for the future to cut about and bury the bodies of those whom they destroyed. As there seems reason to suppose that the goddess Kāli represents the deified tiger, on which she rides, she was eminently appropriate as the patroness of the Thugs and in the capacity of the devourer of corpses.

15. The sacred pickaxe.

When the sacred pickaxe used for burying corpses had to be made, the leader of the gang, having ascertained a lucky day from the priest, went to a blacksmith and after closing the door so that no other person might enter, got him to make the axe in his presence without touching any other work until it was completed. A day was then chosen for the consecration of the pickaxe, either Monday, Tuesday, Wednesday or Friday; and the ceremony was performed inside a house or tent, so that the shadow of no living thing might fall on and contaminate the sacred implement. A pit was dug in the ground and over it the pickaxe was washed successively with water, sugar and water, sour milk, and alcoholic liquor, all of which were poured over it into the pit. Finally it was marked seven times with vermilion.

A burnt offering was then made with all the usual ingredients for sacrifice and the pickaxe was passed seven times through the flames. A cocoanut was placed on the ground, and the priest, holding the pickaxe by the point in his right hand, said, 'Shall I strike?' The others replied yes, and striking the cocoanut with the butt end he broke it in pieces, upon which all exclaimed, 'All hail, Devi, and prosper the Thugs.' All then partook of the kernel of the cocoanut, and collecting the fragments put them into the pit so that they might not afterwards be contaminated by the touch of any man's foot. Here the cocoanut may probably be considered as a substituted sacrifice for a human being. Thereafter the pickaxe was called Kassi or Mahi instead of *kudāli*, the ordinary name, and was given to the shrewdest, cleanest and most sober and careful man of the party, who carried it in his waist-belt. While in camp he buried it in a secure place with its point in the direction they intended to go; and they believed that if another direction was better the point would be found changed towards it. They said that formerly the pickaxe was thrown into a well and would come up of itself when summoned with due ceremonies; but since they disregarded the ordinances of Kāli it had lost that virtue. Many Thugs told Colonel Sleeman[1] that they had seen the pickaxe rise out of the well in the morning of its own accord and come to the hands of the man who carried it; and even the several pickaxes of different gangs had been known to come up of themselves from the same well and go to their respective bearers. The pickaxe was also worshipped on every seventh day during an expedition, and it was believed that the sound made by it in digging a grave was never heard by any one but a Thug. The oath by the pickaxe was in their esteem far more sacred than that by the Ganges water or the Koran, and they believed that a man who perjured himself by this oath would die or suffer some great calamity within six days. In prison, when administering an oath to each other in cases of dispute, they sometimes made an image of the pickaxe out of a piece of cloth and consecrated it for the purpose. If the pickaxe at any time fell from the hands of the carrier it was a dreadful

[1] P. 142.

omen and portended either that he would be killed that year or that the gang would suffer some grievous misfortune. He was deprived of his office and the gang either returned home or chose a fresh route and consecrated the pickaxe anew.

16. The sacred *gur* (sugar). After each murder they had a sacrificial feast of *gur* or unrefined sugar. This was purchased to the value of Rs. 1-4, and the leader of the gang and the other Bhurtotes (stranglers) sat on a blanket with the rest of the gang round them. A little sugar was dropped into a hole and the leader prayed to Devi to send them some rich victims. The remainder of the sugar was divided among all present. One of them gave the *jhirni* or signal for strangling and they consumed the sugar in solemn silence, no fragment of it being lost. They believed that it was this consecrated *gur* which gave the desire for the trade of a Thug and made them callous to the sufferings of their victims, and they thought that if any outsider tasted it he would at once become a Thug and continue so all his life. When Colonel Sleeman asked[1] a young man who had strangled a beautiful young woman in opposition to their rules, whether he felt no pity for her, the leader Feringia exclaimed: "We all feel pity sometimes, but the *gur* of the Tuponi (sacrifice) changes our nature. It would change the nature of a horse. Let any man once taste of that *gur* and he will be a Thug, though he knows all the trades and have all the wealth in the world. I never wanted food; my mother's family was opulent, her relations high in office. I have been high in office myself, and became so great a favourite wherever I went that I was sure of promotion; yet I was always miserable while absent from my gang and obliged to return to Thuggee. My father made me taste of that fatal *gur* when I was yet a mere boy; and if I were to live a thousand years I should never be able to follow any other trade."

The eating of this *gur* was clearly the sacrificial meal of the Thugs. On the analogy of other races they should have partaken of the body of an animal god at their sacrificial meal, and if the goddess Kāli is the deified tiger, they should have eaten tiger's flesh. This custom, if it ever existed, had

[1] P. 216.

been abandoned, and the *gur* would in that case be a substitute; and as has been seen the eating of the *gur* was held to confer on them the same cruelty, callousness and desire to kill which might be expected to follow from eating tiger's flesh and thus assimilating the qualities of the animal. Since they went unarmed as a rule, in order to avoid exciting the suspicions of their victims, it would be quite impossible for them to obtain tiger's flesh, except by the rarest accident; and the *gur* might be considered a suitable substitute, since its yellow colour would be held to make it resemble the tiger.

17. Worship of ancestors.

The Thugs also worshipped the spirits of their ancestors. One of these was Dādu Dhira, an ancient Thug of the Barsote class, who was invoked at certain religious ceremonies, when liquor was drunk. Vows were made to offer libations of ardent spirits to him, and if the prayer was answered the worshipper drank the liquor, or if his caste precluded him from doing this, threw it on the ground with an expression of thanks. Another deity was the spirit of Jhora Nāik, who was a Muhammadan. He and his servant killed a man who had jewels and other articles laden on a mule to the value of more than a lakh and a half. They brought home the booty, assembled all the members of their fraternity within reach, and honestly divided the whole as if all had been present. The Thugs also said that Nizām-ud-dīn Aulia, a well-known Muhammadan saint, famed for his generosity, whose shrine is near Delhi, had been a Thug, at any rate in his younger days. He distributed so much money in charity that he was supposed to be endowed with a Dustul Ghīb or supernatural purse; and they supposed that he obtained it by the practice of Thuggee. Orthodox Muhammadans would, however, no doubt indignantly repudiate this.

18. Fasting.

Whenever they set out on a fresh expedition the first week was known as Satha (seven). During this period the families of those who were engaged in it would admit no visitors from the relatives of other Thugs, lest the travellers destined for their own gang should go over to these others; neither could they eat any food belonging to the families of other Thugs. During the Satha period the Thugs engaged in the expedition ate no animal food except fish and nothing cooked with *ghī* (melted butter). They did not shave or bathe or have their clothes washed or indulge in sexual intercourse, or give away anything in charity or throw any part of their food to dogs or jackals. At one time they ate no salt or turmeric, but this rule was afterwards abandoned. But if the Sourka or first murder took place within the seven days they considered themselves relieved by it from all these restraints.

A Thug seldom attained to the office of Bhurtote or strangler until he had been on several expeditions and acquired the requisite courage or insensibility by slow degrees. At first they were almost always shocked or frightened; but after a time they said they lost all sympathy with the victims. They were first employed as scouts, then as buriers of the dead, next as Shamsias or holders of hands, and finally as stranglers. When a man felt that he had sufficient courage and insensibility he begged the oldest and most renowned Thug of the gang to make him his *chela* or disciple. If his proposal was accepted he awaited the arrival of a suitable victim of not too great bodily strength. While the traveller was asleep with the gang at their quarters the *guru* or preceptor took his disciple into a neighbouring field, followed by three or four old members of the gang. Here they all faced in the direction in which the gang intended to move, and the *guru* said, " *Oh Kāli, Kunkāli, Bhudkāli*,[1] *Oh Kāli, Mahā Kāli, Kalkatāwāli!* If it seemeth to thee fit that the traveller now at our lodging should die by the hands of this thy slave, vouchsafe, we pray thee, the omen on the right." If they got this within a certain interval the candidate was considered to be accepted, and if not some other Thug put the traveller to death and he had to wait for another chance. In the former case they returned to their quarters and the *guru* took a handkerchief and tied the slip-knot in one end of it with a rupee inside it. The disciple received it respectfully in his right

19. Initiation of a novice.

---

[1] 'Oh Kāli, Eater of Men, Oh great Kāli of Calcutta.' The name Calcutta signifies Kāli-ghāt or Kāli-kota, that is Kāli's ferry or house. The story is that Job Charnock was exploring on the banks of the Hoogly, when he found a widow about to be burnt as a sacrifice to Kāli. He rescued her, married her, and founded a settlement on the site, which grew into the town of Calcutta.

hand and stood over the victim with the Shamsia or holder by his side. The traveller was roused on some pretence or other and the disciple passed the handkerchief over his neck and strangled him. He then bowed down to his *guru* and all his relations and friends in gratitude for the honour he had obtained. He gave the rupee from the knot with other money, if he had it, to the *guru*, and with this sugar or sweetmeats were bought and the *gur* sacrifice was celebrated, the new strangler taking one of the seats of honour on the blanket for the first time. The relation between a strangler and his *guru* was considered most sacred, and a Thug would often rather betray his father than the preceptor by whom he had been initiated. There were certain classes of persons whom they were forbidden to kill, and they considered that the rapid success of the English officers in finally breaking up the gangs was to be attributed to the divine wrath at breaches of these rules. The original rule [1] was that the Sourka or first victim must not be a Brāhman, nor a Saiyad, nor any very poor man, nor any man with gold on his person, nor any man who had a quadruped with him, nor a washerwoman, nor a sweeper, nor a Teli (oilman), nor a Bhāt (bard), nor a Kāyasth (writer), nor a leper, dancing-woman, pilgrim or devotee. The reason for some of these exemptions is obvious: Brāhmans, Muhammadan Saiyads, bards, religious mendicants and devotees were excluded owing to their sanctity; and sweepers, washermen and lepers owing to their impurity, which would have the same evil and unlucky effect on their murderers as the holiness of the first classes. A man wearing gold ornaments would be protected by the sacred character of the metal; and the killing of a poor man as the first victim would naturally presage a lack of valuable booty during the remainder of the expedition. Telis and Kāyasths are often considered as unlucky castes, and even in the capacity of victims might be held to bring an evil fortune on their murderers.

20. Prohibition of murder of women. Another list is given of persons whom it was forbidden to kill at any time, and of these the principal category was women. It was a rule of all Thugs that women should not be murdered, but one which they constantly

[1] P. 133.

broke, for few large parties consisted solely of men, and to allow victims to escape from a party would have been a suicidal policy. In all the important exploits related to Colonel Sleeman the women who accompanied victims were regularly strangled, with the occasional exception of young girls who might be saved and married to the sons of Thug leaders. The breach of the rule as to the murder of women was, however, that which they believed to be specially offensive to their patroness Bhawāni; and no Thug, Colonel Sleeman states, was ever known to offer insult either in act or speech to the women whom they were about to murder. No gang would ever dare to murder a woman with whom one of its members should be suspected of having had criminal intercourse. The murder of women was especially reprobated by Hindus, and the Muhammadan Thugs were apparently responsible for the disregard of this rule which ultimately became prevalent, as shown by the dispute over the killing of a wealthy old lady,[1] narrated by one of the Thugs as follows: "I remember the murder of Kāli Bībi well; I was at the time on an expedition to Baroda and not present, but Punua must have been there. A dispute arose between the Musalmāns and Hindus before and after the murder. The Musalmāns insisted upon killing her as she had Rs. 4000 of property with her, but the Hindus would not agree. She was killed, and the Hindus refused to take any part of the booty; they came to blows, but at last the Hindus gave in and consented to share in all but the clothes and ornaments which the woman wore. Feringia's father, Parasrām Brāhman, was there, and when they came home Parasrām's brother, Rai Singh, refused to eat, drink or smoke with his brother till he had purged himself from this great sin; and he, with two other Thugs, a Rājpūt and a Brāhman, gave a feast which cost them a thousand rupees each. Four or five thousand Brāhmans were assembled at that feast. Had it rested here we should have thrived; but in the affair of the sixty victims women were again murdered; in the affair of the forty several women were murdered; and from that time we may trace our decline."

Another rule was that a man having a cow with him

P. 173.

21. Other classes of persons not killed.

should not be murdered, no doubt on account of the sanctity attaching to the animal. But in one case of a murder of fourteen persons including women and a man with a cow at Kotri in the Damoh District, the Thugs, having made acquaintance with the party, pretended that they had made a vow to offer a cow at a temple in Shāhpur lying on their road and persuaded the cow's owner to sell her to them for this sacred purpose, and having duly made the offering and deprived him of the protection afforded by the cow, they had no compunction in strangling him with all the travellers. Travellers who had lost a limb were also exempted from death, but this rule too was broken, as in the case of the native officer with his two daughters who was murdered by the Thugs he had befriended; for it is recorded that this man had lost a leg. Pilgrims carrying Ganges water could not be killed if they actually had the Ganges water with them; and others who should not be murdered were washermen, sweepers, oil-vendors, dancers and musicians, carpenters and blacksmiths, if found travelling together, and religious mendicants. The reason for the exemption of carpenters and blacksmiths only when travelling together may probably have been that the sacred pickaxe was their joint handiwork, having a wooden handle and an iron head; and this seems a more likely explanation than any other in view of the deep veneration shown for the pickaxe. Maimed persons would probably not be acceptable victims to the goddess, according to the rule that the sacrifice must be without spot or blemish. The other classes have already been discussed under the exemption of first victims. Among the Deccan Thugs if a man strangled any victim of a class whom it was forbidden to kill, he was expelled from the community and never readmitted to it. This was considered a most dreadful crime.

22. Belief in omens.

The Thugs believed that the wishes of the deity were constantly indicated to them by the appearance or cries of a large number of wild animals and birds from which they drew their omens; and indeed the number of these was so extensive that they could never be at a loss for an indication of the divine will, and difficulties could only arise when the omens were conflicting. As a general rule the omen varied according as it was heard on the left hand, known as Pilhao, or the right, known as Thibao. On first opening an expedition an omen must be heard on the left and be followed by one on the right, or no start was made ; it signified that the deity took them first by the left hand and then by the right to lead them on. When they were preparing to march or starting on a road, an omen heard on the left encouraged them to go on, but if it came from the right they halted. When arriving at their camping-place on the other hand the omen on the right was auspicious and they stayed, but if it came from the left the projected site was abandoned and the march continued. In the case of the calls of a very few animals these rules were reversed, left and right being transposed in each instance. The howl of the jackal was always bad if heard during the day, and the gang immediately quitted the locality, leaving untouched any victims whom they might have inveigled, however wealthy. The jackal's cry at night followed the rule of right and left. The jackal was probably revered by the Thugs as the devourer of corpses. The sound made by the lizard was at all times and places a very good omen ; but if a lizard fell upon a Thug it was bad, and any garment touched by it must be given away in charity. The call of the *sāras* crane was a very important omen, and when heard first on the left and then on the right or vice versa according to the rules given above, they expected a great booty in jewels or money. The call of the partridge followed the same rules but was not of so much importance. That of the large crow was favourable if the bird was sitting on a tree, especially when a tank or river could be seen ; but if the crow was perched on the back of a buffalo or pig or on the skeleton of any animal, it was a bad omen. Tanks or rivers were likely places for booty in the shape of resting travellers, whose death the appearance of the crow might portend ; whereas in the other positions it might prognosticate a Thug's own death. The chirping of the small owlet was considered to be a bad omen, whether made while the bird was sitting or flying ; it was known as *chiraiya*, and is a low and melancholy sound seldom repeated. They considered it a very bad omen to hear the hare squeaking ; this, unless it was averted by sacrifices, signified, they said, that they would perish in the jungles, and the hare or some other animal of the forest would drink water from their skulls. "We know that the hare was used in Brittany as an animal of augury for foretelling the future; and all animals of augury were once venerated."[1] The hare has still some remnant of sanctity among the Hindus. Women will not eat its flesh, and men eat the flesh of wild hares only, not of tame ones. It seems likely that the hare may have been considered capable of foretelling the future on account of its long ears. The omen of the donkey was considered the most important of all, whether it threatened evil or promised good. It was a maxim of augury that the ass was equal to a hundred birds, and it was also more important than all other quadrupeds. If they heard its bray on the left on the opening of an expedition and it was soon after repeated on the right, they believed that nothing on earth could prevent their success during that expedition though it should last for years. The ass is the sacred animal of Sītala, the goddess of smallpox, who is a form of Kālī. The ears and also the bray of the ass would give it importance.

The noise of two cats heard fighting was propitious only during the first watch of the night; if heard later in the night it was known as '*Kālī ki mauj*' or 'Kālī's temper,' and threatened evil, and if during the daytime as '*Dhāmoni*[2] *ki mauj*,' and was a prelude of great misfortune; while if the cats fell from a height while fighting it was worst of all. The above shows that the cat was also the animal of Kālī and is a point in favour of her derivation from the tiger; and on this hypothesis the importance of the omen of the cat is explained. If they obtained a good omen when in company with travellers they believed that it was a direct order from heaven to kill them, and that if they disobeyed the sign and let the travellers go they would never obtain any more victims.[3]

23. Omens and taboos.

If a mare dropped a foal in their camp while they were travelling, they were all contaminated or came under the Itak;

---

[1] *Orphéus*, p. 170.
[2] Dhāmoni is an old ruined fort and town in the north of Saugor District, still a favourite haunt of tigers; and the Thugs may often have lain there in concealment and heard the tigers quarrelling in the jungle.
[3] Sleeman, p. 196.

and the only remedy for this was to return home and start the journey afresh. Various other events [1] also produced the Itak, especially among the Deccan Thugs; these were the birth of a child in a Thug family; the first courses of a Thug's daughter; a marriage in a Thug's family; a death of any member of his family except an infant at the breast; circumcision of a boy; a buffalo or cow giving calf or dying; and a cat or dog giving a litter or dying. If a party fell under the Itak or contamination at a time when it was extremely inconvenient or impossible to return home, they sometimes marched back for a few miles and slept the night, making a fresh start in the morning, and this was considered equivalent to beginning a new journey after getting rid of the contamination. If any member of the party sneezed on setting out on an expedition or on the day's march, it was a bad omen and required expiatory sacrifices; and if they had travellers with them when this omen occurred, these must be allowed to escape and could not be put to death. Omens were also taken from the turban, without which no Thug, except perhaps in Bengal, would travel.[2] If a turban caught fire a great evil was portended, and the gang must, if near home, return and wait for seven days. But if they had travelled for some distance an offering of *gur* (sugar) was made, and the owner of the turban alone returned home. If a man's turban fell off it was also considered a very bad omen, requiring expiatory sacrifices. The turban is important as being the covering of the head, which many primitive people consider to contain the life or soul (*Golden Bough*). A shower of rain falling at any time except during the monsoon period from June to September was also a bad omen which must be averted by sacrifices. Prior to the commencement [3] of an expedition a Brāhman was employed to select a propitious day and hour for the start and for the direction in which the gang should proceed. After this the auspices were taken with great solemnity and, if favourable omens were obtained, the party set out and made a few steps in the direction indicated; after this they might turn to the right or left as impediments or incentives presented themselves. If they heard any one weeping for a death as they

[1] P. 91. [2] P. 67. [3] P. 100.

left the village, it threatened great evil; and so, too, if they met the corpse of any one belonging to their own village, but not that of a stranger. And it was also a bad omen to meet an oil-vendor, a carpenter, a potter, a dancing-master, a blind or lame man, a Fakīr (beggar) with a brown waistband or a Jogi (mendicant) with long matted hair. Most of these were included in the class of persons who might not be killed.

24. Nature of the belief in omens.

The custom of the Thugs, and in a less degree of ignorant and primitive races generally, of being guided in their every action by the chance indications afforded from the voices and movements of birds and animals appears to the civilised mind extremely foolish. But its explanation is not difficult when the character of early religious beliefs is realised. It was held by savages generally that animals, birds and all other living things, as well as trees and other inanimate objects, had souls and exercised conscious volition like themselves. And those animals, such as the tiger and cow, and other objects, such as the sun and moon and high mountains or trees, which appeared most imposing and terrible, or exercised the most influence on their lives, were their principal deities, the spirits of which at a later period developed into anthropomorphic gods. Even the lesser animals and birds were revered and considered to be capable of affecting the lives of men. Hence their appearance, their flight and their cries were naturally taken to be direct indications afforded by the god to his worshippers; and it was in the interpretation of these, the signs given by the divine beings by whom man was surrounded, and whom at one time he considered superior to himself, that the science of augury consisted. "The priestesses of the oracle of Zeus at Dodona called themselves doves, as those of Diana at Ephesus called themselves bees; this proves that the oracles of the temples were formerly founded on observations of the flight of doves and bees, and no doubt also that the original cult consisted in the worship of these animals."[1] Thus, as is seen here, when the deity was no longer an animal but had developed into a god in human shape, the animal remained associated with him and partook of his sanctity; and what could be

[1] *Orphéus* (M. Salomon Reinach), p. 316.

more natural than that he should convey the indications of his will through the appearance, movements and cries of the sacred animal to his human *protégés*. The pseudo-science of omens is thus seen to be a natural corollary of the veneration of animals and inanimate objects.

25. Suppression of Thuggee.

When the suppression of the Thugs was seriously taken in hand by the Thuggee and Dacoity Department under the direction of Sir William Sleeman, this abominable confraternity, which had for centuries infested the main roads of India and made away with tens of thousands of helpless travellers, never to be heard of again by their families and friends, was destroyed with comparatively little difficulty. The Thugs when arrested readily furnished the fullest information of their murders and the names of their confederates in return for the promise of their lives, and Colonel Sleeman started a separate file or *dossier* for every Thug whose name became known to him, in which all information obtained about him from different informers was collected. In this manner, as soon as a man was arrested and identified, a mass of evidence was usually at once forthcoming to secure his conviction. Between 1826 and 1835 about 2000 Thugs were arrested and hanged, transported or kept under restraint; subsequently to this a larger number of British officers were deputed to the work of hunting down the Thugs, and by 1848 it was considered that this form of crime had been practically stamped out. For the support of the approver Thugs and the families of these and others a labour colony was instituted at Jubbulpore, which subsequently developed into the school of industry and was the parent of the existing Reformatory School. Here these criminals were taught tent and carpet-making and other trades, and in time grew to be ashamed of the murderous calling in which they had once taken a pride.

TURI

LIST OF PARAGRAPHS

1. *Origin of the caste.*
2. *Subdivisions.*
3. *Marriage.*
4. *Funeral rites.*
5. *Occupation.*
6. *Social status.*

1. Origin of the caste.

Turi.—A non-Aryan caste of cultivators, workers in bamboo, and basket-makers, belonging to the Chota Nāgpur plateau. They number about 4000 persons in Raigarh, Sārangarh and the States recently transferred from Bengal. The physical type of the Turis, Sir H. Risley states, their language, and their religion place it beyond doubt that they are a Hinduised offshoot of the Munda tribe. They still speak a dialect derived from Mundāri, and their principal deity is Singbonga or the sun, the great god of the Mundas: "In Lohardaga, where the caste is most numerous, it is divided into four subcastes—Turi or Kisān-Turi, Or, Dom, and Domra—distinguished by the particular modes of basket and bamboo-work which they practise. Thus the Turi or Kisān-Turi, who are also cultivators and hold *bhuinhāri* land, make the *sūp*, a winnowing sieve made of *sirki*, the upper joint of *Saccharum procerum*; the *tokri* or *tokiya*, a large open basket of split bamboo twigs woven up with the fibre of the leaves of the *tāl* palm; the *sair* and *nadua*, used for catching fish. The Ors are said to take their name from the *oriya* basket used by the sower, and made of split bamboo, sometimes helped out with *tāl* fibre. They also make umbrellas, and the *chhota dali* or *dāla*, a flat basket with vertical sides used for handling grain in small quantities. Doms make the *harka* and scale-pans (*tarāju*). Domras make the *peti* and fans. Turis frequently reckon in as a fifth subcaste the Birhors, who cut bamboos and make the *sikas* used for carrying loads slung on a shoulder-yoke (*bhangi*), and a kind of basket called *phanda*. Doms and Domras speak Hindi; Turis, Ors and Birhors use among themselves a dialect of Mundāri."[1]

2. Subdivisions.

In Raigarh and Sārangarh of the Central Provinces the above subcastes are not found, and there are no distinct endogamous groups; but the more Hinduised members of the caste have begun to marry among themselves and call themselves Turia, while they look down on the others to whom they restrict the designation Turi. The names of subcastes given by Sir H. Risley appear to indicate that the Turis are an offshoot from the Mundas, with an admixture of Doms and other low Uriya castes. Among themselves the caste is also known as Husil, a term which signifies a worker in bamboo. The caste say that their original ancestor was created by Singbonga, the sun, and had five sons, one of whom found a wooden image of their deity in the Baranda forest, near the Barpahāri hill in Chota Nāgpur. This image was adopted as their family deity, and is revered to the present day as Barpahāri Deo. The deity is thus called after the hill, of which it is clear that he is the personified representative. From the five sons are descended the five main septs of the Turis. The eldest was called Mailuār, and his descendants are the leaders or headmen of the caste. The group sprung from the second son are known as Chardhagia, and it is their business to purify and readmit offenders to caste intercourse. The descendants of the third son conduct the ceremonial shaving of such offenders, and are known as Surennār, while those of the fourth son bring water for the ceremony and are called Tīrkuār. The fifth group is known as Hasdagia, and it is said that they are the offspring of the youngest brother, who committed some offence, and the four other brothers took the parts which are still played by their descendants in his ceremony of purification. Traces of similar divisions appear to be found in Bengal, as Sir H. Risley states that before a marriage can be celebrated the consent of the heads of the Mādalwār and Surinwār sections, who are known respectively as Rāja and Thākur, is obtained, while

[1] *Tribes and Castes of Bengal*, art. Turi.

the head of the Charchāgiya section officiates as priest. The above names are clearly only variants of those found in the Central Provinces. But besides the above groups the Turis have a large number of exogamous septs of a totemistic nature, some of which are identical with those of the Mundas.

3. Marriage.
Marriage is adult, and the bride and bridegroom are usually about the same age; but girls are scarce in the caste, and betrothals are usually effected at an early age, so that the fathers of boys may obtain brides for their sons. A contract of betrothal, once made, cannot be broken without incurring social disgrace, and compensation in money is also exacted. A small bride-price of three or four rupees and a piece of cloth is payable to the girl's father. As in the case of some other Uriya castes the proposal for a marriage is couched in poetic phraseology, the Turi bridegroom's ambassador announcing his business with the phrase: 'I hear that a sweet-scented flower has blossomed in your house and I have come to gather it'; to which the bride's father, if the match be acceptable, replies: 'You may take away my flower if you will not throw it away when its sweet scent has gone.' The girl then appears, and the boy's father gives her a piece of cloth and throws a little liquor over her feet. He then takes her on his lap and gives her an anna to buy a ring for herself, and sometimes kisses her and says, 'You will preserve my lineage.' He washes the feet of her relatives, and the contract of betrothal is thus completed, and its violation by either party is a serious matter. The wedding is performed according to the ritual commonly practised by the Uriya castes. The binding portion of it consists in the perambulation of the sacred pole five or seven times. After each circle the bridegroom takes hold of the bride's toe and makes her kick away a small heap of rice on which a nut and a pice coin are placed. After this a cloth is held over the couple and each rubs vermilion on the other's forehead. At this moment the bride's brother appears, and gives the bridegroom a blow on the back. This is probably in token of his wrath at being deprived of his sister. A meal of rice and fowls is set before the bride-

groom, but he feigns displeasure, and refuses to eat them. The bride's parents then present him with a pickaxe and a crooked knife, saying that these are the implements of their trade, and will suffice him for a livelihood. The bridegroom, however, continues obdurate until they promise him a cow or a bullock, when he consents to eat. The bride's family usually spend some twenty or more rupees on her wedding, and the bridegroom's family about fifty rupees. A widow is expected to marry her Dewar or deceased husband's younger brother, and if she takes somebody else he must repay to the Dewar the expenditure incurred by the latter's family on her first marriage. Divorce is permitted for misconduct on the part of the wife or for incompatibility of temper.

The caste bury the dead, placing the head to the north. They make libations to the spirits of their ancestors on the last day of Phāgun (February), and not during the fortnight of Pitripaksh in Kunwār (September) like other Hindu castes. They believe that the spirits of ancestors are reborn in children, and when a baby is born they put a grain of rice into a pot of water and then five other grains in the names of ancestors recently deceased. When one of these meets the grain representing the child they hold that the ancestor in question has been born again. The principal deity of the caste is Singbonga, the sun, and according to one of their stories the sun is female. They say that the sun and moon were two sisters, both of whom had children, but when the sun gave out great heat the moon was afraid that her children would be burnt up, so she hid them in a *handi* or earthen pot. When the sun missed her sister's children she asked her where they were, and the moon replied that she had eaten them up; on which the sun also ate up her own children. But when night came the moon took her children out of the earthen pot and they spread out in the sky and became the stars. And when the sun saw this she was greatly angered and vowed that she would never look on the moon's face again. And it is on this account that the moon is not seen in the daytime, and as the sun ate up all her children there are no stars during the day.

4. Funeral rites.

5. Occupation.

The caste make and sell all kinds of articles manufactured from the wood of the bamboo, and the following list of their wares will give an idea of the variety of purposes for which this product is utilised: "*Tukna*, an ordinary basket; *dauri*, a basket for washing rice in a stream; *lodhar*, a large basket for carrying grain on carts; *chuki*, a small basket for measuring grain; *garni* and *sikosi*, a small basket for holding betel-leaf and a box for carrying it in the pocket; *dhitori*, a fish-basket; *dholi*, a large bamboo shed for storing grain; *ghurki* and *paili*, grain measures; *chhanni*, a sieve; *taji*, a balance; *pankha* and *bijna*, fans; *pelna*, a triangular frame for a fishing-net; *choniya*, a cage for catching fish; *chatai*, matting; *chhāta*, an umbrella; *chhitori*, a leaf hat for protecting the body from rain; *pinjra*, a cage; *khunkhuna*, a rattle; and *guna*, a muzzle for bullocks.

Most of them are very poor, and they say that when Singbonga made their ancestors he told them to fetch something in which to carry away the grain which he would give them for their support; but the Turis brought a bamboo sieve, and when Singbonga poured the grain into the sieve nearly the whole of it ran out. So he reproved them for their foolishness, and said, '*Khasar, khasar, tīn pasar*,' which meant that, however hard they should work, they would never earn more than three handfuls of grain a day.

6. Social status.

The social status of the Turis is very low, and their touch is regarded as impure. They must live outside the village and may not draw water from the common well; the village barber will not shave them nor the washerman wash their clothes. They will eat all kinds of food, including the flesh of rats and other vermin, but not beef. The rules regarding social impurity are more strictly observed in the Uriya country than elsewhere, owing to the predominant influence of the Brāhmans, and this is probably the reason why the Turis are so severely ostracised. Their code of social morality is not strict, and a girl who is seduced by a man of the caste is simply made over to him as his wife, the ordinary bride-price being exacted from him. He must also feed the caste-fellows, and any money which is received by the girl's father is expended in the same manner. Members of Hindu castes and Gonds may be admitted into the community, but not the Munda tribes, such as the Mundas themselves and the Kharias and Korwas; and this, though the Turis, as has been seen, are themselves an offshoot of the Munda tribe. The fact indicates that in Chota Nāgpur the tribes of the Munda family occupy a lower social position than the Gonds and others belonging to the Dravidian family. When an offender of either sex is to be readmitted into caste after having been temporarily expelled for some offence he or she is given water to drink and has a lock of hair cut off. Their women are tattooed on the arms, breast and feet, and say that this is the only ornament which they can carry to the grave.

Velama, Elama, Yelama.—A Telugu cultivating caste found in large numbers in Vizagapatam and Ganjām, while in 1911 about 700 persons were returned from Chānda and other districts in the Central Provinces. The caste frequently also call themselves by the honorific titles of Naidu or Dora (lord). The Velamas are said formerly to have been one with the Kamma caste, but to have separated on the question of retaining the custom of *parda* or *gosha* which they had borrowed from the Muhammadans. The Kammas abandoned *parda*, and, signing a bond written on palm-leaf to this effect, obtained their name from *kamma*, a leaf. The Velamas retained the custom, but a further division has taken place on the subject, and one subcaste, called the Adi or original Velamas, do not seclude their women. The caste has at present a fairly high position, and several important Madras chiefs are Velamas, as well as the zamīndār of Sironcha in the Central Provinces. They appear, however, to have improved their status, and thus to have incurred the jealousy of their countrymen, as is evidenced by some derogatory sayings current about the caste. Thus the Balijas call them Gūni Sakalvāndlu or hunchbacked washermen, because some of them print chintz and carry their goods in a bundle on their backs.[1] According to another derivation *gūna* is the large pot in which they dye their cloth. Another story is that the name of the caste is Velimāla, meaning those who are above or better than the

1. Origin and social status.

[1] *North Arcot Manual*, i. p. 216.

Dhers, and was a title conferred on them by the Rāja of Bastar in recognition of the bravery displayed by the Velamas in his army. These stories are probably the outcome of the feeling of jealousy which attaches to castes which have raised themselves in the social scale. The customs of the Velamas do not indicate a very high standard of ceremonial observance, as they eat fowls and pork and drink liquor. They are said to take food from Bestas and Dhīmars, while Kunbis will take it from them. The men of the caste are tall and strong, of a comparatively fair complexion and of a bold and arrogant demeanour. It is said that a Velama will never do anything himself which a servant can do for him, and a story is told of one of them who was smoking when a spark fell on his moustache. He called his servant to remove it, but by the time the man came, his master's moustache had been burnt away. These stories and the customs of the Velamas appear to indicate that they are a caste of comparatively low position, who have gone up in the world, and are therefore tenacious in asserting a social position which is not universally admitted. Their subcastes show that a considerable difference in standing exists in the different branches of the caste. Of these the Rācha or royal Velamas, to whom the chiefs and zamīndārs belong, are the highest. While others are the Gūna Velamas or those who use a dyer's pot, the Eku or 'Cotton-skein' who are weavers and carders, and the Tellāku or white leaf Velamas, the significance of this last name not being known. It is probable that the Velamas were originally a branch of the great Kāpu or Reddi caste of cultivators, corresponding in the Telugu country to the Kurmis and Kunbis, as many of their section names are the same as those of the Kāpus. The Velamas apparently took up the trades of weaving and dyeing, and some of them engaged in military service and acquired property. These are now landowners and cultivators and breed cattle, while others dye and weave cloth. They will not engage themselves as hired labourers, and they do not allow their women to work in the fields.

2. Marriage and social customs.

The caste are said to have 77 exogamous groups descended from the 77 followers or spearsmen who attended Rāja Rudra Pratāp of Bastar when he was ousted from

Wārangal. These section names are eponymous, territorial and totemistic, instances of the last kind being Cherukunūla from *cheruku*, sugarcane, and Pasapunūla from *pasapu*, turmeric, and *nūla*, thread. Marriage within the section or *gotra* is prohibited, but first cousins may intermarry. Marriage is usually adult, and the binding portion of the ceremony consists in the tying of the *mangal-sūtram* or happy thread by the bridegroom round the bride's neck. At the end of the marriage the *kankans* or bracelets of the bridegroom and bride are taken off in signification that all obstacles to complete freedom of intercourse and mutual confidence between the married pair have been removed. In past years, when the Gūna Velamas had a marriage, they were bound to pay the marriage expenses of a couple of the Palli or fisherman caste, in memory of the fact that on one occasion when the Gūna Velamas were in danger of being exterminated by their enemies, the Pallis rescued them in their boats and carried them to a place of safety. But now it is considered sufficient to hang up a fishing-net in the house when a marriage ceremony of the Gūna Velamas is being celebrated.[1] The caste do not permit the marriage of widows, and divorce is confined to cases in which a wife is guilty of adultery. The Velamas usually employ Vaishnava Brāhmans as their priests. They burn the bodies of those who die after marriage, and bury those dying before it. Children are named on the twenty-first day after birth, the child being placed in a swing, and the name selected by the parents being called out three times by the oldest woman present. On this day the mother is taken to a well and made to draw a bucket of water by way of declaration that she is fit to do household work.

[1] *Indian Antiquary* (1879), p. 216.

VIDUR

LIST OF PARAGRAPHS

1. *Origin and traditions.*
2. *The Purāds, Golaks and Borals.*
3. *Illegitimacy among Hindustāni castes.*
4. *Legend of origin.*
5. *Marriage.*
6. *Social rules and occupation.*

1. Origin and traditions.

Vidur,[1] Bidur.—A Marātha caste numbering 21,000 persons in the Central Provinces in 1911, and found in the Nāgpur Division and Berār. They are also returned from Hyderābād and Bombay. Vidur means a wise or intelligent man, and was the name of the younger brother of Pāndu, the father of the Pāndava brothers. The Vidurs are a caste of mixed descent, principally formed from the offspring of Brāhman fathers with women of other castes. But the descendants of Panchāls, Kunbis, Mālis and others from women of lower caste are also known as Vidurs and are considered as different subcastes. Each of these groups follow the customs and usually adopt the occupation of the castes to which their fathers belonged. They are known as Kharchi or Khāltātya, meaning 'Below the plate' or 'Below the salt,' as they are not admitted to dine with the proper Vidurs. But the rule varies in different places, and sometimes after the death of their mother such persons become full members of the caste, and with each succeeding generation the status of their descendants improves. In Poona the name Vidur is restricted to the descendants of Brāhman fathers, and they are also known as Brāhmanja or 'Born from Brāhmans.' Elsewhere the Brāhman Vidurs are designated especially as Krishnapakshi, which means

[1] This article is compiled from papers by Mr. W. A. Tucker, Extra Assistant Commissioner, Bhandāra, and Mr. B. M. Deshmukh, Pleader, Chānda.

'One born during the dark fortnight.' The term Krishnapakshi is or was also used in Bengal, and Buchanan defined it as follows : "Men of the Rājpūt, Khatri and Kāyasth tribes, but no others, openly keep women slaves of any pure tribe, and the children are of the same caste with their father, but are called Krishnapakshis and can only marry with each other."[1] In Bastar a considerable class of persons of similar illegitimate descent also exist, being the offspring of the unions of immigrant Hindus with women of the Gond, Halba and other tribes. The name applied to them, however, is Dhākar, and as their status and customs are quite different from those of the Marātha Vidurs they are treated in a short separate article.

2. The Purāds, Golaks and Borals.

Another small group related to the Vidurs are the Purāds of Nāgpur; they say that their ancestor was a Brāhman who was carried away in a flooded river and lost his sacred thread. He could not put on a new thread afterwards because the sacred thread must be changed without swallowing the spittle in the interval. Hence he was put out of caste and his descendants are the Purāds, the name being derived from *pūr*, a flood. These people are mainly shopkeepers. In Berār two other groups are found, the Golaks and Borals. The Golaks are the illegitimate offspring of a Brāhman widow; if after her husband's decease she did not shave her head, her illegitimate children are known as Rand[2] Golaks; if her head was shaved, they are called Mund (shaven) Golaks; and if their father be unknown, they are named Kund Golaks. The Golaks are found in Malkāpur and Bālāpur and number about 400 persons. A large proportion of them are beggars. A Boral is said to be the child of a father of any caste and a mother of one of those in which widows shave their heads. As a matter of fact widows, except among Brāhmans, rarely shave their heads in the Central Provinces, and it would therefore appear, if Mr. Kitts' definition is correct, that the Borals are the offspring of women by fathers of lower caste than themselves; a most revolting union to Hindu ideas. As, however, the Borals are mostly grocers and shopkeepers, it is possible that they may be the same class

[1] Buchanan, *Eastern India*, i. p. 186.   [2] Rand = widow or prostitute.

as the Purāds. In 1881 they numbered only 163 persons and were found in Dārhwa, Mehkar and Chikhli tāluks.

3. Illegitimacy among Hindustāni castes.

There is no caste corresponding to the Vidurs in the Hindi Districts and the offspring of unions which transgress the caste marriage rules are variously treated. Many castes both in the north and south say that they have $12\frac{1}{2}$ subdivisions and that the half subcaste comprises the descendants of illicit unions. Of course the twelve subdivisions are as a rule mythical, the number of subcastes being always liable to fluctuate as fresh endogamous groups are formed by migration or slight changes in the caste calling. Other castes have a Lohri Sen or degraded group which corresponds to the half caste. In other cases the illegitimate branch has a special name; thus the Nīche Pāt Bundelas of Saugor and Chhoti Tar Rājpūts of Nimār are the offspring of fathers of the Bundela and other Rājpūt tribes with women of lower castes; both these terms have the same meaning as Lohri Sen, that is a low-caste or bastard group. Similarly the Dauwa (wet-nurse) Ahīrs are the offspring of Bundela fathers and the Ahīr women who act as nurses in their households. In Saugor is found a class of persons called Kunwar[1] who are descended from the offspring of the Marātha Brāhman rulers of Saugor and their kept women. They now form a separate caste and Hindustāni Brāhmans will take water from them. They refuse to accept *katcha* food (cooked with water) from Marātha Brāhmans, which all other castes will do. Another class of bastard children of Brāhmans are called Dogle, and such people commonly act as servants of Marātha Brāhmans; as these Brāhmans do not take water to drink from the hands of any caste except their own, they have much difficulty in procuring household servants and readily accept a Dogle in this capacity without too close a scrutiny of his antecedents. There is also a class of Dogle Kāyasths of similar origin, who are admitted as members of the caste on an inferior status and marry among themselves. After several generations such groups tend to become legitimised; thus the origin of the distinction between the Khare and Dūsre Srivāstab Kāyasths and

---

[1] The term Kunwar is a title applied to the eldest son of a chief.

the Dasa and Bīsa Agarwāla Banias was probably of this character, but now both groups are reckoned as full members of the caste, one only ranking somewhat below the other so that they do not take food together. The Pārwār Banias have four divisions of different social status known as the Bare, Manjhile, Sanjhile and Lohri Seg or Sen, or first, second, third and fourth class. A man and woman detected in a serious social offence descend into the class next below their own, unless they can pay the severe penalties prescribed for it. If either marries or forms a connection with a man or woman of a lower class they descend into that class. Similarly, one who marries a widow goes into the Lohri Seg or lowest class. Other castes have a similar system of divisions. Among the great body of Hindus cases of men living with women of different caste are now very common, and the children of such unions sometimes inherit their father's property. Though in such cases the man is out of caste this does not mean that he is quite cut off from social intercourse. He will be invited to the caste dinners, but must sit in a different row from the orthodox members so as not to touch them. As an instance of these mixed marriages the case of a private servant, a Māli or gardener, may be quoted. He always called himself a Brāhman, and though thinking it somewhat curious that a Brāhman should be a gardener, I took no notice of it until he asked leave to attend the funeral of his niece, whose father was a Government menial, an Agarwāla Bania. It was then discovered that he was the son of a Brāhman landowner by a mistress of the Kāchhi caste of sugarcane and vegetable growers, so that the profession of a private or ornamental gardener, for which a special degree of intelligence is requisite, was very suitable to him. His sister by the same parents was married to this Agarwāla Bania, who said his own family was legitimate and he had been deceived about the girl. The marriage of one of this latter couple's daughters was being arranged with the son of a Brāhman father and Bania mother in Jubbulpore; while the gardener himself had never been married, but was living with a girl of the Gadaria (shepherd) caste who had been married in her caste but had never lived with her husband.

Inquiries made in a small town as to the status of seventy families showed that ten were out of caste on account of irregular matrimonial or sexual relations; and it may therefore be concluded that a substantial proportion of Hindus have no real caste at present.

4. Legend of origin.

The Vidurs say that they are the descendants of a son who was born to a slave girl by the sage Vyās, the celebrated compiler of the Mahābhārata, to whom the girl was sent to provide an heir to the kingdom of Hastināpur. This son was named Vidur and was remarkable for his great wisdom, being one of the leading characters in the Mahābhārata and giving advice both to the Pāndavas and the Kauravas.

5. Marriage.

As already stated, the Vidurs who are sprung from fathers of different castes form subcastes marrying among themselves. Among the Brāhman Vidurs also, a social difference exists between the older members of the caste who are descended from Vidurs for several generations, and the new ones who are admitted into it as being the offspring of Brāhman fathers from recent illicit unions, the former considering themselves to be superior and avoiding intermarriage with the latter as far as possible. The Brāhman Vidurs, to whom this article chiefly relates, have exogamous sections of different kinds, the names being eponymous, territorial, titular and totemistic. Among the names of their sections are Indurkar from Indore; Chaurikār, a whisk-maker; Achārya and Pānde, a priest; Menjokhe, a measurer of wax; Mīne, a fish; Dūdhmānde, one who makes wheaten cakes with milk; Goihe, a lizard; Wadābhāt, a ball of pulse and cooked rice; Diwāle, bankrupt; and Joshi, an astrologer. The Brāhman Vidurs have the same sect groups as the Marātha Brāhmans, according to the Veda which they especially revere. Marriage is forbidden within the section and in that of the paternal and maternal uncles and aunts. In Chānda, when a boy of one section marries a girl of another, all subsequent alliances between members of the two sections must follow the same course, and a girl of the first section must not marry a boy of the second. This rule is probably in imitation of that by which their caste is formed, that is from the union of a man of higher with a woman of lower caste. As already stated, the reverse form of connection is considered most disgraceful by the Hindus, and children born of it could not be Vidurs. On the same analogy they probably object to taking both husbands and wives from the same section. Marriage is usually infant, and a second wife is taken only if the first be barren or if she is sickly or quarrelsome. As a rule, no price is paid either for the bride or bridegroom. Vidurs have the same marriage ceremony as Marātha Brāhmans, except that Purānic instead of Vedic *mantras* or texts are repeated at the service. As among the lower castes the father of a boy seeks for a bride for his son, while with Brāhmans it is the girl's father who makes the proposal. When the bridegroom arrives he is conducted to the inner room of the bride's house; Mr. Tucker states that this is known as the *Gaurighar* because it contains the shrine of Gauri or Pārvati, wife of Mahādeo; and here he is received by the bride who has been occupied in worshipping the goddess. A curtain is held between them and coloured rice is thrown over them and distributed, and they then proceed to the marriage-shed, where an earthen mound or platform, known as Bohala, has been erected. They first sit on this on two stools and then fire is kindled on the platform and they walk five times round it. The Bohala is thus a fire altar. The expenses of marriage amount for the bridegroom's family to Rs. 300 on an average, and for the bride's to a little more. Widows are allowed to remarry, but the second union must not take place with any member of the family of the late husband, whose property remains with his children or, failing them, with his family. In the marriage of a widow the common *pāt* ceremony of the Marātha Districts is used. A price is commonly paid to the parents of a widow by her second husband. Divorce is allowed on the instance of the husband by a written agreement, and divorced women may marry again by the *pāt* ceremony. In Chānda it is stated that when a widower marries again a silver or golden image is made of the first wife and being placed with the household gods is daily worshipped by the second wife.

The Vidurs employ Marātha Brāhmans for religious and ceremonial purposes, while their *gurus* are either Brāhmans 6. Social rules and occupation.

or Bairāgis. They have two names, one for ceremonial and the other for ordinary use. When a child is to be named it is placed in a cradle and parties of women sit on opposite sides of it. One of the women takes the child in her arms and passes it across the cradle to another saying, 'Take the child named Rāmchandra' or whatever it may be. The other woman passes the child back using the same phrase, and it is then placed in the cradle and rocked, and boiled wheat and gram are distributed to the party. The Vidurs burn the dead, and during the period of mourning the well-to-do employ a Brāhman to read the Garud Purān to them, which tells how a sinner is punished in the next world and a virtuous man is rewarded. This, it is said, occupies their minds and prevents them from feeling their bereavement. They will take food only from Marātha Brāhmans and water from Rājpūts and Kunbis. Brāhmans will, as a rule, not take anything from a Vidur's hand, but some of them have begun to accept water and sweetmeats, especially in the case of educated Vidurs. The Vidurs will not eat flesh of any kind nor drink liquor. The Brāhman Vidurs did not eat in kitchens in the famine. Their dress resembles that of Marātha Brāhmans. The men do not usually wear the sacred thread, but some have adopted it. In Bombay, however, boys are regularly invested with the sacred thread before the age of ten.[1] In Nāgpur it is stated that the Vidurs like to be regarded as Brāhmans.[2] They are now quite respectable and hold land. Many of them are in Government service, some being officers of the subordinate grades and others clerks, and they are also agents to landowners, patwāris and shopkeepers. The Vidurs are the best educated caste with the exception of Brāhmans, Kāyasths and Banias, and this fact has enabled them to obtain a considerable rise in social status. Their aptitude for learning may be attributed to their Brāhman parentage, while in some cases Vidurs have probably been given an education by their Brāhman relatives. Their correct position should be a low one, distinctly beneath that of the good cultivating castes. A saying has it, ' As the *amarbel* creeper has no roots, so the Vidur has no ancestry.' But owing to

[1] *Bombay Gazetteer*, vol. xviii. p. 185.   [2] *Nāgpur Settlement Report*, p. 27.

their education and official position the higher classes of Vidurs have obtained a social status not much below that of Kāyasths. This rise in position is assisted by their adherence in matters of dress, food and social practice to the customs of Marātha Brāhmans, so that many of them are scarcely distinguishable from a Brāhman. A story is told of a Vidur Tahsīldār or Naib-Tahsīldār who was transferred to a District at some distance from his home, and on his arrival there pretended to be a Marātha Brāhman. He was duly accepted by the other Brāhmans, who took food with him in his house and invited him to their own. After an interval of some months the imposture was discovered, and it is stated that this official was at a short subsequent period dismissed from Government service on a charge of bribery. The Vidurs are also considered to be clever at personation, and one or two stories are told of frauds being carried out through a Vidur returning to some family in the character of a long-lost relative.

Wāghya,[1] Vāghe, Murli.—An order of mendicant devotees of the god Khandoba, an incarnation of Siva; they belong to the Marātha Districts and Bombay where Khandoba is worshipped. The term Wāghya is derived from *vāgh*, a tiger, and has been given to the order on account of the small bag of tiger-skin, containing *bhandār*, or powdered turmeric, which they carry round their necks. This has been consecrated to Khandoba and they apply a pinch of it to the foreheads of those who give them alms. Murli, signifying 'a flute' is the name given to female devotees. Wāghya is a somewhat indefinite term and in the Central Provinces does not strictly denote a caste. The order originated in the practice followed by childless mothers of vowing to Khandoba that if they should bear a child, their first-born should be devoted to his service. Such a child became a Wāghya or Murli according as it was a boy or a girl. But they were not necessarily severed from their own caste and might remain members of it and marry in it. Thus there are Wāghya Telis in Wardha, who marry with other Telis. The child might also

---

[1] This article is partly based on a paper by Pandit Pyāre Lāl Misra, ethnographic clerk.

be kept in the temple for a period and then withdrawn, and nowadays this is always done. The children of rich parents sometimes simply remain at home and worship Khandoba there. But they must beg on every Sunday from at least five persons all their lives. Another practice, formerly existing, was for the father and mother to vow that if a child was born they would be swung. They were then suspended from a wooden post on a rope by an iron hook inserted in the back and swung round four or five times. The sacred turmeric was applied to the wound and it quickly healed up. Others would take a Wāghya child to Mahādeo's cave in Pachmarhi and let it fall from the top of a high tree. If it lived it was considered to be a Rāja of Mahādeo, and if it died happiness might confidently be anticipated for it in the next birth. Besides the children who are dedicated to Khandoba, a man may become a Wāghya either for life or for a certain period in fulfilment of a vow, and in the latter case will be an ordinary member of his own caste again on its termination. The Wāghyas and Murlis who are permanent members of the order sometimes also live together and have children who are brought up in it. The constitution of the order is therefore in several respects indefinite, and it has not become a self-contained caste, though there are Wāghyas who have no other caste.

The following description of the dedication of children to Khandoba is taken from the *Bombay Gazetteer*.[1] When parents have to dedicate a boy to Khandoba they go to his temple at Jejuri in Poona on any day in the month of Chaitra (March-April). They stay at a Gurao's house and tell him the object of their visit. The boy's father brings offerings and they go in procession to Khandoba's temple. There the Gurao marks the boy's brow with turmeric, throws turmeric over his head, fastens round his neck a deer- or tiger-skin wallet hung from a black woollen string and throws turmeric over the god, asking him to take the boy. The Murlis or girls dedicated to the god are married to him between one and twelve years of age. The girl is taken to the temple by her parents accompanied by the Gurao priest and other Murlis. At the temple she is bathed and her body rubbed with turmeric,

[1] Vol. xx. pp. 189-190.

WĀGHYA MENDICANTS.

with which the feet of the idol are also anointed. She is dressed in a new robe and bodice, and green glass bangles are put on her wrists. A turban and sash are presented to the god, and the *guru* taking a necklace of nine cowries (shells) fastens it round the girl's neck. She then stands before the god, a cloth being held between them as at a proper wedding, and the priest repeats the marriage verses. Powdered turmeric is thrown on the heads of the girl and of the idol, and from that day she is considered to be the wife of Khandoba and cannot marry any other man. When a Murli comes of age she sits by herself for four days. Then she looks about for a patron, and when she succeeds in getting one she calls a meeting of her brethren, the Wāghyas, and in their presence the patron says, 'I will fill the Murli's lap.' The Wāghyas ask him what he will pay and after some haggling a sum is agreed on, which thirty years ago varied between twenty-five and a hundred rupees. If it is more than Rs. 50 a half of the money goes to the community, who spend it on a feast. With the balance the girl buys clothes for herself. She lives with her patron for as long as he wishes to keep her, and is then either attached to the temple or travels about as a female mendicant. Sometimes a married woman will leave her home and become a Murli, with the object as a rule of leading a vicious life.

A man who takes a vow to become a Wāghya must be initiated by a *guru*, who is some elder member of the order. The initiation takes place early on a Sunday morning, and after the disciple is shaved, bathed and newly clad, the *guru* places a string of cowries round his neck and gives him the tiger-skin bag in which the turmeric is kept. He always retains much reverence for his *guru*, and invokes him with the exclamation, 'Jai Guru,' before starting out to beg in the morning. The following articles are carried by the Wāghyas when begging. The *dapdi* is a circular single drum of wood, covered with goat-skin, and suspended to the shoulder. The *chouka* consists of a single wire suspended from a bar and passing inside a hollow wooden conical frame. The wire is struck with a stick to produce the sound. The *ghāti* is an ordinary temple bell; and the *kutumba* is a metal saucer which serves for a begging-bowl. This is considered sacred, and sandalwood is applied to it before starting out in the morning. The Wāghyas usually beg in parties of four, each man carrying one of these articles. Two of them walk in front and two behind, and they sing songs in praise of Khandoba and play on the instruments. Every Wāghya has also the bag made of tiger-skin, or, if this cannot be had, of deer-skin, and the cowrie necklace, and a *seli* or string of goat-hair round the neck. Alms, after being received in the *kutumba* or saucer, are carried in a bag, and before setting out in the morning they put a little grain in this bag, as they think that it would be unlucky to start with it empty. At the end of the day they set out their takings on the ground and make a little offering of fire to them, throwing a pinch of turmeric in the air in the name of Khandoba. The four men then divide the takings and go home. Marāthas, Murlis and Telis are the castes who revere Khandoba, and they invite the Wāghyas to sing on the Dasahra and also at their marriages. In Bombay the Wāghyas force iron bars through their calves and pierce the palms of their hands with needles. To the needle a strip of wood is attached, and on this five lighted torches are set out, and the Wāghya waves them about on his hand before the god.[1] Once in three years each Wāghya makes a pilgrimage to Khandoba's chief temple at Jejuri near Poona, and there are also local temples to this deity at Hinganghāt and Nāgpur. The Wāghyas eat flesh and drink liquor, and their social and religious customs resemble those of the Marāthas and Kunbis.

Yerūkala.—A vagrant gipsy tribe of Madras of whom a small number are returned from the Chānda District. They live by thieving, begging, fortune-telling and making baskets, and are usually treated as identical with the Koravas or Kuravas, who have the same occupations. Both speak a corrupt Tamil, and the Yerūkalas are said to call one another Kurru or Kura. It has been supposed that Korava was the Tamil name which in the Telugu country became Yerukalavāndlu or fortune-teller. Mr. (Sir H.) Stewart thought there could be no doubt of the identity of the two castes,[2] though Mr. Francis points out differences

---

[1] *Bombay Gazetteer*, vol. xxii. p. 212.   [2] *Madras Census Report* (1891).

between them.¹ The Yerūkalas are expert thieves. They frequent villages on the pretence of begging, and rob by day in regular groups under a female leader, who is known as Jemādārin. Each gang is provided with a bunch of keys and picklocks. They locate a locked house in an unfrequented lane, and one of them stands in front as if begging; the remainder are posted as watchers in the vicinity, and the Jemādārin picks the lock and enters the house. When the leader comes out with the booty she locks the door and they all walk away. If any one comes up while the leader is in the house the woman at the door engages him in conversation by some device, such as producing a silver coin and asking if it is good. She then begins to dispute, and laying hold of him calls out to her comrades that the man has abused her or been taking liberties with her. The others run up and jostle him away from the door, and while they are all occupied with the quarrel the thief escapes. Or an old woman goes from house to house pretending to be a fortune-teller. When she finds a woman at home alone, she flatters and astonishes her by relating the chief events in her life, how many children she has, how many more are coming, and so on. When the woman of the house is satisfied that the fortune-teller has supernatural powers, she allows the witch to cover her face with her robe, and shuts her eyes while the fortune-teller breathes on them, and blows into her ears and sits muttering charms. Meanwhile one or two of the latter's friends who have been lurking close by walk into the house and carry away whatever they can lay their hands on. When they have left the house the woman's face is uncovered and the fortune-teller takes her fee and departs, leaving her dupe to find out that her house has been robbed.² The conjugal morals of these people are equally low. They sell or pledge their wives and unmarried daughters, and will take them back on the redemption of the pledge with any children born in the interval, as though nothing out of the ordinary had happened. When a man is sentenced to imprisonment his wife selects another partner for the period

---

¹ *Madras Census Report* (1901).
² *Bombay Gazetteer*, vol. xxi. pp. 170, 171.

of her husband's absence, going back to him on his release with all her children, who are considered as his. Mr. Thurston gives the following story of a gang of Koravas or Yerūkalas in Tinnevelly: "One morning, in Tinnevelly, while the butler in a missionary's house was attending to his duties, an individual turned up with a fine fowl for sale. The butler, finding that he could purchase it for about half the real price, bought it, and showed it to his wife with no small pride in his ability in making a bargain. But he was distinctly crestfallen when his wife pointed out that it was his own bird, which had been lost on the previous night. The seller was a Korava."[1] In Madras they have also now developed into expert railway thieves. They have few restrictions as to food, eating cats and mice, though not dogs.[2] The Yerūkalas practised the custom of the Couvade as described by the Rev. John Cain, of Dumagudem:[3] "Directly the woman feels the birth-pangs she informs her husband, who immediately takes some of her clothes, puts them on, places on his forehead the mark which the women usually place on theirs, retires into a dark room where there is only a very dim lamp, and lies down on the bed, covering himself up with a long cloth. When the child is born it is washed and placed on the cot beside the father. Asafoetida, jaggery and other articles are then given, not to the mother but to the father. During the days of ceremonial impurity the man is treated as other Hindus treat their women on such occasions. He is not allowed to leave his bed, but has everything needful brought to him.

"The Yerūkalas marry when quite young. At the birth of a daughter the father of an unmarried little boy often brings a rupee and ties it in the cloth of the father of a newly-born girl. When the girl is grown up he can then claim her for his son."

[1] *Tribes and Castes of Southern India*, art. Korava.
[2] *North Arcot Manual*, p. 247.
[3] *Ind. Ant.* vol. iii., 1874, p. 157.

THE END